THE THEORY OF COMMUNICATIVE ACTION

Volume 1

REASON AND THE RATIONALIZATION OF SOCIETY

THE THEORY OF COMMUNICATIVE ACTION

Volume 1

REASON AND THE RATIONALIZATION OF SOCIETY

Jürgen Habermas

Translated by Thomas McCarthy

Beacon Press   Boston

For Ute Habermas–Wesselhoeft

Beacon Press
25 Beacon Street
Boston, Massachusetts 02108-2800

Beacon Press books
are published under the auspices of
the Unitarian Universalist Association of Congregations.

© 1984 by Beacon Press
Originally published as *Theorie des Kommunikativen Handelns,
Band I: Handlungsrationalität und gesellschaftliche
Rationalisierung,* © 1981 by Suhrkamp Verlag, Frankfurt am Main
Printed in the United States of America

96 95 94 93 92 91 90 89   10 9 8 7 6 5 4 3

Library of Congress Cataloging-in-Publication Data
Habermas, Jürgen
   The theory of communicative action.
   Translation of: Theorie des kommunikativen Handelns.
   Includes bibliographical references and index.
   Contents: v. 1. Reason and the rationalization of society.
   1. Sociology – Philosophy – Collected works.
2. Rationalism – Collected works.   3. Social Action –
Collected works.   4. Communication – Philosophy –
Collected works.   5. Functionalism – Collected works.
I. Title.
HM24.H3213 1983   301'.01   82-72506
ISBN 0-8070-1506-7 (v. 1)
ISBN 0-8070-1507-5 (v. 1) (pbk.)

Contents

Volume 1: Reason and the Rationalization of Society

Contents

Volume 2. Lifeworld and System: A Critique of Functionalist Reason

Translator's Introduction

Since the beginning of the modern era the prospect of a limitless advance of science and technology, accompanied at each step by moral and political improvement, has exercised a considerable hold over Western thought. Against this the radicalized consciousness of modernity of the nineteenth century voiced fundamental and lasting doubts about the relation of "progress" to freedom and justice, happiness and self-realization. When Nietzsche traced the advent of nihilism back to the basic values of Western culture—"because nihilism represents the ultimate logical conclusion of our great values and ideas"—he gave classic expression to a stream of cultural pessimism that flows powerfully again in contemporary consciousness. Antimodernism is rampant today, and in a variety of forms; what they share is an opposition to completing "the project of modernity" insofar as this is taken to be a matter of rationalization. There are, of course, good reasons for being critical of the illusions of the Enlightenment. The retreat of "dogmatism" and "superstition" has been accompanied by fragmentation, discontinuity and loss of meaning. Critical distance from tradition has gone hand in hand with anomie and alienation, unstable identities and existential insecurities. Technical progress has by no means been an unmixed blessing; and the rationalization of administration has all too often meant the end of freedom and self-determination. There is no need to go on enumerating such phenomena; a sense of having exhausted our cultural, social, and political resources is pervasive. But there is a need to subject these phenomena to careful analysis if we wish to avoid a precipitate abandonment of the achievements of modernity. What is called for, it might be argued, is an enlightened suspicion of enlightenment, a reasoned critique of Western rationalism, a careful reckoning of the profits and losses entailed by "progress." Today, once again, reason can be defended only by way of a critique of reason.

Jürgen Habermas has been called "the last great rationalist," and in a certain sense he is. But his is a rationalism with important differences; for, in good dialectical fashion, he has sought to incorporate into it the central insights of the critique of rationalism. *Theorie des kommunikativen Handelns*, published in two volumes in 1981, represents the culmination to date of his efforts.[1] *Reason and the Rationalization of Society* is a translation, with minor revisions, of the first volume; a translation of the second volume, *System and Lifeworld: A Critique of Functionalist Reason*, will follow.

There are both advantages and disadvantages to publishing the two volumes separately. On the positive side, the Anglo-American reception of a major work in twentieth-century social theory can get underway sooner, at a time when the questions it treats are moving rapidly to the center of intellectual interest. As the English-language discussion of these issues has not yet congealed into hard and fast patterns, the appearance of this volume at this time may well play a significant role in structuring it. On the negative side, there is the fact that Habermas sustains a continuous line of thought across the nearly 1,200 pages of the two volumes. The part of the argument deployed in Volume 1, while certainly intelligible and interesting in its own right, might well be misconstrued when detached from that larger context. In this introduction I hope to reduce that danger by sketching the argument of the book as a whole, especially the points developed in Volume 2.

In the preface, and elsewhere, Habermas tells us that *The Theory of Communicative Action* has three interrelated concerns: (1) to develop a concept of rationality that is no longer tied to, and limited by, the subjectivistic and individualistic premises of modern philosophy and social theory; (2) to construct a two-level concept of society that integrates the lifeworld and system paradigms; and, finally, (3) to sketch out, against this background, a critical theory of modernity which analyzes and accounts for its pathologies in a way that suggests a redirection rather than an abandonment of the project of enlightenment. Part I of this introduction deals with the first of these concerns; part II considers the lifeworld/system question and its relevance for a theory of contemporary society. But first, one general remark on Habermas's approach: He develops these themes through a somewhat unusual combination of theoretical constructions with historical reconstructions of the ideas of "classical" social theorists. The thinkers discussed—Marx, Weber, Durkheim, Mead, Lukacs, Horkheimer, Adorno, Parsons—are, he holds, still very much alive. Rather than regarding them as so many corpses to be dissected exegetically, he treats them as virtual dialogue partners from whom a great deal that is of contemporary significance can still be learned. The aim of his "historical reconstructions with systematic intent" is to excavate and incorporate their positive contributions, to criticize and overcome their weaknesses, by thinking with them to go beyond them.

Interspersed throughout these critical dialogues with the classics are numerous excurses and two chapter-length *Zwischenbetrachtungen*, or intermediate reflections, devoted to systematic questions. The concluding chapter attempts to combine the fruits of his historical reconstructions with the results of his systematic reflections in sketching a critical theory of modernity.

For reasons that Habermas sets forth in the text and that I briefly mention below, he holds that an adequate theory of society must integrate methods and problematics previously assigned exclusively to *either* philosophy *or* empirical social science. In the first portion of this introduction I consider some of the more "philosophical" aspects of the theory of communicative action; in the second part, I turn to more "sociological" themes.

I

The Cartesian paradigm of the solitary thinker—*solus ipse*—as the proper, even unavoidable, framework for radical reflection on knowledge and morality dominated philosophical thought in the early modern period. The methodological solipsism it entailed marked the approach of Kant at the end of the eighteenth century no less than that of his empiricist and rationalist predecessors in the two preceding centuries. This monological approach preordained certain ways of posing the basic problems of thought and action: subject versus object, reason versus sense, reason versus desire, mind versus body, self versus other, and so on. In the course of the nineteenth century this Cartesian paradigm and the subjectivistic orientation associated with it were radically challenged. Early in the century Hegel demonstrated the intrinsically historical and social character of the structures of consciousness. Marx went even further, insisting that mind is not the ground of nature but nature that of mind; he stressed that human consciousness is essentially embodied and practical and argued that forms of consciousness are an encoded representation of forms of social reproduction. In establishing the continuity of the human species with the rest of nature, Darwin paved the way for connecting intelligence with self-preservation, that is, for a basically functionalist conception of reason such as we find in American Pragmatism. Nietzsche and Freud disclosed the unconscious at the heart of consciousness, the role of the preconceptual and nonconceptual within the conceptual realm. Historicism exhibited in detail the historical and cultural variability of categories of thought and principles of action. The end result was, in Habermas's phrase, a "desublimation of spirit" and, as a consequence, a "disempowering of philosophy."

But the history of ideas is full of surprises; and twentieth-century philosophy bore witness to the continued power of the Cartesian model, in a variety of forms—from Edmund Husserl's openly Cartesian phenomenology to the Cartesianism lying just below the surface of logical empiricism. More recently, however, the critique of this model has been vigorously renewed. Thus we are said to be living in a "post-Heideggerian," "post-Wittgensteinian," "poststructuralist" age. The spirit has once again been desublimated. Subjectivity has been shown to be "infiltrated with the world" in such a way that "otherness is carried to the very heart of selfhood."[2] This "twilight of subjectivity" is not merely an intraphilosophic affair, a reminder to philosophers that they are not after all the high priests of culture.[3] It is the theoretical center of the stream of antimodernist thought I mentioned at the outset; thus it has implications that go well beyond the confines of academic philosophy. The critique of "rootless rationalism" goes hand in hand with an unmasking of the anthropocentric, egoistic, possessive, and domineering aspects of Western individualism; together they frequently serve as a prologue to the rejection of central concepts of European humanism. We cannot ignore the question of whether, in the absence of an archimedean point outside the world, anything can be salvaged from these emphatic concepts and the universalist claims connected with them. And if the subject is desublimated, can we really expect much more from general social "theory" than a historicist contemplation of the variety of forms of life in the *musée imaginaire* of the past; or a hermeneutic dialogue with other cultures and epochs about the common concerns of human life; or, perhaps, a genealogical unmasking of any pretense to universal validity?

Habermas's response to the decline of the paradigm of consciousness is an explicit shift to the paradigm of language—not to language as a syntactic or semantic system, but to language-in-use or speech. Thus he develops the categorial framework and normative foundations of his social theory in the form of a general theory of communicative action. "If we assume that the human species maintains itself through the socially coordinated activities of its members and that this coordination is established through communication—and in certain spheres of life, through communication aimed at reaching agreement—then the reproduction of the species *also* requires satisfying the conditions of a rationality inherent in communicative action" (1:397).

In the atomistic perspective of much of modern thought, the subject stands over against a world of objects to which it has two basic relations: representation and action. Accordingly, the type of rationality associated with this model is the "cognitive-instrumental" rationality of a subject capable of gaining knowledge about a contingent environment and putting it to effective use in intelligently adapting to and manipulating that environment. By stressing the fact that the goal-directed actions of different individuals are socially coordinated, Habermas shifts our attention to the broader context of individual purposive actions, to the structures of social interaction in which teleological actions are located.

> The communicative model of action does not equate action with communication. Language is a means of communication which serves mutual understanding, whereas actors, in coming to an understanding with one another so as to coordinate their actions, pursue their particular aims...Concepts of *social action* are distinguished by how they specify this coordination among the goal-directed actions of different participants—as the interlacing of egocentric calculations of utility, as a socially integrating consensus about norms and values instilled through cultural tradition and socialization, or as reaching understanding in the sense of a cooperative process of interpretation...The interpretive accomplishments on which cooperative processes [of situation definition] are based represent the mechanism for *coordinating* action; communicative action is not exhausted by the act of reaching understanding...(1:101)

This shift of attention from the teleological to the communicative dimension of social action makes an analysis of language, as the basic medium of communication, essential to laying the foundations of social theory. Drawing on linguistics and the philosophy of language, as well as on cognitive developmental psychology, Habermas sets forth (especially in Chapters I and III) the basic ideas of his theory of communicative competence. As this was developed in earlier writings and has already been widely discussed,[4] we can limit ourselves here to the aspects that are directly relevant to the theory of social action.

Habermas argues that our ability to communicate has a universal core—basic structures and fundamental rules that all subjects master in learning to speak a language. *Communicative competence* is not just a matter of being able to produce grammatical sentences. In speaking we relate to the world about us, to other subjects, to our own intentions, feelings, and desires. In each of these dimensions we are constantly making claims, even if usually only implicitly, concerning the validity of what we are saying, implying, or presupposing—claims, for instance, regarding the truth of what we say in relation to the objective world; or claims concerning the rightness, appropriateness, or legitimacy of our speech acts in relation to the shared values and norms of our social lifeworld; or claims to sincerity or authenticity in regard to the manifest expressions of our intentions and feelings. Naturally, claims of these sorts can be contested and criticized, defended and revised. There are any number of ways of settling disputed claims—for example, by appeal to authority, to tradition or to brute force. One way, the giving of reasons-for and reasons-against has traditionally been regarded as fundamental to the idea of rationality. And it is, in fact, to the experience of achieving mutual understanding in communication that is free from coercion that Habermas looks in developing his idea of rationality.

The key to his notion of reaching understanding (*Verständigung*) is the possibility of using reasons or grounds to gain intersubjective recognition for criticizable validity claims.[5] This possibility exists in each of the three dimensions mentioned above. It is not only claims to propositional truth and to the effectiveness of means for attaining ends that can be criticized and defended with reasons; the claim that an action is right or appropriate in relation to a certain normative context, or that such a context deserves to be recognized as legitimate, can also be discussed in this way; as can the claim that an utterance is a sincere or authentic expression of one's own subjective experiences. That is, in each of these dimensions it is possible to reach agreement about disputed claims by way of argument and insight and without recourse to force other than that of reasons or grounds. In each dimension there exists a "reflective medium" for dealing with problematic validity claims—that is, modes of argumentation or critique that enable us to thematize contested validity claims and to attempt to vindicate or criticize them. "The rationality proper to the communicative practice of everyday life points to the practice of argumentation as a court of appeal that makes it possible to continue communicative action with other means when disagreement can no longer be headed off by everyday routines and yet is not to be settled by the direct or strategic use of force" (1:17-18).

Because validity claims can be criticized, there is a possibility of identifying and correcting mistakes, that is, of learning from them. If this is carried through at a reflective level, forms of argumentation take shape which may be transmitted and developed within a cultural tradition and even embodied in specific cultural institutions. Thus, for instance, the scientific enterprise, the legal system, and the institutions for producing, disseminating, and criticizing art represent enduring possibilities of hypothetically examining the truth of statements, the rightness of actions and norms, or the authenticity of expressions, and of productively assimilating our negative experiences in these dimensions. Through this connection with cultural traditions and social institutions the concept of communicative action becomes serviceable for social theory.

At the same time, the turn to the sociocultural matrix of individual action orientations brings Habermas face to face with the cultural and historical variability of lifeworld structures. If the variety of worldviews and forms of life entails an irreducible plurality of standards of rationality, then the concept of communicative rationality could not claim universal significance and a theory of society constructed upon it would be limited from the start to a particular perspective. Habermas deals with this problem from a number of different angles. In section 2 of Chapter I he highlights the types of structural differences in question through a comparison of "mythical and modern ways of understanding the world." Then, in a careful reconstruction of the recent rationality debates among English anthropologists and philosophers, he argues that the case for relativism is by no means conclusive. In the end, the claim that the concept of communicative rationality has universal significance can be decided only by the empirical-theoretical fruitfulness of the research programs based on it—in different domains from the construction of a formal pragmatics of language and the reconstruction of the ontogenesis of communicative competence to the development of theories of anthropogenesis and social evolution.[6]

This last line of inquiry is one of Habermas's principal preoccupations in the present work, particularly in the form of the question, whether and in what respects modernization can be viewed as rationalization. This question has dominated concept and theory formation in modern sociology: "Sociology arose as the theory of bourgeois society; to it fell the task of explaining the course of the capitalist modernization of traditional societies and its anomic side effects. This problem...was the reference point from which sociology worked up its foundations as well. On a *metatheoretical* level, it chose basic concepts [of action theory] that were tailored to the growth of rationality in the modern lifeworld...On a *methodological* level, the problem of gaining access to the object domain of symbolic objects through understanding (*Verstehen*) was dealt with accordingly: Understanding rational action orientations became the reference point for understanding all action orientations...Finally, [these concerns] were connected with the *empirical* question, whether and in what respects the modernization of society can be described from the standpoint of cultural and societal rationalization" (1:5-6).

Habermas wants to argue that this is no historical accident, that any sociology that aspires to a general theory of society has to confront the rationality problematic on all three levels. His own contributions on the meta- or action-theoretical level can be found here in Chapters I and III; they issue in a theory of communicative action that is further developed in Chapters V (Mead and Durkheim) and VI (Lifeworld and System) of Volume 2, and is elaborated and shaded throughout the book. The methodology of *Sinnverstehen* and its relation to the rationality of action is the explicit theme of section 4 of Chapter I; it is the implicit theme of the discussion of the internal relation between meaning and validity in Chapter III; and it turns up repeatedly in the reconstruction of classical approaches to social inquiry. Finally, the question of how to comprehend modernity, and in particular the capitalist modernization of society, dominates the work as a whole. It is the axis around which the discussions of Weber and Western Marxism turn in this volume, the motivation behind the lifeworld/system discussion in Volume 2, and the central theme of the concluding chapter, in which the different lines of argument converge on a theory of modernity. I shall consider his treatment of this last question in part II below; but for now, there are several additional aspects of his views on metatheory and methodology that should be mentioned.

In section 3 of Chapter I Habermas examines four influential concepts of social action—teleological, normatively regulated, dramaturgical, and communicative action—with an eye to their presuppositions and implications regarding rationality. He argues that only the last of these fully incorporates language as a medium for reaching understanding in the negotiation of common definitions of situations: "A definition of the situation establishes an order . . . A situation definition by another party that prima facie diverges from one's own presents a problem of a peculiar sort; for in cooperative processes of interpretation no participant has a monopoly on correct interpretation. For both parties the interpretive task consists in incorporating the other's interpretation of the situation into one's own in such a way that . . . the divergent situation definitions can be brought to coincide sufficiently" (1:100). In section 4 of the same chapter Habermas goes on to develop his principal point concerning the logic of *Verstehen*. In the model of communicative action, social actors are themselves outfitted with the same interpretive capacities as social-scientific interpreters; thus the latter cannot claim for themselves the status of neutral, extramundane observers in their definitions of actors' situations. They are, whether consciously or not, virtual participants whose only plausible claim to objectivity derives from the reflective quality of their participation. But this reflexivity is in principle open to the actual participants as well; it does not exempt the social scientist from having to take a position—however reflective and however implicit—on the validity claims relevant to the definition of the situation.

> In order to understand an utterance in the paradigm case of a speech act oriented to reaching understanding, the interpreter has to be familiar with the conditions of its validity; he has to know under what conditions the validity claim linked with it is acceptable or would have to be

REASON AND THE RATIONALIZATION OF SOCIETY

acknowledged by a hearer. But where could the interpreter obtain this knowledge if not from the context of the observed communication or from comparable contexts?. . . Thus the interpreter cannot become clear about the semantic content of an expression independently of the action contexts in which participants react to the expression with a "yes" or "no" or an abstention. And he does not understand these yes/no positions if he cannot make clear to himself the implicit reasons that move the participants to take the positions they do. . . But if, in order to understand an expression, the interpreter must bring to mind the reasons with which a speaker would, if necessary and under suitable conditions, defend its validity, he is himself drawn into the process of assessing validity claims. For reasons are of such a nature that they cannot be described in the attitude of a third person. . . One can understand reasons only to the extent that one understands why they are or are not sound (1:115-16).

This very strong claim, which supports the methodological thesis that "communicative action requires an interpretation that is rational in approach," is grounded at another level in Chapter III. There Habermas attempts to expand the truth-conditional approach to semantics into a general theory of the internal relationships between meaning and validity. This involves shifting the level of analysis from semantics to pragmatics, extending the concept of validity to include types of claims other than truth, identifying the validity conditions for the different types of claims, and establishing that, in these other cases as well, the meaning of an utterance is inherently connected with the conditions for redeeming the validity claims raised by it. If these methodological and language-theoretical arguments for the inseparability of meaning, intelligibility, and understanding from validity, rationality, and assessment could be sustained, Habermas would have gone a long way toward setting the foundations of a *critical* social theory.

In any case, because the object domain of social inquiry is symbolically prestructured, antecedently constituted by the interpretive activities of its members, the social scientist can gain access to social objects only via *Sinnverstehen* or interpretive understanding—be these "objects" social actions themselves, their sedimentations in texts, traditions, cultural artifacts and the like, or such organized configurations as institutions, systems, and structures. On the other hand, social reality is not exhausted by the ideas embodied in it; and these ideas change in response to forces and factors that cannot be explained in terms of inner logic. It is with this duality in mind that Weber, for instance, adopted his two-sided approach to the study of modernization: "from above," that is, with a view to the ideas embodied in cultural value spheres, in personality structures, and in social institutions; and "from below," with a view to the empirical factors that condition this embodiment—such as the interests and conflicts of interest of relevant social groups, the organization of authority and the struggle for political power, the process and problems of economic reproduction, and so on.

Habermas is also interested in developing an approach to social research that combines "internalist" and "externalist" perspectives. This methodological concern is in fact one of the central motifs of the lifeworld/system discussion that occupies so much of Volume 2. We shall be considering that discussion below; at present it is important to note that the internalist side of Habermas's two-level approach turns essentially on the related notions of *developmental logic* and *learning process.* As he did earlier in *Communication and the Evolution of Society,* he argues here that changes in social structure cannot be comprehended solely from the outside, in terms of external, contingent factors; there are features of social evolution that must be understood as advances in different types of "knowledge." While learning processes "have to be explained with the help of empirical mechanisms," they are "conceived at the same time as problem solutions" that can be internally reconstructed, that is, "insightfully recapitulated from the perspective of participants" (1:66-67). It is, in fact, this combination of conceptual and empirical analysis that distinguishes the disciplines which now lay claim to the heritage of philosophy as a theory of rationality.

> Philosophical thought that has surrendered the relation to totality loses its self-sufficiency. The goal of formally analyzing the conditions of rationality can be connected neither with ontological hopes . . . nor with transcendental-philosophical hopes. All attempts at discovering ultimate foundations, in which the intentions of First Philosophy live on, have broken down. In this situation, the way is opening up to a new constellation of philosophy and the sciences. As can be seen [for example] in the history and philosophy of science, formal explications of the conditions of rationality

and empirical analysis of the embodiment and historical development of rationality structures mesh in a peculiar way. Theories of modern empirical science . . . make a normative and universalist claim . . . that can be tested against the evidence of counterexamples; and it can hold up in the end only if reconstructive theory proves itself capable of distilling out internal aspects of the history of science and, in conjunction with empirical analysis, systematically explaining the actual, narratively documented history of science . . . Cognitive developmental psychology provides [another] example of this. In the tradition of Piaget, cognitive development in the narrower sense, as well as socio-cognitive and moral development, are conceptualized as internally reconstructible sequences of stages of competences (1:2-3).[7]

Such rationally reconstructive enterprises serve Habermas as models for the type of cooperation between conceptual and empirical analysis that is required to develop an adequate theory of society. Combining the "philosophical" with the "scientific," they eschew the apriorism of traditional philosophy and advance proposals that, however universal their claims, retain the hypothetical character of conjectures open to empirical refutation. It is thus that he seeks to renew the original program of critical theory (developed in the 1930s), which Horkheimer envisioned as a form of critical social research integrating philosophy and the various human sciences in an "interdisciplinary materialism."[8] As we shall soon see, Habermas's relation to critical theory as it developed in the 1940s, epitomized by Horkheimer's and Adorno's *Dialectic of Enlightenment,* is decidedly more ambivalent.

II

The Enlightenment's belief in progress rested on an idea of reason modeled after Newtonian physics, which, with its reliable method and secure growth, was thought to provide a paradigm for knowledge in general. The impact of the advance of science on society as a whole was not envisioned in the first instance as an expansion of productive forces and a refinement of administrative techniques but in terms of its effect on the cultural context of life. In particular, the belief—for us, today, rather implausible— that progress in science was necessarily accompanied by progress in morality, was based not only on an assimilation of the logics of theoretical and practical questions but also on the historical experience of the powerful reverberations of early modern science in the spheres of religion, morals, and politics. The cultural rationalization emanating from the diffusion of scientific knowledge and its emancipatory effect on traditional habits of thought—the progressive eradication of inherited "superstitions, prejudices, errors"—formed the center of an encompassing rationalization of social life, which included a transformation of political and economic structures as well. The embodiment of reason in the political realm meant the establishment of a republican form of government with guarantees of civil liberties and an institutionally secured public sphere, so that political power could be rationalized through the medium of public discussion to reflect the general will and common interest. On the other hand, the embodiment of reason in the economic sphere meant the establishment of a social space for the free pursuit of one's own self-interest, so far as it was compatible with a like pursuit by all other individuals. The global result of this would be a continuous increase in the general wealth of society and a growing equality of the shares falling to its individual members.

The first classical social theorist Habermas discusses in this book, Max Weber, directly challenged all these tenets of the Enlightenment faith in reason and progress in ways that remain relevant for us today. In his view, the rationality that defines modernity is at bottom a *Zweckrationalität,* a purposive or means/ends rationality, the inherent aim of which is the mastery of the world in the service of human interests. As a consequence, the growth and spread of reason does not, as Enlightenment thinkers supposed it would, furnish a new, nonillusory center of meaning to modern culture. It does, to be sure, gradually dissolve traditional superstitions, prejudices and errors; but this "disenchantment of the world," as Weber calls it, does not replace traditional religious worldviews with anything that could fulfill the functions of, for instance, giving meaning and unity to life. Rather, the disenchanted world is stripped of all ethical meaning; it is devalued and objectified as the material and setting for purposive-rational pursuit of interests. The gain in control is paid for with a loss of meaning. And the control that we gain is itself value-neutral—an instrumental potential that can be harnessed from any one of an unlimited number of value perspectives. This subjectivization of "ultimate" ends means that the unity of the world has fallen to pieces. In place of the one God or the unitary ground of being, we have an irreducible plurality of competing, often irreconcilable values, and as Weber says, "over these gods and their struggles it is fate, and certainly not any "science," that holds sway"(1:246-47).

Because in the final analysis values cannot be rationally grounded but only chosen, there are at the core of life rationally unjustifiable commitments through which we *give* the disenchanted world meaning and unity. Correspondingly, the sphere of politics has to be understood as a sphere of decision and power and not of reason: Legitimacy is not a question of rational justification but of de facto acceptance of an order of authority by those subject to it;[9] and law is not an expression of rational will but a product of enactment by duly constituted authorities according to established procedures. Weber's views on economy and society are equally antithetical to Enlightenment hopes regarding the institutionalization of reason. The progress of societal rationalization was indeed well along by the end of the nineteenth century; but what this progress turned out to be, according to Weber, was the ascendency of *purposive* rationality, of technique and calculation, of organization and administration. The triumph of reason brings with it not a reign of freedom but the dominion of impersonal economic forces and bureaucratically organized administrations—a "vast and mighty cosmos" that "determines with irresistible force the lifestyles of all the individuals who are born into (it)" (1:247). Nor would the advent of socialism improve the situation; it would, says Weber, merely mean the final and complete victory of bureaucracy. The realization of reason that the eighteenth-century philosophers envisioned as a Kingdom of God on earth has turned out to be an "iron cage" in which we are henceforth condemned to live. Disenchantment and rationalization are irreversible, as are the loss of meaning and the loss of freedom that accompany them.

The undeniable power of this analysis has, of course, often been harnessed for conservative purposes. What interests Habermas, however, is the immediate and profound impact it had on Western Marxism from Lukacs onwards. Writing in the early 1940s, Max Horkheimer and Theodor Adorno surrendered, in effect, to the force of Weber's diagnosis. The rise of fascism in Europe, with the complicity of some segments of the working class; the degeneration of socialism into Stalinism, with its bloody suppression of any dissent from party rule; and the apparently seamless integration of the American populace, including the working class, into what appeared to be a thoroughly commodified and totally administered society—left them, they felt, no realistic basis for hope. In analyzing this hopeless situation, Horkheimer and Adorno keyed in on a factor that Weber had singled out: the spread of formal, means/ends rationality, which they called instrumental reason. In doing so, they completely revised Marx's positive evaluation of scientific-technological progress. What for him represented an unambiguously emancipatory potential, for them was the core of a domination generalized to all spheres of life. Subjects who, in Horkheimer's words, "have to form themselves, body and soul, in relation to the technical apparatus" are no longer potential subjects of revolution (1:353). This was empirically borne out by the collapse of the revolutionary labor movement in all industrial societies and by the disappearance of the proletariat into the pores of consumer society. Thus the scientific-technological progress that Marx connected with the unleashing of productive forces and the overthrow of capitalism had for Horkheimer and Adorno the ironic effect of immobilizing the very subjective forces that were supposed to accomplish this overthrow. As Horkheimer put it, "All life today tends to be increasingly subjected to rationalization and planning . . . The individual's self-preservation presupposes his adjustment to the requirements for the preservation of the system" (1:353). Given this pessimistic diagnosis, it is not surprising that they saw little hope of changing things. Critical theory became resignative, contemplative. It could, at best, disclose the unreason at the heart of what passes for reason, without offering any positive account of its own.

In Habermas's view, the dead end in which critical theory thus found itself is by no means unavoidable. To avoid it requires, however, a fundamental shift of paradigm away from the philosophy of consciousness, in which the critique of rationalization as reification from Lukacs to Adorno remained rooted in spite of itself. There are two steps to this shift: first a move from the (monological) teleological concept of action to the concepts of communicative action and lifeworld; and second a joining of the lifeworld perspective to that of systems theory. In Chapter V, which opens Volume 2, Habermas approaches these tasks through a consideration of the work of George Herbert Mead and Emile Durkheim. In the former he finds the essential elements of a communications-theoretic reformulation of social-action theory; in the latter, the lineaments of a theory that links social integration with system integration.

There is no need here for a detailed summary of his splendid discussion of Mead. In essence, he uses the theory of communication developed in Volume 1 to reconstruct Mead's account of the conceptual or logical genesis of self and society; and this reconstruction in turn makes that theory serviceable for sociological analysis. Along the way, one finds another twist in the critique of strictly individualistic models of social action. Habermas argues that individuation processes are simultaneously socialization processes (and conversely), that motivations and repertoires of behavior are symbolically restructured in the course of identity formation, that individual intentions and interests, desires and feelings are not essentially private but tied to language and culture and thus inherently susceptible of interpretation, discussion and change. At the end, one finds an attempt to explicate the ideas of freedom and reconciliation that Adorno alluded to without being able to elaborate in a categorial framework still tied to the philosophy of the subject. The explication draws heavily upon the theory of communicative rationality, particularly on the ideas of a rationally binding force that accrues to illocutionary acts by virtue of their internal connection with reasons, and the corresponding possibility of intersubjective recognition based on insight rather than on external force. Habermas maintains that this utopian perspective is ingrained in the very conditions of the communicative sociation of individuals, is built into the linguistic medium of the reproduction of the species. He supports this thesis by reconstructing Mead's notion of universal discourse. "Reconciliation" is fleshed out in terms of an intersubjectivity based on mutual understanding and free recognition; "freedom" in terms of an identity that takes shape within the structures of such an intact intersubjectivity—sociation without repression.[10] This approach aims to integrate the universalism of ethical notions of rational self-determination (e.g., Kant's categorical imperative) with the particularism of psychological notions of self-realization.

> The idea [of universal discourse] actually contains two utopian projections...Imagine individuals being socialized as members of such an ideal community; they would be acquiring identities with two complementary aspects: the universal and the particular. On the one hand...they would learn to orient themselves within a universalistic framework, that is, to act autonomously [in Kant's sense]; on the other

hand, they would learn to use this autonomy—which makes them equal to every other morally acting subject—in order to develop themselves in their subjectivity and uniqueness. Mead ascribes both autonomy and the power of spontaneous self-development to persons who, as participants in universal discourse, free themselves from the fetters of habitual concrete forms of life. Membership in such an ideal community is, in Hegel's terms, constitutive for both the I as universal and the I as individual (2:148).

To put this another way, Habermas is after a notion of ego identity that centers around the ability to realize *oneself* under conditions of *communicatively shared intersubjectivity.* The moment of universality requires that actors maintain a reflective relation to their own affective and practical natures, that is, that they act in a self-critical attitude.[11]

For all its groundbreaking insights, Mead's account of the genesis of behavior mediated by language and guided by norms suffers from several major deficiencies. He reconstructs the development of role behavior from the ontogenetic perspective of the growing child; particularly in his account of the transition to the final stage, he neglects the phylogenetic line of questioning, presupposing on the part of the adults the level of role behavior to be acquired by the child. The crucial mechanism in this transition then is the child's "taking the attitude of the generalized other" toward itself. What remains inadequately accounted for is precisely the genesis of this generalized other. Habermas undertakes to complete the picture by exploiting the affinities with Durkheim's idea of a collective consciousness that is constitutive for group identity. But even if Mead's reconstructive account is filled out in this way, it can be only part of the explanation: developmental logic has to be supplemented by developmental dynamics. Mead does not give adequate consideration to the external factors that influence the actual course of development; he does not give the functional aspects equal play with the structural aspects; he generally neglects the constraints that issue from the material reproduction of society and reach right into the action orientations of sociated individuals. In attempting to make good this deficiency, Habermas looks first to Durkheim's account of how the forms of social solidarity change with the division of labor and then to Talcott Parsons' theory of the social system.

In his study of "The Elementary Forms of Religious Life" Durkheim suggests that the moral authority of social norms has its roots in the sacred. The oldest sacred symbols express a normative consensus that is established and regenerated in ritual practice. This ritually secured and symbolically mediated normative consensus is the archaic core of collective identity—in Mead's terms, of the generalized other. Accordingly, the task of explaining the phylogenesis of the generalized other becomes that of providing an account of the structural transformation of that archaic fund of social solidarity formed in the medium of religious symbolism and interpreted in the semantics of the sacred. The guiding thread in Habermas's account is "the linguistification of the sacred" (*die Versprachlichung des Sakralen*): "To the degree that the rationality potential ingrained in communicative action is set free, the archaic core of the normative dissolves and gives way to the rationalization of worldviews, the universalization of law and morality, and accelerated processes of individuation. It is upon this evolutionary trend that Mead bases his idealistic projection of a communicatively rationalized society" (2:74–75).

Taking Durkheim's analysis of the shift from mechanical to organic solidarity as his point of departure, Habermas examines the process whereby social functions originally fulfilled by ritual practice and religious symbolism gradually shift to the domain of communicative action. This disenchantment means a growing sublimation of the spellbinding and terrifying power of the sacred (*die bannende Kraft des Heiligen*) into the rationally binding/bonding force of criticizable claims to validity (*die bindinde Kraft kritisierbarer Geltungsansprüche*). In virtue of this "communicative liquifaction" of the basic religious consensus, the structures of action oriented to reaching understanding become more and more effective in cultural reproduction, social integration, and personality formation. The authority of tradition is increasingly open to discursive questioning; the range of applicability of norms expands while the latitude for interpretation and the need for reasoned justification increases; the differentiation of individual identities grows, as does the sphere of personal autonomy. Consequently, the conditions of communicative rationality, of rationally motivated intersubjective recognition of norms, gain greater empirical significance for processes of societal reproduction. "The continuation of traditions, the maintenance of legitimate orders, and the continuity of the life histories of individual persons become more and more dependent on attitudes that point in problematic cases to yes/no positions on criticizable validity claims (2:164). As Habermas sums up, the linguistification of the sacred means a rationalization of the lifeworld.[12]

The idea of the lifeworld is introduced as a necessary complement to the concept of communicative action. It links that concept firmly to the concept of society; and by directing our attention to the "context-forming horizon" of social action, it takes us another step away from the subjectivistic biases of modern social theory. Moreover, it makes it possible to construe rationalization primarily as a transformation of implicitly known, taken-for-granted structures of the lifeworld rather than of explicitly known, conscious orientations of action.

Habermas announces his basic approach to the lifeworld theme in the introductory chapter of Volume 1; but it is only in Volume 2, in the second *Zwischenbetrachtung*, that the concept of the "lifeworld" is determined more precisely, distinguished from that of "system," and integrated with it in a two-level concept of society. The specification of the concept proceeds by way of a review, critique, and synthesis of existing approaches. The guiding intention behind this tour de force is to capture the structural complexity of the lifeworld and to show how it is symbolically produced and reproduced through the medium of communicative action. Habermas criticizes existing approaches as typically "selective," "one-sided." The phenomenological approach stemming from Husserl and Schutz suffers from a "culturalistic abridgement," that is, an overemphasis on the reproduction and renewal of cultural knowledge and a relative neglect of the formation and transformation of group memberships and personal identities. In the tradition going back to Durkheim and Parsons, the concept appears with an "institutionalistic bias" in which the aspect of social integration predominates. And the symbolic interactionism inspired by Mead tends to treat the lifeworld from the standpoint of socialization, primarily as a sociocultural milieu for the self-formative processes in which individuals are involved through role playing, role taking, and so on.

Habermas seeks to develop a multidimensional concept of the lifeworld in which these different aspects are integrated; the key to his construction is the multidimensionality of the communicative action through which the lifeworld is symbolically

reproduced. He begins his discussion by examining phenomenological notions of the *Lebenswelt* as the ever-present *horizon*
of social action, as its *Verweisungszusammenhang,* as the taken-
for-granted *background* that is "always already" there when we
act. Finding these formulations still too strongly tied to the
philosophy of consciousness, he turns to reformulations in which
the lifeworld is represented as a "culturally transmitted and linguistically organized stock of interpretive patterns." In the form
of "language" and "culture" this reservoir of implicit knowledge
supplies actors with unproblematic background convictions upon
which they draw in the negotiation of common definitions of
situations. Individuals cannot "step out" of their lifeworlds; nor
can they objectify them in a supreme act of reflection. Particular
segments of the lifeworld relevant to given action situations can,
of course, be problematized; but this always takes place against
an indeterminate and inexhaustible background of other unques-
tioned presuppositions, a shared global preunderstanding that
is prior to any problems or disagreements.[13]

Even when reformulated in communication-theoretic terms,
the phenomenological concept of the lifeworld is inadequate. To
begin with, it retains a culturalistic bias. The taken-for-granted
background of social action comprises norms and subjective experiences, social practices and individual skills , as well as cultural
convictions. Not only culture but also institutional orders and
personality structures should be seen as basic components of the
lifeworld.

To develop a more adequate framework Habermas returns
to the communicative practice of everyday life, the medium of
symbolic reproduction:

> In coming to an understanding with one another about their
> situation, participants in communication stand in a cultural
> tradition which they use and at the same time renew; in coor-
> dinating their actions via intersubjective recognition of
> criticizable validity claims, they rely on memberships in
> social groups and at the same time reinforce the integration
> of the latter; through participating in interaction with compe-
> tent reference persons, growing children internalize the
> value orientations of their social groups and acquire gen-
> eralized capabilities for action . . . Under the functional aspect
> of *reaching understanding* communicative action serves the
> transmission and renewal of cultural knowledge; under the
> aspect of *coordinating action,* it serves social integration and

the establishment of group solidarity; under the aspect of *socialization,* it serves the formation of personal identities (2:208).

Thus, to the different structural components of the lifeworld (culture, society, personality) there correspond reproduction processes (cultural reproduction, social integration, socialization) based on the different aspects of communicative action (understanding, coordination, sociation), which are rooted in the structural components of speech acts (propositional, illocutionary, expressive). These structural correspondences permit communicative action to perform its different functions and to serve as a suitable medium for the symbolic reproduction of the lifeworld. When these functions are interfered with, there arise disturbances in the reproduction process and corresponding crisis manifestations: loss of meaning, withdrawal of legitimation, confusion of orientations, anomie, destabilization of collective identities, alienation, psychopathologies, breakdowns in tradition, withdrawal of motivation.[14]

Habermas argues that the concept of communicative action and the lifeworld concept developed as a complement to it can serve as basic categories of general social theory: They establish the framework within which concrete historical lifeworlds vary. Although these structural limitations tell us nothing about the dynamics of development, they do account for the developmental-logical effect of a *directional variation* in the structures of the lifeworld. The "linguistification of the sacred" can be internally reconstructed as a learning process in which the "prejudgemental power" of the lifeworld over the communicative practice of everyday life progressively diminishes, in the sense that communicative actors increasingly owe their mutual understanding to their own interpretive accomplishments, to their own yes/no positions on criticizable validity claims. This involves a growing differentiation of lifeworld structures and of the processes through which they are maintained, a sharper separation of questions of content from those of form or procedure, and a "reflective refraction" of processes of symbolic reproduction (e.g., in science, law, art, democratic institutions, educational systems).

For questions of developmental dynamics, on the other hand, we have to turn to contingent historical conditions, particularly to the interdependence of sociocultural transformations on the one hand, and changes in the form of material reproduction on the other. Once again Durkheim furnishes important clues, in this case through his study of how the growing "division of labor" is connected with changing forms of social solidarity and why it leads in the modern period to symptoms of social disintegration. From this point of departure Habermas seeks to reconstruct a Marxist approach that traces pathological forms of symbolic reproduction not to the rationalization of the lifeworld itself (as do conservative critics of bourgeois culture) but to constraints issuing from processes of material reproduction. The key to his reconstruction is the distinction between lifeworld and system, which he presents as a distinction between two fundamentally different ways of approaching the study of society.

From one point of view, society is conceptualized as the lifeworld of a social group in which actions are coordinated through harmonizing action orientations. From another point of view, society is conceptualized as a self-regulating system in which actions are coordinated through functional interconnections of action consequences. Habermas considers either of these conceptual strategies, taken by itself, to be one-sided. The theory of society requires a combination of the two—of the internalist perspective of the participant with the externalist perspective of the observer, of hermeneutic and structuralist analysis with systems-theoretic and functionalist analysis, of the study of social integration with the study of system integration. Because social action is symbolically mediated, structural patterns of action systems that are integral to their continued existence have to be grasped hermeneutically; we have to understand and reconstruct the meaning of symbolic structures. Moreover, the self-maintenance of *social* systems is subject to internal limitations resulting from the "inner logic" of symbolic reproduction. For the medium of such reproduction is communicative action; therefore, the validity claims built into that medium, and the constraints under which they stand, have empirical significance—they are social facts. On the other hand, the lifeworld approach, taken by itself, runs the risk of a "hermeneutic idealism" that conceptualizes society from the perspective of participants and remains blind to causes, connections, and consequences that lie beyond the horizon of everyday practice. It implicitly relies on such idealizing fictions as the autonomy of actors, the independence of culture, and the transparency of communicative interaction—that is, the absence of systematic distortions. In this perspective the reproduction of society appears to be only a question of maintaining the symbolic structures of the lifeworld; processes of material reproduction, through which the social system secures its physical existence in relation to nature and to other social systems, fade into the background.

To remedy both forms of one-sidedness, Habermas proposes that we combine the two perspectives and conceive of society as a "system that has to satisfy the conditions of maintenance of sociocultural lifeworlds," or as a "systemically stabilized nexus of action of socially integrated groups." The key to this two-level construction is a *methodological objectification* of the lifeworld as a boundary-maintaining system.

> The material reproduction of the lifeworld cannot be represented as the intended result of collective labor. Normally it takes place as the fulfillment of latent functions that go beyond the action orientations of participants...These reflections suggest a change of method and of conceptual perspective, namely an objectivating view of the lifeworld as a system...Survival imperatives require a functional integration of the lifeworld that takes effect in and through the symbolic structures of the lifeworld and cannot be grasped directly from the perspective of participants. It calls instead for a counterintuitive analysis from the standpoint of an observer who objectivates the lifeworld. From this *methodological point of view* we can separate the two aspects under which the integration problems of a society can be analyzed. Whereas social integration presents itself as part of the symbolic reproduction of the lifeworld—which depends not only on the reproduction of memberships (or solidarities) but also on cultural traditions and socialization processes—functional integration amounts to a material reproduction of the lifeworld that can be conceived as system maintenance. The transition from one problem area to the other is tied to a change of methodological attitude and conceptual apparatus. Functional integration only comes into view when the lifeworld is objectified as a boundary-maintaining system" (2:348–49).[15]

Neither point of view is merely a point of view; each is a response to something in the social object, in the one case to the fundamentally symbolic nature of social action, in the other to the latent functions it fulfills. The lifeworld perspective enjoys a certain priority, as it corresponds to the basic structures of a communicatively mediated reality—and it is at least conceptually possible for all of the functions of action to be manifest, that is, perceptible within the horizon of the lifeworld. On the other hand, the course of social evolution itself has enhanced the importance of the system perspective: Functions of material reproduction have increasingly shifted to mechanisms (e.g., the market) that are differentiated off from the lifeworld and require the counterintuitive approach of systems theory.

In section 2 of his second set of intermediate reflections (Chapter VI), Habermas presents a view of social evolution as a two-level process of differentiation. On one level, there is a growing differentiation between the lifeworld and system aspects of society, a "decoupling of system and lifeworld." The mechanisms of functional integration are increasingly detached from the lifeworld structures responsible for social integration, until, as Weber diagnosed, they congeal into quasi-autonomous subsystems of economic and administrative activity. On another level, there is a progressive differentiation within the dimensions of lifeworld and system themselves. We have discussed the former under the rubric "the rationalization of the lifeworld"; the latter takes the form of newly emerging systemic mechanisms that make possible higher levels of system complexity and enhance society's capacity to steer itself. The two levels do not simply lie parallel to one another, they are interconnected: systemic mechanisms have to be anchored in the lifeworld, that is, institutionalized. More specifically, the rationalization of the lifeworld—particularly of law and morality—is a necessary condition for the institutionalization of new mechanisms of system integration—in the modern era, of formally organized subsystems of purposive-rational economic and administrative action.

The material reproduction of society requires that the purposive activities of different individuals be effectively coordinated. To the extent that economy of effort and efficacy of means are measures of success, there is pressure in the direction of a cooperative division of labor, that is, a functional specification of activities with a corresponding differentiation of their results or products. This requires in turn that these activities be somehow coordinated and these products be somehow exchanged. "The competent combination of specialized performances requires a delegation of the authority to direct, or of *power*, to persons who take on the tasks of organization; and the functional exchange of products requires the establishment of exchange relations" (2:239). Thus the division of labor goes hand in hand with the development of organizational power and exchange relations. In tribal societies this transpires through institutions that are still linked to social integration—for example, status differentiations based on sex, generation, and ancestry; the circulation of goods via marriage relations; the reciprocity of services built into the normative requirements of social roles; and the ritual exchange of valuable objects. This interlocking of system and social integration gives way in the course of social evolution to a gradual separation of mechanisms that serve to heighten system complexity and adaptive capacity from those mechanisms that secure the social solidarity of collectives via normative consensus and the achievement of mutual understanding. Systemic mechanisms become less tied to pregiven social structures, such as kinship relations; they are increasingly linked to spheres of action that are already functionally specified—for example, the organization of exchange relations in a market economy, the institutionalization of political power in the modern state. As these spheres become increasingly independent of the normative structures of the lifeworld, they assume the form of quasi-autonomous subsystems.

One of the preconditions for this development is a "postconventional" level of moral and legal consciousness—at which values and norms are generalized and social action is released from concrete traditional patterns of behavior, at which distinctions are drawn between contexts of instrumental or strategic action and those that rest on or aim at normative consensus. As the rationalization of the lifeworld progresses, so does the risk of disagreement among the parties to interaction. The less the need for mutual understanding is covered in advance by traditions that pre-decide which validity claims are to be recognized, the greater the burden placed on actors themselves to achieve common definitions of situations, and the greater the danger of deficits or failures in coordination. Different types of mechanisms have developed for reducing these risks by reducing the burden placed on communicative action. One type in particular is basic to the structure of modern society: The medium for coordinating action in certain domains has changed over from language to "delinguistified" steering media. By decoupling action in certain ways from yes/no responses to validity claims, these media neutralize the usual lifeworld requirements for consensus formation. They "encode" certain forms of purposive-rational activity, symbolically generalize certain categories of rewards and punishments, and make it possible to exercise strategic influence on action by nonlinguistic means. Further, media-steered interactions can link up in more and more complex functional networks, without anyone commanding an overview of the latter or being responsible for them. The clearest instance of such a medium is money.

With the advent of capitalism the economy was differentiated out as a functionally specified subsystem by the institutionalization of money in bourgeois civil law, particularly property and contract law. This meant a monetarization not only of the relations of different economic units among themselves, but also of the exchange relations between the economy and its noneconomic environments:

> The institutionalization of wage labor and of the modern tax-based state was just as constitutive of the new mode of production as the rise of the capitalist enterprise. Only when money became an intersystemic medium of exchange did it produce structure-forming effects. The economy could constitute itself as a monetarily steered subsystem only to the extent that it regulated its exchange with its social environments through the medium of money. Complementary environments were formed as production was converted to wage labor and the state apparatus was connected back to production through the taxes of the employed. The government apparatus became dependent on the media-steered economic subsystem; this forced it to reorganize in such a way that political power took on the structure of a steering medium—it was assimilated to money (2:256).

As this last sentence indicates, Habermas wants to treat power as a second steering medium, through which government administration also takes the shape of a subsystem decoupled in important respects from the lifeworld. Reviewing Parsons's media theory, he examines the analogies and the disanalogies between money and other claimed steering media. In the case of power, he finds that despite the undeniable differences— for instance, the exercise of power is typically tied to positions in hierarchical organizations and requires legitimation (and thus is more susceptible to risks of disagreement and more

dependent on consensus at another level)—there are sufficient similarities to warrant treating it as a steering medium.
In the other cases, he argues, the structural analogies are so vague
and the conceptual determinations so imprecise as tó render the
use of the term "medium" almost metaphorical. Specifically, he
argues that subsystems can be differentiated out by way of
steering media only for functions of material reproduction and
not for those of symbolic reproduction; the latter cannot be
"mediatized" without sociopathological results.[16]

With this contrast between the lifeworld and those domains
of social interaction that are formally organized and steered by
media, we are in a position to sketch Habermas's account of
modernity. It turns on the following alternative:

> From the mere fact that system integration and social inte-
> gration become largely decoupled, we cannot yet infer linear
> dependencies in one or the other direction. Both are
> conceivable: the institutions that anchor steering mechan-
> isms like money and power in the lifeworld might channel
> either the influence of the lifeworld on formally organized
> domains of action or, conversely, the influence of the system
> on communicatively structured contexts of action. In one
> case they would function as the institutional framework that
> subordinated system maintenance to the normative restric-
> tions of the lifeworld, in the other case as the basis that
> subordinated the lifeworld to the systemic constraints of
> material reproduction (2:275–76).

Habermas attributes the "paradoxes of modernity" to the pre-
dominance of the latter state of affairs (despite the promise of
democracy to ensure the opposite): "The rationalized lifeworld
makes possible the rise and growth of subsystems whose independent imperatives strike back at it in a destructive fashion"
(2:277). It is not the competition between mechanisms of system
and social integration nor the "interference" thereby produced
that is per se pathological. The "mediatization of the lifeworld"
turns into a "colonization of the lifeworld" only when symbolic
reproduction is at stake, that is, when systemic mechanisms drive
out mechanisms of social integration from domains in which they
cannot be replaced.

The principal points of reference for Habermas's theory
of modernity are Marx and Weber. He alternately characterizes

his approach as a "second attempt to appropriate Weber in the spirit of Western Marxism," a "reformulation of the reification problematic in terms of systemically induced lifeworld pathologies" and as a reconstruction and generalization of Marx's analysis of the "real abstraction" involved in the transformation of concrete labor into the abstract commodity "labor power." The phenomena Weber pointed to in his vision of an "iron cage" and Marxists have dealt with in terms of "reification" are here traced back to the exchange relations between system and lifeworld that crystallize in the roles of employee and consumer, citizen and client of the state. Through these channels the lifeworld is subordinated to system imperatives, moral-practical elements are driven out of the private and public spheres, and everyday life is increasingly "monetarized" and "bureaucratized." To the extent that the economic system subjects private households, employees, and consumers to its imperatives,

> consumerism and possessive individualism, motives of performance and competition gain the force to shape conduct. The communicative practice of everyday life is one-sidedly rationalized into a specialist-utilitarian lifestyle; and this media-induced shift to purposive-rational action orientations calls forth the reaction of a hedonism freed from the pressures of rationality. As the private sphere is undermined and eroded by the economic system, so is the public sphere by the administrative system. The bureaucratic disempowering and dessication of spontaneous processes of opinion- and will-formation expands the scope for mobilizing mass loyalty and makes it easier to decouple political decisions from concrete, identity-forming contexts of life (2:480).

Whereas "reification" can be traced back to the colonization of the lifeworld—the subversion of socially integrated spheres of symbolic reproduction and their assimilation into formally organized domains of economic and bureaucratic action—parallel phenomena of "cultural impoverishment" are a consequence of the professionalization that has increasingly separated the development of expert cultures from the communicative infrastructure of everyday life. Processes of mutual understanding are cut off from important cultural resources, while the blind, naturelike traditions upon which everyday practice still draws steadily dry up.

This reappropriation of Weber's reflections on the paradoxes of rationalization does not in itself account for the dynamics behind the colonization process. For this, Habermas turns again to Marx, particularly to his analysis of the dual character of labor in capitalist society. As a concrete action it belongs to the lifeworld of the producer; as an abstract performance organized according to imperatives of capital realization it belongs to the economic system. The commodification of labor power via the institutionalization of the wage-labor relation neutralizes the lifeworld context of labor and renders it abstract. As the Marxian analysis of "real abstraction" relates problems of system integration (crises of capital accumulation) to problems of social integration (class struggle), it restricts itself to what is, on Habermas's view, only one—however central—case of a more general phenomenon: the subordination of the lifeworld to systemic imperatives. He argues here, as he did earlier in *Legitimation Crisis,* that the economy cannot be treated as a closed system; to begin with, it is essentially interconnected with an administrative subsystem that fulfills market-complementing and market-replacing functions. Problems arising in the process of capital accumulation can be transferred to the political system and dealt with administratively; conversely, problems arising in the political sphere can be dealt with through the distribution of economically produced values. Thus Habermas proposes a model of two complementary subsystems that are based on two different media and involved in exchange relations with both the private and public spheres of the lifeworld. He seeks to demonstrate that this model can make good the failure of orthodox Marxism to comprehend central features of advanced capitalism—in particular, government interventionism, mass democracy, and the social-welfare state. In developed capitalist societies, class conflict has been "institutionalized" and the world of labor "tamed" through a "normalization" of occupational roles and an enhancement of consumer roles; the political realm has been "pacified" through "neutralizing" the possibilities for political participation opened up with the universalized role of citizen and inflating the role of the client of the state. "The burdens that result from institutionalizing an alienated mode of political participation are shifted to the role of client, just as the burdens of normalizing alienated labor are shifted to that of consumer" (2:515). Both are paid for in the coin of economically produced value. As long as capital continues to expand under political protection, as long as there is an adequate supply of compensatory use-values that can be channeled into the roles of consumer and client, economic and political alienation does not develop explosive force.

But social-welfare state, mass democracy is an arrangement marked by structural dilemmas and beset by crisis tendencies (as Habermas elaborated in *Legitimation Crisis,* albeit from a somewhat different perspective). In particular, the inner dynamic of capitalist growth means a continuous increase in systemic complexity, an expansion of the "monetary-bureaucratic complex" into ever new areas of life. This leads to conflicts within the lifeworld when communicatively structured domains of action are transformed into formally organized domains—a process that takes the form of *Verrechtlichung,* juridification or legal regulation.[17] For purposes of illustrating the kind of empirical research relevant to his thesis of the internal colonization of the lifeworld, Habermas considers the legal regulation of communicatively structured spheres of action, in particular the social-welfare measures that are an integral part of developed capitalism. "The social-welfare policies of the state were marked from the start by the ambivalence of securing freedom on the one hand and cancelling it on the other . . . The net of social-welfare guarantees is supposed to head off the [negative] effects of a production process based on wage labor. The tighter this net is drawn, however, the more pronounced is the ambivalence . . . that results from the very structure of legal regulation. The means of guaranteeing freedom themselves threaten the freedom of those who are to benefit" (2:531). In other words, the legal-bureaucratic-monetary *form* of administratively dealing with certain problems itself works against their resolution. For one thing, it necessitates a redefinition of life situations in ways that are counterproductive.

> The situation to be regulated, which is embedded in the context of a life-history and a concrete form of life, has to be subjected to violent abstraction, not only because it has to be subsumed under the law but also in order that it can be dealt with administratively . . . Furthermore, the life risks in question [e.g. sickness, old age, unemployment] are usually met with compensation in the form of money . . . As the social-welfare state spreads the net of client relationships over private spheres of life, it increasingly produces the pathological side effects of a juridification that is simultaneously a bureaucratization and monetarization of core domains of the lifeworld. This has the structure of a

dilemma, in that the social-welfare guarantees are supposed
to serve the ends of social integration and yet they foster
the disintegration of those life contexts (2:532–34).

In this way, the increasingly complex economic-political system
penetrates ever deeper into the symbolic reproduction of the lifeworld, drawing ever-new spheres of communicatively structured
interaction into the vortex of capitalist growth.

In Habermas's view, one of the important advantages of a
critical social theory that analyzes processes of real abstraction
in this way is that it puts us in a much better position to comprehend the new potentials for conflict that now "overlie" the traditional politics of economic, social, and military security. For it
is precisely along the "seams between system and lifeworld" that
these new potentials for emancipation, resistance and withdrawal
have developed.

> In advanced Western societies conflicts have developed in
> the last ten to twenty years that deviate in various respects
> from the social-welfare-state pattern of institutionalized
> conflict over distribution. They do not flare up in areas of
> material reproduction; they are not channeled through
> parties and associations; and they are not allayed by com-
> pensations that conform to the system. Rather, these new
> conflicts arise in areas of cultural reproduction, of social inte-
> gration and of socialization; they are carried out in subinsti-
> tutional, or at least extraparliamentary, forms of protest; and
> the deficits that underlie them reflect a reification of com-
> municatively structured domains of action, which cannot be
> gotten at via the media of money and power. It is not pri-
> marily a question of compensations that the social-welfare
> state can provide, but of protecting and restoring endangered
> ways of life or of establishing reformed ways of life. In short,
> the new conflicts do not flare up around problems of dis-
> tribution but around questions concerning *the grammar of
> forms of life* (2:576).

Habermas is thinking here of such phenomena as the ecology
and antinuclear movements, the limits-to-growth debate, the
peace movement, the women's movement, experiments with
communal and rural living—with alternative lifestyles generally,
gay liberation, conflicts over regional and cultural autonomy,
protests against "big government," religious fundamentalism

and the proliferation of religious sects, the multifarious "psycho-scene," the proliferation of support groups, and the like. He maintains that a proper classification, comprehension, and assess-ment of this confusing variety of "new social movements" requires the adoption of the theoretical perspective of internal colonization. They cluster around those roles through which the imperatives of the system are channeled into the lifeworld; and they can be understood in large part as a reaction to the processes of real abstraction that are institutionalized in them.

What does all this tell us about enlightenment and the dialectic of enlightenment with which we began? Habermas is arguing, in effect, that Weber, because he construed rationaliza-tion in terms of the increasing dominance of purposive rationality, did not adequately grasp the *selectivity* of capitalist rationaliza-tion or its causes. Following him in essential respects, Horkheimer and Adorno were led to deny any trace of reason in the struc-tures and institutions of modern life. In Habermas's view, this diagnosis misinterprets the very real distortions of modernity and underestimates its equally real accomplishments and as-yet unrealized potentials. The utopian content of Enlightenment thought, to which the realities of a society delivered up to the uncontrolled dynamic of economic growth gave the lie, was certainly ideological. But it was no mere illusion:

> To the extent that the validity basis of action oriented to reaching understanding replaces the sacred bases of social interaction, there appears the form of a posttraditional everyday communication that stands on its own feet, that sets limits to the inner dynamic of independent subsystems, that bursts open encapsulated expert cultures—and thus that avoids the dangers both of reification and of desolation. Para-doxically, the rationalization of the lifeworld does both— makes possible a systemically induced reification *and* opens up the utopian perspective from which capitalist modern-ization has always been faulted for dissolving traditional forms of life without salvaging their communicative sub-stance. It destroys these life-forms but does not transform them in such a way that the interconnection of cognitive-instrumental elements with moral-practical and expressive elements, which obtained in everyday practice before it was rationalized, could be retained at a higher level of differentiation (2:486–87).

The discontents of modernity are not rooted in rationalization as such, but in the failure to develop and institutionalize all the different dimensions of reason in a balanced way. Owing to the absence of institutions that could protect the private and public spheres from the reifying dynamics of the economic and administrative subsystems, communicatively structured interaction has been increasingly pushed to the margin; due to the lack of feedback relations between a differentiated modern culture and an impoverished everyday practice, the lifeworld has become increasingly desolate. In Habermas's view, the constant attack on the communicative infrastructure of society poses a growing threat to the welfare-state compromise that obtains today in advanced capitalism. For it instrumentalizes spheres of action that have to be structured communicatively if they are to perform their functions in the reproduction of social life. The more deeply these spheres are penetrated by systemic imperatives, the greater the danger of collapse.

The continuous development and balanced institutionalization of the different aspects of reason demands a decolonization of the lifeworld, but not in the sense of insulating it altogether from processes of modernization. There is a type of rationalization proper to the lifeworld, namely an expansion of the areas in which action is coordinated by way of communicatively *achieved* agreement. A communicatively rationalized lifeworld would have to develop institutions out of itself through which to set limits to the inner dynamic of media-steered subsystems and to subordinate them to decisions arrived at in unconstrained communication. Central among these institutions are those that secure an effectively functioning public sphere, in which practical questions of general interest can be submitted to public discussion and decided on the basis of discursively achieved agreement. The Enlightenment's promise of a life informed by reason cannot be redeemed so long as the rationality that finds expression in society is deformed by capitalist modernization. Nor is its ultimate redemption guaranteed by any laws of history. It remains, as Habermas once put it, a "practical hypothesis" from which critical social theory takes its start.

Author's Preface

More than a decade ago, in the preface to *Zur Logik der Sozialwissenschaften*, I held out the prospect of a theory of communicative action. In the meantime, the methodological interest I then connected with a "language-theoretic foundation of the social sciences" has given way to a substantive interest. The theory of communicative action is not a metatheory but the beginning of a social theory concerned to validate its own critical standards. I do not conceive of my analysis of the general structures of action oriented to reaching understanding as a continuation of the theory of knowledge with other means. In this respect the action theory developed by Talcott Parsons in 1937 in *The Structure of Social Action*, with its combination of conceptual analyses and reconstructions of the history of social theory, certainly provided me with a model; at the same time, however, it led me astray because of its methodological orientation. In good Hegelian terms, the formation of basic concepts and the treatment of substantive issues belong inseparably together.

My initial expectation, that I had only to work out the Christian Gauss lectures I had delivered at Princeton University in 1971 (and which I shall publish separately), turned out to be mistaken. The deeper I penetrated into the theories of action, meaning, speech acts, and other similar domains of analytic philosophy, the more I lost sight in the details of the aim of the whole endeavor. The more I sought to satisfy the explicative claims of the philosopher, the further I moved from the interests of the sociologist, who has to ask what purpose such conceptual analysis should serve. I was having difficulty finding the right level of presentation for what I wanted to say; and, as we have known since Hegel and Marx, problems of presentation are not extrinsic to substantive problems.[1] In this situation, the advice of Thomas McCarthy, who encouraged me to make a new start, was important.

With the exception of one semester as a visiting professor in the United States, I have been writing this book in its present form, without interruption, for the last four years. The concept of communicative action is developed in the first set (Chapter III) of "Intermediate Reflections" [Zwischenbetrachtung], which provides access to three intertwined topic complexes: first, a concept of communicative rationality that is sufficiently skeptical in its development but is nevertheless resistant to cognitive-instrumental abridgments of reason; second, a two-level concept of society that connects the "lifeworld" and "system" paradigms in more than a rhetorical fashion; and finally, a theory of modernity that explains the type of social pathologies that are today becoming increasingly visible, by way of the assumption that communicatively structured domains of life are being subordinated to the imperatives of autonomous, formally organized systems of action. Thus the theory of communicative action is intended to make possible a conceptualization of the social-life context that is tailored to the paradoxes of modernity.

In the "Introduction" (Chapter I), I attempt to establish the thesis that the rationality problematic is not brought to sociology from the outside. *Every* sociology that claims to be as theory of society encounters the problem of employing a concept of rationality—which always has a normative content—at three levels: It can avoid neither the metatheoretical question concerning the rationality implications of its guiding concepts of action nor the methodological question concerning the rationality implications of gaining access to its object domain through an understanding of meaning; nor, finally, can it avoid the empirical-theoretical question concerning the sense, if any, in which the modernization of societies can be described as rationalization.

A systematic appropriation of the history of (sociological) theory helped me to find the level of integration on which the philosophical intentions unfolded from Kant through Marx can be made scientifically fruitful today. I treat Weber, Mead, Durkheim, and Parsons as classics, that is, as theorists of society who still have something to say to us. The excurses I scatter throughout these (historical-reconstructive) chapters are, like the "Introduction" and the two sets of "Intermediate Reflections" (Chapters III and VI), devoted to systematic questions. In "Concluding Reflections" (Chapter VIII) I then bring the historical and the systematic investigations together. I attempt, on the one hand, to render the proposed interpretation of modernity plausible in connection with the tendencies toward regulation by law [Verrechtlichung] and, on the other hand, to spell out the tasks with which critical theory of society is faced today.

An investigation of this kind, which uses the concept of communicative reason without blushing, is today suspect of having fallen into the snares of foundationalism. But the alleged similarities of the formal-pragmatic approach to classical transcendental philosophy lead one down the wrong trail. I would recommend that the reader who harbors this suspicion read the conclusion first.[2] We would not be able to ascertain the rational internal structure of action oriented to reaching understanding if we did not already have before us—in fragmentary and distorted form, to be sure—the existing forms of a reason that has to rely on being symbolically embodied and historically situated.[3]

The contemporary-historical motive behind the present work is obvious. Since the end of the 1960s, Western societies have been approaching a state in which the heritage of Occidental rationalism is no longer accepted without argument. The stabilization of internal conditions that has been achieved on the basis of a social-welfare-state compromise (particularly impressively, perhaps, in the Federal Republic of Germany) now exacts increasing sociopsychological and cultural costs. And we have become more conscious of the instability of the relations among the superpowers, which was temporarily repressed but never mastered. The theoretical discussion of these phenomena touches the very substance of Western traditions and inspirations.

Neoconservatives want to hold at any price to the capitalist pattern of economic and social modernization. They give highest priority to the economic growth that the social-welfare-state compromise fosters—and increasingly also constricts. They seek refuge from the socially disintegrative side effects of this growth in uprooted but rhetorically affirmed traditions of a *biedermeierlichen* culture. It is difficult to see how relocating problems that, since the end of the nineteenth century, and for good reasons, have been shifted from the market to the state—that is, how shoving problems back and forth between the media of money and power—is going to give us new impetus. It is even less plausible to attempt to renew, with an historically enlightened consciousness, the traditional padding that capitalist modernization has devoured.

Neoconservative apologetics are countered by a critique of growth—sometimes sharpened in antimodernist fashion—that is directed against the hypercomplexity of economic and administrative action systems, as well as against an arms race that has become autonomous. Experiences of the colonization of the lifeworld, which the neoconservatives want to head off and muffle in a traditionalistic manner, lead on this side to radical opposition.

When this opposition sharpens into a demand for de-differentiation at whatever price, an important distinction is lost. Restricting the growth of monetary-administrative complexity is by no means synonymous with surrendering modern forms of life. In structurally differentiated lifeworlds a potential for reason is marked out that cannot be conceptualized as a heightening of system complexity.

To be sure, these remarks touch upon only the motivational background to this work and not its actual theme.[4] I have written this book for those who have a professional interest in the foundations of social theory.

I would like to express my gratitude to Inge Pethran, who typed the different versions of the manuscript and put together the bibliography. This is only one link in a 10-year chain of close cooperation, without which I would have been helpless. I am also grateful to Ursula Hering, who helped me to obtain necessary literature, as well as to Freidhelm Herborth of Suhrkamp Verlag.

This book is based in part on courses I gave at the universities of Frankfurt, Pennsylvania, and California at Berkeley. I owe a debt of thanks to my students for stimulating discussions, and to my colleagues at these places, above all to Karl-Otto Apel, Richard Bernstein, and John Searle.

If, as I hope, my presentation has strongly discursive traits, this merely reflects the milieu of argumentation in our section of the Max Planck Institute at Starnberg. Various parts of the manuscript were discussed, in a way that was fruitful for me, at the Thursday colloquia in which Manfred Auwärter, Wolfgang Bonss, Rainer Döbert, Klaus Eder, Günter Frankenberg, Edit Kirsch, Sigrid Meuschel, Max Miller, Gertrud Nunner-Winkler, Ulrich Rödel and Ernst Tugendhat participated. To Ernst Tugendhat I am also indebted for a profusion of comments. I also learned much from discussions with colleagues who had longer stays at the Institute—Johann Paul Arnasson, Seyla Benhabib, Mark Gould, and Thomas McCarthy— or who visited us regularly—Aaron Cicourel, Helmut Dubiel, Lawrence Kohlberg, Claus Offe, Ulrich Oevermann, and Charles Taylor.

J.H.
Max Planck Institute for Social Sciences
Starnberg, August 1981

I

Introduction:
Approaches to the Problem
of Rationality

The rationality of beliefs and actions is a theme usually dealt with in philosophy. One could even say that philosophical thought originates in reflection on the reason embodied in cognition, speech, and action; and reason remains its basic theme.[1] From the beginning philosophy has endeavored to explain the world as a whole, the unity in the multiplicity of appearances, with principles to be discovered in reason—and not in communication with a divinity beyond the world nor, strictly speaking, even in returning to the ground of a cosmos encompassing nature and society. Greek thought did not aim at a theology nor at an ethical cosmology, as the great world religions did, but at an ontology. If there is anything common to philosophical theories, it is the intention of thinking being or the unity of the world by way of explicating reason's experience of itself.

In speaking this way, I am drawing upon the language of modern philosophy. But the philosophical tradition, insofar as it suggests the possibility of a philosophical worldview, has become questionable.[2] Philosophy can no longer refer to the whole of the world, of nature, of history, of society, in the sense of a totalizing knowledge. Theoretical surrogates for worldviews have been devalued, not only by the factual advance of empirical science but even more by the reflective consciousness accompanying it. With this consciousness philosophical thought has

1

withdrawn self-critically behind itself; in the question of what it can accomplish with its reflective competence *within the frame-work* of scientific conventions, it has become metaphilosophy.[3] Its theme has thereby changed, and yet it remains the same. In contemporary philosophy, wherever coherent argumentation has developed around constant thematic cores—in logic and the theory of science, in the theory of language and meaning, in ethics and action theory, even in aesthetics—interest is directed to the formal conditions of rationality in knowing, in reaching understanding through language, and in acting, both in everyday contexts and at the level of methodically organized experience or systematically organized discourse. The theory of argumentation thereby takes on a special significance; to it falls the task of reconstructing the formal-pragmatic presuppositions and conditions of an explicitly rational behavior.

If this diagnosis points in the right direction, if it is true that philosophy in its postmetaphysical, post-Hegelian currents is converging toward the point of a *theory of rationality,* how can sociology claim any competence for the rationality problematic? We have to bear in mind that philosophical thought, which has surrendered the relation to totality, also loses its self-sufficiency. To the goal of formally analyzing the conditions of rationality, we can tie neither ontological hopes for substantive theories of nature, history, society, and so forth, nor transcendental-philosophical hopes for an aprioristic reconstruction of the equipment of a nonempirical species subject, of consciousness in general. All attempts at discovering ultimate foundations, in which the intentions of First Philosophy live on, have broken down.[4] In this situation, the way is opening to a new constellation in the relationship of philosophy and the sciences. As can be seen in the case of the history and philosophy of science, formal explication of the conditions of rationality and empirical analysis of the embodiment and historical development of rationality structures mesh in a peculiar way. Theories of modern empirical science, whether along the lines of logical empiricism, critical rationalism, or constructivism, make a normative and at the same time universalistic claim that is no longer covered by fundamental assumptions of an ontological or transcendental-philosophical nature. This claim can be tested only against the evidence of counterexamples, and it can hold up in the end only if reconstructive theory proves itself capable of distilling internal aspects of the history of science and systematically explaining, in con-

junction with empirical analyses, the actual, narratively documented history of science in the context of social development.[5]
What is true of so complex a configuration of cognitive rationality
as modern science holds also for other forms of objective spirit,
that is, other embodiments of rationality, be they cognitive and
instrumental or moral-practical, perhaps even aesthetic-practical.

Empirically oriented sciences of this kind must, as regards
their basic concepts, be laid out in such a way that they can link
up with rational reconstructions of meaning constellations and
problem solutions.[6] Cognitive developmental psychology provides
an example of that. In the tradition of Piaget, cognitive
development in the narrow sense, as well as socio-cognitive and
moral development, are conceptualized as internally reconstructible sequences of stages of competence.[7] On the other
hand, if the validity claims against which we measure problem
solutions, rational-action orientations, learning levels, and the like
are reinterpreted in an empiricist fashion and defined away—as
they are in behaviorism—processes of embodying rationality
structures cannot be interpreted as learning processes in the strict
sense, but at best as an increase in adaptive capacities.

Among the social sciences sociology is most likely to link
its basic concepts to the rationality problematic. There are
historical and substantive reasons for this, as a comparison with
other disciplines will show. *Political science* had to free itself from
rational natural law; even modern natural law started from the
old-European view that represented society as a politically constituted community integrated through legal norms. The new
concepts of bourgeois formal law made it possible to proceed constructively and, from normative points of view, to project the
legal-political order as a rational mechanism.[8] An empirically
oriented political science had to dissociate itself radically from
that view. It concerned itself with politics as a societal subsystem
and absolved itself of the task of conceiving society as a whole.
In opposition to natural-law normativism, it excluded moral-
practical questions of legitimacy from scientific consideration,
or it treated them as empirical questions about descriptively
ascertainable beliefs in legitimacy. It thereby broke off relations
to the rationality problematic.

The situation is somewhat different in *political economy.* In
the eighteenth century it entered into competition with rational
natural law and brought out the independence of an action system
held together through functions and not primarily through

norms.[9] As political economy, economics still held fast at the start to the relation to society as a whole that is characteristic of crisis theories. It was concerned with questions of how the dynamic of the economic system affected the orders through which society was normatively integrated. Economics as a specialized science has broken off that relation. Now it too concerns itself with the economy as a subsystem of society and absolves itself from questions of legitimacy. From this perspective it can tailor problems of rationality to considerations of economic equilibrium and questions of rational choice.

In contrast, *sociology* originated as a discipline responsible for the problems that politics and economics pushed to one side on their way to becoming specialized sciences.[10] Its theme was the changes in social integration brought about within the structure of old-European societies by the rise of the modern system of national states and by the differentiation of a market-regulated economy. Sociology became the science of crisis par excellence; it concerned itself above all with the anomic aspects of the dissolution of traditional social systems and the development of modern ones.[11] Even under these initial conditions, sociology could have confined itself to one subsystem, as the other social sciences did. From the perspective of the history of science, the sociologies of religion and law formed the core of the new discipline in any case.

If I may—for illustrative purposes and, for the time being, without further elaboration—refer to the schema of functions proposed by Parsons, the correlations between *social-scientific disciplines* and *subsystems of society* readily emerge (*see* Figure 1).

Figure 1

	A			G
Economics	Economy		Polity	Political Science
Cultural Anthropology	Culture		Societal Community	Sociology
	L			I

A: adaptation, G: goal-attainment,
I: integration, L: pattern-maintenance

To be sure, there has been no lack of attempts to make sociology a specialized science for social integration. But it is no accident—rather a symptom—that the great social theorists I shall discuss are fundamentally sociologists. Alone among the disciplines of social science, sociology has retained its relations to problems of society as a whole. Whatever else it has become, it has always remained a theory of society as well. As a result, sociology could not, as other disciplines could, shove aside questions of rationalization, redefine them, or cut them down to small size. As far as I can see, there are two reasons for that.

The first concerns *cultural anthropology* and sociology equally. The correlation of basic functions with social subsystems conceals the fact that social interactions in the domains important to cultural reproduction, social integration, and socialization are not at all specialized in the same way as interactions in the economic and political domains of action. Both sociology and cultural anthropology are confronted with the whole spectrum of manifestations of social action and not with relatively clear-cut types of action that can be stylized to variants of purposive-rational action with regard to problems of maximizing profit or acquiring and using political power. Both disciplines are concerned with everyday practice in lifeworld contexts and must, therefore, take into account *all* forms of symbolic interaction. It is not so easy for them to push aside the basic problem of action theory and of interpretation. They encounter structures of a lifeworld that underlie the other subsystems, which are functionally specified in a different way. We shall take up below the question of how the paradigmatic conceptualizations "lifeworld" and "system" relate to one another.[12] Here I would like only to stress that the investigation of societal community and culture cannot be as easily detached from the lifeworld paradigm as the investigation of the economic and political subsystems can. That explains the stubborn connection of sociology to the theory of society.

Why it is sociology and not cultural anthropology that has shown a particular willingness to take up the problem of rationality can be understood only if we take into consideration a circumstance mentioned above. Sociology arose as the theory of bourgeois society; to it fell the task of explaining the course of the capitalist modernization of traditional societies and its anomic side effects.[13] This problem, a result of the objective historical situation, formed the reference point from which sociology worked out its foundational problems as well. On a *metatheoretical level* it chose basic concepts that were tailored to the growth of rationality in the modern lifeworld. Almost without exception, the classical figures of sociological thought attempted to lay out their action theory in such a way that its basic categories would capture the most important aspects of the transition from "community" to "society."[14] On a *methodological level* the problem of gaining access to the object domain of symbolic objects through "understanding" was dealt with correspondingly; understanding rational orientations of action became the reference point for understanding all action orientations.

This connection between (a) the *metatheoretical* question of a framework for action theory conceived with a view to the rationalizable aspects of action, and (b) the *methodological* question of a theory of interpretive understanding [*Sinnverstehen*] that clarifies the internal relation between meaning and validity (between explicating the meaning of a symbolic expression and taking a position on its implicit validity claim), was connected with (c) the *empirical* question—whether and in what sense the modernization of a society can be described from the standpoint of cultural and societal rationalization. This connection emerged with particular clarity in the work of Max Weber. His hierarchy of concepts of action is designed with an eye to the type of purposive-rational action, so that all other actions can be classified as specific deviations from this type. Weber also analyzes the method of *Sinnverstehen* in such a way that complex cases can be related to the limit case of understanding purposive-rational action; understanding action that is subjectively oriented to success requires at the same time that it be objectively evaluated as to its correctness (according to standards of *Richtigkeitstrationalität*). Finally, the connection of these conceptual and methodological decisions with Weber's central theoretical question—how Occidental rationalism can be explained—is evident.

This connection could, of course, be contingent; it could indicate merely that Weber was personally preoccupied with these problems and that this—from a theoretical point of view— contingent interest affected his theory construction down to its foundations. One has only to detach modernization processes from the concept of rationalization and to view them in *other* perspectives, so it seems, in order to free the foundations of action theory from connotations of the rationality of action and to free the methodology of interpretive understanding from a problematic intertwining of questions of meaning with questions of validity. Against that,

I would like to defend the thesis that there were compelling reasons for Weber to treat the historically contingent question of Occidental rationalism, as well as the question of the meaning of modernity and the question of the causes and side effects of the capitalist modernization of society, from the perspectives of rational action, rational conduct of life, and rationalized worldviews. I want to defend the thesis that there are systematic reasons for the interconnection of the precisely three rationality themes one finds in his work. To put it a different way, *any* sociology that claims to be a theory of society has to face the problem of rationality simultaneously on the *metatheoretical, methodological,* and *empirical* levels.

I shall begin (1) with a provisional discussion of the concept of rationality, and then (2) place this concept in the evolutionary perspective of the rise of a modern understanding of the world. After these preliminaries, I shall point out the internal connection between the theory of rationality and social theory: on the one hand, at the metatheoretical level (3) by demonstrating the rationality implications of sociological concepts of action current today; on the other hand, at the methodological level (4) by showing that similar implications follow from approaching the object domain by way of interpretive understanding. This argumentation sketch is meant to demonstrate the need for a theory of communicative action that arises when we want to take up once again, and, in a suitable way, the problematic of societal rationalization, which was largely ousted from professional sociological discussion after Weber.

1. "Rationality"—A Preliminary Specification

When we use the expression "rational" we suppose that there is a close relation between rationality and knowledge. Our knowledge has a propositional structure; beliefs can be represented in the form of statements. I shall presuppose this concept of knowledge without further clarification, for rationality has less to do with the possession of knowledge than with how speaking and acting subjects *acquire and use knowledge.* In linguistic utterances knowledge is expressed explicitly; in goal-directed actions an ability, an implicit knowledge is expressed; this know-how can in principle also be transformed into a know-that.[1] If we seek the grammatical subjects that go with the predicate expression "rational," two candidates come to the fore: persons, who have knowledge, can be more or less rational, as can symbolic expressions—linguistic and nonlinguistic, communicative or noncommunicative actions—that embody knowledge. We can call men and women, children and adults, ministers and bus conductors "rational," but not animals or lilac bushes, mountains, streets, or chairs. We can call apologies, delays, surgical interventions, declarations of war, repairs, construction plans or conference decisions "irrational," but not a storm, an accident, a lottery win, or an illness.

What does it mean to say that persons behave "rationally" in a certain situation or that their expressions can count as "rational"? Knowledge can be criticized as unreliable. The close relation between knowledge and rationality suggests that the rationality of an expression depends on the reliability of the knowledge embodied in it. Consider two paradigmatic cases: an assertion with which *A* in a communicative attitude expresses a belief and a goal-directed intervention in the world with which *B* pursues a specific end. Both embody fallible knowledge; both are attempts that can go wrong. Both expressions, the speech act and the teleological action, can be criticized. A hearer can contest the *truth* of the assertion made by *A*; an observer can dispute the anticipated *success* of the action taken by *B*. In both cases the critic refers to claims that the subjects necessarily attach to their expressions insofar as the latter are intended as assertions or as goal-directed actions. This necessity is of a conceptual nature. For *A* does not make an assertion unless he makes a truth claim for the asserted proposition *p* and therewith indicates his conviction that his statement can, if necessary, be defended. And *B* does not perform a goal-directed action, that is, he does not want to accomplish an end by it unless he regards the action planned as promising and therewith indicates his conviction that, in the given circumstances, his choice of means can if necessary be explained. As *A* claims truth for his statement, *B* claims prospects of success for his plan of action or effectiveness for the rule of action according to which he carries out this plan. To assert this effectiveness is to claim that the means chosen are suited to attain the set goal in the given circumstances. The expected effectiveness of an action stands in internal relation to the truth of the conditional prognoses implied by the plan or rule of action. As *truth* is related to the existence of states of affairs in the world, *effectiveness* is related to interventions in the world with whose help states of affairs can be brought into existence. With his assertion, *A* makes reference to something that *in fact occurs* in the objective world; with his purposive activity, *B* makes reference to something that *should occur* in the objective world. In doing so both raise *claims* with their symbolic expressions, claims that can be criticized and argued for, that is, *grounded.* The rationality of their expressions is assessed in light of the internal relations between the semantic content of these expressions, their conditions of validity, and the reasons (which could be provided, if necessary) for the truth of statements or for the effectiveness of actions.

These reflections point in the direction of basing the rationality of an expression on its being susceptible of criticism and grounding: An expression satisfies the precondition for rationality if and insofar as it embodies fallible knowledge and therewith has a relation to the objective world (that is, a relation to the facts) and is open to objective judgment. A judgment can be objective if it is undertaken on the basis of a *transsubjective* validity claim that has the same meaning for observers and nonparticipants as it has for the acting subject himself. Truth and efficiency are claims of this kind. Thus assertions and goal-directed actions are the more rational the better the claim (to propositional truth or to efficiency) that is connected with them can be defended against criticism. Correspondingly, we use the expression "rational" as a disposition predicate for persons from whom such expressions can be expected, especially in difficult situations.

This proposal to base the rationality of an expression on its criticizability has two obvious weaknesses. On the one hand, the characterization is too abstract, for it does not capture important differentiations. On the other hand, it is too narrow, because we do not use the term "rational" solely in connection with expressions that can be true or false, effective or ineffective. The rationality inherent in communicative practice extends over a broad spectrum. It refers to various forms of argumentation as possibilities of continuing communicative action with reflective means. In what follows I shall take up these points seriatim. Then, because the idea of discursively redeeming validity claims occupies so central a position in the theory of communicative action, I shall insert a lengthy excursus on the theory of argumentation.

A.—To begin with I shall keep to the cognitivist version of rationality defined exclusively with reference to the employment of descriptive knowledge. This concept can be developed in two different directions. If we start from the noncommunicative employment of knowledge in teleological action, we make a prior decision for the concept of *cognitive-instrumental rationality* that has, through empiricism, deeply marked the self-understanding of the modern era. It carries with it connotations of successful self-maintenance made possible by informed disposition over, and intelligent adaptation to, conditions of a contingent environment. On the other hand, if we start from the communicative employment of propositional knowledge in assertions, we make a prior decision for a wider concept of rationality connected with ancient conceptions of *logos*.[2] This concept of *communicative rationality* carries with it connotations based ultimately on the central experience of the unconstrained, unifying, consensus-bringing force of argumentative speech, in which different participants overcome their merely subjective views and, owing to the mutuality of rationally motivated conviction, assure themselves of both the unity of the objective world and the intersubjectivity of their lifeworld.[3]

Let the belief *p* represent an identical store of knowledge at the disposal of A and B. A (as one of several speakers) takes part in communication and puts forward the assertion *p;* B (as an isolated actor) selects means that he regards, on the basis of the belief *p*, as suited in a given situation to achieve a desired effect. *A* and *B* use the *same* knowledge in *different* ways. In one case the relation of the utterance to the facts (and its amenability to grounding) make possible an understanding among participants in communication about something that takes place in the world. It is constitutive of the rationality of the utterance that the speaker raises a criticizable validity claim for the proposition *p*, a claim that the hearer can accept or reject for good reason [*begründet*]. In the other case the relation of the rule of action to the facts (and its ability to be grounded) make possible a successful intervention in the world. It is constitutive of the action's rationality that the actor bases it on a plan that implies the truth of *p*, a plan according to which the projected end can be realized under given conditions. An assertion can be called rational only if the speaker satisfies the conditions necessary to achieve the illocutionary goal of reaching an understanding about something in the world with at least one other participant in communication. A goal-directed action can be rational only if the actor satisfies the conditions necessary for realizing his intention to intervene successfully in the world. Both attempts can fail; the consensus sought can fail to come to pass, the desired effect can fail to take place. But even the nature of these failures shows the rationality of the expressions—failures can be explained.[4]

Along both these lines the analysis of rationality can begin with the concepts of propositional knowledge and the objective world; but the cases differ in the *way* in which the knowledge is *used*. From one perspective the telos inherent in rationality appears to be *instrumental mastery*, from the other *communicative understanding*. Depending on which aspect is the focus of attention, our analysis can lead in different directions. The two positions may be briefly elucidated as follows. The first, which for the sake of simplicity I shall call the "realistic," starts from the ontological presupposition of the world as the sum total of what is the case and clarifies the conditions of rational behavior on this basis. The other, which we can call the "phenomenological," gives a transcendental twist to the question and reflects on the fact that those who behave rationally must themselves presuppose an objective world.

(a) The realist can confine himself to analyzing the conditions that an acting subject must satisfy in order to set and realize ends. On this model rational actions basically have the character of goal-directed, feedback-controlled interventions in the world of existing states of affairs. Max Black lists a series of conditions that an action must satisfy if it is to be able to count as more or less rational ("reasonable") and to admit of critical review ("dianoetic appraisal").

1. Only actions under actual or potential control by the agent are suitable for dianoetic appraisal...

2. Only actions directed toward some end-in-view can be reasonable or unreasonable...

3. Dianoetic appraisal is relative to the agent and to his choice of end-in-view...

4. Judgments of reasonableness are appropriate only where there is partial knowledge about the availability and efficacy of the means...

5. Dianoetic appraisal can always be supported by reasons.[5]

If one develops the concept of rationality along the lines of goal-directed action, that is, problem-solving action, a derivative use of "rational" also becomes comprehensible.[6] We often speak of the "rationality" of a stimulated response, or the "rationality" of a system's change in state. Such reactions can be *interpreted* as solutions to problems, without imputing to the interpolated purposive*ness* of the observed reaction any purposeful *activity* and without ascribing this activity to a subject capable of making decisions and using propositional knowledge, as his action. Behavioral reactions of an externally or internally stimulated organism, and environmentally induced changes of state in a self-regulated system can indeed by understood as *quasi-actions*, that is, as if they were expressions of a subject's capacity for action.[7] But this is to speak of rationality only in a figurative sense, for the susceptibility to criticism and grounding that we require of rational expressions means that the subject to whom they are attributed should, under suitable conditions, *himself* be able to provide reasons or grounds.

(b) The phenomenologist does not rely upon the guiding thread of goal-directed or problem-solving action. He does not, that is, simply begin with the ontological presupposition of an objective world; he makes this a problem by inquiring into the conditions under which the unity of an objective world is constituted for the members of a community. The world gains objectivity only through *counting* as one and the same world *for*

a community of speaking and acting subjects. The abstract concept of the world is a necessary condition if communicatively acting subjects are to reach understanding among themselves about what takes place in the world or is to be effected in it. Through this *communicative practice* they assure themselves at the same time of their common life-relations, of an intersubjectively shared *lifeworld*. This lifeworld is bounded by the totality of interpretations presupposed by the members as background knowledge. To elucidate the concept of rationality the phenomenologist must then examine the conditions for communicatively achieved consensus; he must analyze what Melvin Pollner calls, with reference to Alfred Schutz, "mundane reasoning."

> That a community orients itself to the world as essentially constant, as one which is known and knowable in common with others, provides that community with the warrantable grounds for asking questions of a particular sort of which the prototypical representative is: "How come, he sees it and you do not?"[8]

On this model, rational expressions have the character of meaningful actions, intelligible in their context, through which the actor relates to something in the objective world. The conditions of validity of symbolic expressions refer to a background knowledge intersubjectively shared by the communication community. Every disagreement presents a challenge of a peculiar sort to this lifeworld background.

> The assumption of a commonly shared world (lifeworld) does not function for mundane reasoners as a descriptive assertion. It is not falsifiable. Rather, it functions as an incorrigible specification of the relations which exist in principle among a community of perceivers' experiences of what is purported to be the same world (objective world). . . . In very gross terms, the anticipated unanimity of experience (or, at least of accounts of those experiences) presupposes a community of others who are deemed to be observing the same world, who are physically constituted so as to be capable of veridical experience, who are motivated so as to speak "truthfully" of their experience, and who speak according to recognizable, shared schemes of expression. On the occasion of a disjuncture, mundane reasoners are prepared to call these and other features into question. For a mundane reasoner, a disjuncture is compelling grounds

for believing that one or another of the conditions otherwise thought to obtain in the anticipation of unanimity did not. For example, a mundane solution may be generated by reviewing whether or not the other had a capacity for veridical experience. Thus "hallucination," "paranoia," "bias," "blindness," "deafness," "false consciousness," etc., insofar as they are understood as indicating a faulted or inadequate method of observing the world serve as candidate explanations of disjuncture. The significant feature of these solutions—the feature that renders them intelligible to other mundane reasoners as possible correct solutions—is that they bring into question not the *world's intersubjectivity* but the adequacy of the methods through which the world is experienced and reported upon.[9]

The concept of cognitive-instrumental rationality that emerges from the realist approach can be fit into this more comprehensive concept of communicative rationality developed from the phenomenological approach. That is to say, there are internal relations between the capacity for decentered perception and manipulation of things and events on the one hand, and the capacity for reaching intersubjective understanding about things and events on the other. For this reason, Piaget chooses the model of *social cooperation,* in which several subjects coordinate their interventions in the objective world through communicative action.[10] The contrasts stand out only when one tries, as is usual in empiricist research traditions, to *separate* the cognitive-instrumental rationality based on the monological employment of descriptive knowledge from communicative rationality. This shows up, for example, in concepts like "responsibility" and "autonomy." Only responsible persons can behave rationally. If their rationality is measured by the success of goal-directed interventions, it suffices to require that they be able to choose among alternatives and to control (some) conditions in their environment. But if their rationality is measured by whether processes of reaching understanding are successful, recourse to such capacities does not suffice. In the context of communicative action, only those persons count as responsible who, as members of a communication-community, can orient their actions to intersubjectively recognized validity claims. Different concepts of autonomy can be coordinated with these different concepts of responsibility. A greater degree of cognitive-instrumental rationality produces a greater independence from limitations imposed by the contingent environment on the self-assertion of subjects acting in a goal-directed manner. A greater degree of communicative rationality expands—within a communication-community—the scope for unconstrained coordination of actions and consensual resolution of conflicts (at least to the extent that the latter are based on cognitive dissonance). This last qualification is necessary so long as we are oriented to constative utterances in developing the concept of communicative rationality. Pollner also limits "mundane reasoning" to cases in which there is disagreement about something in the objective world.[11] But the rationality of persons is obviously not exhibited solely by the ability to utter well-grounded factual beliefs and to act efficiently.

B.—Well-grounded assertions and efficient actions are certainly a sign of rationality; we do characterize as rational speaking and acting subjects who, as far as it lies within their power, avoid errors in regard to facts and means-ends relations. But there are obviously *other* types of expressions for which we can have good reasons, even though they are not tied to truth or success claims. In contexts of communicative action, we call someone rational not only if he is able to put forward an assertion and, when criticized, to provide grounds for it by pointing to appropriate evidence, but also if he is following an established norm and is able, when criticized, to justify his action by explicating the given situation in the light of legitimate expectations. We even call someone rational if he makes known a desire or an intention, expresses a feeling or a mood, shares a secret, confesses a deed, etc., and is then able to reassure critics in regard to the revealed experience by drawing practical consequences from it and behaving consistently thereafter.

Normatively regulated actions and *expressive self-presentations* have, like assertions or constative speech acts, the character of meaningful expressions, understandable in their context, which are connected with criticizable validity claims. Their reference is to norms and subjective experiences rather than to facts. The agent makes the claim that his behavior is right in relation to a normative context recognized as legitimate, or that the first-person utterance of an experience to which he has privileged access is truthful or sincere. Like constative speech acts, these expressions can also go wrong. The possibility of intersubjective recognition of criticizable validity claims is constitutive for their rationality too. However, the knowledge embodied in normatively regulated actions or in expressive manifestations does not refer to the existence of states of affairs but to the validity of norms or to the manifestation of subjective experiences. With these expressions the speaker can refer not to something in the objective world but only to something in a common social world or in his own subjective world. For now I shall have to leave the matter with this provisional suggestion that there are communicative actions characterized by other relations to the world and connected with validity claims *different* from truth and effectiveness.

Expressions that are linked with claims to normative rightness or subjective truthfulness in a way similar to that in which other acts are linked with claims to propositional truth and to efficiency satisfy the central presupposition of rationality: they can be defended against criticism. This holds true even for a type of expression that is not invested with a clear-cut validity claim, namely evaluative expressions, which are not simply expressive—that is, manifesting a merely private feeling or need—nor do they lay claim to be normatively binding—that is, to be in agreement with normative expectations. And yet there can be good reasons for such evaluations. The agent can, with the help of value judgments, explain to a critic his desire for a vacation, his preference for autumn landscapes, his rejection of the military, his jealousy of colleagues. Standards of value or appreciation neither have the generality of norms of action nor are they merely private. We distinguish between a reasonable and an unreasonable employment of those standards with which the members of a culture and language community interpret their needs. Richard Norman makes this clear with the following example.

> To want simply a saucer of mud is irrational, because some further reason is needed for wanting it. To want a saucer of mud because one wants to enjoy its rich river-smell is rational. No further reason is needed for wanting to enjoy the rich river-smell, for to characterize what is wanted as "to enjoy the rich river-smell" is itself to give an acceptable reason for wanting it, and therefore this want is rational.[12]

Actors are behaving rationally so long as they use predicates such as "spicy," "attractive," "strange," "terrible," "disgusting," and so forth, in such a way that other members of their lifeworlds can recognize in these descriptions their own reactions to similar situations. If, on the other hand, they use evaluative standards in such a peculiar way that they can no longer count on a culturally established understanding, they are behaving idiosyncratically. Among such private evaluations there may be some which have an innovative character. These are distinguished by their authentic expression (for example, by the conspicuous aesthetic form of a work of art). As a rule, however, idiosyncratic expressions follow rigid patterns; their semantic content is not set free by the power of poetic speech or creative construction and thus has a merely privatistic character. The spectrum ranges from harmless whims, such as a special liking for the smell of rotten apples, to clinically noteworthy symptoms, such as a horrified reaction to open spaces. Someone who explains his libidinous reaction to rotten apples by referring to the "infatuating," "unfathomable," "vertiginous" smell, or who explains his panicked reaction to open spaces by their "crippling," "leaden," "sucking" emptiness, will scarcely meet with understanding in the *everyday* contexts of most cultures. The *justificatory* force of the cultural values appealed to is not sufficient for these reactions, which are experienced as deviant. These extreme cases only confirm that the partialities and sensibilities of the desires and feelings that can be expressed in value judgments also stand in internal relations to reasons and arguments. Anyone who is so privatistic in his attitudes and evaluations that they cannot be explained and rendered plausible by appeal to standards of evaluation is not behaving rationally.

To sum up, we can say that actions regulated by norms, expressive self-presentations, and also evaluative expressions, supplement constative speech acts in constituting a communicative practice which, against the background of a lifeworld, is oriented to achieving, sustaining, and renewing consensus —and indeed a consensus that rests on the intersubjective recognition of criticizable validity claims. The rationality inherent in this practice is seen in the fact that a communicatively achieved agreement must be based *in the end* on reasons. And the rationality of those who participate in this communicative practice is determined by whether, if necessary, they could, *under suitable circumstances,* provide reasons for their expressions. Thus the rationality proper to the communicative practice of everyday life points to the practice of argumentation as a court of appeal that makes it possible to continue communicative action with other means when disagreements can no longer be repaired with every-day routines and yet are not to be settled by the direct or strategic use of force. For this reason I believe that the concept of communicative rationality, which refers to an unclarified systematic interconnection of universal validity claims, can be adequately explicated only in terms of a theory of argumentation.

We use the term *argumentation* for that type of speech in which participants thematize contested validity claims and attempt to vindicate or criticize them through arguments. An *argument* contains reasons or grounds that are connected in a systematic way with the *validity claim* of a problematic expression. The "strength" of an argument is measured in a given context by the soundness of the reasons; that can be seen in, among other things, whether or not an argument is able to convince the participants in a discourse, that is, to motivate them to accept the validity claim in question. Against this background, we can also judge the rationality of a speaking and acting subject by how he behaves as a participant in argumentation, should the situation arise.

> Anyone participating in argument shows his rationality or lack of it by the manner in which he handles and responds to the offering of reasons for or against claims. If he is "open to argument," he will either acknowledge the force of those reasons or seek to reply to them, and either way he will deal with them in a "rational" manner. If he is "deaf to argument," by contrast, he may either ignore contrary reasons or reply to them with dogmatic assertions, and either way he fails to deal with the issues "rationally."[13]

Corresponding to the openness of rational expressions to being explained, there is, on the side of persons who behave rationally, a willingness to expose themselves to criticism and, if necessary, to participate properly in argumentation.

In virtue of their criticizability, rational expressions also admit of improvement; we can correct failed attempts if we can successfully identify our mistakes. The concept of *grounding* is interwoven with that of *learning*. Argumentation plays an important role in learning processes as well. Thus we call a person rational who, in the cognitive-instrumental sphere, expresses reasonable opinions and acts efficiently; but this rationality remains accidental if it is not coupled with the ability to learn from mistakes, from the refutation of hypotheses and from the failure of interventions.

The medium in which these negative experiences can be productively assimilated is *theoretical discourse,* that is, the form of argumentation in which controversial truth claims are thematized. The situation is similar in the moral-practical sphere. We call persons rational who can justify their actions with reference to existing normative contexts. This is particularly true of those who, in cases of normative conflict, act judiciously, that is, neither give in to their affects nor pursue their immediate interests but are concerned to judge the dispute from a moral point of view and to settle it in a consensual manner. The medium in which we can hypothetically test whether a norm of action, be it actually recognized or not, can be impartially justified is *practical discourse;* this is the form of argumentation in which claims to normative rightness are made thematic.

In philosophical ethics, it is by no means agreed that the validity claims connected with norms of action, upon which commands or "ought" sentences are based, can, analogously to truth claims, be redeemed discursively. In everyday life, however, no one would enter into moral argumentation if he did not start from the strong presupposition that a grounded consensus could in principle be achieved among those involved. In my view, this follows with conceptual necessity from the *meaning* of normative validity claims. Norms of action appear in their domains of validity with the claim to express, in relation to some matter requiring regulation, an interest *common to all* those affected and thus to *deserve* general recognition. For this reason valid norms must be capable in principle of meeting with the rationally motivated approval of everyone affected under conditions that neutralize all motives except that of cooperatively seeking the truth.[14] We rely on this intuitive knowledge whenever we engage in moral argument; the "moral point of view" is rooted in these presuppositions.[15] This need not mean that these lay intuitions could also be reconstructively justified; in regard to these basic questions of ethics I am myself inclined, however, to a cognitivist position, according to which practical questions can in principle be settled by way of argumentation.[16] To be sure, if we are to have any prospect of defending this position successfully, we shall have to avoid rashly assimilating practical discourse, which is characterized by an internal relation to the interpreted needs and wants of *those affected* in a given instance, to theoretical discourse, with its relation to the interpreted experiences of *observers.*

There is a reflective medium not only for the cognitive-instrumental and moral-practical domains, but for evaluative and expressive manifestations as well. We call a person rational who interprets the nature of his desires and feelings [*Bedürfnisnatur*] in the light of culturally established standards of value, but especially if he can adopt a reflective attitude to the very value standards through which desires and feelings are interpreted. Cultural values do not appear with a claim to universality, as do norms of action. At most, values are *candidates* for interpretations under which a circle of those affected can, if occasion arises, describe and normatively regulate a common interest. The circle of intersubjective recognition that forms around cultural values does not yet in any way imply a claim that they would meet with general assent within a culture, not to mention universal assent. For this reason arguments that serve to justify standards of value do not satisfy the conditions of discourse. In the prototypical case they have the form of *aesthetic criticism*.

This is a variation of a form of argumentation in which the adequacy of value standards, the vocabulary of our evaluative language generally, is made thematic. To be sure, in the discussions of art, music, and literary criticism, this happens in an indirect way. In this context reasons have the peculiar function of *bringing us to see* a work or performance in such a way that it can be perceived as an authentic expression of an exemplary experience, in general as the embodiment of a claim to authenticity.[17] A work validated through aesthetic experience can then in turn take the place of an argument and promote the acceptance of precisely those standards according to which it counts as an authentic work. In practical discourse reasons or grounds are meant to show that a norm recommended for acceptance expresses a generalizable interest; in aesthetic criticism grounds or reasons serve to guide perception and to make the authenticity of a work so evident that this aesthetic experience can itself become a rational motive for accepting the corresponding standards of value. This provides a plausible explanation of why we regard aesthetic arguments as less conclusive than the arguments we employ in practical or, even more so, in theoretical discourse.

Something similar holds for the argument of a psychotherapist who specializes in training the analysand to adopt a reflective attitude toward his own expressive manifestations. We also apply the term "rational"—even with a special emphasis—to the be-

havior of a person who is both willing and able to free himself
from illusions, and indeed from illusions that are based not on
errors (about facts) but on self-deceptions (about one's own subjective experiences). We are dealing here with the expression of
one's own desires and inclinations, feelings and moods, which
appear with the claim to truthfulness or sincerity. In many
situations an actor has good reason to conceal his experiences
from others or to mislead someone with whom he is interacting
about his "true" experiences. In such cases he is not raising a
claim to truthfulness but at most simulating one while behaving
strategically. Expressions of this kind cannot be objectively criticized because of their insincerity; they are to be judged rather
according to their intended results as more or less effective.
Expressive manifestations can be appraised on the basis of their
sincerity only in the context of communication aimed at reaching
understanding.

Anyone who systematically deceives himself about himself
behaves irrationally. But one who is capable of letting himself
be enlightened about his irrationality possesses not only the
rationality of a subject who is competent to judge facts and who
acts in a purposive-rational way, who is morally judicious and
practically reliable, who evaluates with sensitivity and is aesthetically open-minded; he also possesses the power to behave reflectively in relation to his subjectivity and to see through the irrational limitations to which his cognitive, moral-practical, and
aesthetic-practical expressions are subject. In such a process of
self-reflection, reasons and grounds also play a role. Freud
examined the relevant type of argumentation in his model of the
therapeutic dialogue between analyst and patient.[18] In the analytic
dialogue the roles are asymmetrically distributed; the analyst and
the patient do not behave like proponent and opponent. The presuppositions of discourse can be satisfied only after the therapy
has been successful. I shall call the form of argumentation that
serves to clarify systematic self-deception *therapeutic critique.*

Finally, on another (but still reflective) level, there are the
modes of behavior of an interpreter who sees himself called upon
by stubborn difficulties in understanding to make the very means
of reaching understanding the object of communication in order
to provide relief. We call a person rational if he is ready to come
to an understanding and reacts to disturbances by reflecting on
linguistic rules. This is a question, on the one hand, of checking
the comprehensibility or well-formedness of symbolic expres-

sions, that is, of asking whether symbolic expressions are produced according to rule, in conformity with the corresponding system of generative rules; linguistic inquiry may serve as a model here. On the other hand, it is a question of explicating the meaning of expressions; that is, of asking whether and, if so, how the language of the interpretandum can be clarified—a hermeneutic task for which the practice of translation provides a suitable model. One behaves irrationally if one employs one's own symbolic means of expression in a dogmatic way. On the other hand, *explicative discourse* is a form of argumentation in which the comprehensibility, well-formedness, or rule-correctness of symbolic expressions is no longer naively supposed or contested but is thematized as a controversial claim.[19]

We can summarize the above as follows: Rationality is understood to be a disposition of speaking and acting subjects that is expressed in modes of behavior for which there are good reasons or grounds. This means that rational expressions admit of objective evaluation. This is true of all symbolic expressions that are, at least implicitly, connected with validity claims (or with claims that stand in internal relation to a criticizable validity claim). Any explicit examination of controversial validity claims requires an exacting form of communication satisfying the conditions of argumentation. Argumentation makes possible behavior that counts as rational in a specific sense, namely learning from explicit mistakes. Whereas the openness of rational expressions to criticism and to grounding merely *points* to the possibility of argumentation, learning processes—through which we acquire theoretical knowledge and moral insight, extend and renew our evaluative language, and overcome self-deceptions and difficulties in comprehension—themselves *rely on* argumentation (*see* Figure 2).

C.—An Excursus on the Theory of Argumentation The concept of rationality that I have introduced in a rather intuitive way refers to a system of validity claims that, as Figure 2 indicates, has to be elucidated in terms of a theory of argumentation. Notwithstanding a venerable tradition going back to Aristotle, however, this theory is still in its beginnings. The logic of argumentation does not refer to deductive connections between semantic units (sentences) as does formal logic, but to nondeductive relations between the pragmatic units (speech acts) of which arguments are composed. Thus it also appears under the name of "informal

Figure 2
Types of Argumentation

Reference Dimensions / Forms of Argumentation	Problematic Expressions	Controversial Validity Claims
Theoretical discourse	Cognitive-instrumental	Truth of propositions; efficacy of teleological actions
Practical discourse	Moral-practical	Rightness of norms of action
Aesthetic criticism	Evaluative	Adequacy of standards of value
Therapeutic critique	Expressive	Truthfulness or sincerity of expressions
Explicative discourse	—————	Comprehensibility or well-formedness of symbolic constructs

logic."[20] The organizers of the first international symposium on questions of informal logic mentioned in retrospect the following reasons and motives behind their efforts:

- Serious doubt about whether deductive logic and the standard inductive logic approaches are sufficient to model all, or even the major, forms of legitimate argument.

- A conviction that there are standards, norms, or advice for argument evaluation that are at once logical—not purely rhetorical or domain-specific—and at the same time not captured by the categories of deductive validity, soundness and inductive strength.

- A desire to provide a complete theory of reasoning that goes beyond formal deductive and inductive logic.

- A belief that theoretical clarification of reasoning and logical criticism in non-formal terms has direct implications for such other branches of philosophy as epistemology, ethics and the philosophy of language.

- An interest in all types of discursive persuasion, coupled with an interest in mapping the lines between the different types and the overlapping that occurs among them.[21]

These convictions are characteristic of a position that Steven Toulmin developed in his pioneering examination of *The Uses of Argument*,[22] and which he took as his point of departure in his investigations—drawing upon the history of science—of *Human Understanding*.[23]

On the one side, Toulmin criticizes absolutist views that base theoretical knowledge, moral-practical insight, and aesthetic evaluation on deductively conclusive arguments or empirically compelling evidence. To the extent that arguments are conclusive in the sense of logical inference, they do not bring anything new to light; and to the extent that they have any substantive content at all, they rest on insights and needs that can be variously interpreted in terms of changing frameworks or "languages," and that, therefore, do not provide any ultimate foundations. On the other side, Toulmin is just as critical of relativistic views that do not explain the peculiarly constraint-free force of the better argument and cannot account for the universalistic connotations of validity claims such as the truth of propositions or the rightness of norms.

Toulmin argues that neither position is reflexive; that is, neither position can account for its "rationality" within its own framework. The absolutist cannot call upon another First Principle to secure the status of the doctrine of First Principles. On the other hand, the relativist is in the peculiar (and self-contradictory) position of arguing that his doctrine is somehow above the relativity of judgments he asserts exists in all other domains.[24]

But if the validity of arguments can be neither undermined in an empiricist manner nor grounded in an absolutist manner, then we are faced with precisely those questions to which the *logic of argumentation* is supposed to provide the answers: How can problematic validity claims be supported by good reasons? How can reasons be criticized in turn? What makes some arguments, and thus some reasons, which are related to validity claims in a certain way, stronger or weaker than other arguments?

We can distinguish three aspects of argumentative speech. First, considered as a *process,* we have to do with a form of communication that is improbable in that it sufficiently approximates ideal conditions. In this regard, I tried to delineate the general pragmatic presuppositions of argumentation as specifications of an ideal speech situation.[25] This proposal may be unsatisfactory in its details; but I still view as correct my intention to reconstruct the general symmetry conditions that every competent speaker must presuppose are sufficiently satisfied insofar as he intends to enter into argumentation at all. Participants in argumentation have to presuppose in general that the structure of their communication, by virtue of features that can be described in purely formal terms, excludes all force—whether it arises from within the process of reaching understanding itself or influences it from the outside—except the force of the better argument (and thus that it also excludes, on their part, all motives except that of a cooperative search for the truth). From this perspective argumentation can be conceived as *a reflective continuation, with different means, of action oriented to reaching understanding.*

Second, as soon as one considers argumentation as a *procedure,* we have to do with a form of interaction *subject to special rules.* The discursive process of reaching understanding, in the form of a cooperative division of labor between proponents and opponents, is normatively regulated in such a way that participants

- thematize a problematic validity claim and,
- relieved of the pressure of action and experience, in a hypothetical attitude,
- test with reasons, and only with reasons, whether the claim defended by the proponents rightfully stands or not.

Finally, argumentation can be viewed from a third standpoint: it has as its aim to *produce* cogent *arguments* that are convincing in virtue of their intrinsic properties and with which validity claims can be redeemed or rejected. Arguments are the means by which intersubjective recognition of a proponent's hypothetically raised validity claim can be brought about and opinion thereby transformed into knowledge. Arguments possess a general structure, which Toulmin characterizes as follows. An argument is composed of the problematic utterance for which a certain validity claim is raised (conclusion), and of the reason (ground) through which the claim is to be established. The ground is obtained by means of a rule—a rule of inference, a principle, a law (warrant). This is based on evidence of different kinds (backing). If need be, the validity claim has to be modified or restricted (modifier).[26] This proposal too is in need of improvement, especially as regards the differentiation of various levels of argumentation; but every theory of argumentation faces the task of specifying general properties of cogent arguments, and for this task formal-semantic descriptions of the sentences employed in arguments are indeed necessary but not sufficient.

The three analytical aspects distinguished above can provide the theoretical perspectives from which the familiar disciplines of the Aristotelian canon can be delimited: Rhetoric is concerned with argumentation as a *process,* dialectic with the pragmatic *procedures* of argumentation, and logic with its *products.* As a matter of fact, from each of these perspectives a different structure of argumentation stands out: the structures of an ideal speech situation immunized against repression and inequality in a special way; then the structures of a ritualized competition for the better arguments; finally the structures that determine the construction of individual arguments and their interrelations. At no single one of these analytical levels can the very idea intrinsic to argumentative speech be adequately developed. The fundamental intuition connected with argumentation can best be characterized from the process perspective by the intention of convincing a *universal audience* and gaining general assent for an utterance; from the procedural perspective, by the intention of ending a dispute about hypothetical validity claims with a *rationally motivated agreement;* and from the product perspective by the intention of grounding or *redeeming* a validity claim with arguments. Interestingly enough, however, it turns out that in the attempt to analyze the corresponding basic concepts in the theory of argumentation—such as "the assent of a universal audience,"[27] or "the attainment of a rationally motivated agreement,"[28] or "the discursive redemption of a validity claim"[29] —the separation of the three analytical levels cannot be maintained.

I would like to illustrate this point in connection with a recent attempt to approach the theory of argumentation on only one of these abstract levels, namely that of argumentation as process. Wolfgang Klein's approach has the advantage of giving a consistently empirical-scientific twist to questions concerning rhetoric.[30] Klein chooses the external perspective of an observer who wants to describe and explain processes of argumentation. In doing so he does not proceed objectivistically in the sense of regarding only the observable behavior of participants as acceptable [data]; under strictly behaviorist assumptions, we could not discriminate argumentative behavior from verbal behavior in general. Klein opens himself up to the sense of argumentation; but he wants to investigate it in a strictly descriptivist attitude, without objective evaluation of the arguments employed. He distances himself not only from Toulmin, who starts from the position that the sense of an argumentation cannot be disclosed without at least implicitly evaluating the arguments employed in it; he also distances himself from the tradition of rhetoric, which is interested more in speech that convinces than in its truth content.

> Toulmin's schema is in a certain respect much closer to actual argumentation than the formal approaches he criticizes; but it is a schema of *correct* argumentation. He has not set up an empirical investigation into how people actually do argue. This is true of Perelman/Olbrechts-Tyteca as well, though of all the philosophical approaches they come closest to real argumentation. But the *auditoire universel,* one of their central concepts, is certainly not a group of actually existing people, for instance the earth's present population; it is some court or other—not easy to pin down in other respects. . . . I am not concerned with what rational, reasonable or correct argumentation is, but with how people, dumb as they are, actually argue.[31]

I want to show how Klein, in his attempt to adopt an external perspective in order to separate clearly ''de facto'' from ''valid'' argumentation, gets involved in instructive contradictions.

He begins by defining the domain of argumentative speech: ''In argumentation there is an attempt to transform something collectively problematic into something collectively valid [*geltend*] by drawing upon what is already collectively valid.''[32] Participants in argumentation want to decide problematic validity claims by adducing reasons; and in the final analysis these reasons draw their power to convince from a collectively shared, unproblematic knowledge. Klein's empiricist truncation of the sense of argumentation can be seen in how he uses the concept of ''collectively valid." By this he understands only those views that are actually shared by specific groups at specific times; he screens out all internal relations between what is *de facto* accepted as valid [*geltend*] and what should have validity [*Gültigkeit*] in the sense of a claim transcending local, temporal, and social limitations: "The *valid* and the *questionable* are thus relative to persons and times."[33]

In restricting "what is collectively valid" to the convictions that are actually expressed and accepted at a given time and place, Klein puts forward a description of argumentation that foreshortens attempts to convince by an essential dimension. According to his description, it is indeed reasons that motivate participants in argumentation to let themselves be convinced of something; but these *reasons are conceived of as opaque incentives for changing attitudes.* His description neutralizes all standards that would make it possible to evaluate the rationality of reasons; it closes off to the theoretician the internal perspective from which he could adopt his own standards of judgment. To the extent that we draw upon the concepts proposed by Klein, one argument counts as much as any other, if only it leads to "the direct acceptance of a justification."[34]

Klein himself recognizes the danger that has to arise for a *logic* of argumentation when the concept of validity is replaced by that of *acceptance:* "One might think that in this approach we drop truth and the relation to reality, with which argumentation should possibly also be concerned. It seems as if this way of looking at things focuses only on who gets his way, but not on who is right. But that would indeed be a serious error . . ."[35] The logic of argumentation requires a conceptual framework that permits us to take into account the phenomenon of the peculiarly constraint-free force of the better argument.

> The unfolding of such an argument is by no means a friend-ly agreement on some view or other. What is collectively valid can in some cases be pragmatically very unpleasant for a participant; but if it follows from what is valid by way of valid transitions, then it just is valid—whether he wants it to be or not. One cannot very well defend oneself against thinking. Transitions from what is valid take place in us whether or not we like them.[36]

On the other hand, relativistic consequences are unavoidable if what is collectively valid is conceived only as a social fact, that is, without any internal relation to the rationality of reasons.

> It appears to be . . . arbitrary whether this or that comes to
> be valid for an individual or a collective; some believe this,
> others that, and what wins out depends on contingencies,
> on greater rhetorical skill or on physical force. This leads
> to consequences that are scarcely satisfying. One would then
> have to accept the fact that for one individual "love your
> neighbor as yourself" is valid, while for another it is "slay
> your neighbor if he gives you trouble." It would also be
> difficult to see why then one continued to pursue research
> or strove to gain knowledge at all. Some hold that the earth
> is a disc, others that it is a sphere, or that it is a turkey; the
> first collective is the largest, the third the smallest, the second
> the most aggressive; one cannot accord a greater "right" to
> any of them (although the second view is undoubtedly
> correct).[37]

The dilemma consists in the fact that Klein does not want
to take relativistic consequences into the bargain, but yet does
want to maintain the external perspective of the observer. He
is unwilling to distinguish between the *social currency* [*Geltung*]
and the *validity* [*Gültigkeit*] of arguments: "Concepts of 'true' and
'probable' which abstract from the knowing individuals and the
way in which they gain their knowledge may therefore have some
use; but they are irrelevant for argumentation. There it is a
question of what is valid for the individual."[38]

Klein looks for a curious way out of this dilemma: "The
touchstone for differences in what is valid is not their differences
in truth content—for who could decide this?—but the immanently
effective logic of argumentation."[39] The term "effectiveness" is
systematically ambiguous in this context. If arguments are valid,
then insight into the internal conditions of their validity can have
a rationally motivating force and a corresponding effect. But arguments can also have an influence on the attitudes of addressees
independently of their validity—when they are expressed in
external circumstances that guarantee their acceptance. Whereas
the "effectiveness" of arguments can be explained in the second
case by means of a psychology of argumentation, explanation in
the first case calls for a logic of argumentation. Klein postulates,
however, a third aspect, namely a logic of argumentation that
investigates *validity connections as lawlike empirical regularities.*
Without having recourse to concepts of objective validity, it is

supposed to depict the laws to which participants in argumentation are subject, in some cases against their inclinations and in opposition to external influences. Such a theory has to analyze what *appear* to participants as internal connections between valid utterances as external connections between events linked nomologically.

Klein is able to pass off the dilemma that he himself sees only at the cost of a (deliberate?) category mistake: He requires of the logic of argumentation a task that could only be carried out by a nomological theory of observable behavior.

> I believe that in the systematic analysis of actual argumentation—as in every *empirical analysis*—relatively fixed *regularities* can be found, according to which people argue: precisely the logic of argumentation. And I believe, furthermore, that this concept covers much of what is usually understood by the "rationality of argumentation."[40]

Klein wants to cultivate the logic of argumentation as a nomological theory and thus he has to assimilate rules to causal regularities, reasons to causes.[41]

Paradoxical consequences of this kind arise from the attempt to sketch the logic of argumentation *exclusively* from the perspective of the flow of communication processes and to avoid also analyzing consensus-forming processes from the start as the achievement of rationally motivated agreement and as the discursive redemption of validity claims. As a consequence of this *restriction to the level of abstraction of rhetoric*, the internal perspective of reconstructing validity connections is neglected. There is lacking a concept of rationality that would make it possible to establish internal relations between their standards and ours, between what is valid "for them" and what is valid "for us."

Interestingly, Klein supports the elimination of the truth relation of arguments by pointing out that not all validity claims that can be contested in argumentation can be reduced to truth claims. Many arguments are "not at all (concerned) with statements that one has to decide are 'true' or 'false,' but with questions like, for example, what is good, what is beautiful, or what one ought to do. It is clear that we are here concerned more than ever with what is valid, with what is valid for certain people at certain times."[42] The concept of propositional truth is in fact too narrow to cover everything for which participants in argument claim validity in the logical sense. For this reason the theory of argumentation must be equipped with a more comprehensive concept of validity that is not restricted to validity in the sense of truth. But it does not at all follow from this that we have to renounce concepts of validity analogous to truth, to expunge every counterfactual moment from the concept of validity and to equate validity with context-dependent acceptability.

For me the advantage of Toulmin's approach lies precisely in the fact that he allows for a plurality of validity claims while not denying the critical sense of a validity transcending spatio-temporal and social limitations. Nevertheless this approach also suffers from a failure to mediate clearly the logical and empirical levels of abstraction. Toulmin chooses a starting point in ordinary language that does not necessitate his distinguishing between these two levels. He assembles examples of attempts to influence the attitudes of partners in interaction by means of arguments. This can take place in any number of ways—by handing over information, raising a legal claim, raising objections to the adoption of a new strategy (e.g., a business policy) or a new technique (e.g., in the slalom or in steel production), by criticizing a musical performance, defending a scientific hypothesis, supporting a candidate in competition for a job, and so forth. What is common to these cases is the form of argumentation: We try to support a claim with good grounds or reasons; the quality of the reasons and their relevance can be called into question by the other side; we meet objections and are in some cases forced to modify our original position.

Of course, the arguments can be distinguished according to the *kind of claim* that the proponent wishes to defend. These claims vary with the contexts of action. To begin with, we can characterize the latter by referring to institutions, for instance to law courts, scholarly congresses, meetings of boards of directors, medical consultations, university seminars, parliamentary hearings, discussions among engineers in settling on a design, and so on.[43] The multiplicity of contexts in which arguments can appear can be analyzed in terms of functions and reduced to a few social arenas or "fields." Corresponding to these are different types of claims and just as many different types of argumentation. Thus Toulmin distinguishes the general schema, in which he holds fast to the field-invariant properties of argumentation, from the particular, field-dependent rules of argumentation which are constitutive for the language games or life-orders of law, medicine, science, politics, art criticism, business enterprise, sport, and so on. We are unable to judge the strength of arguments and to understand the category of validity claims that are supposed to be redeemed by them if we do not understand the sense of the enterprise that is supposed to be advanced through argumentation.

What gives judicial arguments their force in the context of actual court proceedings?. . . The status and force of those arguments—as *judicial* arguments—can be fully understood only if we put them back into their practical contexts and recognize what functions and purposes they possess in the actual enterprise of the law. Similarly the arguments advanced in a scientific discussion must be presented in an orderly and relevant manner if the initial claims are to be criticized in a rational manner, open to all concerned. But what finally gives strength and force to those arguments is, once again, something more than their structure and order. We shall understand their status and force fully only by putting them back into their original contexts and recognizing how they contribute to the larger enterprise of science. Just as judicial arguments are sound only to the extent they serve the deeper goals of the legal process, scientific arguments are sound only to the extent that they can serve the deeper goal of improving our scientific understanding. The same is true in other fields. We understand the fundamental force of medical arguments only to the extent that we understand the enterprise of medicine itself. Likewise for business, politics, or any other field. In all these fields of human activity, reasoning and argumentation find a place as central elements within a larger human enterprise. And to mark this feature—the fact that all these activities place reliance on the presentation and critical assessment of "reasons" and "arguments"—we shall refer to them all as rational enterprises.[44]

There is to be sure an ambiguity in this attempt to trace the multiplicity of validity claims and types of argument back to different "rational enterprises" and "fields of argument." It remains unclear whether these totalities of law and medicine, science and management, art and engineering can be delimited only functionally, for example in sociological terms, or in terms of the logic of argumentation as well. Does Toulmin conceive these "rational enterprises" as institutional expressions of forms of argument that are to be characterized internally, or does he differentiate the fields of argument only according to institutional criteria? Toulmin inclines to the latter alternative, which entails a lesser burden of proof.

If we call upon the distinction introduced above among process, procedure, and product aspects, Toulmin's logic of argument makes do with the third level of abstraction, at which he pursues the construction and connection of individual arguments. He then tries to grasp this differentiation into various fields of argument from the viewpoint of institutionalization. In doing so he distinguishes at the procedural level among *patterns of organization,*[45] and at the level of process among *functionally specified contexts of action* in which argumentative speech is embedded as a problemsolving mechanism. These various fields of argument have to be investigated indirectly; they are accessible only to an empirically generalizing analysis. Toulmin singles out five *representative* fields of argument, namely law, morality, science, management, and art criticism: "By studying them we shall identify most of the characteristic modes of reasoning to be found in different fields and enterprises, and we shall recognize how they reflect the underlying aims of those enterprises."[46]

His declaration of intention is, to be sure, not quite so unequivocal as my presentation of it. It is true that Toulmin develops his program in such a way that he always distills the same argumentation schema out of the field-dependent modes of agumentation; to this extent the five fields of argument could be conceived as *institutional differentiations of a general conceptual framework* for argumentation as such. On this way of viewing the matter, the task of a logic of argumentation would be limited to explicating a framework for possible argumentation. Such different enterprises as law and morality, science, management, and art criticism would owe their rationality to this common core. But in other contexts Toulmin is decidedly opposed to such a universalist view; he doubts that direct access to a fundamental and unchangeable framework of rationality is possible. So he sets a historical-reconstructive investigation of concept and paradigm change over against the unhistorical procedures of a normative theory of science of the Popperian sort. The concept of rationality is said to be accessible only to an historically oriented empirical analysis of change in rational enterprises.

On this way of viewing the matter the logic of argumentation would have to deal above all with those substantial concepts that, in the course of history, constitute *at any given time* the rationality of enterprises like science, technology, law, medicine, and so forth. Toulmin aims at a "critique of collective reason" that avoids both an a priori delimitation of arguments and abstractly introduced definitions of science or law or art.

> When we use such categorial terms as "science" and "law," we do so to refer neither to the timeless pursuit of abstract ideals, defined without reference to our changing grasp of men's actual needs and problems, nor to what the men of each separate milieu themselves happen to give the names of "science" and "law." Rather, we work with certain broad, "open-textured" and historically developing conceptions of what the scientific and judicial enterprises *are there to achieve.* These substantive conceptions are arrived at in the light of the empirical record, both about the goals which the men of different milieus have set themselves, in their own cultivation of those rational enterprises, and about the kinds of success they in fact achieved in the pursuit of those goals.[47]

At the same time Toulmin does not want to pay the price of relativism for shunning aprioristic standards of reason. In the change of rational enterprises and their standards of rationality, what participants take to be "rational" at a given time is not the *only* thing that counts. The historian who proceeds with a reconstructive intent has to orient himself to a critical standard of his own if he wants "to compare rationally" the forms of objective spirit. Toulmin identifies this as the "impartial standpoint of rational judgment," which he would like, of course, not to presuppose arbitrarily but to obtain by conceptually appropriating the human species' collective enterprise of reason, as Hegel did in the *Phenomenology.*

Unfortunately Toulmin makes no attempt to analyze the quite generally conceived *standpoint of impartiality* and therefore opens himself to the objection that he delivers up the logic of argumentation—which he develops only on the level of the general schema for argumentation and not on the levels of procedure and process—to *preexisting* notions of rationality. So long as Toulmin does not clarify the general pragmatic presuppositions and procedures of the cooperative search for truth, he is not in a position to specify what it means for a participant in argumentation to adopt an impartial standpoint. This impartiality is to be found not in the construction of the arguments employed; it can be explained only in connection with the conditions for discursively redeeming validity claims. And this basic concept of the theory of argument points in turn to the basic concepts of rationally motivated agreement and the assent of a universal audience.

> Although Toulmin recognizes that the validity of a claim . . . is ultimately established by community-produced consensual decisions, he only implicitly recognizes the critical difference between warranted and unwarranted consensually achieved decisions. Toulmin does not clearly differentiate between these distinct types of consensus.[48]

Toulmin does not push the logic of argument far enough into the domains of dialectic and rhetoric. He doesn't draw the proper lines between accidental *institutional differentiations of argumentation,* on the one hand, and the *forms of argumentation* determined by internal structure, on the other.

This holds first of all for Toulmin's typological demarcation between conflict-oriented and agreement-oriented organization of arguments. Legal proceedings and the working out of compromises can serve as examples of argumentation organized as *disputation;* scientific and moral discussions, as well as art criticism can serve as examples of argumentation set up as a *process of reaching agreement.* In fact, however, the models of conflict and consensus do not stand side by side as forms of organization with equal rights. Negotiating compromises does not at all serve to redeem validity claims in a strictly discursive manner, but rather to harmonize nongeneralizable interests on the basis of balanced positions of power. Arguments in a court of law (like other kinds of judicial discussions, for example, judiciary deliberation, examination of legal tenets, commentaries on the law, and so forth) are distinguished from general practical discourses through being bound to existing law, as well as through the special restrictions of an order of legal proceedings that takes into account the need for an authorized decision and the orientation to success of the contesting parties.[49] At the same time argument in the law court contains essential elements that can be grasped only on the model of moral argument, generally of discussion concerning the rightness of normative standards. Thus *all* arguments, be they related to questions of law and morality or to scientific hypotheses or to works of art, require the *same* basic form of organization, which subordinates the eristic means to the end of developing intersubjective conviction by the force of the better argument.

It is especially evident in his classification of fields of argument that Toulmin does not clearly distinguish the internally motivated differentiation of various *forms of argumentation* from the institutional differentiation of various *rational enterprises*. In my view, his mistake lies in not clearly separating *conventional claims,* which are context-dependent, from *universal validity claims.* Let us consider a few of his preferred examples:

1. The Oakland Raiders are a certainty for the Super Bowl this year.
2. The epidemic was caused by a bacterial infection carried from ward to ward on food-service equipment.
3. The company's best interim policy is to put this money into short-term municipal bonds.
4. I am entitled to have access to any papers relevant to dismissals in our firm's personnel files.
5. You ought to make more efforts to recruit women executives.
6. The new version of *King Kong* makes more psychological sense than the original.
7. Asparagus belongs to the order of Liliaceae.

Sentences (1) to (7) represent utterances with which a proponent can raise a claim vis-à-vis an opponent. The kind of claim usually springs from the context. If one sports fan makes a bet with another and utters (1) in the process, it is not at all a question of a validity claim that can be redeemed by argument, but of a claim about winning that will be decided according to conventional rules of betting. However, if (1) is uttered in a debate among sports cognoscenti, it might be a matter of a prognosis that could be supported or contested with reasons. Even in cases in which it is already clear from the sentences employed that they could be uttered only in connection with discursively redeemable validity claims, it is the context that decides *what kind* of validity claim is involved. Thus interested laypersons or biologists could argue about the botanical classification of asparagus and utter (7) in the process. In this case the speaker is raising a claim to the truth of a proposition. However, if a teacher is explaining Linnaean taxonomy in a biology class and corrects a pupil who has incorrectly classified asparagus, in uttering (7) he raises a claim concerning the correctness of a semantic rule.

It is, further, by no means the case that fields of argument discriminate adequately among the various kinds of validity claims. Although (4) and (5) can be assigned to different fields of argument, namely to law and to morality, in normal circumstances a speaker could only be raising normative validity claims with both of these utterances. In each case he is appealing to a norm of action; in the case of (4) the norm is presumably covered by a firm's organizational regulations and thus has a legal character.

Moreover, the same validity claim, be it propositional truth or normative rightness, can appear in modalized form. We can understand assertions that are formed with the aid of simple predicative sentences, general propositions, or existential sentences, and promises or commands that are formed with the aid of singular or general ought-sentences, as paradigmatic for the *basic modes* of utterances that can be true or right. It is clear, however, in connection with predictions like (1), explanations like (2), or classificatory descriptions like (7), and with justifications like (4) or admonitions like (5) that the *mode* of an utterance normally refers to something more specific; it also expresses the spatio-temporal or substantive perspective from which the speaker relates to a validity claim.

Fields of argument such as medicine, business, politics, and the like are essentially related to expressions that admit of truth; but they differ in their relation to practice. A recommendation of strategies (or technologies) as in (3) is directly connected with a claim to the efficacy of the measures recommended; it rests on the truth of corresponding prognoses, explanations, or descriptions. An utterance like (2), on the other hand, presents an explanation from which technical recommendations can readily be derived in practical contexts, for instance in the public health system, with the help of an imperative to check the spread of an epidemic.

These and similar considerations speak against any attempt to take the institutional differentiations into fields of argument as the guiding thread for a logic of argumentation. The external differentiations build rather on internal differentiations between various forms of argument, which remain closed to a view that shunts everything into functions and goals of rational enterprises. The forms of argument are differentiated according to universal validity claims, which are often *recognizable* only in connection with the context of an utterance, but which are not first *constituted* by contexts and domains of action.

If this is correct, a considerable burden of proof is placed upon the theory of argumentation; it has to be in a position to specify a *system of validity claims*.[50] To be sure, it does not have to provide a derivation for such a system in the sense of a transcendental deduction; a reliable procedure for testing corresponding reconstructive hypotheses suffices. I shall confine myself here to a preliminary observation on this point. A validity claim can be raised by a speaker vis-à-vis a hearer (or hearers). Normally this takes place implicitly. In uttering a sentence the speaker makes a claim which, were he to make it explicitly, might take the form: "It is true that *p*," or "It is right that *a*," or "I mean what I say when I here and now utter *s*" (where *p* stands for a proposition, *a* for the description of an action, and *s* for a first-person sentence). A *validity claim* is equivalent to the assertion that the *conditions for the validity* of an utterance are fulfilled. Whether the speaker raises a validity claim implicitly or explicitly, the hearer has only the choice of accepting or rejecting the validity claim or leaving it undecided for the time being. The permissible reactions are taking a "yes" or "no" position or abstaining. Of course, not every "yes" or "no" to a sentence uttered with communicative intent amounts to a position on a criticizable validity claim. If we call normatively unauthorized— that is, arbitrary—demands "imperatives," then a "yes" or "no" to an imperative likewise expresses assent or rejection, but only in the sense of the willingness or refusal to comply with the expression of another's will. These yes/no reactions to *power claims* are themselves the expression of *arbitrary choice [Willkür]*. By contrast, yes/no positions on validity claims mean that the hearer agrees or does not agree with a criticizable expression and does so *in light of reasons or grounds;* such positions are the expression of *insight or understanding [Einsicht]*.[51]

If we now go through our list of sample sentences from the standpoint of what a hearer could in each case say "yes" or "no" to, we find the following validity claims. If (1) is meant in the sense of a prediction, with his "yes" or "no" the hearer is taking a position on the *truth of a proposition*. The same holds for (2).

A "yes" or "no" to (4) means taking a position on a legal claim, more generally on a claim to *the normative rightness of a way of acting.* The same holds for (5). Taking a position on (6) means that the hearer regards the application of a value standard as *appropriate or inappropriate.* Depending on whether (7) is used in the sense of a description or as an explication of a semantic rule, the hearer, in taking a position, refers either to a truth claim or to a claim that an expression is comprehensible or well formed.

The basic modes of these utterances are determined according to the validity claims implicitly raised with them, claims to truth, rightness, appropriateness or comprehensibility (or well-formedness). *The semantic analysis of sentence forms* leads to the same modes. Descriptive sentences, which serve to ascertain facts in the broadest sense, can be accepted or rejected from the standpoint of the truth of a proposition; normative sentences (or ought-sentences), which serve to regulate actions, from the standpoint of the rightness (or justice) of a way of acting; evaluative sentences (or value judgments), which serve to appraise something, from the standpoint of the appropriateness or adequacy of value standards (or the "good");[52] and explications, which serve to explain operations like speaking, classifying, calculating, deducing, judging, and so on, from the standpoint of the comprehensibility or well-formedness of symbolic expressions. *Starting from* the analysis of sentence forms, we can go on to clarify the semantic conditions under which a corresponding sentence is *valid.* As soon, however, as the analysis advances to the possibilities of backing or "grounding" the validity of statements, the *pragmatic implications* of the concept of validity come to the fore. What *grounding* means, can be explained only in connection with the conditions for discursively redeeming validity claims. Because descriptive, normative, evaluative, explicative, and, moreover, expressive sentences are distinguished by their form, semantic analysis makes us aware that the meaning of "grounding" changes in specific ways with changes in the sentence form. "Grounding" descriptive statements means establishing the existence of states of affairs; "grounding" normative statements, establishing the acceptability of actions or norms of action; "grounding" evaluative statements, establishing the preferability of values; "grounding" expressive statements, establishing the transparency of self-presentations; and "grounding" explicative statements, establishing that symbolic expressions have been produced correctly. The meaning of the correspondingly differentiated validity claims can be explicated through specifying in each case the logical (in the sense of the logic of argumentation) conditions under which these can be established.

I cannot further pursue here these formal-semantic points of connection for systematizing validity claims, but I would like to note two important limitations: Validity claims are not *only* contained in communicative utterances; and not *all* validity claims contained in communicative utterances have a direct connection with corresponding forms of argumentation.

Sentence (6) is an example of an aesthetic evaluation; this evaluative statement refers to the value of a film. The film is thereby regarded as a work that itself appears with a claim, let us say, to be an authentic representation, an instructive embodiment of exemplary experiences. We could imagine that in a discussion concerning the comparatively positive evaluation of the remake— which, in the speaker's opinion, subtly develops the ambivalence in the relations between King Kong and his victim— the standard of value that is at first naively applied might itself be called into question and thus rendered thematic. A similar shift takes place in moral argument when a norm that has been introduced to justify a problematic action is itself placed in doubt. Thus sentence (5) could also be understood in the sense of a general ought-sentence or a norm for whose validity claim a sceptical hearer is demanding a justification. Similarly, a discourse connected with sentence (2) could shift to the underlying theoretical assumptions concerning infectious diseases. When cultural systems of action like science, law, and art are differentiated out, arguments that are institutionally stabilized and professionally organized, carried out by experts, relate to such *higher-level validity claims*, which are attached not to individual communicative utterances but to cultural objectivations—to works of art, to moral and legal norms, to theories. It is at this level of culturally stored and objectivated knowledge that we also find technologies and strategies in which theoretical or professional knowledge is organized with a view to specific practical contexts such as medicine and public health, military technology, business management, and the like. Despite this difference in level, the analysis of individual expressions uttered with communicative intent remains a heuristically productive starting point for systematizing validity claims, since no validity claim appears at the level of cultural objectivations that would not *also* be contained in communicative utterances.

On the other hand, it is no accident that among the examples of criticizable utterances that can, so to speak, be taken up in argumentation, we do not find any sentences of the type:

8. I must confess that I am upset by the poor condition my colleague has been in since leaving the hospital.

At first glance, this is rather remarkable, since expressive sentences uttered in the first person are certainly connected with a validity claim. For example, a second colleague could pose the question: "Do you really mean that, or aren't you also somewhat relieved that he's no competition for you at the moment?" Expressive sentences that serve to manifest subjective experiences can be accepted or rejected from the standpoint of the truthfulness or sincerity of the speaker's self-presentation. Of course, the claims to sincerity connected with expressive utterances is not such that it could be directly redeemed through argument as can truth or rightness claims. At most the speaker can show in the consistency of his actions whether he really meant what he said. The sincerity of expressions cannot be *grounded* but only *shown;* insincerity can be *revealed* by the lack of consistency between an utterance and the past or future actions internally connected with it.

A therapist's critique of his patient's self-deceptions can, of course, also be understood as an attempt to influence attitudes by means of arguments, that is, to *convince* the other. The patient, who does not recognize himself in his desires and feelings, who is trapped in illusions about his experiences, is indeed meant to be brought by argument in the analytic dialogue to the point of seeing through the heretofore unnoticed untruthfulness of his expressive utterances. Nevertheless, there is not the relation here between a problematic validity claim and discourse proper. Argumentation does not connect up in the same way with the validity claim contained in the communicative utterance in this case. In a therapeutic dialogue directed to self-reflection, some important presuppositions for discourse in the strict sense are not fulfilled: the validity claim is not regarded as problematic from the start; the patient does not take up a hypothetical attitude toward what is said; on his side, it is by no means the case that all motives except that of cooperatively seeking the truth are put out of play; the relations between the partners in dialogue are not symmetrical, and so on. Nonetheless, in the psychoanalytic view, the healing power of analytic dialogue owes *something* to the convincing force of the arguments employed in it. To begin with, I would like to take account of these special circumstances by always speaking of "critique" instead of "discourse" when arguments are employed in situations in which participants need not *presuppose* that the conditions for speech free of external and internal constraints are fulfilled.

The situation with discussions of value standards, for which aesthetic criticism provides a model, is somewhat different.[53] Even in disputes about questions of taste, we rely upon the rationally motivating force of the better argument, although a dispute of this kind diverges in a characteristic way from controversies concerning questions of truth and justice. If the description suggested above is accurate,[54] the peculiar role of arguments in this case is to open the eyes of participants, that is, to *lead* them to an authenticating aesthetic experience. Above all, however, the type of validity claim attached to cultural values does not transcend local boundaries in the same way as truth and rightness claims. Cultural values do not count as universal; they are, as the name indicates, located within the horizon of the lifeworld of a specific group or culture. And values can be made plausible only in the context of a particular form of life. Thus the critique of value standards presupposes a shared pre-understanding among participants in the argument, a preunderstanding that is not at their disposal but constitutes and at the same time circumscribes the domain of the thematized validity claims.[55] Only the truth of propositions and the rightness of moral norms and the comprehensibility or well-formedness of symbolic expressions are, by their very meaning, universal validity claims that can be tested in discourse. Only in theoretical, practical, and explicative discourse do the participants have to start from the (often counterfactual) presupposition that the conditions for an ideal speech situation are satisfied to a sufficient degree of approximation. I shall speak of "discourse" only when the meaning of the problematic validity claim conceptually forces participants to suppose that a rationally motivated agreement could in principle be achieved, whereby the phrase "in principle" expresses the idealizing proviso: if only the argumentation could be conducted openly enough and continued long enough.[56]

2. *Some Characteristics of the Mythical and the Modern Ways of Understanding the World*

Our excursus into the outer court of the theory of argumentation was meant to supplement our provisional specification of the concept of rationality. We took the use of the expression "rational" as a guideline in elucidating conditions of rationality both for speaking and acting subjects and for their expressions. Naturally, owing to its individualistic and unhistorical stamp, this concept is not directly serviceable from a sociological point of view.

Even when we are judging the rationality of individual persons, it is not sufficient to resort to this or that expression. The question is, rather, whether *A* or *B* or a group of individuals behaves rationally *in general;* whether one may systematically expect that they have good reasons for their expressions and that these expressions are correct or successful in the cognitive dimension, reliable or insightful in the moral-practical dimension, discerning or illuminating in the evaluative dimension, or candid and self-critical in the expressive dimension; that they exhibit understanding in the hermeneutic dimension; or indeed whether they are "reasonable" in all these dimensions. When there appears a systematic effect in these respects, across various domains of interaction and over long periods (perhaps even over the space of a lifetime), we also speak of the rationality of a *conduct of life.* And in the sociocultural conditions for such a conduct of life there is reflected perhaps the rationality of a lifeworld shared not only by individuals but by collectives as well.

In order to elucidate the difficult concept of a rationalized *lifeworld,* we shall take up the concept of communicative rationality and examine the structures of the lifeworld that make rational orientations of action possible for individuals and groups. The concept of the lifeworld is of course too complex to explicate satisfactorily in the framework of an introduction.[1] Rather than attempt to do so, I shall take up the cultural interpretive systems or worldviews that reflect the background knowledge of social groups and guarantee an interconnection among the multiplicity of their action orientations. Thus I shall first inquire into the conditions that the structures of action-orienting worldviews must satisfy if a rational conduct of life is to be possible for those who share such a worldview. This way of proceeding offers two advantages: on the one hand, it forces us to turn from conceptual to empirical analysis and to seek out the rationality structures embodied in worldviews; and, on the other hand, it keeps us from supposing without further ado that the rationality structures specific to the modern understanding of the world are generally valid and forces us instead to consider them in an historical perspective.

In attempting to elucidate the concept of rationality through appeal to the use of the expression "rational," we had to rely on a *preunderstanding* anchored in modern orientations. Hitherto we have naively presupposed that, in this modern understanding of the world, structures of consciousness are expressed that belong to a rationalized lifeworld and make possible in principle a rational conduct of life. We are implicitly connecting a claim to *universality* with our *Occidental understanding of the world.* In determining the significance of this claim, it would be well to draw a comparison with the mythical understanding of the world. In archaic societies myths fulfill the unifying function of world-views in an exemplary way—they permeate life-practice. At the same time, within the cultural traditions accessible to us, they present the sharpest contrast to the understanding of the world dominant in modern societies. Mythical worldviews are far from making possible rational orientations of action in our sense. With respect to the conditions for a rational conduct of life in this sense, they present an antithesis to the modern understanding of the world. Thus the heretofore unthematized presuppositions of modern thought should become visible in the mirror of mythical thinking.

The earlier discussion of Levy-Bruhl's theses on the mentality of "nature peoples"[2] showed that we cannot postulate a "prelogical" stage of knowing and acting for the "savage mind."[3] The well-known investigations of Evans-Pritchard concerning the belief in witchcraft among the African Azande confirmed the view that the differences between mythical and modern thought do not lie at the level of logical operations.[4] The degree of rationality of worldviews evidently does not vary with the stage of cognitive development of the individuals who orient their action within them. Our point of departure has to be that adult members of primitive tribal societies can acquire basically the same formal operations as the members of modern societies, even though the higher-level competences appear less frequently and more selectively in them; that is, they are applied in more restricted spheres of life.[5] The rationality of worldviews is not measured in terms of logical and semantic properties but in terms of the formal-pragmatic basic concepts they place at the disposal of individuals for interpreting their world. We could also speak of the "ontologies" built into worldviews, providing that this concept, which stems from the tradition of Greek metaphysics, is not restricted to a special world-relation, that is, to the cognitive relation to the world of existing things [Seienden]. There is no corresponding concept in philosophy that includes relations to the social and the subjective worlds as well as to the objective world. The theory of communicative action is also meant to remedy this lack.

I shall begin with (A) a rough characterization of the mythical understanding of the world. For the sake of simplicity I shall confine myself to the results of Lévi-Strauss' structuralist investigations, above all to those stressed by M. Godelier. (B) Against this background the basic concepts constitutive of the modern understanding of the world, and thus intuitively familiar to us, begin to stand out. In this way we can, from a cultural-anthropological distance, link up again with the concept of rationality introduced above. (C) The discussion sparked by Peter Winch's provocative essay on the conventional character of scientific rationality will provide us with an opportunity to clarify the sense in which the modern understanding of the world can claim universality. (D) Finally, I shall take up Piaget's concept of decentration in order to indicate the evolutionary perspective we can adopt if we want, with Max Weber, to posit a world-historical process of rationalization of worldviews. This process issues in an understanding of the world that opens the way to a rationalization of the lifeworld.

A.—The deeper one penetrates into the network of a mythical interpretation of the world, the more strongly the totalizing power of the "savage mind" stands out.[6] On the one hand, abundant and precise information about the natural and social environments is processed in myths: that is, geographical, astronomical, and meteorological knowledge; knowledge about flora and fauna; about economic and technical matters; about complex kinship relations; about rites, healing practices, waging war, and so on. On the other hand, this information is organized in such a way that every individual appearance in the world, in its typical aspects, resembles or contrasts with every other appearance. Through these *contrast and similarity relations* the multiplicity of observations is united in a totality. Myth constructs

> a gigantic mirror-effect, where the reciprocal image of man and the world is reflected ad infinitum, perpetually decomposing and recomposing in the prism of nature-culture relations... By analogy the whole world makes sense, everything is significant, everything can be explained within a symbolic order, where all the positive known facts... may take their place with all their rich abundance of detail.[7]

Structuralists explain this synthetic accomplishment through the fact that the "savage mind" fastens in a *concretistic way* upon the perceptual surface of the world and orders these perceptions by drawing analogies and contrasts.[8] Domains of phenomena are interrelated and classified from the vantage points of *homology* and *heterogeneity*, equivalence and inequality, identity and contrariety. As Lévi-Strauss has put it, the world of myths is both *round and hollow.* Analogical thought weaves all appearances into a single network of correspondence, but its interpretations do not penetrate the surface of what can be grasped perceptually.

The concretism of thought that is tied to perception and the establishment of similarity and contrast relations are two formal aspects under which "savage thought" can be compared with ontogenetic stages of cognitive development.[9] The categories or basic concepts of mythical worldviews, however, originate in domains of experience that have to be analyzed sociologically. On the one hand, the reciprocity structures of kinship systems, the relations of give-and-take between families, sexes, and generations provide an interpretive schema that can be applied in multifarious ways. "The fact that the imaginary societies where mythical ideal characters live, die and are eternally resuscitated are invested with an organization based on relationships of blood and alliance can have its origin neither in the 'pure principles' of thought nor in any models found in nature."[10] On the other hand, the categories of action acquire constitutive significance for mythical worldviews. Actor and the capacity for action, intention and goal-setting, success and failure, active and passive, attack and defense—these are the categories in which a fundamental experience of archaic societies is expressed: the experience of being delivered up unprotected to the contingencies of an unmastered environment.[11]

In the undeveloped state of their productive forces these risks cannot be brought under control. Thus arises the need to check the flood of contingencies—if not in fact at least in imagination—that is, to interpret them away. Through analogy,

> the invisible causes and forces which give rise to and regulate the non-human world (nature) or the human world (culture) assume the attributes of man, i.e. present themselves spontaneously in consciousness as beings endowed with *consciousness, will, authority and power,* therefore as beings analogous to men, but different in that they know what man does not know, they do what man cannot do, they control what he cannot control; they are different from man and are superior to him.[12]

If one considers how these *categories,* which are derived from the model of the kinship system and used to interpret experiences of interacting with an overwhelming nature, work together with the *operations* of a concretistic and analogical mode of thought, the familiar magical-animistic characteristics of mythical worldviews can be understood somewhat better. What *we* find most astonishing is the peculiar leveling of the different domains of reality: nature and culture are projected onto the same plane. From this reciprocal assimilation of nature to culture and conversely culture to nature, there results, on the one hand, a nature that is outfitted with anthropomorphic features, drawn into the communicative network of social subjects, and in this sense humanized, and on the other hand, a culture that is to a certain extent naturalized and reified and absorbed into the objective nexus of operations of anonymous powers. From the perspective of enlightened thought, the "savage mind" gives rise to

> a double illusion, an illusion about the world and an illusion about itself; an illusion about itself because the mind endows idealities with an existence outside of man and independent of him; these idealities are engendered spontaneously and thus the mind alienates itself by its own representations; an illusion about the world because the mind peoples it with imaginary beings similar to man, capable of understanding his needs and responding to them in a favorable or hostile fashion.[13]

Such an interpretation of the world, in which each appearance is in correspondence with every other appearance through the influence of mythical powers, makes possible not only a theory that explains the world narratively and renders it plausible, but also a practice through which the world can be controlled in an imaginary way. The technique of magically influencing the world is a logical inference from the mythical interrelation of perspectives between man and world, between culture and nature.

After this rough sketch of some basic features of mythical thought, I would like to return to the question of why these worldview structures do not allow action orientations that might be called rational by the implicit standards of today.

B.—What irritates us members of a modern lifeworld is that in a mythically interpreted world we cannot, or cannot with sufficient precision, make certain differentiations that are fundamental to our understanding of the world. From Durkheim to Lévi-Strauss, anthropologists have repeatedly pointed out the peculiar *confusion between nature and culture.* We can understand this phenomenon to begin with as a mixing of two object domains, physical nature and the sociocultural environment. Myths do not permit a clear, basic, conceptual differentiation between things and persons, between objects that can be manipulated and agents —subjects capable of speaking and acting to whom we attribute linguistic utterances. Thus it is only consistent when magical practices do not recognize the distinction between teleological and communicative action, between goal-directed, instrumental intervention in objectively given situations, on the one hand, and the establishment of interpersonal relations, on the other. The *ineptitude* to which the technical or therapeutic failures of goal-directed action are due falls into the same category as the *guilt* for moral-normative failings of interaction in violation of existing social orders. Moral failure is conceptually interwoven with physical failure, as is *evil* with the *harmful,* and *good* with the *healthy* and the *advantageous.*

On the other hand, the demythologization of worldviews means the desocialization of nature and the denaturalization of society. This process—which is easily accessible on an intuitive level and often treated in descriptive terms, but which is by no means well and thoroughly analyzed—apparently leads to a basic conceptual *differentiation between the object domains* of nature and culture. This way of looking at the matter does not take into consideration the fact that the categorial distinction between object domains depends, for its part, on a process of differentiation that can better be analyzed in terms of *basic attitudes toward worlds.* The mythical concept of powers and the magical concept of conjuring systematically impede the separation of an objectivating attitude to a world of existing states of affairs from a conformist or nonconformist attitude to a world of legitimately regulated interpersonal relations. Regarded as object domains, nature and culture belong to the world of facts about which true statements are possible; but as soon as we are to specify explicitly wherein things are distinct from persons, causes from motives, happenings from actions, and so forth, we have to go beyond differentiating object domains to differentiating between a basic attitude toward the objective world of what is the case and a basic attitude toward the social world of what can legitimately be expected, what is commanded or ought to be. We make the correct conceptual separations between causal connections of nature and normative orders of society to the extent that we become conscious of the changes in perspective and attitude that we effect when we pass from observing or manipulating to following or violating legitimate expectations.

To be sure, the confusion of nature and culture by no means signifies only a conceptual blending of the objective and social worlds, but also a—by our lights—deficient differentiation between *language and world;* that is, between speech as the medium of communication and that about which understanding can be reached in linguistic communication. In the totalizing mode of thought of mythical worldviews, it is apparently difficult to draw with sufficient precision the familiar (to us) semiotic distinctions between the sign-substratum of a linguistic expression, its semantic content, and the referent to which a speaker can refer with its help. The magical relation between names and designated objects, the concretistic relation between the meaning of expressions and the states-of-affairs represented give evidence of systematic confusion between *internal connections of meaning* and *external connections of objects.* Internal relations obtain between symbolic expressions, external relations between entities that appear in the world. In this sense the logical relation between ground and consequence is internal, the causal relation between cause and effect is external (symbolic *versus* physical causation). Mythical interpretation of the world and magical control of the world can intermesh smoothly because internal and external relations are still conceptually integrated. Evidently there is not yet any precise concept for the nonempirical validity that we ascribe to symbolic expressions. Validity is confounded with empirical efficacy. I am not referring here to special validity claims—in mythical thought diverse validity claims, such as propositional truth, normative rightness, and expressive sincerity are not yet differentiated. But even the diffuse concept of validity in general is still not freed from empirical admixtures. Concepts of validity such as morality and truth are amalgamated with empirical ordering concepts, such as causality and health. Thus a linguistically constituted worldview can be identified with the world-order itself to such an extent that it cannot be perceived *as* an interpretation of the world that is subject to error and open to criticism. In this respect the confusion of nature and culture takes on the significance of a reification of worldview.

Linguistic communication and the cultural tradition that flows into it are only set off as a reality in their own right from the reality of nature and society to the degree that formal world-concepts and nonempirical validity claims are differentiated. In communicative action we today proceed from those *formal presuppositions of intersubjectivity* that are necessary if we are to be able to refer to something in the one objective world, identical for all observers, or to something in our intersubjectively shared social world. The claims to propositional truth or normative rightness actualize these presuppositions of commonality for particular utterances. Thus the truth of a proposition signifies that the asserted state of affairs exists as something in the objective world; and the rightness of an action in respect to an existing normative context signifies that the interpersonal relation established merits recognition as a legitimate element of the social world. Validity claims are in principle open to criticism because they are based on formal world-concepts. They presuppose a world that is identical for *all possible* observers, or a world intersubjectively shared *by members,* and they do so in an abstract form freed of all specific content. Such claims call for the rational response of a partner in communication.

Actors who raise validity claims have to avoid materially prejudicing the relation between language and reality, between the medium of communication and that about which something is being communicated. Under the presupposition of formal world-concepts and universal validity claims, the contents of a linguistic worldview have to be detached from the assumed world-order itself. Only then can we form the concept of a cultural tradition, of a temporalized culture, whereby we become aware that interpretations vary in relation to natural and social reality, that beliefs and values vary in relation to the objective and social worlds. By contrast, mythical worldviews prevent us from categorially uncoupling nature and culture, not only through conceptually mixing the objective and social worlds but also through reifying the linguistic worldview. As a result the concept of the world is dogmatically invested with a specific content that is withdrawn from rational discussion and thus from criticism.

Hitherto we have used the formula "confusing nature and culture" with reference only to *external* nature or the objective world. But an analogous mixing of domains of reality can be shown as well for the relationship of culture and *internal* nature or the subjective world. Only to the extent that the formal concept of an *external world* develops—of an objective world of existing states of affairs and of a social world of norms—can the complementary concept of the *internal world* or of subjectivity arise, that is, a world to which the individual has privileged access and to which everything is attributed that cannot be incorporated in the external world. Only against the background of an objective world, and measured against criticizable claims to truth and efficacy, can beliefs appear as systematically false, action intentions as systematically hopeless, and thoughts as fantasies, as mere imaginings. Only against the background of a normative reality that has become autonomous, and measured against the criticizable claim to normative rightness, can intentions, wishes, attitudes, feelings appear as illegitimate or merely idiosyncratic, as nongeneralizable and merely subjective. To the degree that mythical worldviews hold sway over cognition and orientations for action, a clear demarcation of a domain of subjectivity is apparently not possible. Intentions and motives are just as little separated from actions and their consequences as feelings are from their normatively fixed, stereotyped expressions. In this connection it has been observed that the members of archaic societies tie their own identities in large measure to the details of the collective knowledge set down in myths and to the formal specifications of ritual prescriptions. They do not have at their disposal a formal concept of the world that could secure the identity of natural and social reality in the face of the changing interpretations of temporalized cultural traditions; nor can the individual rely on a formal concept of the ego that could secure his own identity in the face of a subjectivity that has become independent and fluid.

Relying on ordinary language, in which we employ the symmetrical concepts of an internal and external world, I am speaking of the subjective world in distinction from the objective and social worlds. To be sure, the expression "world" might easily lead to misunderstandings in this connection. The domain of subjectivity is complementary to the external world, which is defined by its being shared with others. The objective world is presupposed in common as the totality of facts, where "fact" signifies that a statement about the existence of a corresponding state of affairs, p, can count as true. And a social world is presupposed in common as the totality of all interpersonal relations that are recognized by members as legitimate. Over against this, the subjective world counts as the totality of experiences to which, in each instance, only one individual has privileged access. The expression "subjective *world*" is justified inasmuch as here too we are dealing with an abstract concept which, in the form of common presuppositions, delimits from the objective and social worlds a domain for each member of *what is not common*. The concept of the subjective world has a status similar to that of its complementary concepts. That can also be seen from the fact that it can be analyzed with reference to an additional basic attitude and an additional validity claim.

The expressive attitude of a subject who reveals a thought, makes known a wish, expresses a feeling, who exposes a bit of his subjectivity before the eyes of others, is distinct in a characteristic way from the objectivating attitude of a manipulating or observing subject toward things and events and from the conformative (or nonconformative) attitude of a participant in interaction toward normative expectations. Moreover, we also connect expressive utterances with a criticizable validity claim, namely the claim to truthfulness or sincerity. Thus subjective worlds, as domains of noncommonality with privileged access, can also be drawn into public communication.

Hitherto we have discussed the "closedness" of mythical worldviews from two points of view: the insufficient differentiation among fundamental attitudes to the objective, social, and subjective worlds; and the lack of reflexivity in worldviews that cannot be identified *as* worldviews, as cultural traditions. Mythical worldviews are not understood by members as interpretive systems that are attached to cultural traditions, constituted by internal interrelations of meaning, symbolically related to reality, and connected with validity claims—and thus exposed to criticism and open to revision. In this way we can in fact discover through the quite contrasting structures of "the savage mind" important presuppositions of the modern understanding of the world. Of course, this does not yet prove that the supposed rationality expressed in our understanding of the world is more than a reflection of the particular features of a culture stamped by science, that it may rightfully raise a claim to universality.

C.—This question became pressing toward the end of the nineteenth century as reflection on the foundations of the historical *Geisteswissenschaften* set in. The discussion was carried out basically under two aspects. From a methodological point of view it was concentrated around the question of the objectivity of *Verstehen* or interpretive understanding. With Gadamer's investigations in philosophical hermeneutics this aspect of the discussion has drawn to a certain close.[14] At the same time, under the rubric of the problem of historicism, concern was directed above all to the substantive question of the uniqueness or commensurability of civilizations and worldviews. Toward the end of the 1920s, this part of the discussion did not so much come to an end as break down, because the problem could not be given a sufficiently sharp formulation.[15] This may be due in part to the fact that the object domain of the *Geisteswissenschaften*—above all, intellectually elaborated testimonies from the golden ages of civilizations, passed on in written form—did not—as did mythical traditions, rites, magic, and so forth—force a *radical* confrontation on the one fundamental question: whether and in what respect the standards of rationality by which the investigator was himself at least intuitively guided might claim universal validity. In cultural anthropology this question played a big role from the start. Since the 1960s it has once again stood at the center of a discussion carried on among social scientists and philosophers,[16] a discussion prompted by two publications of Peter Winch.[17] I shall pursue only one line of argument which is important in the present context.[18] For the sake of simplicity, rather than following the actual course of the discussion I shall construe it as a series of six pairs of arguments for and against a universalistic position.

  (a) The first round is still situated at the perimeter of the discussion. Steven Lukes has pointed to a prior decision that could obviate the controversy itself:

When I come across a set of beliefs which appear *prima facie* irrational, what should be my attitude towards them? Should I adopt a critical attitude, taking it as a fact about the beliefs that they *are* irrational and seek to explain how they came to be held, how they manage to survive unprofaned by rational criticism, what their consequences are, etc.? Or should I treat such beliefs *charitably:* should I begin from the assumption that what appears to me to be irrational may be interpreted as rational when fully understood in its context? More briefly, the problem comes down to whether or not there *are alternative standards of rationality.*[19]

Lukes seems to suppose that the anthropologist, when faced with an incomprehensible, prima facie impenetrable and opaque expression, has the choice of whether or not to renounce the attempt at a hermeneutic elucidation of its meaning. He goes on to state that the decision for a hermeneutic procedure is implicitly based on the assumption of alternative standards of rationality. Winch can contest both theses on good grounds.

If an expression that is irrational for the time being stubbornly resists attempts at interpretation, the interpreter can certainly switch to explaining the inaccessible expression, in the sense of the occurrence of an empirical event, with the help of causal hypotheses and initial conditions—for example, in psychological or sociological terms. This position is defended, for instance, by Alasdair MacIntyre in his critique of Winch.[20] Read in this way, in terms of research strategy, Lukes' argument is unobjectionable; but in a strictly methodological sense the alternative posited by Lukes does not exist. Symbolic expressions of speaking and acting subjects can be identified only under descriptions that refer to the action orientations (and the possible reasons) of an actor. The interpreter has therefore no other choice than to test whether an obscure expression—one that is not simply unintelligible but unintelligible in certain aspects—would not after all appear as rational if one clarified the presuppositions from which the agent proceeds in his context.

Notice that in ascribing irrationality to him we should be pointing to the incoherence and incompatibility between the beliefs and criteria which he already possessed and his new behavior. It is not just that his behavior would be at odds with what we believe to be appropriate; it would be at odds with what we know him to believe to be appropriate.[21]

For the interpreter it is not a question of hermeneutic *charity* but a methodological precept that he proceed from the presumptive rationality of the questionable expression in order, if necessary, to assure himself step by step of its irrationality. In doing so, only hermeneutic *severity* in relation to his own presuppositions can preserve him from exercising criticism without self-criticism and falling prey to just the error that Winch rightfully chalks up to Victorian anthropologists such as Frazer and Tyler, namely the error of simply imposing the supposedly universal rationality standards of one's own culture upon alien cultures.

This methodological position does not at all result in a prior decision on alternative standards of rationality, as Lukes asserts. When the interpreter takes up the reasons that an actor gives —or would under suitable circumstances give—for his expression, he is moving to a level where he has to take a positive or negative position on criticizable validity claims. What counts in any instance as a good reason obviously depends on criteria that have changed in the course of history (including the history of science). The context-dependence of the criteria by which the members of different cultures at different times judge differently the validity of expressions does not, however, mean that the ideas of truth, of normative rightness, of sincerity, and of authenticity that underlie (only intuitively, to be sure) the choice of criteria are context-dependent in the same degree. At any rate, a hermeneutic approach to the object domain does not prejudice this question in an affirmative sense. But we can answer it in the sense of the universalistic position that Lukes wants to defend only if we get to the roots of the problematic of understanding meaning [*Sinnverstehen*]. I shall return to this below.

(b) Evans-Pritchard's study of witchcraft, oracles, and magic in the African tribe of the Azande is one of the best examples showing that one can exhibit a high degree of hermeneutic charity toward obscure expressions without drawing the relativistic consequences that Lukes sees connected with this manner of proceeding. I would like to open the second round with an argument from Evans-Pritchard, who clarifies the belief in witches, and thereby also the reasons for the corresponding magical practices, in such a way that his readers can recognize the coherence of the Zande worldview. At the same time, as an anthropologist he holds fast to the standards of scientific rationality when it is a question of objectively assessing the views and techniques of this tribe. Evans-Pritchard distinguishes between the logical require-

ment of consistency, which the Zande belief in witches largely satisfies, and the methodological requirements that (in our view) empirical knowledge about material processes and technical intervention into them are supposed to satisfy. In this latter respect mythical thought is obviously inferior to modern.

> Scientific notions are those which accord with objective reality both with regard to the validity of their premises and to the inferences drawn from their propositions...Logical notions are those in which according to the rules of thought inferences would be true were the premises true, the truth of the premises being irrelevant...A pot has broken during firing. This is probably due to grit. Let us examine the pot and see if this is the cause. That is logical and scientific thought. Sickness is due to witchcraft. A man is sick. Let us consult the oracles to discover who is the witch responsible. That is logical and unscientific thought.[22]

In interpreting the expressions of natives, the anthropologist relates them both to other expressions and to something in the world. In the first dimension he can rely on a system of rules, on intuitively mastered principles of formal logic that hold for both sides in the same way. As to the dimension of relation to the world, in doubtful cases the anthropologist must have recourse to basic expressions (e.g., color predicates) whose rules of use are more or less unproblematic. In doing so, he supposes that everyone involved is starting from the same concept of a world of entities, that in a given situation the natives perceive more or less the same thing as he does himself, that they interpret the situation more or less in the same way he does.[23] To be sure, the different parties cannot have recourse here, as they can in the case of logic, to an unambiguous set of intersubjectively valid rules of interpretation. I understand Evans-Pritchard to be saying that where there is disagreement about the truth of propositions and the efficacy of interventions, the anthropologist must rely on methods of testing that we came to recognize as universally valid only after they had been highly stylized in a scientific manner within the framework of our culture.

Winch bases his objections to Evans-Pritchard on a culturalistic concept of language inspired by Wittgenstein. "Languages" he understands as linguistically articulated worldviews and correspondingly structured forms of life. Worldviews store the cultural knowledge with the help of which a language community interprets the world. Each culture establishes in its language a relation to reality. To this extent, "real" and "unreal," "true" and "untrue" are indeed concepts that are inherent in all languages and not ones that can, say, be present in this language and absent in that. But each culture draws this categorial distinction *within* its own language system.

> Reality is not what gives language sense. What is real and what is unreal shows itself *in* the sense that language has. Further, both the distinction between the real and the unreal and the concept of agreement with reality, themselves belong to our [i.e. to each different, J.H.] language...If then we wish to understand the significance of these concepts, we must examine the use they actually do have—*in* the language.[24]

Now the Azande and the anthropologists obviously speak different languages; this is already evident from the large amount of interpretive energy that the anthropologists have to expend. And Evans-Pritchard himself makes clear that the Zande language reflects a coherent worldview. Like the modern understanding of the world, but in a different way, this worldview lays down the categorial distinctions between "real" and "unreal" and determines how one decides whether or not a conception or proposition is in agreement with reality. According to Winch, it is therefore senseless to suppose that both sides are starting from the same concept of the world. The anthropologist has no right to judge the belief in witches and magic by the standards of scientific rationality. Evans-Pritchard can claim this right for himself only because he proceeds from the untenable assumption

> that the conception of "reality" must be regarded as intelligible and applicable *outside* the context of scientific reasoning itself, since it is that to which scientific notions do, and unscientific notions do not, have a relation. Evans-Pritchard, although he emphasizes that a member of scientific culture has a different conception of reality from that of a Zande believer in magic, wants to go beyond merely registering this fact and making the differences explicit, and to say, finally, that the scientific conception agrees with what reality actually is like, whereas the magical conception does not.[25]

(c) Before exposing, in the third round, the weakness in Winch's argument, we have first to explain its strength. "Language," "linguistically articulated worldview," and "form of life" are concepts that refer on the one hand to something particular; for languages, worldviews, and forms of life appear in the plural. On the other hand, they refer to totalities; for members of the same culture the limits of their language are the limits of the world. They can broaden the horizon of their form of life in an ad hoc manner, but they cannot step out of it; to this extent, every interpretation is also a process of assimilation. Inasmuch as worldviews refer to totalities, we cannot get behind them as articulations of an understanding of the world, even if they can be revised. In this respect they are like a portrait that claims to represent a person as a whole. A portrait is neither a *mapping* that can be exact or inexact, nor a *rendering of facts* in the sense of a proposition that can be true or false. A portrait offers rather an angle of vision from which the person represented appears in a certain way. Thus there can be numerous portraits of the same person; they can make the character appear in quite different aspects, and yet they can all be experienced as accurate, authentic, or adequate. Similarly, worldviews lay down the framework of fundamental concepts within which we interpret everything that appears in the world in a specific way as something. Worldviews can no more be true or false than can portraits.[26]

On the other hand, worldviews differ from portraits in that they in turn *make possible* utterances that admit of truth. To this extent they have a relation, albeit indirect, to truth; and it is this fact Winch does not take into account. Owing to their reference to totality, worldviews are indeed removed from the dimension in which a judgment of them according to criteria of truth makes sense; even the choice of criteria according to which the truth of statements is to be judged may depend on the basic conceptual context of a worldview. But this does not mean that the idea of truth might itself be understood in a particularistic way. Whatever language system we choose, we always start intuitively from the presupposition that truth is a universal validity claim. If a statement is true, it merits universal assent, no matter in which language it is formulated. Thus it can be objected against the thesis developed by Winch that worldviews can be compared with one another not only from the quasiaesthetic and truth-indifferent standpoints of coherence, depth, economy, completeness, and the like, but also from the standpoint of *cognitive adequacy.* The adequacy of a linguistically articulated worldview is a function of the true statements that are possible in this language system.[27]

Of course, Winch might reject this point in the first place as a cognitivistic misunderstanding. Linguistically articulated worldviews are interwoven with forms of life—that is, with the everyday practice of sociated individuals—in such a way that they cannot be reduced to the functions of knowing and mastering external nature.

> Language games are played by men who have lives to live—lives involving a wide variety of different interests, which have all kinds of different bearings on each other. Because of this, what a man says or does may make a difference not merely to the performance of the activity upon which he is at present engaged, but to his life and to the lives of other people. . . What we may learn by studying other cultures are not merely possibilities of different ways of doing things, other techniques. More importantly we may learn different possibilities of making sense of human life, different ideas about the possible importance that the carrying out of certain activities may take on for a man, trying to contemplate the sense of his life as a whole.[28]

In the framework of their worldview the members of a language community come to an understanding on central themes of their personal and social lives. If we wish to compare standards of rationality built into different cultural interpretive systems, we ought not to confine ourselves to the dimension of science and technology suggested by *our* culture and take as the measure of their rationality the extent to which true statements and effective techniques are made possible. Worldviews are comparable only in respect to their potency for conferring meaning. They throw light on existential themes recurrent in every culture—birth and death, sickness and need, guilt, love, solidarity and loneliness. They open equally primordial possibilities of "making sense of human life." They thereby structure forms of life that are *incommensurable in their value.* The rationality of forms of life cannot be reduced to the cognitive adequacy of the worldviews underlying them.

(d) With this argument Winch sidesteps toward aspects of content, though the rationality of worldviews and forms of life would have to be found in their formal properties. We can open the next round of argumentation by showing in what sense

Winch misses the problem at issue. The cognitive adequacy of worldviews—that is, the coherence and the truth of the statements possible in them as well as the effectiveness of the plans of action dependent on them—is *also* reflected in the practice of conducting life. Winch himself picks up Evans-Pritchard's observation that while the Azande can explain apparent contradictions—for example, between two oracles, or between the oracle's prediction and the event that occurs—by drawing on the belief in witches, they can do so only to a certain extent. Using the example of Zande ideas concerning the inheritance of magical powers, Evans-Pritchard discusses contradictions that inevitably arise from certain fundamental assumptions of their animistic worldview. And he leaves no doubt that the Azande themselves experience unavoidable absurdities as disagreeable as soon as they enter upon a stubborn consistency check such as the anthropologist undertakes. But a demand of this kind is *brought* to bear upon them; it does not arise within the framework of their own culture; and when an anthropologist confronts them with it, they generally evade it. But isn't this refusal, this higher tolerance for contradiction, a sign of a more irrational conduct of life? Must we not call action orientations that can be stabilized only at the cost of suppressing contradictions irrational? Winch disputes this. He refers to Evans-Pritchard's remark that the Azande have no theoretical interest in pursuing such problems when they are constrained to notice them.

> It might now appear as though we had clear grounds for speaking of the superior rationality of European over Zande thought, in so far as the latter involves a contradiction which it makes no attempt to remove and does not even recognize: one, however, which is recognizable as such in the context of European ways of thinking. But does Zande thought on this matter really involve a contradiction? It appears from Evans-Pritchard's account that the Azande do not press their ways of thinking about witches to a point at which they would be involved in contradictions.[29]

Winch holds that it is illegitimate to press the demand for consistency further than the Azande of *themselves* do; he comes to the conclusion "that it is the European, obsessed with pressing Zande thought where it would not naturally go—to a contradiction—who is guilty of misunderstanding, not the Azande. The European is in fact committing a category mistake."[30] A belief in witches ought not to be confused with a quasitheory; for the

Azande do not intend with it to comprehend processes in the world in the same objectivating attitude as does a modern physicist or a physician trained in the natural sciences.

(e) The charge of a category mistake raised against the European anthropologist can be understood in a strong and in a weak sense. If it says merely that the scientist should not impute to the natives his own interest in resolving inconsistencies, the question naturally arises, whether this lack of a theoretical interest may not be traced back to the fact that the Zande worldview imposes less exacting standards of rationality and is in this sense less rational than the modern understanding of the world. With this, the next to last round of the controversy has begun.

Taking up Popper's distinction between "closed" and "open" mentalities and the corresponding forms of life of tradition-bound and modern societies, Robin Horton develops this argument. He accepts Winch's view that the structures of worldviews are expressed in forms of life, but insists on the possibility of evaluating worldviews, if not by the degree of their cognitive adequacy, then by the degree to which they hinder or promote cognitive-instrumental learning processes. "For the progressive acquisition of knowledge, man needs both the right kind of theories *and* the right attitude to them."[31]

Horton and Winch base their arguments upon almost the same passages in Evans-Pritchard's report on the uncritical behavior of the Azande; but Horton does not attribute this behavior to a rationality peculiar to the Zande worldview and equally as valid in principle as scientific rationality. Rather, the belief in witches exhibits a structure that binds the Zande consciousness more or less blindly to inherited interpretations and does not permit consciousness of the possibility of alternative interpretations to arise.

> In other words, absence of any awareness of alternatives makes for an absolute acceptance of the established theoretical tenets, and removes any possibility of questioning them. In these circumstances, the established tenets invest the believer with a compelling force. It is this force which we refer to when we talk of such tenets as sacred . . . Here, then, we have two basic predicaments: the "closed"—characterized by lack of awareness of alternatives, sacredness of beliefs, and anxiety about threats to them; and the "open"—characterized by awareness of alternatives, diminished sacredness of beliefs and diminished anxiety about threats to them.[32]

This dimension of "closed" *versus* "open" seems to provide a *context-independent standard for the rationality of worldviews*. Of course, the point of reference is again modern science, for Horton traces the "sacred," that is, identity-securing character of closed worldviews, back to an immunization against alternative interpretations; this stands in contrast to the readiness to learn and the openness to criticism that are the outstanding features of the scientific spirit. Horton does not, it is true, simply subject the belief in witches to the demands of protoscience; but he judges its structure only from the standpoint of the incompatibility of the mythical-magical world of representation with that reflective basic attitude in the absence of which scientific theories cannot arise. Thus the objection that the modern European is here committing a category mistake can be renewed at another level. Even if we are willing to admit that readiness to learn and openness to criticism are by no means idiosyncratic features only of our own culture, it is at least *one-sided* to judge worldviews according to whether they inhibit or promote a scientific mentality. On this point, MacIntyre is in agreement with Winch.

> It is right to wonder whether, sophisticated as we are, we may not sometimes at least continue to make Frazer's mistake, but in a more subtle way. For when we approach the utterances and activities of an alien culture with a well-established classification of genres in our mind and ask of a given rite or other practice "Is it a piece of applied science? Or a piece of symbolic and dramatic activity? Or a piece of theology?" we may in fact be asking a set of questions to which any answer may be misleading...For the utterances and practices in question may belong, as it were, to all and to none of the genres that we have in mind. For those who engage in the given practice the question of how their utterances are to be interpreted—in the sense of "interpretation" in which to allocate a practice or an utterance to a genre is to interpret it, as a prediction, say, rather than as a symbolic expression of desire, or vice versa—may never have arisen. If we question them as to how their utterances are to be interpreted, we may therefore receive an answer which is sincere and yet we may still be deceived. For we may, by the very act of asking these questions, have brought them to the point where they cannot avoid beginning to construe their own utterances in one way rather than another. But perhaps this was not so until we asked the question. Perhaps before that time their utterances were poised in ambiguity...Myths

would then be seen as perhaps potentially science *and* as literature *and* theology; but to understand them as myths would be to understand them as actually yet none of these. Hence the absurdity involved in speaking of myths as misrepresenting reality; the myth is at most a possible misrepresentation of reality, for it does not aspire, while still only a myth, to be a representation.[33]

Horton defines the "closedness" and "openness" of worldviews in terms of a sense for theoretical alternatives. He calls a worldview closed to the degree that it regulates our dealings with external reality, with what can be perceived or handled in the objective world, in such a way as to exclude alternatives. This setting of worldviews against a reality with which they can be more or less in harmony already suggests the idea that their primary meaning lies in the construction of theories. In fact, however, the structures of worldviews determine a life-practice that is by no means exhausted in cognitive-instrumental interaction with external reality. Rather, worldviews are constitutive *across the whole breadth* of processes of understanding and socialization, in which participants relate as much to the orders of their common social world and to the experiences of their respective subjective worlds as to happenings in the one objective world. If mythical thought *does not yet permit* a categorial separation between cognitive-instrumental, moral-practical, and expressive relations to the world, if the expressions of the Azande are for us full of ambiguities, this is a sign that the "closedness" of their animistic worldview cannot be described solely in terms of attitudes toward the objective world; nor can the modern understanding of the world be described solely in terms of formal properties of the scientific mentality.

(f) This objection is already somewhat off Winch's line of argument; for its aim is not to upset the universalist position but to provide it with a more subtle defense. Thus at the start of the sixth and last round of argument, this position enjoys a certain point advantage. In his critique of Horton, Ernest Gellner warns that to view the closedness and openness of worldviews in terms of a "sense for theoretical alternatives" is to conceive the matter too narrowly.[34] The phenomena that Horton adduces in this regard cannot be pressed into this single dimension; they call instead for a more complex system of reference that can grasp the simultaneous differentiation of *three* formal world-concepts. The observations of Horton and Gellner[35] fit easily into the formal-

pragmatic viewpoints from which I characterized the closedness of mythical worldviews and the openness of the modern understanding of the world.[36] Under the catchwords: "mixed vs. segregated motives" and "low vs. high cognitive division of labor," the two authors provide concurring descriptions of the increasing categorial separation among the objective, social, and subjective worlds, of the specialization of cognitive-instrumental, moral practical, and expressive types of questions, and above all of the differentiation of the aspects of validity under which these problems can be dealt with. Horton and Gellner then stress the increasing differentiation between linguistic worldview and reality. They discuss different aspects under the catchwords: "magical vs. non-magical attitudes to words," "ideas bound to occasion vs. ideas bound to ideas" (a characteristic that has to do with the separation of internal connections of meaning from external connections of things and that reappears in Gellner under the catchword "the use of idiosyncratic norms"). Finally, the contrast of "unreflective vs. reflective thinking" refers to those "second-order intellectual activities" that make possible not only formal scientific disciplines like mathematics, logic, grammar, and the like, but also the systematic treatment and formal construction of symbol systems in general.

However, worldviews are constitutive not only for processes of reaching understanding but for the social integration and the socialization of individuals as well. They function in the formation and stabilization of identities, supplying individuals with a core of basic concepts and assumptions that cannot be revised without affecting the identity of individuals and social groups. This *identity-securing knowledge* becomes more and more formal along the path from closed to open worldviews; it attaches to structures that are increasingly disengaged from contents that are open to revision. Gellner speaks of "entrenched constitutional clauses," which shrink to a formal minimum in modern thought.

> There is a systematic difference in the distribution of the entrenched clauses, of the sacred, in this sense, as between savage and modern thought-systems. In a traditional thought-system, the sacred or the crucial is more extensive, more untidily dispersed, and much more pervasive. In a modern thought-system, it is tidier, narrower, as it were economical, based on some intelligible principle, and tends not to be diffused among the detailed aspects of life. Fewer hostages are given to fortune; or, looking at it from the other end, much

less of the fabric of life and society benefits from rein-
forcement from the sacred and entrenched convictions.[37]

Horton brings this development under the catchword
"protective vs. destructive attitudes"; and in this connection he
comprehends taboo as an institution that protects the categorial
foundations of a worldview wherever there is a danger of dis-
sonant experiences regularly arising and obliterating fundamental
distinctions.[38]

If we analyze Horton's and Gellner's anthropologically informed use of Popper's pair of concepts "closed vs. open," we
come upon a perspective from which Winch's misgivings concerning the hypostatization of scientific rationality can be
rendered intelligible and at the same time freed from precipitate
conclusions. Scientific rationality belongs to a complex of
cognitive-instrumental rationality that can certainly claim validity
beyond the context of particular cultures. Nevertheless, after
Winch's arguments have been examined and defused, something
of his pathos survives, to which we have not given its due: "My
aim is not to engage in moralizing, but to suggest that the concept of 'learning from' which is involved in the study of other
cultures is closely linked with the concept of *wisdom*."[39] Can't
we who belong to modern societies learn something from understanding alternative, particularly premodern forms of life?
Shouldn't we, beyond all romanticizing of superseded stages of
development, beyond exotic stimulation from the contents of alien
cultures, recall the losses required by our own path to the modern
world? Horton too does not at all regard this question as senseless.

> As a scientist it is perhaps inevitable that I should at certain
> points give the impression that traditional African thought
> is a poor shackled thing when compared with the thought
> of the sciences. Yet as a man, here I am living by choice in
> a still-heavily-traditional Africa rather than in the scientifical-
> ly oriented Western subculture I was brought up in. Why?
> Well, there may be lots of queer, sinister, unacknowledged
> reasons. But one certain reason is the discovery of *things lost*
> at home. An intensely poetic quality in everyday life and
> thought, and a vivid enjoyment of the passing moment—
> both driven out of sophisticated Western life by the quest
> for purity of motive and the faith in progress.[40]

In the expression "quest for purity of motive" there rings once again that differentiation of world-concepts and validity aspects from which the modern understanding of the world issued. In adding to his remark the sentence "How necessary these are for the advance of science; but what a disaster they are when they run wild beyond their appropriate bounds!" Horton gives a *self-critical emphasis* to the universalist position. What seems to belong to the idiosyncratic traits of Western culture is not scientific rationality as such, but its hypostatization. This suggests a pattern of cultural and societal rationalization that helps cognitive-instrumental rationality to achieve a one-sided dominance not only in our dealings with external nature, but also in our understanding of the world and in the communicative practice of everyday life.

The course of our argumentation can perhaps be summarized as follows: Winch's arguments are too weak to uphold the thesis that inherent to every linguistically articulated worldview and to every cultural form of life there is an incommensurable concept of rationality; but his strategy of argumentation is strong enough to set off the justified claim to universality on behalf of the rationality that gained expression in the modern understanding of the world from an uncritical self-interpretation of the modern world that is fixated on knowing and mastering external nature.

D.—The rationality debate carried on in England suggests that the modern understanding of the world is indeed based on general structures of rationality but that modern Western societies promote a distorted understanding of rationality that is fixed on cognitive-instrumental aspects and is to that extent particularistic. I shall conclude this section of the introduction by pointing out a few implications of such a conception.

If the rationality of worldviews can be judged in the formal-pragmatically specified dimension of closedness/openness, we are reckoning with systematic changes in worldviews that cannot be explained solely in psychological, economic, or sociological terms—that is, by means of external factors—but that can also be traced to an internally reconstructible growth of knowledge. Of course, learning processes must for their part be explained with the help of empirical mechanisms; but they are conceived at the same time as problem solutions, in such a way that they are open to systematic evaluation in the light of *internal validity conditions.* The universalistic position forces one to the assumption that the rationalization of worldviews takes place through

learning processes. This by no means implies that the development of worldviews must have taken place in a continuous or
linear way, or that it was necessary in the sense of an idealistic
causality; questions of the *dynamics* of development are not pre-
judged by this assumption. If we are to conceive historical transitions between differently structured systems of interpretation
as learning processes, however, we must satisfy the demand for
a formal analysis of meaning constellations that makes it possible to reconstruct the empirical succession of worldviews as a
series of steps in learning that can be insightfully recapitulated
from the perspective of a participant and can be submitted to
intersubjective tests.

MacIntyre has objected that Winch would have to *reinterpret cognitive developments* as discontinuous structural leaps.

> I refer to those transitions from one system of beliefs to
> another which are necessarily characterized by raising ques-
> tions of the kind that Winch rejects. In seventeenth-century
> Scotland, for example, the question could not but be raised,
> "But are there witches?" If Winch asks, but within what way
> of social life, under what system of belief was this question
> asked, the only answer is that it was asked by men who
> confronted alternative systems and were able to draw out
> of what confronted them independent criteria of judgment.
> Many Africans today are in the same situation.[41]

The other side of this objection is, of course, the burden of proof
that MacIntyre places on the universalistic position. On this
account, we would have to assume that the scientist who belongs
to a modern society could not seriously understand the Zande
belief in witches, or even the crucifixion of Jesus, unless he had
(broadly speaking) reconstructed those learning processes that
made possible the transition from myth to world religion or the
transition from a religious-metaphysical worldview to the modern
understanding of the world.[42]

In discussing Weber's sociology of religion in the next
chapter, I shall attempt to make the development of religious
worldviews comprehensible from the aspect of a development
of formal world-concepts, that is, as a learning process. In doing
so I shall be making tacit use of a concept of learning that Piaget
expounded for the ontogenesis of structures of consciousness.

As is well known, Piaget distinguishes among stages of cognitive development that are characterized not in terms of new contents but in terms of structurally described levels of learning ability. It might be a matter of something similar in the case of the emergence of new structures of worldviews. The caesurae between the mythical, religious-metaphysical, and modern modes of thought are characterized by changes in the system of basic concepts. With the transition to a new stage the interpretations of the superseded stage are, no matter what their content, *categorially devalued.* It is not this or that reason, but the *kind* of reason, which is no longer convincing. A devaluation of the explanatory and justificatory potentials of entire traditions took place in the great civilizations with the dissolution of mythological-narrative figures of thought, in the modern age with the dissolution of religious, cosmological, and metaphysical figures of thought. These *devaluative shifts* appear to be connected with socio-evolutionary transitions to new levels of learning, with which the conditions of possible learning processes in the dimensions of objectivating thought, moral-practical insight, and aesthetic-expressive capacity are altered.

Piaget's theory is useful not only for distinguishing between the learning of structures and the learning of content but also for conceptualizing a development that extends to worldviews as a whole, that is, to different dimensions of world-understanding simultaneously. Cognitive development in the narrower sense, the development of intelligence, refers to structures of thought and action that the growing child acquires constructively in active confrontation with external reality, with processes in the objective world.[43] But Piaget follows this development of intelligence in connection with the "construction of the external and internal universes"; there gradually emerges "a demarcation through the construction of the universe of objects and of the internal universe of the subject."[44] The growing child works out for himself, equiprimordially, the concepts of the external and internal worlds in dealing practically with objects and with himself. Piaget also draws a distinction between dealing with physical objects and dealing with social objects, that is, "reciprocal action between a subject and objects and reciprocal action between a subject and other subjects."[45] Correspondingly the external universe is differentiated into the world of perceptible and manipulable objects on the one hand and the world of normatively regulated interpersonal relations on the other. Whereas contact with external nature, which is established through instrumental action, mediates the constructive acquisition of the "system of intellectual norms," interaction with other persons opens the way to growing constructively into the socially recognized "system of moral norms." The learning mechanisms of assimilation and accommodation operate through both of these types of action in a specific way: "If reciprocal actions between subject and object modify both, it is a fortiori evident that every reciprocal action between individual subjects mutually modifies them. Every social relation is thus a totality in itself which creates new properties while transforming the individual in his mental structure."[46]

Thus for Piaget there is cognitive development in a wider sense, which is not understood solely as the construction of an external universe but also as the construction of a reference system for the *simultaneous* demarcation of the objective and social worlds from the subjective world. Cognitive development signifies in general *the decentration of an egocentric understanding of the world.* Only to the extent that the formal reference system of the three worlds is differentiated can we form a reflective concept of "world" and open up access to the world through the medium of common interpretive efforts, in the sense of a cooperative negotiation of situation definitions. The concept of a subjective world permits us to contrast not only our own internal world, but also the subjective worlds of others, with the external world. Ego can consider how certain facts (what he regards as existing states of affairs in the objective world) or certain normative expectations (what he regards as legitimate elements of the common social world) look from the perspective of another, that is, as elements of alter's subjective world. He can further consider that alter is for his part considering how what he regards as existing states of affairs and valid norms look from ego's perspective, that is, as a component of ego's subjective world. The subjective worlds of the participants could serve as mirror surfaces in which the objective, the normative, and the subjective-for-another are reflected any number of times. The function of the formal world-concepts, however, is to prevent the stock of what is common from dissolving in the stream of subjectivities repeatedly reflected in one another. They make it possible to adopt in common the perspective of a third person or a nonparticipant.

Every action oriented to reaching understanding can be conceived as part of a cooperative process of interpretation aiming at situation definitions that are intersubjectively recognized. The concepts of the three worlds serve here as the commonly supposed system of coordinates in which the situation contexts can be ordered in such a way that agreement will be reached about what the participants may treat as a fact, or as a valid norm, or as a subjective experience. I can introduce here the concept of the *Lebenswelt* or lifeworld, to begin with as the correlate of processes of reaching understanding. Subjects acting communicatively always come to an understanding in the horizon of a lifeworld. Their lifeworld is formed from more or less diffuse, always unproblematic, background convictions. This lifeworld background serves as a source of situation definitions that are presupposed by participants as unproblematic. In their interpretive accomplishments the members of a communication community demarcate the one objective world and their intersubjectively shared social world from the subjective worlds of individuals and (other) collectives. The world-concepts and the corresponding validity claims provide the formal scaffolding with which those acting communicatively order problematic contexts of situations, that is, those requiring agreement, in their lifeworld, which is presupposed as unproblematic.

The lifeworld also stores the interpretive work of preceding generations. It is the conservative counterweight to the risk of disagreement that arises with every actual process of reaching understanding; for communicative actors can achieve an understanding only by way of taking yes/no positions on criticizable validity claims. *The relation between these weights changes with the decentration of worldviews.* The more the worldview that furnishes the cultural stock of knowledge is decentered, the less the need for understanding is covered *in advance* by an interpreted lifeworld immune from critique, and the more this need has to be met by the interpretive accomplishments of the participants themselves, that is, by way of risky (because rationally motivated) agreement, the more frequently we can expect rational action orientations. Thus for the time being we can characterize the rationalization of the lifeworld in the dimension "normatively ascribed agreement" *versus* "communicatively achieved understanding." The more cultural traditions predecide which validity claims, when, where, for what, from whom, and to whom must be accepted, the less the participants themselves have the possibility of making explicit and examining the potential grounds on which their yes/no positions are based.

If we assess cultural systems of interpretation from this standpoint, we can see why mythical worldviews represent an instructive limit case. To the degree that the lifeworld of a social group is interpreted through a mythical worldview, the burden of interpretation is removed from the individual member, as well as the chance for him to bring about an agreement open to criticism. To the extent that the worldview remains sociocentric in Piaget's sense,[47] it does not permit differentiation between the world of existing states of affairs, valid norms and expressible subjective experiences. The linguistic worldview is reified as the world order and cannot be seen as an interpretive system open to criticism. Within such a system of orientation, actions cannot reach that critical zone in which communicatively achieved agreement depends upon autonomous yes/no responses to criticizable validity claims. Against this background it becomes clear which formal properties cultural traditions have to exhibit if rational action orientations are to be possible in a lifeworld interpreted correspondingly, if they are to be able to consolidate into a rational conduct of life.

a) The cultural tradition must make available formal concepts for the objective, social, and subjective worlds; it must permit differentiated validity claims (propositional truth, normative rightness, subjective truthfulness) and stimulate a corresponding differentiation of basic attitudes (objectivating, norm-conformative, and expressive). Symbolic expressions can then be produced on a formal level at which they are systematically connected with reasons and accessible to objective assessment.

b) The cultural tradition must permit a reflective relation to itself; it must be so far stripped of its dogmatism as to permit in principle that interpretations stored in tradition be placed in question and subjected to critical revision. Then internal interconnections of meaning can by systematically elaborated and alternative interpretations can be methodically examined. Cognitive activities of the second order emerge: learning processes guided by hypotheses and filtered through arguments in the domain of objectivating thought, moral-practical insight, and aesthetic perception.

c) In its cognitive, moral, and evaluative components the cultural tradition must permit a feedback connection with specialized forms of argumentation to such an extent that the corresponding learning processes can be socially institutionalized.

In this way cultural subsystems can arise—for science, law and morality, music, art, and literature—in which traditions take shape that are supported by arguments rendered fluid through permanent criticism but at the same time professionally secured.

d) Finally, the cultural tradition must interpret the lifeworld in such a way that action oriented to success can be freed from the imperatives of an understanding that is to be communicatively renewed over and over again and can be at least partially uncoupled from action oriented to reaching understanding. This makes possible a societal institutionalization of purposive-rational action for generalized goals, for example, the formation of subsystems, controlled through money and power, for rational economics and rational administration. As we shall see below, Max Weber regards the formation of the subsystems mentioned under c) and d) above as a differentiation of spheres of value that represent for him the core of the cultural and societal rationalization in the modern age.

If we employ Piaget's concept of decentration as a guiding thread in this way, in order to clarify the internal connection between the structure of a worldview, the lifeworld as the context of processes of understanding, and the possibilities of a rational conduct of life, we again encounter the concept of communicative rationality. This concept relates a decentered understanding of the world to the possibility of discursively redeeming criticizable validity claims. Albrecht Wellmer characterizes this concept (in connection with the anthropologically inspired debate about rationality) as follows:

> "Discursive rationality" is not a "relational" conception of rationality in the same sense as the "minimal" notions of rationality advanced by Winch, MacIntyre, Lukes and others are. Such minimal conceptions of rationality are simple derivatives of the law of non-contradiction and can be expressed in the form of a postulate of coherence. Now "discursive rationality" does not just signify a specific standard of rationality which would be "parasitic" on the minimal standard of rationality, as are, for example, the specific standards of rationality which are operative in primitive magic or in modern economic systems. "Discursive rationality" rather signifies (a) a *procedural* conception of rationality, i.e., a *specific* way of coming to grips with incoherences, contradictions and dissension, and (b) a formal standard of rationality which operates on a "meta-level" vis-à-vis all those

"substantive" standards of rationality which are "parasitic"
on a minimal standard of rationality in Lukes' sense.[48]

Wellmer considers such a concept of rationality complex enough
to admit Winch's justified misgivings as lines of questioning—
both his scepticism in regard to the one-sidedly cognitive-
instrumental self-understanding of modern rationality and his
motive of learning from other cultures in order to develop an
awareness of this one-sidedness of the modern self-understanding.

If one understands the concept of egocentrism as broadly
as that of decentration and assumes that egocentrism is renewed at each stage, learning processes are accompanied by the
shadow of systematic error.[49] It could very well be the case that
even with a decentered understanding of the world there arises
a special illusion—namely, the idea that the differentiation of an
objective world means totally excluding the social and the subjective worlds from the domains of rationally motivated
agreement.

This illusion of *reifying* thought will be discussed below. A
complementary error of modernity is the *utopianism* which thinks
it possible to derive the "ideal of a completely rational form of
life" directly from the concepts of a decentered world understanding and of procedural rationality.[50] Forms of life do not consist only of worldviews that can be ranked from structural perspectives as more or less decentered, nor only of institutions that
fall under the viewpoint of justice. Winch is right to insist that
forms of life represent concrete "language games," historical configurations of customary practices, group memberships, cultural
patterns of interpretation, forms of socialization, competences,
attitudes, and so forth. It would be senseless to want to judge
such a conglomeration as a whole, *the totality of a form of life,*
under individual aspects of rationality. If we do not want
altogether to relinquish standards by which a form of life might
be judged to be more or less failed, deformed, unhappy, or
alienated, we can look if need be to the model of sickness and
health. We tacitly judge life forms and life histories according
to standards of normality that do not permit an approximation
to ideal limit values. Perhaps we should talk instead of a balance
among non–self-sufficient moments, an equilibrated interplay of
the cognitive with the moral and the aesthetic-practical. But the
attempt to provide an equivalent for what was once intended by
the idea of the good life should not mislead us into deriving this

idea from the formal concept of reason with which modernity's decentered understanding of the world has left us.

> For this reason we can only specify certain formal conditions of a rational life—such as a universalistic moral consciousness, universalistic law, a reflexive collective identity, and the like. But insofar as we are dealing with the possibility of a rational life or a rational identity in the substantial sense, there is no ideal limit value that could be described in terms of formal structures. There is, rather, only the success or failure of the endeavor to realize a form of life in which unconstrained individual identities, together with unconstrained reciprocity among individuals, become a palpable reality.[51]

In speaking of a "rational life in the substantial sense," Wellmer does not, of course, mean to suggest that we resort to the conceptual framework of substantively rational worldviews. But if we have to renounce that, there remains only the critique of deformations inflicted, in two ways, on the life forms of capitalistically modernized societies: through devaluation of their traditional substance and through subjection to the imperatives of a one-sided rationality limited to the cognitive-instrumental.[52]

A critique of this sort can indeed be based on the procedural concept of communicative rationality if it can be shown that the decentration of world understanding and the rationalization of the lifeworld are necessary conditions for an emancipated society. It is only the confusion of a highly developed infrastructure of *possible* forms of life with the concrete historical totality of a *successful* form of life that is utopian.

3. *Relations to the World and Aspects of Rationality in Four Sociological Concepts of Action*

The concept of communicative rationality that emerged from our provisional analysis of the use of the linguistic expression "rational" and from our review of the anthropological debate concerning the status of the modern understanding of the world is in need of a more precise explication. I shall pursue this task only indirectly, by way of a formal-pragmatic clarification of the concept of communicative action, and only within the limits of a systematic look at certain positions in the history of social theory. We can begin with the claim that the concept of communicative rationality has to be analyzed in connection with achieving understanding in language. The concept of reaching an understanding suggests a rationally motivated agreement among participants that is measured against criticizable validity claims. The validity claims (propositional truth, normative rightness, and subjective truthfulness) characterize different categories of a knowledge embodied in symbolic expressions. These expressions can be more closely analyzed in two ways—with respect to how they can be defended and with respect to how actors relate through them to something in a world. The concept of communicative rationality points, on the one side, to different forms of discursively redeeming validity claims (thus Wellmer speaks also of discursive rationality); on the other side, it points to relations to the world that communicative actors take up in raising validity claims for their expressions. Thus the decentration of our understanding of the world proved to be the most important dimension of the development of worldviews. I shall pursue no further the discussion of the theory of argumentation. However, if we return to the thesis introduced at the outset—that every sociology with theoretical pretensions faces the problem of rationality on both the metatheoretical and methodological planes—we come upon the path of examining formal concepts of the world.

I would like to support the first part of my thesis by drawing out the "ontological"—in the broader sense—presuppositions of *four action concepts* relevant to theory formation in the social sciences. I shall analyze the rationality implications of these concepts in connection with the *relations between actor and world* presupposed by each. Generally the connection between social action and actor-world relations is not explicitly established in sociological theories of action. One exception is I. C. Jarvie, who makes interesting use of Popper's three-world theory.[1] In order to clarify the concepts of the objective, social, and subjective worlds that I have introduced in a provisional way, I shall (a) examine Popper's theory of the third world, and then (b) analyze the concepts of teleological, normatively regulated, and dramaturgical action in terms of actor-world relations. This reconstruction will then make it possible to (c) introduce the concept of communicative action.

A.—In his 1967 address, "Epistemology Without a Knowing Subject," Popper makes an unexpected proposal:

> We may distinguish the following three worlds or universes: first the world of physical objects or physical states; secondly, the world of states of consciousness, or of mental states, or perhaps of behavioral dispositions to act; and thirdly, the world of *objective contents of thought,* especially of scientific and poetic thoughts and of works of art.[2]

Later Popper speaks generally about the world of "the products of the human mind."[3] He stresses that those internal relations between symbolic formations that still wait for discovery and explication by the human mind also have to be included in the third world.[4] In the present context we are not interested in the special epistemological considerations that induced Popper to fasten on to Frege's concept of *Gedanken,* to take up Husserl's critique of psychologism, and to claim a status independent of mental acts and states for the semantic contents of symbolic—as a rule, linguistically objectivated—productions of the human mind; nor are we interested in the proposed solution to the problem of the relation between mind and body that he develops with the help of the concept of the third world.[5] It is, however, of interest that in both cases Popper is criticizing the fundamental empiricist conception of a subject that confronts the world in an unmediated way, receives impressions from it through sense perceptions, or influences states in it through actions.

This problem context explains why he understands his doctrine of objective mind as a critical extension of the empiricist concept and introduces both objective and subjective mind as "worlds," that is, as special totalities of entities. The older theories of objective mind or spirit developed in the historicist and neo-Hegelian traditions from Dilthey to Theodor Litt and Hans Freyer start from an active mind that expounds itself in the worlds it constitutes. By contrast, Popper holds fast to the primacy of the world in relation to mind and construes the second and third worlds analogously to the first, in *ontological* terms. In this regard, his construction of the third world is reminiscent of Nicolai Hartmann's theory of mental being [*geistigen Seins*].[6]

The world counts as the totality of what is the case; and what is the case can be stated in the form of true propositions. Starting from this general concept of the world, Popper specifies the concepts of the first, second, and third worlds by the way in which states of affairs exist. The entities belonging to each of these three worlds have a specific mode of being: physical objects and events, mental states and episodes, and semantic contents of symbolic formations.

As Nicolai Hartmann distinguished between objectivated and objective *Geist,* Popper distinguishes between explicit semantic contents that are already *embodied* in phonemes and written signs, in color or stone, in machines, and so forth, on the one hand, and those implicit semantic contents that are not yet "discovered," not yet objectified in carrier objects of the first world, but are simply inherent in already embodied meanings.

These "unembodied world 3 objects"[7] are an important indicator of the independence of the world of objective mind. Symbolic formations are, it is true, generated by the productive human mind; but though they are themselves products, they confront subjective mind with the objectivity of a problematic, uncomprehended complex of meaning that can be opened up only through intellectual labor. The *products* of the human mind immediately turn against it as *problems.*

These problems are clearly autonomous. They are in no sense made by us; rather, they are discovered by us; and in this sense they exist, undiscovered, before their discovery. Moreover, at least some of these unsolved problems may be insoluble. In our attempts to solve these or other problems we may invent new theories. These theories, again, are produced by us: they are the product of our critical and creative thinking in which we are greatly helped by other established theories inhabiting the third world.

Yet the moment we have produced these theories, they create new, unintended and unexpected problems, autonomous problems, problems to be discovered. This explains why the third world, which in its origin is our product, is *autonomous* in what may be called its ontological status. It explains why we can act upon it and add to it or help its growth, even though no one can master even a small corner of this world. All of us contribute to its growth, but almost all of our individual contributions are vanishingly small. All of us try to grasp it, and none of us could live without being in contact with it, for all of us make use of speech, without which we would hardly be human. Yet the third world has grown far beyond the grasp not only of any individual but even of all individuals (as shown by the existence of insoluble problems).[8]

Two noteworthy consequences follow from this description of the third world. The first concerns *interaction between the worlds*, the second *the cognitivistically abridged interpretation of the third world*. In Popper's view the first and second worlds are in immediate interchange, as are the second and third. By contrast, the first and third worlds interact only through the mediation of the second. This entails a renunciation of two fundamental empiricist conceptions. On the one hand, the entities of the third world cannot be reduced—as forms of expression of subjective mind—to mental states, that is, to entities of the second world. On the other hand, the relations between entities of the first and second worlds cannot be conceived exclusively in terms of the causal model that holds for relations between entities of the first world themselves. Popper bars the way both to a psychologistic conception of objective mind and to a physicalistic conception of subjective mind. The autonomy of the third world guarantees instead that knowledge of, as well as intervention into, states of the objective world are mediated through discovery of the independence of internal meaning connections. "And [thus] it is impossible to interpret either the third world as a mere expression of the second, or the second as the mere reflection of the third."[9]

In other respects Popper remains tied to the empiricist context from which he is distancing himself. Cognitive-instrumental relations between the knowing and acting subject on the one hand, and things and events appearing in the world on the other, are so much the center of his attention that they dominate the exchange between subjective and objective mind. The process of bringing forth, externalizing, penetrating, and assimilating products of the human mind primarily serves the growth of *theoretical knowledge* and the expansion of *technically utilizable knowledge*. The development of science, which Popper understands as a cumulative feedback process involving initial problems, creative formation of hypotheses, critical testing, revision, and discovery of new problems, not only serves as the model for subjective mind's grasp of the world of objective mind; according to Popper, the third world is *essentially made up* of problems, theories, and arguments. He does also mention, in addition to theories and tools, social institutions and works of art as examples of entities in the third world; but he sees in them only variant forms of embodiment of propositional contents. Strictly speaking, the third world is the totality of Fregean *Gedanken*, whether true or false, embodied or not: "Theories, or propositions, or statements are the most important third-world linguistic entities."

Popper not only conceives of the third world in ontological terms as a totality of entities with a specific mode of being; within this framework he also understands it in a one-sided manner, from the conceptual perspective of the development of science: the third world encompasses the scientifically processed, cognitive components of the cultural tradition.

Both aspects prove to be severe restrictions in the attempt to make Popper's concept of the third world useful for the foundations of sociology. I. C. Jarvie starts from the phenomenological sociology of knowledge inspired by Alfred Schutz, which conceives of society as a social construction of the everyday world that issues from the interpretive processes of acting subjects and congeals to objectivity.[10] But he analyzes the ontological status of the social life-context, which is produced by the human mind and yet preserves a relative independence in relation to it, on the model of the third world.

> We have argued, then, that the social is an independent realm between the hard physical world and soft mental world: This realm, reality, world, whatever we choose to call it, is very diverse and complex and people in society are constantly striving by trial and error to come to terms with it; to map it; to coordinate their maps of it. Living in an unmanageably large and changing society permits neither perfect mapping, nor perfect coordination of maps. This means that the members of the society are constantly

> learning about it; both the society and its members are in
> a constant process of self-discovery and of self-making.[11]

This proposal throws light on the interesting connection between a sociological concept of action and the relations of actor to world presupposed therein. On the other hand, carrying Popper's three-world theory over from epistemological to action-theoretic contexts makes the weaknesses of the construction visible. In adopting Popper's concept of the third world to characterize social relations and institutions, Jarvie has to represent socially acting subjects on the model of theory-forming and problem-solving scientists: in the lifeworld everyday theories compete in a way similar to scientific theories in the community of investigators.

> People living in a society have to find their way around it,
> both to accomplish what they want and to avoid what they
> do not want. We might say that to do this they construct in
> their minds a conceptual map of the society and its features,
> of their own location among them, of the possible paths
> which will lead them to their goals, and of the hazards along
> each path. The maps are in a way "softer" than geographic
> maps—like dream maps they create the terrain they are map-
> ping. Yet in a way this is a harder reality: geographical maps
> are never real but sometimes reflect real terrains, yet social
> maps *are* terrains to be studied and mapped by other
> people.[12]

There are at least three difficulties with this proposal.

a) In the first place, Jarvie blurs the distinction between a performative and a hypothetical-reflective attitude toward cultural tradition. In communicative everyday practice, the agent draws on the available cultural store of background knowledge to arrive at situation definitions capable of consensus. In the process, disagreements can arise that make it necessary to revise individual interpretive patterns; but the application of traditional knowledge from the background is not equivalent to the hypothetical treatment of knowledge that is systematically questioned. Under the pressure for decision in a given action situation, the layman takes part in interactions with the intention of coordinating the actions of participants through a process of reaching understanding, that is, by employing common cultural knowledge. Certainly the scientist takes part in interactions as well;

but in his case the cooperative processes of interpretation serve the end of testing the validity of *problematic* items of knowledge. The aim is not the coordination of actions, but the criticism and growth of knowledge.

b) Further, Jarvie neglects the elements of cultural tradition that cannot be reduced to *Gedanken* or propositions admitting of truth. He limits the objective complexes of meaning that acting subjects both produce and discover to *cognitive interpretations* in the narrow sense. In this respect Popper's model of the third world is particularly implausible, for the action-orienting power of cultural values is at least as important for interactions as that of theories. Either the status of societal entities is assimilated to that of theories—and then we can't explain how social structures can shape motives for action; or, in view of the fact that descriptive, normative, and evaluative meanings interpenetrate in everyday theories, the model of scientific theories is not meant to be taken so seriously—and then we can conceive an interrelation between motives and third-world concepts; however this approach would make it necessary to expand Popper's version of the third world in such a way that the normative reality of society would owe its independence vis-á-vis subjective mind not only—and not even primarily—to the autonomy of truth claims, but to the binding character of values and norms. That raises the question of how the components of cultural tradition that are relevant to social integration can be understood as systems of knowledge and connected with validity claims *analogous* to truth.

c) In my view, the most serious weakness in Jarvie's proposal is that it permits no distinction between cultural values and the institutional embodiment of values in norms. Institutions are supposed to issue from processes of reaching understanding among acting subjects (and to solidify as objective meaning complexes in relation to them) in a way similar to that in which, on Popper's view, problems, theories, and arguments issue from cognitive processes. With this model we can, it is true, explain the conceptual nature and the relative independence of social reality, but not the specific resistance and *coercive* character of established norms and existing institutions through which societal formations are distinguished from cultural. Jarvie himself remarks at one point: "Unlike a true idea the status of which is not threatened even by universal disbelief, social entities can be jeopardized by universal disbelief—a widespread disinclination to treat them seriously."[13] Thus it makes sense to distinguish, as Parsons does, the domain of institutionalized values from the domain of free-floating cultural values. The latter do not have the same obligatory character as legitimate norms of action.

Jarvie's strategy of employing Popper's three-world theory is instructive in that it reveals the ontological presuppositions that enter into sociological concepts of action. If we wish to avoid the weaknesses in Jarvie's proposal, it will be necessary, however, to revise the three-world theory on which he bases it. It is indeed true that cultural objectivations can be reduced neither to the generative activity of knowing, speaking, and acting subjects, nor to spatio-temporal, causal relations between things and events. For this reason Popper conceives the semantic contents of symbolic formations as entities of a "third world." He bases this concept on the ontological concept of "world" introduced to refer to a totality of entities. Before the concept of a world can become fruitful for action, it has to be modified in the three respects mentioned above.

(ad a) To begin with, I would like to replace the ontological concept of "world" with one derived from the phenomenological tradition and to adopt the pair of concepts "world" and "lifeworld." Sociated subjects, when participating in cooperative processes of interpretation, themselves employ the concept of the world in an implicit way. Cultural tradition, which Popper introduces under the catchphrase "products of the human mind," plays different roles depending on whether it functions from behind as a cultural stock of knowledge from which the participants in interaction draw their interpretations or is itself made the topic of intellectual endeavor. *In the first case,* the cultural tradition shared by a community is constitutive of the lifeworld which the individual member finds already interpreted. This intersubjectively shared *lifeworld* forms the background for communicative action. Thus phenomenologists like Alfred Schutz speak of the lifeworld as the unthematically given horizon within which participants in communication move in common when they refer thematically to something in the *world. In the second case,* individual elements of the cultural tradition are themselves made thematic. The participants must thereby adopt a reflective attitude toward cultural patterns of interpretation that ordinarily *make possible* their interpretive accomplishments. This change in attitude means that the validity of the thematized interpretive pattern is suspended and the corresponding knowledge rendered problematic; at the same time, the problematic element of the

cultural tradition is brought under the category of a state of affairs to which one can refer in an objectivating manner. Popper's theory of the third world explains how cultural semantic contents and symbolic objects can be understood as something in the world, and can at the same time be distinguished as higher-level objects from (observable) physical and (experienciable) mental episodes.

(ad b) Further, I would like to replace the one-sidedly cognitivistic interpretation of the concept "objective mind" with a concept of cultural knowledge differentiated according to several validity claims. Popper's third world encompasses higher-level entities, which are accessible in a reflective attitude and which retain a relative autonomy in relation to subjective mind because they form, on the basis of their relation to truth, a network of problem complexes open to investigation. We could say in the language of neo-Kantianism that the third world enjoys the independence of a sphere of validity. The entities of this world that admit of truth stand in a peculiar relation to the first world. The problems, theories, and arguments attributed to the third world serve in the final analysis to describe and explain events and persons within the first world. And both are mediated in turn through the world of subjective mind, through acts of knowing and doing. The noncognitive elements of culture thereby slip into a peculiar marginal position. But precisely these elements are of significance for a sociological theory of action. From the perspective of action theory, the activities of the human mind are not easily limited to the cognitive-instrumental confrontation with external nature; social actions are oriented to cultural values and these do not have a truth relation. Thus we are faced with the following alternative: either we deny to the noncognitive elements of the cultural tradition the status that third world entities occupy by virtue of being embedded in a sphere of validity connections, and classify them in an empiricist manner as forms of expression of subjective mind, or we seek equivalents for the missing truth relation.

As we shall see, Max Weber chose the second way. He distinguishes several cultural spheres of value—science and technology, law and morality, as well as art and criticism. The noncognitive spheres of value are also spheres of validity. Legal and moral representations can be criticized and analyzed from the standpoint of normative rightness and works of art from that of authenticity (or beauty); that is, they can be treated as autonomous problem domains. Weber understands cultural tradition *in toto* as a store of knowledge out of which special spheres of value and systems of knowledge are formed under different validity claims. He would thus include in the third world the evaluative and expressive components of culture as well as the cognitive-instrumental. If one adopts this alternative, one must of course explain what "validity" and "knowledge" can mean in regard to the noncognitive components of culture. They cannot be correlated in the same way as theories and statements with entities of the first world. Cultural values do not fulfill a representational function.

(ad c) These shifts provide us with an opportunity to rid the concept of world from its narrow ontological connotations. Popper introduces different world concepts to demarcate regions of being *within* the one objective world. In his later works he deems it important to speak not of different worlds, but of *one* world with the indices "1," "2," and "3."[14] I would like, on the contrary, to continue speaking of three worlds (which are in turn to be distinguished from the lifeworld). Of these, only one, namely the objective world, can be understood as the correlate of the totality of true propositions; only this concept retains the strictly ontological significance of a totality of entities. On the other hand, taken together the worlds form a reference system that is mutually presupposed in communication processes. With this reference system participants lay down what there can possibly be understanding about *at all.* Participants in communication who are seeking to come to an understanding with one another about something do not take up a relation only to the one objective world, as is suggested by the precommunicative model dominant in empiricism. They by no means refer only to things that happen or could happen or could be made to happen in the objective world, but to things in the social and subjective worlds as well. Speakers and hearers operate with a *system* of several equally primordial worlds. That is, with propositionally differentiated speech they have mastered not only a level on which they can describe states of affairs—as is suggested by Popper's classification into lower and higher functions of language; rather, all three functions—the "descriptive," the "signalling" and the "self-expressive"—lie in one and the same evolutionary plane.

B.—In what follows I shall no longer employ the Popperian terminology. My purpose in reviewing Jarvie's action-theoretic translation of Popper's three-world theory was only to prepare the way for the thesis that with the choice of a specific sociological concept of action we generally make specific "ontological" assumptions. And the aspects of possible rationality of an agent's actions depend, in turn, on the world relations that we thereby impute to him. The profusion of action concepts employed (for the most part, implicitly) in social-scientific theories can be reduced in essence to four basic, analytically distinguishable concepts.

Since Aristotle the concept of *teleological action* has been at the center of the philosophical theory of action.[15] The actor attains an end or brings about the occurrence of a desired state by choosing means that have promise of being successful in the given situation and applying them in a suitable manner. The central concept is that of a *decision* among alternative courses of action, with a view to the realization of an end, guided by maxims, and based on an interpretation of the situation.

The teleological model of action is expanded to a *strategic* model when there can enter into the agent's calculation of success the anticipation of decisions on the part of at least one additional goal-directed actor. This model is often interpreted in utilitarian terms; the actor is supposed to choose and calculate means and ends from the standpoint of maximizing utility or expectations of utility. It is this model of action that lies behind decision-theoretic and game-theoretic approaches in economics, sociology, and social psychology.[16]

The concept of *normatively regulated action* does not refer to the behavior of basically solitary actors who come upon other actors in their environment, but to members of a social group who orient their action to common values. The individual actor complies with (or violates) a norm when in a given situation the conditions are present to which the norm has application. Norms express an agreement that obtains in a social group. All members of a group for whom a given norm has validity may expect of one another that in certain situations they will carry out (or abstain from) the actions commanded (or proscribed). The central concept of *complying with a norm* means fulfilling a generalized expectation of behavior. The latter does not have the cognitive sense of expecting a predicted event, but the normative sense that members are *entitled* to expect a certain behavior. This normative model of action lies behind the role theory that is widespread in sociology.[17]

The concept of *dramaturgical action* refers primarily neither to the solitary actor nor to the member of a social group, but to participants in interaction constituting a public for one another, before whom they present themselves. The actor evokes in his public a certain image, an impression of himself, by more or less purposefully disclosing his subjectivity. Each agent can monitor public access to the system of his own intentions, thoughts, attitudes, desires, feelings, and the like, to which only he has privileged access. In dramaturgical action, participants make use of this and steer their interactions through regulating mutual access to their own subjectivities. Thus the central concept of *presentation of self* does not signify spontaneous expressive behavior but stylizing the expression of one's own experiences with a view to the audience. The dramaturgical model of action is used primarily in phenomenologically oriented descriptions of interaction; but it has not yet been developed into a theoretically generalizing approach.[18]

Finally the concept of *communicative action* refers to the interaction of at least two subjects capable of speech and action who establish interpersonal relations (whether by verbal or by extraverbal means). The actors seek to reach an understanding about the action situation and their plans of action in order to coordinate their actions by way of agreement. The central concept of *interpretation* refers in the first instance to negotiating definitions of the situation which admit of consensus. As we shall see, language is given a prominent place in this model.[19]

The teleological concept of action was first rendered fruitful for an economic theory of choice by the founders of neoclassical economics, and then for a theory of strategic games by von Neumann and Morgenstern. The concept of normatively regulated action gained paradigmatic significance for theory formation in the social sciences through Durkheim and Parsons, that of dramaturgical action through Goffman, that of communicative action through Mead and later Garfinkel. I cannot carry out a detailed explication of these concepts here. My concern is rather with the rationality implications of the corresponding conceptual strategies. At first glance, only the teleological concept of action seems to open up an aspect of the rationality of action. Action represented as purposeful activity can be viewed under the aspect of purposive rationality. This is a point of view from which actions can be more or less rationally planned and carried out, or can be judged by a third person to be more or less rational. In elementary cases of purposeful activity the plan of action can be represented in the form of a practical syllogism.[20] The other three models of action appear at first not to place action in the perspective of rationality and possible rationalization. That this appearance is deceiving becomes evident when we represent to ourselves the "ontological"—in the broad sense—presuppositions that are, as a matter of conceptual necessity, connected with these models of action. In the sequence teleological, normative, dramaturgical, the presuppositions not only become increasingly complex; they reveal at the same time stronger and stronger implications for rationality.

(a) The concept of teleological action presupposes relations between an actor and a world of existing states of affairs. This objective world is defined as the totality of states of affairs that either obtain or could arise or could be brought about by purposeful intervention. The model equips the agent with a "cognitive-volitional complex," so that he can, on the one hand, form *beliefs* about existing states of affairs through the medium of perception, and can, on the other hand, develop *intentions* with the aim of bringing desired states of affairs into existence. At the semantic level such states of affairs are represented as propositional contents of sentences expressing beliefs or intentions. Through his beliefs and intentions the actor can take up basically two types of rational relation to the world. I call these relations rational because they are open to objective appraisal depending on the "direction of fit."[21] In one direction the question arises whether the actor has succeeded in bringing his perceptions and beliefs into agreement with what is the case in the world; in the other direction the question is whether he succeeds in bringing what is the case in the world into agreement with his desires and intentions. In both instances the actor can produce expressions susceptible of being judged by a third person in respect to "fit and misfit"; he can make assertions that are *true* or *false* and carry out goal-directed interventions that succeed or fail, that *achieve* or *fail to achieve* the intended effect in the world. These relations between actor and world allow then for expressions that can be judged according to criteria of *truth* and *efficacy*.

With regard to ontological presuppositions, we can classify *teleological* action as a concept that presupposes *one* world, namely the objective world. The same holds for the concept of *strategic action*. Here we start with at least two goal-directed acting subjects who achieve their ends by way of an orientation to, and influence on, the decisions of other actors.[22] Success in action is also dependent on other actors, each of whom is oriented to his own success and behaves cooperatively only to the degree that this fits with his egocentric calculus of utility.[23] Thus strategically acting subjects must be cognitively so equipped that for them not only physical objects but decision-making systems can appear in the world. They must expand their conceptual apparatus for what can be the case; but they do not need any richer *ontological presuppositions.* The concept of the objective world does not itself become more complex with the growing complexity of innerworldly entities. Even purposeful activity differentiated to include strategic action remains, as regards its ontological presuppositions, a *one-world concept.*

   (b) By contrast, the concept of normatively regulated action presupposes relations between an actor and exactly two worlds. Besides the objective world of existing states of affairs there is the social world to which the actor belongs as a role-playing subject, as do additional actors who can take up normatively regulated interactions among themselves. A social world consists of a normative context that lays down which interactions belong to the totality of legitimate interpersonal relations. And all actors for whom the corresponding norms have force (by whom they are accepted as valid) belong to the same social world. As the meaning of the objective world can be elucidated with reference to the existence [*Existieren*] of states of affairs, the meaning of the social world can be elucidated with reference to the "existence" [*Bestehen*] of norms. It is important here that we do *not* understand the "existence" of norms in the sense of existence sentences stating that there are social facts of the type: normative regulations. The sentence "It is the case that *q* is commanded" obviously has a different meaning than the sentence "It is commanded that *q*." The latter sentence expresses a norm or a specific command when it is uttered in suitable form with the claim to normative rightness, that is, such that it claims *validity* for a circle of addressees. And we say that a norm exists, is in force, or enjoys social currency [*Geltung*] when it is recognized as valid [*gültig*] or justified by those to whom it is addressed. Existing states of affairs are represented by true statements, "existing" norms by general ought-sentences or commands that count as justified among the addressees. That a norm is ideally *valid* means that it *deserves* the assent of all those affected because it regulates problems of action in their common interest. That a norm is *de facto established* means by contrast that the validity claim with which it appears is recognized by

those affected, and this intersubjective recognition grounds the *social force or currency* of the norm.

We do not attach such a normative validity claim to cultural values; but values are candidates for embodiment in norms—they *can* attain a general binding force with respect to a matter requiring regulation. In the light of cultural values the needs [*Bedürfnisse*] of an individual appear as plausible to other individuals standing in the same tradition. However, plausibly interpreted needs are transformed into legitimate motives of action only when the corresponding values become, for a circle of those affected, normatively binding in regulating specific problem situations. Members can then expect of one another that in corresponding situations each of them will orient his action to values normatively prescribed for all concerned.

This consideration is meant to make comprehensible the fact that the normative model of action equips the agent not only with a "cognitive" but also with a "motivational complex" that makes norm-conformative behavior possible. Moreover this model of action is connected with a learning model of value internalization.[24] According to this model, existing norms gain action-motivating force to the degree that the values embodied in them represent the standards according to which, in the circle of addressees, needs are interpreted and developed through learning processes into need dispositions.

Under these presuppositions the actor can again take up relations to the world, here to the social world, which are open to objective evaluation according to the "direction of fit." In one direction the question is whether the motives and actions of an agent are in accord with existing norms or deviate from these. In the other direction the question is whether the existing norms themselves embody values that, in a particular problem situation, give expression to generalizable interests of those affected and thus deserve the assent of those to whom they are addressed. In the one case, actions are judged according to whether they are in accord with or deviate from an existing normative context, that is, whether or not they are right with respect to a normative context recognized as legitimate. In the other case, norms are judged according to whether they can be justified, that is, whether they deserve to be recognized as legitimate.[25]

With regard to its ontological—in the broad sense —presuppositions, we can classify *normatively regulated action* as a concept that presupposes *two worlds,* the objective world and a social world. Norm-conformative action presupposes that the agent can distinguish the factual from the normative elements of an action situation, that is, conditions and means from values. The point of departure for the normative model of action is that participants can simultaneously adopt both an objectivating attitude to something that is or is not the case, and a norm-conformative attitude to something that is commanded (whether rightly or not). But as in the teleological model, action is represented *primarily* as a relation between the actor and a world—there, as a relation to the objective world over against which the actor as knower stands and in which he can goal-directly intervene; here, as a relation to the social world to which the actor in his role as a norm-addressee belongs and in which he can take up legitimately regulated interpersonal relations. Neither here nor there is the actor *himself* presupposed as a world toward which he can behave reflexively. It is the concept of dramaturgical action that requires the additional presupposition of a subjective world to which the actor relates when in acting he puts himself "on stage."

(c) The concept of dramaturgical action is less clearly developed in social-science literature than are those of teleological and normatively guided action. Goffman first explicitly introduced it in 1959 in his investigation of "the presentation of self in everyday life."[26] From the perspective of dramaturgical action we understand social action as an encounter in which participants form a visible public for each other and perform for one another. "Encounter" and "performance" are the key concepts. The performance of a troupe before the eyes of third persons is only a special case. A performance enables the actor to present himself to his audience in a certain way; in bringing something of his subjectivity to appearance, he would like to be seen by his public in a particular way.

The dramaturgical qualities of action are in a certain way parasitic; they rest on a structure of goal-directed action.

> For certain purposes people control the style of their actions . . . and superimpose this upon other activities. For instance work may be done in a manner in accordance with the principles of dramatic performance in order to project a certain impression of the people working to an inspector or manager . . . In fact what people are doing is rarely properly described as *just* eating, or *just* working, but has stylistic features which have certain conventional meanings associated with recognized types of personae.[27]

Of course, there are special roles tailored to virtuoso self-staging: "The roles of prizefighters, surgeons, violinists, and policemen are cases in point. These activities allow so much dramatic self-expression that exemplary practitioners—whether real or fictional—become famous and are given special places in the commercially organized fantasies of the nation."[28] The trait that is here stylized into an element of the professional role, namely the reflexive character of self-presentation before others, is, however, constitutive for social interactions in general insofar as they are regarded only under the aspect of persons encountering one another.

In dramaturgical action the actor, in presenting a view of himself, has to behave toward his own subjective world. I have defined this as the totality of subjective experiences to which the actor has, in relation to others, a privileged access.[29] To be sure, this domain of subjectivity deserves to be called a "world" only if the significance of the subjective world can be explicated in a way similar to that in which I explained the significance of the social world, through referring to an "existence" of norms analogous to the existence of states of affairs. Perhaps one can say that the subject is represented by truthfully uttered experiential sentences in nearly the same way as are existing states of affairs by true statements and valid norms by justified ought-sentences. We should not understand subjective experiences as mental states or inner episodes, for we would thereby assimilate them to entities, to elements of the objective world. We can comprehend having subjective experiences as something analogous to the existence of states of affairs without assimilating the one to the other. A subject capable of expression does not "have" or "possess" desires and feelings in the same sense as an observable object has extension, weight, color, and similar properties. An actor has desires and feelings in the sense that he can at will express these experiences before a public, and indeed in such a way that this public, if it trusts the actor's expressive utterances, attributes to him, as something subjective, the desires and feelings expressed.

Desires and feelings have a paradigmatic status in this connection. Of course, cognitions, beliefs, and intentions also belong to the subjective world; but they stand in internal relation to the objective world. Beliefs and intentions come to consciousness *as* subjective only when there is in the objective world no corresponding state of affairs that exists or is brought to exist. It becomes a question of "mere," that is, "mistaken" belief as soon as the corresponding statement turns out to be untrue. It is a matter merely of "good," that is, of "ineffectual" intentions as soon as it turns out that the corresponding action was either left undone or failed. In a similar way, feelings of, say, obligation, shame, or guilt stand in internal relation to the social world. But in general feelings and desires can *only* be expressed as something subjective. They cannot be expressed *otherwise*, cannot enter into relation with the external world, whether the objective or the social. For this reason the expression of desires and feelings is measured only against the reflexive relation of the speaker to his inner world.

Desires and feelings are two aspects of a partiality rooted in needs.[30] Needs have two faces. They are differentiated on the volitional side into inclinations and desires; and on the other side, the intuitive, into feelings and moods. Desires are directed toward situations of need satisfaction; feelings "perceive" situations in the light of possible need satisfaction. Needs are, as it were, the background of a partiality that determines our subjective attitudes in relation to the external world. Such predilections express themselves both in the active striving for goods and in the affective perception of situations (so long as the latter are not objectivated into something in the world and thus lose their situational character). The partiality of desires and feelings is expressed at the level of language in the interpretation of needs, that is, in evaluations for which evaluative expressions are available. One can gain clarity about the meaning of value judgments by examining the dual, descriptive-prescriptive content of these evaluative, need-interpreting expressions. They serve to make predilection understandable. This component of justification[31] is the bridge between the subjectivity of experience and that intersubjective transparency that experience gains in being truthfully expressed and, on this basis, attributed to an actor by onlookers. For example, in characterizing an object or a situation as splendid, ample, elevating, auspicious, dangerous, forbidding, dreadful, and so forth, we are trying to express a predilection and at the same time to justify it, in the sense of making it plausible by appeal to general standards of evaluation that are widespread at least in our own culture. Evaluative expressions or standards of value have justificatory force when they characterize a need in such a way that addressees can, in the framework of a common cultural heritage, recognize in these interpretations their own needs. This explains why attributes of style, aesthetic expression, formal qualities in general, have such great weight in dramaturgical action.

In the case of dramaturgical action the relation between actor and world is also open to objective appraisal. As the actor is oriented to his own subjective world in the presence of his public, there can be *one* direction of fit: In regard to a self-presentation, there is the question whether at the proper moment the actor is expressing the experiences he has, whether he *means* what he *says,* or whether he is merely feigning the experiences he expresses. So long as we are dealing here with beliefs or intentions, that is, with cognitive acts, the question of whether someone says what he means is clearly a question of truthfulness or sincerity. With desires and feelings this is not always the case. In situations in which accuracy of expression is important, it is sometimes difficult to separate questions of sincerity from those of authenticity. Often we lack the words to say what we feel; and this in turn places the feelings themselves in a questionable light.

According to the dramaturgical model of action, a participant can adopt an attitude to his own subjectivity in the role of an actor and to the expressive utterances of another in the role of a public, but only in the awareness that ego's inner world is bounded by an external world. In this external world the actor can certainly distinguish between normative and nonnormative elements of the action situation; but Goffman's model of action does not provide for his behaving toward the social world in a norm-conformative attitude. He takes legitimately regulated interpersonal relations into account only as social facts. Thus it seems to me correct also to classify *dramaturgical action* as a concept that presupposes *two worlds,* the internal world and the external. Expressive utterances present subjectivity in demarcation from the external world; the actor can in principle adopt only an objectivating attitude toward the latter. And in contrast to the case of normatively regulated action, this holds not only for physical but for social objects as well.

In virtue of this option, dramaturgical action can take on latently strategic qualities to the degree that the actor treats his audience as *opponents* rather than as a public. The scale of self-presentations ranges from sincere communication of one's own intentions, desires, moods, etc., to cynical management of the impressions the actor arouses in others.

At one extreme, one finds that the performer can be fully taken in by his own act; he can be sincerely convinced that the impression of reality which he stages is the real reality.

> When his audience is also convinced in this way about the
> show he puts on—and this seems to be the typical case—
> then for the moment at least, only the sociologist or the
> socially disgruntled will have doubts about the "realness"
> of what is presented. At the other extreme... the performer
> may be moved to guide the conviction of his audience only
> as a means to other ends, having no ultimate concern with
> the beliefs of his audience; we may call him cynical, reserv-
> ing the term "sincere" for individuals who believe in the
> impression fostered by their own performance.[32]

The manipulative production of false impressions—Goffman
investigates techniques of "impression management," from
harmless segmentation to long-term information control—is by
no means identical with strategic action. It too remains dependent on a public that takes itself to be present at a performance
and fails to recognize its strategic character. Even a strategically
intended self-presentation has to be capable of being understood
as an expression that appears with the claim to subjective truthfulness. As soon as it is judged only according to criteria of success by the audience as well, it no longer falls under the description of dramaturgical action. We then have a case of strategic interaction in which participants have conceptually enriched their
objective world in such a way that opponents can appear in it
who are capable not only of purposive-rational action but of subjective expressions as well.

C.—With the concept of communicative action there comes
into play the additional presupposition of a *linguistic medium*
that reflects the actor-world relations as such. At this level of
concept formation the rationality problematic, which until now
has arisen only for the social scientist, moves into the perspective
of the agent himself. We have to make clear in what sense achieving understanding in language is thereby introduced as a mechanism for coordinating action. Even the strategic model of action
can be understood in such a way that participants' actions,
directed through egocentric calculations of utility and coordinated
through interest positions, are mediated through speech acts. In
the cases of normatively regulated and dramaturgical action we
even *have to* suppose a consensus formation among participants
that is in principle of a linguistic nature. Nevertheless, in these
three models of action language is conceived *one-sidedly* in different respects.

The teleological model of action takes language as one of several media through which speakers oriented to their own success can influence one another in order to bring opponents to form or to grasp beliefs and intentions that are in the speakers' own interest. This concept of language—developed from the limit case of indirect communication aimed at *getting* someone to form a belief, an intention, or the like—is, for instance, basic to intentionalist semantics.[33] The normative model of action presupposes language as a medium that transmits cultural values and carries a consensus that is merely reproduced with each additional act of understanding. This culturalist concept of language is widespread in cultural anthropology and content-oriented linguistics.[34] The dramaturgical model of action presupposes language as a medium of self-presentation; the cognitive significance of the propositional components and the interpersonal significance of the illocutionary components are thereby played down in favor of the expressive functions of speech acts. Language is assimilated to stylistic and aesthetic forms of expression.[35] Only the communicative model of action presupposes language as a medium of uncurtailed communication whereby speakers and hearers, out of the context of their preinterpreted lifeworld, refer simultaneously to things in the objective, social, and subjective worlds in order to negotiate common definitions of the situation. This interpretive concept of language lies behind the various efforts to develop a formal pragmatics.[36]

The one-sidedness of the first three concepts of language can be seen in the fact that the corresponding types of communication singled out by them prove to be limit cases of communicative action: *first,* the indirect communication of those who have only the realization of their own ends in view; *second,* the consensual action of those who simply actualize an already existing normative agreement; and *third,* presentation of self in relation to an audience. In each case only one function of language is thematized: the release of perlocutionary effects, the establishment of interpersonal relations, and the expression of subjective experiences. By contrast, the communicative model of action, which defines the traditions of social science connected with Mead's symbolic interactionism, Wittgenstein's concept of language games, Austin's theory of speech acts, and Gadamer's hermeneutics, takes all the functions of language equally into consideration. As can be seen in the ethnomethodological and hermeneutic approaches, there is a danger here of reducing social

action to the interpretive accomplishments of participants in communication, of assimilating action to speech, interaction to conversation. In the present context I can introduce this concept of communicative action only in a provisional way. I shall restrict myself
to remarks concerning: (a) the character of independent actions;
and (b) the reflective relation to the world of actors in processes
of understanding.

(a) In order to avoid mislocating the concept of communicative action from the start, I would like to characterize the level
of complexity of speech acts that simultaneously express a propositional content, the offer of an interpersonal relationship, and
the intention of the speaker. In the course of the analysis it will
become evident how much this concept owes to investigations
in the philosophy of language stemming from Wittgenstein. Precisely for this reason it might be well to point out that the concept of following a rule with which analytic philosophy of
language begins does not go far enough. If one grasps linguistic
conventions only from the perspective of rule following, and explains them by means of a concept of intentions based on rule
consciousness, one loses that aspect of the *threefold relation to
the world* of communicative agents that is important to me.[37]

I shall use the term "action" only for those symbolic expressions with which the actor takes up a relation to at least one world
(but always to the objective world *as well*)—as is the case in the
previously examined models of teleological, normatively regulated, and dramaturgical action. I shall distinguish from actions
the bodily movements and operations that are *concurrently executed* and can acquire the independence of actions only *secondarily,* through being *embedded, for instance, in play or teaching* practices. This can easily be shown through the example of bodily
movements. Under the aspect of observable events in the world,
actions appear as bodily movements of an organism. Controlled
by the central nervous system, these movements are the substratum in which actions are carried out. With his actions the
agent changes something in the world. We can, of course, distinguish the movements with which a subject intervenes in the
world (acts instrumentally) from those with which a subject embodies a meaning (expresses himself communicatively). In both
cases the bodily movements bring about a physical change in the
world; in the one case this is of causal relevance, in the other
of semantic relevance. Examples of causally relevant bodily movements are straightening the body, spreading the hand, lifting

the arm, bending the leg, and so forth. Examples of semantically relevant bodily movements are movements of the larynx, tongue, lips, etc. in the generation of phonetic sounds; nodding the head; shrugging the shoulders; finger movements while playing the piano; hand movements while writing, drawing; and so on.

Arthur Danto has analyzed these movements as "basic actions."[38] This has given rise to a broad discussion which is biased by the idea that bodily movements do not represent the substratum through which actions enter into the world but are themselves primitive actions.[39] In this view, a complex action is characterized by the fact that it is performed "through" carrying out another action: "through" flicking the light switch I turn on the light; "through" raising my right arm I greet someone; "through" forcefully kicking a ball I score a goal. These are examples of actions performed "through" a basic action. A basic action is characterized in turn by the fact that it cannot be performed by means of an additional act. I regard this conceptual strategy as misleading. In a certain sense, actions are realized through movements of the body, but only in such a way that the actor, in following a technical or social rule, *concomitantly executes* these movements. Concomitant execution means that the actor intends an action but not the bodily movements with the help of which he realizes it.[40] *A bodily movement is an element of an action but not an action.*

As far as their status as nonindependent actions is concerned, *bodily* movements are similar to just those *operations* from which Wittgenstein developed his concepts of rules and rule following. Operations of thought and speech are always only executed concomitantly in *other* actions. If need be, they can be *rendered independent* within the framework of a training exercise—for instance, when a Latin teacher, in the course of a lesson, demonstrates the passive transformation with a sample sentence formed in the active voice. This explains the special heuristic utility of the model of social games. Wittgenstein preferred to elucidate operational rules with reference to chess. He did not see that this model has only limited value. We can certainly understand speaking or doing sums as practices constituted by the grammar of a particular language or the rules of arithmetic, in a way similar to that in which chess playing is constituted by the familiar rules of the game. But the two cases are as distinct as is the concomitantly executed arm movement from the gymnastic exercise that is carried out by means of the same movement. In applying arithmetical or grammatical rules we generate symbolic objects such as sums or sentences; but they do not lead an independent existence. We normally carry out *other* actions by means of sums and sentences—for example, schoolwork or commands. Operatively generated structures can, taken by themselves, be judged as more or less correct, in conformity with a rule, or wellformed; but they are not, as are actions, open to criticism from the standpoints of truth, efficacy, rightness, or sincerity, for they acquire relations to the world only as the infrastructure of other actions. *Operations do not have to do with the world.*

This can be seen in the fact that operational rules can serve to identify an operatively generated structure as more or less well formed, that is, to make it *comprehensible* but not to *explain* its appearance. They permit an answer to the question of whether certain scrawled-out symbols are sentences, measurements, computations, etc.; and if they are, say, a computation, just which one it is. To show that someone has calculated, and indeed correctly, does not, however, explain *why* he carried out this computation. If we wish to answer *this* question, we must have recourse to a rule of *action*; for example, to the fact that a pupil used this sheet of paper to solve a mathematical problem. With the help of arithmetic rules, we can, it is true, state the reason why he continues the number series 1,3,6,10,15 . . . with 21,28,36, and so forth; but we cannot *explain* why he writes this series on a piece of paper. We are explicating the meaning of a symbolic structure and not giving a rational explanation for its coming to be. Operational rules do not have explanatory power; following them does not mean, as does following rules of action, that the actor is relating to something in the world and is thereby oriented to validity claims connected with action-motivating reasons.

(b) This should make clear why we cannot analyze communicative utterances in the same way as we do the grammatical sentences with the help of which we carry them out. For the communicative model of action, language is relevant only from the pragmatic viewpoint that speakers, in employing sentences with an orientation to reaching understanding, take up relations to the world, not only directly as in teleological, normatively regulated, or dramaturgical action, but in a reflective way. Speakers integrate the three formal world-concepts, which appear in the other models of action either singly or in pairs, into a system and presuppose this system in common as a framework of interpretation within which they can reach an understanding. They no

longer relate *straightaway* to something in the objective, social, or subjective worlds; instead they relativize their utterances against the possibility that their validity will be contested by other actors. Reaching an understanding functions as a mechanism for coordinating actions only through the participants in interaction coming to an agreement concerning the claimed *validity* of their utterances, that is, through intersubjectively recognizing the *validity claims* they reciprocally raise. A speaker puts forward a criticizable claim in relating with his utterance to at least one "world"; he thereby uses the fact that this relation between actor and world is in principle open to objective appraisal in order to call upon his opposite number to take a rationally motivated position. The concept of communicative action presupposes language as the medium for a kind of reaching understanding, in the course of which participants, through relating to a world, reciprocally raise validity claims that can be accepted or contested.

With this model of action we are supposing that participants in interaction can now mobilize the rationality potential—which according to our previous analysis resides in the actor's three relations to the world—expressly for the cooperatively pursued goal of reaching understanding. If we leave to one side the well-formedness of the symbolic expressions employed, an actor who is oriented to understanding in this sense must raise at least three validity claims with his utterance, namely:

1. That the statement made is true (or that the existential presuppositions of the propositional content mentioned are in fact satisfied);

2. That the speech act is right with respect to the existing normative context (or that the normative context that it is supposed to satisfy is itself legitimate); and

3. That the manifest intention of the speaker is meant as it is expressed.

Thus the speaker claims truth for statements or existential presuppositions, rightness for legitimately regulated actions and their normative context, and truthfulness or sincerity for the manifestation of subjective experiences. We can easily recognize therein the three relations of actor to world presupposed *by the social scientist* in the previously analyzed concepts of action; but in the concept of communicative action they are ascribed to the perspective of *the speakers and hearers themselves.* It is the actors themselves who seek consensus and measure it against truth, rightness, and sincerity, that is, against the "fit" or "misfit" between the speech act, on the one hand, and the three worlds to which the actor takes up relations with his utterance, on the other. Such relations hold between an utterance and;

1. The objective world (as the totality of all entities about which true statements are possible);

2. The social world (as the totality of all legitimately regulated interpersonal relations);

3. The subjective world (as the totality of the experiences of the speaker to which he has privileged access).

Every process of reaching understanding takes place against the background of a culturally ingrained preunderstanding. This background knowledge remains unproblematic as a whole; only that part of the stock of knowledge that participants make use of and thematize at a given time is put to the test. To the extent that definitions of situations are negotiated by participants *themselves,* this thematic segment of the lifeworld is at their disposal with the negotiation of each new definition of the situation.

A definition of the situation establishes an order. Through it, participants in communication assign the various elements of an action situation to one of the three worlds and thereby incorporate the actual action situation into their preinterpreted lifeworld. A definition of the situation by another party that prima facie diverges from one's own presents a problem of a peculiar sort; for in cooperative processes of interpretation no participant has a monopoly on correct interpretation. For both parties the interpretive task consists in incorporating the other's interpretation of the situation into one's own in such a way that in the revised version "his" external world and "my" external world can—against the background of "our" lifeworld—be relativized in relation to "the" world, and the divergent situation definitions can be brought to coincide sufficiently. Naturally this does not mean that interpretation must lead in every case to a stable and unambiguously differentiated assignment. Stability and absence of ambiguity are rather the exception in the communicative practice of everyday life. A more realistic picture is that drawn by ethnomethodologists—of a diffuse, fragile, continuously revised and only momentarily successful communication in which participants rely on problematic and unclarified presuppositions and feel their way from one occasional commonality to the next.

To avoid misunderstanding I would like to repeat that the communicative model of action does not equate action with communication. Language is a medium of communication that serves understanding, whereas actors, in coming to an understanding with one another so as to coordinate their actions, pursue their particular aims. In this respect the teleological structure is fundamental to *all* concepts of action.[41] Concepts of *social action* are distinguished, however, according to how they specify the *coordination* among the goal-directed actions of different participants: as the interlacing of egocentric calculations of utility (whereby the degree of conflict and cooperation varies with the given interest positions); as a socially integrating agreement about values and norms instilled through cultural tradition and socialization; as a consensual relation between players and their publics; or as reaching understanding in the sense of a cooperative process of interpretation. In all cases the teleological structure of action is presupposed, inasmuch as the capacity for goal-setting and goal-directed action is ascribed to actors, as well as an interest in carrying out their plans of action. But only the strategic model of action *rests content* with an explication of the features of action oriented directly to success; whereas the other models of action specify conditions under which the actor pursues his goals—conditions of legitimacy, of self-presentation, or of agreement arrived at in communication, under which alter can "link up" his actions with those of ego. In the case of communicative action the interpretive accomplishments on which cooperative processes of interpretation are based represent the mechanism for *coordinating* action; communicative action is *not exhausted* by the act of reaching understanding in an interpretive manner. If we take as our unit of analysis a simple speech act carried out by *S*, to which at least one participant in interaction can take up a "yes" or "no" position, we can clarify the conditions for the communicative coordination of action by stating what it means for a hearer to understand what is said.[42] But communicative action designates a type of interaction that is *coordinated through* speech acts and does *not coincide with* them.

4. *The Problem of Understanding Meaning in the Social Sciences*

The same rationality problematic that we encounter in examining sociological concepts of action appears in another light when we pursue the question What does it mean to understand social actions? There is an interdependence between the basic concepts of social action and the methodology of understanding social actions. Different models of action presuppose different relations of actor to world; and these world-relations are constitutive not only for aspects of the rationality of action, but also for the rationality of interpretations of action by, say, social-scientific interpreters. With a formal world-concept an actor becomes involved in suppositions of commonality that, from his perspective, point beyond the circle of those immediately involved and claim to be valid for outside interpreters as well. This connection can easily be made clear in the case of teleological action. The concept of the objective world—in which the actor can intervene in a goal-directed manner—which is presupposed with this model of action must hold in the same way for the actor himself and for any other interpreter of his actions. Thus Max Weber could construct for teleological action the ideal type of purposive-rational action and set up the standard of "the rationality of objective correctness" for interpreting purposive-rational actions.[1]

Weber terms subjectively purposive-rational a goal-directed action "which is exclusively oriented to means that are (subjectively) considered adequate for ends that are (subjectively) clearly apprehended."[2] The action orientation can be described in terms of the schema for practical inferences (as suggested by G. H. von Wright).[3] An interpreter can go beyond this *subjectively* purposive-rational orientation and compare the actual course of action with the constructed case of a corresponding *objectively* purposive-rational course of action. The interpreter is able to construct this ideal-typical case in a nonarbitrary manner since the agent relates in a subjectively purposive-rational way to a world that is, for categorial reasons, identical for actor and observer, that is, cognitively and instrumentally accessible to both in the same way. The interpreter needs only to ascertain "how the action *would have* gone, given knowledge of all the circumstances and all the intentions of those involved, and given a strictly purposive-rational choice of means in light of what appears *to us* as valid experience."[4]

The more clearly an action corresponds to the objectively purposive-rational course, the less we need additional *psychological* considerations to explain it. In the case of objectively purposive-rational action, the description of an action (with the help of a practical syllogism) has at the same time explanatory power in the sense of an explanation by intentions.[5] To be sure, even if the objective purposive-rationality of an action is established, this does not at all mean that the agent must also have behaved subjectively in a purposive-rational manner; on the other hand, a subjectively purposive-rational action can of course prove to be less than optimal when judged objectively.

> We confront the de facto course of action with that which, viewed "teleologically" in the light of general causal rules of experience, is rational; we can then *either* determine a rational motive which *could* have guided the agent and which we intend to elicit—we make this determination by showing his de facto actions to be suitable means to an end which he "could" have pursued—*or* we can make understandable why a motive of the agent known to us had, in consequence of his choice of means, a *different* result from that which the agent subjectively expected.[6]

An action can be interpreted as more or less purposive-rational if there are standards of judgment which both the agent and his interpreter equally accept as valid, that is, as standards of an objective or impartial appraisal. In advancing what Weber calls a rational interpretation, the interpreter himself takes a position on the claim with which purposive-rational actions appear; he relinquishes the attitude of a third person for the performative attitude of a participant who is examining a problematic validity claim and, if need be, criticizing it. Rational interpretations are undertaken in a performative attitude, since the interpreter presupposes a basis for judgment that is shared by all parties, including the actors.

The other two world-relations provide a similar basis. Normatively regulated and dramaturgical actions also admit of rational interpretation. Of course, in these cases the possibility of rationally reconstructing action orientations is not so evident, and in fact not so uncomplicated, as in the case of teleological action considered above.

In normatively regulated actions the actor, by entering into an interpersonal relation, takes up a relation to something in the social world. An actor's behavior is subjectively "right" (in the sense of normative rightness) if he sincerely believes himself to be following an existing norm of action; his behavior is objectively "right" if the norm in question is in fact regarded as justified among those to whom it applies. At this level the question of a rational interpretation does not yet arise, since an observer can ascertain descriptively whether an action accords with a given norm and whether or not the norm in turn enjoys social currency. According to the presuppositions of this model of action, however, an actor can comply with (or violate) only norms that he subjectively regards as valid or justified; and with this recognition of normative validity claims he exposes himself to an objective judgment. He challenges the interpreter to examine not only the actual norm-*conformity* of his action, or the de facto currency of the norm in question, but the rightness of this norm itself. The interpreter can in turn accept the challenge or, from a standpoint sceptical of values, dismiss it as senseless.

If the interpreter adopts such a sceptical standpoint, he will explain, with the help of a noncognitive variety of ethics, that the actor is deceiving himself in regard to the possibility of justifying norms, and that instead of reasons he could at best adduce empirical motives for the recognition of norms. Whoever argues in this way has to regard the concept of normatively regulated action as theoretically unsuitable; he will try to replace a description initially drawn in concepts of normatively regulated action with another one given, for example, in causal-behavioristic terms.[7] On the other hand, if the interpreter is convinced of the theoretical fruitfulness of the normative model of action, he has to get involved in the suppositions of commonality that are accepted with the formal concept of the social world and allow for the possibility of testing the *worthiness* to be recognized of a norm held by an actor to be right. Such rational interpretation of normatively regulated action is based on comparing the social currency of a given normative context with its counterfactually constructed validity. I shall not here go into the methodological problems of a practical discourse carried out by the interpreter as a representative of acting subjects (i.e., as their advocate).[8] The moral-practical appraisal of norms of action   certainly places an interpreter in even greater difficulties than monitoring the success of rules of purposive-rational action. At the moment, however, I am concerned only to show that normatively regulated actions, like teleological actions, can be rationally interpreted.

A similar consequence follows from the dramaturgical model of action. Here the actor, in revealing something of himself before a public, refers to something in his subjective world. Again, the formal world-concept provides a basis for judgment that is shared by the agent and his interpreter. An interpreter can interpret an action rationally in such a way that he thereby captures elements of deception or self-deception. He can expose the latently strategic character of a self-presentation by comparing the manifest content of the utterance, that is, what the actor says, with what the actor means. The interpreter can, furthermore, uncover the systematically distorted character of processes of understanding by showing how the participants express themselves in a subjectively truthful manner and yet objectively say something other than what they (also) mean (unbeknownst to themselves). The depth-hermeneutic procedure of interpreting unconscious motives again involves difficulties different from those connected with judging objectively ascribed interest positions in the role of advocate or with examining the empirical content of technical and strategic rules of action. Drawing on the example of therapeutic critique, however, we can make clear the possibility of rationally interpreting dramaturgical action.[9]

The procedures of rational interpretation enjoy a questionable status in the social sciences. The critique of "model-Platonism" in economics shows that some contest the empirical content and the explanatory fruitfulness of models of rational choice; objections to cognitivist approaches in ethics, and reservations with regard to the critique of ideology developed in the Hegelian-Marxist tradition, show that others doubt the possibility of providing moral-practical justification for norms of action and of setting off particular from generalizable interests; and the widespread critique of the scientific character of psychoanalysis shows that many regard as problematic the very *conception* of the unconscious, the concept of the latent/manifest double meaning of experiential expressions. In my view these objections are themselves based on empiricist assumptions that are open to question.[10] There is no need to go into this controversy here, as it is not my intention to demonstrate the *possibility* and theoretical fruitfulness of rational interpretations; I want rather to give reasons for the stronger claim that access to the object domain of social action through the understanding of meaning of itself makes the rationality problematic *unavoidable.* Communicative actions always require an interpretation that is rational in approach.

The relations of strategic, normatively regulated, and dramaturgical actors to the objective, social, and subjective worlds are in principle open to objective appraisal, both for the individual actor and for an observer. In communicative action, the very outcome of interaction is even made to depend on whether the participants can come to an agreement among themselves on an *intersubjectively valid* appraisal of their relations to the world. On this model of action, an interaction can succeed only if those involved arrive at a consensus among themselves, a consensus that depends on yes/no responses to claims potentially based on grounds. I shall be analyzing below this *rational infrastructure of action oriented to reaching understanding.* In the present context we are dealing with the question of whether, and if so how, this internal structure of the actors' understanding among themselves is represented in the understanding of an interpreter. Does not the task of describing complexes of communicative action consist only in giving as precise as possible an explication of the meaning of the symbolic expressions that make up the observed sequence? And is not this explication of meaning entirely independent of the (in principle testable) rationality of those opinions and attitudes that carry the interpersonal coordination of action? This would be the case only if the interpretation of action oriented to reaching understanding could allow a strict separation between questions of meaning and questions of validity; and this is precisely the problem. To be sure, we have to distinguish the interpretive accomplishments of an observer who wants to understand the meaning of a symbolic expression from those of participants in interaction who coordinate their actions through the mechanism of reaching understanding. Unlike those immediately involved, the interpreter is not striving for an interpretation on which there can be a consensus in order to harmonize his own action plans with those of other actors. But perhaps the interpretive accomplishments of observer and participant differ only in their function and not in their structure. The yes/no position of the interpreter by which, as we have seen, rational interpretations of idealtypically simplified courses of action are characterized, must enter incipiently even into the mere description, the semantic explication of a speech act. Communicative actions can only be interpreted "rationally" in a sense still to be explained. I would like to develop this disquieting thesis in connection with the problematic of *Sinnverstehen*, or understanding meaning, in the social sciences. I shall treat it first from the perspective of the theory of science, and then from that of the phenomenological, ethnomethodological, and hermeneutic schools of interpretive sociology.

A.—In the tradition stemming from Dilthey and Husserl, understanding [*Verstehen*] has been characterized *ontologically* by Heidegger in *Being and Time* (1927) as a basic feature of human existence, and reaching understanding [*Verständigung*] by Gadamer in *Truth and Method* (1960) as a basic feature of historical life. It is not at all my intention to rely systematically on this approach, but I would like to point out that the *methodological* discussions of recent decades concerning the foundations of the social sciences have led to similar results.

> The generation of descriptions of acts of everyday actors is not incidental to social life as ongoing *Praxis* but is absolutely integral to its production and inseparable from it, since the characterization of what others do, and more narrowly their intentions and reasons for what they do, is what makes possible the intersubjectivity through which the transfer of communicative intent is realized. It is in these terms that *verstehen* must be regarded: not as a special method of entry to the social world peculiar to the social sciences, but as the ontological condition of human society as it is produced and reproduced by its members.[11]

Sociology must seek a *verstehenden*, or interpretive, access to its object domain, because it already finds there processes of reaching understanding through which and in which the object domain is antecedently constituted (that is, before any theoretical grasp of it). The social scientist encounters *symbolically prestructured objects;* they embody structures of the pretheoretical knowledge with the help of which speaking and acting subjects produced these objects. The inner logic of a symbolically prestructured reality, which the social scientist runs up against in constituting his object domain, resides in the generative rules according to which the speaking and acting subjects that appear in the object domain produce the social context of life, directly or indirectly. The object domain of the social sciences encompasses everything that falls under the description "element of a lifeworld." What this expression means can be clarified intuitively by reference to those symbolic objects that we produce in speaking and acting, beginning with immediate expressions (such as speech acts, purposive activities, and cooperative actions), through the sedimentations of these expressions (such as texts, traditions, documents, works of art, theories, objects of material culture, goods, techniques, and so on), to the indirectly generated configurations that are self-stabilizing and susceptible of organization (such as institutions, social systems, and personality structures).

Speech and action are the unclarified fundamental concepts to which we have recourse when we wish to elucidate, even in a preliminary way, what it is to belong to, to be an element of a socio-cultural lifeworld. The problem of *Verstehen* is of methodological importance in the humanities and social sciences primarily because the scientist cannot gain access to a symbolically prestructured reality through *observation* alone, and because *understanding meaning [Sinnverstehen]* cannot be methodically brought under control in the same way as can observation in the course of experimentation. The social scientist basically has no other access to the lifeworld than the social-scientific layman does. He must already belong in a certain way to the lifeworld whose elements he wishes to describe. In order to describe them, he must understand them; in order to understand them, he must be able in principle to participate in their production; and participation presupposes that one belongs. As we shall see, this circumstance prohibits the interpreter from separating questions of meaning and questions of validity in such a way as to secure for the understanding of meaning a purely descriptive character. I would like to make four observations in this regard.

(a) The *Verstehen* problematic bears within itself the seeds of a dualistic view of science. Historicism (Dilthey, Misch) and Neo-Kantianism (Windelband, Rickert) constructed a dualism for the natural and human sciences at the level of the contrast between explanation and understanding. This "first round" of the explanation/understanding controversy is no longer alive today.[12] With the reception of phenomenological, language-analytic, and hermeneutic approaches in sociology, however, a discussion has arisen in connection with Husserl and Schutz, Wittgenstein and Winch, and Heidegger and Gadamer, in which a case has been

made for the special status of the social sciences vis-à-vis proto-typical natural sciences such as physics in respect to the method-ological role of communicative experience. Opposed to this case, the empiricist theory of science has defended the concept of the unity of scientific method that was already developed in the Neo-Positivism of Vienna. This discussion can be regarded as over, the few remaining echoes notwithstanding.[13] The critics, basing themselves primarily on arguments of Theodor Abel,[14] misun-derstood *Verstehen* as empathy, as a mysterious act of transpos-ing oneself into the mental states of another subject. Under em-piricist presuppositions they were forced to reinterpret commu-nicative experience in terms of an empathy theory of *Verstehen*.[15] The next phase of the discussion was introduced with the post-empiricist turn of the analytic theory of science.[16] Mary Hesse has argued that the usual contrast of the natural with the social sciences is based on a concept of the natural sciences, indeed of the empirical-analytic sciences in general, that is now out of date. In her view, the debate concerning the history of modern physics that was touched off by Kuhn, Popper, Lakatos, and Feyerabend has shown: first, that the data against which theories are tested cannot be described independently of the theory lan-guage in question; and, second, that theories are constructed not according to the principles of falsificationism but in dependence on paradigms that—as can be seen in the attempt to render inter-theoretic relations precise—relate to one another in a manner similar to particular forms of life.

> I take it that it has been sufficiently demonstrated that data are not detachable from theory, and that their expression is permeated by theoretical categories; that the language of theoretical science is irreducibly metaphorical and unformal-izable, and that the logic of science is circular interpretation, reinterpretation, and self-correction of data in terms of theory, theory in terms of data.[17]

Hesse infers from this that theory formation in the natural sciences is no less dependent on interpretations than it is in the social sciences—interpretations that can be analyzed in terms of the hermeneutic model of *Verstehen*. From the point of view of the *Verstehen* problematic, then, it appears that no case can be made for the social sciences having a special status.[18]

In opposition to this, Anthony Giddens rightly points out

that there is a specific, namely a *double* hermeneutic task in the social sciences.

> The mediation of paradigms of widely discrepant theoretical schemes in science is a hermeneutic matter like that involved in the contacts between other types of meaning-frames. But sociology, unlike natural science, deals with a pre-interpreted world where the creation and reproduction of meaning-frames is a very condition of that which it seeks to analyze, namely human social conduct: this is why there is a double hermeneutic in the social sciences.[19]

Giddens speaks of a "double" hermeneutic because in the social sciences problems of interpretive understanding do not come into play only through the theory-dependency of data description and the paradigm-dependency of theory languages; there is already a problem of understanding below the threshold of theory construction, namely in *obtaining* data and not first in *theoretically describing* them; for the everyday experience that can be *transformed* into scientific operations is, for its part, already symbolically structured and inaccessible to mere observation.[20] If the paradigm-dependent theoretical description of data calls for a stage 1 of interpretation that confronts all sciences with structurally similar tasks, then we can demonstrate for the social sciences an unavoidable stage 0 of interpretation at which there arises a *further* problem for the relation of observation language and theory language. It is not only that the observation language is dependent on the theory language; *prior* to choosing any theory-dependency, the social-scientific "observer," as a participant in the processes of reaching understanding through which alone he can gain access to his data, has to make use of the language encountered in the object domain. The *specific Verstehen problematic* lies in the fact that the social scientist cannot "use" this language "found" in the object domain as a neutral instrument. He cannot "enter into" this language without having recourse to the pretheoretical knowledge of a member of a lifeworld—indeed of his own—which he has intuitively mastered as a layman and now brings unanalyzed into every process of achieving understanding.

This is, of course, not a new insight; it is precisely the thesis that critics of the unity of scientific method had always put forward. It has merely been placed in a new light because the analytic theory of science has, with its recent postempiricist turn, *rediscovered* in its own way the critical insight that was held up to it by the *Verstehen* theorists (and that was to be found in any case along the path of the pragmatist logic of science from Peirce to Dewey[21]).

(b) Wherein consists then the special methodological difficulties of understanding in the sciences that must gain access to their object domains through interpretation? H. Skjervheim already dealt with this problem in 1959.[22] He is among those who reopened the debate concerning social-scientific objectivism, a discussion that has come to a provisional close with the comprehensive examination by Richard Bernstein, *The Restructuring of Social and Political Theory* (1976). Under the spectacular impression of Peter Winch's book, *The Idea of Social Science* (1958), it was not sufficiently noticed that Skjervheim was the one who had first worked out the methodologically shocking consequences of the *Verstehen* problematic; had worked out, that is, what is problematic about *Verstehen*.

Skjervheim begins with the thesis that understanding meaning is a mode of experience. If *meaning* is allowed as a basic theoretical concept, symbolic meanings must be regarded as data: "What is of interest for us. . .is that *meanings*—the meanings of written and spoken words—*must be regarded as belonging to that which is given*. . .In other words, what we propose is a perceptual theory of meaning and of our knowledge of other minds."[23] The analysis of the "perception" of symbolic expressions makes clear how understanding meaning differs from perceiving physical objects: it requires taking up an *intersubjective relation* with the subject who brought forth the expression. The so-called perceptual theory of meaning explains the concept of communicative experience and thereby runs into a "forgotten theme" in the analytic theory of science: the intersubjectivity that is established between ego and alter ego in communicative action. Skjervheim stresses the difference between two basic attitudes. One who, in the role of a *third person,* observes something in the world or makes a statement about something in the world adopts an objectivating attitude. By contrast, one who takes part in a communication and, in the role of the *first person* (ego), enters into an intersubjective relation with a *second person* (who, as the alter ego, behaves to ego in turn as to a second person) adopts a nonobjectivating, or as we would now say, a performative attitude.

Observations are made by each for himself, and the observation statements of another observer are checked once again by each for himself (if need be, against the results of measurement).

If this process leads to stated agreement among different observers —in principle, any observers whatever—the objectivity of an observation may count as sufficiently guaranteed. By contrast, intersubjective understanding, because it is a communicative experience, cannot be carried out in a solipsistic manner. Understanding [*Verstehen*] a symbolic expression fundamentally requires participation in a process of reaching understanding [*Verständigung*]. Meanings—whether embodied in actions, institutions, products of labor, words, networks of cooperation, or documents—can be made accessible only *from the inside*. Symbolically prestructured reality forms a universe that is hermetically sealed to the view of observers incapable of communicating; that is, it would have to remain incomprehensible to them. The lifeworld is open only to subjects who make use of their competence to speak and act. They gain access to it by participating, at least virtually, in the communications of members and thus becoming at least potential members themselves.

In so proceeding, the social scientist has to draw on a competence and a knowledge that he has intuitively at his disposal as a layman. So long, however, as he does not identify and thoroughly analyze this pretheoretical knowledge, he cannot control the extent to which, and the consequences with which, he also *influences* as a participant—and thereby alters—the process of communication into which he *entered* only to understand. The process of understanding is bound up in an unclarified way with a process of bringing something about. The *Verstehen* problematic can thus be expressed in the brief question: How can the *objectivity of understanding* be reconciled with the performative attitude of one who participates in a process of reaching understanding?

Skjervheim goes on to analyze the methodological significance of alternating between an objectivating and a performative attitude. In his view, this alternation is linked with an ambiguity in the social sciences,

> which is the result of the fundamental ambiguity of the human situation: that the other is there both as an object for me and as another subject with me. This dualism crops up in one of the major means of intercourse with the other— the spoken word. We may treat the words that the other utters as sounds merely; or if we understand their meaning we may still treat them as facts, registering the fact that he says what he says; or we may treat what he says as a

knowledge claim, in which case we are not concerned with what he says as a fact of his biography only, but as something which can be true or false. In both the first cases the other is an object for me, although in different ways, while in the latter he is a fellow-subject who concerns me as one on an equal footing with myself, in that we are both concerned with our common world.[24]

Skjervheim draws our attention here to the interesting fact that the performative attitude of a first person in relation to a second means at the same time an orientation to validity claims. In this attitude ego cannot treat a truth claim raised by alter as something that appears in the objective world; ego encounters this claim *frontally;* he has to take it seriously, to react to it with a "yes" or "no" (or to leave to one side, as not yet decided, the question of whether the claim rightly stands). Ego has to grasp the utterance of alter as symbolically embodied knowledge. This follows from the nature of processes of reaching understanding. Those who wish to come to an understanding have to suppose that there are common standards in the light of which participants can decide whether a consensus has been reached. But if participation in communication processes means that one must take a position on the validity claims of the other, the social scientist, even when he is *gathering* communicative experiences, does not have the option of apprehending the utterance of his opposite number as a mere fact. This raises the question of whether we can at all treat separately the two cases distinguished by Skjervheim as cases two and three: understanding the semantic content of an utterance and reacting to the validity claim connected with it. Skjervheim's analysis is still unsatisfactory; but his observations already point to consequences that are important in the present context.

(c) If understanding meaning is conceived as a mode of experience, and if communicative experience is possible only in the performative attitude of a participant in interaction, then the observing social scientist who is gathering language-dependent data has to assume a status similar to that of the layman. How far does the structural similarity between their interpretive accomplishments extend? In answering this question it is useful to recall that speaking and acting are not the same. Those immediately involved in the communicative practice of everyday life are pursuing aims of *action;* their participation in cooperative

processes of interpretation serves to establish a consensus on the basis of which they can coordinate their plans of action and achieve their aims. The social-scientific interpreter does not pursue aims of action *of this kind*. He participates in processes of reaching understanding for the sake of understanding and not for the sake of an end that requires coordinating the goal-oriented action of the interpreter with the goal-oriented actions of those immediately involved. The action system in which the social scientist moves *as an actor* lies on a different plane; it is as a rule a segment of the scientific system; in any case, it does not coincide with the action system under observation. In concentrating, as a speaker and hearer, exclusively on the process of reaching understanding, the social scientist takes part in the observed action system *subject to the withdrawal,* as it were, *of his qualities as an actor.*

This can be made clear in connection with the model of the philologist who deciphers transmitted documents, translates texts, interprets traditions, and so on. In this case, those involved in the original processes of reaching understanding cannot even perceive the virtual participation of the interpreter, who approaches from a temporal distance. This example also throws light on the contrasting model of the participant-observer, whose active presence unavoidably alters the original scene. Even in this case the actions with which the interpreter tries, more or less inconspicuously, to enter into the given context have only the *auxiliary function* of assisting participation in the process of reaching understanding, which is the key to understanding the actions of *other* agents; this participation is pursued as an end in itself. I shall leave the expression "auxiliary function"—in need as it is of clarification—to one side and speak of merely "virtual" participation because the interpreter, viewed in his capacity as an actor, pursues goals that are not related to the given context but to *another* system of action. To this extent, the social scientist does not pursue any aims *of his own* within the observed context.

What does the *role of virtual participant* mean now for the question of the objectivity of the social-scientific interpreter's understanding? Consider the alternative posed by Skjervheim. If the interpreter confines himself to observations in the strict sense, he perceives only the physical substrata of utterances without understanding them. In order to have communicative experience he must adopt a performative attitude and participate, be it only virtually, in the original process of reaching understanding. In doing so, can he, as Skjervheim assumes, confine himself to grasping descriptively the semantic contents of utterances, as if they were mere facts, without reacting to the validity claims that participants raise with their utterances? Can the interpreter wholly abstract from his judgment of the validity of the utterances that are to be captured descriptively?

In order to understand an utterance in the paradigm case of a speech act oriented to reaching understanding, the interpreter has to be familiar with the conditions of its validity; he has to know under what conditions the validity claim linked with it is acceptable, that is, would have to be acknowledged by a hearer. But where could the interpreter obtain this knowledge if not from the context of the observed communication or from comparable contexts? He can understand the meaning of communicative acts only because they are embedded in contexts of *action* oriented to reaching understanding—this is Wittgenstein's central insight and the starting point for his use theory of meaning.[25] The interpreter observes under what conditions symbolic expressions are accepted as valid and when the validity claims connected with them are criticized and rejected; he notices when the action plans of participants are coordinated through consensus formation and when the connections among the actions of different agents fall apart due to lack of consensus. Thus the interpreter cannot become clear about the semantic content of an expression independently of the action contexts in which participants react to the expression in question with a "yes" or a "no" or an abstention. And he does not understand these yes/no positions if he cannot make clear to himself the implicit reasons that move the participants to take the positions they do. For agreement and disagreement, insofar as they are judged in the light of reciprocally raised validity claims and not merely caused by external factors, are based on reasons that participants supposedly or actually have at their disposal. These (most often implicit) reasons form the axis around which processes of reaching understanding revolve. But if, in order to understand an expression, the interpreter must *bring to mind the reasons* with which a speaker would if necessary and under suitable conditions defend its validity, he is *himself* drawn into the process of assessing validity claims. For reasons are of such a nature that they cannot be described in the attitude of a third person, that is, without reactions of affirmation or negation or abstention. The interpreter would not have understood what a "reason" is if he did not reconstruct it with its claim to provide grounds; that is, if he did not give it a *rational interpre-tation* in Max Weber's sense. The *description* of reasons demands *eo ipso* an *evaluation*, even when the one providing the descrip-tion feels that he is not at the moment in a position to judge their soundness. One can understand reasons only to the extent that one understands *why* they are or are not sound, or why in a given case a decision as to whether reasons are good or bad is not (yet) possible. An interpreter cannot, therefore, interpret expressions connected through criticizable validity claims with a potential of reasons (and thus represent knowledge) without taking a posi-tion on them. And he cannot take a position without applying his *own* standards of judgment, at any rate standards that he has made his own. These relate critically to other, divergent stan-dards of judgment. In taking a position on a validity claim rais-ed by alter, standards are applied that the interpreter does not simply light upon; he must have accepted them as correct. In this respect, a merely virtual participation does not free the in-terpreter of the obligations of one who is immediately involved; on this point, which is decisive for the objectivity of under-standing, the same kind of interpretive accomplishment is re-quired of both the social-scientific observer and the layman.

These reflections should make it clear that the method of interpretive understanding places the usual type of objectivity of knowledge in question, because the interpreter, though without aims of action of his own, has to become involved in participating in communicative action and finds himself confronted with the validity claims arising in the object domain itself. He has to meet the rational internal structure of action oriented to validity claims with an interpretation that is rational in conception. The inter-preter could neutralize the latter only at the cost of assuming the objectivating status of an observer; but from that standpoint in-ternal interrelations of meaning are entirely inaccessible. There is then a *fundamental connection between understanding communica-tive actions and constructing rational interpretations.* This connec-tion is fundamental because communicative actions cannot be interpreted in two stages—first understood in their actual course and only then compared with an ideal-typical model. Rather, an interpreter who participates virtually, without his own aims of action, can descriptively grasp the meaning of the actual course of a process of reaching understanding only under the presup-position that he judges the agreement and disagreement, the validity claims and potential reasons with which he is confronted, on a common basis *shared* in principle by him and those immediately involved. At any rate, this participation is imperative for a social-scientific interpreter who bases his descriptions on the communicative model of action. As I shall attempt to show, this follows from the ontological—in the broadest sense—presuppositions of the model.

(d) When we describe behavior as teleological action, we suppose that the agent makes certain ontological presuppositions, that he reckons with an objective world in which he can know something and in which he can purposefully intervene. We who observe him simultaneously make ontological presuppositions in respect to the subjective world of the actor. We distinguish between "the" world and the world as it appears from the agent's standpoint. We can descriptively ascertain what the actor *takes* to be true in contradistinction to what *is* (in our opinion) true. The choice between a descriptive and a rational interpretation consists in either ignoring or taking seriously the truth claim that the actor connects with his opinions and the truth-related claim to success that he connects with his teleological actions. If we ignore them as validity claims, we treat opinions and aims as something subjective, that is, as something that, when brought forth by the actor as his opinion or his aim, when disclosed or brought to expression before a public, has to be ascribed to his subjective world. In this case we neutralize the claims to truth and success by treating opinions and aims as expressive utterances; and these can be objectively judged only from the standpoints of their sincerity and authenticity. These standpoints, however, are not applicable to the teleological action of an in-principle solitary actor without a public, so to speak. If on the other hand we take seriously the actor's claims exactly in the way he rationally intends them, we subject his (supposed) prospects of success to a critique that is based on *our* knowledge and our comparison of the actual course of action with an ideal-typically projected, purposive-rational course of action. Naturally the agent could *respond* to this critique only if we were to equip him with competences other than those permitted by the teleological model of action. *Mutual* critique would be possible only if the agent could for his part take up interpersonal relations, act communicatively, and even participate in the special form of communication (loaded with presuppositions) that we have called "discourse."

We could construct an analogous thought-experiment for the

case in which we describe behavior as normatively regulated action. We thereby suppose that the actor reckons with a second world, the social world, in which he can distinguish norm-conformative from deviant behavior. And again, as observers we simultaneously make ontological presuppositions in respect to the subjective world of the actor, so that we can distinguish between the social world as it appears to the actor, the social world as it appears to other members, and *the* social world as it appears *to us.* Here too the choice between a rational and a descriptive interpretation consists in deciding whether, *mutatis mutandis,* to take seriously the normative validity claim the actor connects with his actions or to reinterpret it as something merely subjective. Here too the descriptive construction rests on reinterpreting what the actor, in following a norm recognized as legitimate, rationally intends. Here too there remains, in the case of a rational interpretation, an asymmetry between us and an actor who, within the limits of the normative model of action, is not equipped with the ability to debate the validity of norms in a hypothetical attitude as a participant in discourse.

The asymmetry is still there when we describe behavior as dramaturgical action and equip the actor with the corresponding world-concepts. In the case of a rational interpretation, we the observers claim a capacity of judgment against which the actor himself could lodge no appeal. We have to believe ourselves capable, if need be, of criticizing as self-deception—on the basis of certain indicators—an expressive utterance that the actor himself performs with a claim to sincerity; while within the limits of the dramaturgical model of action, the actor would not be in a position to defend himself against our rational interpretation.

The basic concepts of teleological, normatively regulated, and dramaturgical action ensure a methodologically relevant gap between the level of the action interpretation and that of the interpreted action. As soon, however, as we describe behavior in terms of communicative action, our own ontological presuppositions are no longer more complex than those we ascribe to the actors themselves. The difference between the conceptual level of communicatively coordinated action and that of the interpretation we make of it as observers no longer functions as a protective filter. For according to the presuppositions of the communicative model of action, the agent possesses just as rich an interpretive competence as the observer himself. The actor is now not only equipped with three world-concepts, he can also apply them reflectively. The success of the communicative action depends, as we have seen, on a process of interpretation in which participants come to a common definition of the situation within the reference system of the three worlds. Every consensus rests on an intersubjective recognition of criticizable validity claims; it is thereby presupposed that those acting communicatively are *capable of mutual criticism.*

But as soon as we equip the actors with *this* capability, we lose our privileged position as observers in relation to the object domain. We no longer have the choice of giving either a descriptive or a rational interpretation to an observed sequence of inter-action. As soon as we ascribe to the actors *the same* judgmental competence that we claim for ourselves as interpreters of their utterances, we relinquish an immunity that was until then methodologically guaranteed. We find ourselves forced to participate, in a performative attitude (albeit without our own action intentions), in the process of reaching understanding that we would like to describe. We thereby expose our interpretation in principle to the same critique to which communicative agents must mutually expose their interpretations. But this means that the distinction between descriptive and rational interpretations becomes meaningless at this level. Or better: that interpretation that is rational in conception is here the only way to gain access to the de facto course of communicative action. It cannot have the status of an ideal type constructed ad hoc (that is, of a post-factum rational model) because independently of it there can be no description of the actual course of action with which it could be compared.

From here light falls retrospectively on the rational interpretations of the first-level types of action. Comparison of the actual course of action with models, each of which stylizes action under a single aspect of rationality (propositional truth, effectiveness or instrumental success, normative rightness, authenticity or sincerity), requires a description of action that is *independent* of rational interpretation. But this prior hermeneutic accomplishment is not thematized in the first-level models of action; it is naively presupposed. The description of a de facto course of action calls for a complex interpretation that already implicitly makes use of the conceptual apparatus of communicative action and, like everyday interpretations themselves, bears the features of an interpretation that is rational in approach. The

possibility of choosing between a descriptive and a rational interpretation arises only when one of the noncommunicative models
of action commits the observer to an abstraction, that is, to stressing only one aspect of the complex of interaction proceeding by
way of validity claims.

B.—If we conceptually enrich the first-level models of action to
the point where interpretation and understanding appear as basic
features of social action itself, the question of how the interpretive
accomplishments of the social-scientific observer are connected
with the natural hermeneutics of the everyday practice of communication, of how communicative experiences can be transformed into data, can no longer be trimmed down to the size of
a technical subproblem in research. In ethnomethodology[26] and
philosophical hermeneutics[27] this insight has been revived and
is upsetting the conventional self-understanding of sociology
determined by the postulate of value-freedom.[28] In these discussions[29]—of which it is difficult to gain an overview—it is only
recently that the proposal on which I shall concentrate has clearly
emerged: the very situation that gives rise to the problem of
understanding meaning can also be regarded as the key to its
solution.[30]

If the social scientist has to participate virtually in the interactions whose meaning he wants to understand, and if, further,
this participation means that he has implicitly to take a position
on the validity claims that those immediately involved in communicative action connect with their utterances, then the social
scientist will be able to link up his own concepts with the
conceptual framework found in the context of action only in the
same way as laymen themselves do in the communicative practice
of everyday life. He is moving within the same structures of
possible understanding in which those immediately involved
carry out their communicative actions. However, the most general
structures of communication that speaking and acting subjects
have learned to master not only open up access to specific
contexts; they not only make it possible to link up with and
develop contexts which draw participants passively—so it may
seem at first—under the spell of the merely particular. These same
structures also simultaneously provide the critical means to
penetrate a given context, to burst it open from within and to
transcend it; the means, if need be, to push beyond a de facto
established consensus, to revise errors, correct misunderstand-

ings, and the like. The same structures that make it possible to reach an understanding also provide for the possibility of a reflective self-control of this process. It is this potential for critique built into communicative action itself that the social scientist, by entering into the contexts of everyday action as a virtual participant, can systematically exploit and bring into play outside these contexts and against their particularity. I would like to sketch briefly how this insight was finally established in the methodological discussion that has accompanied interpretive sociology from the start.

(a) In the context of German sociology of the 1920s, Alfred Schutz thought through most consistently the implications of a *sinnverstehenden* access to symbolically prestructured reality.[31] He saw that with the choice of basic action-theoretic concepts we are making at least three provisional methodological decisions: *first,* the decision to describe social reality in such a way that it is conceived as a construction of the everyday world issuing from the interpretive accomplishments of those directly participating.

> The social world . . . has a particular meaning and relevance structure for the human beings living, thinking, and acting therein. They have preselected and preinterpreted this world by a series of common-sense constructs of the reality of daily life, and it is these thought objects which determine their behavior, define the goals of their action, the means available for attaining them.[32]

Understanding meaning is the privileged mode of experience for members of a lifeworld. To be sure, the social scientist must also make use of this mode of experience; he obtains his data through understanding meanings. This is the *second* decision to which Schutz (along with Max Weber and W. I. Thomas) gives the form of a postulate.

> In order to explain human actions the scientist has to ask what model of an individual mind can be constructed and what typical contents must be attributed to it in order to explain the observed facts as the result of the activity of such a mind in an understandable relation. The compliance with this postulate warrants the possibility of referring all kinds of human action or their result to the subjective meaning such action or result of an action had for the actor.[33]

But for Schutz this postulate is significant not only for the technique of research; rather, there follows from it, *third,* a specific limitation on theory construction. The theoretical concepts in which the social scientist forms his hypothesis must connect up in a certain way with the pretheoretical concepts in which members interpret their situation and the context of action in which they are participating. Schutz does not present a detailed argument showing why such an internal interconnection of theory to the everyday understanding of the participants whose expressions are to be explained with the help of the theory follows conclusively from the "double-hermeneutic" task of the social sciences. He simply postulates:

> Each term in a scientific model of human action must be constructed in such a way that a human act performed within the life-world by an individual actor in the way indicated by the typical construct would be understandable for the actor himself as well as for his fellow-men in terms of common-sense interpretation of everyday life. Compliance with this postulate warrants the consistency of the constructs of the social scientist with the constructs of commonsense experience of the social reality.[34]

The language games the social scientist encounters in his object domain, and in which he has to participate at least virtually, are of a particular nature. How can a social-scientific theory simultaneously link up with the conceptual apparatus of a concrete lifeworld and yet free itself of its particularity? Schutz believes that the social-scientific observer adopts a *theoretical attitude* that enables him to raise himself above the lifeworld perspectives of both his own everyday practice and that under investigation. Whereas we, as members of a lifeworld, enter into "we-relations," occupy places specific to ego and group within the space-time coordinate system of the lifeworld, behave as ego to alter or alius, distinguish predecessors from contemporaries and successors, and so on, the social-scientific observer breaks with this *natural* (or performative) *attitude* and takes up a position beyond his or any other lifeworld—that is, an extramundane position.

> Having no "here" within the social world the social scientist does not organize this world in layers around himself as the center. He can never enter as a consociate in an inter-

action pattern with one of the actors on the social scene without abandoning, at least temporarily, his scientific attitude. The participant observer or field worker establishes contact with the group studied as a man among fellow-men; only his system of relevance which serves as the scheme of his selection and interpretation is determined by the scientific attitude, temporarily dropped in order to be resumed again.[35]

The theoretical attitude is characterized as that of the "disinterested" observer; it is supposedly capable of generally creating a distance from the biographically rooted interests of everyday life. Since Schutz cannot appeal—as did Husserl—to a special method of withholding judgment, *epoché,* he has to explain the neutralization of the lifeworld perspective in another way. He explains it through a specific alteration of systems of relevance. The decision of the scientist to put the value system of the sciences in the place of the value system of his everyday life ("by establishing the life-plan for scientific work") is supposed to be sufficient to bring about *the change from the natural to the theoretical attitude.* This explanation is not really satisfactory. If the theoretical attitude were determined only by the values of the scientific subsystem, Schutz would have to explain the methodological role of these special value orientations. He would have to show why just these help to solve the problem of linking theory formation to the communicatively accessible, pretheoretical knowledge that the social scientist finds in the object domain, without at the same time tying the validity of his statements to the lifeworld context—either the one encountered or the one carried along.

Schutz makes a remark in passing that suggests the starting point for a solution: "Verstehen is by no means a private affair of the observer which cannot be controlled by the experiences of other observers. It is controllable at least to the same extent to which the private sensory perceptions of an individual are controllable by any other individual under certain conditions."[36] If the possible correctives for confused communicative experiences are, so to speak, built into communicative action itself, the social scientist cannot guarantee the objectivity of his cognition by slipping into the fictive role of a "disinterested observer" and thus fleeing to a utopian spot outside the communicatively accessible context of life. Rather, he will have to seek the conditions of the objectivity of understanding [*Verstehen*] in the general structures of the processes of reaching understanding [*Verständigung*] into which he enters; he will then have to ascertain whether, in the knowledge of these conditions, he can reflectively grasp the implications of his participation.

(b) In the short history of ethnomethodology this is the central question about which there is a division of opinion.[37] On the one hand, ethnomethodologists stress the processual and merely particular character of the everyday practice interpretively generated by participants; on the other hand, they draw the methodological consequences from the fact that the social scientist has in principle the status of a participant. They highlight both aspects more precisely than did Schutz, from whom they take their start. This gives rise to a dilemma that cannot be resolved so long as cooperative processes of interpretation are not conceived as processes of reaching understanding that are oriented to validity claims.

With every sequence of interaction, communicative actors renew the appearance of a normatively structured society; but in fact they are groping from one problematic, momentary consensus to the next. If all concepts and action orientations impinging on the situation have to be negotiated anew each time, the occasionalism of the particular dominates the general, so that the appearance of continuity across a number of action sequences can be secured only through reference to the given context.[38] This view explains why Garfinkel and his disciples are interested in the context-dependency of everyday communication and the role of indexical expressions in this connection. The meaning of sentences in which terms such as "I" and "you," "here" and "now," "this" and "that" appear varies with the situation of speech. The references made with the help of such expressions can be understood only in cognizance of the speech situation. The interpreter must either already know, as a participant in interaction, the context on which the speaker is relying, or he must demand of the speaker that he expressly formulate his presuppositions. To meet this demand, the speaker would have to replace the situation-related indexical expressions with situation-independent expressions, for example, with space-time specifications or other characterizations. Such efforts to make contextual knowledge partly explicit and to remove misunderstandings about presuppositions are altogether common in everyday communication. But these attempts lead to a regress: each additional explication is dependent in turn on presuppositions. In the framework of everyday communication we can clarify the context of speech step by step, but we cannot in principle get behind it.

Garfinkel rightly stresses that utterances in which indexical expressions appear do not at all need to be "put in order," because context-dependency is not a defect but a necessary condition for the normal use of our language. Of course, he dramatizes this trivial observation in a peculiar way and uses it to throw into overly bold relief the exploratory and creative moments of the interpretive process, the *projection* and cooperative *production* of an occasional commonality. This throws light on the hermeneutic ties of the interpreter to his initial situation.

In everyday communication an utterance never stands alone; a semantic content accrues to it from the context the speaker presupposes that the hearer understands. The interpreter too must penetrate that context of reference as a participating partner in interaction. The exploratory moment oriented to knowledge cannot be detached from the creative, constructive moment oriented to producing consensus. For the interpreter cannot acquire a preunderstanding of a context—upon which the understanding of an utterance situated within it depends—without participating in the process of shaping and developing that context. The social scientist also has no privileged access to the object domain; he must draw upon the intuitively mastered interpretive procedures that he has "naturally" acquired as a member of his social group.

So long as the sociologist is not conscious of this situation he shares naively the status of a social-scientific layman and, like the latter, hypostatizes social reality to something existing in itself. Thus the conventional sociologist takes no account of the fact that he can objectivate a context of action of which he is making an object of study only through previously drawing upon it as a source of information. He does not see that he has already contributed, as a participant in interaction, to establishing the context of action that he then analyzes as an object. Ethnomethodological critique produces ever-new variations on this theme of confusing "resource and topic." It attempts to demonstrate that the usual constructions of social science have at bottom the same status as the everyday constructions of lay members. They remain bound to the social context they are supposed to explain because they fall prey to the objectivism of everyday consciousness.

If at this most fundamental level the only way an observer can identify what actions have occurred is through documentary interpretation, then description of interaction is not intersubjectively verifiable in any strong sense, since the interpretations of different individuals will necessarily agree only when they are able to negotiate a common social reality; nor are such descriptions independent of context. In describing interaction interpretively, the observer necessarily imputes an underlying pattern that serves as the essential context for seeing what the situation and actions are, while these same situations and actions are a necessary resource for seeing what the context is.[39]

Of course, this critique of method also becomes a problem for ethnomethodologists themselves as soon as they set about developing social-scientific theories. In the ethnomethodological camp we find primarily *three* reactions to this difficulty.

The *radical self-application* of this methodological critique leads to the conclusion that interpretive sciences must give up the claim to produce objective knowledge at all. The insight that interpretation of an action context presupposes participation in, and constructive influence upon, this context merely brings a dilemma to consciousness; it does not resolve it. Insight into the unavoidably self-referential character of research practice does not open a way to context-independent knowledge. Thus social research should count only as one particular form of life alongside of others. Theoretical work is, like religion or art, an activity distinguished by reflexivity; the fact that it makes an explicit theme of the interpretive processes on which the researcher draws does not dissolve its situational ties. The universality of the claim to truth is an illusion; what is accepted as true at any given time is a matter of convention.

We must accept that there are no adequate grounds for establishing criteria of truth except the grounds that are employed to grant or concede it—truth is conceivable only as a socially organized upshot of contingent courses of linguistic, conceptual, and social behavior. The truth of a statement is not independent of the conditions of its utterance, and so to study truth is to study the ways truth can be methodically conferred. It is an ascription ...Actually, this principle applies to any phenomenon of social order.[40]

In order to avoid the consequences of a self-destructive relativism, others attempt to defuse the dilemma through *trivialization*. Representatives of conventional sociology unhesitatingly take up a challenge that is anyhow in line with their ideals of objectivity: research methods have to be improved in such a way that everyday theories no longer flow unreflectedly into measurements. There are two versions of this argument. Either one admits in principle the dependency of *all* social-scientific interpretation on the preunderstanding of the participants (then it must be shown that the consequences are harmless); or one treats the context-dependency of social-scientific interpretations from the outset as a pragmatic research question, as a question of degree and not of principle.[41] A few ethnomethodologists adopt this reaction with the intent of taking into methodological consideration the performative attitude of the interpreter—that is, his participation in the text he wants to understand—and reforming social research in such a way that it can satisfy its own ideals of objectivity better than previously. It is in this spirit that Cicourel, for instance, endeavors to develop new imaginative designs that avoid the objectivism of interview and survey methods.[42] Of course, ethnomethodology thereby gives up its claim to replace conventional action theories with a new paradigm. But the orthodox disciples of Garfinkel do insist upon a *change of paradigm*.

Garfinkel wants to carry out the phenomenological program of grasping the general structures of lifeworlds as such by searching out in the interpretive activities of everyday routine action the practices through which individuals renew the objective appearance of social order. He makes "common sense knowledge of social structure" the object of analysis in order to show how the "routine grounds of everyday activities" come to be as a result of concerted accomplishments in everyday action. *A theory of the construction and reproduction of action situations in general aims at the invariant features of the interpretive procedures used by participants in communicative action.* The object of interest is primarily universal features of the reference system for speaker-hearer relations: that is, the narrative organization of temporal sequences, the interpersonal organization of spatial distances, the objectivity of a common world, fundamental normalcy expectations, understanding for the context-dependency of communicative utterances and their need for interpretation, and so on.[43]

To the extent that ethnomethodology no longer presents itself only as a critique of method but as a theory in its own right, the outlines of a program of formal pragmatics become visible. But then the question again arises: how can this type of research into universals be carried out at all if social-scientific interpretations are context dependent in the same way as everyday interpretations?

> If interpretative practices are to be opened up as a topic for investigation, then "interpretive" methods can scarcely provide the appropriate means for so doing...On the contrary, any explanation of invariant features of interactions will need to be through a language other than that of the everyday actor, and in terms which will be decidedly revelatory to him.[44]

Zimmerman parries this objection in the style of Alfred Schutz: "The ethnomethodologist treats the fact that he lives and acts within the same social world that he investigates in quite a different way than do the varieties of traditional sociologists."[45] Thus the critical sociologist supposedly gives up the natural attitude that prevents the layman and the conventional sociologist alike from treating the normative reality of society as *appearance*— that is, as produced consciousness. In doing so, he orients himself above all to the naiveté of his less enlightened colleagues because they reproduce the everyday naiveté of laymen in a methodical form easier to grasp. But it remains unclear how this reflection on the general presuppositions of communication can be secured methodologically. Zimmerman would either have to claim a privileged access to the object domain—to specify, for example, an equivalent for Husserl's *epoché* and transcendental reduction[46]—or he would have to show how social-scientific analysis can take up everyday interpretations, reflectively penetrate them, and transcend the given context to such an extent that a reconstruction of *general* presuppositions of communication is possible. If I am not mistaken, most ethnomethodologists remain undecided in the face of this alternative. They *cannot* choose the first way without contradicting their critical methodological insights; they do not wish to choose the second way because it would require that they push on to the rational internal structure of action oriented to validity claims.

Garfinkel treats as *mere phenomena* the validity claims, on whose intersubjective recognition every communicatively achieved agreement does indeed rest—however occasional, feeble, and fragmentary consensus formation may be. He does not distinguish between a valid consensus for which participants could if necessary provide reasons, and an agreement without validity—that is, one that is established de facto on the basis of the threat of sanctions, rhetorical onslaught, calculation, desperation, or resignation. Garfinkel treats standards of rationality like all other conventions, as the result of *contingent* interpretive practices that can be described but not systematically evaluated on the basis of the standards intuitively applied by participants themselves. The ethnomethodologically enlightened sociologist regards validity claims that point beyond local, temporal, and cultural boundaries as something that participants merely *take to be* universal.

> Thus, a leading policy is to refuse serious consideration to the prevailing proposal that efficiency, efficacy, effectiveness, intelligibility, consistency, planfulness, typicality, uniformity, reproducibility of activities—i.e., that *rational properties* of practical activities—be assessed, recognized, categorized, described by using a rule or a standard obtained outside actual settings within which such properties are recognized, used, produced, and talked about by settings' members. All procedures whereby *logical* and *methodological* properties of the practices and results of inquiries are assessed in their general characteristics by rule are of interest as *phenomena* for ethnomethodological study but not otherwise...All "logical" and "methodological" properties of action, every feature of an activity's sense, facticity, objectivity, accountability, communality is to be treated as a *contingent accomplishment of socially organized common practices.* The policy is recommended that any social setting be viewed as self-organizing with respect to the intelligible character of its own appearances as either representations of or as evidences of a social order. Any setting organizes its activities to make its properties as an organized environment of practical activities detectable, countable, recordable, reportable, tell-a-story-aboutable, analyzable—in short, *accountable.*[47]

But if Garfinkel is serious about this recommendation, he has to reserve for the ethnomethodologist the privileged position of a "disinterested" observer who watches how those immediately involved formulate their utterances in such a way that others can understand them and how they interpret as intelligible the utterances of others. The ethnomethodologist who credits himself with this position, claims for his own statements standards of validity that *a fortiori* lie outside the domain of those applied by the participants themselves. If he does not credit himself with such an extramundane position, he cannot claim a theoretical status for his statements. At best he can allow for an additional type of criterion of validity in the language games theoreticians play among themselves; the rationality standards of science would be just as particular as the other types of criteria of validity that function in their own ways in the various departments of life.[48]

Garfinkel could escape this dilemma of either a Husserlian absolutism or the confessed relativism of Blum and McHugh only if he would take seriously the claim to universality implicitly built into the ideas of truth and rightness as pointing to *the validity basis of speech.* The social-scientific interpreter, in the role of an at-least virtual participant, must in principle orient himself to the *same* validity claims to which those immediately involved also orient themselves; for this reason, and to this extent, he can start from the always implicitly shared, immanent rationality of speech, take seriously the rationality claimed by the participants for their utterances, and at the same time critically examine it. In thematizing what the participants merely presuppose and assuming a reflective attitude to the interpretandum, one does not place oneself *outside* the communication context under investigation; one deepens and radicalizes it in a way that is in principle open to *all* participants. In natural contexts this path from communicative action to discourse is often blocked; but it is always ingrained in the very structure of action oriented to reaching understanding.

(c) The ethnomethodologist is interested in the interactive competence of adult speakers because he wants to investigate how actions are coordinated through cooperative processes of interpretation. He is concerned with interpretation as an *ongoing accomplishment* of participants in interaction, that is, with the microprocesses of interpreting situations and securing consensus, which are highly complex even when the participants can effortlessly begin with a customary understanding of the situation in a stable context of action; under the microscope *every* understanding proves to be occasional and fragile. By contrast, philosophical hermeneutics investigates the interpretive competence of adult speakers from the perspective of how speaking and acting subjects make incomprehensible utterances in an alien environment comprehensible. Hermeneutics is concerned with

interpretation as an *exceptional accomplishment,* which becomes necessary only when relevant segments of the lifeworld become problematic, when the certainties of a culturally stable background break down and the normal means of reaching understanding fail; under the "macroscope" understanding appears to be endangered only in the extreme cases of penetrating a foreign language, an unfamiliar culture, a distant epoch or, all the more so, pathologically deformed areas of life. From our point of view this hermeneutic approach has an advantage, for in the test case of disturbed communication a problem that is set aside in the two variants of interpretive sociology discussed above can no longer be neglected: Can questions of meaning explication be divorced in the final analysis from questions arising in a reflection on validity?

Communication will be said to be disturbed when (some of) the presuppositions of direct understanding between (at least) two participants in an interaction are not satisfied. Let us begin with the clear case in which participants employ grammatical sentences of a shared (or easily translatable) language. The paradigm case for hermeneutics is the interpretation of a traditional text. The interpreter appears at first to understand the sentences of the author; in going on, he then has the unsettling experience that he does not really understand the text so well that he could, if need be, respond to the questions of the author. The interpreter takes this to be a sign that he is wrongly embedding the text in a context other than the author himself did, that he is starting with other questions.[49]

The task of interpretation can now be specified as follows: the interpreter learns to differentiate his own understanding of the context—which he at first believed to be shared by the author but in fact falsely imputed to him—from the author's understanding of the context. His task consists in gaining access to the definitions of the situation presupposed by the transmitted text through the lifeworld of its author and his audience.

As we have seen, a lifeworld forms the horizon of processes of reaching understanding in which participants agree upon or discuss something in the one objective world, in their common social world, or in a given subjective world. The interpreter can tacitly presuppose that he shares these formal world-relations with the author and his contemporaries. He seeks to understand *why* the author—in the belief that certain states of affairs obtain, that certain values and norms are valid, that certain experiences can be attributed to certain subjects—has made certain assertions in his text, observed or violated certain conventions, expressed certain intentions, dispositions, feelings, and the like. Only to the extent that the interpreter grasps the *reasons* that allow the author's utterances to appear as *rational* does he understand what the author could have *meant*. Against the background of this insight into the basically rational structure of the utterance, individual idiosyncrasies can be identified if necessary—that is, passages that do not become comprehensible even on the presuppositions of the lifeworld that the author shared with his contemporaries.

Thus the interpreter understands the meaning of a text only to the extent that he sees why the author felt himself entitled to put forward (as true) certain assertions, to recognize (as right) certain values and norms, to express (as sincere) certain experiences. The interpreter has to clarify the context that must have been presupposed as common knowledge by the author and the contemporaneous public if the difficulties with which the text presents us today did not arise at that time, and if *other* difficulties could arise for contemporaries that now appear trivial to us. The meaning of the text can be disclosed only against the background of the cognitive, moral, and expressive elements of the cultural store of knowledge from which the author and his contemporaries constructed their interpretations; and the posthumous interpreter cannot identify these presuppositions without again, at least implicitly, taking a position on the validity claims connected with the text.

This is explained by the immanent rationality the interpreter must impute to all utterances, however opaque they may be to start with, insofar as he ascribes them to a subject whose responsibility he has no reason to doubt. The interpreter cannot understand the semantic content of a text if he is not in a position to present to himself the reasons that the author might have been able to adduce in defense of his utterances under suitable conditions. And because it is not the same thing for reasons to be sound as for them to be taken to be sound—be they reasons for asserting facts, for recommending norms and values, or for giving expression to experiences—the interpreter absolutely cannot present reasons to himself without judging them, without taking a positive or negative position on them. It may be that the interpreter leaves certain validity claims undecided, that he chooses not to regard certain questions as decided, as the author did, but to treat them as problems. But if he *would not so much as* enter upon a systematic assessment, if he were not only to suspend taking a position, however implicitly, with respect to the reasons that the author could have adduced for his text, but were to regard this position as incompatible with the descriptive character of his enterprise, he would not be able to treat reasons as that which they are intended to be. In this case the interpreter would *not be taking his subject seriously* as a responsible subject.

An interpreter can elucidate the meaning of an opaque expression only by explaining how this opacity arises, that is, why the reasons which the author might have been able to give in his context are no longer acceptable to us. If the interpreter would not so much as pose questions of validity, one might rightfully ask him whether he is interpreting at all; that is, whether he is making an effort to set in motion once again the disturbed communication between the author, his contemporaries, and us. In other words, the interpreter is obliged to retain the performative attitude he assumes as a communicative actor even (and precisely) when he is inquiring into the presuppositions underlying an incomprehensible text.[50] Gadamer speaks in this connection of an "anticipation of completeness" [*Vorgriff auf Vollkommenheit*]. The interpreter has to assume that the transmitted text, notwithstanding its initial inaccessibility for him, represents a reasonable expression, one that could be grounded under certain presuppositions.

> The reader is guided not only by the assumption of an immanent unity of meaning; his understanding is also constantly guided by transcendent expectations of meaning that arise from the relation of what is being said to the truth. Just as the recipient of a letter understands the news that it contains and sees things at first through the eyes of the letter writer, that is, takes what he has written for the truth—and does not, for instance, try to comprehend the peculiar opinions of the letter writer as such—so too do we understand transmitted texts on the basis of expectations of meaning that are drawn from our own previous understanding of the subject matter . . . It is only when the attempt to accept what is said as true fails that we try to "understand" the text as the opinion of another—psychologically or historically. Thus the prejudgment of completeness comprises not only the formal element that a text should fully express its meaning, but also that what it says is the whole

truth. Here too it proves to be the case that understanding means primarily to understand the subject matter and only secondarily to isolate and understand another's opinion as such. Hence the first of all hermeneutic conditions remains the preunderstanding that springs from having to do with the same subject matter.[51]

Gadamer uses "truth" here in the traditional philosophical sense of a rationality encompassing propositional truth, normative rightness, authenticity, and sincerity. We credit all subjects with rationality who are oriented to reaching understanding and thereby to universal validity claims, who base their interpretive accomplishments on an intersubjectively valid reference system of worlds, let us say, on a decentered understanding of the world. This underlying agreement, which unites us before the fact and in the light of which every actually attained agreement can be criticized, grounds the hermeneutic utopia of universal and unlimited dialogue in a commonly inhabited lifeworld.[52] Every successful interpretation is accompanied by the expectation that the author and his audience, if only they would bridge the "temporal distance" (separating them from us) through a learning process complementary to our interpretive process, could share our understanding of their text. In such a fictive, time-overcoming process of reaching understanding, the actor would have to detach himself from his contemporary horizon in a way similar to that in which we, as interpreters, broaden our own horizon by entering into a text. For this process Gadamer employs the image of horizons fusing with one another.

To be sure, Gadamer gives the interpretive model of *Verstehen* a peculiarly *one-sided twist.* If in the performative attitude of virtual participants in conversation we start with the idea that an author's utterance has the presumption of rationality, we not only admit the possibility that the interpretandum may be exemplary *for us,* that we may learn something from it; we *also* take into account the possibility that the author could learn *from us.* Gadamer remains bound to the experience of the philologist who deals with classical tests: "The classic is that which stands up in the face of historical criticism."[53] The knowledge embodied in the text is, Gadamer believes, fundamentally superior to the interpreter's.

In opposition to this stands the anthropologist's experience that the interpreter by no means always assumes the position of a subordinate in relation to a tradition. To understand the Zande belief in witches satisfactorily, a modern interpreter would have to reconstruct the learning processes that separate us from them and that could explain wherein mythical and modern thought differ. Here the task of interpretation expands to what is actually the theoretical task of discovering patterns of development of rationality structures. Only a systematic history of rationality would keep us from falling into sheer relativism or naively positing our own standards as absolute.

The methodological contribution of philosophical hermeneutics can be summed up as follows:

1. The interpreter can elucidate the meaning of a symbolic expression only as a virtual participant in the process of reaching understanding among those immediately involved;

2. This performative attitude does bind him to the preunderstanding of the hermeneutic initial situation;

3. But this binding does not have to detract from the validity of his interpretation;

4. Because he can avail himself of the rational internal structure of action oriented to reaching understanding and reflectively lay claim to the competence for judgment of a responsible participant in communication,

5. In order to place the lifeworld of the author and his contemporaries systematically in relation to his own lifeworld,

6. And to reconstruct the meaning of the interpretandum as the at least implicitly judged content of a criticizable utterance.

Gadamer endangers his fundamental hermeneutic insight because hidden behind his preferred model of philological concern with canonical texts lies the really problematic case of the *dogmatic interpretation of sacred scriptures*. Only against this background is he able to analyze interpretation exclusively along the lines of *application*, that is, from the perspective that "every understanding of a text represents an actualizing appropriation of the meaning of the text by the interpreter with a view to possible situations in his world."[54] Philosophical hermeneutics rightly asserts an internal connection between questions of meaning and questions of validity. To understand a symbolic expression means to know under what conditions its validity claim would have to be accepted; but it does *not* mean assenting to its validity claim without regard to context. This identification of understanding and agreement is (at least) abetted by Gadamer's hermeneutics-with-a-traditionalist-turn.

> Being in agreement is by no means a necessary condition for a dialogical attitude toward that which is to be understood. One can also behave dialogically toward an expressed meaning whose claim one understands without in the end accepting . . . To understand oneself as being addressed by a claim does not mean that one has to accept the claim; it does mean that one has to take it seriously. One who examines the justification for a claim also takes it seriously— that is, one who argues and does not straight away apply. In undertaking an argumentative examination, a discourse for the purpose of passing a well-grounded judgment, one also behaves dialogically at the level of validity . . . *Mere* application lacks dialogical correspondence, since a claim can be acknowledged *as* a validity claim only in discourse. For a validity claim contains the assertion that something is *worthy of acknowledgment.*[55]

Our discussions of the basic concepts of action theory and of the methodology of *Verstehen* have shown that the rationality problematic does not come to sociology from the outside but breaks out within it. It is centered around a concept of reaching understanding that is basic from both a metatheoretical and a methodological point of view. This concept has been of interest to us both under the aspect of the coordination of action and under that of an interpretive access to the object domain. Processes of reaching understanding are aimed at a consensus that depends on the intersubjective recognition of validity claims; and these claims can be reciprocally raised and fundamentally criticized by participants in communication. In the orientation to validity claims the actors' world-relations are actualized. In referring with their utterances to something in one or another world, subjects presuppose formal commonalities that are constitutive for reaching any understanding at all. If this rationality problematic cannot be avoided in the basic concepts of social action and in the method of understanding meaning, how do things stand with respect to the substantial question of whether, and if so how, modernization processes can be viewed from the standpoint of rationalization?

Sociology, which arose as the theory of society, has occupied itself with this theme since its beginnings. This is a reflection of preferences which, as I mentioned above, have to do with the conditions under which this discipline arose; these preferences can be explained historically. Beyond this, however, there is an *internal* relation between sociology and the theory of rationalization. In the investigation that follows I shall introduce the theory of communicative action in connection with this theme.

If *some* concept of rationality is unavoidably built into the action-theoretic foundations of sociology, then theory formation is in danger of being limited from the start to a particular, culturally or historically bound perspective, unless fundamental concepts are constructed in such a way that the concept of rationality they implicitly posit is encompassing and general, that is, satisfies universalistic claims. The demand for such a concept of rationality also emerges from methodological considerations. If the understanding of meaning has to be understood as communicative experience, and if this is possible only in the performative attitude of a communicative actor, the experiential basis of an interpretive [*sinnverstehenden*] sociology is compatible with its claim to objectivity only if hermeneutic procedures can be based at least intuitively on general and encompassing structures of rationality. From both points of view, the metatheoretical and the methodological, we cannot expect objectivity in social-theoretical knowledge if the corresponding concepts of communicative action and interpretation express a merely particular perspective on rationality, one interwoven with a particular cultural tradition.[56]

We have, by way of anticipation, characterized the rational internal structure of processes of reaching understanding in terms of (a) the three world-relations of actors and the corresponding concepts of the objective, social, and subjective worlds; (b) the validity claims of propositional truth, normative rightness, and sincerity or authenticity; (c) the concept of a rationally motivated agreement, that is, one based on the intersubjective recognition of criticizable validity claims; and (d) the concept of reaching understanding as the cooperative negotiation of common definitions of the situation. If the requirement of objectivity is to be satisfied, this structure would have to be shown to be *universally valid* in a specific sense. This is a very strong requirement for someone who is operating without metaphysical support and is also no longer confident that a rigorous transcendental-pragmatic program, claiming to provide ultimate grounds, can be carried out.

It is, of course, obvious that the type of action oriented to reaching understanding, whose rational internal structure we sketched above in very rough outline, is by no means everywhere and always encountered as the normal case in everyday practice.[57] I have myself pointed to contrasts between the mythical and the modern understandings of the world, to contrasts between action orientations that typically appear in archaic and in modern societies. In claiming universal validity—with, however, many qualifications—for *our* concept of rationality, without thereby adhering to a completely untenable belief in progress, we are taking on a sizable burden of proof. Its weight becomes completely clear when we pass from sharp and oversimplified contrasts supporting a superiority of modern thought to the less glaring oppositions disclosed by intercultural comparison of the modes of thought of the various world religions and world civilizations. Even if this multiplicity of systematized and highly differentiated worldviews could still be placed in a hierarchical relation to the modern understanding of the world, we would encounter within the modern period, at the latest, a pluralism of belief systems from which it is not so easy to extract a universal core.

If one is at all still willing today to venture to expound the universality of the concept of communicative rationality, without falling back upon the guarantees of the great philosophical tradition, basically three ways present themselves. The *first* way is the formal-pragmatic development of the concept of communicative action introduced above in a propaedeutic fashion. Linking up with formal semantics, speech-act theory, and other approaches to the pragmatics of language, this is an attempt at rationally reconstructing universal rules and necessary presuppositions of speech actions oriented to reaching understanding. Such a program aims at hypothetical reconstructions of that pretheoretical knowledge that competent speakers bring to bear when they employ sentences in actions oriented to reaching understanding. This program holds out no prospect of an equivalent for a transcendental deduction of the communicative universals described. The hypothetical reconstructions must, however, be capable of being checked against speakers' intuitions, scattered across as broad a sociocultural spectrum as possible. While the universalistic claim of formal pragmatics cannot be conclusively redeemed (in the sense of transcendental philosophy) by way of rationally reconstructing natural intuitions, it can be rendered plausible in this way.[58]

Second, we can try to assess the empirical usefulness of formal-pragmatic insights. For this purpose, there are above all three relevant areas of research: the explanation of pathological patterns of communication, the evolution of the foundations of sociocultural forms of life, and the ontogenesis of capabilities for action.

a) If formal pragmatics reconstructs universal and necessary conditions of communicative action, it must be possible to obtain from this reconstruction nonnaturalistic standards for normal, that is, undisturbed communication. Disturbances in communication could then be traced back to violations of normalcy conditions marked out by formal pragmatics. Hypotheses of this type could be examined in the light of the material concerning patterns of systematically distorted communication that heretofore has been gathered primarily in pathogenic families from clinical points of view and evaluated in terms of the theory of socialization.

b) Anthropogenesis should also be capable of throwing light on whether the universalistic claims of formal pragmatics can be taken seriously. We would have to be able to find the formal-pragmatically described structures of action oriented to success and to understanding in the emergent properties that appear in the course of hominization and that characterize the form of life of socioculturally sociated individuals.

c) Finally, the universalistic claims of formal pragmatics can be examined in the light of the material that developmental psychology presents in regard to the acquisition of communicative and interactive capabilities. The reconstruction of action oriented to reaching understanding would have to be suitable for describing the competences whose ontogenesis has already been investigated from universalistic points of view in the Piagetian tradition.

It would obviously require a great effort to fill in these three research perspectives, even if only through secondary evaluation of the empirical research in these areas. A *third*, somewhat less demanding way would be to work up the sociological approaches to a theory of societal rationalization. Here we could link up with a well-developed tradition of social theory. This is the path I shall follow—not with the intention of carrying out historical investigations; rather, I shall take up conceptual strategies, assumptions, and lines of argument from Weber to Parsons with the systematic aim of laying out the problems that can be solved by means of a theory of rationalization developed in terms of the basic concept of communicative action. What can lead us to this goal is not a history of ideas but a history of theory with a systemic intent. I am hoping that the flexible exploration and deliberate exploitation of important theories constructed for explanatory purposes will allow us to proceed in a fruitful, problem-oriented way. And I want to ascertain the systematic yield, from the theoretical perspectives developed in this introduction, in a series of excurses and intermediate reflections [*Zwischenbetrachtungen*].

The path of a history of theory with a systemic intent recommends itself not by reason of a false convenience that always creeps in when we cannot yet deal with a problem frontally. In my view, this alternative—escape into the history of theory versus systematic treatment—is based on a false assessment of the status of social theory, in two respects. For one thing, the competition of paradigms has a different significance in the social sciences than in modern physics. The originality of great social theorists like Marx, Weber, Durkheim, and Mead consists—as it does for Freud and Piaget—in their having introduced paradigms that, in a certain way, still compete on equal footing today. These theorists have remained contemporaries; at any rate,they have not become "historical" in the same sense as Newton, Maxwell, Einstein, or Planck, who achieved advances in theoretically exploiting a single fundamental paradigm.[59] For another thing, social-scientific paradigms are internally connected with the social contexts in which they emerge and become influential. In them is reflected the world- and self-understanding of various collectives; mediately they serve the interpretation of social-interest situations, horizons of aspiration and expectation.[60] Thus for any social theory, linking up with the history of theory is also a kind of test; the more freely it can take up, explain, criticize, and carry on the intentions of earlier theory traditions, the more impervious it is to the danger that particular interests are being brought to bear unnoticed in its own theoretical perspective. Moreover, reconstructions of the history of theory have the advantage that we can move back and forth between basic action-theoretic concepts, theoretical assumptions, and the illustrative use of empirical evidence, and can at the same time hold fast to the fundamental problem that is our point of reference, namely the question of whether, and if so how, capitalist modernization can be conceived as a process of one-sided rationalization.

I shall take the following path: Max Weber's theory of rationalization extends, on the one side, to the structural changes in religious worldviews and the cognitive potential of the differentiated value spheres of science, morality, and art, and, on the other side, to the selective pattern of capitalist rationalization (Chapter II). The aporetic course of the Marxist reception of Weber's rationalization thesis from Lukacs to Horkheimer and Adorno shows the limits of approaches based on a theory of consciousness and the reasons for a change of paradigm from purposive activity to communicative action (Chapter IV). In this light, Mead's foundation of the social sciences in a theory of communication and Durkheim's sociology of religion fit together in such a way that the concept of interaction mediated by language and regulated by norms can be given an explanation in the sense of a conceptual genesis. The idea of the linguistification of the sacred [*Versprachlichung des Sakralen*] provides a perspective from which Mead's and Durkheim's assumptions regarding the rationalization of the lifeworld converge (Chapter V).

The problem of linking the basic concepts of systems theory with those of action theory can be analyzed in connection with the theoretical development of Talcott Parsons. At the same time, the results of the intermediate reflections devoted to systematic questions will be taken up (Chapter VII). The first set of intermediate reflections takes Weber's theory of action as its point of departure in order to set out the formal pragmatic approach of a theory of communicative action (Chapter III). The second set of intermediate reflections first develops the concept of the lifeworld and then follows the evolutionary trend toward a decoupling of system and lifeworld, to a point at which Weber's rationalization thesis can be reformulated and applied to contemporary conditions (Chapter VI). The concluding reflections bring together the explorations from the history of theory and the systematic investigations. They are intended, on the one hand, to make the proposed interpretation of modernity accessible to a test in connection with tendencies toward regulation by law [*Verrechtlichung*], and, on the other hand, to render more precise the tasks that a critical theory of society is faced with today (Chapter VIII).

II

Max Weber's Theory of Rationalization

Among the classical figures of sociology, Max Weber is the only one who broke with both the premises of the philosophy of history and the basic assumptions of evolutionism and who nonetheless wanted to conceive of the modernization of old-European society as the result of a universal-historical process of rationalization. He opened up rationalization processes to an encompassing empirical investigation without reinterpreting them in an empiricist manner so that precisely the aspects of rationality of societal learning processes would disappear. Weber left his work behind in a fragmentary state; nevertheless, using his theory of rationalization as a guideline, it is possible to reconstruct his project as a whole. This was once the dominant perspective of interpretation in the largely philosophical discussions of the twenties;[1] it was then displaced by a strictly sociological interpretation oriented to *Economy and Society*; in the most recent Weber research, it has once again come to the fore.[2] The inconsistencies in his work appear more clearly from a perspective that views it as a whole. Weber analyzes the *process of disenchantment in the history of religion,* which is said to have fulfilled the necessary internal conditions for the appearance of Occidental rationalism; in doing so he employs a complex, but largely unclarified concept of rationality. On the other hand, in his analysis of *societal rationalization* as it makes its way in the modern period, he allows himself to be guided by the restricted idea of purposive rationality [*Zweckrationalität*]. Weber shares this

143

concept with Marx, on the one hand, and with Horkheimer and Adorno, on the other. To begin with, I shall make the perspective of my line of questioning clear by means of a rough comparison of these three positions.[3]

According to Marx, the rationalization of society takes place directly in the development of productive forces, that is, in the expansion of empirical knowledge, the improvement of production techniques, and the increasingly effective mobilization, qualification, and organization of socially useful labor power. On the other hand, relations of production, the institutions that express the distribution of social power and regulate a differential access to the means of production, are revolutionized only under the pressure of rationalization of productive forces. Max Weber views the institutional framework of the capitalist economy and the modern state in a different way—not as relations of production that fetter the potential for rationalization, but as subsystems of purposive-rational action in which Occidental rationalism develops at a societal level. Of course, he is afraid that bureaucratization will lead to a reification of social relationships, which will stifle motivational incentives to a rational conduct of life. Horkheimer and Adorno, and later Marcuse, interpret Marx in this Weberian perspective. Under the sign of an instrumental rationality that has become autonomous, the rationality of mastering nature merges with the irrationality of class domination. Fettered forces of production stabilize alienated relations of production. The *Dialectic of Enlightenment* removes the ambivalence that Weber still entertained in relation to rationalization processes, and it abruptly reverses Marx's positive assessment. Science and technology—for Marx an unambiguously emancipatory potential —themselves become the medium of social repression.

At this point I am not interested in which of the three positions might be in the right; I am interested rather in the theoretical weakness they share. On the one hand, Marx, Weber, Horkheimer, and Adorno identify societal rationalization with expansion of the instrumental and strategic rationality of action contexts; on the other hand, they all have a vague notion of *an encompassing societal rationality*—whether in the concept of an association of free producers, in the historical model of an ethically rational conduct of life, or in the idea of fraternal relations with a resurrected nature—and it is against this that they measure the relative position of empirically described processes of rationalization. But this encompassing concept of rationality would have to be confirmed at the same level as forces of production, sub-systems of purposive-rational action, totalitarian carriers of in-strumental reason. This does not happen. In my view, the reason for this lies, on the one hand, in action-theoretic bottlenecks: The action concepts that Marx, Weber, Horkheimer, and Adorno take as basic are not complex enough to capture all those aspects of social actions to which societal rationalization can attach;[4] on the other hand, it lies as well in the confusion of basic action-theoretic and systems-theoretic concepts—The rationalization of action orientations and lifeworld structures is not the same as the expan-sion of the "rationality," that is, complexity of action systems.[5]

However, I would like to make clear at the start that Weber took up the rationality theme in a scientific context that had already discharged the mortgages from philosophy of history and the nineteenth-century evolutionism encumbered by it. The theory of rationalization does not belong to that speculative heritage from which sociology as a science had to free itself. As sociology developed in the wakes of Scottish moral philosophy and early socialism, with its own lines of questioning and its own theoretical approaches, as a discipline concerned with the origin and development of modern society,[6] it found the theme of societal rationalization already at hand. This theme had been dealt with in the eighteenth century by philosophy of history and had been taken up and transformed in the nineteenth century by evo-lutionary theories of society. I would like briefly to recall this prehistory in order to characterize the problem situation with which Weber was confronted.

The most important motifs of the philosophy of history are contained in Condorcet's *Sketch for a Historical Picture of the Progress of the Human Mind* of 1794.[7] The model of rationality is provided by the mathematical sciences of nature. Their core is Newtonian physics; it has discovered the "true method of studying nature." "Observation, experiment, calculation" are the three tools with which physics unlocks the secrets of nature. Like Kant, Condorcet too is impressed by the "sure course" of this science. It becomes a paradigm for knowledge in general because it follows a method that raises the knowledge of nature above the scholastic debates of philosophers and reduces all previous philosophy to the status of mere opinion. "The mathematical and physical sciences formed one large division by themselves. As they are based on calculation and observation, and as their findings are indifferent in just those matters on which the various sects were divided, they became separated from philosophy, over which the various sects still reigned."[8]

Condorcet does not, as Kant does, attempt to elucidate the foundations of this methodical knowledge and, therewith, the conditions of the rationality of science; he is interested in what Weber will call the "cultural significance" of science, that is, in the question of what effects the methodically secured growth of theoretical knowledge has on the development of the human mind and of the cultural context of life as a whole. Condorcet wants to conceive the history of mankind on the model of the history of modern science, that is, as a process of rationalization. Basically he pursues four lines of reflection.

(a) To begin with, he reinterprets the concept of perfection according to the model of scientific progress. Perfection no longer means, as it does in the Aristotelian tradition, the realization of a telos found in the nature of a thing; it signifies instead a process of improvement that does have a direction but is not teleologically limited in advance. Perfection is interpreted as progress. In his work Condorcet wants to explain "that nature has set no term to the perfection of human faculties (perfectionnement des facultés humaines); that the perfectibility of man is truly indefinite; and that the progress of this perfectibility . . . has no other limit than the duration of the globe upon which nature has cast us."[9]

The advances of the human mind are not limited by a telos inherent in it; and they are achieved under contingent conditions. The concept of progress is connected with the idea of learning. The human mind owes its advances not to approaching a telos, but to the unimpeded operation of its intelligence, that is, to a learning mechanism. Learning means intelligently overcoming obstacles. Condorcet characterizes the "constitution of our understanding" through "the connection between our means of discovering the truth and the resistance that [nature] offers to our efforts."[10]

(b) To this resistance of nature belongs prejudice, superstition. The concept of knowledge developed on the model of the natural sciences devalues, as if with one blow, inherited religious, philosophical, moral, and political opinions. In the face of the power of this tradition, the sciences take on the function of enlightenment. At the close of the eighteenth century, the institutionalization of science as a subsystem independent from theology and humanistic rhetoric is so far advanced that the organization of the discovery of truth can become a model for the organization of state and society. Enlightenment becomes a political concept for emancipation from prejudice through the diffusion of scientific knowledge with its many practical consequences—in Condorcet's terminology, for the effects of philosophy on public opinion. Scientific progress can be transposed into a rationalization of social life if only scientists take up the task of public education with the aim of making the principles of their own work principles of social intercourse in general. In his function as a representative of enlightenment, the scientist seeks "to proclaim aloud" the right that he enjoys, the right "to submit all opinions to his own reason...Soon there was formed in Europe a class of men who were concerned less with the discovery or development of the truth than with its propagation, men who whilst devoting themselves to the tracking down of prejudices in the hiding places where the priests, the schools, the governments, and all long-established institutions had gathered and protected them, made it their life-work to destroy popular errors rather than to drive back the frontiers of human knowledge." And Condorcet, himself in prison, adds: "an indirect way of aiding the progress [of knowledge], which was not less fraught with peril, nor less useful."[11]

(c) The concept of enlightenment functions as a bridge between the idea of scientific progress and the conviction that the sciences also serve the moral perfection of human beings. In the battle against the traditional powers of church and state, enlightenment requires the courage to make use of one's own reason, that is, autonomy or maturity [Mündigkeit]. Moreover, the sublime passion of enlightenment can derive support from the experience that moral-practical prejudices have in fact been shaken by the critical force of the sciences. "All errors in politics and morals are based on philosophical errors and these in turn are connected with scientific errors. There is not a religious system nor a supernatural extravagance that is not founded on ignorance of the laws of nature."[12]

Thus it was quite natural for Condorcet not only to trust the sciences in regard to critique, but also to expect help from them in answering normative questions: "Just as the mathematical and physical sciences tend to improve the arts that we use to satisfy our simplest needs, is it not also part of the necessary order of nature that the moral and political sciences should exercise a similar influence upon the motives that direct our feelings and our actions?"[13]

In moral-practical no less than in cognitive questions, Condorcet counts on the possibility of learning and of scientifically organizing learning processes. As man is capable of "acquiring moral concepts," he shall also succeed in bringing the moral sciences up to the level already attained by the natural sciences. "The sole foundation for belief in the natural sciences is this idea, that the general laws directing the phenomena of the universe, known or unknown, are necessary and constant. Why should this principle be any less true for the development of the intellectual and moral faculties of man than for the other operations of nature?"[14]

(d) If enlightenment can rely upon human sciences, whose progress in knowledge is methodically secured in the same way as that of the natural sciences, we may expect progress not only in the morality of individual men but in the forms of civilized association. Like Kant, Condorcet sees the progress of civilization along the lines of a republic that guarantees civil liberties, an international order that establishes a perpetual peace, a society that accelerates economic growth and technical progress and does away with or compensates for social inequalities. Among other things, he expects "the complete annihilation of the prejudices that have brought about an inequality of rights between the sexes";[15] he expects the elimination of criminality and degeneration, the conquest of misery and sickness through hygiene and medicine; he believes "that the day will come when death will be due only to extraordinary accidents."[16] In other words, Condorcet believes in eternal life before death.

This conception is representative of eighteenth-century philosophy of history, even if it could receive such a pointed formulation only from a contemporary of the French Revolution. Precisely this radical quality makes the cracks in the type of thinking characteristic of philosophy of history stand out. There are, above all, four presuppositions that subsequently became problematic and gave impetus to the transformation of the historico-philosophical interpretation of the modern age.

I am thinking *first* of the presuppositions that Condorcet has to make when he bases a linear conception of progress on the scientific progress represented by the modern natural sciences. He presupposes that the history of physics and of the sciences modelled after it can be reconstructed as a continuous path of development. Against this, postempiricist philosophy of science today stresses the dependency of theory construction on paradigms; it makes us aware that the continuum of scientific rationality does not establish itself directly at the level of theory construction but at the level of intertheoretic relations, that is, the obscure relations between different paradigms. But even more risky is the additional presupposition that all problems to which religious and philosophical doctrines previously supplied answers can be either transposed into scientifically manageable problems—and in this sense rationally resolved—or seen through as illusory problems and made to disappear. Condorcet's expectation that death could be done away with is not simply a curiosity. Behind it lies the view that the experiences of contingency and problems of meaning that were previously interpreted in religious terms and worked off in cult practices can be radically defused. Otherwise there would remain a rationally irresolvable residual problem, which would mean, in spite of everything, that the value of a problem-solving capability based on science alone would be palpably relativized. This is the starting point for Weber's attempt to pursue the process of societal rationalization along the lines, not of scientific development but of the development of religious worldviews.

Second, Condorcet, a child of the eighteenth century, is not fully aware of the import of the universalistic claim he is making when he conceives the unity of human history from the reference point of a rationality represented by modern science. He has no doubt that *all* nations will one day "attain that state of civilization which the most enlightened, the freest and the least burdened by prejudices, such as the French and the Anglo-Americans, have attained already."[17] In the final analysis, he justifies this conviction with the view that the rationality that has broken through in the natural sciences does not merely reflect standards peculiar to Western civilization but is inherent in the human mind in general. The presupposition of a universal reason was placed in question first by the historical school and later by cultural anthropology; it is still a controversial theme today, as the rationality debate dealt with in the introduction demonstrates. For the development of the philosophy of history in the nineteenth century, however, two further presuppositions were of even greater significance.

Third, as we have seen, Condorcet connects the cognitive aspects of scientific progress with the moral-practical aspects of coming-of-age, in the sense of liberation from dogmatism and from quasi-natural authority. He is thereby operating with a precritical concept of nature, which reappears in a reflective way in Kant's writings on history; they both presuppose the unity of theoretical and practical reason. In Condorcet this is not treated as a problem, although it was clear since Hume that the normative propositions of moral and political theory could not be inferred from propositions of empirical science. This theme was first worked through in philosophy from Kant to Hegel. The dialectical mediation of theoretical and practical reason that Hegel carried through in his philosophy of right then gained entrance into social theory through Marx in two ways. On the one hand, Marx criticized the self-sufficiency of retrospectively oriented philosophical reflection. From his temporalization of the Hegelian dialectic in terms of contemporary history there emerged the permanent theme of mediating theory and practice. The questions that fell under the jurisdiction of practical reason were no longer to admit of resolution by philosophical means; they ranged beyond the horizon of mere argumentation—the weapons of critique stood in need of the critique of weapons. Not much of a general nature could be said about the continuation of theory with other, namely practical, means; what could be said about this was a matter for the theory of revolution.[18]

On the other hand, Hegel's influence on Marx also took the form of an uncritical appropriation of the dialectical conceptual apparatus; the unity of theory and practice was inserted into the basic concepts of the critique of political economy in such a way that the normative foundations of Marxian theory have been obscured till today. In Marxism this obscurity has been in part by-passed, in part concealed, but not really cleared up: by-passed through splitting Marxian social theory into social research and ethical socialism (Adler), concealed both through orthodox ties to Hegel (Lukacs, Korsch) and through assimilation to more strongly naturalistic, nineteenth-century theories of development (Engels, Kautsky). These theories formed the bridges over which the rationalization thematic dealt with in the philosophy of history passed into sociology.[19]

It is above all the *fourth* presupposition on which Condorcet developed his conception of history that has become relevant for these theories. Condorcet could base the progress of civilization on the progress of the human mind only by counting on the empirical efficacy of an ever-improving theoretical knowledge. Every interpretive approach that places historical phenomena in the perspective of rationalization is committed to the view that the argumentative potential of cognitions and insights becomes *empirically effective*. But Condorcet neither investigates the learning mechanisms and the conditions through and under which learning processes take place, nor does he explain how knowledge is transposed into technical progress, economic growth, or a rational organization of society; nor does he consider the possibility that knowledge can be effective by way of nonintended side effects. He relies on an automatic efficacy of the mind, that is, on the belief that human intelligence is disposed to the accumulation of knowledge and brings about advances in civilization through a diffusion of this knowledge per se. This automatism appears in two aspects, which stand in an inverse relation to one another. From the *practical* perspective of those involved, the civilizing advances appear to be the results of a practice of disseminating knowledge, of the influence of philosophers on public opinion, of the reform of the schools, of popular education, and so on. However, this practice of the enlighteners, which aims at further advances of the human mind, is for its part an offspring of the philosophy of history; for it is the latter that first brings the process of humanity to the theoretical awareness of those who can practically advance it. From the *theoretical* perspective of the scientist, the civilizing advances present themselves as phenomena that can be explained by laws of nature. Thus: from the practical perspective, rationalization appears as a communicative practice carried on with will and consciousness; from the theoretical perspective, it appears as a cognitive process flowing along in a lawlike way. Both aspects stand side by side unmediated; they can be combined unproblematically only when the human mind is conceived idealistically as a power that unfolds according to its own inner logic and at the same time spontaneously, of its own accord.

It is at this point that the developmental theories of the nineteenth century, culminating in Spencer, undertook a decisive revision of the rationalization thematic: they interpreted advances in civilization in a Darwinian manner, as the development of quasi-organic systems.[20] The paradigm for the interpretation of cumulative changes was no longer the theoretical progress of science but the natural evolution of the species. With this, the thematic of rationalization was transformed into that of social evolution. This change in perspective also made it possible to take better account of the key historical experiences of the nineteenth century:

- With the Industrial Revolution the development of productive techniques came into prominence as an important dimension of societal evolution. The development of productive forces, which did not at first take place through the implementation of scientific knowledge, provided a model on which societal progress could be better conceived empirically than on that of the development of the modern natural sciences.

- The situation was similar in regard to the political upheavals that set in with the French Revolution and led up to the creation of bourgeois constitutions. Progress could more palpably be found in the processes whereby civil liberties were institutionalized than in the development of the human sciences, which was questionable anyway.

- Finally, with capitalist growth the economy came to the fore as a functionally autonomous subsystem and was represented in the political economy of the time by models of circulation. This brought into play both holistic perspectives, in which the phenomena of the social division of labor needed no longer be reduced to aggregates of individuals, and functionalist perspectives, in which societies could be regarded on an analogy with organisms as self-maintaining systems.

The first two motifs promoted the empiricist reinterpretation of rationalization processes as growth processes, whereas the third facilitated the assimilation of the history of society to the evolutionary models established by Darwin for the history of nature. Thus Spencer could put forward a theory of social evolution that did away with the unclear idealism of the philosophy of history, that regarded advances in civilization as a continuation of natural evolution and thereby subsumed them unambiguously under laws of nature.

In this way, trends such as scientific development, capitalist growth, the establishment of constitutional states, the rise of modern administrations, and the like could be treated directly as empirical phenomena and conceived as results of the structural differentiation of social systems. They no longer had to be interpreted as empirical indicators of an internal history of the spirit based on learning processes and the accumulation of knowledge, as signs of a rationalization in the sense of the philosophy of history.

With a view to the four basic presuppositions of the philosophy of history illustrated above in connection with Condorcet, Victorian theories of social evolution can be characterized in a simplified manner as follows: They questioned neither the rationalism nor the universalism of the Enlightenment and were thus not yet sensitive to the dangers of Eurocentrism; they repeated the naturalistic fallacies of the philosophy of history, albeit less blatantly, for they at least suggested interpreting theoretical statements about evolutionary advances in the sense of value judgments about practical-moral progress; on the other hand, they were more strongly oriented in a social-scientific direction and filled in the gaps left open by the philosophy of history—with its rather idealistically meant talk of historical laws—with a concept of evolution inspired by biology and having, so it seemed, the status of empirical science.

From the standpoint of the history of science, the situation in which Max Weber took up the rationalization thematic again and turned it into a problem that could be dealt with sociologically was defined by the critique of these nineteenth-century theories of evolution. The main points of critical attack can be laid out schematically with reference to the immediately preceding remarks. In doing so, I shall go through in reverse order the fundamental assumptions mentioned above (which are implicitly still related to the philosophy of history): the points of attack are evolutionary determinism and ethical naturalism, as well as the universalism and rationalism of developmental theories.

Evolutionary Determinism. The rise of the *Geisteswissenschaften* that took place within the framework of the Historical School from the time of Ranke and Savigny was accompanied by methodological reflections.[21] With Dilthey at the latest, these took on a systematic form—as historicism. The historicist critique was directed equally against dialectical and evolutionist theories of history and society. In the present context we are primarily interested in one result of this debate, namely the discrediting of any attempt to discover laws of development for a naturalistically interpreted culture. Historicism worked out the peculiar character of culture as an object domain that is constituted by interconnections of meaning and that exhibits structural, but not nomological—still less evolutionary—regularities. Ironically, just this historical separation of the cultural sciences from biological models, from natural-scientific prototypes in general, induced Max Weber to pose the problem of the origins and development of modern societies once again from the wholly nonhistoricist viewpoint of rationalization. If one took the historicist critique seriously, then directional, cumulatively effective changes would have to be traced back to the inner logic of meaning complexes or ideas and not to evolutionary mechanisms of social systems; they would have to be explained in structuralist terms and not on the basis of laws of social evolution. On the other hand, this historicist heritage generally prevented Weber from doing justice to systems-functionalism in its methodologically less dubious aspects.

Ethical Naturalism. Weber himself stands in the tradition of Southwest German Neo-Kantianism.[22] In the theory of the *Geisteswissenschaften* and cultural sciences, Windelband and Rickert represented positions similar to that of Dilthey and other philosophers of the Historical School. Beyond its dualistic philosophy of science, Neo-Kantianism gained special significance for the critique of evolutionist approaches in the social sciences because of its theory of value. It brought to bear at the methodological level a distinction between "is" and "ought," between statements of fact and judgments of value, and in practical philosophy it emphatically criticized all varieties of ethical naturalism. This is the background to Weber's position in the controversy over value judgments in social science. He is critical of concepts of progress and evolution precisely when they play an implicitly normative role in empirical science. Sharpened on Kant and the Neo-Kantian philosophy of value, this sensitivity to naturalistic fallacies in the ethical sphere, to the confusion of descriptive and evaluative statements in general, has of course another side to it. In Weber it is combined with a wholly un-Kantian, plainly historicist mistrust of the argumentative capacity of practical reason. On the methodological level, he rejects ethical cognitivism just as emphatically as he does ethical naturalism.

Universalism. Nineteenth-century research in the *Geisteswissenschaften* and the cultural sciences had developed a sense for the variability of social life-forms, values, and norms. Historicism had sharpened this basic experience of the relativity of traditions and modes of thought to the problem of whether even the standards of rationality presupposed in the empirical sciences were elements of a regionally and temporally limited culture, the modern European, and thus had to forfeit their naively raised claim to universal validity. But historicism had made things too easy in regard to the question of whether there resulted from the pluralism of cultures an epistemological relativism as well. Whereas in the *Geisteswissenschaften*—which were essentially occupied with the traditions of written cultures—it was easy to gain an intuitive impression of the equality in principle of different civilizations, cultural anthropology—which concerned itself with primitive societies—could not so easily overlook the developmental gradient between archaic and modern societies. Furthermore, in functionalistically oriented cultural anthropology there was never a danger of dismissing, together with evolutionary determinism, every form of nomological analysis aimed at discovering regularities and of drawing relativistic inferences from this. As we shall see below, Max Weber adopted in this controversy a cautiously universalistic position; he did not regard rationalization processes as a phenomenon peculiar to the Occident, although the rationalization demonstrable in all world religions led at first only in Europe to a form of rationalism that exhibited both particular, Occidental features and general features, that is, features characteristic of modernity as such.

  Rationalism. In philosophies of history science and technology served as patterns of rationalization. There are good reasons for their paradigmatic character, which Weber did not deny. However, to serve as models for concepts of progress, science and technology have to be evaluated in the sense of enlightenment or of positivism; that is, they have to be characterized as problem-solving mechanisms with an important impact on the history of the species. The bourgeois cultural criticism of the late nineteenth century, which had its most influential representatives in Nietzsche and the contemporary *Lebensphilosophen,* was directed against this surrogate-metaphysical revaluation. Weber too shares in the pessimistic appraisal of scientific civilization.[23] He mistrusts the rationalization processes set loose and detached from ethical value orientations, which he observes in modern societies—so much so that in his theory of rationalization, science and technology forfeit their paradigmatic status. Weber's research is focused on the moral-practical bases of the institutionalization of purposive-rational action.

  From the four points of view mentioned above, the situation in the social sciences is favorable to taking up once again—in an empirical manner but without the empiricist constrictions—the question of how the emergence and development of modern societies can be conceived as a process of rationalization. First (1) I shall examine the phenomena that Weber interprets as signs of societal rationalization, in order then to clarify the different concepts of rationality on which he bases, often only implicitly, his investigation. Weber's theory covers religious and societal rationalization—that is, the universal-historical emergence of modern structures of consciousness, on the one hand, and the embodiment of these rationality structures in social institutions, on the other. I shall reconstruct these complex interconnections from a systematic point of view, in such a way as (2) to work out the logic of the rationalization of worldviews from Weber's studies in the sociology of religion. I shall then go on (3) to derive from this a structural model for the rationalization of society, in order to deal first with the role of the "Protestant ethic" and then (4) with the rationalization of law.

1. *Occidental Rationalism*

In the famous *"Vorbemerkung"* to his studies in the sociology of religion,[1] Weber identifies in retrospect the "universal-historical problem" on which he endeavored throughout his life to shed light: the question of why, outside of Europe, "Neither scientific, nor artistic, nor political, nor economic development entered upon that path of rationalization peculiar to the Occident?"[2] In this connection he enumerates a wealth of phenomena that indicate "the specific and peculiar rationalism of Western culture."[3] The list of original achievements of Western rationalism is long. Weber points first to modern natural science, which puts theoretical knowledge in mathematical form and tests it with the help of controlled experiments; he adds to this the systematic specialization of scientific activity in university settings. He mentions the printed products of literature produced for the market, and the institutionalization of art in theaters, museums, periodicals, and so on; harmonious music in the form of sonatas, symphonies, and operas, and the orchestral instruments (organ, piano, violin); the use of linear and aerial perspective in painting, and the constructive principles of the great architecture. He further lists scientific jurisprudence, institutions of formal law, and the administration of justice through legally trained, specialized officials; modern state administration, with a rational organization of civil servants, operating on the basis of enacted laws. Further, he mentions calculable commerce under civil law and profit-oriented capitalist enterprise, which presupposes the separation of household and business (that is, the legal distinction between personal and corporate wealth), which has at its disposal rational bookkeeping, which organizes formally free labor from the standpoint of efficiency, and which uses scientific knowledge for improving the production plant and business organization. Finally, Weber points to the capitalist economic ethic, which is part of a rational conduct of life—"for just as the development of economic rationalism is dependent on rational technique and rational law, so it is also dependent on the ability and disposition of men to adopt certain types of practically rational conduct."[4]

This enumeration of the forms of appearance of Western rationalism is confusing. In order to gain a first overview, I shall in what follows pursue two different paths: (A) a classification of these phenomena according to content, and (B) a conceptual clarification of them; I shall then go on (C) to examine whether Weber conceives Western rationalism as a cultural peculiarity or as a phenomenon with universal significance.

A.   The Manifestations of Western Rationalism.   In the following classification I shall make use of the customary (since Parsons) division into (a) society, (b) culture, and (c) personality.

(a) Like Marx, Weber conceives the *modernization of society* as the *differentiation* of the capitalist economy and the modern state. They complement one another in their functions so as to mutually stabilize one another. The organizational nucleus of the capitalist economy is the capitalist enterprise, which

1. is separated from the household and,
2. with the help of capital accounting (rational bookkeeping),
3. orients investment decisions to the opportunities of the commodity, capital, and labor markets,
4. efficiently sets in action formally free labor power, and
5. makes technical use of scientific knowledge.

The organizational nucleus of the state is the rational public institution, which,

1. on the basis of a centralized and permanent tax system,
2. has at its disposal a centrally commanded, standing military force,
3. has a monopoly on setting laws and legitimately using force, and
4. organizes administration bureaucratically, that is, in the form of rule by specialized officials.[5]

Formal law, based on the principle of enactment, serves as a means for organizing the capitalist economy and the modern state as well as the interaction between them. These three elements, examined above all in *Economy and Society,* are constitutive for the rationalization of *society.* Weber views this as an expression of

Western rationalism and at the same time as the central phenomenon in need of explanation. He distinguishes it from phenomena on the levels of culture and personality. Western rationalism comes to light in these too; but in the construction of his theory they do not, as does the rationalization of society, assume the status of explananda.

(b) Weber sees cultural rationalization in modern science and technology, in autonomous art, and in a religiously anchored ethic guided by principles. He designates as rationalization every expansion of empirical knowledge, of predictive capacity, of instrumental and organizational mastery of empirical processes. In modern science, learning processes of this type become reflective and can be institutionalized in the scientific enterprise. In his writings on methodology and the theory of science, Weber does develop a clear, normative concept of science. However, he treats rather in passing the phenomenon of the rise of the modern sciences. These sciences are characterized by the methodical objectivation of nature; they come to be through an improbable concurrence of scholastically trained discursive thought, mathematical theory construction, an instrumental attitude toward nature, and an experimental treatment of it. Somewhat later, technical innovation is also connected with scientific development. Only this "methodical involvement of the natural sciences in the service of the economy is one of the copestones in that general development of a 'method of life' to which certain influences from the Renaissance and Reformation contributed."[6] Weber considers "the history of modern science and of its practical relations to the economy, which first developed in the modern period, to be 'fundamentally different' from the history of the modern conduct of life in its practical significance for the economy."[7] And in his material investigations he was interested only in the latter. The history of science and technology is certainly an important aspect of Western culture; but in his *sociological* attempt to *explain* the origins of modern society, Weber treats it rather as a boundary condition.

This subordinate role of scientific development in the causal-genetic dimension stands in peculiar contrast to the central role that the *structure* of scientific thought plays in the *analytical comprehension of forms of rationality*. The scientific understanding of the world generated by the sciences is the reference point of that universal-historical process of disenchantment, at the end of which stands an "unbrotherly aristocracy based on the possession of rational culture."[8]

> Wherever rational, empirical knowledge has consistently
> brought about the disenchantment of the world and its trans-
> formation into a causal mechanism, a definitive pressure
> arises against the claims of the ethical postulate that the
> world is a divinely ordered, that is, somehow ethically
> *meaningful* cosmos. For the empirical mode of viewing the
> world—and most completely, the mathematically oriented
> mode—develops in principle a rejection of every approach
> that inquires in any way about a "meaning" of what happens
> in the world.[9]

In this respect Weber understands modern science as the fateful
power of rationalized society.

Weber regards not only science but *autonomous art* as a form
of manifestation of cultural rationalization. Artistically stylized
expression, which was first integrated into the religious cult in
the form of adornments for church and temple, ritual dance and
song, the performance of significant episodes, sacred texts, and
the like, gained independence first under the conditions of artistic
production for court and patron and later under bourgeois capitalist conditions. "Art becomes a cosmos of more and more consciously grasped, independent values which exist in their own
right."[10] Gaining independence means, to begin with, that the
"inner logic [*Eigengesetzlichkeit*] of art" can develop. Naturally
Weber does not view this primarily from the standpoint of the
establishment of a traffic in art (with the institutionalization of
the art-enjoying public and of the art critic as a mediator between
producers and recipients of art). He focuses rather on the effects
that a conscious grasp of independent aesthetic values has on the
material mastery of art production, that is, on its techniques. In
his posthumous work on "The Rational and Social Foundations
of Music" Weber investigates the development of modern
harmony, of modern musical notation, and of instrument construction (especially of the piano as the specifically modern keyed
instrument).

Adorno analyzed avant garde artistic development along
these lines and showed how the processes and means of artistic
production became reflexive, how modern art turned the procedures of material mastery themselves into themes for artistic
representation. He remained sceptical of this "autonomization
of method vis-à-vis subject matter."

> Without question there are advances in historical materials
> and their mastery, i.e. technique. The broadest examples of
> this are inventions like that of perspective in painting or of
> polyphony in music. Beyond this, there is undeniable
> progress within set modes of procedure as well, their con-
> sistent and full development—for example, the differentia-
> tion of harmonic awareness from the time of thorough bass
> to the threshold of recent music, or the transition from
> impressionism to pointillism. Such unmistakable progress
> is [however] not automatically progress in quality. One
> would have to be blind to deny the gains in means of painting
> from Giotto and Cimabue to Piero de la Francesca; but to
> infer from this that Piero's paintings were better than the
> frescos of Assisi would be pedantic.[11]

Weber would have said that rationalization extends to the techniques of realizing values, not to the values themselves.

All the same, art's becoming autonomous means that the
inner logic of the aesthetic value sphere is set free, making
possible a rationalization of art and, therewith, a cultivation of
experiences in dealing with inner nature, that is, the methodical-
expressive interpretation of a subjectivity freed from the everyday
conventions of knowledge and action. Weber traces this tendency
in bohemianism as well, in life-styles that correspond to the
development of modern art. He speaks of the consistent autonomization and stylization of a "consciously cultivated and thereby
extra-ordinary sphere" of sexual love, of an eroticism that can be
heightened to "orgiastic ecstasy" or to "pathological obsession."

For Weber the development of art plays as little a role in
the *sociological* explanation of the rationalization of society as the
history of science does. Unlike science that has become a productive force, art cannot even speed up these processes. Autonomous art and the expressive self-presentation of subjectivity stand
rather in a complementary relation to the rationalization of everyday life. They take on the compensatory function of "an innerworldly *deliverance* from everyday life and above all from the
increasing pressure of theoretical and practical rationalism."[12]
The development of the aesthetic sphere of value and of the subjectivism held up as an example in bohemianism forms a counter-
world to the "objectified [*versachlichten*] cosmos" of toil in one's
vocation.

Aesthetically imbued counterculture belongs, together with
science and technology on the one hand, and with *modern legal*

and moral representations on the other, to the whole of rationalized culture. The complex that is taken to be central to the rise of modern society is, however, this ethical and juridical rationalism. Thus Weber uses the term "rationalization" also to designate the growing autonomy of law and morality, that is, the detachment of moral-practical insights, of ethical and legal doctrines, of basic principles, of maxims and decision rules, from the world-views in which they were at first embedded. At any rate, cosmological, religious, and metaphysical worldviews are structured in such a way that internal distinctions between theoretical and practical reason cannot yet come into their own. The path of growing autonomy of law and morality leads to formal law and to profane ethics of conviction and responsibility. At almost the same time as the modern natural sciences, both of these were systematized within the framework of practical philosophy: as rational natural law and as formal ethics. To be sure, even this growing autonomy still made its way within religious interpretive systems. Radicalized salvation prophecies led to a sharp dichotomy between, on the one hand, a quest for salvation oriented to inner, spiritually sublimated, sacred values and means of redemption and, on the other hand, the knowledge of an external, objectivated world. Weber shows how the beginnings of an ethic of conviction [*Gesinnungsethik*] developed out of this religiosity of conviction [*Gesinnungsreligiousität*]. "This follows from the meaning of salvation and from the substance of the prophetic teachings as soon as these develop into . . . a rational ethics oriented to *inward* sacred values as means of salvation."[13]

This ethic is distinguished, from a formal point of view, in that it is *based on principles and is universalistic.* The soteriological religiosity of congregations grounds an abstract ethic of brotherliness that, with "one's neighbor" as a point of reference, supersedes the separation between in-group and out-group morality (characteristic of the ethics of the sib, the locality, or the state). "Its ethical demand has always lain in the direction of a universalist brotherhood which goes beyond all barriers of societal associations, often including that of one's own faith."[14]

Corresponding to this is a radical break with the traditionalism of the legal heritage. From the perspective of a formal ethic based on general principles, legal norms (as well as the creation and application of laws) that appeal to magic, sacred traditions, revelation, and the like are devalued. Norms now count as mere conventions that can be considered hypothetically and enacted positively. The more strongly legal representations are developed as complementary to an ethic of conviction, the more legal norms, procedures, and materials become the subject of rational discussions and profane decision. I am emphasizing *both* the principle of having to justify norms and the principle of enactment. Of course Weber, in line with the legal positivism of his time, particularly stressed the second moment, that is, the basic idea that any law whatever can be created and modified by formal enactment. From this follows the most important characteristics of legal domination; Bendix summarizes these as follows:

1. Any norm may be enacted as law with the claim and expectation that it will be obeyed by all those who are subject to the authority of the political community.

2. The law as a whole constitutes a system of abstract rules, which are usually the result of enactment, and the administration of justice consists in the application of these rules to particular cases. Governmental administration is likewise bound by rules of law and conducted in accordance with generally formulated principles that are approved or at least accepted.

3. The people who occupy positions of authority are not personal rulers, but superiors who temporarily hold an office by virtue of which they possess limited authority.

4. The people who obey the legally constituted authority do so as citizens, not as subjects, and obey the "law" rather than the official who enforces it.[15]

Just as important as the principle of enacted law is the basic idea that every legal decision needs to be grounded. From this it follows that (among other things) "the state is not allowed to interfere with life, liberty, or property without the consent of the people or their duly elected representatives. Hence any law in the substantive sense...must have its basis in an act of the legislature."[16]

We might summarize the above as follows: The cultural rationalization from which the structures of consciousness typical of modern societies emerge embraces cognitive, aesthetic-expressive, and moral-evaluative elements of the religious tradition. With science and technology, with autonomous art and the values of expressive self-presentation, with universal legal and moral representations, there emerges a differentiation of

three value spheres, each of which follows its own logic. In the
process, not only do the "inner logics" of the cognitive, expressive, and moral elements of culture come into consciousness but
also the tension between these spheres grows along with their
differentiation. While ethical rationalism retains at first a certain
affinity to the religious context from which it emerges, both ethics
and religion come into opposition with the other value spheres.
Weber sees in this "a very general, and for the history of religion
very important consequence of the development of innerworldly
and otherworldly values towards rationality, towards conscious
endeavor, and towards sublimation by *knowledge*."[17] And this in
turn is the starting point for a dialectic of rationalization that
Weber will develop (as we shall see) in the form of a diagnosis
of the times.

(c) Corresponding to cultural rationalization, we find at the
level of the personality system that *methodical conduct of life* whose
motivational bases were the chief object of Weber's interest,
because he believed himself to be grasping here a—if not *the*—
most important factor in the rise of capitalism. In the value orientations and behavioral dispositions of that style of life, he discovered the correlate in personality of a religiously anchored,
principled, universalistic ethic of conviction which had taken hold
of the strata that bore capitalism. In the first place, then, ethical
rationalism penetrates from the level of culture to that of the
personality system. In fact, the concrete form of the Protestant
ethic, centered around vocational conceptions, means that ethical
rationalism provides the foundation for a cognitive-instrumental
attitude to innerworldly happenings, in particular to social interactions in the domain of social labor. Even cognitive and legal
rationalization enter into the value orientations of this life-style
insofar as they relate to the vocational sphere. By contrast, the
aesthetic-expressive elements of a rationalized culture find their
parallels at the level of personality in behavioral dispositions and
value orientations that are contrary to the methodical conduct
of life.

Weber investigates the religious foundations of the rational
conduct of life in the everyday consciousness of its exemplary
bearers, in the ideas of Calvinists, Pietists, Methodists, and the
sects that arose from the Anabaptist movements. He energeti-
cally works up the following principal features:

1. Radical repudiation of magical measures and all sacraments

as means in the quest for salvation—the definitive disenchantment of religion;

2. Relentless isolation of the individual believer in a world where
   the dangers of creature idolatry threaten, and in the midst of
   a soteriological community that denies any visible identification of the elect;

3. The idea of a calling or vocation, based to begin with on the
   teachings of Luther, according to which the believer proves
   himself to be an obedient instrument of God in the world
   through the worldly fulfillment of the duties of his vocation;

4. The transformation of the Judaeo-Christian rejection of the
   world into an innerworldly asceticism of restless labor in one's
   calling; outward success does not, it is true, represent the real
   basis of the individual redemptory fate, but it does represent
   a basis for knowing it;

5. Finally, the methodical rigor of a principled, self-controlled,
   autonomous conduct of life, which penetrates every domain
   of life because it stands under the idea of assuring oneself of
   salvation.

To this point I have been arranging the manifestations of
rationalization listed by Weber (in the foreword to his collection
of studies on the sociology of religion) in an order according to
whether they lie at the level of society, culture, or personal life-
style; and I have been commenting upon them accordingly. Before
examining in what sense we may speak here of "rational" and
"rationality," I would like to present in a schematic fashion the
empirical interconnections that Weber establishes among the
various manifestations of Occidental rationalism. For this purpose
I shall distinguish (1) the *cultural spheres of value:* science and
technology, art and literature, law and morality, as the elements
of culture that were, with the transition to modernity, differentiated out from the traditional residues of religious-metaphysical
worldviews transmitted by the Greek and above all the Judaeo-
Christian traditions—a process that begins in the sixteenth century
and comes to a conclusion in the eighteenth; (2) *the cultural systems
of action* in which traditions are systematically dealt with under
particular aspects of validity: the scientific enterprise (universities and academies), the artistic enterprise (with institutions for
producing, distributing, and receiving art, and with the mediation of art criticism), the legal system (with specialized juridical
training, scientific jurisprudence, public justice), and finally the

religious congregation (in which a principled ethic with its universalistic demands is taught and lived, that is, institutionally embodied); (3) *the central systems of action that establish the structure of society:* the capitalist economy, the modern state, and the nuclear family; and (4) at the level of the *personality system,* the behavioral dispositions and value orientations that are typical of the methodical conduct of life and its subjective antithesis.

Figure 3 singles out the capitalist economy and the modern state as the phenomena that Weber would like to *explain* with the help of a theory of societal rationalization. Only in Western societies does the differentiation of these two, complementarily interrelated subsystems lead so far that modernization can disengage itself from its initial constellations and continue on in a self-regulating way. Weber can *describe* this modernization as societal rationalization because the capitalist enterprise is tailored to rational economic action and the modern state to rational administration; that is, both are tailored to the type of action he calls purposive-rational. But this is only one aspect; there is a second and, viewed methodologically, more important aspect that cannot be neglected. Weber wants above all to *explain* the institutionalization of purposive-rational action in terms of a process of rationalization. It is from this rationalization process, which takes on the role of explanans in the explanatory scheme, that the diffusion of purposive-rational action arises. With regard to the *initial conditions* of modernization, two moments above all are important: the methodical conduct of life, along the lines of a vocational ethic, on the part of entrepreneurs and government officials; and the organizational measures of formal law. Considered formally, both are based on the same structures of consciousness: posttraditional legal and moral representations. Modern legal representations, which were systematized in the form of rational natural law, entered into the judicial system and the juridical organization of economic commerce and government administration through legal training, professionally inspired public justice, and so on. On the other hand, through the socializing agencies of the congregation and the religiously inspired family, the Protestant ethic was transposed into professional-ascetic orientations for action and thus motivationally anchored, if only in the classes that bore capitalism. Moral-practical structures of consciousness were embodied along both paths, in institutions on the one side and in personality systems on the other. This process led to the spread of purposive-rational action orienta-

Figure 3

Forms of Manifestation of Occidental Rationalism in the Emergence of Modernity

	Cognitive Elements	Evaluative Elements		Expressive Elements
Culture	Modern Natural Science	Rational Natural Law	Protestant Ethic	Autonomous Art
Society	Scientific enterprise (universities, academies, laboratories)	University-based jurisprudence, specialized legal training	Religious associations	Artistic enterprise (production, trade, reception, art criticism)
	Capitalist economy	Modern governmental institutions	Bourgeois nuclear family	
Personality	Behavioral Dispositions and Value Orientations			
	of the methodical conduct of life		of the countercultural life-style	

tions, above all in economic and administrative spheres of life; to this extent it has *a relation to* purposive rationality. What is decisive for Weber, however, is that this process, which lends institutional and motivational embodiment to structures of consciousness, is *itself* a rationalization process. In the same way as modern science and autonomous art, ethical and juridical rationalism is the result of a differentiation of value spheres that is in turn the result of a process of disenchantment reflected at the level of worldviews. Occidental rationalism is preceded by religious rationalization. And Weber deliberately brings this universal-historical process of the disenchantment of mythical interpretive systems under the concept of rationalization as well.

We can distinguish the two great advances in rationalization that Weber investigates both in his studies on the economic ethics of the world religions and in his studies on the origin and development of the capitalist economy and of the modern state (including those on the Protestant ethic). He is interested, on the one hand, in *the rationalization of worldviews;* he has to clarify the structural aspects of disenchantment and the conditions under which cognitive, normative, and expressive problems can be systematically detached and developed in accord with their inner logics. On the other hand, he is interested in the institutional embodiment of the modern structures of consciousness that developed along the path of religious rationalization, that is, in *the transposition of cultural rationalization into societal rationalization.* Here he has to clarify the structural aspects of law and morality insofar as (a) they make possible the organization of legal domination and the interaction under civil law of strategically acting subjects, or (b) they generate the intrinsic motivation for a methodical conduct of life oriented to disciplined and constant labor in one's calling.

B.—Concepts of Rationality. Weber reminds us again and again that "rationalism" may mean very different things. "It means one thing if we think of the kind of rationalization the systematic thinker performs on the image of the world: an increasing theoretical mastery of reality by means of increasingly precise abstract concepts. Rationalism means another thing if we think of the methodical attainment of a definite, given, practical end by way of an increasingly precise calculation of the adequate means. These types of rationalism are very different, in spite of the fact that ultimately they belong inseparably together."[18]

To begin with, then, Weber draws a distinction between theoretical and practical mastery of reality. Of course, he is chiefly interested in *practical rationality,* in the sense of the standards according to which acting subjects learn to control their environment. "Action is purposive-rational [*zweckrational*] when it is oriented to ends, means, and secondary results. This involves rationally weighing the relations of means to ends, the relations of ends to secondary consequences, and finally the relative importance of different possible ends. Determination of action either in affectual or traditional terms is thus incompatible with this type."[19] The concept of purposive-rational action is the key to *the complex concept of rationality* (viewed to begin with in its practical aspects). But this more encompassing rationality, which underlies the "type of bourgeois rationalization of life that has been at home in the Occident since the sixteenth and seventeenth centuries," is by no means equivalent to purposive rationality. I shall now reconstruct in five steps the way in which Weber constructs the complex concept of "practical rationality."[20]

(a) Weber starts with a broad concept of "technique" [Technik] in order to make clear that the aspect of regulated employment of means, in a very abstract sense, is relevant to the rationality of behavior. "Rational technique" is a use of means "consciously and systematically oriented to experience and reflection."[21] So long as we do not specify the techniques, their domain of application, and the experiential basis on which their efficacy can be tested, the concept of "technique" remains very general. Every rule or system of rules that permits reliably reproducible action, whether methodical or customary, that can be predicted by participants in interaction and calculated from the perspective of the observer, is a technique in this sense. "Thus there are techniques of every conceivable type of action: techniques of prayer, of asceticism, of thought and research, of memorizing, of education, of exercising political or hierocratic domination, of administration, of making love, of making war, of musical performances, of sculpture and painting, of arriving at legal decisions. And all these are capable of the widest variation in degree of rationality. The presence of a "technical question" always means there is some doubt over the choice of the most rational means to an end."[22] In this sense, then, even mystical illumination, which is objectively not testable, and the ascetic mastery of desires and emotions have been "rationalized." The only criterion by which "technical" rationalization in the broadest sense is measured is the rule-governedness of reproducible behavior to which others can adapt themselves in a calculating manner.[23]

(b) Weber qualifies this broad meaning of "technique" and "rationalization of means" by way of specifying the means. If we consider only means with which an acting subject can realize set ends through intervention in the objective world, the evaluative criterion of success comes into play. The rationality of employing means is measured by the objectively testable efficacy of an intervention (or of a purposeful omission). This permits us to distinguish between "subjectively purposive-rational" and "objectively correct" actions. We can also speak of a "progressive rationality of means" in an objective sense. "If human behavior (of whatever kind) becomes in any respect 'more correctly' oriented from a technical point of view, then we have a 'technical advance.'''[24] This concept of technique is also a broad one; it extends not only to instrumental rules for mastering nature, but also to rules for artistically mastering materials, or, for example, to techniques for 'dealing with human beings politically, socially, educationally, propagandistically.'[25] We can speak of techniques in this sense whenever the ends that can be causally realized with their help are conceived as elements of the objective world. Even social techniques can apply to social relations, interactions, arrangements, and symbols only if these are presupposed in an objectivating attitude as items of possible manipulation. 'In the special area usually referred to as 'technology,' but also in the areas of commercial techniques and legal techniques, we can speak of 'progress' (in the sense of the progressive technical rationality of means), *if* we take as our starting point a clearly determined state of a concrete structure.'[26]

(c) So far Weber is considering rationality only from the standpoint of employing means. He then differentiates this concept by distinguishing two aspects of the rationality of goal-directed actions: not only the means and the way they are applied can be more or less rational, i.e., effective in relation to given ends; even the ends themselves can be more or less rational, i.e., chosen correctly, in an objective sense, in view of given values, means, and boundary conditions. To the conditions of purposive-rational action there belongs not only an *instrumental rationality* of means, but a *rationality of choice* in setting ends selected in accord with values. From this standpoint an action can be rational only to the degree that it is not blindly controlled by affects or guided by sheer tradition. *"One* essential aspect of the 'rationalization' of action is the replacement of the unthinking acceptance of ancient customs by deliberate adaptation to situations in terms of self-interest."[27] Such rationalization can take place at the expense of affectual as well as of traditional action.

The important distinction between *formal and substantive rationality* belongs in this context. Weber's own formulations are not very clear. Formal rationality relates to the decisions of subjects acting rationally as regards choice, subjects who try to pursue their interests in accord with clear preferences and given decision maxims, paradigmatically in economic action.

The term *"formal rationality* of economic action" will be used to designate the extent of *calculation* that is technically possible and actually applied. . . The concept of *"substantive rationality,"* on the other hand. . .conveys only. . .that certain *demands* are made, be they ethical, political, utilitarian, hedonistic, feudal [*ständisch*], egalitarian, or whatever, and that the results of the economic action—however formally "rational," i.e., calculated, it may be—are measured against these in respect to *value-rationality* or *substantive* purposive rationality.[28]

As soon as subjects are released from the bonds of tradition or from control by affects, to the extent that they become conscious of their preferences and can choose their goals on the basis of clarified preferences, action can be evaluated from two points of view: from the instrumental standpoint of efficacy of means and from the standpoint of the correctness with which goals are inferred in view of given preferences, means, and boundary conditions. Weber calls these two aspects of *instrumental rationality and the rationality of choice,* taken together, "formal rationality," in contradistinction to substantive evaluation of the value systems underlying the preferences.

(d) From the standpoint of formal rationality, we can demand only that the actor be aware of his preferences, that he make precise the underlying values and check them for consistency, that he place them, if possible, in a transitive ordering, and so on. In normative questions Weber is a sceptic; he is convinced that the decision between different value systems (however clarified analytically) cannot be grounded, cannot be rationally justified. Strictly speaking there is no *rationality of value postulates* or belief systems as regards their content. Nevertheless, the *way* in which the actor grounds his preferences, in which he is oriented to values, is for Weber an aspect under which an action can be viewed as rationalizable. "Actions are *purely* value-rational when the agents, regardless of foreseeable consequences, act according to their convictions of what seems to them to be required by duty, honor, beauty, a religious call, piety, or the importance of some 'cause,' no matter in what it consists. Value-rational action is always action in accordance with 'commands' or 'demands' which the actor believes himself to be placed under."[29] The rationality of the values underlying action preferences is not measured by their material content but by formal properties, that is, by whether they are so fundamental that they can ground *a mode of life based on principles.* Only values that can be abstracted and *generalized* into principles, internalized

largely as *formal* principles, and applied *procedurally,* have so intensive a power to orient action that they can cut across various particular situations and, in the extreme case, systematically penetrate all spheres of life and bring an entire biography, or even the history of social groups, under a unifying idea.

The distinction between *interests* and *values* is relevant in this context. Interest positions change, whereas generalizable values are always valid for more than merely one type of situation. Utilitarianism does not take into account this categorial difference worked out by the neo-Kantians; it makes a vain attempt to *reinterpret* interest orientations into ethical principles, to hypostatize purposive rationality itself as a value. Thus in Weber's view the utilitarian doctrine can never attain the status and the power of an ethic based on principles.

(e) Weber differentiates the concept of practical rationality from the three perspectives of *employing means, setting ends,* and *being oriented to values.* The instrumental rationality of an action is measured by effective planning of the application of means for given ends; the rationality of choice of an action is measured by the correctness of the calculation of ends in the light of precisely conceived values, available means, and boundary conditions; and the normative rationality of an action is measured by the unifying, systematizing power and penetration of the value standards and the principles that underlie action preferences. Weber calls actions that satisfy the conditions of rationality of means and choice "purposive-rational," and those that satisfy the conditions of normative rationality "value-rational." These two aspects can vary independently. Advances in the dimension of purposive rationality can "take place in favor of a morally sceptical, purely purposive-rational type of action, [and] at the expense of action tied to value-rationality."[30] In fact it is in this direction that rationalized Western culture seems to be developing. But there is also evidence of the converse case: rationalization of value orientations while purposive-rational action is simultaneously impeded. This is the case, for instance, with early Buddhism, which Weber considers to be a rationalized ethic "in the sense of constant, alert mastery of all natural instinctive drives,"[31] but which at the same time leads (its adherents) away from getting hold of the world in a disciplined way.

The combination of purposive-rational and value-rational action yields a type of action that satisfies the conditions for *practical rationality in its entirety.* When persons and groups generalize this type over time and across social spheres, Weber speaks of a *methodical-rational conduct of life*. And he sees the first historical approximation to this ideal type in the Protestant vocational asceticism of Calvinism and the early Puritan sects.

> Only the vocational ethic of ascetic Protestantism produced a principled, systematic and unbroken unity of an inner-worldly vocational ethic with the assurance of religious salvation. For only here does the world, with all its creaturely depravity, possess an exclusively religious significance as the object through which one fulfills one's duties by rational action in accord with the will of an absolutely transcendent God. The rational, sober, purposive character of action not submitting to the world, and its success, are signs of God's blessing thereupon. This innerworldly asceticism had a number of characteristics and consequences not found in any other religion. It demanded of the believer not celibacy, as in the case of the monk, but the elimination of all erotic pleasure or desire; not poverty, but the elimination of all idle enjoyment of unearned wealth and income, and the avoidance of all feudalistic, life-loving ostentation of wealth; not the ascetic death-in-life of the cloister, but an alert, rationally controlled conduct of life and the avoidance of all surrender to the beauty of the world, to art, or to one's own moods and emotions. The clear and uniform goal of this asceticism was the disciplining and methodical organization of conduct. Its typical representative was the "man of vocation" or "professional" [*Berufsmensch*]; and its specific result was the rational, functional organization of social relations.[32]

The methodically rational conduct of life is distinguished by the fact that it establishes the complex type of action which aims at rationality and its increase under *all three aspects* and that combines these rationality structures with one another so that they are mutually stabilizing, in that successes in one dimension in part presuppose, in part stimulate, successes in the other dimensions. Methodically rational conduct of life makes possible and places a premium upon the success of action simultaneously

1. From the standpoint of instrumental rationality, in the solution of technical tasks and in the construction of effective means;

2. From the standpoint of the rationality of choice, in the consistent choice among alternative lines of action (we speak of

strategic rationality when the decisions of rational opponents must be considered in the process); and finally

3. From the standpoint of normative rationality, in the solution of moral-practical tasks within the framework of an ethic of principle.

Different categories of knowledge can be coordinated with these three aspects of the rationality of action. Both empirical and analytical knowledge enter into the orientations of purposive-rational action via techniques and strategies; this knowledge can in principle take the precise form of scientifically corroborated knowledge. On the other hand, moral-practical knowledge (as well as aesthetic-expressive knowledge) enter into the orientations of value-rational action through competences and motives; this knowledge is rendered precise and improved at two stages of development: first within religious worldviews, later within the framework of the autonomous value spheres of law, morality, and art. At this point it becomes evident that the rationalization of actions and forms of life, and the rationalization of worldviews "ultimately belong inseparably together."[33]

The complex concept of practical rationality, which Weber introduces as an ideal type in connection with the methodical conduct of life in Protestant sects, is still partial. It points to a concept of rationality that encompasses *both* theoretical and practical rationality. At any rate, Weber derives such a concept from structures of consciousness that find expression not directly in actions and forms of life, but primarily in cultural traditions, in symbol systems. The two catchphrases under which Weber investigates a corresponding *cultural rationalization* are "the systematization of worldviews" and "the inner logics of value spheres." They refer to additional concepts of rationality that are not, as are those previously dealt with, oriented to action theory, but are based instead on a theory of culture.

(f) Weber terms "rational" the formal organization of symbol systems, of religious systems in particular, as well as of legal and moral representations. He attributes great significance to the intellectual strata both in the development of dogmatically rationalized religions of salvation[34] and in the development

of formal law. Intellectuals specialize in shaping and improving, from formal points of view, traditional symbol systems as soon as they are fixed in writing. This is a matter of rendering meanings precise, of explicating concepts, of systematizing thought motifs, of consistency among sentences, of methodical construction, of simultaneously increasing the complexity and specificity of teachable knowledge. This *rationalization of worldviews* attaches to the *internal relations* of symbol systems. However, there are two different sides to the improvement of formal qualities that Weber accentuates as the result of the intellectuals' labors. On the one side, rationalized worldviews satisfy to a greater degree the *requirements of formal-operational thought.* This aspect of rationalization can be studied, for example, in connection with the formalization, scientific systematization, and professional specialization of the specialized juridical knowledge which was, to begin with, a matter of practical training in a profession.[35] On the other side, however, rationalized worldviews also satisfy to a greater degree the *requirements of a modern understanding of the world,* which categorially presupposes the *disenchantment of the world.* Weber investigates this aspect of rationalization primarily in connection with the "ethical rationalization" of religions of salvation. With regard to "all kinds of practical ethics that are systematically and unambiguously oriented to fixed goals of salvation," Weber applies the term "rational" (in the sense of a categorially disenchanted world) to "the differentiation between the normatively "valid" and the empirically given."[36] He sees in the overcoming of magical beliefs the essential achievement of the great world religions as regards rationalization. The categorial breakthrough to a modern disenchanted concept of the world also expresses itself in a formal-operational reworking of elements of tradition, but it is not identical with it.

Weber himself blurs this distinction, for instance at the beginning of his study on ancient Judaism, where, in respect to the degree of rationalization of this worldview, he makes note of the following questions: "whether specific conceptions of the Israelites appear... more or less intellectualized and rationalized (in the sense of casting off magical ideas), or more or less uniformly systematized, or more or less turned (sublimated) in the direction of an ethic of conviction."[37] Whereas the first and the last questions concern categories of world-understanding, the question of systematization refers to the formal structuring of a religious symbol system. Frequently these two aspects are not clearly separated by Weber's interpreters either.

J. Weiss characterizes the rationalization of worldviews as the "consequent thinking through to the end of given meaning or value contents. Thinking through to the end means both going back to the ultimate basic principles and developing the furthest consequences or the totality of implications."[38] Weiss separates this achievement of rationalization from what he calls ethical rationalism. By contrast, W. Schluchter identifies the two. "Rationalism means . . . systematizing complexes of meaning, intellectually working through and consciously sublimating the 'aims of meaning.' It is a consequence of the 'inner compulsion' of civilized beings not only to grasp the world as a meaningful cosmos but also to take a position on it; it is thus metaphysical-*ethical* rationalism in the broadest sense."[39] This lack of clarity disappears if we (1) analytically separate the aspect of formal restructuring of worldviews from that of categorial differentiation of world-concepts, and (2) with the help of Piaget's genetic psychology, explain why the consistent application of formal operations to worldviews is perhaps a necessary, but not a sufficient condition for the breakthrough to the modern understanding of the world. Evidently "taking things back to their principles" means something different than "the systematization of belief contents"—not merely a generalization of the domain of application of formal operations of thought, but a decentration of world-perspectives that is impossible without a simultaneous change in deep-seated, moral-practical structures of consciousness.[40]

(g) To the degree that the rationalization of worldviews leads to a differentiation of cognitive, evaluative, and expressive elements of culture, and in this sense to a modern understanding of the world, it satisfies the initial conditions for *cultural rationalization* in the narrower sense. This sets in when "the internal and autonomous logics" of the value spheres, "the spheres of external and internal, religious and secular values . . . come to *consciousness* with all [their] implications."[41]

To the degree that individual value spheres are "separated out in their rational consistency," we become conscious of the universal validity claims against which cultural advances or "enhancements of value" are measured. Weber distinguishes progress in the technical rationality of means from "value enhancement" [*Wertsteigerung*]. As soon as science, morality, and art have been differentiated into autonomous spheres of values,

each under *one* universal validity claim—truth, normative rightness, authenticity or beauty—objective advances, improvements,
enhancements become possible in a sense specific to each. "Value-
enhancing" rationalization comprehends not only the cognitive
(in the narrower sense) elements of cultural tradition, but the
socially integrative as well. It extends to empirical-theoretical
knowledge of external nature, moral-practical knowledge of
society by its members, and aesthetic-expressive knowledge by
individuals of their own subjectivity or inner nature.

What "value enhancement" means in the domain of modern
science is unproblematic at first glance: progress in knowledge
in the sense of an expansion and improvement of theoretical
knowledge. Value enhancement in the sphere of legal and moral
representations is more problematic. Here Weber reckons with
a change in structures, an ever more precise working out of the
universalistic principles of legal and moral theory—otherwise he
could not set up a hierarchy among traditionbound legalistic
ethics, ethics of conviction, and ethics of responsibility. Moreover,
the "improvement" of knowledge in this instance is closely linked
to its implementation. With regard finally to value enhancement
in the aesthetic domain, the idea of progress fades into that of
renewal and rediscovery, an innovative revivification of authentic
experiences. In the aesthetic-expressive sphere, advances from
the viewpoint of purposive rationality have to be distinguished
from enhancements of value rationality just as carefully as in the
moral-practical sphere. Weber stresses

> that the use of a certain technique, however "advanced,"
> says nothing at all about the *aesthetic* value of the work of
> art. Works of art with very "primitive" techniques—for
> example, paintings in the absence of perspective—can,
> aesthetically viewed, be absolutely the equal of those created
> in the most consummate manner on the basis of rational
> technique, provided that the artistic intention has been
> limited to those forms which are adequate to the "primitive"
> technique. The creation of new technical means signifies in
> the first instance only increasing differentiation; and it
> provides only the *possibility* of an increasing "richness" of
> art in the sense of value enhancement. In fact, it often has
> the opposite effect of "impoverishing" the feeling for form.[42]

"Advances" in the domain of autonomous art move in the

direction of an increasingly radical and pure—that is, purified of theoretical and moral admixtures—working out of basic aesthetic experiences. Avant garde art achieved this value enhancement in part by way of becoming reflective in its artistic techniques; the enhanced instrumental rationality of an art that makes its own production processes transparent enters here into the service of enhancing aesthetic value.

Our journey through the different concepts of rationality (a–g) shows that Weber approaches the problematic of rationality on the level of structures of consciousness—speaking with Parsons we could say, on the level of personality and culture. On the one hand, he derives the *concept of practical rationality* from a type of action represented in the historical form of the Protestant-ethical conduct of life, which combines means-ends rationality and value rationality. On the other hand, he contrasts *the rationality of action orientations* with *the rationality of world-perspectives and spheres of value.* He finds the reference points for *cultural* rationalization in modern science, in posttraditional legal and moral consciousness, and in autonomous art. The rationalization phenomena that he wants to *explain,* however, lie on the level of *society*: "Our European-American social and economic life is, in a specific way and in a specific sense, 'rationalized.' To explain this rationalization . . . is one of the chief tasks of our discipline."[43] We shall see how Weber brings these phenomena of *societal rationalization*—above all the establishment of the capitalist economy and the modern state—under concepts he has first elucidated in connection with other phenomena, with manifestations of motivational and cultural rationalization.

In concluding this section, I would like to clarify one more conceptual point: In which respects is what Weber calls "Occidental rationalism" a peculiarity of modern European-American culture, and in which respects is it an expression of universal features of "civilized man"?

C.—As is well known, Max Weber opens his famous *Vorbemerkung* to the *Gesammelte Aufsätze zur Religionssoziologie* with an ambiguous question.

A product of modern European civilization studying the problem of universal history is bound to ask himself, and rightly so, to what combination of circumstances the fact should be attributed that in Western civilization, and in

> Western civilization only, cultural phenomena have appeared
> which (at least as we like to think) lie on a line of develop-
> ment having *universal* significance and validity.[44]

This formulation is ambiguous because it leaves open the question
of whether the process of rationalization, from the perspective
of which *we*, the children of the modern world, view the development of civilizations, has, or merely *appears to us* to have, a
universal validity. I want to defend the thesis that a universalist
position follows from Weber's conceptual approach as we have
developed it so far. Nevertheless, Weber himself did not draw
universalistic consequences without reservations. As can be seen
in his diagnosis of the times, in the prescientific context of his
everyday experience he adopted a highly ambivalent position
regarding Western rationalism. It is for this reason that he sought
a point of reference from which the ambivalent rationalization
of society could be relativized as a *special case* of cultural
development. He regarded rationalism as "Occidental" not only
in the sense that it was in Europe that those historical
constellations emerged in which an essentially general phenomenon could appear for the first time; he also uses the expression "rationalism" for features of this particular Western culture.
        On the other hand, Weber does not straightforwardly defend
a culturalist position; instead he revokes the "universal significance and validity" of Occidental rationalism on the level of
methodological reflection. As Schluchter puts it:

> The rationalism of mastering the world is *our* perspective;
> we use it like a search-light to illuminate a segment of world
> history; and it has for *us* a claim to correctness insofar as
> *we* are concerned with continuity. It belongs to *our* her-
> meneutic initial situation, which not only arose contingently
> but remains particular. However, modern Occidental culture
> is at the same time of such a kind that *all* civilized men could
> take an interest in it. For it brought a new, historically
> previously unknown, interpretation of civilized humanity.
> This not only makes it a special phenomenon but gives it
> a special status. And because this is the case, it poses a
> universal-historical problem and is of universal significance
> and validity. Even the civilized man who does not choose
> this alternative for himself is forced to recognize in it a
> possible interpretation of civilized humanity, an interpreta-
> tion against which he need not relativize his own choice,

but to which he must relate it, insofar as he wants to live
consciously. Thus the point of view Weber singles out, the
criterion of correctness he sets forth, does in fact constitute
a result. However, to the extent that the latter is loaded not
only with heuristic claims but also with claims to correctness, it remains a result *for us.*[45]

This characterization by Schluchter may well capture
Weber's self-understanding; but this understanding only appears
to mediate the two opposed positions on the claim to universality
of the modern understanding of the world. If we do not frame
Occidental rationalism from the conceptual perspective of
purposive rationality and mastery of the world, if instead we take
as our point of departure the rationalization of worldviews that
results in a decentered understanding of the world, then we have
to face the question, whether there is not a formal stock of universal structures of consciousness expressed in the cultural value
spheres that develop, according to their own logics, under the
abstract standards of truth, normative rightness, and authenticity.
Are or are not the structures of scientific thought, posttraditional
legal and moral representations, and autonomous art, as they have
developed in the framework of Western culture, the possession
of that "community of civilized men" that is present as a
regulative idea? The universalist position does not have to deny
the pluralism and the incompatibility of historical versions of
"civilized humanity"; but it regards this multiplicity of forms
of life as limited to *cultural contents,* and it asserts that every
culture must share certain *formal properties* of the modern understanding of the world, if it is at all to attain a certain degree of
"conscious awareness" or "sublimation." Thus the universalist
assumption refers to a few necessary structural properties of
modern life forms as such. If, however, we regard this universalist view as itself cogent only *for us,* the relativism that was
rejected at the theoretical level returns at the metatheoretical
level. I do not think that relativism, whether of the first or second
order, is compatible with the conceptual framework in which
Weber accounts for the rationality problematic. Certainly he had
his relativistic reservations. They derived from a source that
would have disappeared had he traced the peculiarity of Occidental rationalism not to a cultural singularity, but to the selective pattern that rationalization processes assumed under the
conditions of modern capitalism.

With an eye to the manifestations of Occidental rationalism enumerated in the *Vorbemerkung* to his *Religionssoziologie,* Weber remarks:

> For in all the above cases it is a question of the specifically constituted "rationalism" of Western culture. Now by this term very different things may be understood, as the discussions below will repeatedly show. There are, for example, "rationalizations" of mystical contemplation, that is, of behavior which, viewed from other departments of life, is specifically "irrational," just as much as there are rationalizations of economic life, technique, scientific research, education, war, jurisprudence and administration. Furthermore, each of these fields may be rationalized from very different ultimate points of view and ends, and what is "rational" from one [point of view] may well be "irrational" from another. Hence rationalizations of the most varied character have existed in the various departments of life in all cultures. To characterize their differences from the point of view of cultural history, it is necessary to know what spheres are rationalized and in what direction. Hence it is our first concern to work out and to explain genetically the special *peculiarity* of Occidental rationalism, and within this of modern Occidental rationalism.[46]

This key sentence, which seems to express a culturalistic position, reappears almost verbatim in the essay on the Protestant ethic: "Life may be rationalized from very different basic points of view and in very different directions."[47] Whether and, if so, how *the relativism of value contents* affects *the universal character of the direction of the rationalization process,* depends then on the level at which the pluralism of "basic points of view" is set. The culturalist position requires that for every *form* of rationality it is possible to specify *on the same level* at least one abstract point of view from which this form could at the same time be described as "irrational." It is precisely this that Weber apparently wants to maintain concerning the concepts of rationality that we have run through. But he cannot sustain this view. In what follows, I shall be referring to the enumeration presented in the preceding section.

(ad a) Rationality in the sense of technically rationalizing actions, which are made reproducible by methodical guidance and which thereby take on a regular or even a systematic character. As examples of the irrationality of actions that are ra-

tionalized in this way, Weber mentions "methods of mortificatory or of magical asceticism or contemplation, in their most consistent forms, for instance in *yoga* or in the manipulation of the prayer machines of later Buddhism."[48] What are the abstract points of view from which such technical discipline may be judged "irrational"? From the viewpoint of a modern understanding of the world, one could certainly criticize the religious worldviews that give a definite meaning to ascetic exercises, to mystical illuminations, to *yoga,* and the like as irrational. However, this criticism does not refer to the technical rationalization of the actions itself but to the religious interpretation of ritual actions; moreover, it would provide support for relativistic assumptions only if it could be shown that the modern understanding of the world may, from formal points of view as well, be placed at the same level as worldviews that are still tied to magical modes of thought.

(ad b) and (c) Formal rationality. Weber points to rationalizations of economic life, of technique, scientific research, education, war, jurisprudence, and administration, which may appear as "specifically irrational (when) viewed from other departments of life."[49] However, this criticism does not refer to the technologies and strategies with the help of which such domains of action are rationalized but to the relative significance of these domains in the whole of a culture. If and to the extent that a domain of action is to be rationalized at all, progress is measured by the culture-invariant criteria of successful disposition over natural and social processes encountered as something in the objective world.

(ad d) Value rationality. Within individual spheres of life, such as the economic, religious, educational, and so on, the value patterns under which one acts rationally in a means-ends sense can vary. In each case these values have a concrete historical form; they are of a particular nature and provide points of reference for what Weber misleadingly calls substantive [*materiale*] rationality. Perhaps the most striking example of a pluralism of "ultimate" value postulates are the ideas of salvation found in the world religions. "The nature of sacred values has been strongly influenced by the nature of the external interest situation and the corresponding way of life of the ruling strata, and thus by social stratification itself. But the reverse also holds: the direction of the whole way of life, wherever it has been systematically rationalized, has been profoundly determined by the ultimate values to which this rationalization was oriented."[50]

However, the abstract *standards of value,* that is, the formal points of view from which Weber investigates the rationality of salvation religions, lie at a different level than these *value contents.* The former count as universal. All ethics of conviction owe their penetrating, systematizing power to a type of principled reasoning. And this establishes the dimension in which worldviews can be more or less rationalized ethically.

(ad f) and (g) The modern understanding of the world and the inner logics of the spheres of value. When Weber speaks of "ultimate points of view" from which life can be rationalized, he does not always understand by this cultural values, that is, the contents that develop in historical configurations *within* a sphere of life; sometimes he is referring to those abstract ideas that are decisive for the inner logics of value spheres as such, ideas such as truth and success in the cognitive sphere of value; justice, normative rightness in general in the moral-practical sphere of value; beauty, authenticity, sincerity in the expressive sphere of value. These ideas (or validity aspects) should not be confused with material values, the particular *contents* of individual spheres of value. According to Weber, the cultural spheres of value are important for the development of modern societies because they steer the differentiation of societal subsystems or spheres of life. From the perspective of each particular sphere of life, the rationalization of every other sphere can, of course, appear as "irrational" in a certain sense. This is the thesis Weber develops in his essay on "Religious Rejections of the World." He is convinced that the "distillation of the specific peculiarity of every sphere that crops up in the world" brings out ever harsher incompatibilities and conflicts that are grounded in the inner logics of the value spheres. But this critique refers not to the differentiation of the inner logics of individual value spheres but to some value spheres becoming predominant at the expense of others. We must at least regard it as an empirical question, whether the tensions among the ever more rationalized spheres of life go back in fact to an incompatibility of abstract standards of value and aspects of validity, or rather to a partial and therefore *imbalanced rationalization*—for example, to the fact that the capitalist economy and modern administration expand at the expense of other domains of life that are structurally disposed to moral-practical and expressive forms of rationality and squeeze them into forms of economic or administrative rationality. Whatever the answer, we may not in any case place the aspects of validity—under which both the value

spheres that have developed independently in the modern period
and the social subsystems corresponding to them have been formally rationalized—on a level with any value contents whatever,
with any historically changing particular patterns of value. Rather,
those validity claims form a system—however fraught with
internal tensions—that did indeed first appear in the form of Occidental rationalism, but that, beyond the peculiarity of this specific culture, lays claim to a universal validity binding on *all*
"civilized men."

(ad e) The rationality of the methodical conduct of life.
Weber pointed often to the irrational core of the Protestant ethic
of vocation; and, intuitively speaking, there is no denying that
he is right in a certain way. He wanted "to find out whose spiritual
child the particular, concrete form of 'rational' thought and life
was, from which that idea of a calling and that devotion to labor
in the calling has grown, which is . . . so irrational from the standpoint of self-interest, but which has been and still is one of the
characteristic elements of our capitalistic culture. We are particularly interested here in the origin of that *irrational* element
which lies in this, as in every, conception of a 'calling.'"[51] The
repression which this innerworldly asceticism imposes on the
individual in his dealings, both with his own subjective nature
and with interaction partners, even with fellow-believers, corresponds to the blindness of obedience to the quite irrational
decrees of God concerning the salvation of his soul. This psychic
repression is at least partially functional for the motivational basis
of purposive-rational action in the occupational sphere; but it also
makes clear the price that has to be paid for satisfying the requirements of this ethic of conviction—a price that can be calculated
in terms of moral and expressive rationality. L. Brentano, for
example, correctly remarked that this discipline has to be conceived as "rationalization toward an irrational mode of life" rather
than as training in a methodical-rational mode of life. Weber's
response to this objection is not very convincing. "He [Brentano]
is in fact quite correct. A thing is never 'irrational' in itself but
only from a particular 'rational' *point of view.* For the unbeliever,
every religious way of life is 'irrational,' as is every ascetic way
of life for the hedonist; it makes no difference whether they count
as 'rationalization' when measured against their ultimate values.
If this essay ["The Protestant Ethic and the Spirit of Capitalism"]
makes any contribution at all, may it be to bring out the complexity of the only superficially simple concept of the rational."[52]

But Brentano's objection is not directed against the Protestant ethic of vocation as an ethical form of life in competition with other, utilitarian or aesthetic, forms of life. Brentano is inquiring about the internal consistency of a mode of life that Weber regards as the exemplary form in which, for the first (and only) time in history, the complex type of action that systematically combines means-ends and value rationality was realized. In Weber's view, the methodical way of life represents a form of life that embodies the three general aspects of practical rationality simultaneously; to this extent, what it expresses is not merely a cultural peculiarity. If this form of life nevertheless bears irrational features, then they lie in fact at the same level as the rationality for which Weber singles out this life form in his analysis. As we shall see, this contradiction can be resolved only through demonstrating the selective character of this particular form of ethical rationalization.

2. *The Disenchantment of Religious-Metaphysical World-views and the Emergence of Modern Structures of Consciousness*

We have now gained a first overview of Occidental rationalism and of the conceptual means that Weber employed to analyze this phenomenon. We saw that Weber regarded the differentiation of cultural value spheres as a key to the explanation of Occidental rationalism and that he conceived this differentiation in turn as the result of an internal history, namely of the rationalization of religious worldviews. This theoretical approach can be understood only against the background of the neo-Kantian philosophy of value, even though Weber himself made no attempt to order systematically and to analyze from formal points of view the value spheres that he gleaned inductively and treated in a descriptive attitude. We would fail from the start to grasp Weber's theory of rationalization if we did not explain the sociological concept of an order of life [*Lebensordnung*] with the help of the philosophical concept of the actualization of value [*Wertverwirklichung*]. From the theoretical perspective of the scientist, there arises a strict distinction between the spheres of being and of validity and, correspondingly, between descriptive and evaluative statements. Of course, not only valuation but knowledge retains its relation to a sphere of validity through the truth claim connected with descriptive statements. Like every other scientist, the sociologist distinguishes between these spheres; but the segment of reality with which he has to deal is distinguished by the fact that the spheres of the "is" and the "ought" interpenetrate in a peculiar way; in Rickert's view, culture is formed through *Wertbeziehungen*, the relation of its facts to a system of values.[1] In their social actions, individual agents and groups are oriented to values; values are actualized in cultural objects and institutional orders. Hence the sociologist must take into consideration that the reality he analyzes in a descriptive attitude *can also* be viewed under aspects of validity, and that individuals who appear in this object domain normally do view their world under such aspects—whenever they are oriented to concrete values or to abstract validity claims. The sociologist can make use of this value-relatedness of objects by combining the descriptive grasp of orders of social life with a reconstruction of the ideas or values embodied in them.

Weber could not have put forth a theory of rationalization had he not been convinced as a neo-Kantian that he could view processes of value actualization from the outside and from the inside simultaneously, that he could investigate them both as empirical processes and as objectivations of knowledge, that he could tie together the aspects of reality and validity. The disenchantment of religious-metaphysical worldviews calls for an analysis of just this kind. Thus Schluchter is right to stress that:

> Weber tends to survey spheres of value and orders of life descriptively; and he views validity in a historical-empirical attitude primarily under the aspect of efficacy. However, in the background of this analysis stands a theory of value in which the historical-empirical investigations must be anchored. And in my view this is especially true for the historical-empirical theory of rationalization.[2]

Weber does not make this value-theoretical background explicit, but he is relying on it when he (A) places ideas and interests in relation to one another, and (B) in the analysis of worldviews connects an external examination with an internal one. I shall deal with these briefly below, and then go on (C) to characterize the rationalization of worldviews itself, both from the point of view of content and (D) from that of structural change. Finally, I shall (E) indicate a few of the conditions that had to be satisfied before the structures of the disenchanted religious understanding of the world could be effective at the level of social institutions.

A.—Ideas and Interests. The rationalization of culture becomes empirically effective only when it is transposed into a rationalization of action orientations and life orders. Weber conceives of this transposition of culturally stored knowledge into the life conduct of individuals and groups and into social forms of life (or "spheres" or "orders" of life, as Weber says instead of "social subsystems") as a transfer between ideas and interests. He starts from the view that "civilized men" [*Kulturmenschen*] or sociated individuals have needs directed to satisfaction; on the other hand, they find themselves in complexes of meaning that call for interpretation and the creation of meaning. Correspondingly there

are *material* and *ideal* interests. The former are directed to worldly
goods like prosperity, security, health, longevity, and so forth;
the latter to sacred values [*Heilsgüter*] like grace, redemption,
eternal life, or—innerworldly—to overcoming loneliness, sickness,
fear of death, and so forth. In the case of material privations,
there arise *problems of external need;* in the case of ideal privations, there arise *problems of inner need.* These empirical-anthro-
pological determinations reflect the dichotomizing concept formation of the Kantian and neo-Kantian theory of knowledge. Between ideas and interests there are both conceptual and empirical relations. Conceptually, ideal needs are directed immediately
to ideas and values, and material needs have to be interpreted
with the help of ideas. Empirically, ideas and interests enter into
empirical relation to one another both in the life orders of society and in the personality structures of its members.

Orders of life can be viewed from two sides. On the one
side, they regulate the appropriation of goods, that is, the satisfaction of material and ideal interests; on the other side, they
actualize ideas or values. And the two are interconnected:
Interests can be satisfied through norms of social intercourse in
the long run only if they are connected with ideas that serve to
provide reasons for them; and ideas in turn cannot establish themselves empirically if they are not connected with interests that
supply them with power.

This general perspective—which Marx had already
formulated in the *Deutsch-Französische Jahrbücher*—takes a slightly
idealist turn in Weber's hands. Reinhard Bendix attests to this
by citing a characteristic utterance of Otto Hintze:

> Wherever interests are vigorously pursued, an ideology tends
> to be developed also to give meaning, reenforcement and
> justification to these interests. And this ideology is as "real"
> as the real interests themselves, for ideology is an indis-
> pensable part of the life-process which is expressed in action.
> And conversely: wherever ideas are to conquer the world,
> they require the leverage of real interests, although fre-
> quently ideas will more or less detract these interests from
> their original aim.[3]

Weber starts from a model that Parsons later worked out (in a
version influenced by Durkheim): social action systems or "life
orders" integrate both ideas and interests in such a way that they
organize legitimate opportunities for satisfying material and ideal

interests. The interpenetration of ideas and interests and their reciprocal stabilization serve to regulate the appropriation of material and ideal goods and to anchor this regulation in the motives and value orientations of those involved, in such a way that there exists a sufficient chance that the norms in question will be followed on the average. Interests have to be tied to ideas if the institutions in which they are expressed are to be lasting; for only through ideas can an order of life acquire legitimacy.

This can be seen in comparison with a "validity-free" order that is upheld only de facto. Apart from the unstable case of an openly repressive, coercive order based on intimidation and fear,[4] there is the case of "regularity in the course of social action that is determined by custom or self-interest."[5] Weber employs the term *custom* for "habituation in accustomed action" which is so "numb" that the normative internal structure of the habit has shrivelled up and there remains only sheer habituation, unconsciously functioning compliance with rules. On the other hand, an instrumental order based on self-interest rests only on the "purposive-rational weighing of advantages and disadvantages" by strategically acting subjects, such that their complementary interest-orientated expectations are mutually stabilizing. However, an order that rested "*only* on such foundations" (as repression, custom or self-interest) would be "relatively unstable."[6] Thus the normal case is that of an order that expresses interest positions and is at the same time viewed as legitimate.

Weber speaks of normative validity and legitimacy when an order is subjectively recognized as binding. This recognition rests *directly* on ideas that harbor a potential for grounding and justification, and not on self-interest.

> The meaningful content of a social relationship will be called an "order" only if the conduct is, approximately and on the average, oriented to determinable maxims. This order will be called "valid" [gelten] only if the de facto orientation to these maxims occurs, among other reasons, *also* because (in some appreciable way) it is regarded by the actor as somehow valid—obligatory or exemplary—for action. Naturally, in concrete cases the orientation of an action to an order involves a wide variety of motives. But the circumstance that, along with the other sources [of conformity], the order is also held by at least part of the actors to be exemplary or binding—and thus as one that *ought* to obtain—naturally increases the probability that action will in fact be oriented to it, and

often to a very considerable degree. An order which is ad-
hered to only from motives of purposive rationality is generally much less stable than one upheld on a purely customary basis through the fact that the corresponding
behavior has become habitual. The latter is much the most
common type of subjective attitude. But even this type of
order is in turn much less stable than an order which enjoys
the prestige of being considered exemplary or binding, or
as we shall say, "legitimate."[7]

To the extent that the continued existence of an action system
or an order of life depends on its legitimacy, it rests in fact on
"consensual validity" [Einverständnisgeltung]. The consensual
character of social action consists in the fact that the members
of a group recognize the binding force of their norms of action
and know about one another that they feel mutually obliged to
observe these norms. For the rationalization problematic, what
is first of all important in this concept of a legitimate order is
that while ideas are joined together with interests in a very
incomplete way, they do nevertheless lend *factual efficacy to
reasons and validity claims* through this integration.

A sphere of value to which socially influential ideas belong
can generally be only incompletely embodied in a legitimate
order. This can be seen in the force [Gewalt] that is built into the
structure of action norms despite their "consensual character."
Norms require sanctions, either external sanctions (disapproval
by members in the case of *conventions,* an organization's coercive
apparatus in the case of *legal norms*[8]) or inner sanctions (such as
shame and guilt in the case of *ethical norms*). Weber clarifies the
relation between normative validity claims and the empirical
validity of norms of action resting on de facto consensus through
the example of a legally organized economic order.

It is obvious. . . that the ideal legal order of legal theory has
nothing directly to do with the world of real economic conduct, since each exists on a different level. One exists in the
ideal realm of the "ought," the other in the real world of
events. If it is nevertheless said that the economic and legal
orders are very intimately related to one another, the latter
is understood not in the legal but in the sociological sense,
i.e., as being *empirically* valid. In this context "legal order"
thus assumes a totally different meaning. It refers not to a
realm of norms of logically demonstrable correctness, but
to a complex of actual determinants of real human conduct.[9]

Two consequences follow from this distinction between ideal and empirical validity: first a methodological consequence that has been the focus of attention since the debates concerning value judgments [in social science]. In his exchange with Stammler, Weber, in the tradition of neo-Kantianism, stresses two differentiations: the difference between de facto regularities of behavior and normative regulations of conduct and the difference between the meaning of a normative validity claim and the fact of its actual recognition. Weber then criticizes the confusion of descriptive statements about accepted standards of evaluation and established norms with statements that recommend, express, or justify norms. "Above all, Stammler confuses the *ideal* validity of a norm with the actual influence of a norm on empirical conduct through its assumed validity. The former can be systematically deduced by legal theorists or moral philosophers; the latter ought to be the subject of empirical observation."[10]

Questions regarding the ideal validity of norms, whether for the theoretician or for those involved themselves, can be posed only in the performative attitude of an actor (or of a participant in discourse), whereas questions concerning the social "validity" or currency of norms, questions of whether norms and values are or are not actually recognized within a group, have to be dealt with in the objectivating attitude of a third person. Corresponding to this at the semantic level is the distinction between value judgments and judgments of fact. Weber rightly insists that statements of the one type cannot be inferred from statements of the other type. This interest of Weber-the-methodologist has to this day largely concealed the *other* interest that Weber-the-sociologist also registers in the same context.

The problematic of societal rationalization arises from the fact that "ideas of the validity of norms" are supported with reasons and can thus also be influenced by the intellectual treatment of internal relations of meaning, by what Weber calls "intellectualization." The stability of legitimate orders depends on, among other things, the fact of recognition of normative validity claims. And as this social validity stands in internal relation to reasons, (in general to the potential for justification inherent in interpretive systems, worldviews, and cultural traditions), the systematization and elaboration of worldviews carried on by intellectuals has empirical consequences. Intellectual engagement with cultural interpretive systems leads as a rule to learning processes that the social scientist can *recapitulate and appraise* if he adopts the same performative attitude as the intel-lectuals who are influential in the object domain. In this rational reconstruction of processes of cultural (and societal) rational-ization, the social scientist can *not* confine himself to describing de facto views; he can understand the empirical power of con-vincing new ideas, and the devaluation, the loss of the power to convince, of old ideas only to the degree that he becomes aware of the *reasons or grounds* with which the new ideas established themselves. The social scientist does not have to be convinced by these reasons himself in order to understand them; but he will not understand them if he does not, at least implicitly, take a position regarding them (that is, know whether he shares them and, if not, why he cannot do so, or why he is leaving the matter unresolved). The methodological side of rational reconstruction does not need to concern us here; but I would like to make clear that the distinction between the ideal validity and the social validity or social currency of (values and) norms has a conse-quence that is of greater importance in the present context than the postulate of freedom from value judgments. Processes of rationalization can attach to societal orders of life only because the stability of legitimate orders depends on the de facto recog-nition of validity claims that can be attacked internally, that is, shaken by critique, new insights, learning processes, and the like.

In traditional societies (but not only in them), new ideas, new grounds, and new levels of justification do not arise in the form of regulated argumentation.

> We must ask how anything new can arise in this world, oriented as it is toward the "regular" as that which is valid? No doubt innovations have been induced from the outside, that is, by changes in the external conditions of life. But the response to external change may just as well be the extinc-tion of life as its orientation. Furthermore, external change is by no means a necessary precondition for innovation; in some of the most significant cases, it has not even been a contributing factor in the establishment of a new order.[11]

Weber explains innovations rather through the "inspiration" of charismatically influential figures who possess to a special degree the capacity to create meaning. The great world religions all go back to founding figures who were masters of the prophetic word and lent force to their ideas by an exemplary conduct of life. Of course, later the intellectual work of priests, monks, and teachers of wisdom was needed to shape these new ideas and modes of life into dogma and to "rationalize" them into a doctrine capable of being passed on as tradition. It is at this level that the motifs, interpretive patterns, and structures of grounding of the earlier, mythological understanding of the world are dealt with intellectually.

> Religious interpretations of the world and religious ethics created by intellectuals and meant to be rational have been strongly exposed to the imperative of consistency. However little in the individual case they may have complied with the demand for consistency, and however much they might integrate points of view into their ethical postulates which could not be rationally deduced, the effect of the *ratio*—especially of a teleological deduction of practical postulates—is nevertheless in some way, and often very strongly, noticeable in all of them.[12]

With the help of these considerations, we can grasp the relation between interests and ideas somewhat more precisely. In the introduction to "The Economic Ethics of World Religions" we find the famous passage that refers implicitly to Marx's preface to "A Contribution to the Critique of Political Economy": "Not ideas, but material and ideal interests directly govern men's conduct. Yet very frequently the 'world images' created by 'ideas' have, like switchmen, determined the tracks along which action has been pushed by the dynamic of interest."[13] Insofar as we explain social action with reference to legitimate orders (conventions and legal norms), we are supposing:

1. That the "dynamic of interests" is the motor force behind conduct;

2. That this dynamic usually takes effect, however, within the bounds of de facto valid, normative regulations;

3. That the validity of normative regulations rests on the power to convince inherent in the ideas that can be brought forward in their support; and

4. That the de facto power of these ideas to convince *also* depends on the potential—which is susceptible to objective appraisal—for grounding and justification that these ideas afford in a given context.

The stability of legitimate orders is also subject to structural limitations arising from the legitimation potential of available ideas and worldviews. This potential changes both with the actual (external) conditions of credibility and with the rational (internal) conditions of validity. *To the degree* that the facticity of recognized validity claims is dependent on internal conditions of "worthiness to be recognized"—or of validity—the internal rationalization of worldviews according to criteria of validity is empirically effective, in the sense of a "switchman" for the tracks along which interests can be combined with ideas in a legitimate order.

Weber also uses this theoretical assumption to support his method.

> We may hope to facilitate the presentation of an otherwise immensely multifarious subject matter by expediently constructed rational types. To do this we must extract the internally most "consistent" forms of practical conduct that can be deduced from fixed and given presuppositions. Above all, such an essay in the sociology of religion necessarily aims at contributing to the typology and sociology of rationalism. This inquiry therefore proceeds from the most rational forms reality *can* assume; it attempts to find out how far certain rational conclusions, which can be established theoretically, have been drawn in reality and, if necessary, why they have not.[14]

This does not mean that Weber equates rationally reconstructible worldviews with the systems of orientation that are directly effective in everyday life; he uses them as a means of pushing through to the structures of everyday consciousness, particularly to economic ethics.

> This term ["economic ethic of a religion"] is not meant to focus our attention on the ethical theories of theological compendia; for however important such compendia may be under certain circumstances, they merely serve as tools of knowledge. It directs us rather to the practical impulses for action which are founded in the psychological and pragmatic contexts of religions.[15]

B.—Internal and External Factors in the Development of Worldviews.
It is not only at the level of society that ideas and interests combine; we can observe an interplay of ideas and interests at the

level of culture as well. In the analysis of the development of religious and metaphysical worldviews, it is especially important to separate constellations of validity from constellations of causality in such a way that we can relate the *logic of the developmental possibilities* circumscribed by worldviews to the *dynamics of worldview development*—that is, to the factors selectively influencing worldviews from the outside—and can do so without confusing the two.

F. H. Tenbruck has rightly stressed that Weber, in his studies on "The Economic Ethics of World Religions," did not intend merely to buttress his Protestantism thesis by comparative means. Tenbruck shows that the real theme is the universal-historical process of disenchantment: "Obviously, his concern was not merely with the question of whether in other cultures no rational economic disposition could form owing to the absence of inner-worldly asceticism; the issue was, rather, the much more general question of how rationality is produced and takes effect in the interplay of ideas and interests."[16] In this connection, Tenbruck makes three observations that had not been sufficiently stressed in previous Weber research. First of all, he sees that with his thesis about the unidirectional rationalization of *all* world religions, Weber, despite his scepticism in regard to laws of progress, "suddenly finds himself in the camp of the contemporary evolutionism so far as matters of religion are concerned."[17] He points out, furthermore, that Weber concedes empirical effectiveness to the internal validity claims of religious worldviews and their inner-logical development. In Weber's view, "their development is supposed to follow predominantly rational constraints; the genesis of religion is thus supposed to comprise a progress in rationality ...He drew the proof of their quasi-real validity from the empirical findings on the economic ethics of world religions."[18] Finally, Tenbruck identifies the substantive problem to which Weber relates the "learning process" that extends through all world religions: "The rational constraints that religion is supposed to follow arise from the need to have a rational answer to the problem of theodicy; and the stages of religious development are increasingly explicit conceptions of this problem and its solutions."[19] Tenbruck offers the following characterization of the line along which the mythical thought of archaic tribal religions was rationalized step-by-step and transformed finally into a universalistic ethic of conviction, that is, was "ethically rationalized" [*ethisiert*].

When men no longer regarded the forces that mysteriously confronted them in the unmastered environment as powers immanent in the things themselves, but represented them as beings lying behind the things, then for Weber a new idea was born; and when they made personal beings out of them, that was once again a new idea. Likewise for Weber, the monotheistic concept of a transcendent God was a new idea which first had to be born, but which once accepted had far-reaching consequences. Then it was a completely new idea that this was a rewarding and punishing God, especially when this further gave rise to the idea that the destiny of men in this world and in the next depended essentially on keeping such ethical commandments. Another new idea came into the world with emissary prophecy, that is with Judaism, because now men had to understand themselves as God's instruments working in the world. And it was again a new idea when Protestantism added predestination to this.[20]

Robert Bellah and Rainer Döbert have taken up this religious rationalization in a systematic way.[21] Döbert's investigations have made it clear that Weber (and, following him, Tenbruck) does not distinguish sufficiently between the *substantive* problematic that guides rationalization and the *structures* of consciousness that result from the ethical rationalization of worldviews. Whereas the contents of worldviews reflect various resolutions of the theodicy problem, the structural aspects appear, as we shall see, in the "attitudes toward the world" which are determined by formal world-concepts. If one separates structure from content in this way, the interplay of ideas and interests can be analyzed quite well in connection with the material Weber laid out.

In the first place, Weber's investigations can be used to substantiate the view that all the paths of religious rationalization branching through civilizations, from the beginnings in myth to the threshold of the modern understanding of the world, (a) start from the same problem, that of theodicy, and (b) point in the same direction, that of a disenchanted understanding of the world purified of magical ideas (although only the Occidental path of development leads to a completely decentered understanding of the world). If we then assume that the *direction* of religious development can be explained through the inner logic of the core problem and of the structures of worldviews, whereas the *substantive articulation* of structurally circumscribed possibilities must be traced back to external factors, there results a clear methodological demarcation: the work of rational reconstruction concerns itself with internal relations of meaning and validity, with the aim of placing the structures of worldviews in a developmental-logical order and of arranging the contents in a typology; on the other hand, empirical—that is, sociological—analysis is directed to the external determinants of the contents of worldviews and to questions concerning the dynamics of development, such as, for example, the following:

1. What the conflicts that overload the structurally limited interpretive capacity of an existing worldview look like, and how they can be identified;

2. In which historically caused conflict situations a theodicy problematic typically arises;

3. Who the social carriers are that establish or rationalize a new worldview;

4. In which social strata a new worldview is adopted, in which sectors and how broadly it affects the orientation of everyday conduct;

5. To what extent new worldviews have to be institutionalized in order to make legitimate orders possible—merely in elites or in entire populations;

6. Finally, how the interests of the carrier strata guide the selection of the contents of worldviews?

Before taking up Weber's analysis of worldviews, I would like to indicate the two perspectives from which this analysis is carried out. What *first* strikes one is that Weber limits the rationalization of worldviews to the standpoint of ethical rationalization [*Ethisierung*]; he traces the development of a religiously grounded ethic of conviction—more generally, the development of posttraditional legal and moral representations. As he is interested in the rational presuppositions for the maintenance of legitimate orders, particularly in the rational conditions of social integration in the transition to modern societies, this limitation seems plausible. But the rationalization of worldviews could have been traced equally well in two additional dimensions; Weber could also have investigated the transformation of cognitive and expressive elements looking back from the perspective of modern science and autonomous art. He did not do this, even though he presupposed a differentiation of all three value spheres in the rationalization of society that set in with the modern age.

Second, Weber examines the process of the disenchantment of religious worldviews from a concrete historical reference point. He does not reconstruct the history of legal and moral representations with a view to the structures of ethics of conviction *generally.* Rather, he traces religious rationalization with a view to the rise of the capitalist economic ethic, because he wants to clarify precisely those cultural conditions under which the transition to capitalism could be accomplished so as to solve the basic evolutionary problem of socially integrating a differentiated subsystem of purposive-rational action. He is solely interested, therefore, in the ideas that make it possible to anchor purposive-rational action in the system of social labor in a value-rational way, that is, to institutionalize it and to provide a motivational base for it.

It is helpful to keep these two limitations in mind. They may explain why, as we shall see, Weber did not exhaust the systematic scope of his theoretical approach. In this approach, the institutionalization of new action orientations and the emergence of legitimate orders are traced back to the interplay of ideas and interests. The interest positions are supposed to explain *both* the impetus behind the development of worldview structures according to an inner logic, *and* the selective filling out of the possibilities opened up by new cognitive structures, that is, the sorts of worldview contents. This theoretical perspective is set in the work of Max Weber as a whole. If we allow ourselves to be guided by it in interpreting Weber's studies in the sociology of religion, there emerges a sharper contrast between the *possibilities* for orientation contained in the modern structures of consciousness that issued from the process of disenchantment and the profile of those parts of this spectrum of possibilities that were actualized, that is, translated in fact into institutions and motivations—a profile characteristic of capitalist society. Weber understands the rationalization of worldviews as a process that (a) takes place *in the same direction* in all world religions, but that (b) for external reasons, is radically brought to a conclusion only along *one* line of tradition, so that (c) in the Occident it sets free the structures of consciousness that make a modern understanding of the world possible. The cognitive and expressive elements of tradition are no less affected by these structures of world understanding than the evaluative; but Weber concentrates on the development of a universalistic ethic of conviction.

The fact that the posttraditional stage of moral consciousness becomes accessible in one—the European—culture is not a sufficient condition for its establishment in the form of the Protestant ethic. It comes to this only when the structures of an ethic of conviction that elevates value-rational action to the principle of the *innerworldly* conduct of life determines the life-style of broad social strata, and in such a way that it can serve to anchor purposive-rational action in a value-rational way.

Weber has to postulate a parallel, if not simultaneous process for modern law. The ethical rationalization of worldviews entails a rationalization of legal consciousness as well; but again, the availability of posttraditional legal representations is not sufficient for the establishment of a modern legal system. It is only on the foundations of rational natural law that legal matters could be reconstructed in basic concepts of formal law in such a way that legal institutions could be created that formally satisfied univer-salistic principles—principles regulating commercial relations among commodity owners and the complementary activity of public administrations.

In Weber's presentation, the parallelism between these two processes—the motivational anchoring and the institutional em-bodiment of posttraditional moral and legal representations—does not clearly emerge. He separates the sociologies of religion and law and relates religious rationalization more strongly to the economic ethic than to the development of law. This may also have something to do with the fact that the emergence of rational natural law cannot be explained solely through the ethical ratio-nalization of worldviews; it depends to a considerable extent on the development of science and thus would have required an analysis of the relation between the cognitive and the moral-practical elements of worldviews.

If we separate the results of religious rationalization—that is, the development of modern structures of consciousness in the dimensions of law and morality—from the process of value ac-tualization [*Wertverwirklichung*] through which a form of social integration specific to modern society came about, the distribu-tion of the burden of proof to internal and external factors becomes clear. We can indicate, in an abstract way, the type of problem that concerns the dynamics of development and that, therefore, cannot be explained by the inner logic of worldview development and the differentiation of value spheres. Only a so-ciological investigation of the interest positions of carrier strata, of social movements, conflicts, and so forth, can explain (a) why it was only in the Judaeo-Christian line of tradition that the rationalization found in all worldviews was carried through to the end; (b) why it was only in the Occident that the conditions for an implementation of universalistic legal and moral structures in institutions and in personalities were fulfilled; and (c) why it was only here that typically occurring system problems were resolved in such a way that the form of social integration characteristic of capitalistic societies emerged (with the methodical conduct of life and the modern judicial system).

Weber's contribution to these sociological (in the narrower sense) analyses of the transition from feudal to modern society is well known. He highlighted many of the external factors that today play an important role in modernization research: the fact of a relatively homogeneous culture; the decentralization of political power; the balanced conflict between church and state; the internal differentiation of the former into the official church, religious orders, and the laity; the peculiar structure of the medieval trading city with its nobility, guilds, and corporations; the tendencies to a commercialization of trade, a bureaucratization of administration; and so on.[22] I shall not be dealing with these factors; my remarks will be confined to the *internal factors* in the rationalization of worldviews and to the *structural aspects* of the embodiment of modern structures of consciousness in the Protestant ethic of the calling and in the modern legal system.

C.—Substantive Aspects.   Weber examined three of the great world religions: the Chinese (Confucianism, Taoism), the Indian (Buddhism, Hinduism), and ancient Judaism; he was not able to carry out the projected investigations of Christianity and Islam. His procedure was throughout comparative; but only in a few places did he consolidate his comparative presentation into a systematic comparison: principally in the introductory essay, "The Social Psychology of World Religions," the intermediate reflections, "Religious Rejections of the World and Their Directions," and the conclusion to *The Religion of China,* "Conclusions: Confucianism and Puritanism."[23] Taking only the most general perspectives into consideration, we see that Weber differentiates worldviews—which have a common theme as their point of departure—primarily in the dimensions of the representation of God (personal lord of creation versus impersonal cosmic order) and of the orientation to salvation (affirmation of the world versus rejection of the world).[24]

(a) The Theme. Rationalization is tied to a theme that is common to all world religions: the question of justifying the unequal distribution of life's goods. This *basic ethical problematic,* which bursts the bounds of myth, arises from a need for a religious explanation of suffering that is perceived as unjust. For personal misfortune to be perceived as unjust, it is first necessary that suffering be revalued, for in tribal societies suffering counts as a symptom of secret guilt. "Individuals continually suffering, mourning, ill, or otherwise unfortunate were, according to the nature of their suffering, believed either to be possessed by a demon or burdened with the wrath of a god whom they had insulted."[25] Moreover, tribal cults were tailored to dealing with collective exigencies and not with the fates of individuals. What is new is the idea that individual misfortune can be undeserved and that the individual may cherish the religious hope of being delivered from all evil, from sickness, need, poverty, even from death. Also new is the formation of communities independent of ethnic associations, the organization of religious communities for the redemptory fates of individuals.

> The annunciation and the promise of religion were naturally addressed to the masses of those in need of deliverance. They and their interests moved to the center of the professional organization of the care of souls which really only originated therewith. The typical service of magicians and priests became the determination of why, or through what, suffering had been brought on—that is, the confession of sins. At first these sins were offenses against ritual commandments. The magician and priest also gave counsel regarding behavior fit to remove the suffering. Their material and ideal interests could thereby actually and increasingly enter the service of specifically *plebian* motives.[26]

This suggests a sociological explanation that Weber did not pursue very far: The revaluation of individual suffering and the appearance of individual needs for salvation—which made the question of the ethical meaning of what is meaningless the point of departure for a religious thought pushing beyond local myths— did not fall from heaven. They are the result of learning processes that set in as the ideas of justice established in tribal societies clashed with the new reality of class societies. Without exception, world religions developed within civilizations, that is, within the framework of societies organized around a state, in which there emerged new modes of production independent of the kinship system and corresponding forms of economic exploitation.[27] To be sure, the potential for conflict had first to be released by prophets in order that the masses, who were "everywhere engulfed in the massive, archaic growth of magic," might be "swept into a religious movement of an ethical character."[28]

(b) *Theocentric versus Cosmocentric Worldviews.* The world religions start from the same basic problem: they attempt to satisfy "the rational interest in material and ideal equalization" in view of the evidently unequal distribution of earthly goods; and they do so by way of offering explanations for this inequality. "Behind them always lies a stand towards something in the actual world which is experienced as specifically 'senseless'; they reflect the demand that the world order in its totality somehow is, or could, or should be, a meaningful 'cosmos.' "[29] The question of the justification of manifest injustices is not, however, treated as a purely ethical question; it is part of the theological, cosmological, metaphysical question concerning the constitution of the world as a whole. This *world order* is so conceived that ontic and normative questions are blended together. In this framework of religious-metaphysical thought about the world order, quite different solutions to the same problem have been found. Weber contrasts above all the two basic conceptual strategies: one, the Occidental, employs the conception of a transcendent, personal Lord of Creation; the other strategy, widespread in the Orient, starts from the idea of an impersonal, noncreated cosmos. Weber also refers to these as transcendent and immanent conceptions of God. The "God of Action" is developed in an exemplary way in the form of Jahweh,[30] the "God of Order" in Brahman.[31] The faithful must enter into a different relationship with the Lord of Creation than they do with the static ground of the cosmic order. They understand themselves as *instruments of God* and not as *vessels of the divine.*[32] In the one case the believer seeks to win God's favor, in the other to participate in the divine.

The religious foundation of ethics is also different in the two traditions; the hope for divine grace stands in contrast to the idea of self-deliverance through knowledge in Asiatic religiosity. Thus the nucleus of speculative world-interpretation is, in the former case, the history of salvation and, in the latter case, the cosmos or being. And although the contrast between the religiosity of virtuosos and that of the masses is everywhere to be found, the

Asiatic religions have a greater affinity to the world outlook and life experience of the intellectual strata.

Thus Weber conceives of the world religions as different solutions to the same basic problem. These solutions move within the basic conceptual space of religious-metaphysical conceptions of world order, which blend together ontic, normative, and expressive aspects. He explains their different contents by means of external factors, the primary object of investigation being "the external and the internal, psychologically conditioned interest positions of those strata that have been the carriers of the way of life in question during the decisive period of its formation."[33] This may be a stratum of officials educated as literati (Confucianism), wandering mendicant monks (Buddhism), a peasantry tied to nature (and to magical thought), a nomadic warrior stratum (Islam), or bourgeois towndwellers, handworkers, merchants, entrepreneurs in cottage industry, and so forth (Protestantism). These sociological (in the narrower sense) points of view determine the dynamics and the extent of the rationalization process, as well as the selection made from the structurally possible contents.

(c) World Affirmation versus World Rejection. Weber distinguishes world religions not only according to whether they are theocentric or cosmocentric in form, but also according to whether they motivate followers to affirm or to reject the world as a whole. This question is independent of whether a life-style is passive or active; it has to do with whether the believers place a basically positive or negative value on "the world," that is, on their society and the surrounding nature, whether or not these have for them an intrinsic value. A negative attitude to the world first became possible through the dualism characteristic of the radical religions of salvation. It required a worldview structure that devalued the world—be it as a historically fleeting earthly realm in relation to a transcendent Lord of Creation, or as a merely phenomenal foreground in relation to the essential ground of all things—and that established a reality behind the appearance, to which the world had sunk, as the reference point of the individual quest for salvation.

To be sure, Weber is inclined to assume that a world-affirming attitude can be maintained only where magical thought has not been radically overcome and where the stage of a dualistic (in the strict sense) interpretation of the world has not been reached. But he could have tested whether or not this was the case only through a comparison of Confucianism and Taoism with Greek philosophy; such a comparison could have determined whether radical disenchantment, a dualistic worldview structure, and affirmation of the world might not also go together. World rejection would then depend more on a radicalization of the thought of salvation, which led in religions of conviction to an accentuation of the dualism found in *all* world religions and to an intensification of the contrasts therein. Weber offers a socio-logical explanation for this as well. He points to the social con-flicts that brought on the appearance of prophets. Emissary prophecies, as in the Judaeo-Christian tradition, promoted a par-ticularly radical split between the here and the hereafter and cor-respondingly consistent forms of world rejection.

The following schema contains the abstract points of view from which Weber differentiates religious worldviews *according to content* within the framework of a common religious-meta-physical conceptual apparatus. He starts from the assumption that these substantially different formations can be explained sociologically, that is, by means of external factors.

Figure 4
Religious-Metaphysical Worldviews According
to Their Typical Contents

Conceptual Strategies / Evaluation of the World as a Whole	Theocentric	Cosmocentric
World Affirmation	——	Confucianism Taoism
World Rejection	Judaism Christianity	Buddhism Hinduism

D.—Structural Aspects. Weber measures the rationalization of a worldview by its eradication of magical thought (disenchantment) on the one hand and by its systematic organization (or "dogmatization," in Rothacker's sense[34]) on the other.

> To judge the level of rationalization a religion represents there are two principle yardsticks, which are in many ways interrelated. One is the degree to which the religion has divested itself of magic; the other is the degree of systematic unity it gives to the relation between God and the world and correspondingly to its own ethical relation to the world.[35]

The fact that Weber places greater stress on overcoming magical practices than on overcoming the mythical modes of thought in which magic is interpreted is to be explained by the sociologist's interest in the influence of worldviews on the practical conduct of life. The transformation of the cognitive elements that religious worldviews inherit from myths is less relevant for the rationality of life conduct than the transformation of the technical-practical and, above all, the moral-practical elements. The magical world of ideas is an impediment to the adoption of an objectivistic attitude toward technical innovation, economic growth, and the like.[36] Above all, in the main cultic domains it blocks the development of a personal communication between the faithful and God or the divine being. The manipulative techniques for compelling God, which live on in the sublime form of the sacrament, dominate in place of worship and prayer.[37] Weber describes the world of the "enchanted garden" by way of (among other things) contrasting superstition and the belief in miracles.[38] I shall demonstrate what disenchantment means from a structural point of view in connection with the *attitudes toward the world* that Weber distinguishes. In doing so, I shall, for systematic reasons, consider not only the ethical rationalization of worldviews but also the transformation of their cognitive components—at least by way of suggestions. I shall then treat the structural aspects of the transition from matured religious-metaphysical worldviews to the modern mode of thought.

(a) Mystical Flight from the World versus Ascetic Mastery of the World. Religious-metaphysical worldviews ground fundamental attitudes toward the world. Each such attitude makes a rationalization possible to the degree that it is directed in a uniform and unifying manner to nature and society as a whole

and thus requires a systematic concept of the world. This is, of course, not yet a matter of a formal world-concept,[39] but only of a concept of a concrete world order that relates the multiplicity of appearances, monotheistically or cosmologically, to a point of unity. This principle is represented as a God of Creation or a Ground of Being that unites in itself the universal aspects of "is" and "ought," essence and appearance. Indeed, worldviews count as the "more rational," the more clearly they make it possible to grasp or to deal with the world—be it as the temporal world or as the world of appearances—under *one* of these aspects, which are still unseparated in the realm of the supramundane. Weber concentrates on the normative aspect of the "ought-to-be" or the "commanded," and, correspondingly, on the moral-practical structures of consciousness that make possible an attitude of the acting subject toward the world as a whole that has been thoroughly systematized from the perspective of an ethic of conviction.

Under this aspect of ethical rationalization [*Ethisierung*], a worldview can count as rationalized to the degree that it distills out "the world" (the temporal realm or the realm of appearances) as the sphere of moral testing under practical principles and *separates this from all other aspects.* An ethically rationalized worldview presents the world (a) as the field of practical activity in general, (b) as a stage upon which the actor can ethically fail, (c) as the totality of situations that are to be judged according to "ultimate" moral principles and mastered in accord with the criteria of moral judgments, and thus (d) as a domain of objects and occasions of ethical conduct. The objectified world stands over against the basic moral norms and the moral conscience of fallible subjects, as something outside, external.

Weber selects the world attitude that corresponds to such an ethical-rational worldview in two steps. *First,* he shows that salvation religions that develop the dualism between God and the world in sharp contrasts satisfy the conditions for an ethical rationalization better than worldviews with a more weakly developed orientation to salvation and a less sharp dualism.[40] A relation of heightened tension between God (or the divine), on the one side, and the profane orders of life, on the other, shifts the believer's search for salvation into a perspective from which the world can be devalued and objectivated solely from the abstract viewpoint of a religious testing.

Prophetic and redemptory religions have lived. . .in a permanent state of tension in relation to the world and its orders. The more the religions have been true religions of salvation, the greater has this tension been. This followed from the meaning of salvation and from the substance of the redemptory teachings as soon as these developed into an ethic that was rational and oriented to *inward* sacred values as means of salvation—and the more principled the way in which they did so, the greater the tension. In the usual terminology, this means that the tension has been greater, the more religion has been sublimated away from ritualism and toward a "religiosity of conviction" [*Gesinnungsreligiosität*]. On the other side, the further the rationalization and sublimation of the external and internal possession of—in the widest sense—"things worldly" has progressed, the stronger has the tension on the part of religion become.[41]

A negative attitude toward the world resulting from an orientation to a sacred value that transcends the world or is hidden in its innermost recesses is not, however, per se conducive to the ethical rationalization of life-conduct. World rejection leads to an objectivation of the world under ethical aspects only when it is connected with an active mode of life turned toward the world and does not lead to a passive turning away from the world. Thus, in a *second* step, Weber selects from the world-rejecting attitudes those which actively aim at mastering the devalued and objectivated world. Within the class of salvation religions aligned with ethics of conviction, what differentiates these two attitudes are the kinds of promise and the privileged paths to salvation. When the believer can understand himself as the tool of a transcendent God, the ascetic forms of an active search for salvation are more likely than when he sees himself as the vessel of a divine ground of being profoundly immanent in the world, when contemplative forms of the mystical search for salvation are more likely.

In our introductory remarks we contrasted, as abnegations of the world, active asceticism, *action* willed by God and carried out as a tool of God, on the one hand, with the contemplative *possession* of the holy as found in mysticism, on the other hand. The latter is a "having" and not a doing; the individual is not a tool but a "vessel" of the divine; action in the world must thus appear as endangering thoroughly irrational and otherworldly sacred powers.[42]

The contemplatively oriented "thought religions" of the Orient do not steer world rejection in the direction of an ethical rationalization of the world, even when, as in Hinduism, they stress the motive of salvation. The mystic's passive search for salvation leads rather to a flight from the world. Only the ascetically oriented "religions of conviction" of the Occident bind religious testing to ethical action, for which a devalued and objectivated world offers ever new situations and occasions. The mystic proves himself through withdrawing from the world, the ascetic through acting in it.[43] Of course, the attitude of ascetic world mastery, which the Christian monk shares with the Puritan, does not of itself signify the spread of an ethically rationalized conduct of life to extrareligious departments of life. The turning toward the world of an active mode of life, which I contrasted with flight from the world and correlated with the ascetic path to salvation, is not yet equivalent to innerworldliness. In order for the ascetic search for salvation—which, while based on a negative attitude toward the world, is at the same time turned toward it—to be able to expand to innerworldly asceticism, an additional step is required. I shall disregard this for the moment (see Figure 5).

(b) Theoretical Contemplation of the World versus Practical Adjustment to the World. Weber analyzes the attitude of world affirmation only in the one form of a practically oriented adjustment to the world. He illustrates this in connection with China. "As with the genuine Hellenes, all transcendental anchorage of ethics, all tension between the imperatives of a supramundane

Figure 5
Attitudes Toward the World Based On the
Rejection of the World in Salvation Religions

Paths to Salvation ⟍ Evaluation of the World as a Whole	Ascetic Turning Towards the World	Mystical Turning Away from the World
World Rejection	Mastery of the World: Judaism Christianity	Flight from the World: Hinduism

God and a creatural world, all orientation toward a goal in the beyond, and all conception of radical evil were absent."[44] Since, in line with his aim to study the economic ethics of world religions, Weber judges Confucianism and Taoism only from the standpoint of ethical rationalization, he arrives at his famous (and controversial) assessment of the lower potential for rationalization in these worldviews.

> This ethic of unconditional affirmation of, and adjustment to, the world presupposed the unbroken and continued existence of purely magical religion. It applied to the position of the emperor, who, by personal qualification, was responsible for the good conduct of spirits and the occurrence of rain and good harvest weather; it applied to ancestor worship, which was equally fundamental for popular and for official religiosity; and it applied to unofficial (Taoist) magical therapy and the other survival forms of animistic compulsion of spirits (i.e., anthropo- and herolatric belief in functional deities).[45]

Thanks to Joseph Needham's pioneering investigations,[46] however, it is now well known that the Chinese, from the first century B.C. to the fifteenth century A.D., were evidently more successful than the West in developing theoretical knowledge and in using this knowledge for practical purposes. Only since the Renaissance has Europe clearly taken the lead in this field. This suggests that the rationalization potential of these traditions might have been studied first of all from the standpoint of cognitive and not of ethical rationalization—all the more so, as Greek philosophy, which shares with the cosmological ethic of the Chinese a world-affirming attitude, also advanced the rationalization of worldviews more in the direction of theoreticization. Moreover, successful Chinese science appears prima facie to have run up against the same limits as the metaphysical view of the world of Greek philosophy: in both cases, the ethically rooted, noninterventionist attitude toward nature and society blocked

> the evolutionary transition from the stage attained by da Vinci to that of Galileo. In medieval China, experimentation was carried out more systematically than was ever attempted by the Greeks, or even by the Europeans of the Middle Ages; however, so long as there was no change in the "bureaucratic feudalism," mathematics, empirical observation of nature,

and experiment could not be combined in such a way as to produce a wholly new approach.[47]

The essentials of a rationalizable worldview are as little lacking in Confucianism and Taoism as they are in Greek philosophy. In the concept of a concrete world-order, the multiplicity of appearances is systematically grasped and related to principles. To be sure, the dominant salvation motif, which sharpens the dualism between the world of appearances and the world-transcending principle, is missing. Nevertheless, the dualistic worldview structure is sufficient to put the world of appearances at such a distance that it can be objectivated under *one* of the aspects (which are not yet differentiated at the level of principles), indeed under the cognitive aspect of being and becoming. Under this aspect, worldviews can count as the more rational, the further the world of appearances is distilled out from abstract points of view as a sphere of the existing or the useful, and is purified of other—normative and expressive—aspects. A cognitively rationalized worldview represents the world as the totality of all forms and processes that can be made contemplatively present to the mind. To the extent that practical needs take precedence here (as Weber emphasizes is the case for the Chinese mind), the fundamental attitude of world affirmation takes the shape of adjustment to the world. On the other hand, world affirmation seems to lead to an objectivation of the world under purely theoretical aspects when it is linked with a theoretical form of life removed from practical need and is placed in the service of contemplation of the world. The stratum of cultivated Chinese could not rely on an "academic" life set apart from praxis and devoted to contemplation—a *bios theoretikos*—in the same way that the Greek philosophers could.

This hypothesis would require detailed examination; here I can only express my suspicion that the Chinese traditions would appear in another light if one considered them primarily from the standpoint of theory rather than of ethics and compared them with the classical Greek traditions. The differentiation of an attitude to the world that promotes the systematic unification of the world under ontic aspects might be dependent on methods of gaining the highest good. This is not a question of paths to salvation, as it is in the case of salvation religions with an ethic of conviction, but of ways of ascertaining or securing the world [*Weltvergewisserung*]. To the active and passive search for salvation of the ascetic and mystic we can counterpose forms of life that serve to secure or ascertain the world in an active or passive manner: the *vita activa* and the *vita contemplativa*. [48] If this hypothesis holds up, one may hope to arrive at four attitudes toward the world, differentiated according to paths of salvation or forms of life (see Figure 6).

If the stance toward the world that is based on cosmological-metaphysical affirmation and differentiated according to *adjustment to* and *contemplation of* the world had a significance for the cognitive rationalization of worldviews like that which, according to Weber, *mastery of* and *flight from* the world had for the ethical rationalization of worldviews, we could assume that cosmocentric worldviews provide the greatest scope for objectivating the world under aspects of being and becoming when they are linked to an attitude of world contemplation. According to this hypothesis, the passive form of ascertaining the world permits a more extensive decentration of those worldviews that are predisposed to cognitive rationalization; on the other hand, the active form of seeking salvation permits a more extensive decentration of worldviews that are predisposed to ethical rationalization. In connection with dimensions of rationalization and attitudes toward the world, this would give us the assessment of the rationalization potential of different worldviews represented in Figure 7. Thus in the Occident the two worldviews that are structured in such a way that the world can be most ex-

Figure 6
Attitudes Toward the World

Ways of Seeking Salvation or of Securing the World / Evaluation of the World as a Whole	Active: Asceticism or the Vita Activa	Passive: Mysticism or the Vita Contemplativa
Rejection of the World	Mastery of the World: Judaism, Christianity	Flight from the World: Hinduism
Affirmation of the World	Adjustment to the World: Confucianism	Contemplation of the World: Greek Metaphysics

tensively objectified [*versachlicht*] from the normative and the ontic standpoints come together.

Figure 7
Rationalization Potential of Worldviews

Ratio- nalization Potential Dimen- sion of Rationalization	High	Low	
Ethical	Mastery of the World: Judaism Christianity	Flight from the World: Hinduism	Salvation Religions
Cognitive	Contemplation of the World: Greek Philosophy	Adjustment to the World: Confucianism	Cosmological-Metaphysical Worldviews
	Occident	Orient	

E.—Disenchantment and the Modern Understanding of the World. Weber judges the rationalization of worldviews by the extent to which magical thinking is overcome. In the dimension of ethical rationalization, he observes disenchantment primarily in the interaction between the believer and God (or the divine being). The more the relation is established as a purely communicative relationship between persons—between the individual in need of salvation and a transcendent, morally demanding sacred authority—the more strictly the individual can systematize his innerworldly relations from the abstract standpoint of a morality to which either only the chosen—the religious virtuosos—or all of the faithful are subject in the same way. This entails (a) the distillation of a world concept, abstracted from a single point of view, for the totality of normatively regulated interpersonal relations; (b) the differentiation of a purely ethical attitude, in which the agent can follow and criticize norms; and (c) the development of a concept of the person that is at once universalistic and individualistic, with its correlates of conscience, moral accountability, autonomy, guilt, and so forth. With this the devout attachment to concrete orders of life secured in tradition can be superseded in favor of a free orientation to universal principles.[49]

In the cognitive dimension, disenchantment of the manipulation of things and events goes along with a demythologization of the knowledge of what is. The more the instrumental intervention into, and the theoretical interpretation of, empirical processes can be separated from one another, the more strictly the individual can in turn systematize his lifeworld relations (in this case from the abstract standpoint of a cosmological-metaphysical order) to the laws of which all phenomena are subject without exception. This entails (a) the distillation of a formal world-concept for the whole of what is, with universals for the lawlike spatiotemporal interconnection of entities in general;[50] (b) the differentiation of a purely theoretical attitude (set off from practice), in which the knower can contemplatively ascertain the truth, make and contest statements;[51] and (c) the development of an epistemic ego in general, which can give itself over to the contemplation of what is, freed from affects, lifeworld interests, prejudices, and the like.[52] With this the fixation on the surface of concrete phenomena that is anchored in myth can be superseded in favor of a disinterested orientation to general laws underlying the phenomena.

In the preceding, I have correlated the ethical dimension of rationalization with salvation religions and the cognitive dimension with cosmological-metaphysical worldviews. This correlation should be understood as proposing merely that certain structures of worldviews and corresponding attitudes toward the world more strongly favor rationalization in one of these two dimensions. Naturally, the Christian religion can just as little be reduced to ethics as Greek philosophy can to cosmology. It is remarkable that the two worldviews with the structurally greatest potential for rationalization came together within the same European tradition. From this there arose a productive relation of tension that marked the history of ideas in the European Middle Ages. The collision led to a polarization, that is, to a radical working out of the basic concepts of, on the one side, a religious ethic of conviction and, on the other, a theoretically grounded cosmology. At the same time, it also necessitated syntheses of the two formal world-concepts developed from ethical and ontological standpoints.

Weber was not able to carry out his plan to include Christianity and Islam in his comparative studies. If he had, then he could have studied the emergence of modern structures of consciousness in late medieval philosophy and theology, in which Arabic, Patristic, and Aristotelian conceptual strategies encountered one another. Nowhere did Weber analyze in greater detail the cognitive structures that crystallized out along the independent paths of rationalization of religious and metaphysical worldviews. For that reason, it did not become sufficiently clear that there is an *additional step* between the results of worldview rationalization and the understanding of the world that is in a specific sense "modern."

The unity of rationalized worldviews that refer, in a theological vein, to the creation, or in a metaphysical vein, to the whole of what exists, is anchored in concepts like "God," "being," or "nature," in ultimate principles or "beginnings"; while all arguments can be traced back to such beginnings, the latter are not themselves exposed to argumentative doubt. In these basic concepts, descriptive, normative, and expressive aspects are still fused; precisely in these "beginnings" there lives on something of mythical thought.[53] This protects the rationalized worldviews, *as* worldviews, from consequences that would endanger the tradition-securing modes of pious belief or reverential contemplation. By contrast, modern modes of thought do not recognize any such preserves, any such exemptions from the critical power of hypothetical thought, either in ethics or in science. In order to remove this barrier, it was first necessary to generalize the level of learning that was attained with the conceptual apparatus of religious-metaphysical worldviews, that is, to apply the modes of thought achieved in ethical and cognitive rationalization consistently to profane domains of life and experience. This was possible in turn only with the reversal of just those uncouplings to which the high forms of religious ethics of conviction and theoretically grounded cosmology owe their emergence. I am referring to the break of the ascetic search for salvation with the profane orders of this world and the separation of contemplative devotion from those same orders.

If Weber's approach is consistently carried through, there are two problems at the threshold of the modern world that had to be resolved before the rationalization potential of the Occidental tradition could be released and cultural rationalization could be transformed into societal rationalization. The religious asceticism that flowered in medieval monastic orders had to penetrate all *extrareligious departments of life,* so that profane actions were also subjected to the maxims of the ethic of conviction (which was at first anchored in religion). Weber locates this process in the emergence of the Protestant ethic of the calling. By contrast, he shows less interest in a parallel development, the emergence of modern science (without which the development of modern law is also incomprehensible). In this area the uncoupling of theory from the *experiential domains of practice*— particularly from those of social labor—had to be overcome. Theoretical argumentation had to be rejoined above all with those experiential domains accessible from the technical perspective of the craftsman. The solution to this second problem came in the form of the experimental natural sciences.[54] The social carriers of those strands of tradition that were combined, amazingly, in modern science—the Scholastics, the Humanists, and above all the engineers and artists of the Renaissance—played a role in releasing for purposes of research practice the potential stored in cognitively rationalized worldviews—a role similar to that played by the Protestant sects in transposing ethically rationalized worldviews into everyday practice.[55]

3. Modernization as Societal Rationalization: The Role of the Protestant Ethic

The cognitive potential that emerged with consistently and thoroughly rationalized worldviews could not have an overall impact on those traditional societies in which the process of disenchantment took place. It was set free only in modern societies; and this process of implementation meant the modernization of society.[1] It involved a combination of external factors, which prompted the differentiation of a market-regulated economic system and a complementary state apparatus,[2] with those structures of consciousness that had emerged from the tension-filled syntheses of the Judaeo-Christian, Arabic, and Greek traditions and were, so to speak, available at the cultural level.

Since Weber regards ideas and interests as equally primary, the process of modernization can be read from "above" and likewise from "below": as the motivational anchoring and embodiment of structures of consciousness, and also as the innovative mastery of conflicts of interest arising from problems of economic reproduction and the struggle for political power. The transition to modern society calls, of course, for a complex explanation that takes into account the interplay of ideas and interests without falling back on a priori assumptions regarding one-sided causal dependencies (in the sense of a naive idealism or materialism). In describing modernization processes—that is, the emergence of capitalist society and of the European system of states and their development since the eighteenth century—as a process of rationalization, Weber adopts the perspective "from above" suggested by his studies in the sociology of religion. He investigates how the cognitive potential arising from the rationalization of worldviews becomes operative at the societal level.

On the one hand, a decentered understanding of the world opens up the possibility of dealing with the world of facts in a cognitively objectified [*versachlicht*] manner and with the world of interpersonal relations in a legally and morally objectified manner; on the other hand, it offers the possibility of a subjectivism freed from imperatives of objectification in dealing with individualized needs, desires, and feelings [*Bedürfnisnatur*]. The transfer of this understanding of the world from the level of cultural tradition to the level of institutionalized social action can be traced along three paths. The first path, which Weber himself largely neglects, was cleared by *social movements* that were inspired by traditionalistic and rather defensive attitudes, as well as by modern conceptions of justice, that is, by ideas of bourgeois and, later, of socialist provenance. The second path leads to *cultural systems of action* specialized in processing the differentiated elements of cultural tradition; by the eighteenth century there had arisen a scientific enterprise organized into academic disciplines, a university-based jurisprudence, and an informal legal public, as well as an artistic enterprise organized through the market. At the same time, the church lost its global responsibility for the interpretation of the world; along with its diaconal functions, it maintained a partial responsibility for moral-practical questions, in competition with secular authorities. Weber's attention to the cultural sociology of modernity is also secondary. He directs his attention to the third path, the royal road of rationalization: between the sixteenth and the eighteenth centuries there arose in Europe a broadly effective *institutionalization of purposive-rational action* with structural effects on society as a whole.

The two institutional complexes in which Weber sees modern structures of consciousness mainly embodied—and which he regards as exemplary for spelling out the process of societal rationalization—are the capitalist economy and the modern state. What is "rational" about these? From his sociologies of economics and politics one gets the impression that when he speaks of societal rationalization Weber has before him the *organizational model* actualized in the capitalist enterprise and in modern governmental institutions. According to Weber, the rationality of these forms of enterprise [*Betrieb*] and institution (or compulsory association, *Anstalt*) consists in the fact that at first entrepreneurs and officials, and then also workers and employees, are obliged to act purposive-rationally. From an organizational point of view, what is characteristic of both capitalist enterprise and modern state administration is "the concentration of the material means of operation" in the hands of the rationally calculating entrepreneur or leader.

> The relative independence of the artisan, the producer under the putting-out system, the free seigneurial peasant, the

traveling associate in a *commenda* relationship, the knight and vassal, rested on their ownership of the tools, supplies, finances and weapons with which they fulfilled their economic, political and military functions and maintained themselves. In contrast, the hierarchical dependence of the wage worker, the administrative and technical employee, the assistant in the academic institute, as well as that of the civil servant and the soldier is due to the fact that in their case the means indispensable for their undertakings and for their economic existence are in the hands of the entrepreneur or the political ruler . . . This all-important economic foundation: the "separation" of the worker from the material means of operation—from the means of production in the economy, from the means of war in the military, from the means of administration in public administration, from the means of research in universities and laboratories, and from financial means in all these cases—is the common and decisive basis of the modern state in its political, cultural and military operations and of the private capitalist economy.[3]

This concentration of material means is a necessary condition for the institutionalization of purposive-rational action. Moreover, an administration that works in a purposive-rational way and is, therefore, calculable is necessary for the purposive-rational decision making of capitalist entrepreneurs.

In a historical perspective too, the "progress" toward the bureaucratic state, adjudicating and administering according to rationally established laws and regulations, is very closely related to modern capitalist development. The modern capitalist enterprise rests (internally) primarily on calculation. It requires for its existence a legal and administrative system whose functioning can be rationally calculated, at least in principle, on the basis of fixed general norms, just like the expected performance of a machine.[4]

The reference point from which Weber investigates *societal* rationalization is, therefore, *the purposive rationality of entrepreneurial activity* as it is institutionalized in the capitalist enterprise. From this he derives additional functional requirements: (a) purposive-rational action orientations on the part of a labor force that is integrated into a systematically organized production process; (b) an economic environment that is calculable for capitalist business enterprise, that is, markets for goods, capital, and labor; (c) a legal system and a state administration that can guarantee this calculability; and therefore (d) a state apparatus that provides sanctions for the law and itself institutionalizes purposive-rational action orientations in public administration. From this point of reference, we get a clear view of the central line of questioning that makes it possible to treat modernization as societal rationalization. How is the *institutionalization* of purposive-rational action orientations in the domain of social labor possible?

Societal rationalization consists in the establishment of subsystems of purposive-rational action and, indeed, in the forms of the capitalist enterprise and the modern governmental institution. What calls for explanation here is not the purposive rationality of economic and administrative action but its institutionalization. And this cannot be explained in turn by reference to purposive-rational regulations; the *normative regulation [Normierung] of purposive-rational action* entails a form of social integration that *anchors* the structures of purposive rationality in the personality system and in the system of institutions. As indicated, this specific form of social integration requires:

1. An ethic of conviction that systematizes all spheres of life and anchors purposive-rational action orientations in the personality system in a value-rational way (Protestant ethic); further,

2. A social subsystem that guarantees cultural reproduction of the corresponding value orientations (religious congregation and family); and

3. A system of compulsory norms that is suited by its formal structure to require of actors, as legitimate behavior, the purposive-rational, exclusively success-oriented pursuit of their own interests in an ethically neutralized domain (civil law).

Weber is of the opinion that these innovations came to pass through an institutional embodiment of those structures of consciousness that had resulted from the ethical rationalization of worldviews. This interpretation distinguishes him from functionalist theorists of modernization.[5]

On the other hand, it is important to see that Weber approaches the modernization problematic from a specific, characteristically restricted point of view. His approach offers advantages from the standpoint of research strategy, but it does not

220   REASON AND THE RATIONALIZATION OF SOCIETY

exhaust the explanatory potential of his own two-stage theory. If we call to mind the systematic construction that underlies Weber's rationalization theory—which he did not himself make sufficiently explicit—the line of questioning suggested by his analysis of world religions becomes clear. I summarized the fruits of this analysis in the following terms: modern structures of consciousness emerged from the universal-historical process of worldview rationalization, that is, from the disenchantment of religious-metaphysical worldviews. These structures were present in a certain way at the level of cultural tradition; but in the feudal society of the European High Middle Ages they penetrated only a relatively small carrier stratum of religious virtuosos, partly within the Church, above all in monastic orders, and later also in the universities. The structures of consciousness locked up in the cloisters needed to be implemented in broader strata before the new ideas could bind, reorient, permeate social interests, and rationalize the profane orders of life. From this perspective the question arises: How did the structures of the lifeworld familiar in traditional societies have to change before the cognitive potential that resulted from religious rationalization could be fully exploited at a societal level and embodied in the structurally differentiated orders of life of a society modernized in this way?

This counterfactual line of inquiry is unusual for an empirical sociologist; but it springs from the approach chosen by Weber—a theory that separates internal and external factors, that reconstructs the internal history of worldviews and encounters the independent logics of culturally differentiated value spheres. For such a theory opens up possibilities of learning that are grounded in a developmental logic and that cannot be described in a third-person attitude, but can only be reconstructed in the performative attitude of participants in argumentation. The theory of rationalization makes it possible to pose counterfactual questions that would, of course—and this is the ineliminable Hegelian element still in Weber—not be accessible *for us* who pursue such a theoretical strategy if we were not able to find heuristic support in the *internal* development of the cultural systems of action—science, law, morality, and art—and if we did not *know* in an exemplary way how the *possibilities* of expanding cognitive-instrumental, moral-practical, and aesthetic-expressive knowledge—possibilities that are grounded *in abstracto* through the modern understanding of the world, that is, in terms of developmental logic—can look *in concreto*.[6]

Against this background, an analysis of the emergence and development of capitalist society, or of modern social systems in general, set out in terms of a theory of rationalization would have to proceed from the question of whether the path of rationalization taken in Europe is one among various systematically possible paths. The question arises, whether the modernization that was established with capitalism should be described as a merely partial realization of modern structures of consciousness, and, if so, how the selective pattern of capitalist rationalization can be explained.

It is interesting that Weber did not pursue the systematic line of his two-stage approach, moving from cultural to societal rationalization. Instead, he began with the fact that the purposive rationality of entrepreneurial activity was institutionalized in the capitalist enterprise and believed that the explanation of this fact provided the key to the explanation of capitalist modernization. Unlike Marx, who proceeds here to reflections on the labor theory of value, Weber explains the institutionalization of purposive-rational economic action first by way of the Protestant vocational culture and subsequently by way of the modern legal system. Because they embody posttraditional legal and moral representations, both of these make possible a societal rationalization in the sense of an expansion of the legitimate orders of purposive-rational action. With them arises a new form of social integration that can satisfy the functional imperatives of the capitalist economy. Weber did not hesitate to equate *this* particular historical form of rationalization with rationalization of society *as such*.

That is to say, Weber takes into consideration the *horizon of possibilities* opened by the modern understanding of the world *only* to the extent that it serves to explain the core phenomenon he identified in advance; he sees in the latter the exemplary form of implementation of socially effective rationality. This assessment of the capitalist enterprise is suggested, for one thing, by the fact that the institutionalization of purposive-rational entrepreneurial activity is, from a functional point of view, actually of central importance for modern societies; on the other hand, however, it is suggested by the place Weber gives to the element of purposive rationality at the level of action orientations. As we shall see, in the transition from cultural to societal rationalization, there is a noticeable and consequential *narrowing* of the concept of rationality in Weber's action theory—which is, in any case, tailored to the type of purposive-rational action. Thus Weber starts *immediately* from the actually existing forms of Occidental rationalism, without viewing them against the counterfactually projected possibilities of a rationalized lifeworld. To be sure, he cannot make the residual problems of his wideranging theoretical approach disappear without a trace. The repressed problems turn up again in his reflections on the state of our times, where he implicitly relies on standards by which he can assess and criticize a rationality that has shrunken to a totalized purposive rationality. Thus the systematic construction behind the two-stage theory of societal rationalization, which is not exhausted by the descriptive elements of *Economy and Society,* reappears in Weber's diagnosis of the present with regard to contemporary capitalism.

I want first (A) to examine the role that Weber ascribes to the Protestant ethic in connection with the rise of capitalism, in order then (B) to formulate some guiding principles for a model of societal rationalization against which the Occidental path of development might be assessed.

A.—According to Weber's own understanding, his studies on the Protestant ethic relate to a key variable in the whole cultural development of the Occident. He regards modern vocational culture not only in general as an offspring of modern structures of consciousness, but as precisely that implementation of the ethic of conviction through which the purposive rationality of entrepreneurial activity was motivationally secured in a way that had important consequences for establishing the capitalist enterprise. From the point of view of his theoretical strategy, the studies on Protestantism occupy a central position. Nonetheless, their position is methodologically restricted in many respects. (a) They serve an analysis "from above," focusing on the motivational anchoring and institutional embodiment of ideas, on the exploitation of a problem-solving potential that had emerged in a developmental-logical process; and thus they stand in need of being complemented by an analysis "from below," by an investigation of external factors and developmental dynamics. (b) Furthermore, these studies are set out in what we would today call a "structuralist" perspective; they do not treat of causal relations but of "elective affinities" between the Protestant ethic and the spirit of capitalism that has congealed in the modern vocational culture. For this reason, they cannot meet Weber's own demand for an analysis of "how Protestant asceticism was in turn influenced in its development and its character by the totality of socio-cultural conditions, especially economic."[7] (c) These studies also fail to allow for comparisons among the different components of the stratified lifeworlds drawn into the whirl of rationalization, and still less for weighing the different life-styles as these are determined in more cognitive-instrumental, more aesthetic-expressive, or more moral-political ways. (d) Of primary importance for our purposes is the fact that these studies do *not* take up the question of how *selectively* that understanding of the world that is expressed in ethically rationalized worldviews finds its way into the Protestant vocational culture. It is only in the context of these *further* questions—to which Weber elsewhere makes references that are today still actual[8]—that the role of the Protestant ethic in the explanation of Occidental rationalism could be determined. I shall leave these questions to one side, with the exception of the last.

As mentioned above, according to Calvinist doctrine successful activity in one's calling does not count directly as a means for *attaining* salvation but as an outward sign for *ascertaining* a state of grace that is in principle uncertain. By means of this ideological connecting link, Weber explains the functional significance that Calvinism gained for the spread of innerworldly-ascetic attitudes, but especially for an objectified, systematized conduct of life centered around purposive-rational activity in one's calling. Weber does not want to explain why the Catholic inhibitions against striving for commercial gain were dropped; he wants rather to explain what made possible the changeover "from economic profit when the occasion arises to an economic *system*," the development "from the romance of economic adventure to a rational economic *method* of life."[9] In Calvinism and in the Protestant sects, Weber discovers the *teachings* that singled out the methodical conduct of life as a path to salvation. In the life of religious congregations, which also served as an inspiration to family upbringing, he finds the *institution* that saw to the influence of those teachings on socialization in the carrier strata of early capitalism.

> The God of Calvinism demanded of his believers not single good works, but a life of good works combined into a unified *system*. There was no place for the very human Catholic cycle of sin, repentance, atonement, release, followed by renewed sin. Nor was there any balance of merit for a life

as a whole which could be adjusted by temporal punishments or the Church's means of grace. The moral conduct
of the average man was thus deprived of its planless and
unsystematic character and subjected to a consistent *method*
for conduct as a whole. It is no accident that the name of
"Methodists" stuck to the participants in the last great
revival of Puritan ideas in the eighteenth century, just as the
term "Precisians," which has the same meaning, was applied
to their spiritual ancestors in the seventeenth century. For
only by a fundamental change in the whole meaning of life
at every moment and in every action could the effects of
grace transforming a man from the *status naturae* to the *status
gratiae* be proved. The life of the saint was directed solely
toward a transcendent end, salvation. But precisely for that
reason it was thoroughly rationalized in this world and
dominated entirely by the aim of adding to the glory of God
on earth.[10]

In this passage Weber emphasizes above all the feature of
Calvinism that constrains its followers to strip everyday practice
of its nonsystematic character, that is, to carry out the search
for salvation in such a way that ethical conviction, principled
morality penetrates *all* spheres and phases of life to the same
extent. The remark about the life of the "saint" alludes to an additional feature of sectarian piety, and it is only this that explains
why the Protestant ethic made possible not only innerworldly
asceticism in general, but, in particular, the action orientations
characteristic of the methodical conduct of life of early capitalist
entrepreneurs: the systematic character of life conduct that comes
about because the layman, unable to rely on priestly sacramental
grace or on the assistance of an official establishment for dis-
pensing grace—and this means, unable to divide up his lifeworld
into those spheres of life relevant to salvation and those not—
regulates his life autonomously according to principles of a postconventional morality.

The conduct of life that Weber calls "methodical" is characterized in particular by the fact that the vocational sphere is
"objectified" [*versachlicht*]; this means that it is morally segmented
and morally superelevated. Interactions *within* the sphere of labor
in one's calling are morally neutralized to the degree that communicative action can be detached from norms and values and
switched over to the success-oriented pursuit of one's own interests. At the same time, success in one's calling is connected with

the individual's redemptory fate in such a way that labor in one's calling, *taken as a whole,* is ethically charged and dramatized. This moral anchoring of a sphere of purposive-rational testing in one's calling—a sphere that is set free from traditional morality—is connected with a feature of the Protestant ethic only alluded to in the quotation above; namely the restriction of the ethic of conviction embodied in salvation religion through a particularism of grace, thus eliminating the Catholic coexistence of monastic piety, priestly and lay ethics in favor of an elitist separation between the religiosity of the virtuosos and that of the masses.

Drawing on Troeltsch's contrast between sects and churches, Wolfgang Schluchter has worked out the ethical consequences of the particularism of grace that was so pronounced in sectarian Protestantism: The inner isolation of the individual and the understanding of one's neighbor as an other who is neutralized in strategic contexts of action are the two most striking consequences.

> Thus ascetic Protestantism formulates for laymen an ethic of religious virtuosos which strikes the normal Catholic as inhuman. . . . Its individualism does not lead back to the godly community of love of primitive Christianity. It does indeed allow for . . . the idea of God's children, but not for that of God's *community.* . . Thus the religious ethic of ascetic Protestantism is a *monological* ethic of individuation with *unbrotherly* consequences. It is precisely in this that I find its developmental potential.[11]

Schluchter sees this potential for development not in an ethical rationalization of the conduct of life per se, but particularly in the objectification of interpersonal relations that is necessary if the capitalist entrepreneur is to be able to act in an ethically neutralized domain in a continuously purposive-rational manner, that is, in an objectivating attitude.

To be sure, Weber supposed that objectification [*Versachlichung*], in the sense of the strategic objectification [*Vergegendständlichung*] of interpersonal relations, is the only possible road to a rational loosening of life-relations that are traditional, habitual, and conventionally regulated. Schluchter is of the same opinion. The passage quoted above continues: The ethic of ascetic Protestantism "not only places the individual's relationship to God above his relations to other men, as do in the final analysis all consistent Christian forms of salvation religion;

it also gives these relations a new meaning—they are no longer interpreted in terms of piety. With this it produces motivation for objectifying first the religious relations between men and then their extrareligious relations."[12] As opposed to this, it is important to keep in mind that the posttraditional legal and moral representations, as soon as they break through to the level of legitimate orders, are per se incompatible with the traditional foundations of substantial life-relations guided by piety. In principle, the spell of traditionalism could also have been broken without separating off an ethically neutralized system of action. As we have seen, ethical rationalization brings with it a formal concept of the world as the totality of legitimately regulated interpersonal relations, within which the autonomously acting individual can morally prove himself. This kind of objectification, which devalues all traditional norms to mere conventions, already destroys the legitimating foundations of piety. For this it is not necessary to have the special kind of objectification that makes possible the segmenting of a legally organized domain of strategic action—though the latter is indeed functionally necessary for capitalist economic relations.

Max Weber explicitly rejected the possibility of a development of this kind. But it is interesting to note that he does not ground this, as one might have expected, by pointing empirically to the developmental dynamics of an economic system whose functional imperatives can be met only by an ethic that provides a value-rational anchor for setting free strategic action in the sphere of social labor. He appeals instead to a developmental-logical fact, namely to the structural incompatibility of such a consistently ethically rationalized religion of salvation with the impersonal orders of a rationalized economy and a secularized politics. Because of the systematic significance of this thesis, I would like to present the argument in some detail.

First, Weber regards the Christian ethic of brotherliness as an exemplary form of a rationally worked out ethic of conviction.

> The more rationally the idea of salvation was construed and the more it was sublimated into an ethic of conviction, the more the imperatives that issue from the ethic of reciprocity among neighbors were heightened, both externally and internally. Externally they were heightened into a communism of loving brethren, internally to the disposition of *caritas*, love for the sufferer as such, for one's neighbor, for mankind, and finally for one's enemy.[13]

The strictly universalistic conception of moral principles, the form of autonomous self-control on the basis of internalized and highly abstract action orientations, and the model of a complete reciprocity of relations among members of an unlimited communication community—these are the features of a religious ethic of brotherliness that emerged from the "new social community" of a "soteriological religion of congregations" created by religious prophecies, wherever the ethical rationalization of salvation religion was pushed forward with great consistency.[14]

The *Zwischenbetrachtung,* "Religious Rejections of the World and Their Directions," can be read as an extended argument for the view that this essentially communicative ethic comes more sharply into contradiction with the "unbrotherly" innerworldly orders of life the more thoroughly the latter are rationalized. "The more the world of the modern, rational, capitalist economy followed its own immanent laws, the less accessible it became to any imaginable relationship with a religious ethic of brotherliness."[15] For here, as in politics, this ethic would have to function as a "restraint on formal rationality." The universalistic ethic of brotherliness clashes with the forms of economic-administrative rationality in which the economy and the state are objectified into an unbrotherly cosmos. "As rational economic and political actions follow laws of their own, so every other rational action within the world remains inescapably bound to the unbrotherly conditions of the world that must serve as its means or its ends; hence all rational action somehow comes into tension with the ethic of brotherliness."[16] This conflict, structurally grounded in the opposition between brotherliness and unbrotherliness, can be defused in only two ways: either through withdrawal into the "acosmic brotherliness" of Christian mysticism, or by taking the path of innerworldly asceticism and thereby entering upon

the paradox of the Protestant ethic of vocation. As a religion of virtuosos, Puritanism renounced the universalism of love and rationally bound all work in this world to serving God's will and testing one's own state of grace. God's positive will, in its ultimate meaning, was quite incomprehensible; yet in this way it could at least be recognized. In this respect, Puritanism accepted the objectification of the economic cosmos, which, with the whole world, it devalued as creaturely and depraved. It regarded this as willed by God and as providing material for fulfilling one's duty. At bottom, this meant renouncing salvation in principle as a goal for

every man, in favor of a groundless and always only particular grace. In truth, this standpoint of unbrotherliness was
no longer a genuine religion of salvation.[17]

The regression of the ascetic ethic of vocation—with its egocentric
foreshortening, particularism of grace, and conformity to the unbrotherliness of the capitalist economy—behind the level already
attained in the communicatively developed ethic of brotherliness,
could scarcely be more bluntly formulated. Yet Weber did not
glean theoretical fruit from this insight, which is even less understandable if one follows his analysis of the subsequent fate of
the Protestant ethic in the course of capitalist development.

The Protestant ethic of the calling fulfills necessary conditions for the emergence of a motivational basis for purposive-
rational action in the sphere of social labor. With the value-
rational anchoring of purposive-rational action orientations, it
satisfies, to be sure, only the *starting* conditions of capitalist
society; it gets capitalism underway, without, however, being able
to secure the conditions for its own stabilization. In Weber's view,
the subsystems of purposive-rational action form an environment
that is destructive of the Protestant ethic in the long run; this
is all the more so, the more these systems develop in accord with
the immanent laws of capitalist growth and of the reproduction
of state power. The moral-practical rationality of the ethic of
conviction cannot itself be institutionalized in the society whose
start it makes possible. In the long run, it is replaced instead by
a utilitarianism that owes its existence to an empiricist reinterpretation of morality, namely to a pseudomoral revaluation of purposive rationality, and that no longer has an internal relation to the
moral sphere of value.

How does Weber explain this self-destructive pattern of
societal rationalization? The Protestant ethic had already stripped
away the element of brotherliness; from then on, only its embed-
dedness in the context of a salvation religion as such could bring
it into opposition with the conditions of modern life. In fact it
is the competition with scientifically rationalized patterns of
interpretation and orders of life that decides the fate of religion
and therewith, Weber believes, the fate of religiously grounded
ethics as well.

The general result of the modern form of thoroughly rationalizing our conception of the world and our way of life—theo-

retically and practically, intellectually and purposively—has been that religion has been shifted into the realm of what is—from the standpoint of the intellectual articulation of a worldview—the irrational; and this has been all the more the case, the further this particular type of rationalization has progressed.[18]

In the *Zwischenbetrachtung*, Weber works out the basis of this conflict in sharper detail.

> The rational knowledge to which ethical religiosity had itself appealed followed its own autonomous and innerworldly norms. It fashioned a cosmos of truths which no longer had anything to do with the systematic postulates of a rational religious ethic—postulates to the effect that the world as a cosmos must satisfy the demands of this ethic or evince some "meaning" or other. On the contrary, rational knowledge had to reject this claim in principle. The cosmos of natural causality and the postulated cosmos of ethical causality stood in irreconcilable opposition. And although the science that created this cosmos seemed unable to answer with certainty the question of its own ultimate presuppositions, it came forward in the name of "intellectual integrity" with the claim of being the only possible form of a reasoned view of the world. Thus, like all cultural values, the intellect also created an unbrotherly aristocracy, based on the possession of rational culture and independent of all personal ethical qualities.[19]

This explanation of the self-destructive pattern of societal rationalization is unsatisfactory because Weber still owes us a demonstration that a moral consciousness guided by principles can survive only in a religious context. He would have to explain why embedding a principled ethic in a salvation religion, why joining moral consciousness to interests in salvation, are just as indispensable for the *preservation* of moral consciousness as, from a genetic standpoint, they undoubtedly were for the *emergence* of this stage of moral consciousness. For this thesis there exist neither (a) convincing empirical evidence, nor (b) strong systematic arguments.

a) Weber's research program, which was to make it possible to estimate "the cultural significance of Protestantism in relation to the other plastic elements of modern culture,"[20] was never carried through. It was supposed to cover, among other things, the socioethical influence of humanism as well as of philosophical and scientific empiricism. Weber would have had to deal with the traditions that flowed into the rationalism of the Enlightenment and promoted a secularized, lay morality in bourgeois strata. And when one considers the effects of an emancipation from the world of Catholic ecclesiastical piety, these traditions were altogether the equivalent of the Protestant ethic. Bernard Groethuysen's well known 1927 study[21] focuses on one such case: the development in the French bourgeoisie of a bourgeois moral consciousness that was autonomous in relation to the Church. He relies for the most part on sermons from the seventeenth and eighteenth centuries, as well as on pedagogical and philosophical treatises from the second half of the eighteenth century. From these sources there emerges a picture of a principled ethic that is removed from religious contexts, and through which the bourgeois strata set themselves off from both the clergy and from the common people caught up in naive piety. The bourgeois "knows very well how to distinguish here: for him, worldly morality and science, for the others, religion."[22] Groethuysen shows how the French bourgeoisie of the time grows away from the Catholic world of ideas and develops the secularized views of life that "are needed to regulate socio-economic life and to bring their demands to bear."[23] Bourgeois morality is self-sufficient. Whether or not the individual bourgeois remains Catholic, ecclesiastical Catholicism loses its action-orienting power over the everyday practice of the bourgeois strata. "The bourgeois found his form of life, his morality, which stood in close connection with the bourgeois conditions of life."[24]

b) The thesis that a moral consciousness at a posttraditional stage cannot be stabilized without being embedded in religion also lacks systematic grounds. If the ethical rationalization of religious worldviews leads to the differentiation of a value sphere specialized in moral-practical questions, we would expect that ethical rationalization would continue within this value sphere, and indeed according to the inner logic of a practical reason set off from descriptive claims and expressive tasks. It is along this line that we find the philosophical, profane ethics of the modern period, which lead through formalistic ethics of the Kantian type to the discourse ethics of the present, which connect up partly with Kant and partly with rational natural law, but also adopt utilitarian perspectives. With a view to Weber, one might call these "cognitivist ethics of responsibility."[25]

Of course, Weber himself, particularly in methodological

contexts, starts from a state of the argument determined by the positivism of his time, according to which ethical value judgments express purely subjective attitudes and are not capable of being grounded in an intersubjectively binding way. This stands in contradiction to his own arguments for the superiority of ethics of responsibility over ethics of conviction. Weber himself assumes the role of an ethical systematist when he attempts to demonstrate the limits of the religious ethic of brotherliness as an ethic of conviction. It provides

> no means of deciding even the very first question: Whence is the ethical value of an act to be determined in the individual case? In terms of success or in terms of some ethically determined intrinsic value of the act itself? That is, whether and to what extent the responsibility of the actor for the results sanctifies the means or, conversely, whether the value of the intention [Gesinnung] that guides the action justifies him in refusing to take responsibility for consequences, in pushing them onto God or to the wickedness and foolishness of the world that are permitted by God? The sublimation of religious ethics into an ethic of conviction will incline men towards the latter alternative: "The Christian does right and leaves success to God."[26]

With these and similar arguments[27] Weber entered upon a philosophical discussion that would have enabled him to work out the intrinsic meaning of moral-practical questions, the logic of justifying norms of action, after morality had become detached from the conceptual framework of religious (and metaphysical) worldviews. If the possibility of a rational moral theory—not in the sense of a scientific theory, but of one compatible with the requirements of modern scientific thought as regards the vindication of claims—cannot be excluded from the start, the cognitive dissonance between a scientifically enlightened everyday consciousness and the Protestant ethic of the calling would have to be explained in other ways, for example, through the special character of the particularism of grace. Then Weber's occasional remarks concerning the irrational character of the doctrine of election and of the form of life based upon it would have been given systematic significance.

The Protestant ethic is by no means the exemplary embodiment of the moral consciousness expressed to begin with in the religious ethic of brotherliness, but a distorted, highly irrational one. Rainer Döbert has given us a good analysis of the double face that the historically influential versions of the ethic of the calling present from a structural point of view.[28] With the Protestant ethic, structures of consciousness that had previously possessed, so to speak, only an extraterritorial significance were anchored in some of the strata bearing capitalism. However, the price of success in institutionalizing them was that a *selective utilization* of the structures of consciousness that had become in principle accessible. Döbert points above all to the particularism of grace of a God whose decrees are inscrutable, and to the merciless uncertainty of grace that had to be made psychologically bearable through auxiliary constructions of a more or less abstruse sort. This selectivity is also evident in the repressive features of religious sociation, as well as in the total inner isolation of the religious virtuoso who adapted himself to instrumental behavior even within his own congregation and in the rigidity of the control of instincts that precluded a free relationship of the individual to his own inner nature. In his essays on the Protestant sects, Weber does not at all conceal these disagreeable but thoroughly systematic features of the methodical-rational conduct of life.[29]

But if the Protestant ethic—both the doctrines that provide its context, as well as the forms of life and structures of personality in which it is embodied—may not be taken simply as the privileged expression of a principled morality, if we take seriously the partial character of this form of ethical rationalization, then those Protestant sects that, like the Anabaptists, wanted to institutionalize the universalistic ethic of brotherliness with fewer reservations—that is, *also* in new forms of social community and of political will-formation—appear in a new light.[30] These social movements, which did not want to divert the potential of ethically rationalized worldviews onto the tracks of disciplined labor *by privatized individuals,* but wanted rather to convert it into social-revolutionary forms of life, failed in this first attempt. For the *radicalized forms of life* did not correspond to the requirements of a capitalist economic ethic. These connections call for a more precise analysis. Nevertheless, our reflections suggest the following questions:

—Whether the methodical conduct of life of those Protestant groups studied by Weber achieved its historical significance only because it actualized a pattern of posttraditional morality that was functional for capitalist enterprise;—

and whether its instability, as observed by Weber, is due to the fact that capitalist development permits posttraditional action orientations only in a restricted form, in the sense that it promotes a pattern of rationalization such that cognitive-instrumental rationality penetrates beyond the economy and state into other spheres of life and there enjoys a preeminence at the expense of moral-practical and aesthetic-practical rationality.[31]

B.   These questions lie along a line of argument that Weber did not pursue, although it arises out of his two-stage theoretical approach. Weber's empirical investigations are focused directly on the problem of the rise of capitalism and the question of how purposive-rational action orientations could in fact be institutionalized in the phase of its emergence. He thereby relates societal rationalization from the start to the aspect of purposive rationality; he does not view the historical profile of this process against the background of what was *structurally possible*. But this more complex line of questioning reappears in his diagnosis of the times. Weber is there troubled by the fact that subsystems of purposive-rational action are breaking loose from their value-rational foundations and becoming independent, following their own dynamics. I shall take up his thesis of a loss of freedom below. Weber connects it with the results of his comparative sociology of religion, namely, with the thesis that the structures of consciousness differentiated into independent cultural value spheres are embodied in correspondingly *antagonistic* orders of life. The theme of the *Zwischenbetrachtung* is those *internally grounded* conflicts that, according to Weber, *have to* arise between a consistent ethic of brotherliness and the secular orders of a structurally differentiated society. I shall put to one side for now Weber's diagnostic reflections on the times which connect up with this theme. I would like first to extract the model of "value spheres" and "life-orders" on which these reflections are based.

The systematic viewpoint from which Weber set about his *Zwischenbetrachtung* is formulated in the famous sentence: "The rationalization and conscious sublimation of our relations to the various spheres of goods—internal and external, religious and secular—have pressed toward making us conscious of the inner logics of the individual spheres and their consequences, thereby letting them come into those tensions with one another that remain hidden in the originally naive relation to the external world."[32] The phrase "inner logics" refers to the "rational closure" of *ideas;* on the other hand, the possession of internal and external, ideal and material goods establishes *interest* positions. So long as we view ideas in themselves, they form *cultural value spheres;* as soon as they are connected with interests, they form *orders of life* that legitimately regulate the possession of goods. I would like now (a) to take up the systematic aspects of these life orders, and then (b) deal with their "inner logics," in order, finally, (c) to reexamine the question of the partial realization of modern structures of consciousness.

(a) In the *Zwischenbetrachtung* Weber does not draw a precise distinction between the level of cultural tradition and that of institutionalized action systems or orders of life. The religious ethic of brotherliness that provides the reference point for the comparison with the "orders and values of the world" is treated primarily in terms of *cultural symbolism,* as corresponds to the context of an analysis of worldviews. On the other hand, science and art appear rather under the aspect of orders of life, that is, as *cultural action systems* that have been differentiated out, together with the *social action systems* of the economy and the state. Nevertheless, the systematic thrust of Weber's basic concepts suggests the following differentiation between the level of cultural tradition and that of cultural actions systems (see Figure 8).

Figure 8
Cultural Complex

Cultural Value Spheres	Cognitive Ideas	Normative Ideas	Aesthetic Ideas
Cultural Action Systems: Possession of Ideal Goods	Scientific enterprise	Religious community	Artistic enterprise

The three cultural systems of action regulate the possession of ideal goods. Weber distinguishes from these the spheres of the possession of *worldly goods.* In modern societies, it is above all the ordinary goods—wealth and power—and the extraordinary goods —sexual (or erotically sublimated) love—which represent values around which orders of life crystallize. Thus there are five life-orders—that is, cultural and (in a narrower sense) social systems of action—with which the religious ethic of brotherliness can come into tension (see Figure 9).

In the *Zwischenbetrachtung* it is Weber's intention to analyze "the relations of tension between religion and the world," with the ethic of brotherliness forming the religious point of reference. On his analysis, conflicts must become all the sharper, the more the "relations of man to the different spheres of possession of external and internal goods" come to consciousness in all their specificity. And the further the orders of life are rationalized, the more clearly this is the case. The conflicts or "relations of tension" that interest Weber here do not arise externally, from incompatible interest positions, but internally, from the incompatibility of different structures. If, rather than directly following the text, we follow the systematic thrust of this line of inquiry, we have to turn first to the cultural value spheres, for these directly follow the intrinsic logics of ideas, whereas in the orders of life, ideas are already fused with interests into legitimate orders.

Figure 9
Life Orders that Come into Tension
with the Religious Ethic of Conviction

Interest in the Possession of / Cultural ideas	Ordinary		Extraordinary
Ideal Goods	Knowledge: scientific enterprise		Art: artistic enterprise
Worldly Goods	Wealth: economy	Power: politics	Love: hedonistic counter-cultures

(b) Weber contrasts science and art with the ethical sphere of value. We can recognize here the cognitive, normative, and expressive elements of culture that are differentiated out, each according to one universal validity claim. In these cultural value spheres are expressed the modern structures of consciousness that emerged from the rationalization of worldviews. As was pointed out above, this rationalization led to the formal concepts

of an objective, a social, and a subjective world, and to the corresponding basic attitudes in relation to a cognitively or morally
objectified external world and to a subjectivized inner world.
Furthermore, we distinguished the objectivating attitude toward
processes of external nature, the norm-conformative (or critical)
attitude toward legitimate orders of society, and the expressive
attitude toward the subjectivity of internal nature. The structures
of a decentered (in Piaget's sense) understanding of the world
that are decisive for modernity can be characterized by the fact
that the acting and knowing subject is able to assume *different
basic attitudes toward elements of the same world.* From the combination of basic attitudes and formal world-concepts there result
nine fundamental relations. The following scheme offers a guiding
thread, taken from the line of Weber's own thought, for the "rationalization of the relations of men to the different spheres" (see
Figure 10).

I cannot systematically examine these formal-pragmatic
relations here; I shall content myself with intuitive indications
of characteristic forms of expression, which can serve as illus-
trations. The cognitive-instrumental relation (1.1) can be exem-
plified by assertions, instrumental actions, observations, and so
forth; the cognitive-strategic relation (1.2) by social actions of the
purposive-rational type; the obligatory relation (2.2) by normatively regulated actions; presentation of self (3.2) by social actions
of the dramaturgical or self-presenting type. An objectivistic
relation to one's self (1.3) can find expression in certain theories
(for instance, of empiricist psychology or utilitarian ethics); a cen-
sorious relation to one's self (2.3) can be illustrated by superego
phenomena such as guilt feelings, as well as by defense reactions;
a sensual-spontaneous relation to one's self (3.3) can be found
in affective expressions, libidinal stirrings, creative performances, and the like. Trivial exemplifications of an aesthetic
relation to a nonobjectivated environment (3.1) are provided by
works of art, phenomena of style in general, but also by theories,
for example, in which a morphological way of looking at nature
finds expression. The phenomena that exemplify a moral-
practical, a "fraternal" relationship with nature are the least clear,
if one does not wish to have recourse to mystically inspired traditions or to taboos (such as vegetarian aversions), to the anthro-
pomorphizing treatment of animals, and so on.

Even this provisional attempt at characterization shows that
only a few of those pragmatic relations between actors and their

Figure 10
Formal-Pragmatic Relations

Worlds / Basic Attitudes	1. Objective	2. Social	3. Subjective
1. Objectivating	Cognitive-instrumental relation	Cognitive-strategic relation	Objectivistic relation to self
2. Norm-Conformative	Moral-aesthetic relation to a nonobjectivated environment	Obligatory relation	Censorious relation to self
3. Expressive		Presentation of self	Sensual-spontaneous relation to self

external or internal environments that became formally accessible through "disenchantment" were selected out and articulated into standardized forms of expression. The reasons for this differential exploitation of formal possibilities could be external or internal. It could reflect a culture-specific and society-specific exploitation of a potential for rationalization given with modern structures of consciousness, that is, a selective pattern of societal rationalization. But perhaps it is the case that only some of the formal-pragmatic relations are suitable for the accumulation of knowledge. Thus we have to try to identify those relations that are sufficiently productive from the standpoint of *acquiring knowledge* to permit, in Weber's terms, a development of cultural value spheres with their own inner logics. As I cannot here vindicate a systematic claim, I shall keep to Weber's statements. He is evidently of the view that only six of the classified actor-world relations can be "rationalized and consciously sublimated" (see Figure 11).

The objectivating attitude toward external nature and society circumscribes a complex of cognitive-instrumental rationality, within which the production of knowledge can take the form of scientific and technical progress (including social technologies). The fact that the area 1.3 (in Figure 11) is empty stands for the assumption that nothing can be learned in an objectivating attitude about inner nature qua subjectivity. The norm-conformative attitude toward society and inner nature circumscribes a

Figure 11
Rationalization Complexes

Worlds / Basic Attitudes	1 Objective	2 Social	3 Subjective	1 Objective
3 Expressive	Art			
1 Objectivating	▲Cognitive-instrumental rationality Science Technology	┆ ┆ Social ┆technologies ▼	X	
2 Norm-conformative	X	▲ Moral-practical rationality Law	┆ ┆Morality ▼	
3 Expressive		X	▲ Aesthetic-practical rationality Eroticism	┆ Art

complex of moral-practical rationality, within which the production of knowledge can take the form of a systematic treatment of legal and moral representations. The fact that the area 2.1 is empty signifies a scepticism concerning the possibility of giving a rational form to fraternal relations with a nonobjectivated nature—for instance, the form of a philosophy of nature that could compete with the modern sciences of nature.[33] Finally, the expressive attitude toward internal and external nature circumscribes a complex of aesthetic-practical rationality, within which the production of knowledge can take the form of authentic interpretations of needs, interpretations that have to be renewed in each historically changed set of circumstances. The fact that the area 3.2 is empty signals that expressively determined forms of interaction (for example, countercultural forms of life) do not form structures that are rationalizable in and of themselves, but are parasitic in that they remain dependent on innovations in the other spheres of value.

These three complexes of rationality, derived in formal-pragmatic terms from basic attitudes and world-concepts, point to just those three cultural value spheres that were differentiated out in modern Europe; but this is not in itself an objection against the systematic status of the schema. According to Weber, modern structures of consciousness are the product of a universal-historical process of disenchantment and thus do not merely reflect idiosyncratic traits of a particular culture. Of course, Weber's historical presentations do not satisfy systematic demands either. Perhaps an independent grounding could be gained from a theory of argumentation. On this point I can for the time being offer only a remark relating to research strategy.

If cultural value spheres are distinguished by a production of knowledge that is differentiated according to validity claims and rendered cumulative; and if the continuity of this knowledge can be guaranteed only by learning processes becoming reflective—that is, being coupled in feedback relations with specialized and institutionalized forms of argumentation—then we should be able to demonstrate, for each historically articulated sphere of value (which we derived from the combinations 1.1, 1.2; 2.2, 2.3; 3.3, 3.1), the existence of plausible relations to a typical form of argumentation specialized in accord with a universal validity claim. Our hypothesis is refuted if we cannot do so or, conversely, if we could in fact locate specialized forms of argumentation for the empty areas marked with an X (1.3, 2.1, 3.2), that is, for the domains of experience represented by them. It also suffices for falsification to show descriptively that there are cultures in which corresponding spheres of value, difficult for us to imagine, do appear with a correspondingly cumulative knowledge production. Weber's assessments of utilitarianism (1.3) and Bohemianism (3.2) are instructive in this connection. He regards both as incapable of stabilization because neither embodies a sphere of value endowed with its own inner logic. And Weber always considered relations with external nature of a moral sort—on the model of interaction (2.1)—merely as [an aspect of] that "enchanted garden" that had to disappear in the wake of the rationalization of other spheres of value and life.

(c) If we start from the view that modern structures of consciousness condense to the three complexes of rationality indicated above, then we can think of the structurally possible

rationalization of society as a combination of the corresponding ideas (from the domains of science and technology, law and morality, art and eroticism) with interests, and their embodiment in correspondingly differentiated orders of life. This (rather risky) model would enable us to state the necessary conditions for a nonselective pattern of rationalization: The three cultural value spheres have to be connected with corresponding action systems in such a way that the production and transmission of knowledge that is specialized according to validity claims is secured; the cognitive potential developed by expert cultures has, in turn, to be passed on to the communicative practice of everyday life and to be made fruitful for social action systems; finally, the cultural value spheres have to be institutionalized in such a balanced way that the life-orders corresponding to them are sufficiently autonomous to avoid being subordinated to laws instrinsic to heterogeneous orders of life. A selective pattern of rationalization occurs when (at least) one of the three constitutive components of the cultural tradition is not systematically worked up, or when (at least) one cultural value sphere is insufficiently institutionalized, that is, is without any structure-forming effect on society as a whole, or when (at least) one sphere predominates to such an extent that it subjects life-orders to a form of rationality that is alien to them.

Of course, Weber did not engage in counterfactual reflections of this sort. But with this as a foil, the systematic content of the *Zwischenbetrachtung* can be made quite clear.

(i) *Cognitive-instrumental rationality* is institutionalized in the scientific enterprise. At the same time, the development, in accord with their own laws, of the economic and political orders of life, which determine the structure of bourgeois society, proceeds according to the standards of formal rationality.

(ii) *Aesthetic-practical rationality* is institutionalized in the artistic enterprise. Of course, autonomous art has just as little structure-forming effect on society as a whole as do the shifting, unstable countercultures that form around this subsystem. On the other hand, the extraordinary values of this sphere form the focus for a hedonistic life-style directed to innerworldly salvation, the life-style of the "sensualist" who is reacting against the "pressure of the theoretical and practical" rationality of the ordinary "specialist," who is established in science, the economy, and the state.

(iii) The *moral-practical rationality* of the ethic of brotherliness found in salvation religions is incompatible with both the specialized and the pleasure-seeking man. The modern world is ruled by orders of life in which the other two complexes of rationality achieve domination and, in a kind of division of labor, establish a "world dominion of unbrotherliness." In the face of this world—objectified in a cognitive-instrumental manner and turned in the direction of the subjectivistic—moral representations that aim at an autonomy rooted in communicative reconciliation do not have a sufficient chance to establish themselves. The ethic of brotherliness finds no foothold in institutions through which it could culturally reproduce itself in the long run.

(iv) Not only the religious ethic of brotherliness, but also the form of ethics adapted to the "lovelessness of the objectified cosmos," namely the *Protestant ethic,* is in the long run ground down between the millstones of the two other complexes of rationality. At first it does come institutionally into force in Protestant vocational culture, so that the starting conditions for modernization are fulfilled; but the modernization process itself reacts back upon and undermines the value-rational foundations of purposive-rational action. According to Weber's diagnosis, the foundation of the vocational orientation in an ethic of conviction is washed away in favor of an instrumental attitude toward work interpreted in utilitarian terms.

In the end, the religiously articulated need that has been the stimulus to all forms of rationalization remains unsatisfied: the demand that "the course of the world, at least insofar as it touches the interests of men, be a somehow 'meaningful' process." What is paradoxical about the rationalization of society is the experience of the "meaninglessness of the purely inner-worldly perfection of self as a man of culture, hence of the ultimate value to which 'culture' has seemed reducible."[34]

If one represents the systematic content of the *Zwischenbetrachtung* in this way, it becomes clear that Weber's intuitions point in the direction of a selective pattern of rationalization, a jagged profile of modernization. Yet Weber speaks of paradoxes and not of the partial character of societal rationalization. In his view, the real reason for the dialectic of rationalization is not an unbalanced institutional embodiment of available cognitive potentials; he locates the seeds of destruction of the rationalization of the world in the very differentiation of independent cultural value spheres that released that potential and made that rationalization possible.

This idea retains a certain plausibility only so long as Weber does not take into account, with respect to the moral-practical complex of rationality, a form of the religious ethic of brotherliness secularized at the same level as modern science and autonomous art, a communicative ethic detached from its foundation in salvation religion; that is, so long as he remains generally fixated instead on the relations of tension between religion and the world.

It is striking, moreover, that modern law is accorded no systematic place in the *Zwischenbetrachtung.* It comes up only in the context of the order of the state, as an organizational means without moral-practical substance.[35] But modern law played a role in the institutionalization of purposive-rational action orientations similar to that played by the Protestant ethic of the calling. Without the legal regulation [*Verrechtlichung*] of capitalist economic relations, it is unimaginable that a subsystem of purposive-rational action, detached from its ethical-motivational basis, would have become automatic or self-stabilizing. For this reason, Weber could carry through the diagnosis of the present set forth in *Zwischenbetrachtung* only if he succeeded in uncoupling the development of modern law from the fate of moral-practical rationality and conceptualizing it as just a further embodiment of cognitive-instrumental rationality.

4. *The Rationalization of Law.*
Weber's Diagnosis of the Times

In Weber's theory of rationalization the development of law occupies a place as prominent as it is ambiguous. The ambiguity consists in the fact that the rationalization of law makes possible—or seems to make possible—both the institutionalization of purposive-rational economic and administrative action and the detachment of subsystems of purposive-rational action from their moral-practical foundations. In contrast, the methodical conduct of life counts per se as an embodiment of moral-practical structures of consciousness; but the principled ethic of the calling remains influential, in Weber's view, only so long as it is embedded in a religious context. As we have seen, the dialectic of scientific and religious development is supposed to provide empirical grounds for the view that, in consequence of the shaking of religious faith, ethical action orientations can no longer be reliably reproduced. This explanation could not hold in an analogous way for modern law, since the latter appeared from the start in secularized form. Thus in his sociology of law Weber pursues a different strategy than he does in his studies on the sociology of religion. Whereas in the case of the Protestant ethic he gives reasons why there can never be an enduring institutionalization of secularized moral-practical structures of consciousness, he *reinterprets* modern law in such a way that it is detached from that evaluative sphere and can appear from the start as an institutional embodiment of cognitive-instrumental rationality. This strategy stands in the context of a diagnosis of the times based on the line of thought sketched in the *Zwischenbetrachtung.* Thus before I take up (B) the rationalization of law, I would like to consider (A) the two most important elements of Weber's diagnosis.

A.—In his diagnosis of the times Weber keeps closer than usual to the theoretical perspective in which modernization is represented as a continuation of the world-historical process of disenchantment. The differentiation of independent cultural value spheres that is important for the phase of capitalism's *emergence,* and the growing autonomy of subsystems of purposive-rational action that is characteristic of the *development* of capitalist society since the late eighteenth century, are the two trends that Weber combines into an existential-individualistic critique of the present age. The first component is represented in the thesis of a *loss of meaning,* the second in the thesis of a *loss of freedom.* These two theses together still determine the underlying ideology—with its scepticism concerning progress—of those neoconservative social scientists who do not want completely to sacrifice their need for a worldview to their declared scientism.[1]

With the differentiation of autonomous cultural spheres of value, we also become aware of their inner logics. In Weber's view, this has two kinds of consequences. On the one hand, it first makes possible a rationalization of symbol systems under one (at a time) abstract standard of value (such as truth, normative rightness, beauty, authenticity); on the other hand, the meaning-giving unity of metaphysical-religious worldviews thereby falls apart. A competition arises among the autonomous value spheres which can no longer be settled from the superordinate standpoint of a divine or cosmological world-order. As soon as systems of action crystallize around those "ultimate ideas," these spheres of life "drift into the tensions with one another which remain hidden in the originally naive relation to the external world."[2] This central idea, which is the point of departure of the *Zwischenbetrachtung,* is illustrated in Figure 11 above.

To the degree that the inner logics of individual value spheres are transposed into the societal structures of correspondingly differentiated orders of life, *differences between validity claims* at the cultural level can become, at the societal level, tensions between institutionalized action orientations, that is, *conflicts of action.* In Figure 11 the arrows pointing in opposite directions designate the contrary basic attitudes that an actor can adopt in relation to the same domain of reality. In relation to external nature, he can adopt not only an objectivating attitude but an expressive one as well; in relation to society, not only a norm-conformative attitude but an objectivating one as well; and in relation to inner nature, not only an expressive attitude but a norm-conformative one as well. These possibilities of "switching over" are characteristic of the degrees of freedom of a decentered understanding of the world. But these same degrees of freedom can become a source of conflict as soon as different cultural value spheres *simultaneously* penetrate the same institutional domains, so that rationalization processes of different types compete with one another in the same place. Cognitive-instrumental, moral-practical, and aesthetic-expressive orientations of action ought not to become so independently embodied in antagonistic orders of life that they overburden the personality system's average capacity for integration and lead to permanent conflicts between life-styles.

The problem of how the unity of the lifeworld can be secured in the multiplicity of structures of social action and spheres of life has of course always existed. Differentiations already arise within segmentary tribal societies. There, antagonisms between different spheres of life can still be held in check by means of a mythical interpretation of the world: Each sphere is represented by a particular primordial power that communicates with all other powers. Polytheism is a late form of this mythical view, which makes it possible to personify the competition among life-problems as a struggle among the gods and to project it into the heavens. At the developmental level of civilizations, society is differentiated according to occupational groups and social strata, so that the unity of the lifeworld can no longer be so readily guaranteed by mythical interpretations of the world. Now religious-metaphysical worldviews carry out this unifying function, and all the more impressively the more they are rationally organized.

It is, however, just this integrative achievement that is placed in question in modern societies by the differentiation of cultural spheres of value. To the degree that the rationalization of worldviews issues in modern structures of consciousness, worldviews *as such* fall to pieces.

> The grandiose rationalism of an ethical-methodical conduct of life, which flows from every religious prophecy, dethroned this polytheism in favor of "the one thing that is needful." And then, faced with the realities of outer and inner life, it saw itself forced into the compromising and relativizing that is familiar to all of us from the history of Christianity. Today however it has become a religious commonplace. Many old gods arise from their graves, disenchanted and in the form of impersonal forces; they strive to gain power over our lives and resume again their eternal struggle with one another. What is hard for modern man, and especially for the younger generation, is to measure up to an everyday life of this kind. All that chasing after "experience" stems from this weakness; for it is a weakness not to be able to view face to face the grave countenance of the fate of our times.[3]

Both ethically rationalized religious worldviews and cognitively rationalized metaphysical worldviews still held together—in principles such as God, Nature, Reason, and the like—the three aspects under which the world can become accessible to rational treatment, as an objective or social or subjective world. They were thus able to impart a unitary sense to the life-conduct of those who oriented themselves according to these worldviews in their thought and action. In "Religious Rejections of the World and Their Directions" and "Science as a Profession," Weber develops the two correlated theses that, in light of the rational inner logics of the modern orders of life, ethical unification of the world in the name of a secularized faith has become just as impracticable as theoretical unification of the world in the name of science. Weber sees the sign of the age in the return of a new polytheism, in which the struggle among the gods takes on the depersonified, objectified form of an antagonism among irreducible orders of value and life. The rationalized world has become meaningless

> because the various value orders of the world stand in insoluble conflict with each other. The elder Mill. . .once said: If one proceeds from pure experience, one arrives at polytheism. This is a superficial formulation and it sounds paradoxical; and yet there is truth in it. If anything, we realize again today that something can be sacred not only in spite of its not being beautiful, but rather *because* and *insofar* as it is not beautiful. You will find this documented in the fifty-third chapter of the book of Isaiah and in the twenty-second Psalm. And since Nietzsche we realize that something can be beautiful, not only in spite of its not being good, but rather in that very respect in which it is not good. You will find this expressed earlier in the *Fleurs du Mal,* as Baudelaire entitled his volume of poems. And it is a commonplace that something can be true although, and in the respect that, it is not beautiful, not sacred, and not good. But these are only the most elementary cases of the struggle among the gods of the separate orders and values. . .It is as it was in the ancient world, which was not yet disenchanted of its gods and demons, only in a different sense. As Hellenic man at times sacrificed to Aphrodite and at other times to Apollo, and above all, everyone sacrificed to the gods of his city, so do we still nowadays, only in a way that is disenchanted and denuded of the mystical but inwardly genuine plasticity of that earlier behavior. And over these gods and their strug-

gles it is fate—and certainly not any "science"—that holds sway.[4]

With the formula of a "new polytheism," Weber gives expression to the thesis of a loss of meaning. In it is reflected an experience typical of his generation, the experience of nihilism that Nietzsche had dramatized so impressively. While the thesis itself is not original with Weber, the way in which he grounds it is more so—by reference to a dialectic that is supposedly inherent in the very process of disenchantment within the history of religion, that is, in the very freeing of modern structures of consciousness: reason splits itself up into a plurality of value spheres and destroys its own universality. Weber interprets this loss of meaning as an existential challenge to the individual to establish the unity which can no longer be established in the orders of society in the privacy of his own biography, with the courage of despair, the absurd hope of one who is beyond all hope. Henceforth the practical rationality that binds purposive-rational action orientations in a value-rational manner and provides them with grounds can find its place, if not in the charisma of new leaders, only in the personality of the solitary individual. This inner autonomy, which is to be heroically maintained, is threatened, because within modern society there is no longer any legitimate order that could guarantee the cultural reproduction of the corresponding value orientations and action dispositions.

The thesis of the growing independence of subsystems of purposive-rational action, as a threat to the freedom of the individual, does not follow without further ado from the first thesis. It is unclear how the two theses—regarding the loss of meaning and the loss of freedom—are connected. The famous passage in which Weber advances the latter thesis runs as follows:

> One of the fundamental elements of the spirit of modern capitalism—and not only of that but of all modern culture—viz. rational conduct on the basis of the idea of calling, was born—this is what this discussion has sought to demonstrate—from the spirit of Christian asceticism . . . for when ascetism was carried out of monastic cells into workaday life and began to dominate worldly morality, it did its part in building the vast and mighty cosmos of the modern economic order, which is bound to the technical and economic conditions of machine production. This cosmos today deter-

mines, with irresistible force, the lifestyles of all the individuals who are born into this mechanism, not only of those directly concerned with economic acquisition. Perhaps it will so determine them until the last ton of fossilized fuel is burnt. In Baxter's view, the concern with external goods should only lie on the shoulders of his saints like a "light cloak, which can be thrown aside at any moment." But fate has decreed that the cloak should become an iron cage. Since asceticism undertook to remodel the world and to work out its ideals in the world, material goods have gained an increasing and finally an inexorable power over the lives of men, as in no previous period of history. Today the spirit of religious asceticism has escaped from this cage—whether finally, who knows? But victorious capitalism, since it rests on mechanical foundations, needs its support no longer . . . No one knows who will live in this cage in the future, or whether at the end of this tremendous development entirely new prophecies will arise, or there will be a powerful rebirth of old ideas and ideals, or, if neither, mechanized petrification, embellished with a sort of convulsive self-importance. For then it might be said of the "last men" of this cultural development: "Specialists without spirit, sensualists without heart"; this nullity imagines that it has attained a level of civilization never before achieved.[5]

Weber treats the emergence and development of capitalism from the standpoint of the institutionalization of purposive-rational action orientations; in doing so, he comes across the roles of the Protestant ethic and modern law. He shows how, with their help, cognitive-instrumental rationality is institutionalized in the economy and the state. However, this does not of itself yield his pessimistic prediction of a reification of the subsystems into an "iron cage." Weber himself felt that this prognosis took him into the area of "judgments of value and of faith."[6] Nevertheless, the late essays ("Politics as a Vocation," "Science as a Vocation," "Religious Rejections of the World and Their Directions") convey the impression that the second thesis might not only be empirically supported, as the statement of a trend, but might be derived as a theoretical statement from the first thesis.[7] This attempt will not stand up under closer examination, as the following two considerations indicate.

To begin with, the first thesis is not plausible. It is, of course, true that with the appearance of modern structures of consciousness the immediate unity of the true, the good, and the perfect, which is suggested by religious and metaphysical basic concepts, falls apart. Even the emphatic concept of reason, which does not so much mediate the cognitive, evaluative, and expressive aspects of the world as make them one, becomes untenable along with the approach of metaphysical thought. To this extent, Weber is right to object to the "charisma of reason"[8] and to insist upon a concept of rationality that divides up into the inner logics of different, mutually irreducible value spheres, as the neo-Kantians would put it. But Weber goes too far when he infers from the loss of the substantial unity of reason a polytheism of gods and demons [*Glaubensmächte*] struggling with one another, with their irreconcilability rooted in a pluralism of incompatible validity claims. The unity of rationality in the multiplicity of value spheres rationalized according to their inner logics is secured precisely at the formal level of the argumentative redemption of validity claims. Validity claims differ from empirical claims through the presupposition that they can be made good by means of arguments. And arguments or reasons have at least this in common, that they, and only they, can develop the force of rational motivation under the communicative conditions of a cooperative testing of hypothetical validity claims. Of course, the differentiated validity claims—to propositional truth, normative rightness, sincerity and authenticity, as well as the claim to well-formedness or intelligibility related to symbolic construction in accordance with rules—call not merely for reasoning in general, but for reasons in a form of argumentation typical of each. Accordingly, the arguments play different roles with different degrees of discursive binding force. As we have seen, even today we lack a pragmatic logic of argumentation that satisfactorily captures the internal connections between *forms* of speech acts. Only such a theory of discourse could explicitly state wherein the unity of argumentation consists and what we mean by procedural rationality after all substantial concepts of reason have been critically dissolved.[9]

Weber did not distinguish adequately between the particular value *contents* of cultural traditions and those universal *standards* of value under which the cognitive, normative, and expressive components of culture became autonomous value spheres and developed complexes of rationality with their own logics. An example of this confusion of value standards, or universal validity claims, with particular value contents can be found in the passage cited above in which Weber works out the differences among

the various validity claims and shows that truth, normative obligation (sacredness), and beauty cannot be reduced to one another;
he goes on to say: "But these are only the most elementary cases
of the struggle among the gods of the various orders and values.
I don't know how one might wish to decide 'scientifically' between the value of French and German culture. Here, too, different gods struggle with one another, now and for all times to
come."[10] The value systems of French and German culture are in
fact good examples of historical configurations of value contents
that cannot be reduced to one another. But the pluralism of value
contents has nothing to do with the differences among the *aspects*
of validity under which questions of truth, justice, and taste can
be differentiated out and rationally dealt with as such.

For this reason, the differentiation of scientific, legal, and
artistic enterprises, in which cultural knowledge is developed
under one or another of these universal aspects of validity, also
need in no way provoke a conflict among irreconcilable orders
of life. These cultural systems of action stand between the cultural spheres of value to which they have direct reference and
those social systems of action that, like the economy and the state,
crystallize around particular values, such as wealth, power,
health, and the like. It is only with this institutionalization of
different value matters that competitive relations among
ultimately irrational action orientations come into play. On the
other hand, rationalization processes that connect up with the
three general complexes of rationality mean an embodiment of
different cognitive structures; at worst, this raises the problem
of where, in the communicative practice of everyday life,
"switching stations" have to be brought into operation so that
individuals can shift their action orientations from one complex
to another.

One of these switching stations has special relevance for the
form of social integration that developed with capitalist society:
that between the cognitive-instrumental and the normative complexes of rationality. We are already familiar with this problem
under the description: "the institutionalization of purposive-
rational action orientations." This brings us back to the question
of how the second thesis—viz. the freedom-endangering autonomy of successfully established life-spheres of purposive-
rational, economic, and administrative action—is connected with
the first thesis (which, for the sake of argument, I shall take as
correct).

The organizational means of formal law, though based on posttraditional legal representations, are not, as are the structurally similar moral orders, exposed to competition from the side of science or art. Rather, the legal system develops along with an increasingly complex economic and administrative system. It even becomes more and more indispensable as the moral sources that supply the necessary motives to the occupational system dry up. Thus Weber stands before the choice: either to de-dramatize his vision of an "iron cage" whose moral-practical substance has dried up, or to assign morality and law to *different* complexes of rationality. He chooses the second alternative and plays down the structural analogies that obtain between moral development and the rationalization of law. Weber considers law primarily as a sphere which, like the provision of material goods or the struggle for legitimate power, is open to formal rationalization. Here, once again, the confusion between value contents and validity claims comes to his aid. For the rationalization of the legal order could be viewed exclusively under the aspect of purposive-rationality—in the same way as the economic and political-administrative orders—only if there existed an internal interconnection between the abstract value standard of the law, that is, the "rightness" of norms, on the one hand, and value matters such as wealth or power, on the other hand.

The model of three value spheres, each rationalized under one abstract aspect of validity in accord with an inner logic, is here replaced by the idea of a variety of unclassified values like truth, wealth, beauty, health, law, power, sacredness, and so on. These values are supposed to be particular and, in the last analysis, irrational; there are conflicts among them which cannot be settled with reasons. When from out of this pool a few values become the crystallizing cores of rationalizable orders of life, the aspect of rationalization can only extend to means-end relations. It is this model that Weber applies, for instance, to the professional practice of scientific medicine, to aesthetics and jurisprudence.

> The general "presupposition" of the medical enterprise is, stated trivially, that it has the task of maintaining life as such and of diminishing suffering as such to the greatest possible degree. Yet this is problematical. By his means the medical man sustains the life of the mortally ill man, even if the patient implores us to relieve him of life, even if his rela-

tives, to whom his life is worthless and to whom the costs of maintaining him grow unbearable, grant his deliverance from suffering. Perhaps a poor lunatic is involved, whose relatives, whether they admit it or not, wish and must wish for his death. Yet the presuppositions of medicine, as well as the penal code, prevent the physician from relinquishing his therapeutic efforts. Whether life is worth living and when—this question is not asked by medicine. Natural science gives us an answer to the question of what we must do if we wish to master life technically. It leaves quite aside, or assumes for its purposes, whether we should and do wish to master life technically, and whether it ultimately makes sense to do so. Or consider a discipline such as aesthetics. The fact that there are works of art is given for aesthetics. It seeks to find out under what conditions this state of affairs obtains, but it does not raise the question whether or not the realm of art is perhaps a realm of diabolical grandeur, a realm of this world and therefore in its core hostile to God, and in its innermost aristocratic spirit hostile to the brotherhood of man. Thus aesthetics does not ask whether there should be works of art. Or consider jurisprudence. It establishes what is valid according to the rules of juristic thought, which is partly bound by logically compelling schemata and partly by conventionally given schemata. Juridical thought obtains when certain legal rules and certain methods of interpreting them are recognized as binding. Whether there should be law and whether one should establish just these rules—such questions jurisprudence does not answer. It can only state: If one wishes this result, according to the norms of our legal thought this legal rule is the appropriate means of getting it.[11]

In this passage, jurisprudence, standing for the sphere of law in general, is represented on the model of an order of life that, like the economy or the state, can be rationalized formally— that is, in terms of means-ends relations—from a particular value standpoint. Of the examples mentioned, however, this model applies unambiguously only to medical care. Here we have a case of the value-oriented application of natural-scientific knowledge, that is, of the rationalization of services in the framework of a professional practice that, as the practice of healing, is directed to a specific value content—the health of patients. Empirically this value is almost universally accepted; nevertheless, it is a matter of a particular pattern of values that is by no means internally connected with one of the universal validity claims. This is, of course, not true of medicine as a scientific discipline; qua research it is oriented not to particular values but to questions of truth. The situation is similar with aesthetics and jurisprudence insofar as they are considered as scientific disciplines. These disciplines can also be transposed into professional practices, for example, aesthetics into art criticism, jurisprudence into the administration of justice or legal journalism. They thereby become components of cultural systems of action: the artistic enterprise or the administration of justice. These systems, however, unlike the professional practice of medicine, are not oriented to particular values, such as "health," but to systems of knowledge that have been differentiated out under one or another of the universal validity claims. In this respect, the artistic enterprise and the administration of justice resemble the scientific enterprise and not the health system. The concern here is to judge the authenticity of works that give expression to exemplary experiences or to deal with normative questions, as the concern in the scientific system is to produce empirical-theoretical knowledge.

Thus it is not permissible to generalize the medical situation of applying empirical-theoretical knowledge, which can be adequately analyzed from the standpoint of the establishment of purposive-rational action orientations, and to conceive societal rationalization in *all* domains of life as a rationalization of means for ends that are selected in accord with particular values. Weber's own theoretical approach attributes central importance to moral-practical rationality in connection with the *institutionalization* of purposive-rational economic and administrative action. It would be astonishing if Weber had not seen that the rationalization of law has to be conceived, in the first instance, from the standpoint of a value-rational transformation of the institutional system, and only in the second instance from the standpoint of the establishment of purposive-rational action orientations. But the interference of the two different lines of questioning along which Weber pursues modernization processes as rationalization processes leads to contradictions in his sociology of law.

These can be traced back to one central contradiction. *On the one hand,* Weber identifies the two innovations to which capitalism owes its rise as the Protestant ethic of the calling and the modern legal system. In them a moral consciousness guided by principles is successfully embodied in the personality and institutional systems. This secures a value-rational anchoring for purposive-rational action orientations. As I have shown, Weber has at his disposal a complex concept of practical rationality that takes the coordination of purposive-rational and value-rational aspects of action as its point of departure. Nevertheless, *on the other hand,* Weber considers societal rationalization explicitly from the perspective of purposive-rationality. At the level of institutions, he does not apply the comprehensive concept of rationality upon which he bases his investigations of cultural tradition. Only the cognitive-instrumental complex of rationality acquires significance for the rationality of action systems. At the level of the economic and political subsystems, only the aspect of purposive-rational, and not that of value-rational action is supposed to have structure-forming effects. From Weber's sociology of the economy, state, and law, one gets the impression that in modern societies rationalization processes attach only to empirical-theoretical knowledge and to the instrumental and strategic aspects of action, whereas practical rationality cannot be institutionalized independently, that is, with an inner logic specific to a subsystem.

B.—These conflicting tendencies are reflected in his sociology of law. On the one hand (a), modern law, like the Protestant ethic, counts as an embodiment of posttraditional structures of moral consciousness. The legal system is an order of life that responds to the forms of moral-practical rationality. On the other hand (b), Weber attempts to view the rationality of law exclusively from the standpoint of purposive-rationality and to construe it as a parallel case to the embodiment of cognitive-instrumental rationality in the economy and the state administration. He succeeds in this only at the cost of an empiricist reinterpretation of the legitimation problematic and a conceptual separation of the political system from forms of moral-practical rationality—he trims back political will-formation to processes of acquiring and competing for power.

(a) First a word on the posttraditional character of bourgeois law. Social actions are institutionalized in the framework of legitimate orders; and the latter rest in part on consensus [*Einverständnis*]. This consensus is grounded in the intersubjective recognition of norms. To the degree that the normative consensus is based on tradition, Weber speaks of conventional social action [*Gemeinschaftshandeln*]. To the degree that conventionally bound action is replaced by action oriented to success, by

purposive-rational action, there arises a problem of how the scopes of actions based on self-interest [*Interessenhandelns*], freed from convention, can in turn be legitimately ordered, that is, demarcated from one another in a normatively binding way. Normative agreement has to shift from a consensus pregiven by tradition to a consensus that is achieved communicatively, that is, agreed upon [*vereinbart*]. In the limit case, what is to count as a legitimate order is formally agreed upon and positively enacted; with this, rationally regulated action [*Gesellschaftshandeln*] takes the place of conventional social action.

> Naturally the transition from consensual action to rationally regulated action is fluid—after all, the latter represents only the special case of regulation by enactment. . .Conversely, almost every associative relationship [*Vergesellschaftung*] tends to give rise to consensual action among consociates which goes beyond the sphere of its rational purposes (this will be called "consensual action conditioned by associative relationship"). . . The more numerous the spheres to which the individual rationally orients his action, and the more varied these are as regards the kind of opportunities constitutive of them, the further "rational societal differentiation" has progressed; the more things take on the character of associative relationship, the further the "rational societal organization."[12]

The ideal-typical case of the normative regulation of purposive-rational action is freely agreed-upon enactment with legal force; an institution based on an order achieved through enactment is an association [*Verein*] or, where a coercive apparatus permanently sanctions the original agreement, a compulsory association [*Anstalt*]. In these concepts Weber describes the tendency to societal rationalization: "On the whole. . .we find that the purposive-rational ordering of consensual action through enactment, and particularly the transformation of organizations [*Verbände*] into purposive-rationally ordered compulsory associations is ever on the increase."[13] In this passage, Weber is not using the term "purposive-rational" in accord with his own definitions; he should have written "value-rational" instead, as the following reflection indicates.

When normative consensus takes the form of a legally sanctioned agreement, only the procedure through which it comes to pass grounds the presumption that it is rationally motivated. Here too, consensus is still related to the validity of a normative regulation that becomes part of the legitimate order and binds agents to certain value orientations in connection with some matter requiring regulation. It is only *within* normatively established limits that legal subjects are permitted to act purposive-rationally without concern for conventions. Thus for the institutionalization of purposive-rational action, a kind of normative consensus is required, which stands under the idea of free (discursive) agreement and autonomous (willed) enactment, and which is characterized by formal properties of value rationality. To be sure, Weber's position in this matter is not unambiguous; the fluctuating terminology is no accident.

In specifying the essential features of the rationality of modern law, Weber points first to its systematic character. Modern law is in a particularly high degree jurists' law. With legally trained judges and officials, the administration of justice and public administration became professionalized. Not only the application of law but the enactment of law became increasingly bound to formal procedures and thereby to the specialized mind of jurists. This situation promoted the systematization of legal propositions, the coherence of legal doctrine, that is to say, the rationalization of law according to internal, purely formal criteria of analytic conceptual structure, deductive rigor, principled explanation and justification, and the like. This tendency can be observed already in late medieval faculties of law; with legal positivism, it is completely established (and explicitly conceptualized, for instance, by Kelsen). This formal structuring of the law, the unrestricted application of formal-operational thought to the professional practical knowledge of legal specialists, is certainly an interesting state of affairs. But the fact that this tendency appears very unevenly in the legal developments of different nations (more pronouncedly in countries within a tradition of Roman law), makes one sceptical regarding any proposal to look for the growth of rationality in modern law primarily in its internal systematization. Rather, this systematization of meaning relations presupposes the transition to posttraditional stages of moral consciousness made possible by the ethical rationalization of worldviews. It is at this stage that we first find a formal concept of the social world as the totality of legitimately regulated interpersonal relations.

In such a world the moral subject of action can orient himself according to principles of the methodical conduct of life; so too, the subject of civil law can feel himself justified in acting, within legal bounds, purely with an orientation to success. The disenchantment of the religious worldview and the decentration of world understanding are the presuppositions for a transformation of sacred legal concepts carried out from the hypothetical perspective of legal associates who are in principle free and equal. According to this conception, legal associates can make agreements concerning which norms will gain or lose validity.

> Originally there was a complete absence of the notion that rules of conduct possessing the character of "law," i.e. rules which are guaranteed by "legal coercion," could be intentionally created as norms...at first, legal decisions altogether lacked the concept of "norm." They were not at all seen as the "application" of fixed and stable "rules," which we today take it for granted that legal judgments are. And where there emerged the conception of norms that were "valid" for action and *binding* in the resolution of disputes, these were at first not viewed as the products, or even as the possible subject matter, of human enactment. Their "legitimate" existence rested rather upon the absolute sacredness of certain usages as such, deviation from which would produce either evil magical effects, the restlessness of the spirits, or the wrath of the gods. They were taken as "tradition" [and thus] at least in theory as immutable. They had to be correctly known and interpreted in accordance with established usage, but they could not be created. Their interpretation was the task of those who had known them longest, i.e. the physically "oldest persons" or the elders of the kinship group or—quite frequently—the magicians and the priests, who alone, in virtue of their specialized knowledge of magical forces, knew, and had to know, the techniques of intercourse with supernatural powers. Nevertheless [on the other hand] norms emerged through conscious *imposition* of new rules. But this could happen in one way only, viz. through new charismatic revelation, which could assume two forms: either the revelation of a merely individual decision as to what was right in a concrete individual case—this is the original form—or the revelation of a general norm that was to govern all similar cases in the future. Revelation of law in these forms was the original revolutionary element opposing the stability of tradition and is the mother of all legal "enactment."[14]

Weber traces the emergence of the *formal qualities of modern law* "from charismatic revelation of law by 'law *prophets*'; to empirical creation and finding of law by legal *honoratiores* (creation of law through cautelary jurisprudence and adherence to precedent); further, to imposition of law by secular or theocratic *powers*; and finally, to the systematic enactment of law and specialized administration of justice by persons with literary and formal-logical training, by persons *educated* in the law (professional jurists)."[15] Schluchter terms the perspective from which Weber investigates the rationalization of law "the disenchantment of the paths to the law"—in analogy with "the disenchantment of the paths to salvation." Weber traces this process from its beginnings in a "magically conditioned formalism," in which the ritualistic observance of the form of legal action guarantees the substantive correctness of the judgment, down to the "logical formalism" of contemporary law, in which the norms of the legal process are distinguished from the matter, that is, the procedure from the content.

Weber constructs a development from revealed, through traditional, to modern law—whether "deduced" or "enacted"; and he does so with a view to the differentiation of various *fields of law*, on the one hand, and to the conceptualization of the *foundations of the validity of law*, on the other. At the stage of primitive law, there is as yet no concept of an objective norm; at the stage of traditional law, norms are taken as given, as conventions that are passed on; only at the stage of modern law can norms be regarded as free enactments and judged in the light of principles that are themselves viewed as hypothetical. The rationalization of law reflects the same series of stages of preconventional, conventional, and postconventional basic concepts that developmental psychology has shown to obtain in ontogenesis. Klaus Eder has examined this thesis in the light of anthropological material;[16] Schluchter illustrates it with Weber's sociology of law.

> The primitive legal process does not yet recognize any "objective" law independent of actions; actions and norms are interwoven. The probability of regularity in social relations rests entirely on usage and custom, or on self-interest. For action is not yet oriented to legal duties recognized "for their own sakes" as "binding" by a group of men. This first takes place in the transition to the traditional legal process, where actions are now judged in the light of given legal norms. Of course, the latter remain particularistic; they are not yet

based on universalistic legal principles. This is the achievement of natural law, which supposes that such principles
can be rationally derived. With this, however, law is given
not only a principled basis, but at the same time a metajuristic basis. Existing law must now be legitimized through
such principles; and it can and must be changed when it contradicts them. With this, the idea of enacting law was given
a decisive impluse. To be sure, law still held fast to the idea
of the giveness of legal principles. Only when this idea was
shattered, when the principles themselves became reflective,
could law become positive in the strict sense. This was
achieved in the modern legal process. Almost all law can
be considered as enacted and thus as open to revision. And
its "anchoring" is therefore shifted from metajuristic to
juristic principles. These now have a merely hypothetical
status, which is an expression of the fact that law has become
autonomous while at the same time retaining its relation to
extralegal contexts.[17]

It is only at this stage of development that modern structures of consciousness can be embodied in a legal system such
as bourgeois private law, which is distinguished primarily by
three formal properties; positivity, legalism, and formality.

POSITIVITY. Modern law is viewed as positively enacted
law. It is not developed by way of interpreting recognized, hal-
lowed traditions; rather it expresses the will of a sovereign law-
giver who regulates social states of affairs conventionally with
juridical means of organization.

LEGALISM. Aside from a general obedience to the law,
modern law does not attribute to legal subjects any moral motives;
it safeguards their private inclinations within sanctioned limits.
It is not evil dispositions that are sanctioned, but behavior
deviating from norms (presupposing accountability and guilt).

FORMALITY. Modern law defines domains in which private
individuals may legitimately exercise free choice [Willkür]. This
freedom of choice of legal subjects in a morally neutralized
domain of private actions connected with legal consequences is
presupposed. Thus interactions under private law can be regulated negatively, by way of restricting the entitlements that are
recognized in principle (instead of being regulated positively,
through concrete duties and substantive precepts). In this domain,
anything that is not legally forbidden is allowed.

These three structural properties refer to the mode of legal validity and legal enactment, to criteria of culpability and the mode of sanction, and finally to the way in which legal action is organized. They define a system of action in which it is assumed that all individuals behave strategically, in that they, first, obey laws as publicly sanctioned agreements that can, however, be legitimately changed at any time; second, pursue their interests without regard to moral considerations; and third, in accord with these interest orientations, make optimal decisions in the framework of existing laws (that is, with regard to calculable legal consequences as well). In other words, it is assumed that legal subjects utilize their private autonomy in a purposive-rational manner.

Positivity, legalism, and formality are general features of a legally binding institutionalization of well-circumscribed domains of strategic action. They make explicit the form in virtue of which modern law can fulfill the functional imperatives of economic commerce regulated through markets. However, this functionality for the system is a *consequence* of legal structures in which purposive-rational action can become universal; it does not *explain* how these structures are themselves possible. The fact that modern law is functional for the institutionalization of purposive-rational action does not, in other words, explain the structural properties in virtue of which it can fulfill these functions. The form of modern law is to be explained, rather, in terms of the posttraditional structures of moral consciousness that it embodies. To this extent, Weber should have understood the modern legal system as an order of life that was correlated with the normative sphere of value and that, like the methodical conduct of life of early capitalist entrepreneurs, could be rationalized under the abstract value standard of normative rightness. But this contradicts the competing attempt to regard the rationalization of law exclusively from the standpoint of purposive rationality.

The positivization, legalization, and formalization of law mean that the validity of law can no longer feed off the taken-for-granted authority of moral traditions but requires an autonomous foundation, that is, a foundation that is not only relative to given ends. Moral consciousness can satisfy such a requirement only at the postconventional level. It is here that there first emerges *the idea that legal norms are in principle open to criticism and in need of justification;* the distinction between norms and principles of action; the concept of producing norms according to principles; the notion of rational agreement on normatively binding rules (as well as that of a compact that first makes contractual relations possible); the insight into the connection between the universality and justifiability of legal norms; the concept of the abstract legal subject's general competency; that of the law-giving power of subjectivity; and so forth. These posttraditional basic concepts of law and morality are first developed and systematized in modern natural law theories. The model for justifying legal norms is an uncoerced agreement, arrived at by those affected, in the role of contractual partners who are in principle free and equal. However the conceptions of justification look in detail, what is important is that an autonomous grounding, independent of tradition, is required—in Weber's terms, that validity based on traditional consensus is replaced by validity based on rational consensus.

The separation of morality and legality effected in modern law brings with it the problem that the domain of legality *as a whole* stands in need of practical justification. The sphere of law, which is independent of the sphere of morality but at the same time demands the readiness of legal subjects to obey the law, must be complemented by a morality grounded on principles. The particular accomplishment of the positivization of the legal order consists in *displacing* problems of justification, that is, in relieving the technical administration of the law of such problems over broad expanses—but not in doing away with them. Precisely the posttraditional structure of legal consciousness sharpens the problem of justification into a question of principle that is shifted to the foundations but not thereby made to disappear. The catalog of basic rights contained in bourgeois constitutions, insofar as they are formally set down, together with the principle of the sovereignty of the people, which ties the competence to make law to the understanding of democratic will-formation, are expressions of this justification that has become structurally necessary.

To be sure, the basic institutions of bourgeois constitutions that are effective for legitimation (as well as those of civil and criminal law) can be understood not *only* as embodiments of posttraditional structures of consciousness; we can "get behind" them with functionalist or ideology-critical lines of questioning. However, the critique of ideology makes use of the functionalist analysis of legal systems only to sue for unredeemed normative validity claims, not to suspend them; otherwise it falls prey to the empty formulae of a Marxist functionalism, which is no better in this respect than a systems functionalism that is running loose. Weber appears to have seen this very clearly. To the degree that modern law becomes an organizational means for political domination, that is, for "legitimate domination," the latter is dependent on a legitimation that satisfies modern law's need for the principled mode of justification. Such legitimation is served, for example, by a constitution that can be understood as the expression of a rational agreement among all citizens: "Our present-day organizations, above all the political ones, belong to the type of 'legal' domination. That is, the legitimacy of the powerholder's giving commands is based on rationally enacted, agreed upon, or imposed rules; and the legitimation to enact these rules rests in turn on a rationally enacted or interpreted 'constitution.'"[18]

To be sure, formulations of this kind obscure Weber's legal positivism. In general, he conceives modern law and legal domination so narrowly that the need for a principled mode of justification is shaded out in favor of sheer positivism. Weber streses precisely the structural properties connected with the formalism of a law that is systematized by specialists and with the positivity of norms that are enacted. He emphasizes the structural features I have elucidated as the positivity, legalism, and formality of law. But he neglects the moment of a need for rational justification; he excludes from the concept of modern law precisely the conceptions of rational justification that arose with modern theories of natural law in the seventeenth century and since then have been characteristic, if not of all particular legal norms, certainly of the legal system as a whole, and especially of the public-legal foundations for political domination. It is in this way that Weber assimilates the law to an organizational means applied in a purposive-rational manner, detaches the rationalization of law from the moral-practical complex of rationality, and reduces it to a rationalization of means-ends relations.

(b) For the most part, Weber describes the rationality of modern law in such a way that the *value-rational anchoring* of purposive-rational economic and administrative action no longer stands in the foreground; this place is occupied instead by the *purposive-rational applicability* of legal means of organization. This can be seen in three characteristic lines of argument: the interpretation of modern natural law theories, the positivistic equation of legality and legitimacy, and the thesis of the threat to the formal qualities of law arising from "substantive rationalization."

ON THE INTERPRETATION OF NATURAL LAW. Rational natural law, in its different versions from Hobbes and Locke through Rousseau and Kant to Hegel, can be understood as a theoretical framework for attempts to ground legally organized constitutions for state and society.[19] As Weber points out, this natural law ties the legitimacy of positive law to formal conditions:

> All legitimate law rests upon enactment, and all enactment in turn rests finally upon rational agreement. This agreement is either real, that is, derived from an actual original contract among free individuals, which also regulates the form in which new law is to be enacted in the future. Or it is ideal, in the sense that only such law is legitimate whose content does not contradict the conception of a reasonable order enacted by free agreement. The "freedoms" are the essential elements of such a natural law, above all the "freedom of contract." The voluntary rational contract became one of the universal formal principles of natural law constructions, either as the real historical basis of all associative relationships, including the state, or at least as the regulative standard of evaluation.[20]

Weber sees in rational natural law "the purest type of value-rational validity" and cites it as an impressive example of the external influence of internal relations of validity. "However limited in comparison to its ideal claims, there is no denying that its logically derived propositions have had a not inconsiderable degree of real influence on action."[21]

Natural law in the modern sense rests on a rational principle of justification and is, in terms of moral-practical rationalization, further advanced than the Protestant ethic, which is still founded on religion. Nevertheless, Weber does not hold it to be purely and simply an element of modern law. He wants to separate it carefully "from revealed, as well as from enacted and from traditional law."[22] Thus he constructs an antithesis between modern law in the strict sense, which rests *only* on the principle of enactment, and the not yet completely "formal" law of modern natural law theories which rests upon principles of grounding (however rational). In his view, modern law is to be understood in a positivistic sense, as law that is enacted by decision and fully disconnected from rational agreement, from ideas of grounding in general, however formal they might be. He has the idea that "there can be no purely formal natural law."

"Nature" and "reason" are the *substantive* criteria for what is legitimate from the standpoint of natural law . . . What ought to be is identified with what actually exists on the average everywhere. The "norms" that are obtained through logical analysis of legal or ethical concepts belong, in the same sense as the "laws of nature," to those universally binding rules which "not even God himself can change," and with which no legal order may come into conflict.[23]

This argument is confusing because it combines, in an opaque manner, an immanent critique of the deficient radicalism of natural law conceptions of grounding that are not yet sufficiently formal with a transcendent critique of the need for principles of justification at all and clothes both in the guise of a criticism of the naturalistic fallacy. One might certainly raise the objection that the concept of natural rights still had strong metaphysical connotations in the seventeenth and eighteenth centuries. However, with the model of a contract through which all legal associates, after rationally weighing their interests, regulate their common life as free and equal partners, modern natural law theorists were the first to meet the demand for a procedural grounding of law, that is, for a justification by principles whose validity could in turn be criticized. To this extent, "nature" and "reason" do not stand in this context for some metaphysical contents or other; rather, they circumscribe formal conditions which an agreement must satisfy if it is to have legitimating force, that is, if it is to be rational. Weber again confuses the formal properties of a postconventional level of justification with particular substantive values. In respect to rational natural law, he also fails to distinguish sufficiently between structural and material aspects, and thus he can equate "nature" and "reason" with value *contents* from which modern law in the strict sense becomes detached as an instrument for realizing any values and interests whatever.

ON THE BELIEF IN LEGALITY. The positivistic concept of law lands Weber in an embarrassing situation in regard to the question of how legal domination can be legitimized. If some form of rational agreement (which natural law contract theories spell out in specific ways) is the "only consistent type of legitimacy of a legal order that can remain once religious revelation and the authority of the sanctity of tradition and its bearers have lost their force,"[24] then we have the following problem: assuming that legitimacy is a necessary condition for the continued existence of *every* type of political domination, how can a legal domination whose legality is based on a law that is viewed purely in decisionistic terms (that is, a law that devalues all grounding in principle) be legitimated at all? Weber's answer, which has found adherents from Carl Schmitt to Niklas Luhmann,[25] runs as follows: through procedure. Legitimation through procedure does not mean here going back to formal conditions for the moral-practical justification of legal norms;[26] it means rather keeping to procedural prescriptions in administering, applying, and enacting law. Legitimacy rests then on "belief in the legality of enacted rules and the right of those elevated to authority under such rules to issue commands."[27] It remains unclear how the belief in legality is supposed to summon up the force of legitimation if legality means only conformity with an actually existing legal order, and if this order, as arbitrarily enacted law, is not in turn open to practical-moral justification. The belief in legality can produce legitimacy only if we already presuppose the legitimacy of the legal order that lays down what is legal. There is no way out of this circle.[28]

In his discussion of "Basic Sociological Terms," Weber puts it in this way: "Legality can be regarded as legitimate in virtue of (i) voluntary agreement among the interested parties, (ii) imposition by an authority which is held to be legitimate and therefore meets with compliance."[29] In neither case is it legality as such that produces legitimation, but either (i) rational agreement that already underlies the legal order, or (ii) the *otherwise* legitimized authority of those who impose the legal order. The transitions between "agreed upon" and "imposed" order are fluid.

Today the most common form of legitimacy is the belief in *legality,* the compliance with enactments that are *formally* correct and that have been made in the accustomed manner. The distinction between an order derived from voluntary agreement and one that has been imposed is only relative. For as soon as the validity of an agreed upon order does not rest on *unanimous* agreement—as has often in the past been held necessary for complete legitimacy—but on de facto compliance with the majority within a given circle by those who hold different views—as is very often the case—then the order is actually imposed on the minority.[30]

Notwithstanding these fluid transitions, the two sources of legitimacy on which the belief in legality depends can certainly be distinguished analytically: *rationally motivated agreement* versus *the imposition of a powerful will.* Weber writes of the latter: "So far as it is not derived merely from fear or from motives of expediency but involves notions of legality, a willingness to submit to an order imposed by one person or a small group always implies a belief in the legitimate—in some sense—authority of the source imposing it."[31]

Belief in the legality of a procedure cannot per se—that is, in virtue of positive enactment—produce legitimacy. This is clear already in the logical analysis of the expressions "legality" and "legitimacy." It is so evident that one asks oneself how Weber came to regard legal domination as an *independent* form of legitimate domination. I can find only one argument—which does not, however, stand up under closer examination. One might regard the belief in legality as a special case of a more general phenomenon. Techniques and regulations that have come about in a rational manner are normally no longer grasped in their inner rationales by those who deal with them on a day-to-day basis.

> The empirical "validity" precisely of a "rational" order rests in turn chiefly upon consensual compliance with the customary, habitual, inculcated, ever-recurring. . . Progress of societal differentiation and rationalization thus means—if not absolutely in every case, certainly as a rule—an increasing distancing overall of those affected by the rational techniques and orders from their rational basis, which is on the whole usually more hidden from them than the sense of the magician's magical procedures are from the "savage." Thus rationalization of social action does not at all mean universalizing knowledge of its conditions and connections; usually it means just the opposite.[32]

Weber is referring here to something like secondary traditionalism, to the gradual disappearance of the problematic aspects of arrangements in which rationality structures are embodied and which are loaded with presuppositions. We might then understand the belief in legality as the expression of such a traditionalizing effect. But in this case it is precisely confidence in the globally assumed rational foundations of the legal order that makes the legality of a decision an *indication* of its legitimacy. Weber sees this himself.

> What gives the situation of the "civilized man," as opposed
> to that of the "savage," its specifically rational quality in this
> respect is the generally instilled belief that the conditions
> of his everyday life—be it the train or the lift or money or
> the court or the military or medicine—are in principle of a
> rational nature, that is, are human artifacts capable of being
> rationally known, created, controlled—and this has some im-
> portant consequences for the character of "consensus."[33]

Thus a legal order also lays claim to validity, in the sense
of rational agreement, when participants start from the assumption that experts alone would be able to give good reasons for
its existence, whereas juristic laymen would not be in a position
to do so ad hoc. From whatever angle one views it, legality based
on positive enactment alone can *indicate* an underlying legitimacy,
but never replace it. Belief in legality is not an independent type
of legitimacy.[34]

ON THE DIALECTIC OF FORMAL AND SUBSTANTIVE RATIONAL-
IZATION. Having adopted a positivistic conception of law and
developed a decisionistic concept of legitimacy through procedure, Weber is able to transpose the rationalization of law to
the cognitive sphere of value and investigate it irrespective of
the viewpoint of ethical rationalization. But as soon as the rationalization of law is reinterpreted as a question of the purposive-
rational organization of purposive-rational economic and administrative action, questions concerning the institutional embodiment
of moral-practical rationality are not only shoved aside but
directly turned into their opposite: they now appear to be the
source of irrationality, at any rate "of motives that weaken the
formal rationalism of law."[35]

Weber confuses an appeal to the need to justify legal domination—that is, an attempt to go back to the legitimating foundation of rational agreement—with an appeal to particular values.
For this reason, the substantive rationalization of law means for
him not, say, progressive ethical rationalization, but destruction
of the cognitive rationality of law.

> With the emergence of modern class problems, there have
> arisen substantive demands upon the law from a part of
> those whose interests are involved (namely labor), on the
> one hand, and from legal ideologists, on the other. They are
> directed precisely against the dominance of standards
> tailored to business ethics, and call for a social law on the

basis of such emotionally colored ethical postulates as "justice" or "human dignity." But this places the formalism of law fundamentally in question.[36]

This perspective makes it possible to incorporate the development of law into the dialectic of rationalization, in an ironic way to be sure.

Weber forcefully works out the formal properties of modern law, on the basis of which it is suited to serve as a means of organization for subsystems of purposive-rational action. But he restricts the concept of law positivistically to such an extent that he can neglect the moral-practical aspect of rationalization (the principle of justification) and take account only of its cognitive-instrumental aspect (the principle of enactment). Weber considers the advances of modern legal development exclusively from the standpoint of formal rationality, that is, of a value-neutral, means-ends, systematic shaping of spheres of action, which is tailored to the type of strategic action. The rationalization of law is then no longer measured against the inner logic of the moral-practical sphere of value, as is that of ethics and life-conduct; it is directly connected to the progress of knowledge in the cognitive-instrumental sphere of value.

Weber specifies empirical indicators for the formal rationalization of law, above all improvement of the formal qualities of law insofar as these can be seen (1) in the analytic systematization of legal propositions and the professional treatment of legal norms by legal experts, and (2) in the reduction of legitimacy to legality, that is, the replacement of problems of grounding with problems of procedure. The secondary traditionalism of laymen in relation to a law that has become opaque but is in principle recognized as "rational" is also characteristic of these two trends.

> Whatever form law and legal procedure may come to assume under the impact of these various influences, it will be inevitable that, as a result of technical and economic developments, the legal ignorance of laymen will increase. The use of jurors and similar lay judges will not suffice to stop the continuous growth of technical elements in the law and hence of its character as a specialists' domain. Nor can it prevent the spread of the notion that the law is a rational technical apparatus which is continually transformable in the light of expediential considerations [zweckrational] and devoid of sanctity of content. This unavoidable fate may

be obscured by the tendency of acquiescence in existing law—which, for general reasons, is increasing in many ways—but it cannot really be stayed.[37]

It is true that ignorance of the law in light of the continuous growth of its technical elements lengthens the path of legitimation and relieves public administration from the immediate pressure of legitimation. But this lengthening of the path to legitimation does not mean that belief in legality can replace belief in the legitimacy of the legal system as a whole. The assumption—which sprang up with legal positivism and was adopted and overextended by social-scientific functionalism—that normative validity claims could be withdrawn, without any noteworthy consequences for the stability of the legal system in the consciousness of the system's members, is empirically untenable. Moreover, this conceptual strategy leads to the highly problematic result that Weber has to disqualify as "substantive rationalization" *all* countermovements against the dilution of modern law into a mere organizational means detached from moral-practical contexts of justification. Under "anti-formalistic tendencies of modern legal development" he subsumes (without distinction) not only tendencies toward reideologizing legal foundations, which actually do attack the posttraditional status of law, but also the push toward an ethical rationalization of law, which means a further embodiment of posttraditional structures of moral consciousness.

This leads to a rather ironic consequence for Weber's diagnosis of the times. He deplores the switch from ethical to purely utilitarian action orientations and conceives of this as a detaching of motivational foundations from the moral-practical sphere of value. Thus he ought to welcome movements that are directed against parallel tendencies in the law. What appears to him in the former context as a growing independence of subsystems of purposive rationality—their becoming an "iron cage of bondage"—should appear to him as no less a danger in this latter context, which has to do with detaching the law, as the socially integrative core of institutional orders, from the same moral-practical sphere of value. The opposite is the case. Weber regards as detracting from the formal qualities of law not only traditionalistic attempts to reideologize it but also progressive efforts to reattach it to procedural requirements for grounding: "In any case, the juristic precision of judicial opinions will be seriously impaired if sociological, economic or ethical arguments take the place of legal concepts. All in all, the movement is one of those characteristic reactions against the dominance of 'specialization' and the rationalism which is in the last analysis its very parent."[38]

Weber is not able to fit both moments into the pattern of partial rationalization of developed capitalist societies so as to safeguard the consistency of his judgments of moral and legal development. It is not my intention to pursue a critique of ideology probing the roots of this inconsistency. I am concerned with the immanent reasons for Weber's inability to carry through his theory of rationalization as it is set up. Only after we have cleared up the errors, which, I think, lie in his theory construction itself, will we be able to reconstruct the systematic content of Weber's diagnosis of the times, so that the potential of his theory for stimulating an analysis of our own present can be exploited. In my opinion, the errors—which are quite instructive—can be found in two places, both important from the standpoint of his theoretical strategy.

First, I want to unearth certain bottlenecks in the concept formation of his action theory. These prevent Weber from examining the rationalization of action systems under aspects other than that of purposive rationality, notwithstanding the fact that he does describe the rationalization of worldviews and the differentiation of cultural spheres decisive for modernity in a conceptual framework that brings into view societal rationalization in all its complexity; that is, which also includes moral-practical and aesthetic-expressive manifestations of Occidental rationalism. This problem will give us occasion to go back to the basic concept of communicative action in connection with a critical analysis of Weber's action theory and to clarify further the concept of communicative reason (in Chapter III, "Intermediate Reflections: Social Action, Purposive Activity, and Communication").

Second, I would like to show that the ambiguity in the rationalization of law cannot be adequately grasped at all within the limits of a theory of action. With the tendencies toward regulation by law [*Verrechtlichung*] formally organized systems of action are established, and this does in fact result in subsystems of purposive-rational action becoming detached from their moral-practical foundations. But this growing autonomy of self-regulated subsystems in relation to the communicatively structured lifeworld has less to do with the rationalization of action orientations than with a new level of system differentiation. This problem will provide us with an occasion, not to expand the action-theoretic approach in the direction of a theory of communicative action, but to combine it with the systems-theoretic approach (in Chapter VI, "Intermediate Reflections: System and Lifeworld"). Only the integration of both approaches makes the theory of communicative action a sound foundation for a social theory with any hope of success in tackling the problem of societal rationalization first dealt with by Max Weber (in Chapter VIII, "Concluding Reflections: From Parsons through Weber to Marx").

III

Intermediate Reflections: Social Action, Purposive Activity, and Communication

If we follow Weber's studies in the sociology of religion, it is an empirical—and thus to begin with an open—question, why all three rationality complexes differentiated out after the disintegration of traditional worldviews have not found a balanced institutional embodiment in the orders of life of modern societies, why they do not determine the communicative practice of everyday life each to the same degree. However, through his basic action-theoretic assumptions Weber prejudiced this question in such a way that processes of societal rationalization could come into view only from the standpoint of purposive rationality. I would like, therefore, to discuss the conceptual bottlenecks in his theory of action and to use this critique as the starting point for analyzing further the concept of communicative action.

In this sketch I shall not be dealing with the analytic theory of action developed in the Anglo-Saxon world.[1] The studies carried out under this title (the results of which I have drawn upon above[2]) by no means represent a unified approach. What is common to them is the method of conceptual analysis and a relatively narrow formulation of the problem. Analytic action theory has been fruitful for clarifying the structures of purposive activity. However, it is limited to the atomistic model of action by an isolated actor and does not consider the mechanisms for coordinating action through which interpersonal relations come about. It conceptualizes action on the presupposition of exactly one world of existing states of affairs and neglects those actor-world relations that are essential to social interaction. As actions are reduced to purposive interventions in the objective world, the rationality of means-ends relations stands in the foreground. Furthermore, analytic action theory understands its task to be a metatheoretical clarification of basic concepts; it is not concerned with the empirical usefulness of basic action-theoretic assumptions and thus is scarcely connected with concept formation in the social sciences. It generates a set of philosophical problems that are too unspecific for the purposes of social theory.

On the field of analytic action theory, empiricism is repeating battles long since fought. Once again there are debates concerning the relation of mind and body (idealism versus materialism), concerning reasons and causes (free will versus determinism), concerning behavior and action (objectivistic versus nonobjectivistic descriptions of action), concerning the logical status of explanations of action, concerning causality, intentionality and so on. To put the matter in a pointed way: Analytic action theory treats the venerable problems of the pre-Kantian philosophy of consciousness in a new perspective, and without pushing through to the basic questions of a sociological theory of action.

From a sociological point of view it makes sense to begin with communicative action. "The necessity for coordinated action generates in society a certain need for communication, which must be met if it is to be possible to coordinate actions effectively for the purpose of satisfying needs."[3] Analytic philosophy, with the theory of meaning at its core, does offer a promising point of departure for a theory of communicative action that places understanding in language, as the medium for coordinating action, at the focal point of interest. This is less true of those approaches to meaning theory that stand closest to action theory in one respect, namely the intentionalist semantics[4] which goes back to studies by Grice,[5] which was further developed by Lewis,[6] and was worked out by Schiffer[7] and Bennett.[8] This nominalistic theory of meaning is not suitable for clarifying the coordinating mechanism of linguistically mediated interaction because it analyzes the act of reaching understanding on a model of action oriented to consequences.

Intentionalist semantics is based on the counterintuitive idea that understanding the meaning of a symbolic expression X can be traced back to understanding the intention of speaker S to give hearer H something to understand by means of a sign. In this way, a derivative mode of reaching understanding, to which speakers can have recourse if the road to direct understanding is obstructed, is stylized into the original mode of reaching understanding. The attempt of intentionalist semantics to base the meaning of the symbolic expression X on what S means by X, or indirectly gives to understand by X, miscarries. For a hearer to understand what S means by X—that is, the meaning of X— and for him to be aware of the intention that S is pursuing in using X—that is, the purpose that S wants to accomplish with his action—are two different things. S will be able to accomplish his intention of giving rise to a certain meaning [*Meinung*] in H only if H recognizes this intention and understands what is meant—understands, that is, the meaning of a corresponding symbolic expression. Solely on the basis of knowing *that* S has the intention of achieving understanding, H will not be able to infer *what* S means and wants to communicate to him.[9]

For a theory of communicative action only those analytic theories of meaning are instructive that start from the structure of linguistic expressions rather than from speakers' intentions. And the theory will have to keep in view the problem of how the actions of several actors are linked to one another by means of the mechanism of reaching understanding, that is, how they can be interlaced in social spaces and historical times. The organon model of Karl Bühler is representative of this communication-theoretic line of inquiry. Bühler starts from the semiotic model of a linguistic sign used by a speaker (sender) with the aim of coming to an understanding with a hearer (receiver) about objects and states of affairs.[10] He distinguishes three functions of the use of signs: the cognitive function of representing a state of affairs, the expressive function of making known experiences of the speaker, and the appellative function of directing requests to addressees. From this perspective the linguistic sign functions simultaneously as symbol, symptom and signal. "It is a *symbol* in virtue of being correlated with objects and states of affairs, a *symptom* (indication, index) in virtue of its dependence on the sender, whose subjectivity it expresses, and a *signal* in virtue of its appeal to the hearer, whose external or internal behavior it steers like other traffic signs."[11]

There is no need here to go into the reception and critique of this model of language in linguistics and psychology[12] since the decisive developments of it have come, with one exception,[13] from the side of language analysis. At least the three most important analytic theories of meaning can be worked into Bühler's model in such a way that communication theory is further articulated from within—through the formal analysis of rules for using linguistic expressions—and not from without—through a cybernetic reformulation of the transmission process. This meaning-theoretic line of development of the organon model leads us away from the objectivistic conception of processes of reaching understanding as information flows between senders and receivers[14] and in the direction of the formal-pragmatic concept of interaction among speaking and acting subjects, interaction that is mediated through acts of reaching understanding.

Starting from the pragmatist theory of signs introduced by Peirce and developed by Morris, Carnap made the symbolic complex, which Bühler had first considered only functionalistically, accessible to an internal analysis from syntactic and semantic points of view. The bearers of meaning are not isolated signs but elements of a language system, that is, sentences whose form is determined by syntactic rules and whose semantic content is determined by relations to designated objects or states of affairs. With Carnap's logical syntax and the basic assumptions of reference semantics, the way was opened to a formal analysis of the representational function of language. On the other hand, Carnap considered the appellative and expressive functions of language as pragmatic aspects that should be left to empirical analysis. On this view, the pragmatics of language is not determined by a general system of rules in such a way that it could be opened up to conceptual analysis like syntax and semantics.

The theory of meaning was finally established as a formal science only with the step from reference semantics to truth semantics. The semantics founded by Frege and developed through the early Wittgenstein to Davidson and Dummett gives center stage to the relation between sentence and state of affairs, between language and the world.[15] With this ontological turn, semantic theory disengaged itself from the view that the representational function can be clarified on the model of names that designate objects. The meaning of sentences, and the understanding of sentence meanings, cannot be separated from language's inherent relation to the validity of statements. Speakers and hearers understand the meaning of a sentence when they know under what conditions it is true. Correspondingly, they understand the meaning of a word when they know what contribution it makes to the capacity for truth of a sentence formed with its help. Thus truth semantics developed the thesis that the meaning of a sentence is determined by its truth conditions. The internal connection between the *meaning* of a linguistic expression and the *validity* of a sentence formed with its help was first worked out, then, for the dimension of the linguistic representation of states of affairs.

This theory is committed to analyzing all sentences on the model of assertoric sentences. The limits of this approach become visible as soon as the different modes of using sentences are brought under formal consideration. Frege had already distinguished between the assertoric or interrogative force of assertions or questions and the structure of the propositional sentences employed in these utterances. Along the line from the later Wittgenstein through Austin to Searle, the formal semantics of sentences was extended to speech acts. It is no longer limited to the representational function of language but is open to an unbiased analysis of the multiplicity of illocutionary forces. The theory of speech acts marks the first step toward a formal pragmatics that extends to noncognitive modes of employment. At the same time, as the attempts at a systematization of speech acts from Stenius through Kenny to Searle show, it remains tied to the narrow ontological presuppositions of truth-conditional semantics. The theory of meaning can attain the level of integration of the communication theory that Bühler advanced in a programmatic way only if it is able to provide a systematic grounding for the appellative and expressive functions of language (and perhaps also for the "poetic" function related to the linguistic means themselves, as this was developed by Jakobson), in the same way that truth-conditional semantics has done for the representational function. I have taken this path with my reflections on universal pragmatics.[16]

Bühler's theory of language functions could be connected with the methods and insights of the analytic theory of meaning and be made the centerpiece of a theory of communicative action oriented to reaching understanding if we could generalize the concept of validity beyond the truth of propositions and identify validity conditions no longer only on the semantic level of sentences but on the pragmatic level of utterances. For this purpose the paradigm change in philosophy of language that was introduced by J. L. Austin—a clear historical account of which has been given by K. O. Apel[17]—must be radicalized in such a way that the break with the "logos characterization of language," that is, with privileging its representational function, also has consequences for the choice of ontological presuppositions in the theory of language. It is not merely a question of admitting other modes of language use on an equal footing with the assertoric; we have to establish validity claims and world-relations for them as was done for the assertoric mode.[18] It is with this in mind that I have proposed that we do not set illocutionary role over against propositional content as an irrational force, but conceive of it as the component that specifies which validity claim a speaker is raising with his utterance, how he is raising it, and for what.

With the illocutionary force of an utterance a speaker can motivate a hearer to accept the offer contained in his speech act and thereby to accede to *a rationally motivated binding* (or bonding: *Bindung) force.* This conception presupposes that acting and speaking subjects can relate to more than only one world, and that when they come to an understanding with one another about something in one world, they base their communication on a commonly supposed system of worlds. In this connection I have proposed that we differentiate the external world into an objective and a social world, and that we introduce the internal world as a complementary concept to the external world. The corresponding validity claims of truth, rightness, and sincerity can then serve as guiding threads in the choice of theoretical perspectives for distinguishing the basic modes of language use, or the functions of language, and classifying the speech acts that vary with individual languages. Bühler's appellative function would accordingly have to be split up into the regulative and imperative functions. In the regulative use of language, participants raise normative validity claims in various ways and relate their utterances to something in their common social world; in the imperative use of language, they relate them to something in the objective world, whereby the speaker raises a claim to power vis-à-vis the addressee in order to get him to act in such a way that the intended state of affairs comes into existence. A theory of communication worked out along these lines in formal-pragmatic terms could be made fruitful for a sociological theory of action if we could show how communicative acts—that is, speech acts or equivalent nonverbal expressions—take on the function of coordinating action and make their contribution to building up interactions.

Finally, communicative action is dependent on situational

contexts, which represent in turn segments of the life-world of the participants in interaction. The connection of action theory to the basic concepts of social theory can be rendered secure by means of the concept of the life-world; this will be introduced as a complementary concept to communicative action via the analyses of background knowledge stimulated by Wittgenstein.[19]

In the compass of these intermediate reflections, I can at best hope to make this program plausible. (A) Starting from two versions of Weber's action theory, I would like first to make clear the central importance of the problem of coordinating actions. (B) following this I shall try to make Austin's distinction between illocutionary and perlocutionary acts fruitful for delimiting action oriented to reaching understanding from action oriented to success. Then I shall examine (C) the illocutionary binding (or bonding) effect of the offers contained in speech acts, and (D) the role of criticizable validity claims. (E) A discussion of competing proposals for classifying speech acts will serve to confirm my views. (F) Finally, I want to examine a few of the transitions from the formal-pragmatic level of analysis to empirical pragmatics, and, in connection with the relation between the literal and context-dependent meanings of speech acts, to explain why the concept of communicative action has to be completed through a concept of the lifeworld.

A.—Two Versions of Weber's Theory of Action. Weber begins by introducing 'meaning' as a basic concept of action theory and with its help distinguishes actions from observable behavior: "Human behavior—be it external or internal, activity, omission or acquiescence—will be called "action" if and insofar as the actor attaches a subjective meaning to it."[20] Weber does not rely here on a theory of meaning but on a theory of consciousness. He does not elucidate "meaning" in connection with the model of speech; he does not relate it to the linguistic medium of possible understanding, but to the beliefs and intentions of an acting subject, taken to begin with in isolation. At this first switchpoint Weber parts company with a theory of communicative action. What counts as fundamental is not the interpersonal relation between at least two speaking and acting subjects—a relation that refers back to reaching understanding in language—but the purposive activity of a solitary acting subject. As in intentionalist semantics, reaching understanding in language is represented on the model of teleologically acting subjects reciprocally influencing one another. "A language community is represented in the ideal-typical, 'purposive-rational' limit case by numerous individual acts . . . which are oriented to the expectation of gaining 'understanding' from others for an intended meaning."[21] Reaching understanding counts as a derivative phenomenon that is to be explained with the help of a concept of intention posited as primitive. Thus Weber starts from a teleological model of action and specifies "subjective meaning" as a (precommunicative) action intention. An agent can either pursue his own interests, such as acquiring power or wealth, or he can attempt to live up to values such as piety or human dignity, or he can seek satisfaction in living out affects and desires. These utilitarian, value-related, or affectual goals, which can be broken down into situation-specific purposes, are forms of the subjective meaning that acting subjects can connect with their goal-directed activity.[22]

Since Weber starts from a monologically conceived model of action, the concept of "social action" cannot be introduced by way of explicating the concept of meaning. Instead he has to expand the model of purposive activity with two specifications so that the conditions of social interaction are satisfied: (a) an orientation to the behavior of other acting subjects, and (b) a reflexive relation of the reciprocal action orientations of several interacting subjects. To be sure, Weber vacillates as to whether he should regard condition (a) as sufficient for social interaction or should also require (b). In section 1 of *Economy and Society* he says only: "That action will be called 'social' which, in its meaning as intended by the actor or actors, takes account of the behavior of others and is thereby oriented in its course."[23] On the other hand, in section 3 Weber stresses that the action orientations of participants have to be *reciprocally* related to one another: "The term 'social relationship' will be used to denote the behavior of a plurality of actors insofar as, in its meaning content, the behavior of each is reciprocally related to that of the others and is thereby oriented."[24]

For the construction of a theory of action, another decision is even more important. Should Weber introduce the aspects of the rationality of action on the basis of the teleological action model, or should the concept of social action serve as basic for that purpose? In the first case, Weber has to limit himself to those aspects of rationality yielded by the model of purposive activity, that is, to the rationality of means and ends. In the second case, the question arises whether there are different kinds of reflexive relations of action orientations and thus also additional aspects under which actions can be rationalized.

(a) The Official Version. Weber distinguishes the types of purposive-rational, value-rational, affectual, and traditional action. This typology is based on categories of action goals to which an actor can orient himself in his purposive activity: utilitarian, value-related, and affectual goals. Then "traditional action" follows as a residual category that is not further determined. This typology is obviously guided by an interest in distinguishing the degrees to which action is rationalizable. Weber does not start from the social relationship. He regards as rationalizable only the means-ends relation of teleologically conceived, monological action. If one adopts this perspective, the only aspects of action open to objective appraisal are the *effectiveness* of a causal intervention into an existing situation and the *truth* of the empirical assumptions that underlie the maxim or the plan of action—that is, the subjective belief about a purposive-rational organization of means. So Weber chooses purposive-rational action as the reference point of his typology:

> Like every action, social action too can be determined (1) *purposive-rationally*—through expectations as to the behavior of objects in the external world and of other men, using these expectations as "conditions" or as "means" for one's own *ends*, weighed and pursued rationally in terms of success—(2) *value-rationally*—through conscious belief in the (ethical, aesthetic, religious or however interpreted) unconditional, *intrinsic* value of a certain mode of behavior, purely as such and independently of success—(3) *affectually*, especially *emotionally*—through present affects and emotional states—(4) *traditionally*—through the habituation of long practice.[25]

If one follows a suggestion for interpretation advanced by Wolfgang Schluchter,[26] this typology can be reconstructed in accord with the formal properties of purposive-rational action. An actor behaves purposive-rationally when he chooses *ends* from a clearly articulated horizon of *values* and organizes suitable *means* in consideration of alternative *consequences*. In the series of types of action proposed by Weber, the range of what the acting subject takes into consideration narrows step by step. In value-rational action the consequences are screened out of the subjective meaning and thus withdrawn from rational control; in affectual action this is true of the consequences and the values; in action that is merely habitual, the ends as well (see Figure 12).

Figure 12
The Official Typology of Action

Types of action in descending order of rationality	Subjective meaning covers the following elements:			
	Means	Ends	Values	Consequences
Purposive-rational	+	+	+	+
Value-rational	+	+	+	−
Affectual	+	+	−	−
Traditional	+	−	−	−

Of course, Weber can accommodate "value-rational" action in this construction only by attaching to it a restrictive significance. This type can include only action orientations of an ethic of conviction and not of an ethic of responsibility. Moreover, it does not take into account the principled character on the basis of which the Protestant ethic, for example, qualifies as a framework for a methodical conduct of life. The postconventional structures of consciousness that Weber finds in ethically rationalized worldviews cannot, on analytic grounds, be included in an action typology that rests on a categorization of *nonsocial* actions; for moral consciousness is related to the consensual regulation of *interpersonal* conflicts of action.

(b) The Unofficial Version. When Weber attempts to set up a typology on the conceptual level of social action, he encounters additional aspects of the rationality of action. Social actions can be distinguished according to the mechanisms for coordinating individual actions, for instance according to whether a social relation is based on *interest positions* alone or on *normative agreement* as well. It is in this way that Weber distinguishes the sheer facticity of an economic order from the social validity [*Geltung*] of a legal order. In the one case, social relations gain stability through the factual intermeshing of interest positions; in the other, through an additional recognition of normative validity claims. A coordination of actions secured only through the comple-

mentarity of interests can, of course, be normatively restructured through the superaddition of "validity based on agreement," that is, through the "belief that a certain behavior is required by law or convention."[27] Weber elucidates this in connection with the development of traditions through the transition from "custom" to "convention": "It is by way of conventional rules that merely factual regularities of action—that is, mere custom—are normally transformed into binding norms, guaranteed primarily by psychological coercion."[28]

Interaction based on *complementarity of interests* exists not only in the form of custom—that is, of insensibly accepted habituation—but also at the level of rational competitive behavior, for example in modern commerce, in which participants have formed a clear consciousness of the complementarity as well as of the contingency of their interest positions. On the other hand, interaction based on *normative consensus* does not only take the form of tradition-bound, conventional action; the modern legal system is dependent on an enlightened belief in legitimation, which rational natural law—in the idea of a basic contract among free and equals—traces back to procedures of rational will-formation. This might have suggested constructing the types of social action (a) according to the kind of coordination and (b) according to the degree of rationality of the social relationship (see Figure 13).

Figure 13
An Alternative Typology of Action

Degree of Rationality of Action / Coordination	Low	High
Through interest positions	De facto customary action[*Sitte*]	Strategic action [*Interessenhandeln*]
Through normative agreement	Conventional action based on agreement [*Gemeinschaftshandeln*]	Postconventional action based on agreement [*Gesellschaftshandeln*]

There are indications of this typology in *Economy and Society*;[29] there is relatively strong evidence for it in the essay "On Some Categories of Interpretive Sociology."[30] But I shall not pursue this here, because Weber did not clearly carry through, at the level of action orientations themselves, the interesting distinction between social relations mediated by interest positions and those determined by normative agreement. (I shall take this up below in discussing the orientations to success and to understanding.) More serious is the fact that while Weber does distinguish between tradition-bound and rational agreement, he explains this rational agreement inadequately, as we have seen above, using the model of arrangements among subjects of private law. At any rate, he does not trace it back to the moral-practical foundations of discursive will-formation. Otherwise it would have become clear in this context that action in society [*Gesellschaftshandeln*] is distinguished from action in community [*Gemeinschaftshandeln*] not through the purposive-rational action orientations of the participants, but through the higher, namely postconventional stage of moral-practical rationality. Because that did not happen, a *specific* concept of value-rationality could not gain the significance for action theory that it would have to have if the ethical rationalization that Weber examined at the level of cultural tradition is to be grasped in terms of its consequences for systems of social action.

Weber was not able to make his unofficial typology of action fruitful for the problematic of societal rationalization. The official version, however, is so narrowly conceived that in its framework social action can be assessed only under the aspect of purposive-rationality. From this conceptual perspective the rationalization of action systems has to be restricted to the establishment and diffusion of the types of purposive-rational action specific to various subsystems. If processes of societal rationalization are to be investigated *in their entire breadth*, other action-theoretical foundations are required.

I would like therefore to take up once again the concept of communicative action expounded in the introduction and, by drawing upon speech act theory, to pursue those aspects of the rationality of action neglected in Weber's official action theory. In this way I hope to capture in action-theoretic terms the complex concept of rationality that Weber did employ in his cultural analyses. I shall be starting from a typology that is modelled on the unofficial version of Weber's action theory, insofar as social actions are distinguished according to two action orientations—corresponding to the coordination of action through interest positions and through normative agreement (see Figure 14).

Figure 14
Types of Action

Action Situation / Action Orientation	Oriented to Success	Oriented to Reaching Understanding
Nonsocial	Instrumental action	———
Social	Strategic action	Communicative action

The model of purposive-rational action takes as its point of departure the view that the actor is primarily oriented to attaining an end (which has been rendered sufficiently precise in terms of purposes), that he selects means that seem to him appropriate in the given situation, and that he calculates other foreseeable consequences of action as secondary conditions of success. Success is defined as the appearance in the world of a desired state, which can, in a given situation, be causally produced through goal-oriented action or omission. The effects of action comprise the results of action (which the actor foresaw and intended, or made allowance for) and the side effects (which the actor did not foresee). We call an action oriented to success *instrumental* when we consider it under the aspect of following technical rules of action and assess the efficiency of an intervention into a complex of circumstances and events. We call an action oriented to success *strategic* when we consider it under the aspect of following rules of rational choice and assess the efficacy of influencing the decisions of a rational opponent. Instrumental actions can be connected with and subordinated to social interactions of a different type—for example, as the "task elements" of social roles; strategic actions are social actions by themselves. By contrast, I shall speak of *communicative* action whenever the actions of the agents involved are coordinated not through egocentric calculations of success but through acts of reaching understanding. In communicative action participants are not primarily oriented to their own individual successes; they pursue their individual goals under the condition that they can harmonize their plans of action on the basis of common situation definitions. In this respect the negotiation of definitions of the situation is an essential element of the interpretive accomplishments required for communicative action.

B.—Orientation to Success versus Orientation to Reaching Understanding. In identifying strategic action and communicative action as types, I am assuming that concrete actions can be classified from these points of view. I do not want to use the terms "strategic" and "communicative" only to designate two analytic aspects under which the same action could be described—on the one hand as a reciprocal influencing of one another by opponents acting in a purposive-rational manner and, on the other hand, as a process of reaching understanding among members of a lifeworld. Rather, social actions can be distinguished according to whether the participants adopt either a success-oriented attitude or one oriented to reaching understanding. And, under suitable conditions, these attitudes should be identifiable on the basis of the intuitive knowledge of the participants themselves.

In the framework of action theory, the conceptual analysis of the two attitudes cannot be understood as a psychological task. It is not my aim to characterize behavioral dispositions empirically, but to grasp structural properties of processes of reaching understanding, from which we can derive general pragmatic presuppositions of communicative action. To explain what I mean by "an attitude oriented to reaching understanding," I have to analyze the concept of "reaching understanding." This is not a question of the predicates an observer uses when describing processes of reaching understanding, but of the pretheoretical knowledge of competent speakers, who can themselves distinguish situations in which they are causally exerting an influence *upon* others from those in which they are coming to an understanding *with* them, and who know when their attempts have failed. Once we are able to specify the standards on which these distinctions are implicitly based, we will be in a position to explain the concept of reaching understanding.

Reaching understanding [*Verständigung*] is considered to be a process of reaching agreement [*Einigung*] among speaking and acting subjects. Naturally, a group of persons can feel at one in a mood which is so diffuse that it is difficult to identify the propositional content or the intentional object to which it is directed. Such a collective like-mindedness [Gleichgestimmtheit] does not satisfy the conditions for the type of agreement [Einverständnis] in which attempts at reaching understanding terminate when they are successful. A communicatively achieved agreement, or one that is mutually presupposed in communicative action, is propositionally differentiated. Owing to this linguistic structure, it cannot be merely induced through outside influence; it has to be accepted or presupposed as valid by the participants. To this extent it can be distinguished from merely de facto accord [Übereinstimmung]. Processes of reaching understanding aim at an agreement that meets the conditions of rationally motivated assent [Zustimmung] to the content of an utterance. A communicatively achieved agreement has a rational basis; it cannot be imposed by either party, whether instrumentally through intervention in the situation directly or strategically through influencing the decisions of opponents. Agreement can indeed be objectively obtained by force; but what comes to pass manifestly through outside influence or the use of violence cannot count subjectively as agreement. Agreement rests on common *convictions.* The speech act of one person succeeds only if the other accepts the offer contained in it by taking (however implicitly) a "yes" or "no" position on a validity claim that is in principle criticizable. Both ego, who raises a validity claim with his utterance, and alter, who recognizes or rejects it, base their decisions on potential grounds or reasons.

If we were not in a position to refer to the model of speech, we could not even begin to analyze what it means for two subjects to come to an understanding with one another. Reaching understanding is the inherent telos of human speech. Naturally, speech and understanding are not related to one another as means to end. But we can explain the concept of reaching understanding only if we specify what it means to use sentences with a communicative intent. The concepts of speech and understanding reciprocally interpret one another. Thus we can analyze the formal-pragmatic features of the attitude oriented to reaching understanding in connection with the model of the attitude of participants in communication, one of whom—in the simplest case—carries out a speech act, to which the other takes a yes or no position (even though utterances in the communicative practice of everyday life usually do not have a standard linguistic form and often have no verbal form at all).

If we approach the task of delimiting actions oriented to success from those oriented to reaching understanding by way of an analysis of speech acts, we encounter the following difficulty. On the one hand, we are regarding the communicative acts with the help of which speakers and hearers come to an understanding about something as a mechanism for coordinating actions. The concept of communicative action is presented in such a way that the acts of reaching understanding, which link the teleologically structured plans of action of different participants and thereby first combine individual acts into an interaction complex, cannot themselves be reduced to teleological actions. In this respect the paradigmatic concept of linguistically mediated interaction is compatible with a theory of meaning which, like intentionalist semantics, tries to conceptualize reaching understanding as the solution to a problem of coordination among subjects acting with an orientation to success. On the other hand, not every linguistically mediated interaction is an example of action oriented to reaching understanding. Without doubt, there are countless cases of indirect understanding, where one subject gives another something to understand through signals, indirectly gets him to form a certain opinion or to adopt certain intentions by way of inferentially working up perceptions of the situation; or where, on the basis of an already habitual communicative practice of everyday life, one subject inconspicuously harnesses another for his own purposes, that is, induces him to behave in a desired way by manipulatively employing linguistic means and thereby instrumentalizes him for his own success. Such examples of the use of language with an orientation to consequences seem to decrease the value of speech acts as the model for action oriented to reaching understanding.

This will turn out not to be the case only if it can be shown that the use of language with an orientation to reaching understanding is the *original mode* of language use, upon which indirect understanding, giving something to understand or letting something be understood, and the instrumental use of language in general, are parasitic. In my view, Austin's distinction between illocutions and perlocutions accomplishes just that.

As is well known, Austin distinguishes locutionary, illocutionary and perlocutionary acts.[31] He applies the term "locutionary" to the content of propositional sentences (p) or of nominalized propositional sentences (that p). Through *locutionary acts* the speaker expresses states of affairs; he says something.

Through *illocutionary acts* the speaker performs an action in saying something. The illocutionary role establishes the mode of a sentence ("M*p*") employed as a statement, promise, command, avowal, or the like. Under standard conditions, the mode is expressed by means of a performative verb in the first person present; the action meaning can be seen particularly in the fact that "hereby" can be added to the illocutionary component of the speech act: "I hereby promise you (command you, confess to you) that *p*." Finally, through *perlocutionary acts* the speaker produces an effect upon the hearer. By carrying out a speech act he brings about something in the world. Thus the three acts that Austin distinguishes can be characterized in the following catch-phrases: to say *something*, to act *in* saying something, to bring about something *through* acting in saying something.

Austin makes his conceptual incisions in such a way that the speech act ("M*p*"), composed of an illocutionary and a propositional component, is presented as a self-sufficient act which the speaker always performs with a communicative intent, that is, so that a hearer may understand and accept his utterance.[32] The self-sufficiency of the speech act is to be understood in the sense that the communicative intent of the speaker and the illocutionary aim he is pursuing follow from the manifest meaning of what is said. It is otherwise with teleological actions. We identify their meaning only in connection with the intentions their authors are pursuing and the ends they want to realize. As *the meaning of what is said* is constitutive for illocutionary acts, *the intention of the agent* is constitutive for teleological actions.

What Austin calls *perlocutionary effects* arise from the fact that illocutionary acts are embedded in contexts of interaction. Speech acts, like actions in general, can produce side effects that the actor did not foresee; these are perlocutionary effects in a trivial sense, which I shall not consider any further. Less trivial are the perlocutionary effects which result from the fact that illocutionary acts sometimes take on roles in contexts of strategic interaction. These effects ensue whenever a speaker acts with an orientation to success and thereby instrumentalizes speech acts for purposes that are only contingently related to the meaning of what is said. This is what Austin has in mind:

> There is a further sense in which to perform a locutionary act, and therein an illocutionary act, may also be to perform an act of another kind. Saying something will often, or even normally, produce certain consequential effects upon the

feelings, thoughts, or actions of the audience, or of the speaker, or of other persons: and it may be done with the design, intention, or purpose of producing them; and we may then say, thinking of this, that the speaker has performed an act in the nomenclature of which reference is made either only obliquely, or even not at all, to the performance of the locutionary or illocutionary act. We shall call the performance of an act of this kind the performance of a *perlocutionary act* or *perlocution*.[33]

The demarcation between illocutionary and perlocutionary acts has given rise to an extended controversy.[34] From it have emerged four criteria of demarcation.

a) The illocutionary aim a speaker pursues with an utterance follows from the very meaning of what is said; speech acts are, in this sense, self-identifying.[35] By means of an illocutionary act a speaker lets a hearer know that he wants what he says to be understood as a greeting, command, warning, explanation, and so forth. His communicative intent does not go beyond wanting the hearer to understand the manifest content of the speech act. By contrast, the perlocutionary aim of a speaker, like the ends pursued with goal-directed actions generally, does not follow from the manifest content of the speech act; this aim can be identified only through the agent's intention. For example, a hearer who understands a request directed to him can just as little know thereby what *else* the speaker has in view in uttering it as an observer who sees an acquaintance hurrying along the street can know why he is in a hurry. The addressee could at best infer the speaker's perlocutionary aims from the context.[36] The three remaining criteria have to do with this character of self-identification of speech acts.

b) From the description of a speech act, as in (1) and (2) below, we can infer the conditions for the corresponding illocutionary success of the speaker, but not the conditions for the perlocutionary results that a speaker acting with an orientation to success might want to achieve, or did achieve, in a given case by carrying out this speech act. Into the description of perlocutions, as in (3) and (4) below, there enter results that go beyond the meaning of what is said and thus beyond what an addressee could directly understand.

1. *S* asserted to *H* that he gave notice to his firm.

S will have achieved illocutionary success with the utterance represented by (1) if H understands his assertion and accepts it as true. The same holds for

2. H warned S not to give notice to his firm.

H will have achieved illocutionary success with the utterance represented by (2) if S understands his warning and accepts it as true or right—depending on whether in a given context it has more the sense of a prognosis or of a moral appeal. In any case, accepting the utterance described in (2) is grounds for certain obligations on the part of the addressee and for corresponding expectations on the part of the speaker. Whether the expected consequences actually come to pass or not has no effect on the illocutionary success of the speaker. If, for instance, S does not give notice, this is not a perlocutionarily achieved effect but the consequence of a communicatively achieved agreement and thus the fulfillment of an obligation the addressee took upon himself with his "yes" to a speech act offer. Consider now:

3. Through informing H that he had given notice to his firm, S gave H a fright (as he intended to do).

From this description it follows that the illocutionary success of the assertion described in (1) is not a sufficient condition for achieving a perlocutionary effect. In another context the hearer could just as well react to the same utterance with relief. The same holds for:

4. H upset S with the warning against giving notice to his firm.

In another context the same warning could just as well strengthen S in his resolve, for instance if S harbors a suspicion that H does not wish him well. The description of perlocutionary effects must therefore refer to a context of teleological action that *goes beyond* the speech act.[37]

c) From considerations of this kind Austin concluded that illocutionary results stand in a *conventionally* regulated or *internal* connection with speech acts, whereas perlocutionary effects remain external to the meaning of what is said. The possible perlocutionary effects of a speech act depend on fortuitous contexts and are not fixed by conventions, as are illocutionary results.[38] Of course, one might use (4) as a counterexample. Only if the addressee takes the warning seriously is being upset a plausible reaction, and only if he doesn't take it seriously is a feeling of being confirmed (in his decision) plausible. In some cases, the meaning conventions of the action predicates with which illocutionary acts are formed exclude certain classes of perlocutionary effects. At the same time, these effects are not connected with speech acts only in a conventional way. When a hearer accepts an assertion of S as true, a command as right, an admission as truthful, he therewith implicitly declares himself ready to tie his further action to certain conventional obligations. By contrast, the feeling of being upset which a friend arouses in S with a warning that the latter takes seriously is a state that may or may not ensue.

d) Similar considerations have motivated Strawson to replace the criterion of conventionality with another criterion of demarcation.[39] A speaker, if he wants to be successful, may not let his perlocutionary aims be known, whereas illocutionary aims can be achieved only through being expressed. Illocutions are expressed openly; perlocutions may not be "admitted" as such. This difference can also be seen in the fact that the predicates with which perlocutionary acts are described (to give a fright to, to cause to be upset, to plunge into doubt, to annoy, mislead, offend, infuriate, humiliate, and so forth) cannot appear among those predicates used to carry out the illocutionary acts by means of which the corresponding perlocutionary effects can be produced. Perlocutionary acts constitute a subclass of teleological actions which must be carried out by means of speech acts, under the condition that the actor does not declare or admit to his aims as such.

Whereas the sense of the division into locutionary and illocutionary acts is to separate the propositional content from the mode of speech acts as analytically different aspects, the distinction between these two types of acts, on the one side, and perlocutionary acts on the other, is by no means analytical in character. Perlocutionary effects can be achieved by way of speech acts only if the latter are *incorporated as means* into actions oriented to success. Perlocutionary acts are an indication of the integration of speech acts into contexts of strategic interaction. They belong to the intended consequences or results of a teleological action which an actor undertakes with the intention of influencing a hearer in a certain way by means of illocutionary successes. Naturally, speech acts can serve this *nonillocutionary aim of influencing hearers* only if they are suited to achieve illocutionary aims. If the hearer failed to understand what the speaker was saying, a strategically acting speaker would not be able to bring the hearer, by means of communicative acts, to behave in the desired way. To this extent, what we initially designated as "the use of language with an orientation to consequences" is not an original use of language but the subsumption of speech acts that serve illocutionary aims under conditions of action oriented to success.

As speech acts by no means always function in this way, however, it must also be possible to clarify the structure of linguistic communication without reference to structures of purposive activity. The teleological actor's orientation to success is not constitutive for the "success" of processes of reaching understanding, particularly not when these are incorporated into strategic actions. What we mean by reaching understanding has to be clarified *solely* in connection with illocutionary acts. From this it also follows that we cannot explain illocutionary success in terms of the conditions for the purposively achieved success of a teleological action. Illocutionary aims are different from those purposes that can be achieved *under the description* of something to be brought about in the world.

Perlocutionary effects, like the results of teleological actions generally, are intended under the description of states of affairs brought about through intervention in the world. By contrast, illocutionary results are achieved at the level of interpersonal relations on which participants in communication come to an understanding with one another about something in the world. In this sense, they are not innerworldly but extramundane. Illocutionary results appear in the lifeworld to which the participants belong and which forms the background for their processes of reaching understanding. They cannot be intended under the description of causally produced effects.

I would like to suggest that we conceive perlocutions as a special class of strategic interactions in which illocutions are employed as means in teleological contexts of action. As Strawson has shown, this employment is subject to certain provisos. A teleologically acting speaker has to achieve his illocutionary aim—that the hearer understand what is said and undertake the obligations connected with the acceptance of the offer contained in the speech act—without betraying his perlocutionary aim. This proviso lends to perlocutions the peculiarly asymmetrical character of concealed strategic actions. These are interactions in which at least one of the participants is acting strategically, while he deceives other participants regarding the fact that he is *not* satisfying the presuppositions under which illocutionary aims can normally be achieved. For this reason as well, this type of interaction is not suitable as the model for an analysis that is supposed to explain the linguistic mechanism of coordinating action by way of the illocutionary binding (or bonding) effect of speech acts. It would be advisable to select for this purpose a type of interaction that is not burdened with the asymmetries and provisos of perlocutions. I have called the type of interaction in which *all* participants harmonize their individual plans of action with one another and thus pursue their illocutionary aims *without reservation* ''communicative action.''

Austin also analyzes speech acts in contexts of interaction. It is precisely the point of his approach to work out the performative character of linguistic utterances in connection with institutionally bound speech acts like baptizing, betting, appointing, and the like, in which the obligations issuing from the performance of the speech act are unambiguously regulated by accompanying institutions or norms of action. However, Austin confuses the picture by not treating these interactions, in connection with which he analyzes the illocutionary binding effect of speech acts, as *different in type* from those interactions in which perlocutionary effects occur. Someone who makes a bet, appoints an officer as supreme commander, gives a command, admonishes or warns, makes a prediction, tells a story, makes a confession, reveals something, and so forth, is acting communicatively and cannot at all produce perlocutionary effects *at the same level of interaction.* A speaker can pursue perlocutionary aims only when he deceives his partner concerning the fact that he is acting strategically—when, for example, he gives the command to attack in order to get his troops to rush into a trap, or when he proposes a bet of $3,000 in order to embarrass others, or when he tells a story late in the evening in order to delay a guest's departure. It is certainly true that in communicative action unintended consequences may appear at any time; but as soon as there is a danger that these will be attributed to the speaker as intended results, the latter finds it necessary to offer explanations and denials, and if need be, apologies, in order to dispel the false impression that these side effects are perlocutionary effects. Otherwise, he has to expect that the other participants will feel deceived and adopt a strategic attitude in turn, steering away from action oriented to reaching understanding. Of course, in complex action contexts a speech act that is directly performed and accepted under the conditions of communicative action can at the same time have a strategic position at *other* levels of interaction, can have perlocutionary effects on *third parties*.

Thus I count as communicative action those linguistically mediated interactions in which all participants pursue illocutionary aims, and *only* illocutionary aims, with their mediating acts of communication. On the other hand, I regard as linguistically mediated strategic action those interactions in which at least one of the participants wants with his speech acts to produce perlocutionary effects on his opposite number. Austin did not keep these two cases separate as different types of interaction, because he was inclined to identify acts of communication, that is, acts of reaching understanding, with the interactions coordinated by speech acts. He didn't see that acts of communication or speech acts function as a coordinating mechanism for *other* actions. "Acts of communication" should not be confused with what I have introduced as "communicative action." Indeed, they have to be disengaged from contexts of communicative action before they can be incorporated into strategic interactions. And this is possible in turn only because speech acts have a certain independence in relation to communicative action, though the meaning of what is said always points to the interaction structures of communicative action. The difference between a speech act and the context of interaction that it constitutes through achieving a coordination of the plans of different actors can be recognized the more easily if one is not fixated on the model of institutionally bound speech acts, as Austin was.[40]

C.—Meaning and Validity. In connection with the controversial relation between illocutionary and perlocutionary acts, I have attempted to show that while speech acts can indeed be employed strategically, they have a constitutive meaning only for communicative action. The latter is distinguished from strategic action by the fact that all participants pursue illocutionary aims without reservation in order to arrive at an agreement that will provide the basis for a consensual coordination of individually pursued plans of action. In what follows, I would like to explicate the conditions that have to be satisfied by a communicatively achieved agreement that is to fulfill functions of coordinating action. In doing so, I shall confine myself to the model of elementary pairs of utterances, each of which consists of the speech act of a speaker and the affirmative response of a hearer. Consider the following examples:[41]

1. I (hereby) promise you that I shall come tomorrow.
2. You are requested to stop smoking.
3. I confess to you that I find your actions loathsome.
4. I can predict (to you) that the vacation will be spoiled by rain.

We can recognize in each case what an affirmative response would mean and what kind of interaction sequence it would ground.

1. Yes, I shall depend upon it.
2. Yes, I shall comply.
3. Yes, I believe you do.
4. Yes, we'll have to take that into account.

With his "yes" the speaker accepts a speech-act offer and grounds an agreement; this agreement concerns the *content of the utterance,* on the one hand, and, on the other hand, certain *guarantees immanent to speech acts* and certain *obligations relevant to the sequel of interaction.* The action potential typical of a speech act finds expression in the claim that the speaker raises for what he says—in an explicit speech act by means of a performative verb. In acknowledging this claim, the hearer accepts an offer made with the speech act. This illocutionary success is relevant to the interaction inasmuch as it establishes between speaker and hearer an interpersonal relation that is effective for coordination, that orders scopes of action and sequences of interaction, and that opens up to the hearer possible points of connection by way of general alternatives for action.

The question now arises, whence do speech acts draw their power to coordinate interactions, when this authority is neither borrowed directly from the social force [*Geltung*] of norms (as it is in the case of institutionally bound speech acts) nor owed to a contingently available potential for sanctions (as it is in the case of imperative expressions of will)? From the perspective of a hearer to whom an utterance is addressed, we can distinguish three levels of reaction to a (correctly perceived) speech act: The hearer *understands* the utterance, that is, he grasps the meaning of what is said; with his "yes" or "no" the hearer *takes a position* on the claim raised with the speech act, that is, he accepts the speech act offer or declines it; and in consequence of an achieved agreement, the hearer directs his action according to *conventionally fixed obligations.* The *pragmatic* level of agreement that is effective for coordination connects the *semantic* level of understanding meaning with the *empirical* level of developing further—in a manner dependent on the context—the accord relevant to the sequel of interaction. How this connection comes about can be explained by means of the theory of meaning; for this purpose, the formal-semantic approach limited to understanding sentences has to be expanded.[42]

The formal-pragmatic approach to meaning theory begins with the question of *what it means to understand an utterance*—that is, a sentence employed communicatively. Formal semantics makes a conceptual cut between the meaning [*Bedeutung*] of a sentence and the meaning [*Meinung*] of the speaker, who, when he uses the sentence in a speech act, can say something other than it literally means. But this distinction cannot be developed into a methodological separation between the formal analysis of sentence meanings and the empirical analysis of speakers' meanings in utterances; for the literal meaning of a sentence cannot be explained at all independently of the standard conditions of its communicative employment. To be sure, formal pragmatics must also take measures to see that in the standard case what is meant does not deviate from the literal meaning of what is said. For this reason, our analysis is limited to speech acts carried out *under standard conditions.* And this is intended to insure that the speaker means nothing else than the literal meaning of what he says.

In a distinct analogy to the basic assumptions of the semantics of truth conditions, I want now to explain understanding an utterance by knowledge of the conditions under which a hearer may accept it. *We understand a speech act when we know what makes it acceptable.* From the standpoint of the speaker, the conditions of acceptability are identical to the conditions for his illocutionary success. Acceptability is not defined here in an objectivistic sense, from the perspective of an observer, but in the performative attitude of a participant in communication. A speech act may be called "acceptable" if it satisfies the conditions that are necessary in order that the hearer be allowed to take a "yes" position on the claim raised by the speaker. These conditions cannot be satisfied one-sidedly, either relative to the speaker or to the hearer. They are rather conditions for the *intersubjective recognition* of a linguistic claim, which, in a way typical of a given class of speech acts, grounds a specified agreement concerning obligations relevant to the sequel of interaction.

From the standpoint of a sociological theory of action, my primary interest has to be in making clear the mechanism relevant to the coordinating power of speech acts. To this end I shall concentrate on those conditions under which a speaker can be motivated to accept the offer contained in a speech act, assuming that the linguistic expressions employed are grammatically well formed and that the general contextual conditions required for a given type of speech are satisfied.[43] A hearer understands the meaning of an utterance when, in addition to grammatical conditions of well-formedness and general contextual conditions,[44] he knows those *essential conditions* under which he could be motivated by a speaker to take an affirmative position.[45] These *acceptability conditions in the narrower sense* relate to the illocutionary meaning that S expresses by means of a performative clause.

But let us take a look first at a grammatically correct imperative formulated as a request [*Aufforderung*]:

5. I am (hereby) requesting that you stop smoking.

Imperatives are often understood on the model of perlocutionary acts, as attempts by an actor S to get H to carry out a certain action a. In this view, S makes an imperative request when he connects with his utterance the intention that H gather from the utterance that S is attempting to get him to bring about some state p by doing a.[46] But this view misconstrues the illocutionary meaning of such requests. In uttering an imperative, a speaker *says* what H is to do. This *direct form* of achieving understanding makes superfluous a speech act by means of which the speaker could indirectly get a hearer to perform a certain action. The illocutionary meaning of imperative requests or demands can be described through the following paraphrases:[47]

  5a. *S* told *H* that he should take care to see that *p* comes
     to pass.
  5b. *S* signified to *H* that he should translate *p* into reality.
  5c. The request uttered by *S* is to be understood in the sense
     that *H* should bring about *p*.

Here *p* designates a state in the objective world that, relative to the time of the utterance, lies in the future and that, other conditions remaining constant, can come into existence through an intervention or omission *a* by the addressee—for instance, the state of not smoking that *H* brings about by putting out his lit cigarette.

A hearer can accept the request (5) by responding affirmatively to it with:

  5'. Yes, I shall do what is required of me.

If we restrict ourselves to conditions of acceptability in the narrower sense, the conditions under which *H* accepts (5) fall into two components.

a) The hearer should understand the illocutionary meaning of imperative requests in such a way that he could paraphrase this meaning with sentences like (5a), (5b), or (5c) and could interpret the propositional content "to stop smoking" as a request directed to him. In fact, the hearer understands the request (5) if he is familiar with the conditions under which *p* would come to pass and if he knows what he himself is supposed to do or not to do in the given circumstances in order that these conditions will be satisfied. As one must know the truth conditions of a proposition to understand it, one must know the conditions under which an imperative would count as fulfilled if one is to understand it. In the framework of a pragmatic theory of meaning, these *conditions of satisfaction*—formulated to begin with in semantic terms—are interpreted in terms of obligations relevant to the sequel of interaction. The hearer understands an imperative if he knows what he must do or not do in order to bring about a state *p* desired by *S*; he thereby also knows how he could link up his actions with those of *S*.

b) As soon as we conceptualize the understanding of imperatives from this perspective, broadened to include the context of interaction, it becomes clear that awareness of "satisfaction conditions" is not sufficient for knowing when an imperative is acceptable. A second component is lacking: awareness of *the conditions of the agreement that first grounds adherence to the obligations* relevant to the interaction sequel. The hearer fully understands the illocutionary meaning of the imperative when he knows why the speaker expects that he might impose his will on him. With his imperative, the speaker raises a claim to power, to which the hearer, if he accepts it, yields. It belongs to the meaning of an imperative that the speaker harbors a *grounded* expectation that his claim to power will carry; and this holds only under the condition that S knows that his addressee has reason to acquiesce in his claim. Since we have so far understood imperatives as sheer expressions of will, these grounds cannot lie in the illocutionary meaning of the speech act itself; they can reside only in a potential for sanctions that is externally connected with the speech act. Thus the *conditions of satisfaction* have to be supplemented with *conditions of sanction* to complete the conditions of acceptability.

A hearer understands the imperative request (5) if he knows (a) the conditions under which an addressee can bring about the desired state (not smoking) and (b) the conditions under which S has good reason to expect that H will see himself constrained to yield to the will of S (for example, the threat of penalties for violating safety regulations). Only by knowing both components (a) and (b) does the hearer know what conditions have to be met if a hearer is to be able to respond affirmatively, as in (5′), to the (imperative) request (5). In knowing these conditions, he knows what makes the utterance acceptable.

This picture is complicated in instructive ways when we pass from genuine or *simple* imperatives to *normatively authorized* imperatives or directions, which can take the form of commands or orders and which can, on the surface, also resemble simple requests and demands. Let us compare (5) with

6. I am (hereby) ordering you to stop smoking.

This utterance presupposes recognized norms (for example, the safety regulations for international air travel) and an institutional framework authorizing those holding certain positions (flight attendants) under certain conditions (preparing to land) to direct a certain class of persons (passengers) to stop smoking by appealing to certain regulations.

Again, the illocutionary meaning can be specified first through the conditions mentioned under (a); but in the case of directions [*Anweisungen*], the illocutionary meaning not only *points to* conditions (b), which have to be added from the context of the speech act; instead, these conditions for accepting the linguistic claim, and thus for agreement between S and H, *spring from* the meaning of the illocutionary act itself. In the case of mere imperative expressions of will, S has good reason to expect that H will yield to his will only if he has at his disposition negative or positive sanctions with which he can perceptibly threaten or entice H. So long as S does not appeal to the validity of norms, it makes no difference whether the potential for sanction is grounded de jure or de facto. For so long as S utters a simple imperative and expresses nothing but his own will, his influence on H's decision is merely empirical—he threatens him with losses or offers him rewards. In this case, the grounds for accepting demands are related to motives of the hearer that the speaker can influence only empirically, in the last analysis by means of weapons or goods. It is otherwise with normatively authorized demands or directions, such as commands and orders. In contrast to (5), with (6) the speaker is appealing to the *validity* of safety regulations and, in issuing directions, is raising a claim to normative validity.

Registering a *validity claim* is not the expression of a contingent will; and responding affirmatively to a validity claim is not merely an empirically motivated decision. Both acts, putting forward and recognizing a validity claim, are subject to conventional restrictions, because such a claim can be rejected only by way of criticism and can be defended against a criticism only by refuting it. One who opposes directions is referred to existing [*geltende*] regulations and not to the mere fact of penalties that can be expected if they are not followed. And one who doubts the validity of the underlying norms has to give *reasons*—whether against the legality of the regulations—that is, against the lawfulness of its social force [*Geltung*]—or against the legitimacy of the regulation—that is, against its claim to be right or justified in a moral-practical sense. Validity claims are *internally* connected with reasons and grounds. To this extent, the conditions for the acceptability of directions can be found in the illocutionary meaning of the speech act itself; they do not need to be completed by *additional* conditions of sanction.

Thus a hearer understands the direction (6) if he knows (a) the conditions under which an addressee could bring about the desired state (not smoking), and (b) the conditions under which S could have convincing reasons to regard an imperative with the content (a) as valid, that is, as normatively justified. The conditions (a) pertain to obligations that arise out of an agreement based on intersubjective recognition of the normative validity claims raised for a corresponding imperative.[48] The conditions (b) immediately pertain to the acceptance of the validity claim itself. We have to distinguish here between the *validity* of an action or of the norm underlying it, the *claim* that the conditions for its validity are satisfied, and the *redemption* of the validity claim raised, that is, the grounding (of the claim) that the conditions for the validity of an action or of the underlying norm are satisfied. We are now in a position to say that a speaker can *rationally motivate* a hearer to accept his speech act offer because—on the basis of an internal connection between validity, validity claim, and redemption of a validity claim—he can assume the *warranty* [*Gewähr*] for providing, if necessary, convincing reasons that would stand up to a hearer's criticism of the validity claim. Thus a speaker owes the binding (or bonding: *bindende*) force of his illocutionary act not to the validity of what is said but to *the coordinating effect of the warranty* that he offers: namely to redeem, if necessary, the validity claim raised with his speech act. In all cases in which the illocutionary role expresses not a power claim but a validity claim, the place of the empirically motivating force of sanctions (contingently linked with speech acts) is taken by the rationally motivating force of accepting a speaker's guarantee for securing claims to validity.

This holds not only for regulative speech acts like (1) and (2), but also for expressive and constative speech acts like (3) and (4). Just as with (1) a speaker *produces* a normative validity claim for his intention to bring about a desired state, and just as with (2) he *raises* a normative validity claim for his imperative that H bring about a state desired by S, so with (3) the speaker makes a claim to truthfulness for a revealed subjective experience, and with (4) a truth claim for a proposition. In (3) it is the disclosure of a previously concealed emotional attitude, in (4) the putting forward of a proposition, for the validity of which the speaker assumes the warranty (offers a guarantee or takes responsibility) in making a confession (3) or a prediction (4). Thus a hearer understands the avowal (3) if he knows (a) the conditions under which a person could experience loathing for p, and (b) the conditions under which S says what he means and thereby accepts responsibility for the consistency of his further behavior with this confession. A hearer understands (4) if he knows (a) the conditions that would make the prediction true, and (b) the conditions under which S could have convincing reasons for holding a statement with the content (a) to be true.

Of course, there are also important asymmetries. Thus the conditions mentioned under (a) do *not*, in the cases of expressive and constative speech acts like (3) and (4), have to do with obligations resulting from the intersubjective recognition of the validity claims in question; they relate only to understanding the propositional content of a first-person sentence or an assertoric sentence for which the speaker claims validity. In the case of regulative speech acts like (1) and (2), the conditions (a) likewise relate to understanding the propositional content of a sentence expressing an intention or a request for which the speaker produces or claims normative validity; but here the content simultaneously circumscribes the obligations relevant to the sequence of interaction that arise for the hearer from acceptance of the validity claim.

In general, obligations result from the meaning of expressive speech acts only in that the speaker specifies what his past or future behavior may not contradict. That a speaker means what he says can be made credible only in the consistency of what he does and not through providing grounds. Thus addressees who have accepted a claim to sincerity can expect a consistency of behavior in certain respects; this expectation follows from the conditions given under (b). Of course, consequences spring from the warranties offered with the validity claims in regulative and constantive speech acts too; but these *validity-related* obligations to provide, if necessary, justification for norms or grounding for propositions are relevant for argumentation, not for the continuation of interaction. Only those obligations to prove trustworthy [*Bewährungsverpflichtungen*] that the speaker takes on with expressive speech acts have direct relevance for the continuation of interaction. They contain an offer to the hearer to check against the consistency of the speaker's past or future sequence of actions whether he means what he says.[49]

In general, no *special* obligations follow from the meaning of constative speech acts. Obligations relevant to the continuation of interaction arise from the satisfaction of the acceptability conditions stated under (a) and (b) only inasmuch as speakers and hearers obligate themselves to base their actions on interpretations that do not contradict statements accepted as true.

We have distinguished genuine imperatives, with which the speaker connects a claim to power, from speech acts with which the speaker raises a criticizable validity claim. Whereas validity claims are internally connected with grounds and give the illocutionary act a rationally motivating force, power claims have to be covered by a potential for sanction if they are to be successful. Imperatives, however, admit of a secondary normativization. This can be illustrated by the relation that holds between intention sentences and declarations of intention. Intention sentences belong in the same category as the request or demand sentences with which imperatives are formed. We can interpret intention sentences as internalized demands addressed by the speaker to himself.[50] Of course, requests or demands are illocutionary acts, whereas intention sentences get an illocutionary role only through being transformed into declarations of intention or announcements. Whereas imperatives have an illocutionary force by nature—albeit one that calls for supplementation by sanctions—intention sentences, which have, so to speak, lost their imperative force *in foro interno*, can get back an illocutionary force through being connected with validity claims, whether in the form of expressive speech acts like

7. I confess that it is my intention to...

or in the form of normative speech acts like

8. I am hereby declaring my intention to...

With announcements like (8) the speaker enters into a weak normative bond to which the addressee can appeal in a similar way as to a promise.

The normativization of intention sentences can serve as a model for grasping the transformation of simple imperatives into normatively authorized imperatives, of mere imperatives into directions. The imperative request (5) can, through being loaded with a normative validity claim, be transformed into the direction (6). With this, the component of the acceptability conditions given under (b) changes; the conditions of sanction accessory to an imperative power claim are replaced by the rationally motivating conditions for accepting a criticizable validity claim. Because these conditions can be derived from the meaning of the illocutionary act itself, normatively authorized imperatives gain an autonomy that is missing from simple imperatives.

This makes it clear once again that only those speech acts with which a speaker connects a criticizable validity claim can move a hearer to accept an offer independently of external forces. In this way they can be effective as a mechanism for coordinating action.[51]

After these reflections, the class of communicative actions, which we introduced in a provisional way, now needs to be defined more cautiously. We began by including in communicative action all interactions in which those involved coordinate their individual plans unreservedly on the basis of communicatively achieved agreement. With the specification "unreservedly pursuing illocutionary aims," we meant to exclude cases of latently strategic action, in which the speaker *inconspicuously* employs illocutionary results for perlocutionary purposes. In the meantime we have learned that simple imperatives are illocutionary acts with which the speaker *openly* declares his aim of influencing the decisions of his opposite number, and in so doing has to base the success of his power claim on supplementary sanctions. Thus with genuine imperatives—requests and demands that lack normative authorization—speakers can unreservedly pursue illocutionary aims and nonetheless act with an orientation to success rather than to understanding.

Not all illocutionary acts are constitutive for communicative action, but only those with which speakers connect criticizable validity claims. In the other cases, when a speaker is pursuing undeclared ends with perlocutionary acts—ends on which the hearer can take no position at all—or when a speaker is pursuing illocutionary aims on which hearers cannot take a grounded position—as in relation to imperatives—the potential for the binding (or bonding) force of good reasons—a potential which is always contained in linguistic communication—remains unexploited.

D.—Validity Claims. After having demarcated communicative actions from all other social actions through their illocutionary binding (or bonding) force, we might consider ordering the multiplicity of acts of communication according to types of speech acts. And as our guideline in classifying speech acts we may take the options open to hearers to adopt rationally motivated "yes" or "no" positions on the utterances of speakers. In our previous examples we have assumed that the speaker raises precisely one validity claim with his utterance. With the promise (1), he connects a validity claim for an announced attention; with the direction (2), a validity claim for an (imperative) request; with the avowal (3), a validity claim for the expression of a feeling; and with the prediction (4), a validity claim for a statement. Correspondingly, with a "no" response, the addressee is contesting the rightness of (1) and (2), the truthfulness of (3), and the truth of (4). This picture is incomplete inasmuch as every speech act in a natural context can be contested (that is, rejected as invalid) under more than one aspect.

Let us assume that a seminar participant understands the following request addressed to him by the professor:

7. Please bring me a glass of water

not as a simple imperative or sheer expression of will but as a speech act carried out in an attitude oriented to understanding. Then he can in principle reject this request under three validity aspects. He can either contest the normative rightness of the utterance:

7.' No. You can't treat me like one of your employees.

or he can contest the subjective truthfulness of the utterance:

7.'' No. You really only want to put me in a bad light in front of the other seminar participants.

or he can deny that certain existential presuppositions obtain:

7.''' No. The next water tap is so far away that I couldn't get back before the end of the session.

In the first case, what is contested is that the action of the professor is right in the given normative context; in the second, that the professor means what he says (because he wants to achieve a certain perlocutionary effect); in the third, the truth of propositions the professor has to presuppose in the given circumstances.

What we have shown in connection with this example holds true for *all* speech acts oriented to reaching understanding. In contexts of communicative action, speech acts can always be rejected under each of the three aspects: the aspect of the rightness that the speaker claims for his action in relation to a normative context (or, indirectly, for these norms themselves); the truthfulness that the speaker claims for the expression of subjective experiences to which he has privileged access; finally, the truth that the speaker, with his utterance, claims for a statement (or for the existential presuppositions of a nominalized proposition). This strong thesis can be tested against numerous cases and made plausible by reflections that take us back to Bühler's model of the functions of language.

The term "reaching understanding" [*Verständigung*] means, at the minimum, that at least two speaking and acting subjects understand a linguistic expression in the same way. The meaning of an elementary expression consists in the contribution that it makes to the meaning of an acceptable speech act. And to understand what a speaker wants to say with such an act, the hearer has to know the conditions under which it can be accepted. In this respect, understanding [*Verständnis*] an elementary expression already points beyond the minimal meaning of the term. When a hearer accepts a speech act, an agreement [*Einverständnis*] comes about between at least two acting and speaking subjects. However, this does not rest only on the intersubjective recognition of a single, thematically stressed validity claim. Rather, an agreement of this sort is achieved simultaneously at three levels. We can identify these intuitively if we keep in mind that in communicative action a speaker selects a comprehensible linguistic expression only in order to come to an understanding *with* a hearer *about* something and thereby to make *himself* understandable. It belongs to the communicative intent of the speaker (a) that he perform a speech act that is *right* in respect to the given normative context, so that between him and the hearer an intersubjective relation will come about which is recognized as legitimate; (b) that he make a *true* statement (or *correct* existential presuppositions), so that the hearer will accept and share the knowledge of the speaker; and (c) that he express *truthfully* his beliefs, intentions, feelings, desires, and the like, so that the hearer will give credence to what is said. The fact that the intersubjective commonality of a communicatively achieved agreement exists at the levels of normative accord, shared propositional knowledge, and mutual trust in subjective sincerity can be explained in turn through the functions of achieving understanding in language.

As the medium for achieving understanding, speech acts serve: (a) to establish and renew interpersonal relations, whereby the speaker takes up a relation to something in the world of legitimate (social) orders; (b) to represent (or presuppose) states and events, whereby the speaker takes up a relation to something in the world of existing states of affairs; (c) to manifest experiences—that is, to represent oneself—whereby the speaker takes up a relation to something in the subjective world to which he has privileged access. Communicatively achieved agreement is measured against exactly three criticizable validity claims; in coming to an understanding about something with one another and thus making themselves understandable, actors cannot avoid embedding their speech acts in precisely three world-relations and claiming validity for them under these aspects. Someone who rejects a comprehensible speech act is taking issue with at least one of these validity claims. In rejecting a speech act as (normatively) wrong or untrue or insincere, he is expressing with his "no" the fact that the utterance has not fulfilled its function of securing an interpersonal relationship, of representing states of affairs, or of manifesting experiences. It is not in agreement with *our* world of legitimately ordered interpersonal relations, or with *the* world of existing states of affairs, or with *the speaker's own* world of subjective experiences.

Although speech acts oriented to reaching understanding are always involved in this way in a complex net of world-relations, the illocutionary role—under standard conditions, the meaning of the illocutionary component—determines the aspect of validity under which the speaker wants his utterance to be understood *first and foremost*. When he makes a statement, asserts, narrates, explains, represents, predicts, discusses something, or the like, he is looking for an agreement with the hearer based on the recognition of a truth claim. When the speaker utters a first-person experiential sentence, discloses, reveals, confesses, manifests something, or the like, agreement can come about only on the basis of the recognition of a claim to truthfulness or sincerity. When the speaker gives an order or makes a promise, appoints or warns somebody, baptizes or weds someone, buys something, or the like, agreement depends on whether those involved admit the action as right. These basic modes appear in all the more purity, the more clearly reaching understanding is oriented to only one dominant validity claim. Considerations of expediency suggest beginning analysis with idealized or *pure cases of speech acts.* I am thinking here of:

  —constative speech acts in which *elementary propositional (assertoric) sentences* are used;

  —expressive speech acts in which *elementary experiential sentences* (in the first person present) appear; and of

  —regulative speech acts in which either *elementary imperative sentences* (as in commands) or *elementary intentional sentences* (as in promises) appear.

In analytic philosophy there is an extended literature on each of these complexes. Instruments have been developed and analyses carried out that make it possible to explain the universal validity claims to which speakers are oriented and to characterize more precisely the basic attitudes that speakers thereby adopt. I am referring here to the *objectivating attitude* in which a neutral observer behaves toward something happening in the world; to the *expressive attitude* in which a subject presenting himself reveals to a public something within him to which he has privileged access; and finally to the *norm-conformative attitude* in which members of social groups satisfy legitimate expectations. To each of these fundamental attitudes there corresponds a concept of "world."

Let Mp represent any explicit speech act, where M stands for the illocutionary component and p for the propositional component;[52] and let M_c designate the cognitive use of language, M_e the expressive, and M_r the regulative. We can, in terms of basic attitudes, distinguish intuitively the senses in which speakers want the propositional components (of their speech acts) to be interpreted. In a valid utterance of the type M_cp, p signifies a state of affairs that *exists* in the objective world; in a valid utterance of the type M_ep, p signifies a subjective experience that is manifested and ascribed to the *internal world* of the speaker; and in a valid utterance of the type M_rp, p signifies an action that is recognized as legitimate in the social world.

This distinction among exactly three basic ways of using language with an orientation to reaching understanding could be grounded only in the form of an elaborated theory of speech acts. I cannot carry out the necessary analyses here, but I would like to take up a few prima facie objections to the proposed program.

A. Leist has formulated my basic thesis as follows: "For all S and all H, in all speech acts which belong to action oriented to reaching understanding and which are illocutionarily and propositionally differentiated and institutionally unbound, it is mutual knowledge that the speaker is required to speak intelligibly, to be truthful or sincere, to take his utterances for true and the norms relevant to his act for right."[53] To begin with, this formulation requires the explanatory comment that, from the standpoint of the theory of interaction, I delimit speech acts "oriented to reaching understanding" from speech acts that are incorporated into strategic action complexes, either because the latter, like genuine imperatives, are connected only with power claims and thus produce no illocutionary binding effect on their own, or because the speaker is pursuing perlocutionary aims with such utterances. Next, I would not use the expression "mutual knowledge," which comes from intentionalist semantics, but speak instead of "common suppositions." Furthermore, the expression "required" suggests a normative sense; I would rather make allowance for weak transcendental connotations and speak of "general conditions" that have to be satisfied if a communicative agreement is to be achieved. Finally, I find lacking here a hierarchical order between the well-formedness or comprehensibility of the linguistic expression as a presupposition of communication, on the one hand, and the claims to sincerity, propositional truth, and normative rightness, on the other hand. Accepting these claims brings about an agreement between S and H that grounds obligations that are relevant to the sequence of interaction. I distinguish from these the warrant that the speaker assumes for the validity claims he raises, as well as the reciprocal obligation that the hearer undertakes with the negation of a validity claim. Reservations have been expressed mainly in regard to the assumptions (a) that with *every* speech act oriented to reaching understanding *exactly three* validity claims are raised; (b) that the validity claims can be *adequately distinguished* from one another; and (c) that validity claims have to be analyzed in *formal-pragmatic terms,* that is, on the level of the communicative employment of sentences.

(ad a) Can we maintain the universality of the claim to truth, even though we obviously cannot raise a truth claim with nonconstative speech acts?[54] It is certainly the case that only with constative speech acts can we raise the claim that an asserted proposition p is true. But all other speech acts also contain a propositional component, normally in the form of a nominalized propositional sentence *that p*. This means that the speaker also relates to states of affairs with nonconstative speech acts, not directly to be sure—that is, not in the propositional attitude of one who thinks or is of the opinion, knows, or believes that p is the case. The propositional attitudes of speakers who employ first-person experiential sentences in expressive speech acts and imperative or intentional sentences in regulative speech acts are of another kind. They are in no way directed to the existence of the state of affairs mentioned in the propositional component. However, in saying with a nonconstative speech act that he desires or detests something, that he wants to bring about something or see it brought about, the speaker *presupposes* the existence of certain states of affairs. It belongs to the concept of an objective world that states of affairs are located in a nexus and do not hang isolated in the air. Therefore, the speaker connects *existential presuppositions* with the propositional component of his speech act; if need be, these presuppositions can be rendered explicit in the form of assertoric sentences. In this respect, nonconstative speech acts have an indirect relation to truth.

Moreover, this holds not only for propositionally differentiated speech acts; illocutionarily abbreviated speech acts—for example, a "hello" uttered as a greeting—are understood as satisfying norms from which the propositional content of the speech act can be supplemented—for example, in the case of a greeting, the well-being of the addressee or the confirmation of his social status. The existential presuppositions of a greeting include, among other things, the presence of a person for whom things can go well or badly, his membership in a social group, and so forth.

The situation is somewhat different with the universality of the claim to rightness. It can be objected to this that no relation to normative contexts can be inferred from the meaning of nonregulative speech acts.[55] However, communications are sometimes "inappropriate," reports "out of place," confessions "awkward," disclosures "offensive." That they can go wrong under this aspect is by no means extrinsic to nonregulative speech acts; it springs rather from their character *as* speech acts. We can see from their illocutionary component that the speaker also enters into interpersonal relations with constative and expressive speech acts; and whether or not these relations agree with an existing normative context, they belong to the social world.

There have also been objections with respect to the completeness of the table of validity claims. If one compares this to the conversational postulates proposed by Grice,[56] for example, one finds not only certain parallels but certain asymmetries as well. Thus there is no counterpart to the postulate that the speaker always wants to make a contribution to the theme which is relevant in the context of conversation. Apart from the fact, however, that such a claim to the relevance of a contribution to conversation is raised by the hearer and related to a text (rather than to an individual speech act)—that is, cannot be subjected to a yes/no test—the universality of such a requirement would be difficult to establish. There are obviously situations—for example, social gatherings, or even entire cultural milieus—in which a certain redundancy of contributions is plainly called for.[57]

(ad b) Reservations have been expressed in regard to the possibility of sharply discriminating between claims to truth and claims to truthfulness. It is not the case that a speaker who truthfully utters the opinion p must simultaneously raise a truth claim for p? It appears to be impossible "to expect of S that he is speaking the truth in any other sense than that S wants to speak the truth—and this means nothing else than being truthful."[58] This objection is not relevant to the class of expressive speech acts in its entirety but only to those utterances whose propositional content contains a cognition verb in the first person present (such as I think, know, believe, suspect, am of the opinion that p). At the same time, there is an internal relation between the propositional attitude that can be expressed by means of cognition verbs and constative speech acts. When someone asserts or ascertains or describes p, he simultaneously knows or believes that p. Moore already pointed out the paradoxical character of expressions like:

9. + It is raining now, but I don't believe that it is raining now.[59]

Despite these internal connections, however, a hearer can be rejecting two *different* validity claims with his rejection of:

9. It is raining now.

In taking a negative position, he can mean both:

9.' No, that isn't true.
     and
9.'' No, you don't mean what you're saying.

In the first case he understands (9) as a constative utterance, in the second as an expressive utterance. Obviously, the negation of the proposition *p* just as little implies the negation of the belief that *p* as, conversely, (9'') does (9'). To be sure, the hearer may suppose that when *S* asserts *p* he also believes that *p*. But this does not change the fact that the truth claim relates to the existence of the state of affairs *p*, whereas the truthfulness claim has to do only with the manifestation of the opinion or the belief that *p*. A murderer who makes a confession can mean what he says and yet, without intending to do so, be saying what is untrue. He can also, without intending to do so, speak the truth although, in concealing his knowledge of the facts of the case, he is lying. A judge who had sufficient evidence at his disposal could criticize the truthful utterance as untrue in the one case, and the true utterance as untruthful in the other.

As against this, Ernst Tugendhat tries to make do with a single validity claim.[60] He takes up the extended discussion connected with Wittgenstein's private language argument in order to show that the same assertoric validity claim is connected with such first-person sentences as:

10. I am in pain.

11. I am afraid of being raped.

as with corresponding third-person sentences:

12. He is in pain.

13. She is afraid of being raped.

where the corresponding personal pronouns in the first and third person are supposed to have the same reference. If Tugendhat's assimilation thesis is correct, the negation of (10) or (11) has the same sense as the negation of (12) or (13). It would be redundant to postulate a truthfulness claim alongside the claim to truth.

Following Wittgenstein, Tugendhat begins with an expressive gesture, the cry "ouch," and imagines that this linguistically rudimentary cry of pain is replaced by an expressive utterance represented at the semantic level by the first-person sentence (10). Wittgenstein denies to such experiential sentences the character of statements.[61] He assumes that there is a continuity between both noncognitive forms of expressing pain, the gesture and the sentence. For Tugendhat, by contrast, the categorial difference consists in the fact that the experiential sentence can be false, but not the gesture. His analysis leads to the result that with the transformation of the cry into an experiential sentence with the same meaning, "an expression is produced which, though it is used according to the same rule as the cry, is true when it is used correctly; and thus there arises the singular case of assertoric sentences which can be true or false but which are nevertheless not cognitive."[62] For this reason, first-person sentences like (10) are *not* supposed to be distinguishable from third-person sentences with the same propositional content like (12) on the basis of the criterion of whether or not they admit of truth. Both can be true or false. Of course, first-person, experiential sentences exhibit the peculiarity of expressing an "incorrigible knowledge"; thus, when they are used according to the rules they *must* be true. Between the sentences (10) and (12) there exists a "verificatory symmetry," in the sense that (12) is true whenever (10) is used in conformity with semantic rules.

Tugendhat explains this connection through the special nature of the singular term "I," with which the speaker *refers* to himself without at the same time *identifying* himself. Even if his thesis is correct, this does not solve the problem of explaining how a sentence can have an assertoric character and thus admit of truth and yet not admit of being employed cognitively, that is, for reporting existing states of affairs.

In general, the semantic rules for employing assertoric sentences indicate a cognition; only in the case of expressive sentences is the correct employment of the linguistic expression also supposed to *guarantee* its truth. But a hearer who wants to ascertain whether a speaker is deceiving him with the sentence (10) has to test whether or not the sentence (12) is true. This shows that expressive sentences in the first person do not primarily serve the purpose of expressing cognitions, that at most they borrow

the truth claim ascribed to them from the corresponding assertoric sentences in the third person; only the latter can *represent*
the state of affairs to whose existence the truth claim refers. Thus
Tugendhat falls into the dilemma of having to characterize in a
contradictory way what a speaker means with first-person experiential sentences. On the one hand, this supposedly has to do
with a knowledge for which the speaker claims validity in the
sense of propositional truth; on the other hand, this knowledge
cannot have the status of a cognition, for cognitions can be
reported only in assertoric sentences which can in principle be
contested as untrue. But this dilemma arises only if the validity
claim to truthfulness—which is *analogous* to truth—is *identified*
with the claim to truth. The dilemma dissolves as soon as one
shifts from the semantic to the pragmatic level and compares
speech acts rather than sentences. Consider

> 14. I have to confess (to you) that I've been in pain for days.
> 15. I can tell you that he's been in pain for days.

where the personal pronoun in the first person in (14) and the
personal pronoun in the third person in (15) are to have the same
reference. It becomes clear at a glance that if (14) is invalid, the
speaker is deceiving the hearer, whereas if (15) is invalid, the
speaker is telling the hearer something that is not true, though
he need not intend to deceive him. Thus it is legitimate to postulate for expressive speech acts a *different* validity claim than
for constative speech acts with the same meaning. Wittgenstein
comes very close to this insight at one point in his *Philosophical
Investigations,* where he is showing, in connection with the
paradigm case of a confession, that expressive utterances do not
have a descriptive meaning—that is, do not admit of truth—and
yet can be valid or invalid.

> The criteria for the truth of the *confession* that I thought such-
> and-such are not the criteria for a true *description* of a process.
> And the importance of the true confession does not reside
> in its being a correct and certain report of a process. It resides
> rather in the special consequences which can be drawn from
> a confession whose truth is guaranteed by the special criteria
> of *truthfulness.*[63]

(ad c) With these arguments we have already touched upon

the third group of objections, which is directed against a formal-pragmatic approach to the analysis of validity claims. Like legal claims, validity claims have to do with relations between persons and are meant to be intersubjectively recognized. They are raised for the validity of symbolic expressions, in the standard case for the validity of a sentence with propositional content that is dependent on an illocutionary component. This suggests that we should regard a validity claim as a complex and derivative phenomenon that can be traced back to the underlying phenomenon of satisfying conditions for the validity of sentences. But then shouldn't we look for their conditions of satisfaction on the semantic level of analyzing assertoric, experiential, impera-tive, and intentional sentences, rather than on the pragmatic level of the employment of these sentences in constative, expressive and regulative speech acts? Isn't a theory of speech acts, which hopes to explain the illocutionary binding effect through a war-rant offered by the speaker for the validity of what he says and through a corresponding rational motivation on the part of the hearer, dependent in turn on a theory of meaning that explains under what conditions the sentences employed are valid?

In this debate we are not concerned with questions of ter-ritorial boundaries or of nominal definitions but with whether *the concept of the validity of a sentence* can be explicated independently of *the concept of redeeming the validity claim raised through the utterance of the sentence.* I am defending the thesis that this is not possible. Semantic investigations of descriptive, expressive, and normative sentences, if only they are carried through consistently enough, force us to change the level of analysis. The very analysis of the conditions of the validity of sentences *itself* compels us to analyze the conditions for the intersubjective recognition of corresponding validity claims. An example of this can be found in Michael Dummett's development of truth-conditional semantics.[64]

Dummett starts from the distinction between the conditions that an assertoric sentence has to satisfy to be true and the knowl-edge that a speaker who asserts the sentence as true has of these conditions—conditions that at the same time determine the meaning of the sentence. Knowing the truth conditions consists in knowing how one ascertains whether or not they are satisfied in a given case. The orthodox version of truth-conditional semantics, which tries to explain understanding the meaning of a sentence in terms of knowing its truth conditions, is based on the unrealistic assumption that for every sentence, or at least for every assertoric sentence, procedures are available for effectively deciding whether or not its truth conditions are satisfied. This assumption rests implicitly on an empiricist theory of knowledge that takes the simple predicative sentences of an observation language to be basic. But not even the argumentation game that Tugendhat postulates for verifying such seemingly elementary sentences consists in a decision procedure that can be applied like an algorithm, that is, in such a way that further demands for grounding could be excluded in principle.[65] This is especially clear in the case of counterfactuals, universal existential sentences, and sentences with a temporal index (in general, any sentences referring to places and times that are actually inaccessible), which lack effective decision procedures. "The difficulty arises because natural language is full of sentences which are not effectively decidable, ones for which there exists no effective procedure for determining whether or not their truth conditions are fulfilled."[66]

Because knowing the truth conditions of assertoric sentences is problematic in many, if not in most cases, Dummett stresses the difference between knowing the conditions that make a sentence true and knowing the grounds that entitle a speaker to assert a sentence as true. Relying on basic assumptions of intuitionism, he goes on to reformulate the theory of meaning as follows:

> ...an understanding of a statement consists in a capacity to recognize whatever is counted as verifying it, i.e. as conclusively establishing it as true. It is not necessary that we should have any means of deciding the truth or falsity of the statement, only that we be capable of recognizing when its truth has been established.[67]

It is part of understanding a sentence that we are capable of recognizing *grounds* through which the *claim* that its truth conditions are satisfied *could be redeemed*. This theory explains the meaning of a sentence only mediately through knowing the conditions of its validity, but immediately through knowing grounds that are objectively available to a speaker for redeeming a validity claim.

Now a speaker might still produce such grounds according to a procedure that can be applied monologically; then an explanation of truth conditions in terms of grounding validity claims would not make it necessary to move from the semantic level of sentences to the pragmatic level of using sentences communicatively. Dummett stresses, however, that the speaker is by no means able to undertake the required verifications in a deductively compelling manner, relying exclusively on rules of inference. The set of grounds available in any given instance is circumscribed by internal relations of a universe of language that can be explored only in and through argumentation. Dummett pursues this idea so far that in the end he gives up entirely the basic idea of verificationism.

> A verificationist theory comes as close as any plausible theory of meaning can do to explaining the meaning of a sentence in terms of the grounds on which it may be asserted; it must of course distinguish a speaker's actual grounds, which may not be conclusive, or may be indirect, from the kind of direct, conclusive grounds in terms of which the meaning is given, particularly for sentences, like those in the future tense, for which the speaker cannot have grounds of the latter kind at the time of utterance. But a falsificationist theory . . . links the content of an assertion with the commitment that a speaker undertakes in making that assertion; an assertion is a kind of gamble that the speaker will not be proved wrong.[68]

This I understand as an indication of the fallibilistic character of the discursive redemption of validity claims. What is important is only that the illocutionary claim the speaker raises for the validity of a sentence be criticizable in principle. In any case, truth-conditional semantics in its revised form takes into consideration the fact that truth conditions cannot be explicated apart from knowing how to redeem a corresponding truth claim. To understand an assertion is to know when a speaker has good grounds to undertake a warrant that the conditions for the truth of the asserted sentences are satisfied.

As with the meaning of assertoric sentences, it can also be shown for expressive and normative sentences that semantic analysis pushes beyond itself. The discussion that stems from Wittgenstein's analysis of first-person sentences makes it clear that the claim connected with expressions is genuinely addressed to others.[69] The intersubjective character of the validity of norms is even clearer. Here too, an analysis that starts from simple predicates for seemingly subjective emotional reactions to violations or impairments of personal integrity leads step-by-step to the intersubjective, indeed transsubjective meaning of basic moral concepts.[70]

E.—On the Classification of Speech Acts. If it is true that the validity of speech acts oriented to reaching understanding can be contested under precisely three universal aspects, we might conjecture that a system of validity claims also underlies the differentiation of types of speech acts. If so, the universality thesis would also have implications for attempts to classify speech acts from theoretical points of view. Up to this point I have been tacitly employing a division into regulative, expressive, and constative speech acts. I would like now to justify this division by way of a critical examination of other classificatory schemes.

As is well known, at the end of his series of lectures on "How to Do Things with Words," Austin had a go at a typology of speech acts. He ordered illocutionary acts in terms of performative verbs and distinguished five types (verdictives, exercitives, commissives, behabitives, and expositives), without denying the provisional character of this division.[71] In fact, it is only for the class of commissives that Austin gives us a clear criterion of demarcation: With promises, threats, announcements, vows, contracts, and the like, the speaker commits himself to carry out certain actions in the future. The speaker enters into a normative bond that obliges him to act in a certain way. The remaining classes are not satisfactorily defined, even if one takes into account the descriptive character of the division. They do not meet the requirements of distinctness and disjunctiveness;[72] we are not forced by Austin's classificatory scheme always to assign different phenomena to different categories nor to assign each phenomenon to at most one category.

The class of verdictives comprises utterances with which "judgments" or "verdicts"—in the sense of appraisals and assessments—are made. Austin does not distinguish here between judgments with descriptive content and those with normative content. Thus there is some overlap with both the expositives and the exercitives. The class of exercitives comprises, to begin with, all declaratives, that is, expressions of institutionally—for the most part, legally—authorized decisions (such as sentencing, adopting, appointing, nominating, resigning). There is overlap with both verdictives (such as naming and awarding) and behabitives (such as protesting). These behabitives in turn form a class that is quite heterogeneous in composition. In addition to verbs for standardized expressions of feeling (such as complaints and expressions of sympathy), it contains expressions for institutionally bound utterances (congratulations, curses, toasts, greetings of welcome) as well as expressions for satisfactions (apologies, thanks, all sorts of making good). Finally, the class of expositives does not discriminate between constatives, which serve to represent states of affairs, and communicatives, which (like asking, replying, addressing, citing, and the like) refer to speech itself. Also to be distinguished from these are the expressions with which we designate the execution of operations (such as deducing, identifying, calculating, classifying, and the like).

Searle has attempted to sharpen Austin's classification.[73] He no longer orients himself to a list of performative verbs differentiated in a specific language, but to the illocutionary aim, the particular "point" or "purpose" that speakers pursue with various types of speech acts, independently of the forms in which they are realized in individual languages. He arrives at a clear and intuitively evident classification: assertive (or constative), commissive, directive, declarative, and expressive speech acts. To start with, Searle introduces assertive (constative, representative) speech acts as a well-defined class. Then he takes over from Austin the class of commissives and contrasts these with the directives. Whereas with the former the speaker commits himself to an action, with the latter he tries to get the hearer to carry out a certain action. Among the directives Searle counts order, command, request, invite, as well as ask, pray, and entreat. He does not discriminate here between normatively authorized imperatives—such as petition, reprimand, order, and the like— and simple imperatives, that is, nonauthorized expressions of will. For this reason, the delimitation of directives from declaratives is also not very sharp. It is true that for declarative utterances we need particular institutions that secure the obligatory character of, for instance, appointing, abdicating, declaring war, and giving notice; but their normative meaning is similar to that of commands and directions. The last class comprises expressive speech acts. These are defined by their illocutionary point: with them the speaker brings sincerely to expression his psychic attitudes. But Searle is uncertain in his application of this criterion; thus the exemplary cases of avowals, disclosures, and revelations are missing. Apologies and expressions of joy and sympathy are mentioned. Apparently Searle has let himself be misled by Austin's characterization of behabitives to tack onto this class institutionally bound speech acts like congratulations and greetings as well.

Searle's sharpened version of Austin's speech act typology marks the starting point of a discussion that has developed in two different directions. The first is characterized by Searle's own efforts to provide an ontological grounding for the five types of speech acts; the other is marked by the attempt to develop the classification of speech acts from the standpoint of empirical pragmatics so as to make it fruitful for the analysis of speech-act sequences in everyday communication.

It is along this latter path that we find the work of linguists and sociolinguists like Wunderlich, Campbell, and Kreckel.[74] In empirical pragmatics social-life contexts are represented as communicative actions that intermesh in social spaces and historical times. The patterns of illocutionary forces realized in particular languages reflect the structures of this network of actions. The linguistic possibilities for performing illocutionary acts—whether in the fixed form of grammatical modes or in the more flexible form of performative verbs, sentence particles, sentence intonations, and the like—provide schemata for establishing interpersonal relations. The illocutionary forces constitute the knots in the network of communicative sociation [*Vergesellschaftung*]; the illocutionary lexicon is, as it were, the sectional plane in which the language and the institutional order of a society interpenetrate. This societal infrastructure of language is itself in flux; it varies in dependence on institutions and forms of life. But these variations *also* embody a linguistic creativity that gives new forms of expression to the innovative mastery of unforeseen situations.[75]

Indicators that relate to the general dimensions of the speech situation are important for a pragmatic classification of speech acts. In the *temporal dimension* there is the question of whether participants are oriented more to the future, the past, or the present, or whether the speech acts are temporally neutral. In the *social dimension* there is the question of whether obligations relevant for the sequence of interaction arise for the speaker, the hearer, or for both parties. And for the *dimension of content* there arises the question of whether the thematic center of gravity lies more with the objects, the actions, or the actors themselves. M. Kreckel uses these indicators to propose a classification on which she bases her analyses of everyday communication (see Figure 15).

Figure 15
Classification According to Three Pragmatic Indicators

	Speaker (S)	Hearer (H)
	Cognition oriented (C)	*Cognition oriented (C)*

Present	Does the speaker indicate that he has taken up the hearer's message?
	
	Examples: agreeing
	        acknowledging
	        rejecting
		Does the speaker try to influence the hearer's view of the world?
		
		Examples: asserting
		        arguing
		        declaring

	Person oriented (P)	*Person oriented (P)*

Past	Does the speaker refer to himself and/or his past action?
	
	Examples: justifying
	        defending
	        lamenting
		Does the speaker refer to the person of the hearer and/or his past action?
		
		Examples: accusing
		        criticizing
		        teasing

	Action oriented (A)	*Action oriented (A)*

Future	Does the speaker commit himself to future action?
	
	Examples: promising
	        refusing
	        giving in
		Does the speaker try to make the hearer do something?
		
		Examples: advising
		        challenging
		        ordering

From: Kreckel (1981), p. 188.

The advantage of this and similar classifications consists in the fact that they provide us with a guideline for ethnolinguistic and sociolinguistic descriptive systems and are more of a match for the complexity of natural scenes than are typologies that start from illocutionary points and purposes rather than from features of situations. But they pay for this advantage by relinquishing the intuitive evidence of classifications that link up with semantic analyses and take account of the elementary functions of language (such as the representation of states of affairs, the expression of experiences, and the establishment of interpersonal relations). The classes of speech acts that are arrived at inductively and

constructed in accordance with pragmatic indicators do not consolidate into intuitive types; they lack the theoretical power to
illuminate our intuitions. Searle takes the step to *a theoretically
motivated typology of speech acts* by giving an ontological characterization of the illocutionary aims and the propositional attitudes
that a speaker pursues or adopts when he performs assertive (or
constative), directive, commissive, declarative, and expressive
speech acts. In doing so he draws upon the familiar model that
defines the world as the totality of states of affairs, sets up the
speaker/actor outside of this world, and allows for precisely two
linguistically mediated relations between actor and world: the
cognitive relation of ascertaining facts and the interventionist
relation of realizing a goal of action. The illocutionary aims can
be characterized in terms of the direction in which sentences and
facts are supposed to be brought into accord. The arrow pointing
downwards says that the sentences are supposed to fit the facts;
the arrow pointing upwards says that the facts are to be fit to
the sentences. Thus the assertoric force of constative speech acts
and the imperative force of directive speech acts appear as
follows:

where *C* stands for cognitions or the propositional attitudes of
thinking, believing, supposing, and the like, and *I* stands for
intentions or the propositional attitudes of wanting, desiring,
intending, and the like. The assertoric force signifies that *S* raises
a truth claim for *p* vis-a-vis *H*, that is, he assumes responsibility
for the agreement of the assertoric sentence with the facts
(↓); the imperative force signifies that *S* raises a power claim vis-a-
vis *H* for seeing to it that "*H* brings about *p*," that is, he assumes
responsibility for having the facts brought into agreement with
the imperative sentence (↑). In describing illocutionary forces by
means of the relations between language and the world, Searle
has recourse to the conditions of satisfaction for assertoric and
imperative sentences. He finds his theoretical standpoint for
classifying speech acts in the dimension of validity. But he restricts
himself to the perspective of the speaker and disregards the
dynamics of the negotiation and intersubjective recognition of
validity claims—that is, the building of consensus. The model of

two linguistically mediated relations between a solitary actor and the one objective world has no place for the intersubjective relation between participants in communication who come to an understanding with one another about something in the world. In being worked out, this ontological concept proves to be too narrow.

The commissive speech acts seem at first to fit easily into the model. With a speech act of this type S assumes vis-a-vis H responsibility for bringing the facts into agreement with the intentional sentence ($\uparrow$):

> Commissive C' $\uparrow$I (S brings about p)

In analyzing the use of intentional sentences in announcements, we saw that the illocutionary force of commissive speech acts cannot be explained through the conditions of satisfaction, that is, the conditions for fulfilling the announced intention. But it is only this that is meant by ($\uparrow$). With commissive speech acts the speaker *binds* his will in the sense of a *normative obligation;* and the conditions for *the reliability of a declaration* of intention are of quite another sort than the conditions that the speaker satisfies when he lives up to his intention as an actor. Searle would have to distinguish conditions of validity from conditions of satisfaction.

In a similar way, we distinguished normatively authorized imperatives such as directions, commands, ordinances, and the like from mere imperatives; with the former the speaker raises a normative validity claim, with the latter an externally sanctioned claim to power. For this reason, not even the full modal meaning of simple imperatives can be explained by the conditions for fulfilling the imperative sentences thereby employed. Even if that would do, Searle would have difficulty in reducing the class of directives to the class of simple imperatives, or in delimiting genuine imperatives from directions, orders, or commands, since his model does not allow for conditions of validity other than those for propositional truth and efficiency. This lack is especially noticeable when Searle tries to accommodate declarative and expressive speech acts in his system.

It is evident that the illocutionary force of a declaration of war, a resignation, the opening of a session, the reading of a bill, or the like cannot be interpreted according to the schema of two directions of fit. In producing institutional facts, a speaker does not at all refer to something in the objective world; rather he acts in accord with the legitimate orders of the social world and at the same time initiates new interpersonal relations. It is purely out of embarrassment that Searle symbolizes this meaning, which belongs to *another* world, by a double arrow coined in respect to the objective world:

declarative $\qquad\qquad\qquad$ D $\updownarrow$ (p)

where no special propositional attitudes are supposed to be required. This embarrassment turns up once again in the case of expressive speech acts, whose illocutionary force can just as little be characterized in terms of an actor's relations to the world of existing states of affairs. Searle is consistent enough to give expression to the inapplicability of his scheme through a neither/nor sign:

expressive speech acts $\qquad\qquad$ E Ø (p)

where any propositional attitude is possible.

We can avoid the difficulties of Searle's attempts at classification, while retaining his fruitful theoretical approach, if we start from the fact that the illocutionary aims of speech acts are achieved through the intersubjective recognition of claims to power or validity, and if, further, we introduce normative rightness and subjective truthfulness as validity claims analogous to truth and interpret them too in terms of actor/world relations. This revision yields the following classification:

—With *imperatives* the speaker refers to a desired state in the objective world, and in such a way that he would like to get H to bring about this state. Imperatives can be criticized only from the standpoint of whether the action demanded can be carried out, that is, in connection with conditions of satisfaction. However, refusing imperatives normally means rejecting a claim to power; it is not based on criticism but itself *expresses a will.*

—With *constative speech acts* the speaker refers to something in the objective world, and in such a way that he would like to represent a state of affairs. The negation of such an utterance means that H *contests* the validity claim raised by S for the proposition stated.

—With *regulative speech acts* the speaker refers to something in a common social world, and in such a way that he would like to establish an interpersonal relation recognized as legitimate. The negation of such an utterance means that *H contests* the normative rightness claimed by *S* for his action (or for an underlying norm).

—With *expressive speech acts* the speaker refers to something in his subjective world, and in such a way that he would like to reveal to a public an experience to which he has privileged access. The negation of such an utterance means that *H doubts* the claim to sincerity of self-representation raised by *S*.

Communicatives constitute another class of speech acts. They can also be understood as that subclass of regulative speech acts—questioning and answering, addressing, objecting, admitting, and the like—that serve *the organization of speech*, its arrangement into themes and contributions, the distribution of conversational roles, the regulation of turn-taking in conversation, and the like.[76] But it is more convenient to regard the communicatives as an independent class instead and to define them through their *reflexive relation to the process of communication*; for then we can also include those speech acts that refer directly to validity claims (affirming, denying, assuring, confirming, and the like).

Finally, there is the class of *operatives,* that is, of speech acts—such as inferring, identifying, calculating, classifying, counting, predicting, and the like—that signify the application of generative rules (of logic, grammar, mathematics, and the like). Operative speech acts have a performative sense but *no genuine communicative intent;* they serve at the same time to *describe* what one does in constructing symbolic expressions in conformity with generative rules.[77]

If one takes this classification as basic, commissives and declaratives, as well as institutionally bound speech acts (betting, marrying, oath-taking) and satisfactives (which relate to excuses and apologies for violating norms, as well as to reparations), must all be subsumed under the same class of regulative speech acts. One can see from this that the basic modes have to be further differentiated. They cannot be used for the analysis of everyday communication until we succeed in developing taxonomies for *the whole spectrum of illocutionary forces* differentiated out in a given language within the boundaries of a specific basic mode.

Only very few illocutionary acts—like assertions and statements, promises and directions, avowals and disclosures—are so general that they can characterize a basic mode as such. Of course, the possibilities of expression standardized in particular languages mark not only the relation to validity claims in general, but the *way* in which a speaker claims truth, rightness, or truthfulness for a symbolic expression. Pragmatic indicators—such as the degree of institutional dependence of speech acts, the orientation to past and future, the speaker/hearer orientation, the thematic focus, and so forth—can now help us to grasp systematically *the illocutionary modifications of validity claims.* Only an empirical pragmatics that is theoretically guided will be able to develop speech-act taxonomies which are informative, that is, which are neither blind nor empty.

The pure types of language-use oriented to reaching understanding are suitable as guidelines for constructing typologies of linguistically mediated interaction. In communicative action the plans of individual participants are coordinated by means of the illocutionary binding (or bonding) effects of speech acts. Thus we might conjecture that constative, regulative, and expressive speech acts also constitute corresponding types of linguistically mediated interaction. This is obviously true of regulative and expressive speech acts, which are constitutive for what we have discussed under the titles of normatively regulated and dramaturgical action. At first glance there seems to be no type of interaction that would correspond in the same way to constative speech acts. However, there are contexts of action that do not *primarily* serve the carrying out of communicatively harmonized plans of action (that is, the purposive activities of the participants) but make communication possible and stabilize it—for instance, chatting, conversing, and arguing—in general conversation that becomes an end in itself. In such cases the process of reaching understanding is detached from the instrumental role of serving as a mechanism for coordinating individual actions, and the discussion of themes becomes independent for purposes of conversation. I shall speak of "conversation" when the weight is shifted in this way from purposive activity to communication; argumentation is perhaps the most important special case of conversation. As interest in the topics discussed is here predominant, we could perhaps say that constative speech acts have constitutive significance for conversations.

Thus our classification of speech acts can serve to introduce

328 REASON AND THE RATIONALIZATION OF SOCIETY

three pure types—or better, *limit cases*—of communicative action: conversation, normatively regulated action, and dramaturgical action. If we further take into account the internal relation of strategic action to perlocutionary acts and imperatives, we get the classification of linguistically mediated interactions in Figure 16.

F.—Formal and Empirical Pragmatics. Even if the program I have outlined for a theory of speech acts were carried out, one might ask what would be gained for a useful sociological theory of action by such a formal-pragmatic approach. The question arises, why would not an empirical-pragmatic approach be better for this, an approach that did not dwell on the rational reconstruction of isolated, highly idealized speech acts but started at once with the communicative practice of everyday life? From the side of linguistics there are interesting contributions to the analysis of stories and texts,[78] from sociology contributions to conversational analysis,[79] from anthropology contributions to the ethnography of speech,[80] and from psychology investigations into the pragmatic variables of linguistic interaction.[81] By comparison, formal pragmatics—which, in its reconstructive intention (that is, in the sense of a theory of competence) is directed to the universal presuppositions of communicative action[82]—seems to be hopelessly removed from actual language use.[83] Under these circumstances, does it make any sense to insist on a formal-pragmatic grounding for an action theory?

I would like to respond to this question by first (a) enumerating the methodological steps through which formal pragmatics gains a connection to empirical pragmatics; then I shall (b) identify the problems that make it necessary to clarify the rational foundations of processes of reaching understanding; finally, I would like (c) to take up a strategically important argument, about which empirical pragmatics has to learn from formal pragmatics if the problem of rationality is not to end up in the wrong place—that is, in the orientations for action, as it does in Max Weber's theory of action—but in the general structures of the lifeworld to which acting subjects belong.

(ad a) The pure types of linguistically mediated interaction can be brought progressively closer to the complexity of natural situations without sacrificing all theoretical perspectives for analyzing the coordination of interactions. This task consists in

Figure 16
Pure Types of Linguistically Mediated Interaction

Formal-Pragmatic Features / Types of action	Characteristic Speech Acts	Functions of Speech	Action Orientations	Basic Attitudes	Validity Claims	World Relations
Strategic Action	Perlocutions Imperatives	Influencing one's opposite number	Oriented to success	Objectivating	(Effectiveness)	Objective world
Conversation	Constatives	Representation of states of affairs	Oriented to reaching understanding	Objectivating	Truth	Objective world
Normatively Regulated Action	Regulatives	Establishment of interpersonal relations	Oriented to reaching understanding	Norm-conformative	Rightness	Social world
Dramaturgical Action	Expressives	Self-representation	Oriented to reaching understanding	Expressive	Truthfulness	Subjective world

reversing step by step the strong idealizations by which we have built up the concept of communicative action:

—In addition to the basic modes, we first admit the concretely shaped illocutionary forces that form the culture-specific net of possible interpersonal relations standardized in each individual language;

—In addition to the standard forms of speech acts, we admit other forms of linguistic realization of speech acts;

—In addition to explicit speech acts, we admit elliptically foreshortened, extraverbally supplemented, implicit utterances, for understanding which the hearer is thrown back upon the knowledge of nonstandardized, contingent contexts;

—In addition to direct speech acts, we admit indirect, transposed, and ambiguous expressions, the meaning of which has to be inferred from the context;

—The focus is enlarged from isolated acts of communication (and yes/no responses) to sequences of speech acts, to texts or conversations, so that conversational implications can come into view;

—In addition to the objectivating, norm-conformative and expressive basic attitudes, we admit an overlapping performative attitude, to take account of the fact that with each speech act participants in communication relate simultaneously to something in the objective, social, and subjective worlds;[84]

—In addition to the level of acts of communication (that is, speech), we bring in the level of communicative action (that is, the coordination of the plans of individual participants);

—Finally, in addition to communicative action, we include in our analysis the resources of the background knowledge (that is, lifeworlds) from which participants feed their interpretations.

These extensions amount to dropping the methodological provisions that we began with in introducing standard speech acts. In the standard case the literal meaning of the sentences uttered coincides with what the speaker means with his speech act.[85] However, the more that what the speaker means with his utterance is made to depend on a background knowledge that remains implicit, the more the context-specific meaning of the utterance can diverge from the literal meaning of what is said. When one drops the idealization of a complete and literal representation of the meaning of utterances, the resolution of another problem is also made easier—namely, distinguishing and identifying in natural situations actions oriented to understanding and actions oriented to success. Here we must take into consideration that not only do illocutions appear in strategic-action contexts, but perlocutions appear in contexts of communicative action as well. Cooperative interpretive processes run through different phases. In the initial phase participants are often handicapped by the fact that their interpretations do not overlap sufficiently for the purpose of coordinating actions. In this phase participants have either to shift to the level of metacommunication or to employ means of indirectly achieving understanding. Coming indirectly to an understanding proceeds according to the model of intentionalist semantics. Through perlocutionary effects, the speaker gives the hearer something to understand which he cannot (yet) directly communicate. In this phase, then, the perlocutionary acts have to be embedded in contexts of communicative action. These strategic *elements* within a use of language oriented to reaching understanding can be distinguished from strategic *actions* through the fact that the entire sequence of a stretch of talk stands—on the part of all participants—under the presuppositions of communicative action.

(ad b) An empirical pragmatics without a formal-pragmatic point of departure would not have the conceptual instruments needed to recognize the rational basis of linguistic communication in the confusing complexity of the everyday scenes observed. It is only in formal-pragmatic investigations that we can secure for ourselves an idea of reaching understanding that can guide empirical analysis into particular problems—such as the linguistic representation of different levels of reality, the manifestation of communication pathologies, or the development of a decentered understanding of the world.

The linguistic *demarcation of the levels of reality* of "play" and "seriousness," the linguistic construction of a fictive reality, wit and irony, transposed and paradoxical uses of language, allusions and the contradictory withdrawal of validity claims at a metacommunicative level—all these accomplishments rest on intentionally confusing modalities of being. For clarifying the mechanisms of deception that a speaker has to master to do this, formal pragmatics can do more than even the most precise empirical description of the phenomena to be explained. With training in the basic modes of language use, the growing child gains the ability to demarcate the subjectivity of his own expressions from the objectivity of an external reality, from the normativity of society, and from the intersubjectivity of the medium of language itself. In learning to deal hypothetically with the corresponding validity claims, he practices drawing the categorial distinctions between essence and appearance, being and illusion, "is" and "ought," sign and meaning. With these modalities of being he gets hold of the deceptive phenomena that first spring from the unwilling confusion between his own subjectivity, on the one hand, and the domains of the objective, the normative, and the intersubjective, on the other. He now knows how one can master the confusions, produce de-differentiations intentionally, and employ them in fiction, wit, irony, and the like.[86]

The situation is similar with manifestations of *systematically distorted communication.* Here too formal pragmatics can contribute to the explanation of phenomena that are first identified only on the basis of an intuitive understanding matured by clinical experience. Such communication pathologies can be conceived of as the result of a confusion between actions oriented to reaching understanding and actions oriented to success. In situations of concealed strategic action, at least one of the parties behaves with an orientation to success, but leaves others to believe that all the presuppositions of communicative action are satisfied. This is the case of manipulation which we mentioned in connection with perlocutionary acts. On the other hand, the kind of unconscious repression of conflicts that the psychoanalyst explains in terms of defense mechanisms leads to disturbances of communication on both the intrapsychic and interpersonal levels.[87] In such cases at least one of the parties is deceiving himself about the fact that he is acting with an attitude oriented to success and is only keeping up the appearance of communicative action. The place of systematically distorted communication within a framework of a theory of communicative action can be seen in Figure 18.

In the present context, the main advantage of a formal pragmatics is that it highlights, in the pure types of linguistically mediated interaction, precisely those aspects under which social actions embody different sorts of knowledge. The theory of communicative action can make good the weaknesses we found in Weber's action theory, inasmuch as it does not remain fixated on purposive rationality as the only aspect under which action can be criticized and improved. Drawing on the types of action

Figure 18

Social Actions

Communicative Action   Strategic Action

Concealed Strategic   Open Strategic
Action   Action

Unconscious   Conscious
Deception   Deception
(Systematically   (Manipulation)
distorted
communication)

introduced above, I would like now to comment briefly on the different aspects of the rationality of action.

Teleological actions can be judged under the aspect of effectiveness. The rules of action embody technically and strategically useful knowledge, which can be criticized in reference to truth claims and can be improved through a feedback relation with the growth of empirical-theoretical knowledge. This knowledge is stored in the form of technologies and strategies.

Constative speech acts, which not only embody knowledge but explicitly represent it and make conversations possible, can be criticized under the aspect of truth. In cases of more obstinate controversy concerning the truth of statements, theoretical discourse offers its services as a continuation, with different means, of action oriented to reaching understanding. When discursive examination loses its ad hoc character and empirical knowledge is systematically placed in question, when quasi-natural learning processes are guided through the sluices of argumentation, there results a cumulative effect—this knowledge is stored in the form of theories.

Normatively regulated speech acts embody moral-practical knowledge. They can be contested under the aspect of rightness. Like claims to truth, controversial claims to rightness can be made thematic and examined discursively. In cases of disturbance of the regulative use of language, practical discourse offers its services as a continuation of consensual action with other means. In moral-practical argumentation, participants can test both the rightness of a given action in relation to a given norm, and, at the next level, the rightness of such a norm itself. This knowledge is handed down in the form of legal and moral representations.

Dramaturgical actions embody a knowledge of the agent's own subjectivity. These expressions can be criticized as untruthful, that is, rejected as deceptions or self-deceptions. Self-deceptions can be dissolved in therapeutic dialogue by argumentative means. Expressive knowledge can be explicated in terms of those values that underlie need interpretations, the interpretations of desires and emotional attitudes. Value standards are dependent in turn on innovations in the domain of evaluative expressions. These are reflected in an exemplary manner in works of art. The aspects of the rationality of action are summarized in Figure 19.

Figure 19
Aspects of the Rationality of Action

Types of Action	Type of Knowledge Embodied	Form of Argumentation	Model of Transmitted Knowledge
Teleological Action: instrumental, strategic	Technically and strategically useful knowledge	Theoretical discourse	Technologies, Strategies
Constative Speech Acts (conversation)	Empirical-theoretical knowledge	Theoretical discourse	Theories
Normatively Regulated Action	Moral-practical knowledge	Practical discourse	Legal and moral representations
Dramaturgical Action	Aesthetic practical knowledge	Therapeutic and aesthetic critique	Works of art

(ad c) This interconnection of action orientations, types of knowledge, and forms of argumentation is, of course, inspired by Weber's idea that in modern Europe, with the development of science, morals, and art, stores of explicit knowledge were differentiated out; these flowed into various domains of institutionalized everyday action and, as it were, put under the pressure of rationalization certain action orientations that had been determined in a traditionalist manner. The aspects of the rationality of action that we found in communicative action should now permit us to grasp processes of societal rationalization across their whole breadth, and no longer solely from the selective viewpoint of the rationalization of purposive-rational action.

In posing the problem in this way, the role of implicit knowledge is not given its due. We are not yet clear about the horizon of everyday action into which the explicit knowledge of cultural experts comes rushing, nor about how the communicative practice of everyday life actually changes with this influx. The concept of action oriented to reaching understanding has the additional—and quite different—advantage of throwing light on this background of implicit knowledge which enters *a tergo* into cooperative processes of interpretation. Communicative action takes place within a lifeworld that remains at the backs of participants in communication. It is present to them only in the prereflective form of taken-for-granted background assumptions and naively mastered skills.

If the investigations of the last decade in socio-, ethno-, and psycholinguistics converge in any one respect, it is on the often and variously demonstrated point that the collective background and context of speakers and hearers determines interpretations of their explicit utterances to an extraordinarily high degree. Searle has taken up this doctrine of empirical pragmatics and criticized the long dominant view that sentences get *literal meaning* only by virtue of the rules for using the expressions contained in them.[88] So far, I have also construed the meaning of speech acts as literal meaning in this sense. Naturally this meaning could not be thought independently of contextual conditions altogether; for each type of speech act there are *general* contextual conditions that must be met if the speaker is to be able to achieve illocutionary success. But these general contextual conditions could supposedly be derived in turn from the literal meaning of the linguistic expressions employed in the standard speech acts. And as a matter of fact, if formal pragmatics is not to lose its object, knowledge of the conditions under which speech acts may be accepted as valid cannot depend *completely* on contingent background knowledge.

However, Searle has now shown—in connection with such simple assertions as "The cat is on the mat" and such imperatives as "Give me a hamburger"—that the truth conditions of the assertoric and imperative sentences employed therein cannot be completely determined independently of implicit contextual knowledge. If we begin to vary relatively deep-seated and trivial background assumptions, we notice that the (only) seemingly context-invariant conditions of validity change meaning and are thus by no means absolute. Searle does not go so far as to deny to sentences and utterances a literal meaning; but he does defend the thesis that the literal meaning of an expression must be completed by the background of an implicit knowledge that participants normally regard as trivial and obvious.

The sense of this thesis is not to reduce the meaning of a speech act to what a speaker means by it in a contingent context. Searle is not maintaining a simple relativism of the meaning of linguistic expressions; for their meaning does not change as we pass from one contingent context to the next. We discover the incompleteness of the literal meaning of expressions only through a sort of problematizing that is not directly under our control. It emerges as a result of problems that appear objectively and have an unsettling effect on our natural worldview. The fundamental background knowledge that must tacitly supplement our knowledge of the acceptability conditions of linguistically standardized expressions if hearers are to be able to understand their literal meanings, has remarkable features: It is an *implicit* knowledge that cannot be represented in a finite number of propositions; it is a *holistically structured* knowledge, the basic elements of which intrinsically define one another; and it is a knowledge that *does not stand at our disposition,* inasmuch as we cannot make it conscious and place it in doubt as we please. When philosophers nevertheless seek to do so, then that knowledge comes to light in the form of the commonsense certainties in which G. E. Moore, for instance, took an interest,[89] and to which Wittgenstein referred in his reflections "On Certainty."

Wittgenstein calls these certainties elements of a worldview that are "anchored in all my questions and answers, so anchored that I cannot touch [them]."[90] Beliefs that do not fit such convictions—convictions that are as beyond question as they are fundamental—appear to be absurd. "Not that I could describe the system of these convictions. Yet my convictions do form a system, a structure."[91] Wittgenstein characterizes the dogmatism of everyday background assumptions and skills in a way similar to that in which Schutz describes the mode of taken-for-grantedness in which the lifeworld is present as a prereflexive background.

> The child learns to believe a host of things. I.e. it learns to act according to these beliefs. Bit by bit there forms a system of what is believed, and in that system some things stand unshakeably fast and some are more or less liable to shift. What stands fast does so, not because it is intrinsically obvious or convincing; it is rather held fast by what lies around it.[92]

Literal meanings are, then, relative to a deep-seated, implicit knowledge, *about* which we normally know nothing, because it is simply unproblematic and does not pass the threshold of communicative utterances that can be valid or invalid. "If the true is what is grounded, then the ground is not true, nor yet false."[93]

Searle encounters this layer of worldview knowledge functioning in everyday life as the background with which a hearer has to be familiar if he is to be able to understand the literal meaning of speech acts and to act communicatively. He thereby directs our gaze to a continent that remains hidden so long as the theoretician analyzes speech acts only from the perspective of the speaker who relates with his utterances to something in the objective, social, and subjective worlds. It is only with the turn back to the context-forming horizon of the lifeworld, from within which participants in communication come to an understanding with one another about something, that our field of vision changes in such a way that we can see the points of connection for social theory within the theory of communicative action: The concept of society has to be linked to a concept of the lifeworld that is complementary to the concept of communicative action. Then communicative action becomes interesting primarily as a principle of sociation [*Vergesellschaftung*]: Communicative action provides the medium for the reproduction of lifeworlds. At the same time, processes of societal rationalization are given a different place. They transpire more in implicitly known structures of the lifeworld than in explicitly known action orientations (as Weber suggested). I shall take up this topic once more in the second set of "intermediate reflections."

IV

From Lukacs to Adorno:
Rationalization as Reification

As we saw above, a critique of the foundations of Weber's action theory can be developed from a line of argument found in his own work. But this critique leads to a demand for a change of paradigm (from teleological to communicative action) that Weber did not envision, let alone accomplish. "Meaning" as a primitive term of communication theory had to remain inaccessible to a neo-Kantian reared in the tradition of the philosophy of consciousness. The same holds for a concept of societal rationalization drawn up from the perspective of action oriented to reaching understanding and referring to the lifeworld as the common background knowledge presupposed in real action. The rationalization of society would then no longer mean a diffusion of purposive-rational action and a transformation of domains of communicative action into subsystems of purposive-rational action. The point of reference becomes instead the potential for rationality found in the validity basis of speech. This potential is never completely stilled, but it can be activated at different levels, depending on the degree of rationalization of the knowledge incorporated into worldviews. Inasmuch as social actions are coordinated through reaching understanding, the formal conditions of rationally motivated agreement specify how participants' relations to one another can be rationalized. As a general principle, they count as rational to the extent that the yes/no decisions that carry a given consensus issue from the interpretive processes of the participants themselves. Correspondingly, a lifeworld can be regarded as rationalized to the extent that it permits interactions that are not guided by normatively *ascribed* agreement but—directly or indirectly—by communicatively *achieved* understanding.

In Weber's view, as we saw above, the transition to modernity is characterized by a differentiation of spheres of value and structures of consciousness that makes possible a critical transformation of traditional knowledge in relation to specifically given validity claims. This is a necessary condition for the institutionalization of correspondingly differentiated knowledge systems and learning processes. Along this line we find (a) the establishment of a scientific enterprise in which empirical-scientific problems can be dealt with according to internal truth standards, independently of theological doctrines and separately from basic moral-practical questions; (b) the institutionalization of an artistic enterprise in which the production of art is gradually set loose from cultic-ecclesiastical and courtly-patronal bonds, and the reception of works of art by an art-enjoying public of readers, spectators, and listeners is mediated through professionalized aesthetic criticism; and finally (c) the professional intellectual treatment of questions of ethics, political theory, and jurisprudence in schools of law, in the legal system, and in the legal public sphere.

To the degree that the institutionalized production of knowledge that is specialized according to cognitive, normative, and aesthetic validity claims penetrates to the level of everyday communication and replaces traditional knowledge in its interaction-guiding functions, there is a rationalization of everyday practice that is accessible only from the perspective of action oriented to reaching understanding—a rationalization of the lifeworld that Weber neglected as compared with the rationalization of action systems like the economy and the state. In a rationalized lifeworld the need for achieving understanding is met less and less by a reservoir of traditionally certified interpretations immune from criticism; at the level of a completely decentered understanding of the world, the need for consensus must be met more and more frequently by risky, because rationally motivated, agreement—be it directly, through the interpretive accomplishments of participants, or through a professionalized expert knowledge that has become customary in a secondary sense. In this way communicative action becomes loaded with expectations of consensus and risks of disagreement that make great demands on reaching understanding as the mechanism for coordinating action. The growing subjectivism of beliefs, obligations, and needs, the reflexivity of the understanding of time, and the mobilization of the consciousness of space can be read in many phenomena. Religious faith is privatized. With the bourgeois family and the decentralized religiosity of the congregation there arises a new sphere of intimacy that is expressed in a deepened culture of reflection and feeling and that alters the conditions of socialization. At the same time, a political public sphere of private persons takes shape, which, as a medium for permanent criticism, alters the conditions for the legitimation of political domination. The consequences of this rationalization of the lifeworld are ambivalent: What some celebrate as institutionalized individualism (Parsons), others abhor as a subjectivism that undermines traditionally anchored institutions, overloads the individual's capacity for decision making, gives rise to a consciousness of crisis, and thereby endangers social integration (Gehlen).

From the conceptual perspective of action oriented to reaching understanding, rationalization appears first as a restructuring of the lifeworld, as a process that exerts an influence on everyday communication by way of the differentiation of knowledge systems, and that thus affects the forms of cultural reproduction, social integration, and socialization. Against this background the rise of subsystems of purposive-rational action occupies a different position than it does in the context of Weber's investigations. On the level of the theory of action, he also depicted the global process of rationalization as a tendency toward replacing communal social action [*Gemeinschaftshandeln*] with rationally regulated action [*Gesellschaftshandeln*]. But only if we differentiate *Gesellschaftshandeln* into action oriented to reaching understanding and action oriented to success can we conceive the communicative rationalization of everyday action and the formation of subsystems of purposive-rational economic and administrative action as *complementary* developments. Both reflect, it is true, the institutional embodiment of rationality complexes; but in other respects they are *counteracting* tendencies.

Unfettering normative contexts and releasing communicative action from traditionally based institutions—that is, from obligations of consensus—loads (and overloads) the mechanism of reaching understanding with a growing need for coordination. On the other hand, in two central domains of action, institutions are replaced by compulsory associations [*Anstalten*] and organizations of a new type; they are formed on the basis of media that uncouple action from processes of reaching understanding and coordinate it via generalized instrumental values such as money and power. These steering media replace language as the mechanism for coordinating action. They set social action loose from integration through value consensus and switch it over to purposive rationality steered by media. Because Weber's action theory is too narrowly gauged, he is unable to see in money and power the media which, *by substituting for language,* make possible the differentiation of subsystems of purposive-rational action. It is these media, and not directly the purposive-rational action orientations themselves, that need to be institutionally and motivationally anchored in the lifeworld. The legitimacy of the legal order and the moral-practical foundation of the realms of action that are regulated by law—that is, formally organized—form the links that connect the economic system (differentiated out via money) and the administrative system (differentiated out via power) to the lifeworld. Weber was right to fix on these two institutional complexes in order to decode modernization as a rationalization harboring contradictions within itself.

Only with the conceptual framework of communicative action do we gain a perspective from which the process of societal rationalization appears as contradictory from the start. The contradiction arises between, on the one hand, a rationalization of everyday communication that is tied to the structures of intersubjectivity of the lifeworld, in which language counts as the genuine and irreplaceable medium of reaching understanding, and, on the other hand, the growing complexity of subsystems of purposive-rational action, in which actions are coordinated through steering media such as money and power. Thus there is a competition *not between the types of action* oriented to understanding and to success, *but between principles of societal integration*—between the mechanism of linguistic communication that is oriented to validity claims—a mechanism that emerges in increasing purity from the rationalization of the lifeworld—and those de-linguistified steering media through which systems of success-oriented action are differentiated out. The paradox of rationalization of which Weber spoke can then be abstractly conceived as follows: The rationalization of the lifeworld makes possible a kind of systemic integration that enters into competition with the integrating principle of reaching understanding and, under certain conditions, has a disintegrative effect on the lifeworld.

I do not want to bring this thesis to bear on Weber from the outside, but rather to arrive at it from the course of the argument as it developed historically. There is something corresponding to the dialectic of societal rationalization already in Marx, in the form of the dialectic of living and dead labor. As the historical passages of *Capital* show, Marx investigates how the accumulation process erodes the lifeworld of those producers who can offer as their only commodity their own labor power. He traces the contradictory process of societal rationalization in the self-destructive movements of an economic system that, on the basis of wage labor, organizes the production of goods as the production of exchange values; it thereby exercises a decisive and disintegrative influence on the conditions of life of the classes involved in these transactions. For Marx, socialism lies on the vanishing line of a rationalization of the lifeworld that was *misguided* by the capitalist dissolution of traditional forms of life. I shall not, however, go into the interesting relations between Weber and Marx,[1] but pick up the argument at the point where representatives of Western Marxism—first Lukacs and then Horkheimer and Adorno—took up Weber's theory of rationalization in ways connected to the dialectic of living and dead labor, of ethical and systemic relations, which Hegel and Marx had studied.

In this tradition we find the two problems that have remained decisive for social theory until the present day. On the one hand, there is the problem of expanding the teleological concept of action and relativizing purposive rationality against a model of reaching understanding, which presupposes not only a transition from the philosophy of consciousness to the philosophy of language, but the development and radicalization of language analysis itself.[2] In addition to this expansion of the action-theoretic approach, there is the problem of integrating action theory and systems theory; this can lead, as it did with Parsons, to a systems-theoretic absorption of action theory unless we are able to separate clearly the rationalization of the lifeworld and the rationalization of societal subsystems. In the former case, rationalization results from the structural differentiation of the lifeworld, in the latter, from the growing complexity of systems of action. Systems theory and action theory are the *disjecta membra* of a dialectical concept of totality employed by Marx himself and then by Lukacs—though they were unable to reconstruct it in terms that might provide an equivalent of the basic concepts of the Hegelian logic they rejected as idealistic.

I shall begin (in Section 1) by examining the Marxist reception of Weber's theory of rationalization in Lukacs, Horkheimer, and Adorno; and then (in Section 2) go on to trace the aporetic course of the critique of instrumental reason in order to show how this problematic bursts the bounds of the philosophy of consciousness.

1. *Max Weber in the Tradition of Western Marxism*

If we take as our point of departure the theoretical positions that Horkheimer and Adorno developed out of critical theory in the early 1940s,[3] convergences become evident between Weber's rationalization thesis and the critique of instrumental reason along the lines of the Marx-Lukacs tradition. This is particularly true of Horkheimer's *Eclipse of Reason,* which he completed in 1946.[4]

Horkheimer shares with Weber the view that formal rationality "underlies our contemporary industrial culture."[5] Under the concept of "formal rationality" Weber summed up the determinations that make possible the "calculability" of actions: under the instrumental aspect, the efficacy of available means; under the strategic aspect, the correctness of the choice of means in the light of given preferences, means, and boundary conditions. It is especially the latter aspect that Weber calls "formal" in contrast to substantive appraisal of the values underlying subjective preferences. He also uses the term as a synonym for purposive rationality. Here it is a question of a structure of action orientations that is determined by cognitive-instrumental rationality without regard to standards of morally or aesthetically practical rationality. Weber emphasizes the *increase* in rationality that comes about when a cognitive (in the narrower sense) value sphere and scientifically organized learning processes are differentiated out. Extended chains of actions can now be systematically appraised under the validity aspects of truth and efficacy and assessed and improved in the sense of formal rationality. By contrast, Horkheimer stresses the *loss* that takes place to the degree that actions can be judged, planned, and justified only under cognitive aspects. This is already expressed in his choice of terms: He equates "purposive rationality" with "instrumental reason." The irony of this usage can be seen in the fact that "reason," which according to Kant referred to the faculty of ideas and included both practical reason and aesthetic judgment, is identified with what Kant carefully distinguished from it, that is, with the "understanding" of the subject that knows and acts in accord with technical imperatives. "When the idea of reason was conceived, it was intended to achieve more than the mere regulation of the relation between means and ends; it was regarded as the instrument for understanding the ends, for *determining* them."[6]

Despite the difference in emphasis, Horkheimer takes up the two theses that are the explanatory elements in Weber's diagnosis of the times: (A) the thesis of the loss of meaning, and (B) the thesis of the loss of freedom. The differences show up in the way they ground these theses; Horkheimer relies on (C) the interpretation of capitalist rationalization as reification, which was proposed by Lukacs.

A.—On the Thesis of the Loss of Meaning. Horkheimer introduces instrumental reason as "subjective reason" and contrasts it with "objective reason." This results in a perspective that goes beyond the unity of a reason differentiated in itself and reaches back to metaphysics: It is not Kant but metaphysics that presents the real contrast to a consciousness that allows as rational only the power of formal rationality, that is, "the ability to calculate probabilities and thereby to coordinate the right means with a given end."[7] The theory of objective reason "did not focus on the coordination of behavior and aim, but on concepts—however mythological they sound to us today—on the idea of the greatest good, on the problem of human destiny, and on the way of realization of ultimate goals."[8] The phrase "objective reason" stands for the ontological thinking that advanced the rationalization of worldviews, that conceived of the human world as part of a cosmological order. "The philosophical systems of objective reason implied the conviction that an all-embracing or fundamental structure of being could be discovered and a conception of human destination derived from it."[9]

The background to the modern history of consciousness, to the development of instrumental reason as the dominant form of rationality, was formed by those metaphysical-religious worldviews in connection with which Weber first traced the process of disenchantment—albeit from the standpoint of ethical rather than theoretical rationalization. Like Weber, Horkheimer sees the result of this development of worldviews in the formation of cultural value spheres that are governed by specific inner logics: "This division of the realm of culture is a corollary to the replacement of universal objective truth by formalized, inherently relativist reason."[10] Corresponding to this subjectivization of reason, morality and art became irrational. The authors of the *Dialectic of Enlightenment*[11]—the systematic content of which Horkheimer is merely summing up in the *Eclipse of Reason*—devoted one chapter to a novel by De Sade in order to show that even in the paradigmatic century of the Enlightenment, the "black writers of the bourgeois world" were conscious of the dissociation of reason and morality in all of its implications. "They did not pretend that formalistic reason was more closely connected with morality than with immorality."[12] Horkheimer holds the same thing to be true in the development of modern art: The dissociation of art and reason "transforms works of art into cultural commodities and their consumption into a series of haphazard emotions divorced from our real intentions and aspirations."[13]

Of course, Horkheimer differs from Weber in his assessment of the separation of cognitive, normative, and expressive spheres of value. Recalling the emphatic concept of truth proper to metaphysics—which Weber, interestingly enough, never systematically examined—Horkheimer dramatizes the inner division of reason in two directions. On the one side, he sees the normative and expressive value spheres robbed of any immanent claim to validity, so that it is no longer possible to speak of moral and aesthetic *rationality*; on the other side, for all his hesitancy, he does credit speculative thought that has been transformed into critique with a restorative power—which Weber would have considered utopian and suspected of the false charisma of reason. Both, however, agree on the thesis that the meaning-giving unity of metaphysical-religious worldviews is falling into ruin and that this places in question the unity of modernized lifeworlds and thereby threatens the identity of socialized subjects and their social solidarity.

For Horkheimer too, modernity is characterized by the fact that the same disenchantment through which religion and metaphysics had superseded the stage of mythical thought has shaken the very core of these rationalized worldviews themselves, namely the credibility of theological and of ontological-cosmological principles. The religious-metaphysical knowledge passed on by teaching is hardened into dogma; revelation and inherited wisdom are transformed into mere tradition; conviction becomes a subjective holding-for-true. The very form of thought of the worldview becomes obsolete; sacred knowledge and worldly wisdom are dissolved into subjectivized objects of belief. Now, for the firt time, phenomena like confessional fanaticism and cultivated traditionalism can appear, and indeed as concomitant manifestations of Protestantism, on the one hand, and of humanism, on the other. As soon as the knowledge of God—in whom the validity aspects of the true, the good, and the perfect are not yet separated—encounters those knowledge systems that are specialized according to standards of propositional truth, normative rightness, and authenticity or beauty, the mode of holding fast to religious convictions loses the unforced quality that comes to a conviction only through good reasons or grounds.

Hereafter religious *faith* is characterized by moments of blindness, of mere belief, and of subjugation—faith and knowledge part ways.

> Faith is a private concept; it is destroyed as faith if it does not constantly accentuate its opposition to knowledge or its agreement with it. As it remains dependent on the limitation of knowledge, it is itself limited. The attempt made within Protestantism to find the transcendental principle of truth—without which faith cannot endure—directly in the word itself, as in the earlier times, and to give back to the word its symbolic power, was paid for with obedience to the word. As faith remains unquestioningly bound to knowledge, as friend or as foe, it perpetuates the separation in the very struggle to overcome it. Its fanaticism is the mark of its untruth, the objective admission that whoever *merely* believes, by that very fact no longer believes.[14]

On the other hand, a cultivated knowledge separates off from modern philosophy (which, as the opponent and at the same time the heir of religion, ambiguously identifies itself with science and thus provisionally rescues itself within the system of science). The justification of this type of knowledge consists primarily in the continuation of traditions. The difficulty with this cultivated traditionalism is expressed in the fact that it has to conceal its own foundations; for the only traditions that are in need of this affirmation are those that lack the authentication of good grounds. Every traditionalism bears the mark of a neotraditionalism.

> What are the consequences of the formalization of reason? Justice, equality, happiness, tolerance, all the concepts that, as mentioned, were in preceding centuries supposed to be inherent in or sanctioned by reason, have lost their intellectual roots. They are still aims and ends, but there is no rational agency authorized to appraise and link them to

an objective reality. Endorsed by venerable historical documents, they may still enjoy a certain prestige, and some are contained in the supreme law of the greatest countries. Nevertheless, they lack any confirmation by reason in its modern sense. Who can say that any one of these ideals is more closely related to truth than its opposite?[15]

The second stage of disenchantment, consciously carried out by historicism, means the ironic return of the demonic powers that had been subdued by the unifying, meaning-bestowing power of religious and metaphysical worldviews. The thesis developed in the *Dialectic of Enlightenment*, that enlightenment reverts to myth, accords with the thesis of Weber's "Religious Rejections of the World and Their Directions." The more sharply "the specific nature of each special sphere existing in the world" comes to the fore, the more powerless does the quest for salvation and for wisdom become in the face of a restrengthened polytheism, a struggle among the gods—which, naturally, is now carried on by subjective reason under the banners of impersonal powers. Because it has been stripped of its mythological form, this new polytheism has lost its binding force and has left to fate—which is deprived of its socially integrative function—only its blindness—that is, the contingent character of a conflict among subjective powers [*Glaubensmächte*] that have become irrational. Even science stands on a precarious foundation, which is no securer than the subjective engagement of those who are resolved to let their lives be nailed to this cross.[16]

For the rest, subjective reason is instrumental reason, that is, a tool for self-preservation. Horkheimer identifies the idea of self-preservation as the principle that drives subjective reason to madness, for the thought of anything that goes beyond the subjectivity of self-interest is robbed of all rationality.

The life of the totemistic tribe, the clan, the church of the Middle Ages, the nation in the era of the bourgeois revolutions, followed ideological patterns shaped through historical developments. Such patterns—magical, religious, or philosophical—reflected current forms of social domination. They constituted a cultural cement even after their role in production had become obsolete; thus they also fostered the idea of a common truth. This they did by the very fact that they had become objectified . . . These older systems had vanished because the forms of solidarity postulated by them proved to be deceptive, and the ideologies related to them became hollow and apologetic.[17]

In the same connection Weber speaks of the world dominion of unbrotherliness.

Thus Weber and Horkheimer agree in the fundamentals of their oddly ambivalent diagnoses of the present age.

a) The credibility of religious and metaphysical worldviews falls prey to a process of rationalization to which they owed their own development; in this respect, the Enlightenment critique of theology and ontology is rational, that is, understandable on internal grounds, and irreversible.

b) The second stage of rationalization after the overcoming of myth makes possible a modern consciousness that is determined by the differentiation of cultural value spheres with their own inner logics; this results in a subjectivization of faith and knowledge; art and morality are split off from claims to propositional truth, whereas science retains a practical relation only to purposive-rational action (and forfeits its relation to communicative practice).

c) Subjective reason functions as a tool for self-preservation in a struggle in which those involved orient themselves to fundamentally irrational and irreconcilable "gods and demons." It is no longer able to bestow meaning; rather, it threatens the unity of the lifeworld, and, therewith, the integration of society.

d) As the power of socially integrative worldviews and the social solidarity they bring about are not simply irrational, the "splitting apart of the cultural realms" of science, morality, and art cannot count simply as rational, even though it is based on learning processes and thus on reason.

B. —On the Thesis of the Loss of Freedom. The thesis of a loss of meaning was inferred from an internally reconstructible process of cultural rationalization; the thesis of a loss of freedom is derived from processes of societal rationalization. To be sure, Weber and Horkheimer select different historical points of reference within the European development: the sixteenth and seventeenth centuries in the one case, and the late nineteenth century in the other. For Weber it is the period in which Protestantism, humanism, and modern science called into question the unity of religious and metaphysical worldviews. For Horkheimer it is the period of "high liberalism," on the threshold of the transition from liberal to organized capitalism.

The take-off of capitalist development drew upon the qualities of a way of life that owed its methodical rationality to the
unifying power of the ascetic ethic that was generalized within
Protestantism. With a slight—psychoanalytically informed—
reservation, Horkheimer shares Weber's view that this principled
ethic is the basis for the cultural reproduction of personal independence and individuality.

> By the very negation of the will to self-preservation on earth
> in favor of the preservation of the eternal soul, Christianity
> asserted the infinite value of each man, an idea that pene-
> trated even non-Christian or anti-Christian systems of the
> Western world. True, the price was the repression of the vital
> instincts and, since such repression is never successful, an
> insincerity that pervades our culture. Nevertheless, this very
> internalization enhances individuality. By negating himself,
> by imitating Christ's sacrifice, the individual simultaneously
> acquires a new dimension and a new ideal on which to
> pattern his life on earth.[18]

Horkheimer repeats in a vaguer form Weber's thesis
concerning the religious-ascetic bases of the economically rational
action of capitalist entrepreneurs; in doing so he refers to the era
of liberalism and not to the phase in which the new mode of production is established.

> Individualism is the very heart of the theory and practice
> of bourgeois liberalism, which sees society as progressing
> through the automatic interaction of diverging interests in
> a free market. The individual could maintain himself as a
> social being only by pursuing his own long-term interests
> at the expense of ephemeral immediate gratifications. The
> qualities of individuality forged by the ascetic discipline of
> Christianity were thereby reinforced.[19]

Horkheimer contents himself with stylizations against which
he can set off the tendency toward a "decline of the individual."
Following Weber again, he grounds this tendency in progressive
bureaucratization, that is, in the growing complexity of the
organizational forms that have come to dominate in the economy
and the state. Adorno's formula of an "administered world" is
an equivalent for Weber's vision of an "iron cage." Subsystems of
purposive-rational action detach themselves from the motiva-

tional bases that Weber studied in connection with the Protestant ethic and Horkheimer described with a view to the individualistic social character. Just what does this "loss of freedom," to which both attest, signify?

Weber conceives of the loss of freedom in terms of action theory. In the methodical conduct of life there is embodied a practical rationality that relates purposive rationality to value rationality; purposive-rational actions are guided by the moral judgment and autonomous will of individuals who are determined by principles (and who act value-rationally in this sense). To the degree that economic and administrative operations are bureaucratized, however, the purposive rationality of actions (or at least the systemic rationality of their output) has to be secured independently of the value-rational judgments and decisions of organization members. Organizations themselves take over the regulation of actions, which now need to be anchored subjectively only in generalized utilitarian motives. This freeing of subjectivity from the determinations of moral-practical rationality is reflected in the polarization of "specialists without spirit" and "sensualists without heart." Weber can imagine a reversal of the tendency only in the wills of charismatic leaders. "As the satisfaction of political and economic needs is increasingly rationalized, the spread of discipline advances inexorably; this universal phenomenon more and more restricts the importance of charisma and of individually differentiated action."[20] If the struggle between creative charisma and a bureaucracy that restricts freedom is to be decided against the seemingly "inexorable" march of rationalization, then it can only be via the organizational model of "the leader with a machine." In the domain of economics, this signifies the voluntarism of authoritarian business leaders; in that of politics, a plebiscitary democracy with charismatic leaders [Führerdemokratie]; and in both domains, an optimal selection of leaders. Wolfgang Mommsen captured Weber's position in the "only seemingly paradoxical" formula: "as much freedom as possible through as much domination as possible."[21]

Horkheimer conceives of the loss of freedom in a similar way, albeit in psychoanalytic rather than in action-theoretic terms. The control of behavior tends to pass from the authority of conscience of associated individuals to the planning authority of societal organizations. It is less and less necessary for subjects to orient themselves by their superegos and more necessary for them to adjust to the imperatives of their environments. (This thesis was later taken up by David Riesman and interpreted as a shift from "inner-directed" to "outer-directed" modes of life, and thereby trivialized.)[22] In Horkheimer's words:

> Just as all life today tends increasingly to be subjected to rationalization and planning, so the life of each individual, including his most hidden impulses, which formerly constituted his private domain, must now take the demands of rationalization and planning into account: the individual's self-preservation presupposes his adjustment to the requirements for the preservation of the system . . . Formerly reality was opposed to and confronted with the ideal, which was evolved by the supposedly autonomous individual; reality was supposed to be shaped in accordance with this ideal. Today such ideologies are compromised and skipped over by progressive thought, which thus unwittingly facilitates the elevation of reality to the status of ideal. Therefore adjustment becomes the standard for every conceivable type of subjective behavior. The triumph of subjective, formalized reason is also the triumph of a reality that confronts the subject as absolute, overpowering.[23]

The expansion of the possibilities of individual choice, which Horkheimer does not deny, goes hand in hand with a "change in the character of freedom."[24] As the process of rationalization advances, the subsystems of purposive-rational action become increasingly independent of the ethically grounded motives of their members and thus make increasingly superfluous any internal behavioral controls related to moral-practical rationality.[25]

The parallels extend only this far. Weber goes directly from his diagnosis of a loss of freedom to his therapeutic reflections; he puts forward an organizational model that, by way of the charisma of leaders, reconnects rationalized domains of action back to the value orientations of eminent individual subjects, orientations interpreted in life-historical terms; and he does this, of course, at the expense of the dominated followers.[26] Horkheimer and Adorno take the analysis a step further. They are interested in what the growing autonomy of subsystems of purposive-rational action means—and, accordingly, in "the self-alienation of individuals who have to form themselves, body and soul, in relation to the technical apparatus."[27] If, however, the control of behavior passes from aspects of personality to the "much smoother operation of automatic ordering mechanisms,"[28] then what now occupies center stage are the *systemic* ordering mechanisms of domains of action organized in the form of enterprises or compulsory associations, as well as the imperatives to adjust that penetrate into the subjectivity of individual members of organizations. Horkheimer and Adorno now have to avoid two forms of one-sidedness. On the one hand, Weber remained within the limits of an action theory, which offers no way of approaching this problem. On the other hand, a systems theory that concentrates *exclusively* on systemic ordering performances ignores questions about the "change in the character of freedom" signified by the dissociation of action systems from the lifeworld, especially from the moral-practical motives of their members. Horkheimer and Adorno are interested precisely in the ironic connection that the rationalization of society seems to establish between the transformation of traditional realms of life into subsystems of purposive-rational action, on the one hand, and the "atrophy of individuality," on the other.

In Horkheimer's view the destruction of the identity that an individual gains from the orientation to "basic intellectual concepts" or principles is directly connected not only with bureaucratization but with the detachment of systems of purposive-rational action from "culture," from a horizon of the lifeworld experienced as rational. The more the economy and the state change into embodiments of cognitive-instrumental rationality and subordinate other departments of life to their imperatives, and the more they push to the fringes anything in which moral-practical and aesthetic-practical rationality can be embodied, the less support processes of individuation find in a domain of cultural reproduction that has been shunted into the irrational or wholly tailored to the pragmatic. In premodern societies, "there was still a cleavage between culture and production. This cleavage left more loopholes than modern superorganization, which virtually reduces the individual to a mere cell of functional response. Modern organizational units, such as the totality of labor, are organic parts of the socio-economic system."[29]

For the analysis of those processes that close up the "cleavage between culture and production," Marxist theory has at hand the basic concept of "reification." Georg Lukacs used this key in *History and Class Consciousness* to detach Weber's analysis of societal rationalization from its action-theoretic framework and relate it to anonymous processes of capital realization within the economic system. He attempted to clarify the connection between the differentiation of a capitalist economy steered through exchange value, on the one hand, and the deformation of the lifeworld, on the other, by drawing on the model of commodity fetishism. I want now to examine the first Marxist reception of Weber,[30] and then to discuss why Horkheimer and Adorno understood their critique of instrumental reason as a "negation of reification"[31] but hesitated nevertheless to follow Lukacs' line of argument, which had stimulated them to undertake this critique.

C.—Lukacs' Interpretation of Weber's Rationalization Thesis. In his central essay on "Reification and the Consciousness of the Proletariat,"[32] published in 1922, Lukacs develops the thesis that "in the structure of the commodity relation [can] be found the model of all the forms of objectivity in bourgeois society, together with all the form of subjectivity corresponding to them."[33] Lukacs uses the neo-Kantian term "form of objectivity" [*Gegenständlichkeitsform*] in a sense coined by Dilthey, as a "form of existence or thought" [*Daseinsform, Denkform*] that has arisen historically and that characterizes the "totality of the stage of development of society as a whole." He conceives of the development of society as "the history of the continuous transformation of the forms of objectivity that shape the existence of human beings." To be sure, Lukacs does not share the historicist view, in which forms of objectivity express the particularity of unique cultures. Rather, the forms mediate "the interaction of human beings with their environment, which determines the objectivity of their inner and outer lives."[34] They retain a relation to the universality of reason; for Lukacs, like Horkheimer,[35] holds onto the Hegelian idea that in the relation of human beings to one another and to nature (to external nature as well as to their own internal nature) reason is objectivated—in however unreasonable a manner. Capitalist society too is determined by a specific form that establishes the way in which its members categorially interpret objective nature, interpersonal relations, and their own subjective natures—that is to say, "the objectivity of their inner and outer lives." In our own terminology: the form of objectivity that predominates in capitalist society prejudices the world-relations, the ways in which speaking and acting subjects can relate to things in the objective, the social, and their own subjective worlds.

Lukacs maintains that we can characterize this prejudice as "reification," as a peculiar assimilation of social relationships and subjective experiences to things, that is, to objects that we can perceive and manipulate. The three worlds are so lopsidedly coordinated that category mistakes are built into our understanding of interpersonal relationships and subjective experiences; we apprehend them under the form of things, as entities that belong to the objective world, although they are really elements of our common social world or of an individual subjective world. To this must be added the following: because understanding and apprehending are constitutive for communicative intercourse itself, a systematically ingrained misunderstanding of this kind affects not only the subjects' "forms of thought" but their "forms of existence" as well. It is the lifeworld itself that is "reified."

Lukacs sees the cause of this deformation in a mode of production that is based on wage labor and that necessitates the "transformation of a human function into a commodity."[36] He grounds this thesis in several steps. (a) First, he examines the reifying effect to which the commodity form gives rise to the degree that it penetrates into the production process; he then goes on to show that the reification of persons and of interpersonal relations in the sphere of social labor is only the other side of the rationalization of this action system. (b) In conceiving rationalization and reification as two aspects of the same process, Lukacs works up two arguments that rest on Weber's analysis and yet are directed against its implications. With his concept of "formal rationality," Weber captures structural analogies to purposive-rational economic action in other departments of life, particularly in the state bureaucracy. According to Lukacs, Weber misconstrues the causal connection; he detaches "the phenomena of reification from the economic basis of their existence" and eternalizes them as "a timeless type of possible human relationship"; but he does show that the processes of societal rationalization acquire a structure-forming significance for capitalist society as a whole. Lukacs takes up this analysis and interprets it in such a way that the commodity form assumes a universal character and becomes the form of objectivity of capitalist society purely and simply. (c) Lukacs makes use of the concept of formal rationality in another way. It constitutes for him a bridge between the commodity form and the forms of the understanding analyzed by Kant. In this way, Lukacs reintroduces the concept of a form of objectivity into the context of the theory of knowledge, from which it was tacitly borrowed, so as to carry out the critique of reification from the philosophical perspective of Hegel's critique of Kant. He takes from Hegel the concept of the totality of a rationally organized life-context and uses it as a standard for the irrationality of societal rationalization. In having recourse to this concept, Lukacs implicitly denies Weber's central assertion to the effect that the metaphysically conceived unity of reason had fallen apart *once and for all* with the separation of cultural value spheres, each with its own inner logic; and that it couldn't be put back together again, not even dialectically.

(ad a) Lukacs develops his concept of reification out of Marx's analysis of the commodity form. He refers to the famous passage in the first volume of *Capital*,[37] where Marx is describing the fetishism of commodities.

> A commodity is therefore a mysterious thing simply because in it the social character of men's labor appears to them as an objective character of the products of that labor, as social natural properties of these things; because the relation of the producers to the sum total of their labor appears to them as a social relation among objects, a relation existing outside of them. Through this quid pro quo the products of labor become commodities—things which are at the same time perceptible and imperceptible to the senses, social things . . . It is only a definite social relation among men that assumes, in their eyes, the fantastic form of a relation among things.[38]

Marx analyzes the double form of the commodity as a use value and an exchange value, as well as the transformation of its natural form into the value form; for this purpose he draws upon Hegel's concept of abstraction and treats the relation between use value and exchange value like that between essence and appearance. Today this presents us with difficulties; we cannot employ unreconstructed basic concepts from Hegel's logic just like that. The extended discussion on the relation of Marx's *Capital* to Hegel's *Logic* has illuminated these difficulties rather than resolved them.[39] I shall therefore not go any deeper into the analysis of the commodity form. Lukacs doesn't either. He is interested only in the reification effects that come about to the degree that the labor power of producers becomes a commodity, in "the split between the worker's labor power and his personality, its metamorphosis into a thing, an object that is sold on the market."[40]

The basic idea is easy to grasp in intuitive form. As long as interactive relations in the sphere of social labor are regulated in a traditional manner, through quasi-natural norms, individuals stand to one another and to themselves in communicative relations that they enter into intentionally. The same would hold if one day social relations could be determined through will-formation in common. But so long as the production of goods is organized as the production of exchange values and the labor power of producers is itself exchanged as a commodity, another medium for coordinating action is in force: Economically relevant action orientations are detached from lifeworld contexts and linked with the medium of exchange value (or money). To the extent that interactions are no longer coordinated through norms and values but through the medium of exchange value, actors have to assume an objectivating attitude to one another (and to themselves). The mechanism for coordinating action is itself encountered as something external. Transactions that proceed through the medium of exchange value fall outside of the inter-subjectivity of reaching understanding through language; they become something that takes place in the objective world—a pseudonature.[41] Marx characterizes the effect of assimilating the normative and the subjective to the status of perceptible and manipulable things as objectivation [*Objektivierung*] or "objectification" [*Versachlichung*]. To the degree that the wage laborer becomes dependent on the market for his entire existence, anonymous valorization processes encroach upon his lifeworld and destroy the ethical order [*Sittlichkeit*] of communicatively established intersubjectivity by turning social relations into purely instrumental relations. The producers, he writes,

> exist for one another only in objectified form [*sachlich*]; and this is merely developed further in the money relationship, where their communal life itself appears as an external and therefore accidental thing standing over against all of them. The fact that the social nexus which arises through the encounter of independent individuals appears to be an objective necessity and, at the same time, an external bond standing over against them, represents precisely their dependence; in this regard, social life is indeed a necessity, but only as a means; thus it appears to the individuals them-selves as something external, even as a palpable thing in [the form of] money. They produce in and for society, as social; at the same time, however, society appears as a mere means by which to objectify their individuality. Since they are not subsumed under a nature-like communal life nor, on the

other hand, do they subsume communal life under themselves as consciously social beings, it must exist for them, the individual subjects, as something similarly independent, external, accidental, objective, standing over against them.[42]

Weber had already learned from Simmel's *Philosophy of Money* about the change of scene that takes place as soon as naturelike communicative relations are translated into "the universal language of money." Lukacs now reaches back behind Simmel to Marx's original analysis in order to grasp the basic phenomenon of societal rationalization in terms of capitalist commodity exchange, which for Weber was only an exemplary expression of a *more general* process. Lukacs' specific achievement consists in bringing Marx and Weber together in such a way that he can view the decoupling of the sphere of social labor from lifeworld contexts simultaneously under two aspects: as reification and rationalization. As acting subjects switch to exchange-value orientations, their lifeworld shrinks to the format of the objective world; they assume toward themselves and others the objectivating attitude of success-oriented action and thereby make themselves into objects to be "handled" by other actors. For the price of reifying interactions, however, they gain the freedom of strategic action oriented to their own success. Reification is, as Marx says in continuing the passage quoted above, "the condition of their [the producers'] standing as independent private persons in a social context."[43] For Marx, the jurist, the subject of civil law who is oriented to the purposive-rational pursuit of his own interests is the model for an acting subject who is sociated [*vergesellschaftet*] through exchange relations. Thus for Lukacs there is a clear relation between the analyses of Marx and Weber: "We are concerned above all with the *principle* at work here: the principle of rationalization based on what is and what can be *calculated*."[44] He conceives of the reification of lifeworld contexts, which sets in when workers coordinate their interactions by way of the de-linguistified medium of exchange value rather than through norms and values, as the other side of a rationalization of their action orientations. In this way he makes the system-forming effects of sociation established through the medium of exchange value intelligible from the perspective of action theory.

As we shall see, in systems theory money also serves as the model from which the concept of a steering medium is developed. Media theory absorbs into its conceptual framework, in an undramatic fashion, the double aspect of reification and rationalization worked out by Lukacs. Here too the switchover of action orientations from linguistic communication to the medium of money will mean a "change in the character of freedom"; in a drastically expanded horizon of possibilities of choice, there arises an automatic process of reciprocal conditioning through offers, one that is independent of processes of consensus formation.[45]

(ad b) The reification of social relations (and of the relations of individuals to themselves) finds its expression in the organizational form of the capitalist enterprise separated from the private household; with this, entrepreneurial activity is institutionalized: calculation of capital, investment decisions oriented to the opportunities of the market, rational organization of labor, technical exploitation of scientific knowledge, and so forth. As we saw above, Max Weber traced the structural analogies that hold between formal-rational economic and administrative action, between the organizational forms of capitalist enterprise and public bureaucracy, between the concentration of material means of operation in the former and in the latter, and between the action orientations of entrepreneurs and officials, of workers and salaried employees. As Lukacs takes only one medium into consideration, viz. exchange value, and traces reification to the "abstraction of exchange" alone, he interprets *all* manifestations of Occidental rationalism as symptoms of a process in which the whole of society is rationalized through and through.[46] Lukacs understands the encompassing character of the societal rationalization diagnosed by Weber as a confirmation of his assumption that the commodity form is establishing itself as the dominant form of objectivity in capitalist society.

> It was capitalism, with its unified economic structure for the whole of society, that first brought into being a—formally—unified structure of consciousness which embraced the whole of society. This unified structure is expressed in the fact that problems of consciousness arising from wage labor are repeated in the ruling class in a refined and spiritualized but, for that reason, intensified form . . . The transformation of the commodity relation into a thing of "ghostly objectivity" cannot therefore content itself with the reduction of all objects for the satisfaction of human needs to commodities. It impresses its structure upon the whole consciousness of man; his qualities and abilities are no longer an organic part of his personality; they appear as "things"

that he can "possess" or "dispose of" like the various objects of the external world. And there is naturally no form of relations among men, no possibility for men to bring their physical and psychic "qualities" into play, that are not being increasingly subjected to this form of objectivity.[47]

To the degree that the commodity form becomes the form of objectivity and rules the relations of individuals to one another as well as their dealings with external nature and with internal subjective nature, the lifeworld has to become reified and individuals degraded—as systems theory foresees—into an "environment" for a society that has become external to them, that has consolidated for them into an opaque system, that has been abstracted from them and become independent of them. Lukacs shares this perspective with Weber, as with Horkheimer; but he is convinced that this development not only can be stopped practically but, for reasons that can be theoretically demonstrated, *has to* run up against internal limits: "This rationalization of the world appears to be complete, it seems to penetrate to the very depths of man's physical and psychic nature; but it finds its limit in the formal character of its own rationality."[48]

The burden of proof that Marx wanted to discharge in political-economic terms, with a theory of crisis, now falls upon a demonstration of the immanent limits to rationalization, a demonstration that has to be carried out in philosophical terms. Lukacs sets about analyzing the properties of formal rationality at the level on which Hegel developed his critique of Kant's theory of knowledge; he projects this concept, which was developed in the context of action theory, onto the level of the theory of knowledge. For him formal rationality finds its most precise expression in modern science; and Kant's critique of knowledge explains the activity of the understanding [*Verstand*] that is expressed in these sciences, prototypically in Newton's physics. The latter "allows its underlying material substratum to rest inviolate and undisturbed in its irrationality (its character of being given, not made), so that it is possible to operate freely with unproblematically applicable categories of the understanding, in the resulting, self-enclosed, methodically purified world."[49] Kantian theory mercilessly tore to shreds the metaphysical illusions of preceding epochs; it undermined the dogmatic pretension of objective reason; but it did so, Lukacs believes, only to justify scientism, that is to say, the similarly dogmatic "assumption that the formalistically rational mode of cognition is the only way of apprehending reality that is possible 'for us.' "[50]

In the final analysis the Kantian critique also reflects only reified structures of consciousness; it is itself an expression in thought of the now universal commodity form.[51] Lukacs follows, in a thoroughly conventional manner, the line of Kant criticism from Schiller to Hegel. Schiller identified in the play instinct the aesthetic principle, in accord with which the human being, "having been socially destroyed, fragmented, and divided among different subsystems, is to be made whole again in thought."[52] And Hegel developed the idea—already present in Rousseau's concept of nature—of a totality of life-relations that "has inwardly overcome, or is in the process of overcoming, the divisions in theory and practice, reason and sense, form and matter; for which the tendency to give form to itself does not mean an abstract rationality that ignores concrete contents; and for which freedom and necessity come together."[53] Lukacs acknowledges that Hegel's logic, which dialectically reestablished the unity of a reason that had fallen apart into its moments, was "still very problematic"[54] and that it has not seriously been further developed since that time; but he does nonetheless rely on the "dialectical method," which is supposed to lead us beyond the type of thinking inherent in bourgeois society. In taking over—unanalyzed—the basic concepts of Hegelian logic, Lukacs is presupposing the unity of theoretical and practical reason at the conceptual level of absolute spirit, whereas Weber saw the paradox of societal rationalization precisely in the fact that the development (and institutional embodiment) of formal rationality is by no means irrational as such; it is linked with learning processes that exclude a *grounded* resumption of metaphysical worldviews no less than they do a dialectical connection with objective reason.

To be sure, Lukacs, despite his affirmative relation to Greek philosophy, to classicism in general,[55] does not directly call for a restoration of forms of objectivity like those reflected in metaphysical-religious ordo-thinking. Even his link with Hegel has a Young-Hegelian twist; it is forged from the perspective of Marx's critique of Hegel: "In terms of developmental history, classical philosophy found itself in the paradoxical position of trying to overcome bourgeois society in thought, of attempting to bring speculatively back to life the human being destroyed in and by that society. In the upshot, however, it succeeded only in completely reproducing bourgeois society in thought, in providing an a priori deduction of it.''[56] As long as the unity of reason is only dialectically *thought*, ascertained within theory, even a philosophy that reaches beyond the limits of formal rationality merely reproduces the reified structure of consciousness that constrains us to adopt a contemplative relation to a world that we have ourselves created. Thus for Lukacs, as for the Marx of the *Deutsch-Französische Jahrbücher*, it is a question of the practical realization of the rational life-relations that Hegel first conceptualized, albeit in a speculative manner. The objectivism of Hegel's theory lies in its contemplative character: that is, in the fact that it wants to put the moments of reason that have split apart back together again only in theory; that it holds on to philosophy as the place where the reconciliation of a totality that has become abstract will both come to pass and find its consummation. In Lukacs's view, Hegel misses here the level of historical practice on which alone the critical content of philosophical insight can become effective.

Marx's specification of the relation between theory and practice was ambiguous on an essential point; in the reading that Lukacs gives to it, the ambiguity becomes obvious. *To begin with*, Lukacs can take up Weber's central insight: Modernity is characterized by the motivational anchoring and institutional embodiment of a formal rationality that issued from the dissolution of the substantial unity of reason and its separation into abstract, for the present unreconciled, moments (validity aspects, value spheres); the theoretical reestablishment of an objective reason *at the level of philosophical thought* is excluded here. *Then* Lukacs can go on to object against Weber that the moments of reason need not enter into implacable opposition to one another on the level of rationalized action systems just because on the level of cultural interpretive systems they can no longer be united into a totality, that is, fused into a basic conceptual foundation for worldviews. It is characteristic of the pattern of rationalization in capitalist societies that the complex of cognitive-instrumental rationality establishes itself at the cost of practical rationality; communicative relations are reified. Thus it makes sense to ask whether the critique of the incomplete character of the rationalization that appears as reification does not suggest taking a complementary relation between cognitive-instrumental rationality, on the one hand, and moral-practical and aesthetic-practical rationality, on the other, as a standard that is inherent in the unabridged concept of practice, that is to say, in communicative

364 REASON AND THE RATIONALIZATION OF SOCIETY

action itself. In metaphysical worldviews this reason was projected as a substantial unity, but the concept of an objective reason itself fell prey in the end to the rationalization of worldviews. In "theory"—this is the point of Marx's critique of Hegel—the reconciliation intended under the title of "reason" remains and—all dialectic notwithstanding—must remain a fiction. Between the differentiated moments of reason there is now only a formal connection, namely the procedural unity of argumentative grounding. What now presents itself merely as a formal connection in "theory"—at the level of cultural interpretive systems—can possibly be realized in "practice"—in the lifeworld. Under the watchword of "philosophy becoming practical," Marx appropriates the perspective of the Young-Hegelian "philosophy of the deed."

Lukacs makes a decisive error—one that is suggested by Marx, to be sure—by bringing in this "becoming practical" on a *theoretical* plane and *representing* it as a revolutionary actualization of philosophy. In doing so, he has to credit theory with more power than even metaphysics had claimed for itself. Now philosophy has to be capable of thinking not only the totality that is hypostatized as the world order, but the world-historical process as well—the historical development of this totality through the self-conscious practice of those who are enlightened by philosophy about their active role in the self-realization of reason. For the work of enlightenment by the avant garde of world revolution, Lukacs has to claim a knowledge that is incompatible with Weber's austere insight into the disintegration of objective reason—in two respects. A metaphysics transformed into a dialectical philosophy of history must not only be capable of a conceptual perspective from which the unity of the abstractly separated moments of reason can be grasped; beyond this, it must believe itself capable of identifying the subjects who will establish this unity practically and of showing them the way. For these reasons, Lukacs supplements his theory of reification with a theory of class consciousness.

This theory amounts to an enthronement of proletarian class consciousness as the subject-object of history as a whole.[57] Nor does Lukacs shy away from drawing the instrumentalist consequences that follow from his historical objectivism with regard to questions concerning the organization of the revolutionary struggle—consequences unveiled in Stalinist terror. But I shall not go into that here.[58] Wellmer provides us with an accurate summary of Lukacs's attempt "to go beyond Weber's abstract concept of 'rationalization' and to make the specific political-economic content of the capitalist industrialization process visible; [this attempt] was part of his larger project to restore the philosophical dimension of Marxism. That his attempt ultimately failed is, I believe, in an ironical way due to the fact that Lukacs's philosophical reconstruction of Marxism was in some important respects equivalent to return to objective idealism."[59]

2. The Critique of Instrumental Reason

The critique of instrumental reason understands itself as a critique of reification that takes up Lukacs' Weber reception without accepting the implications of his objectivistic philosophy of history (which were merely alluded to above.)[1] In attempting this, Horkheimer and Adorno get ensnared in their own difficulties. There is something to be learned from these problems; indeed they furnish us with reasons for a *change of paradigm* within social theory. I shall begin this section with (A) a sketch of how Horkheimer and Adorno, borrowing from Lukacs, transform Weber's rationalization thesis.[2] The version in which Lukacs put forward the theory of reification stood contradicted by the failure of the revolution and the unforeseen integrative accomplishments of advanced capitalist societies. (B) It can also be criticized theoretically for its affirmative ties to Hegel's objective idealism. Thus Horkheimer and Adorno see themselves forced (C) to sink the foundations of the reification critique still deeper and to expand instrumental reason into a category of the world-historical process of civilization as a whole, that is, to project the process of reification back behind the capitalist beginnings of the modern age into the very beginnings of hominization. With this, however (D), the contours of the concept of reason are in danger of becoming blurred. On the one hand, the theory takes on features of a rather traditional "contemplation" that renounces its relations to practice; at the same time, it cedes to art the competence to represent a reason that is now appealed to only indirectly. The aporias of the negative-dialectical self-transcendence of philosophical thought give rise to the question (E), whether this situation is not merely the consequence of an approach that remains rooted in the philosophy of consciousness, fixated on the relation of subjectivity and self-preservation.

A.—As Helmut Dubiel has shown,[3] three historical experiences were decisive above all others for the development of critical theory; all three experiences converged in the disappointment of revolutionary expectations. The Soviet development confirmed by and large Weber's prognosis of an accelerated bureaucratization; and the Stalinist practice provided a bloody confirmation of Rosa Luxemburg's critique of the Leninist theory of organization and its historico-objectivistic foundations. Fascism demonstrated the ability of advanced capitalist societies to respond in critical situations to the danger of revolutionary change by restructuring the political system and its capacity to absorb the opposition of organized labor. Finally, developments in the United States showed in another way the integrating powers of capitalism: without open repression, mass culture bound the consciousness of the broad masses to the imperatives of the status quo. The Soviet-Russian perversion of the humane content of revolutionary socialism, the collapse of the social-revolutionary labor movement in all industrial societies, and the socially integrative accomplishments of a rationalization that had penetrated into cultural reproduction—these were the basic experiences that Horkheimer and Adorno attempted to work through theoretically in the early 1940s. They stand in contrast to the central assumptions of the theory of reification that Lukacs had put forward in the early 1920s.

Marx regarded the productive forces unleashed by capitalism as an objective presupposition for overcoming it; he was thinking here primarily of increases in productivity brought about through scientific-technical progress, qualification of labor power, and improved organization of the labor process. Among the productive forces that were to come into "contradiction" with the relations of production, he also included, of course, the subjective potential of workers insofar as this found expression (not merely in productive activity but also) in critical-revolutionary activity. Capitalism, Marx assumed, would create not only the objective conditions, but also the "essential subjective preconditions for the self-emancipation of the proletariat."[4] Lukacs holds fundamentally the same position, but he revises Marx's assessment of modern science. It is true that the sciences are increasingly interconnected with the development of productivity by way of technical progress; however, with the formation of a scientistic self-understanding, which identifies the limits of objectivating knowledge with the limits of knowledge as such, the sciences simultaneously take on an ideological role. The positivistically narrowed conception of science is a particular expression of those general tendencies toward reification that Lukacs is criticizing. This is the start of that line of argument which Horkheimer and Adorno (and, in a more pronounced way, Marcuse)[5] take so far that the scientific-technical forces of production appear to them to merge with the relations of production and to lose entirely their power to burst the system. The rationalized world contracts to a "false" totality.

In contrast to this, Lukacs insists that the "seemingly complete" rationalization of the world, though it "penetrates to the very depths of man's physical and psychic nature," runs up against an inner limit—it is limited "by the formal character of its own rationality."[6] Thus Lukacs counts on there being some reservation within the subjective nature of human beings that is resistant to reification. Precisely because the individual worker is forced to split off his labor power—as a function—from his total personality and to objectivate it as a commodity—as something that is literally alienable, saleable—his now abstract, empty subjectivity is roused to resistance: "In virtue of the split between objectivity and subjectivity that arises within human beings who objectivate themselves as commodities, the situation is one of which they can also become conscious."[7] This assertion is implicitly based on Hegel, who construed the self-movement of the spirit as a logical necessity in a specific sense. If we drop this presupposition and regard Lukacs' statement as an empirical one, then we obviously need other grounds to make it plausible that the individual wage laborer will rise above his role as an object, that the proletariat as a whole will develop a consciousness with which and in which the self-exposure of a society based on commodity production can be achieved. Lukacs merely assures us that "while the process by which the worker is reified and becomes a commodity—so long as he does not consciously offer resistance to it—dehumanizes him and cripples and atrophies his 'soul,' it remains true that precisely his human nature is not changed into a commodity. He can, therefore, inwardly objectivate himself completely against this existence of his."[8] Horkheimer and Adorno, who no longer trust in the Hegelian logic just as it is, contest this assertion on empirical grounds. Because they hold to the theory of reification, they have to explain the historical experiences that so clearly speak for the fact that the subjective nature of the masses was sucked into the whirl of societal rationalization without offering resistance and that it accelerated rather than retarded this process.

They develop theories of fascism and of mass culture which deal with the socio-psychological aspects of a deformation that penetrates into the deepest regions of subjectivity and takes hold of the motivational foundations of the personality, which explains cultural reproduction from the perspective of reification. Whereas the theory of mass culture[9] starts from the view that the commodity form takes hold of culture too—and thus has a tendency to take over *all* of the functions of human beings—the theory of fascism[10] involves a deliberate refunctionalization (that is, one intended by political elites) of the resistance that subjective nature opposes to rationalization. Horkheimer interprets the increasingly shrill discontent within the culture as a rebellion of subjective nature against reification, as a "revolt of nature": "The more loudly the idea of rationality is proclaimed and acknowledged, the stronger is the growth in the minds of people of conscious or unconscious resentment against civilization and its agency within the individual, the ego."[11] Horkheimer already has in view the phenomena that have since been thematized by Foucault, Laing, Basaglia and others.[12]

The socio-psychological costs of a rationalization restricted to the cognitive-instrumental dimension—costs that are externalized by society and shifted to individuals—appear in different guises, ranging from clinically treated mental illnesses through neuroses, phenomena of addiction, psychosomatic disturbances, educational and motivational problems, to the protest actions of aesthetically inspired countercultures, religious youth sects, and marginal criminal groups (now also including anarchistic terrorism). Horkheimer interprets fascism as a successful refunctionalization, as a utilization of the revolt of inner nature on behalf of the societal rationalization against which it is directed. In fascism

> rationality has reached a point at which it is no longer satisfied with simply repressing nature; rationality now exploits nature by incorporating into its own system the rebellious potentialities of nature. The Nazis manipulated the suppressed desires of the German people. When the Nazis and their industrial and military backers launched their movement, they had to enlist the masses, whose material interests were not theirs. They appealed to the backward strata doomed by industrial development, that is, squeezed out by the techniques of mass production. Here, among the peasants, middle-class artisans, retailers, housewives, and small manufacturers, were to be found the protagonists

of repressed nature, the victims of instrumental reason. Without the active support of these groups, the Nazis could never have gained power.[13]

This thesis explains not only the class basis on which fascism came to power but also the historical function that it took on—namely, to accelerate processes of societal modernization in a "belated nation."[14]

> The revolt of natural man—in the sense of the backward strata of the population—against the growth of rationality has actually furthered the formalization of reason, and has served to fetter rather than to free nature. In this light, we might describe fascism as a satanic synthesis of reason and nature—the very opposite of that reconciliation of the two poles that philosophy has always dreamed of.[15]

Horkheimer and Adorno investigate empirically the psychic mechanisms by means of which the revolt of inner nature is refunctionalized into strengthening the forces against which it is directed. Stimulated by the early work of Erich Fromm,[16] they consider above all the ideological pattern of antisemitism and the sadomasochistic drive structure of the authoritarian character.[17] (In the meantime these studies have led to inquiries into political prejudice that have moved away from psychoanalytic assumptions and abandoned relations to the conceptual apparatus of a critical theory of reification.)

The theory of mass culture deals with the less spectacular manifestations of a social integration of consciousness through the mass media. Adorno investigates the "new style of commodity fetishism" in connection with the fetishizing of works of art into cultural goods and the regression of the enjoyment of art into consumption and managed entertainment. He is convinced that the sadomasochistic character of the petit bourgeois who allows himself to be mobilized for the total state, on the one side, and "those who accept present-day mass art," on the other, represent "the same thing from different sides." Lukacs had already conceded that the further the process of reification moved away from the sphere of production and the everyday experiences of the proletarian lifeworld, and the more it changed the qualitative nature of thoughts and feelings, the less accessible it became to self-reflection.[18] Adorno connects up with these reflections in his work "On the Fetish Character in Music and the Regression of Listening."[19]

To be sure, exchange value establishes itself in a special way in the realm of cultural goods. For in the world of commodities this realm appears to be exempted from the power of exchange...and it is to this illusion that cultural goods owe their exchange value...If a commodity always combines exchange value and use value, then pure use value—the illusion of which cultural goods have to preserve in a thoroughly capitalist society—is replaced by pure exchange value, which, precisely as exchange value, deceptively takes on the function of use value. The specific fetish character of music lies in this quid pro quo; the affects directed to the exchange value create the illusion of the unmediated, at the same time as the lack of a relation to the object belies it.... It has been asked what the cement is that holds capitalist society together. One part of the explanation may be this transfer of the use value of consumer goods to their exchange value within a total order such that every pleasure which emancipates itself from exchange value takes on subversive features. The appearance of exchange value in commodities has taken over a specific cementing function.[20]

Adorno elucidates this statement in connection with the changed conditions of production of mass culture, the de-differentiation of the forms of cultural goods produced in standardized ways, the changed mode of reception in art enjoyment fused with entertainment, and finally the function of adapting to an everyday life put forward as paradise: "In the culture industry jovial denial takes the place of the pain that is present in ecstasy and in asceticism...In every exhibit of the culture industry, the permanent denial imposed by civilization is once again unmistakably demonstrated to, and inflicted upon, those affected by it."[21]

I shall not go any further into this theory; it has remained of interest more in virtue of its general line of questioning than through its detailed hypotheses. Adorno adopted a culture-critical perspective that made him sceptical—and rightly so—of Benjamin's somewhat precipitous hopes for the emancipatory power of mass culture—at that time chiefly of film.[22] On the other hand, as we shall see, he had no clear concept of the thoroughly ambivalent character of social control exercised through the mass media. An analysis that starts from the commodity form assimilates the new means of mass communication to the medium of exchange value, even though the structural similarities do not extend this far. Whereas the medium of money *replaces* understanding in language as a mechanism for coordinating action, the media of mass communication remain dependent on achieving understanding in language. They technically amplify linguistic communication, bridge over spatial and temporal distances, multiply possibilities of communication and intensify the network of communicative action, without, however, uncoupling action orientations from lifeworld contexts as such. Of course, this pronounced expansion of communication potential is neutralized for the present by organizational forms that establish one-way— that is, nonreversible—communication flows. But whether a mass culture tailored to mass media develops into a regressive integration of consciousness depends in the first instance on whether "communication (brings about) the assimilation of human beings by isolating them"[23] and *not* on whether the laws of the market exert an increasingly decisive influence on cultural production itself.[24]

B.—Horkheimer and Adorno radicalize Lukacs' theory of reification in socio-psychological terms; they do this so as to explain the stability of advanced capitalist societies without having to give up the approach of the critique of commodity fetishism. Their theory is supposed to explain why capitalism simultaneously heightens the forces of production and immobilizes the forces of subjective resistance. Lukacs had assumed the validity of a logic according to which the process of the reification of consciousness *had to* lead to its own overcoming [*Selbstaufhebung*] in proletarian class consciousness. Horkheimer and Adorno put Hegel's logic to one side and try to explain empirically the evidence that refutes this prediction. They are in agreement with Weber—the "arch-positivist"—on one point: Objective reason cannot be restored, not even in dialectical concepts.

In his critique of Hegel, which points beyond Lukacs, Adorno takes up and sharpens one of Lukacs' arguments. It has to do with the question of the relation between mind and matter, which Lukacs poses in the epistemological context of the "thing-in-itself" problematic. In this connection he cites a line from Emil Lask: "For subjectivity it is not self-evident but rather the whole aim of its investigations [to ascertain] the category into which logical form in general is differentiated when some determinate individual matter is to be grasped categorially—or, to put it another way, [to ascertain] the individual matter that everywhere constitutes the material domain of individual categories."[25]

Whereas Lukacs assumes that this problem arises only for thinking at the level of the understanding, and that it can be resolved by way of a dialectical mediation of form and content, Adorno sees the same problem turn up again at the heart of dialectical thought.[26] *All* conceptual thought that stands apart from mere *intuition*—and this includes dialectical thought—proceeds by way of identification and betrays the utopian element in cognition. "That element of truth encountered through concepts, beyond their abstract compass, can show itself only in that which is suppressed, despised and discarded by concepts. It is the utopian hope of cognition to open up what is conceptless by means of concepts without (thereby) assimilating it to them. Such a notion of dialectic raises doubts as to its possibility."[27]

There is no need to discuss here how Adorno works out these programmatic ideas—or rather displays them in their unworkability—in the form of a "negative dialectics."[28] In the present context, what is important is the argument with which he rejects—in an almost existentialist fashion—the logic of Hegel.

> Cognition aims at the particular and not at the universal. It seeks its true object in the possible determination of the difference between that very particular and the universal, which it criticizes as nevertheless unavoidable. But if the mediation of the universal through the particular and of the particular through the universal is put into the abstract normal form of mediation pure and simple, then the particular has to pay—to the point of being dismissed in an authoritarian manner in the material sections of Hegel's system.[29]

In terms of Hegel's own concepts, the dialectical reconciliation of the universal and the particular remains metaphysical because it does not give its due to what is "non-identical" in the particular.[30] The structure of reified consciousness continues on in the very dialectic that is offered as a means of overcoming it, because everything that is of the nature of a thing counts for it as radically evil: "Whoever wants to 'dynamize' everything that is into pure activity tends to be hostile toward the other, the alien, whose name we are reminded of, and not without good reason, in alienation, the non-identity for which not only consciousness but a reconciled humanity is to be made free."[31]

But if negative dialectics presents itself as the only possible path of reconstruction—a path that cannot be traversed discursively—how then can we explicate the idea of reconciliation in the light of which alone Adorno is able to make the shortcomings of the idealist dialectic visible? From the beginning, critical theory labored over the problem of giving an account of its own normative foundations; since Horkheimer and Adorno made their turn to the critique of instrumental reason early in the 1940s, this problem has become drastically apparent. Horkheimer first takes up two positions that react in opposite ways to the replacement of objective reason by subjective reason, to the disintegration of religion and metaphysics. In the chapter of the *Eclipse of Reason* entitled "Conflicting Panaceas," he develops a position with two fronts: one against approaches in contemporary philosophy that are oriented to the tradition and the other against scientism; these fronts have remained decisive for the intraphilosophical arguments of critical theory until the positivism debate. The actual situation to which Horkheimer refers is a controversy between representatives of logical positivism and certain currents of neo-Thomism.[32] Neo-Thomism stands here for any attempt to link up with Plato or Aristotle so as to renew the ontological claim of philosophy to comprehend the world as a whole, whether precritically or under the banner of objective idealism, and to put back together again metaphysically the moments of reason that separated out in the modern development of the spirit—the different aspects of validity: the true, the good, and the beautiful. "Today there is a general tendency"—and this tendency actually continues into the present[33]—

> . . . to revive past theories of objective reason in order to give some philosophical foundation to the rapidly disintegrating hierarchy of generally accepted values. Along with pseudo-religious or half-scientific mind cures, spiritualism, astrology, cheap brands of past philosophies such as yoga, Buddhism, or mysticism, and popular adaptations of classical objectivistic philosophies, medieval ontologies are recommended for modern use. But the transition from objective to subjective reason was not an accident, and the process of development of ideas cannot arbitrarily at any given moment be reversed. If subjective reason in the form of enlightenment has dissolved the philosophical basis of beliefs that have been an essential part of Western culture, it has been able to do so because this basis proved to be too weak. Their revival, therefore, is completely artificial. . . The absolute becomes itself a means, objective reason a scheme for subjective purposes.[34]

With his critique of traditional approaches Horkheimer is not, of course, placing himself on the side of logical empiricism. What he opposes to metaphysics is not at all based on positivism's false equation of science with reason. Rather, he attacks the false complementarity between a positivistic understanding of science and a metaphysics that merely elevates itself above scientific theories without contributing to our understanding of them. Horkheimer regards both neopositivism and neo-Thomism as limited truths that "try to assume a despotic role in the realm of thought."[35] Like traditionalism, logical empiricism has to have recourse to self-evident first principles; only it is the scientific method, the foundations of which remain unclarified, that the latter absolutizes in place of God, Nature, or Being. Positivism is unwilling to ground the identity of science and truth that it asserts. It limits itself to analyzing the procedures of established scientific practice. This may be an expression of reverence for institutionalized science; but why certain precedures may be recognized as scientific is something that requires normative justification: "To be the absolute authority, science must be justified as an intellectual principle, not merely deduced from empirical procedures and then made absolute as truth on the basis of dogmatic criteria of scientific success."[36]

One is naturally anxious to hear Horkheimer's explanation of the standard on which he bases his own critique of the "limited truth" of scientism. Either he has to take this standard from a theory that elucidates the foundations of the modern natural, social, and cultural sciences within the horizon of more encompasing concepts of truth and knowledge; or, supposing there is not—or not yet—any such theory, he has to enter upon the rocky path of immanent critique of science and obtain the desired standard from a self-reflection that reaches down into the lifeworld foundations, the structures of action and the contexts of discovery, underlying scientific theory-construction or objectivating thought in general.[37] In respect to these alternatives, the following passage is unclear:

> Modern science, as positivists understand it, refers essentially to statements about facts, and therefore presupposes the reification of life in general and of perception in particular. It looks upon the world as a world of facts and things and fails to connect the transformation of the world into facts and things with the social process. The very concept of "fact"

is a product—a product of social alienation; in it, the abstract object of exchange is conceived as a model for all objects of experience in the given category. The task of critical reflection is not merely to understand the various facts in their historical development—and even this has immeasurably wider implications than positivist scholasticism has ever dreamed of—but also to see through the notion of fact itself, in its development and therefore in its relativity. The so-called facts ascertained by quantitative methods, which the positivists are inclined to regard as the only scientific ones, are often surface phenomena that obscure rather than disclose the underlying reality. A concept cannot be accepted as the measure of truth if the ideal of truth that it serves in itself presupposes social processes that thinking cannot accept as ultimates.[38]

On the one hand, the reminiscence of Lukacs' critique of scientific objectivism is clear; on the other hand, we know that Horkheimer does not want to accept without reservation the basic assumptions of the Hegelian (or Hegelian-Marxist) critique of Kant. He agrees with Weber that the split between theoretical and practical reason, the splitting up of rationality into the validity aspects of truth, normative rightness, and authenticity or sincerity, cannot be undone by having recourse—however dialectical or materialistic—to the lost totality, to the whole of what is.

Thus the appeal to critical reflection cannot be understood as a disguised call to retreat to a Marxistically restored Hegel; it can only be understood as a first step toward a self-reflection of the sciences—which has since actually been carried out. For one thing, the self-criticism developed within the framework of the analytic theory of science has, with admirable consistency, led to the—ambiguous—positions of so-called postempiricism (Lakatos, Toulmin, Kuhn, Hesse, Feyerabend). For another, in the debate concerning the methodological foundations of the social sciences, the program of a unified science has been abandoned under the influence of phenomenology, hermeneutics, ethnomethodology, linguistic philosophy—and critical theory as well—without any clear alternative coming into view.[39] It is by no means the case that these two lines of argument have led to an unambiguous resumption of the rationality problematic; they have left room for sceptical and, above all, relativistic conclusions (Feyerabend, Elkana). Viewed retrospectively, therefore, it does not look as if Horkheimer could safely have left critical reflection to the "cunning" of scientific development. Besides, this perspective was quite alien to him. Nevertheless, Horkheimer and Adorno did not consider their task to be a substantive critique of science; they did not take it upon themselves to start from the situation of the disintegration of objective reason, to follow the thread of a subjective reason externalized in its objects as it displayed itself in the practice of the most advanced sciences, to develop a "phenomenological" concept of knowledge expanded through self-reflection, in order thereby to open up one (not the only) avenue of access to a differentiated but encompassing concept of rationality.[40] Instead, they submitted subjective reason to an unrelenting critique from the ironically distanced perspective of an objective reason that had fallen irreparably into ruin.

C.—This paradoxical step was motivated, on the one hand, by the conviction that "great" philosophy, of which Hegel was the culmination and endpoint, could no longer of itself systematically develop and ground the idea of reason, the idea of a universal reconciliation of spirit and nature, and that in this respect it had perished together with metaphysical-religious worldviews. On the other hand, however, the time had passed for the realization of philosophy that was once possible, as Marx had proclaimed; as a result, philosophy remained, so to speak, the only memorial to the promise of a humane social life. In this respect, under the ruins of philosophy there lay buried the only truth from which thought could draw its negating, reification-transcending power. "Philosophy, which once appeared to have been superseded, remains alive because the moment for its realization was missed." With this sentence *Negative Dialectics* gets underway.[41]

Horkheimer and Adorno face the following problem. On the one hand, they do not agree with Lukacs' view that the seemingly complete rationalization of the world has its limit in the formal character of its own rationality; they criticize this thesis empirically, by reference to the forms of manifestation of a penetrating reification of culture and inner nature, and theoretically, by showing that even the objective idealism developed in Hegelian Marxism simply carries on the line of identity thinking and reproduces in itself the structures of reified consciousness. On the other hand, Horkheimer and Adorno radicalize Lukacs' critique of reification. They do not consider the rationalization of the world to be only "seemingly complete"; and thus they need a conceptual apparatus that will allow them nothing less than to denounce the whole as the untrue. They cannot achieve this aim by way of an immanent critique of science, because a conceptual apparatus that could satisfy their desiderata would still share the pretensions of the great philosophical tradition. But this tradition—and this is the Weberian thorn still in critical theory—cannot simply be renewed with its systematic pretensions; it has "outlived" its own claims; in any case, it cannot be renewed in the form of philosophy. I shall try to make clear how the authors of the *Dialectic of Enlightenment* attempt to resolve this difficulty—and at what cost.

First of all, Horkheimer and Adorno generalize the category of reification. This can be laid out in three steps, if we keep in view their implicit starting point, namely the theory of reification developed by Lukacs in *History and Class Consciousness.*

a) Lukacs derived the form of objectivity specific to capitalist society from an analysis of the wage-labor relation, which is characterized by the commodity form of labor power; he further derived from this the structures of reified consciousness as these are expressed in the *Verstandesdenken* of the modern sciences, particularly in Kant's philosophical interpretation of them. By contrast, Horkheimer and Adorno regard these structures of consciousness—what they refer to as subjective reason and identifying thought—as fundamental. The abstraction of exchange is only the historical form in which identifying thought develops its world-historical influence and determines the forms of intercourse of capitalist society. The occasional references to real abstractions that have become objective in exchange relations cannot conceal the fact that Horkheimer and Adorno do not— like Lukacs (and Sohn Rethel)—derive the form of thought from the commodity form. Identifying thought, whose force Adorno sees at work rather in first philosophy than in science, lies deeper historically than the formal rationality of the exchange relation, although it does first gain its universal significance through the differentiation of the medium of exchange value.[42]

b) After this, if you will, "idealist" retranslation of the concept of reification into the context of the philosophy of consciousness, Horkheimer and Adorno give such an abstract interpretation of the structures of reified consciousness that it covers not only the theoretical form of identifying thought but even the confrontation of goal-oriented acting subjects with external nature. This confrontation comes under the idea of the self-preservation of the subject; thought is in the service of technical mastery over, and informed adaptation to, an external nature that is objectivated in the behavioral circuit of instrumental action. It is "instrumental reason" that is at the basis of the structures of reified consciousness. In this way, Horkheimer and Adorno anchor the mechanism that produces the reification of consciousness in the anthropological foundations of the history of the species, in the form of existence of a species that has to reproduce itself through labor. With this they take back in part the abstraction they made at first, namely the detachment of thought from the context of reproduction. Instrumental reason is set out in concepts of subject-object relations. The interpersonal relation between subject and subject, which is decisive for the model of exchange, has no constitutive significance for instrumental reason.[43]

c) This abstraction from the dimension of society is rescinded in a last step, but in a curious way. Horkheimer and Adorno do not understand "the mastery of nature" as a metaphor; they reduce the control of external nature, the command over human beings, and the repression of one's own internal nature to a common denominator, under the name of "domination." "Domination of nature involves domination of man."[44] This sentence is almost analytically true if one starts from the view that the same structure of exercising force recurs in a subject's mastering an objectified nature as in the mastery of a subject who makes an object of another subject or of himself. Identifying thought, first expanded into instrumental reason, is now further expanded into a logic of domination over things *and* human beings. Left to itself, instrumental reason makes "the domination of nature, without and within, into the absolute aim of life";[45] it is the motor force behind a "self-assertion gone wild."

Lukacs used the concept of reification to describe that peculiar compulsion to assimilate interhuman relations (and subjectivity) to the world of things, which comes about when social actions are no longer coordinated through values, norms, or linguistic understanding, but through the medium of exchange value. Horkheimer and Adorno detach the concept not only from the special historical context of the rise of the capitalist economic system but from the dimension of interhuman relations altogether; and they generalize it temporally (over the entire history of the species) and substantively (the same logic of domination is imputed to both cognition in the service of self-preservation and the repression of instinctual nature). This double generalization of the concept of reification leads to a concept of instrumental reason that shifts the primordial history of sub-jectivity and the self-formative process of ego identity into an encompassing historico-philosophical perspective.

The ego, which is formed in coming to grips with the forces of outer nature, is the product of successful self-assertion, the result of the accomplishments of instrumental reason, and in two respects: It is the subject that irresistibly charges ahead in the process of enlightenment, that subjugates nature, develops the forces of production, disenchants the surrounding world; but at the same time it is the subject that learns to master itself, that represses its own nature, that advances self-objectification within itself and thereby becomes increasingly opaque to itself. Victories over outer nature are paid for with defeats of inner nature. This dialectic of rationalization is to be explained by the structure of a reason that is instrumentalized for the purpose of self-preservation, which is posed as an absolute end. We can see in the history of subjectivity how this instrumental reason marks every advance that it brings about with the stamp of irrationality.

> As soon as man cuts off his consciousness of himself as nature, all the ends for which he keeps himself alive—social progress, the heightening of all his natural and spiritual powers, even consciousness itself—are nullified; the en-thronement of means as ends, which in late capitalism has taken on the character of open madness, is already per-ceptible in the primordial history of subjectivity. Man's domination over himself, which grounds his selfhood, is vir-tually always the destruction of the subject in whose service it takes place; for the substance which is dominated, sup-pressed and undone by self-preservation is none other than that very life for which the accomplishments of self-preser-vation are supposed to be functional; it is in fact just what is supposed to be preserved.[46]

Now what is the role of this thesis in connection with the task mentioned at the outset, viz. to rehabilitate an encompassing concept of reason without having recourse to the "totality" thinking of a philosophy that has in a certain sense "outlived itself"? This philosophy of history opens up a catastrophic view of a relation between spirit and nature that has been distorted beyond recognition. But we can speak of distortion only insofar as the original relation of spirit and nature is secretly conceived in such a way that the idea of truth is connected with that of a universal reconciliation—where reconciliation includes the interaction of human beings with nature, with animals, plants, and minerals.[47]

If spirit is the principle that brings external nature under control only at the price of suppressing internal nature, if it is the principle of a self-preservation that is at the same time self-destruction, then subjective reason, which presupposes the dialectic of spirit and nature, is as much entangled in error as objective reason, which maintains the original unity of the two.

> Such hypostatization results from the basic contradiction in the human condition. On the one hand, the social need of controlling nature has always conditioned the structure and forms of man's thinking and thus given primacy to subjective reason. On the other hand, society could not completely repress the idea of something transcending the subjectivity of self-interest, to which the self could not help aspiring. Even the divorcing and formal reconstruction of the two principles as separate rest on an element of necessity and historical truth. By its self-critique, reason must recognize the limitations of the two opposite concepts of reason; it must analyze the development of the cleavage between the two, perpetuated as it is by all the doctrines that tend to triumph ideologically over the philosophical antinomy in an antinomic world.[48]

Horkheimer understands his attempt to demonstrate the complementary limitations of positivism and ontology to be such a self-critique.

> The fundamental issue discussed in this book, the relation between the subjective and the objective concepts of reason, must be treated in the light of the foregoing reflections on spirit and nature, subject and object. What has been referred to in chapter one as subjective reason is that attitude of consciousness that adjusts itself without reservation to the alienation between subject and object, the social process of reification, out of fear that it may otherwise fall into irresponsibility, arbitrariness, and become a mere game of ideas. The present-day systems of objective reason, on the other hand, represent attempts to avoid the surrender of existence to contingency and blind hazard. But the proponents of objective reason are in danger of lagging behind

industrial and scientific developments, of asserting meaning
that proves to be an illusion, and of creating reactionary
ideologies.[49]

This dialectic makes us aware of the untruth of both
positions, and this raises the question of their mediation. The
thesis developed in *Dialectic of Enlightenment* does not direct our
thought to the path that is nearest at hand, a path which leads
through the inner logics of the different complexes of rationality
and through processes of societal rationalization divided up
according to universal aspects of validity, and which suggests a
unity of rationality beneath the husk of an everyday practice that
has been simultaneously rationalized and reified. Rather Horkheimer and Adorno follow the (largely effaced) path that leads
back to the origins of instrumental reason, so as to *outdo* the
concept of objective reason: "From the time when reason became
the instrument for domination of human and extrahuman nature
by man—that is to say, from its very beginnings—it has been
frustrated in its intention of discovering the truth."[50] On the one
hand, this reflection suggests a concept of truth that can be interpreted via the guiding idea of a universal reconciliation, an emancipation of man through the resurrection of nature; a reason that
pursues its aim of discovering truth will, "by being the instrument
of reconciliation, be more than an instrument."[51] On the other
hand, Horkheimer and Adorno can only suggest this concept of
truth; for if they wanted to explicate those determinations that,
on their view, cannot inhere in instrumental reasons, they would
have to rely on a reason that is before reason (which was from
the beginning instrumental). As the placeholder for this
primordial reason that was diverted from the intention of truth,
Horkheimer and Adorno nominate a capacity, *mimesis,* about
which they can speak only as they would about a piece of uncomprehended nature. They characterize the mimetic capacity,
in which an instrumentalized nature makes its speechless accusa-
tion, as an "impulse."[52]

The paradox in which the critique of instrumental reason
is entangled, and which stubbornly resists even the most supple
dialectic, consists then in this: Horkheimer and Adorno would
have to put forward a *theory* of mimesis, which, according to their
own ideas, is impossible. Thus they are only being consistent
when they do not attempt to explicate "universal reconciliation"
as Hegel had done, as the unity of the identity and nonidentity

of spirit and nature, but let it stand as a code, almost in the manner of *Lebensphilosophie*. At most, we can circle around this idea, drawing on images from Judaeo-Christian mysticism; the formula of the young Marx regarding the dialectical interconnection between the humanization of nature and the naturalization of humans already referred back to this tradition.[53] The "dialectic of enlightenment" is an ironic affair: It shows the self-critique of reason the way to truth, and at the same time contests the possibility "that at this stage of complete alienation the idea of truth is still accessible."[54]

D.—This raises the question of the status that Horkheimer and Adorno can still claim for a theory that no longer wants to rely on philosophy and science critically working together. On the one hand, it shares with the tradition of great philosophy (which, in however refracted a manner, it continues) certain essential features: It adheres to contemplation, to a theory diverted from practice; it aims at the totality of nature and the human world; it turns back to the beginning in an effort to get beyond the break of culture with nature; it even shares a concept of truth that Horkheimer once defined as the correspondence of language with reality: "Philosophy is the conscious effort to knit all our knowledge and insight into a linguistic structure in which all things are called by their right names."[55] On the other hand, Horkheimer and Adorno regard the systems of objective reason as ideologies that have no chance of standing up against a critique that ceaselessly moves back and forth between subjective and objective reason.

Horkheimer considers it to be the business of philosophy to give things their right names; but we have to look at what he and Adorno say about the act of naming.

> Even though laughter is still the sign of force, an outburst of blind and callous nature, it also has within it the opposite element: In laughter, blind nature precisely becomes aware of itself as such and therewith renounces destructive force. This double meaning of laughter is akin to that of the name, and perhaps names are nothing but frozen laughter, as nicknames still are today—the only names in which something of the primordial act of name-giving lives on. [56]

The critique of instrumental reason aims at being critique in the sense that the reconstruction of instrumental reason's incessant operation reminds us of what has been sacrificed, of the mimetic impulses of a suppressed nature—of external nature, but, above all, of subjective nature.

> Through such mindfulness [*Eingedenken*] of nature in the subject, in the achievement of which lies enclosed the misunderstood truth of all culture, enlightenment is opposed to domination as such; and the call to put a stop to enlightenment resounded even in the time of Vanini less from fear of exact science than from hatred of undisciplined thought which leaves the spell of nature in acknowledging itself to be nature's own trembling before itself. [57]

It is the task of critique to recognize domination as unreconciled nature even within thought itself. But even if thought had mastered the idea of reconciliation, even if it were not in the position of having to let this idea come to it from without, how could it transform mimetic impulses into insights, discursively, in its own element, and not merely intuitively, in speechless "mindfulness"? How could it do so if thought is always identifying thought, tied to operations that have no specifiable meaning outside the bounds of instrumental reason—all the more so today when, with the triumphal procession of instrumental reason, the reification of consciousness seems to have become universal?

Unlike Marcuse,[58] Adorno no longer wanted to get out of his aporia—and in this he was more consistent than Horkheimer. "Negative Dialectics" is both an attempt to circumscribe what cannot be said discursively and an admonition to seek refuge nonetheless in Hegel in this situation. It is the "Aesthetic Theory" that first seals the surrender of all cognitive competence to art in which the mimetic capacity gains objective shape. Adorno withdraws the theoretical claim: Negative dialectics and aesthetic theory can now only "helplessly refer to one another."[59]

Adorno had already seen in the early thirties that philosophy had to learn "to renounce the question of totality" and "to get along without the symbolic function in which up to now, at least in idealism, the particular seemed to represent the universal."[60] At that time, referring to Benjamin's concept of the allegorical,[61] he had already methodically appropriated the motif of "awakening the enciphered, the petrified" in a history that had become a second nature,[62] and he had proposed a program of "interpreting what is without intention" through "assembling the most minute and insignificant details," a program that forswore the self-certainty of "autonomous ratio." It was a matter of setting up models "with which ratio, scrutinizing and testing, approaches a reality which denies itself to the law, but which the schema of the model may always imitate, provided that the latter is correctly formed."[63]

Later, as he is attempting to break away from the dialectic of enlightenment, Adorno returns to these tentative attempts to avoid the shadow of identifying thought, with the aim of radicalizing them. Negative dialectics is now to be understood only as an exercise, a drill. In reflecting dialectical thought once more, it exhibits what we can only catch sight of in this way: the aporetic nature of the concept of the nonidentical.[64] It is by no means the case that "aesthetics is one step further removed from the truth content of its objects than negative dialectics, which already has to do with concepts."[65] Rather, because it has to do with concepts, critique can only show why the truth that escapes theory finds a refuge in the most advanced works of modern art—out of which we surely could not coax it without an aesthetic theory.

Axel Honneth has shown that even as a theoretician Adorno assimilated his mode of presentation to the aesthetic mode;[66] it is guided by the "idea of the happiness of a freedom in relation to the object which gives the latter more of its due than when it is mercilessly incorporated into the order of ideas."[67] Adorno's theory takes its ideal of presentation "from the mimetic achievement of the work of art, not from the principle of grounding of modern science."[68] In the shadow of a philosophy that has outlived itself, philosophical thinking intentionally retrogresses to gesticulation. As opposed as the intentions behind their respective philosophies of history are, Adorno is in the end very similar to Heidegger as regards his position on the theoretical claims of objectivating thought and of reflection: The mindfulness [Eingedenken] of nature comes shockingly close to the recollection [Andenken] of being.[69]

If one looks back from Adorno's late writings to the intentions that critical theory initially pursued, one can weigh the price that the critique of instrumental reason had to pay for the aporias it consistently owns up to. A philosophy that withdraws behind the lines of discursive thought to the "mindfulness of nature" pays for the wakening powers of its exercises by renouncing the goal of theoretical knowledge, and thus by renouncing that program of "interdisciplinary materialism" in whose name the critical theory of society was once launched in the early thirties. Horkheimer and Adorno had already given up this goal by the beginning of the forties, without, however, acknowledging the practical consequences of relinquishing a connection to the social sciences; otherwise they would not have been in a position to rebuild the Institute for Social Research after the War. Nevertheless, as the foreword to *Dialectic of Enlightenment* clearly explains, they had given up the hope of being able to redeem the promise of early critical theory.[70]

Against this, I want to maintain that the program of early critical theory foundered not on this or that contingent circumstance, but from the exhaustion of the paradigm of the philosophy of consciousness. I shall argue that a change of paradigm to the theory of communication makes it possible to return to the undertaking that was *interrupted* with the critique of instrumental reason; and this will permit us to take up once again the since-neglected tasks of a critical theory of society. In the following section I would like to illustrate the limits of the philosophy of consciousness and indicate some of the motifs in Horkheimer and Adorno that already push beyond them.

E.—Referring to Heidegger, Dieter Henrich once characterized the philosophical self-interpretation of modernity—under which the critique of instrumental reason can also be classified—as follows:

> It accepts the view that subjectivity can determine its accomplishments only on the basis of its own structures, that is, not on the basis of insight into more universal purposive systems. At the same time, however, it also claims to recognize that subjectivity and reason themselves have only the status of means or functions which serve to reproduce a process that is self-maintaining but indifferent to consciousness. This position was first enunciated in modern materialism by Hobbes. It explains the impression made and the influence exercised upon modern consciousness by Darwin and Nietzsche, Marx and Freud. Of course, in Marx's thought there are elements of the metaphysics of reconciliation that came to him via Hegel and Feuerbach.[71]

Horkheimer and Adorno are also guided by the idea of reconciliation; but they would rather renounce entirely any explication of it than fall into a *metaphysics* of reconciliation. As we saw, this leads them into the aporias of a critique that some-how retracts any claim to theoretical knowledge. The critique of instrumental reason conceptualized as negative dialectics renounces its theoretical claim while operating with the means of theory.

This fear of a fall back into metaphysics is appropriate only so long as one moves within the horizon of the modern philosophy of the subject. The idea of reconciliation cannot plausibly be accommodated in the basic concepts of the philosophy of con-sciousness from Descartes to Kant; and in the concepts of objective idealism from Spinoza and Leibniz to Schelling and Hegel, it can only be given an extravagant formulation. Hork-heimer and Adorno know this, but they remain fixated on this conceptual strategy in the very attempt to break its spell. They do not, to be sure, analyze in detail how subjective reason functions; but they do rely upon model representations that connect the basic notions of an idealistic theory of knowledge with those of a naturalistic theory of action. On these models, subjective reason regulates exactly two fundamental relations that a subject can take up to possible objects. Under "object" the philosophy of the subject understands everything that can be represented as existing; under "subject" it understands first of all the capacities to relate oneself to such entities in the world in an objectivating attitude and to gain control of objects, be it theoretically or practically. The two attitudes of mind are representation and action. The subject relates to objects either to represent them as they are or to produce them as they should be. These two functions of mind are intertwined: knowledge of states of affairs is structurally related to the possibility of intervention in the world as the totality of states of affairs; and successful action requires in turn knowledge of the causal nexus in which it intervenes. The epistemological connection between knowing and acting became all the clearer along the way from Kant through Marx to Peirce, the more a naturalistic concept of the subject gained ground. The concept of the subject developed in empiricism and rationalism and restricted to contemplative behavior, that is, to theoretically grasping objects, was transformed in such a way as to absorb the concept of self-preservation developed in the modern period.

On the metaphysical worldview, self-preservation meant that every being strives to realize the end that is immutably intrinsic to its essence according to a natural order. Modern thought detached the concept of self-preservation from such a system of highest ends; the concept became "intransitive."[72] According to the basic assumptions of Newtonian physics, every body maintains itself in a state of rest or uniform motion in a straight line unless acted upon by some outside force. According to the basic assumptions of bourgeois social philosophy and economics, each individual socially maintains his life by rationally pursuing his own, clearly understood interests. According to the basic assumptions of Darwinian biology and of contemporary systems theory, an organism, population, or system maintains itself through demarcation from and adaptation to a changeable, hypercomplex environment.[73]

From this perspective, the attributes of mind—knowing, acting for an end—are transformed into functions of the self-maintenance of subjects that, like bodies and organisms, pursue a single "abstract" end: to secure their continued (and contingent) existence. In this way, Horkheimer and Adorno conceive of subjective reason as instrumental reason. Objectivating thought and purposive-rational action serve to reproduce a "life" that is characterized by the knowing and acting subject's devotion to a blind, self-directed, intransitive self-preservation as his only "end."

> The fact that the bourgeois has always defined "reason" through its relation to individual self-preservation seems to run counter to Locke's exemplary determination, according to which "reason" designates the management of intellectual activity, no matter which ends are served by this activity. But reason is far from leaving the jurisdiction of monadic self-interest with this dissociation from every particular end; rather, it merely develops procedures with which it can all the more obligingly serve any arbitrary monadic end. The growing formal universality of bourgeois reason does not mean a growing consciousness of universal solidarity.[74]

Horkheimer illustrates the meaning of "solidarity"—namely, the "presence of the universal in the particular interest"—by reference to Plato and Aristotle, that is, to a metaphysics with a conceptual apparatus that can no longer measure up to the experiences of modernity: "These metaphysical systems express, in partly mythological form, the insight that self-preservation can be achieved only in a supra-individual order, that is to say, through social solidarity."[75] Horkheimer and Adorno cannot demythologize the idea of social solidarity because they think that it is possible to transcend the now-universal process of reification only from the inside, and they believe that even the critique of instrumental reason remains tied to the model that instrumental reason itself follows.

The societal subject behaves in relation to nature just as the individual subject does in relation to objects: Nature is objectivated and dominated for the sake of reproducing the life of society. The resistance of the law-governed nexus of nature, on which the societal subject toils in knowing and acting, thereby continues on in the formation of society and of its individual members. "The resistance of external nature, to which the pressure can ultimately be traced back, continues on within society through its classes, and affects every individual from childhood on as the harshness of his fellow men."[76] The relations between subject and object regulated by instrumental reason determine not only the relationship between society and external nature that is expressed historically in the state of productive forces, particularly of scientific-technical progress. The structure of exploiting an objectivated nature that is placed at our disposal repeats itself within society, both in interpersonal relations marked by the suppression of social classes and in intrapsychic relations marked by the repression of our instinctual nature.

But the conceptual apparatus of instrumental reason is set up to make it possible for subjects to exercise control over nature and *not* to tell an objectivated nature what is to be done to it. Instrumental reason is also "subjective" in the sense that it expresses the relations between subject and object from the vantage point of the knowing and acting subject and not from that of the perceived and manipulated object. For this reason, it does *not* provide the explicative tools needed to explain what the instrumentalization of social and intrapsychic relations means from the perspective of the violated and deformed contexts of life. (Lukacs wanted to glean this aspect from societal rationalization by means of the concept of reification.) Thus the appeal to social solidarity can merely indicate *that* the instrumentalization of society and its members destroys something; but it cannot say explicitly *wherein* this destruction consists.

The critique of instrumental reason, which remains bound to the conditions of the philosophy of the subject, denounces as a defect something that it cannot explain in its defectiveness because it lacks a conceptual framework sufficiently flexible to capture the integrity of what is destroyed through instrumental reason. To be sure, Horkheimer and Adorno do have a name for it: *mimesis*. And even though they cannot provide a theory of mimesis, the very name calls forth associations—and they are intended: Imitation designates a relation between persons in which the one accommodates to the other, identifies with the other, empathizes with the other. There is an allusion here to a relation in which the surrender of the one to the example of the other does not mean a loss of self but a gain and an enrichment. Because the mimetic capacity escapes the conceptual framework of cognitive-instrumentally determined subject-object relations, it counts as the sheer opposite of reason, as impulse. Adorno does not simply deny to the latter any cognitive function. In his aesthetics he attempts to show what the work of art owes to the power of mimesis to unlock, to open up. But the rational core of mimetic achievements can be laid open only if we give up the paradigm of the philosophy of consciousness—namely, a subject that represents objects and toils with them—in favor of the paradigm of linguistic philosophy—namely, that of intersubjective understanding or communication—and puts the cognitive-instrumental aspect of reason in its proper place as part of a more encompassing *communicative rationality.*

This change of paradigm lies near at hand in the few passages in which Adorno does decide to provide some explication of the complementary ideas of reconciliation and freedom; but he does not carry it through. At one point he illustrates the idea of reconciliation with a reference to Eichendorff's saying about the "beautiful alien": "The state of reconciliation would not annex what is unfamiliar or alien with philosophical imperialism; instead, it would find its happiness in the fact that the latter, in the closeness allowed, remains something distant and different, something that is beyond being either heterogeneous or proper."[77] Adorno describes reconciliation in terms of an intact intersubjectivity that is only established and maintained in the reciprocity of mutual understanding based on free recognition. George Herbert Mead had already elevated symbolically mediated interaction to the new paradigm of reason and had based reason on the communicative relation between subjects, which is rooted in the mimetic act of role-taking—that is, in ego's making his own the expectations that alter directs to him. I shall be coming back to Mead's basic ideas below.

The situation with the complementary concept of freedom is similar to that with the idea of a reconciliation made possible through intersubjectivity free of coercion. Like Mead,

Horkheimer and Adorno start from the idea that individuation is possible only by way of socialization, so that the "emancipation of the individual" would *not* be an emancipation *from* society, but "the deliverance of society from atomization," that is, from an isolation of subjects that "may reach its peak in periods of collectivization and mass culture."[78] Adorno develops this implicitly in the following passage:

> On the Kantian model, subjects are free insofar as they are conscious of themselves, identical with themselves; and in this identity they are also unfree insofar as they are subject to its compulsion and perpetuate it. As non-identical, as diffuse nature, they are unfree; and yet as such they are free, because in the impulses that overcome them—and the non-identity of the subject with itself means just that—they are also rid of the compulsive character of identity. Personality is a caricature of freedom. The ground of this aporia is to be found in the fact that the truth that lies beyond the compulsion to identity would not be simply different from it, but would be mediated through it.[79]

Adorno is here proposing the perspective of an ego-identity that takes shape only in forms of an intact intersubjectivity. His interpretation of Kant takes its inspiration from Freud's structural model. The forms of interpersonal understanding that are established in a society determine the superego formation that emerges from the child's interactions with his reference persons; and the shape of the forms of intrapsychic understanding, the ways in which the ego can deal with the reality of outer nature and of its own inner nature depend in turn on this foundation.

Adorno cannot elucidate the mimetic capacity by means of an abstract opposition to instrumental reason. The structures of reason to which Adorno merely alludes first become accessible to analysis when the ideas of reconciliation and freedom are deciphered as codes for a form of intersubjectivity, however utopian it may be, that makes possible a mutual and constraint-free understanding among individuals in their dealings with one another, as well as the identity of individuals who come to a compulsion-free understanding with themselves—sociation without repression. This means, on the one hand, a change of paradigm within action theory: from goal-directed to communicative action, and, on the other hand, a change of strategy in an effort to reconstruct the modern concept of rationality that became possible with the decentration of our understanding of the world. The phenomena in need of explication are no longer, in and of themselves, the knowledge and mastery of an objective nature, but the intersubjectivity of possible understanding and agreement—at both the interpersonal and intrapsychic levels. The focus of investigation thereby shifts from cognitive-instrumental rationality to communicative rationality. And what is paradigmatic for the latter is not the relation of a solitary subject to something in the objective world that can be represented and manipulated, but the intersubjective relation that speaking and acting subjects take up when they come to an understanding with one another about something. In doing so, communicative actors move in the medium of a natural language, draw upon culturally transmitted interpretations, and relate simultaneously to something in the one objective world, something in their common social world, and something in each's own subjective world.

In contrast to *representation* or *cognition, coming to an understanding* requires the rider *uncoerced,* because the expression is meant to be used here as a normative concept. From the perspective of the participants, coming to an understanding is not an empirical event that causes de facto agreement; it is a process of mutually convincing one another in which the actions of participants are coordinated on the basis of motivation by reasons. "Coming to an understanding" refers to communication aimed at achieving a valid agreement. It is only for this reason that we may hope to obtain a concept of rationality by clarifying the formal properties of action oriented to reaching understanding—a concept expressing the interconnection of those moments of reason that became separated in the modern period, no matter whether we look for these moments in cultural value spheres, in differentiated forms of argumentation, or in the communicative practice of everyday life, however distorted that may be.

If we assume that the reproduction of social life is tied not only to the conditions of cognitive-instrumental dealings with external nature (by individuals or by groups united in cooperation) and to the conditions of cognitive-strategic dealings of individuals and groups with one another; and we assume that sociation stands just as much under conditions of the intersubjectivity of understanding among participants in interaction; then we also have to reformulate the naturalistic concept of self-preservation—but not in the same way that Dieter Henrich does in the course of a controversy with Hans Blumenberg and others.[80]

Henrich defends the thesis that what is constitutive for the position of modern consciousness is not an intransitive self-preservation that is posited absolutely but an interconnection of subjectivity and self-preservation. In his view, subjective reason is not identical with instrumental reason because the self-reference of the acting subject, the self of self-preservation, has to be thought together with the self-reference of the knowing subject, with self-consciousness. The process of conscious life is a "continuous act of self-preservation also by virtue of the fact that it has to orient itself in relation to its own non-actualized possibilities for constructing a unity."[81] Because the subject relates to its objects through both acting and knowing, it can maintain its existence only if it also relates to itself reflexively as the knowing subject. The unity of self-preservation and self-consciousness prohibits, however, the instrumentalization of consciousness in the service of *mere* self-preservation.

> What modern thought expects and what it hopes for is only this: that the self, concerned with its existence in view of its own criteria of rightness, may find in the end an internal ground of its own possibility which would not be as alien and indifferent to it as the aspect of nature against which it has to direct the energy of self-preservation. Self-consciousness expects [to find] a reason of its own essence and achievement in the context that grounds it, knowing at the same time that it would be senseless to represent the latter as another context of objectivity that can be mastered.[82]

As Lukacs did before him, Henrich wants to focus attention on an internal limit built into subjectivity itself, which stands in the way of a complete self-objectivation of consciousness; he wants to get from self-consciousness a characterization that explains in what way subjectivity *cannot* be exhausted in carrying out the imperatives of self-preservation.

Henrich tries to establish this thesis—which is directed against Heidegger and, implicitly, also against Horkheimer and Adorno—by means of a theory of self-consciousness.[83] But this does not lead to an alternative self-interpretation of modernity because Henrich starts from the very model of the philosophy of consciousness that his opponents also take as basic. According to this model, the subject, both in representing and in acting, relates in an objectivating attitude to objects or states of affairs. Epistemic *self*-consciousness is supposed to be decisive for the subjectivity of a subject that relates in this way to objects. As a subject it is essentially characterized by the fact that it has knowledge not only of objects but also and equiprimordially of itself. This knowledge the subject has of itself, in which knowing and what is known coincide, has to be thought on the model of the knowledge of objects. The self-knowledge constitutive for self-consciousness has to be explicated in such a way that the subject relates to itself as to any object and gives a description of its experiences as of any states of affairs—but with the intuitively penetrating certainty of being identical with this object or these states. The constraints of this conceptual strategy lead us in a circle, which Henrich himself draws out as clearly as one might wish. Tugendhat describes this circle as follows:

> Self-consciousness is supposed to be consciousness of an "I." But, we are told, something is an I only when it has the structure of the identity of knowing and what is known. Now if, according to the theory of reflection, self-consciousness is achieved in a turning back on itself, then the identity of knowing with what is known is first established in this turning back. On the other hand, the subject upon which the act turns back is already supposed to be an I. Thus, on the one hand, in turning back the act is supposed to represent the I; on the other hand, according to the concept of the I, it is first constituted in this act. As Henrich shows, this results in a circle. In starting with a subject that is already available, the theory of reflection presupposes something that is supposed to be actually constituted only in relation to itself.[84]

Henrich attempts to get out of this difficulty by assuming that self-consciousness is based on an ego-less consciousness which is no longer distinguished by a self-relation but is still marked by a kind of original intimacy or familiarity with itself as with something impersonal. He constructs a concept of consciousness that is supposed, on the one hand, to be rid of all traces of a self that can get hold of itself only as an object, and, on the other hand, to retain something like subjectivity this side of self-objectivation.

> At most, a self-relation can be attributed to consciousness insofar as we arrive at an understanding concerning it: It is

> consciousness and awareness of consciousness at once, and thus—in a manner of speaking that is difficult to avoid but easy to misunderstand—awareness of self. The knowing relation-to-self that we find in reflection is not a basic state of affairs but an isolating explication—not under the presupposition of an implied self-consciousness of whatever sort, but under that of a (–n implicit) selfless consciousness of self.[85]

This concept is no less paradoxical than a concept of the non-identical that is thought in an identifying manner, and for the same reasons. But whereas Adorno wanted only to show that the paradox was unavoidable, Henrich believes that with his construction he can specify the conditions for a "thematization of self and consciousness that is free of contradictions." He does not succeed in this.[86]

The ambiguity of reducing self-consciousness to a depersonalized, anonymous consciousness can already be seen in the way that Henrich ties the concept of an ego-less consciousness to two contrary theoretical lines. On the one side, the idea that the self is secondary to the basic structure of an impersonal consciousness builds a bridge to the acosmism of Oriental mysticism: "Self-overcoming is the royal road to self-knowledge."[87] On the other side, the idea that self-awareness, in the sense of reflexivity, cannot be constitutive for consciousness builds a bridge to those body-mind theories that conceive of consciousness as an objective process: "Perhaps an explanation within the framework of . . . neurology could show the indissoluble connection between two processes that correspond to consciousness and awareness of consciousness."[88] Both of these ways out, mysticism and objectivism, reflect the paradoxical structure of the concept of an ego-less consciousness that produces such alternatives. If one wants to hold onto the model of a subject that relates to objects and yet get behind the reflexive structure of consciousness, the only consistent solution is the one that Henrich wants to avoid: the subsumption of consciousness under categories of self-preservation. This is what Horkheimer and Adorno maintain: From the reflexivity of an objectified relation we cannot derive any "intrinsic criteria of rightness" except those for cognitive-instrumental self-maintenance.

Thus it is not difficult for Luhmann to depict the reflexivity of the two relations permitted by the subject-object model in systems-theoretic terms. Systems theory replaces "subject" with "system," "object" with "environment," and conceptualizes the subject's ability to know and to deal with objects as systemic achievements that consist in registering and reducing the complexity of the environment. When systems learn to relate reflexively to their own systemic unity, this is merely an additional step in heightening their own complexity in order to be a better match for the hypercomplexity of the environment; this "self-consciousness" also remains within the logical sphere of the self-maintenance of systems.[89] The specific quality that Henrich rightly wants to bring out in the self-preservation of self-conscious subjects—by way of contrast to the self-maintenance that instrumentalizes reason, that "goes wild"—cannot be salvaged within the framework of a philosophy of the subject that systems theory undermines with an irresistible irony. Henrich thinks "that 'self-preservation' is more than a word in our language with which we can successfully describe the behavior of systems and organisms. There must remain connected with this word the right and the claim adequately to grasp the true character of a process which, as the basic process of *conscious* life, can at the same time be experienced by itself."[90] However, Adorno's despair derives precisely from the fact that nothing more than instrumental reason is retained when we think through "the basic process of conscious life" radically enough in the categories provided by the philosophy of consciousness.

The transition from the philosophy of consciousness to language analysis that was accomplished by formal semantics in the wake of Frege and Wittgenstein is, to be sure, only a first step. This becomes clear precisely in connection with the phenomenon of self-consciousness. Experiential sentences in the first-person singular do provide a methodologically reliable starting point for analyzing the concept of the "I" as the experience of self-knowledge that is accessible only intuitively. Ernst Tugendhat has also shown that the above-mentioned problem with egological theories of consciousness dissolves if we reformulate its initial question in semantic terms.[91] At the same time, however, a language analysis restricted to the semantic point of view loses sight of the full meaning of the relation-to-self that is present in the performative use of the expression "I"; for this type of analysis replaces the relation between subject and object or system and environment with *another two-term relation*—that between sentence and state of affairs—and thus remains within the confines of a model that foreshortens the relation-to-self in an epistemic way. Once again the *experiences* that the ego affirms of itself in experiential sentences are represented as *states of affairs* or inner episodes to which it has privileged access, and are thereby assimilated to entities of the world. One only gets hold of that relation-to-self that has traditionally been thematized—and distorted—as self-consciousness if one extends the semantic line of inquiry in a pragmatic direction. Thus it is the analysis of the meaning of the performative—and not of the referential—use of the expression "I" within the system of personal pronouns that offers a promising approach to the problematic of self-consciousness.

I shall be coming back to the connection between subjectivity and linguistically established intersubjectivity. The theme of self-consciousness merely presents an occasion to show that the phenomena that, within the limits of the traditional conceptual apparatus, lead to acknowledged and unacknowledged paradoxes of a nonidentical or a nonreflexive consciousness can be captured in language-analytic terms only if one draws upon the *three-term model* of sign use that goes back to Bühler and, from the very start, relates the analysis of linguistic meaning to the idea of participants in communication coming to an understanding about something in the world.[92] This model has ushered in a *communications-theoretic turn* that goes beyond the linguistic turn of the philosophy of the subject. What interests me in the present context is not the philosophical significance of this turn, but the caesura that the end of the philosophy of the subject means for the theory of society.

If we assume that the human species maintains itself through the socially coordinated activities of its members and that this coordination has to be established through communication—and in certain central spheres through communication aimed at reaching agreement—then the reproduction of the species *also* requires satisfying the conditions of a rationality that is inherent in communicative action. These conditions have become perceptible in the modern period with the decentration of our understanding of the world and the differentiation of various universal validity claims. To the extent that religious-metaphysical worldviews lose their credibility, the concept of self-preservation changes, but not only in the respect emphasized by Blumenberg. It does, as he argues, lose its teleological alignment with objective ends, so that a self-preservation that has become absolute can move up to the rank of an ultimate end for cognition and success-oriented action. At the same time, to the degree that the normative integration of everyday life is loosened up, the concept of self-preservation takes a direction that is at once universalistic and individualistic. A process of self-preservation that has to satisfy the rationality conditions of communicative action becomes dependent on the integrative accomplishments of subjects who coordinate their action via criticizable validity claims. Thus, what is characteristic of the position of modern consciousness is less the unity of self-preservation and self-consciousness than the relation expressed in bourgeois philosophy of history and society: The social-life context reproduces itself *both* through the media-controlled purposive-rational actions of its members *and* through the common will anchored in the communicative practice of all individuals.[93]

A subjectivity that is characterized by communicative reason resists the denaturing of the self for the sake of self-preservation. Unlike instrumental reason, communicative reason cannot be subsumed without resistance under a blind self-preservation. It refers neither to a subject that preserves itself in relating to objects via representation and action, nor to a self-maintaining system that demarcates itself from an environment, but to a symbolically structured lifeworld that is constituted in the interpretive accomplishments of its members and only reproduced through communication. Thus communicative reason does not simply encounter ready-made subjects and systems; rather, it takes part in structuring what is to be preserved. The utopian perspective of reconciliation and freedom is ingrained in the conditions for the communicative sociation of individuals; it is built into the linguistic mechanism of the reproduction of the species.

On the other hand, societal imperatives of self-preservation establish themselves not only in the teleology of individual members' actions but also in the functional interconnection of the aggregated effects of action. The integration of members of society that takes place via processes of reaching understanding is limited not only by the force of competing interests but also by the weight of systemic imperatives of self-preservation that develop their force objectively in operating through the action orientations of the actors involved. The problem of reification arises less from a purposive rationality that has been absolutized in the service of self-preservation, from an instrumental reason that has gone wild, than from the circumstance that an unleashed functionalist reason of system maintenance disregards and over-rides the claim to reason ingrained in communicative sociation and lets the rationalization of the lifeworld run idle.

The reception of Weber's theory of rationalization from Lukacs to Adorno makes it clear that the rationalization of society has constantly been thought of as a reification of consciousness. The paradoxes to which this leads show, however, that this theme cannot be adequately treated with the conceptual means of the philosophy of consciousness. I shall take up the problematic of reification again in Volume 2 and reformulate it in terms of communicative action, on the one hand, and of the formation of subsystems via steering media, on the other. Before doing so, I shall develop these concepts in the context of the history of social theory. Whereas the problematic of rationalization/reification lies along a "German" line of social-theoretical thought determined by Kant and Hegel, and running from Marx through Weber to Lukacs and critical theory, the paradigm change that interests me was prepared by George Herbert Mead and Emile Durkheim. Mead (1863–1931) and Durkheim (1858–1917) belong, like Weber (1864–1920), to the generation of the founding fathers of modern sociology. Both developed basic concepts in which Weber's theory of rationalization can be taken up and freed from the aporias of the philosophy of consciousness: Mead with his communica-tions-theoretic foundation of sociology, Durkheim with his theory of social solidarity that interrelates social integration and system integration.

Notes

Abbreviations Used in Notes

DoE   Max Horkheimer and Theodor Adorno, *Dialectic of Enlightenment* (New York, 1972)

EoR   Max Horkheimer, *Eclipse of Reason* (New York, 1974)

ES   Max Weber, *Economy and Society,* G. Roth and C. Wittich, eds., 2 vols. (Berkeley, 1978)

HCC   Georg Lukacs, *History and Class Consciousness* (Cambridge, Mass., 1971)

RRW   Max Weber, "Religious Rejections of the World and Their Directions," in H. H. Gerth and C. W. Mills, eds., *From Max Weber* (New York, 1958), pp. 323–359.

PE   Max Weber, *The Protestant Ethic and the Spirit of Capitalism* (New York, 1958).

SPWR   Max Weber, "The Social Psychology of the World Religions," in *From Max Weber*, pp. 267–301.

Notes to Translator's Introduction

1. Page references given in parentheses in the text and notes of this introduction are to the present translation, in the case of Volume 1, and to the German original, in the case of Volume 2. Thus, for example, (1:168) refers to page 168 of this volume and (2:270) refers to page 270 of Volume 2 of the German original.
2. These phrases are taken from Fred R. Dallmayr, *Twilight of Subjectivity* (Amherst, Mass., 1981).
3. Cf. Richard Rorty, *Philosophy and the Mirror of Nature* (Princeton, 1979).
4. For an overview see Thomas McCarthy, *The Critical Theory of Jürgen Habermas* (Cambridge, Mass., 1978), chap. 4.
5. Habermas uses the terms *begründen* and *Begründung* in this weak sense of giving reasons or grounds for a claim, supporting it with evidence and argument, defending it against criticism—and *not* in the foundationalist sense of grounding a claim on some irrefragable basis.
6. The explicitly nontranscendental character of Habermas's theory of communication has been ignored by many critics.
7. This notion of internally reconstructible sequences of stages in the acquisition of various species-wide competences is Habermas's version of universalism—Hegelian rather than Kantian in form, empirical rather than transcendental or ontological in intention.
8. Cf. the essays by Seyla Benhabib, Wolfgang Bonss, and Axel Honneth in *Sozialforschung als Kritik,* W. Bonss and A. Honneth, eds. (Frankfurt, 1982); and Helmut Dubiel, *Theory and Politics: Studies in the Development of Critical Theory* (Cambridge, Mass.: MIT Press, forthcoming).
9. Correspondingly, Weber distinguishes between the "ideal validity" of a norm and its de facto validity, i.e. its "actual influence on conduct through its assumed validity." The concern of the sociologist should be with the latter, which Weber also refers to as "empirical" or "social" validity. By contrast, Habermas uses "validity" only in

403

the normative sense, that is, in such a way as to distinguish it from de facto acceptance (Weber's empirical validity). This raises some problems of translation in chap. II, where Habermas is discussing Weber. I have translated Weber's *Geltung* as "validity" when the context makes it clear whether empirical (social) or ideal validity is intended—for instance, when they are being contrasted. In other contexts, where de facto acceptance and influence is in question and this may not be clear from the context, I have translated it as "currency" or "force"—as in "the social currency (force) of norms." The same convention is followed in the "Excursus" on argumentation in Chapter one.

10. Following Simmel's translators (Kurt Wolff, in particular) I have rendered *Vergesellschaftung* as "sociation." Habermas generally uses it in the same broad way to denote the development of stable patterns of social relations through social interaction or the integration into or adaptation to such patterns. At times, when he is dealing specifically with the *Vergesellschaftung* of individuals, he tends to use it as a synonym for "socialization," and I have sometimes translated it as such.

11. Habermas's position on the essential interdependence of ego identity and intact intersubjectivity provides a basis for responding to criticisms of his moral universalism in the name of individual self-realization—conceived in aesthetic, religious, existential, or psychological terms. The "socialized" version of ethical formalism does not call for the suppression of concrete subjectivity to ensure that the individual is identical with the universal. Rather, it *presupposes* different individuals, with different needs and wants, emotions and feelings, life histories and anticipated futures—in short, with different personal identities. What is required is that, *in those areas of common life subject to binding social norms,* the latter be agreed upon in communication free from domination. Differences are not suppressed but discussed, so that any eventual agreement involves a mediation of the particular and the general. The "ego and its own" critics often simply ignore the very thorny question of how the actions and orientations of different individuals are to be coordinated, a central question of *social* and *political* theory.

12. It is important to note—once again—that the idea of a communicatively rationalized lifeworld does not serve Habermas as a premise for a resurrected philosophy of history but as an interpretive foil for empirical social inquiry. There is nothing inevitable about rationalization processes; they are empirically conditioned on every side (as was made clear in *Communication and the Evolution of Society,* pp. 140ff.); to get at these conditions we need to go beyond structural descriptions within the framework of a developmental

logic. Furthermore, rationalization cannot simply be equated with progress:

> Opposing developments are connected in social evolution, namely the cumulative learning process without which history could not be interpreted as evolution (i.e., as a directional process) and, on the other hand, the exploitation which is intensified in class societies...We are maintaining the existence of developmental stages both for productive forces and for the forms of social integration. But the extent of exploitation and repression by no means stands in inverse proportion to these levels of development...New levels of learning mean not only expanded ranges of options but also new problem situations...new categories of burdens...new dimensions of scarcity. (Communication and the Evolution of Society, pp. 163–65.)

In interpreting societal change we must attend not only to what we have learned but also to what we have unlearned, to what has fallen apart as well as to what has come together (2:588). Further, the idea of discursive rationality cannot be used as a standard by which to judge concrete forms of life or life histories as "better" or "worse," "successes" or "failures." "It would make no sense to want to judge the totality of a form of life from the standpoint of individual aspects of rationality...The attempt to specify an equivalent for what was once meant by the good life ought not to mislead us into inferring an idea of the good life from the formal concept of reason with which the decentered understanding of the world in the modern age has left us"; that is, the "ideal speech situation" is not the image of a concrete form of life (Habermas: Critical Debates, John Thompson and David Held, eds. [Cambridge, Mass., 1982], p. 262; see also 1:173 and 2:166).

If, contrary to the assumptions of many critics, the notion of communicative rationality does not serve Habermas as the telos of a philosophy of history, or as the equivalent of progress, or as the standard for the good life, then what end does it serve? Speaking very generally, it has both a theoretical and a practical point. Theoretically it serves as the fundamental concept in an interpretive framework for critical social research; the entire edifice of his theories of individual and social development are built upon it. Practically it provides the key to diagnosing the sociopathologies of modernity and a way of sorting out proposed remedies to these ills. What many critics have simply overlooked is Habermas's left-Hegelianism. He is not seeking to demonstrate conceptually that what is rational is (or will be) real and what is real is (or will be) rational, but to identify empirically the actually existing possibilities for embodying rationality structures in concrete forms of life.

13. This is not altered by modern reflexivity and the development of a critical tradition. What does change is that fewer elements of the cultural tradition are exempted from problematization and that this problematization increasingly takes place in methodical and reflective form within specialized cultural spheres.

14. It is clear from the tables on pp. 214, 215 of Vol. 2 that each of the reproductive processes contributes to the maintenance of all three structural components of the lifeworld; a disturbance in any one of them leads to crisis manifestations in all three dimensions.

15. This strategy is to be distinguished from Parsons's treatment of culture, society, and personality as action systems that form environments for one another. Habermas examines at some length Parsons's various attempts to integrate action theory and systems theory (chap. VIII). While he finds much to learn there, he concludes that Parsons failed to integrate the two approaches: Whereas he consistently maintained that social-action theory was logically prior to social-systems theory, his later work clearly cedes conceptual hegemony to the latter. As a result, he was unable to project a concept of society from the perspective of action theory and play it off against the systems-theoretical concept.

16. There is, however, another type of medium that also serves to reduce the amount of interpretive energy needed in particular action situations and thus to enhance coordination and reduce risks; it does so by "condensing" rather than replacing consensus formation in language. Although they remain tied in the end to lifeworld contexts, these "generalized forms of communication" can be technologically enhanced and organizationally mediated. Thus writing, the printing press, the electronic media make it possible to free communication from narrow spatio-temporal limitations and to employ it in multiple contexts; such mass media play a central role in the formation of various "public spheres," with both authoritarian and emancipatory potential (2:573).

17. "The expression *Verrechtlichung* refers quite generally to the tendency toward an increase of statutory law. We can distinguish here between the *expansion* of law, that is the legal regulation of new social situations, which were previously regulated informally, and the *intensification* of law, as specialists further break down global statutory definitions into individual definitions" (2:524).

Author's Preface

1. *See* Michael Theunissen, *Sein und Schein* (Frankfurt, 1978).
2. Parts of this chapter have been published in English translation as "New Social Movements," *Telos* 49 (1981): 33–37.
3. On the relationship between truth and history, *see* Cornelius Cas-

toriadis, *Les Carrefours du Labyrinthe* (Paris, 1978); English transl. MIT Press, forthcoming.
4. *See* Jürgen Habermas, interview with Axel Honneth, Eberhard Knödler-Bunte, and Arno Widmann in *Telos* 49(1981): 5-31.

Chapter I. Introduction: Approaches to the Problem of Rationality

1. *See* Bruno Snell, *Die Entdeckung des Geistes* (Hamburg, 1946); Hans-Georg Gadamer, "Platon und die Vorsokratiker," in *Kleine Schriften* (Tübingen, 1977), 4:14ff. and "Mythos und Vernunft," 4:48ff.; W. Schadewalt, *Die Anfänge der Philosophie bei den Griechen* (Frankfurt, 1978).
2. *See* Jürgen Habermas, "Does Philosophy Still Have a Purpose?," in *Philosophical-Political Profiles* (MIT Press, forthcoming).
3. *See* Richard Rorty, ed., *The Linguistic Turn* (Chicago, 1967) and *Philosophy and the Mirror of Nature* (Princeton, N.J., 1979).
4. On the critique of First Philosophy, *see* Theodor Adorno, *Against Epistemology* (Cambridge, Mass., 1983); for an opposed view, *see* Karl-Otto Apel, "Das Problem der philosophischen Letzbegründung im Lichte einer transzendentalen Sprachpragmatik," in B. Kanitschneider, ed., *Sprache und Erkenntnis* (Innsbruck, 1976), pp. 55ff.
5. *See* the discussions in connection with Thomas Kuhn's *The Structure of Scientific Revolutions* (Chicago, 1972), above all: I. Lakatos and A. Musgrave, eds., *Criticism and the Growth of Knowledge* (Cambridge, 1970); W. Diedrich, ed., *Beiträge zur diachronischen Wissenschaftstheorie* (Frankfurt, 1974); and R. Bubner, "Dialektische Elemente einer Forschungslogik," in *Dialektik und Wissenschaft* (Frankfurt, 1973), pp. 129ff.
6. *See* Ulrich Oevermann, "Programmatische Überlegungen zu einer Theorie der Bildungsprozesse und einer Strategie der Sozialisationsforschung," in K. Hurrelmann, ed., *Sozialisation und Lebenslauf* (Hamburg, 1976), pp. 34ff.
7. *See* R. Döbert, J. Habermas, and G. Nunner-Winkler, eds., *Entwicklung des Ichs* (Köln, 1977).
8. *See* W. Hennis, *Politik und praktsiche Philosophie* (Neuwied, 1963); H. Maier, *Die ältere deutsche Staats- und Verwaltungslehre* (Neuwied, 1966); and J. Habermas, "The Classical Doctrine of Politics in Relation to Social Philosophy," in *Theory and Practice* (Boston, 1973), pp. 41-81.
9. *See* F. Jonas, "Was heisst ökonomische Theorie? Vorklassisches und klassisches Denken," in *Schmollers Jahrbuch* 78(1958); and H. Neuendorff, *Der Begriff des Interesses* (Frankfurt, 1973).
10. *See* F. Jonas, *Geschichte der Soziologie,* vols. I-IV (Reinbek, 1968/69); R. W. Friedrichs, *A Sociology of Sociology* (New York, 1970); and

T. Bottomore and R. Nisbet, *A History of Sociological Analysis* (New York, 1978).

11. Jürgen Habermas, "Kritische und konservativen Aufgaben der Soziologie," in *Theorie und Praxis* (Frankfurt, 1971), pp. 290–306.

12. *See* Chap. VI, Vol. 2.

13. *See* H. Neuendorff, "Soziologie," in *Evangelisches Staatslexikon* (Stuttgart, 1975), pp. 2424ff.

14. On the paired concepts of the older sociology, *see* J. Habermas, "Technology and Science as 'Ideology,'" in *Toward a Rational Society* (Boston, 1970), pp. 81–122; and C. W. Mills, *The Sociological Imagination* (Oxford, 1959).

Section I.1: "Rationality"—A Preliminary Specification

1. *See* Gilbert Ryle, *The Concept of Mind* (London, 1949); Eike von Savigny, *Die Philosophie der normalen Sprache* (Frankfurt, 1974), pp. 97ff.; D. Carr, "The Logic of Knowing How and Ability," *Mind* 88(1979):394ff.

2. For relevant conceptual history, *see* Karl-Otto Apel, *Die Idee der Sprache in der Tradition des Humanismus von Dante bis Vico* (Bonn, 1963).

3. For a Wittgensteinian perspective, *see* D. Pole, *Conditions of Rational Inquiry* (London, 1961) and "The Concept of Reason," in R. F. Dearden, D. H. Hirst, and R. S. Peters, eds., *Reason* (London, 1972), 2:1ff. The aspects under which Pole explicates the concept of rationality are, above all, objectivity, publicity and interpersonality, truth, the unity of reason, and the ideal of rational agreement. On Wittgenstein's concept of rationality, *see* Stanley Cavell, *Must We Mean What We Say?* (Cambridge, 1969), and *The Claims of Reason* (Oxford, 1979).

4. Of course, reasons play different *pragmatic roles* according to whether they are meant to explain a disagreement among conversation partners or a failed intervention. A speaker who makes an assertion has to have a "reserve supply" of good reasons at his disposal in order to be able, if necessary, to convince his conversation partners of the truth of his statement and bring about a rationally motivated agreement. On the other hand, for the success of an instrumental action it is not necessary that the actor be able to ground the rule of action he is following. In the case of teleological actions, reasons serve only to explain the fact that the application of a rule in certain circumstances was or was not successful, could or could not have been successful. In other words, there does exist an internal connection between the validity (efficacy) of a technical or strategic rule of action and the explanations that can be given for its validity; but knowledge of this connection is not a necessary subjective condition for successfully applying the rule.

5. Max Black, "Reasonableness," in Dearden et al, eds., *Reason*, 2.
6. For an overview, *see* W. Stegmüller, *Probleme und Resultate der Wissenschaftstheorie und Analytischen Philosophie* (Heidelberg, 1965), 1:335ff.
7. *See* Niklas Luhmann, *Zweckbegriff und Systemrationalität* (Tübingen, 1968).
8. Melvin Pollner, "Mundane Reasoning," *Philosophy of the Social Sciences* 4(1974):40.
9. Pollner, pp. 47–48.
10. Jean Piaget, *Introduction à l'épistemologie génétique* (Paris, 1950), 3:202. Two types of reciprocal action are combined in social cooperation: the "reciprocal action between the subject and objects," which is mediated through teleological action, and the "reciprocal action between the subject and other subjects," which is mediated through communicative action.
11. Pollner selects empirical examples from the area of traffic law, in "Mundane Reasoning," pp. 49ff.
12. Richard Norman, *Reasons for Actions* (New York, 1971), pp. 63–64. On pp. 65ff. Norman discusses the status of evaluative expressions which, owing to their partly normative and partly descriptive meanings, have been called Janus-words by such authors as Hare and Nowell-Smith.
13. S. Toulmin, R. Rieke, and A. Janik, *An Introduction to Reasoning* (New York, 1979), p. 13.
14. *See* A. R. White, *Truth* (New York, 1970), pp. 57ff.; G. Patzig, *Tatsachen, Normen, Sätze* (Stuttgart, 1981), pp. 155ff.
15. Kurt Baier, *The Moral Point of View* (Ithaca, 1964).
16. Compare John Rawls, *A Theory of Justice* (Cambridge, Mass., 1971) and the collection of critical essays on Rawls edited by O. Höffe, *Über Rawls Theorie der Gerechtigkeit* (Frankfurt, 1977); John Rawls, "Kantian Constructivism in Moral Theory," *Journal of Philosophy* 77(1980):515ff. On the constructivist approach, *see* O. Schwemmer, *Philosophie der Praxis* (Frankfurt, 1971); F. Kambartel, ed., *Praktische Philosophie und konstruktive Wissenschaftstheorie* (Frankfurt, 1975). On the transcendental-hermeneutic approach, *see* Karl-Otto Apel, *Towards a Transformation of Philosophy* (London, 1980), pp. 225ff., and "Sprechakttheorie und transzendentale Sprachpragmatik, zur Frage ethischer Normen," in Apel, ed., *Sprachpragmatik und Philosophie* (Frankfurt, 1976), pp. 10–173. On the discourse-theoretical approach, *see* J. Habermas, "Wahrheitstheorien," in H. Fahrenbach, ed., *Wirklichkeit und Reflexion* (Pfullingen, 1973), pp. 211–65; R. Alexy, *Theorie juristischer Argumentation* (Frankfurt, 1978) and "Eine Theorie des praktischen Diskurses," in W. Oelmüller, ed. *Normenbegründung, Normendurchsetzung* (Paderborn, 1978), pp. 22ff.; W. M. Sullivan, "Communication and the Recovery

of Meaning," *International Philosophical Quarterly* 18(1978):69ff. For an overview, *see* R. Wimmer, *Universalisierung in der Ethik* (Frankfurt, 1980); R. Hegselmann, *Normitivität und Rationalität* (Frankfurt, 1979).

17. Compare R. Bittner, "Ein Abschnitt sprachanalytischer Ästhetik," in R. Bittner and P. Pfaff, *Das ästhetische Urteil* (Köln, 1977), p. 271: "What matters is one's own perception of the object, and aesthetic judgments seek to guide it, to provide pointers and open perspectives for it. Stuart Hampshire formulates this as follows: It is a question of bringing someone to perceive the special attributes of the special object. Isenberg gives it a negative formulation: Without the presence or direct recollection of the object discussed, aesthetic judgment is superfluous and meaningless. These two determinations are not contradictory. In the terminology of speech acts, the situation can be described as follows: The illocutionary act normally carried out with utterances like 'The drawing x is particularly balanced' belongs to the species of statements, whereas the perlocutionary act which is as a rule carried out with such utterances is to guide someone to his own perception of the object's aesthetic qualities. I make a statement and thereby guide someone in his aesthetic perception, in just the same way that one can make a statement and thereby make him cognizant of the relevant facts, or that one can ask a question and thereby remind someone of something." Bittner is here picking up a line of argument traced through the works of M. MacDonald, A. Isenberg, and S. Hampshire; *see* the bibliography he provides on pp. 281ff.

18. *See* Chapters 10–12 of my *Knowledge and Human Interests* (Boston, 1971); Paul Ricoeur, *Freud and Philosophy* (New Haven, Conn., 1970), Book 3; W. A. Schelling, *Sprache, Bedeutung, Wunsch* (Berlin, 1978).

19. On the nature of explicative discourse, *see* H. Schnädelbach, *Reflexion und Diskurs* (Frankfurt, 1977), pp. 277ff.

20. For literature in German, *see* the research report by P. L. Völzing, "Argumentation," *Zeitschrift für Literaturwissenschaft und Linguistik* 10(1980):204ff.

21. J. A. Blair and R. H. Johnson, eds., *Informal Logic* (Inverness, Calif., 1980), p. x.

22. S. Toulmin, *The Uses of Argument* (Cambridge, Eng., 1958).

23. S. Toulmin, *Human Understanding* (Princeton, N.J., 1972).

24. B. R. Burleson, "On the Foundations of Rationality," *Journal of the American Forensic Association* 16(1979):113.

25. J. Habermas, "Wahrheitstheorien."

26. Toulmin has developed this analysis in Toulmin, Rieke, and Janik, *An Introduction to Reasoning.* He summarizes it as follows: "It must be clear just what *kind* of issues the argument is intended to raise (aesthetic rather than scientific, say, or legal rather than psychi-

atric) and what its underlying *purpose* is. The *grounds* on which it
rests must be relevant to the *claim* made in the argument and must
be sufficient to support it. The *warrant* relied on to guarantee this
support must be applicable to the case under discussion and must
be based on solid *backing*. The *modality,* or strength, of the resulting
claim must be made explicit, and the possible *rebuttals* or exceptions
must be well understood" (p. 106).

27. Ch. Perelman and L. Olbrechts-Tyteca, *La nouvelle rhétorique*
(Brussels, 1970).
28. *See* my "Wahrheitstheorien." The important concept of rational
motivation is certainly not yet sufficiently analyzed. *See* H.
Aronovitch, "Rational Motivation," *Philosophy and Phenomenological
Research* 15(1979):173ff.
29. Toulmin, *Uses of Argument.*
30. W. Klein, "Argumentation und Argument," *Zeitschrift für
Literaturwissenschaft und Linguistik* 38/39(1980):9ff. This approach
has been applied by Max Miller (with a somewhat different emphasis) to group discussions of moral questions by children and
adolescents; *see* Max Miller, "Zur Ontogenese moralischer Argu-
mentationen," *Zeitschrift für Literaturwissenschaft und Linguistik*
38/39(1980):58ff. and "Moralität und Argumentation," in *Newsletter
Soziale Kognition* 3(Technische Universität, Berlin, 1980).
31. W. Klein, "Argumentation," p. 49; *see also* M. A. Finocchiaro, "The
Psychological Explanation of Reasoning," *Philosophy of the Social
Sciences* 9(1979):277ff.
32. Klein, "Argumentation," p. 19.
33. Ibid., p. 18. For purposes of illustration, Klein refers to a sectarian
group that grounds the statement that religion is harmful to the
people by pointing out that this assertion can be found in Lenin's
writings. In this group, appeal to the authority of Lenin suffices
to transform something "collectively problematic" into something
"collectively valid." He intentionally uses these concepts in such
a way as to leave aside the question of what grounds these people,
who may appear sectarian to us, could give, if the situation arose,
in order to convince others that the theoretical explanations Lenin
offers for relevant phenomena are superior to competing
explanations, say to those of Durkheim or Weber.
34. Ibid., p. 16.
35. Ibid., p. 40.
36. Ibid., pp. 30–31.
37. Ibid., pp. 47–48.
38. Ibid., p. 47.
39. Ibid., p. 48.
40. Ibid., pp. 49–50.
41. This explains why, for instance, Klein compares (in a highly im-

plausible manner) pathological deviations from rules of argument with the overdetermination of physical phenomena: "Of course, in argumentation other lawlike regularities are at work besides its logic, and not everything that is said in an argument corresponds to the latter. Just as falling apples do indeed follow the law of gravitation, and one can study this law in connection with falling apples and other bodies moving relative to one another; but the movement of apples is also determined by other laws. I mention this because I would consider a reference to argumentation among the insane no more of an objection to the explication advanced above than throwing an apple would be considered an objection against the law of gravitation" (p. 50).

42. Ibid., p. 47.
43. Toulmin et al., *Introduction to Reasoning*, p. 15.
44. Ibid., p. 28.
45. Ibid., pp. 279ff.
46. Ibid., p. 200.
47. Toulmin, *Human Understanding*, p. 498.
48. B. R. Burleson, "On the Foundations of Rationality," p. 112. Compare W. R. Fischer, "Toward a Logic of Good Reasons," *Quarterly Journal of Speech* 64(1978):376ff.
49. Because of this, I earlier regarded court proceedings as a form of strategic action (see J. Habermas and N. Luhmann, *Theorie der Gesellschaft oder Sozialtechnologie* (Frankfurt, 1971), pp. 200–201; English translation, Columbia University Press, forthcoming.) I have since been persuaded by Robert Alexy that juridical argumentation in all its institutional varieties has to be conceived of as a special case of practical discourse: R. Alexy, *Theorie der juristischen Argumentation* (Frankfurt, 1978), pp. 263ff.
50. On the connection between the theory of validity claims and the logic of argumentation, see V. L. Völzing, *Begründen, Erklären, Argumentieren* (Heidelberg, 1979), pp. 34ff.
51. This important distinction is neglected by Ernst Tugendhat, *Vorlesungen zur Einführung in die sprachanalytische Philosophie* (Frankfurt, 1976), pp. 219ff; English transl., *Traditional and Analytical Philosophy: Lectures in the Philosophy of Language* (Cambridge, Eng., 1982).
52. I am referring here only to "genuine" value judgments that are based on value standards of a nondescriptive sort. Evaluations that serve to rank something according to descriptively applicable criteria can be formulated as statements susceptible of truth and do not belong to value judgments in the narrower sense. In this vein P. W. Taylor distinguishes between "value grading" and "value ranking": "In order to make clear the difference between value gradings and value rankings, it is helpful to begin by consid-

ering the difference between two meanings of the word 'good.' Suppose we are trying to decide whether a certain president of the United States was a good president. Do we mean good as far as presidents usually go? Or do we mean good in an absolute sense, with an ideal president in mind? In the first case, our class of comparison is the thirty-five men who have actually been president. To say that someone was a good president in this sense means that he was *better than average.* It is to claim that he fulfilled certain standards to a higher degree than most of the other men who were president. 'Good' is being used as a ranking word. In the second case, our class of comparison is not the class of actual presidents but the class of all possible (imaginable) presidents. To say that a certain president was good in this sense means that he fulfilled to a high degree those standards whose complete fulfillment would define an ideal president. 'Good' is here used as a grading word. It is not possible to specify exactly to what degree the standards must be fulfilled for a man to be graded as a good president rather than as mediocre or bad. That depends on what standards one is appealing to (that is, what conception of an ideal president one has in mind), how clearly those standards are defined, to what extent the degrees to which they can be fulfilled are measurable, and how distant from reality is one's ideal." [*Normative Discourse* (Englewood Cliffs, N.J., 1961), pp. 7–8.]

53. J. Zimmermann, *Sprachanalytische Ästhetik* (Stuttgart, 1980), pp. 145ff.
54. *See* above, this volume, p. 20.
55. *See* the conference report, *Werte in kommunikativen Prozessen,* G. Grossklaus and E. Oldemeyer, eds. (Stuttgart, 1980).
56. On this formal-pragmatic theory of truth, which goes back to Peirce, *see* the recent study by H. Scheit, *Studien zur Konsensustheorie der Wahrheit* (Habilitation, University of Munich, 1981).

Section I.2: Some Characteristics of the Mythical and the Modern Ways of Understanding the World

1. *See* Vol. 2, Chap. VI, sect. 1, below.
2. L. Levy-Bruhl, *La Mentalité primitive* (Paris, 1922).
3. E. Cassirer, Philosophy of Symbolic Forms, vol. 2 (New Haven, 1955); Robin Horton, "Levy-Bruhl, Durkheim and the Scientific Revolution," in R. Horton and R. Finnegan, eds., *Modes of Thought* (London, 1973), pp. 249ff.
4. *See* E. E. Evans-Pritchard, *Oracles and Magic among the Azande* (Oxford, 1937). In his "Levy-Bruhl's Theory of Primitive Mentality," *Bulletin of the Faculty of the Arts* 2(1934):1ff., Evans-Pritchard summarizes his critique of Levy-Bruhl as follows: "The fact that we at-

tribute rain to meteorological causes alone while savages believe that Gods or ghosts or magic can influence the rainfall is no evidence that our brains function differently from their brains . . . I did not come to this conclusion myself by observation and inference and have, in fact, little knowledge of the meteorological process that leads to rain. I merely accept what everybody else in my society accepts, namely that the rain is due to natural causes . . . Likewise a savage who believes that under suitable natural and ritual conditions the rainfall can be influenced by use of appropriate magic is not on account of this belief to be considered of inferior intelligence. He did not build up this belief from his own observations and inferences but adopted it in the same way as he adopted the rest of his cultural heritage, namely by being born into it. He and I are both thinking in patterns of thought provided for us by the societies in which we live. It would be absurd to say that the savage is thinking mystically and that we are thinking scientifically about rainfall. In either case like mental processes are involved and, moreover, the content of thought is similarly derived. But we can say that the social content of our thought about rainfall is scientific, is in accord with objective facts, whereas the social content of savage thought about rainfall is unscientific because it is not in accord with reality and may also be mystical where it assumes the existence of supra-sensible forces."

5. M. Cole, J. Gay, J. Glick, and D. Sharp, *The Cultural Concept of Learning and Thinking* (New York, 1971); P. R. Dasen, "Cross-Cultural Piagetian Research," *Journal of Cross-Cultural Psychology* 3(1972):23ff.; and B. B. Lloyd, *Perception and Cognition* (Harmondsworth, Eng., 1972).

6. *See* Claude Lévi-Strauss, *Structural Anthropology,* vols. 1 and 2 (New York, 1963, 1976) and *The Savage Mind* (Chicago, 1966); and W. Lepenies and H. H. Ritter, eds., *Orte des wilden Denkens* (Frankfurt, 1970).

7. Maurice Godelier, "Myth and History: Reflections on the Foundations of the Primitive Mind," in *Perspectives in Marxist Anthropology* (Cambridge, Eng., 1977), p. 213.

8. On the analogical character of the "savage mind" *see* S. J. Tambiah, "Form and Meaning of Magical Acts," in Horton and Finnegan, eds., *Modes of Thought,* pp. 199ff.

9. J. Piaget, *The Child's Conception of Physical Causality* (London, 1930).

10. Godelier, "Myth and History," p. 212.

11. B. Malinowski stresses this theme in *Argonauts of the Western Pacific* (New York, 1922). Malinowski showed that the fishermen of the Trobriand Islands employ magical practices primarily on occasions when they experience the shortcomings of their knowledge and recognize the limits of their rational methods; *see also* his *Magic, Science and Religion* (Glencoe, Ill., 1948).

12. Godelier, "Myth and History," p. 208.
13. Ibid., pp. 208–209.
14. Hans-Georg Gadamer, *Truth and Method* (New York, 1975).
15. E. Troeltsch, *Der Historismus und seine Probleme* (Tübingen, 1922); K. Mannheim, "Historismus," *Archiv für Sozialpolitik* 52(1924):1ff. and *Ideology and Utopia* (New York, 1955); for an overview *see* J. Rüsen, *Für eine erneuerte Historik* (Stuttgart, 1976).
16. Bryan Wilson, ed., *Rationality* (Oxford, 1970); Horton and Finnegan, eds., *Modes of Thought;* Kai Nielsen, "Rationality and Relativism," *Philosophy of the Social Sciences* 4(1974):313ff.; E. Fales, "Truth, Tradition, Rationality," *Philosophy of the Social Sciences* 6(1976):97ff.; I. C. Jarvie, "On the Limits of Symbolic Interpretation in Anthropology," *Current Anthropology* (1976):687ff.; R. Horton, "Professor Winch on Safari," *European Journal of Sociology* 17(1976):157–80; K. Dixon, "Is Cultural Relativism Self-Refuting?" *British Journal of Sociology* (1977):75ff.; J. Kekes, "Rationality and Social Sciences," *Philosophy of Social Sciences* 9(1979):105ff.; and L. Hertzberg, "Winch on Social Interpretation," *Philosophy of Social Sciences* 10(1980):151ff.
17. Peter Winch, *The Idea of a Social Science* (London, 1958) and "Understanding a Primitive Society," in Wilson, ed., *Rationality*, pp. 78–111.
18. Here I shall be following Thomas McCarthy, "The Problem of Rationality in Social Anthropology," *Stony Brook Studies in Philosophy*, 1(1974):1ff. and *The Critical Theory of Jürgen Habermas* (Cambridge, Mass., 1978), pp. 317ff. I am particularly indebted for a number of essential ideas to an unpublished manuscript by Albrecht Wellmer, "On Rationality," vols. I–IV (1977).
19. Steven Lukes, "Some Problems about Rationality," in Wilson, ed., *Rationality*, p. 194.
20. Alasdair MacIntyre, "The Idea of a Social Science," in *Against the Self-Images of the Age* (London, 1971), pp. 211ff. and "Rationality and the Explanation of Action," ibid., pp. 244ff.
21. MacIntyre, "Rationality," pp. 251–52.
22. Cited by Winch in "Understanding a Primitive Society," p. 80.
23. Martin Hollis provides an accurate characterization of these suppositions of commonality in "The Limits of Rationality," in Wilson, ed., *Rationality*, pp. 214ff.
24. Winch, "Understanding a Primitive Society," p. 82.
25. Ibid., p. 81.
26. I owe this comparison to a manuscript by Patrick Burke (who is evidently taking his inspiration from Wittgenstein here) made available to me by Richard Rorty: "Truth and Worldviews" (1976). On page 3 it reads: "Worldviews, like portraits, are cases of 'seeing as.' We have a worldview when we succeed in seeing the sum total

of things as something or other. It is not necessary that we give an account of all the items in the world individually, but of the whole as the whole. So in one sense a worldview must embrace everything, but in another sense not."

27. I introduced the criterion of adequacy in this sense to characterize theoretically useful language systems in "Wahrheitstheorien," pp. 245ff.
28. Winch, "Understanding a Primitive Society," pp. 105–106.
29. Ibid., p. 92.
30. Ibid., p. 93.
31. Robin Horton, "African Traditional Thought and Western Science," in Wilson, ed., Rationality, p. 153.
32. Ibid., pp. 154–55.
33. MacIntyre, "Rationality," pp. 252–53.
34. Ernest Gellner, "The Savage and the Modern Mind," in Horton and Finnegan, eds., Modes of Thought, pp. 162ff.
35. On the following, compare Horton, "African Traditional Thought," pp. 155ff. and Gellner, "The Savage and Modern Mind," pp. 162ff.
36. See the concluding paragraph of Section B, pp. 52–53 above.
37. Gellner, "The Savage and the Modern Mind," p. 178.
38. Horton, "African Traditional Thought," p. 178: "Perhaps the most important occasion of taboo reaction in traditional African cultures is the commission of incest. Incest is one of the most flagrant defiances of the established category-system; for he who commits it treats mother, daughter or sister like a wife. Another common occasion for taboo reaction is the birth of twins. Here, the category distinction involved is that of human beings versus animals—multipie births being taken as a characteristic of animals as opposed to men. Yet another very generally tabooed object is the human corpse, which occupies, as it were, a classificatory no-man's land between the living and the inanimate. Taboo reactions are often given to occurrences that are radically strange or new; for these too (almost by definition) fail to fit into the established category system."
39. Winch, "Understanding a Primitive Society," p. 106.
40. Horton, "African Traditional Thought," p. 170.
41. MacIntyre, "The Idea of a Social Science," p. 228.
42. On this assumption, the belief in witches that spread in early modern Europe would have to be regarded as a regression. On this point see R. Döbert, "The Role of Stage-Models within a Theory of Social Evolution, Illustrated by the European Witchcraze," in R. Harré and U. J. Jensen, eds., Studies in the Concept of Evolution (Brighton, Eng., 1981).
43. For an overview see J. Piaget, The Principles of Genetic Epistemology (New York, 1972); J. H. Flavell, The Developmental Psychology of

Jean Piaget (Princeton, 1963); H. G. Furth, *Piaget and Knowledge* (Chicago, 1981); B. Kaplan, "Meditation on Genesis," *Human Development* 10(1967):65ff.; and N. Rotenstreich, "An Analysis of Piaget's Concept of Structure," *Philosophy and Phenomenological Research* 37(1977):368ff.

44. J. Piaget, *Introduction à l'épistémologie génétique*, 3(Paris, 1950):189ff.
45. Ibid., p. 202; compare John Broughton, "Genetic Metaphysics," in R. W. Rieber, ed., *Body and Mind* (New York, 1980), pp. 177ff.
46. Ibid., pp. 202–03.
47. Ibid., pp. 245–46.
48. Wellmer, "On Rationality," 4:12ff.; *see also* K. O. Apel, "The Common Presuppositions of Hermeneutics and Ethics," in J. Bärmark, ed., *Perspectives on Metascience* (Göteborg, 1980), pp. 39ff.
49. David Elkind has given an impressive description of the stage-specific forms of egocentrism in the ontogenetic sphere, in "Egocentrism in Adolescence," *Child Development* 38(1967):1025–34. On pp. 1032–33 we find the following summary: "In infancy, egocentrism corresponds to the impression that objects are identical with the perception of them, and this form of egocentrism is overcome with the appearance of representation. During the pre-school period, egocentrism appears in the guise of a belief that symbols contain the same information as the objects which they represent. With the emergence of concrete operations, the child is able to discriminate between symbol and referent, and so overcome this type of egocentrism. The egocentrism of the school-age period can be characterized as the belief that one's own mental constructions correspond to a superior form of perceptual reality. With the advent of formal operations and the ability to construct contrary-to-fact hypotheses, this kind of egocentrism is dissolved because the young person can now recognize the arbitrariness of his own mental constructions. Finally, during early adolescence, egocentrism appears as the belief that the thoughts of others are directed toward the self. This variety of egocentrism is overcome as a consequence of the conflict between the reactions which the young person anticipates and those which actually occur."
50. Albrecht Wellmer, "Thesen über Vernunft, Emanzipation und Utopie" (unpubl. Ms, 1979), p. 32.
51. Ibid., p. 53.
52. *See* my "Reply to My Critics," in J. Thompson and D. Held, eds., *Habermas: Critical Debates* (Cambridge, Mass., 1982), pp. 219–83.

Section I.3: Relations to the World and Aspects of
Rationality in Four Sociological Concepts of Action

1. I. C. Jarvie, *Concepts and Society* (London, 1972), pp. 147ff.
2. K. R. Popper, *Objective Knowledge* (Oxford, 1972), p. 106.

3. K. R. Popper and J. C. Eccles, *The Self and Its Brain* (New York, 1977), p. 38.
4. K. R. Popper, "Reply to My Critics," in P. A. Schilp, ed., *The Philosophy of Karl Popper* (La Salle, Ill., 1974), p. 1050.
5. Popper and Eccles, *The Self and Its Brain*, pp. 100ff.
6. Nicolai Hartmann, *Das Problem des geistigen Seins* (Berlin, 1932).
7. Popper and Eccles, *The Self and Its Brain*, pp. 41ff.
8. Popper, *Objective Knowledge*, pp. 180–81.
9. Ibid., pp. 168–69.
10. Peter Berger and Thomas Luckmann, *The Social Construction of Reality* (New York, 1966).
11. Jarvie, *Concepts and Society*, p. 165.
12. Ibid., p. 161.
13. Ibid., p. 153.
14. Popper, "Reply to My Critics," p. 1050. Popper takes this terminology from J. C. Eccles, *Facing Realities* (New York, 1970).
15. R. Bubner, *Handlung, Sprache und Vernunft* (Frankfurt, 1976), pp. 66ff.
16. On decision theory, *see* H. Simon, *Models of Man* (New York, 1957); G. Gäfgen, *Theorie der wirtschaftlichen Entscheidung* (Tübingen, 1968). On game theory, *see* R. D. Luce and H. Raiffa, *Games and Decisions* (New York, 1957); M. Shubik, *Spieltheorie und Sozialwissenschaften* (Frankfurt, 1965). On exchange-theoretical approaches in social psychology, *see* P. P. Ekeh, *Social Exchange Theory* (London, 1964).
17. T. R. Sarbin, "Role Theory," in G. Lindsey, ed., *Handbook of Social Psychology*, vol. 1 (Cambridge, Mass., 1954), pp. 223–58; Talcott Parsons, "Social Interaction," in *International Encyclopedia of Social Science*, 7:1429–41; Hans Joas, *Die gegenwärtige Lage der Rollentheorie* (Frankfurt, 1977), pp. 68ff.
18. G. J. McCall and J. L. Simmons, *Identity and Interactions* (New York, 1966); E. Goffman, Frame Analysis (Harmondsworth, Eng., 1975), *Relations in Public* (Harmondsworth, Eng., 1971), *Interaction Ritual* (Harmondsworth, Eng., 1957); R. Harré and P. F. Secord, *Explanation of Behavior* (Totowa, N.J., 1972); R. Harré, *Social Being* (Oxford, 1979).
19. One can get an overview of symbolic interactionism and ethnomethodology from, for instance, the reader put together by the Arbeitsgruppe Bielefelder Soziologen, *Alltagswissen, Interaktion und gesellschaftliche Wirklichkeit*, 2 vols. (Hamburg, 1973); *see also* H. Steinert, "Das Handlungsmodell des symbolischen Interaktionismus," in H. Lenk, ed., *Handlungstheorien*, 4(Munich, 1977):79ff.
20. G. H. von Wright, *Explanation and Understanding* (London, 1971), pp. 96ff. Von Wright's point of departure is G. E. M. Anscombe, *Intention* (Oxford, 1957).

21. J. L. Austin speaks of the "direction of fit" or the "onus of match," which Anthony Kenny elaborates as follows: "Any sentence whatever can be regarded as—*inter alia*—a description of a state of affairs . . . Now let us suppose that the possible state of affairs described in the sentence does not, in fact, obtain. *Do we fault the sentence or do we fault the facts?* If the former, then we shall call the sentence assertoric, if the latter, let us call it for the moment imperative." *Will, Freedom and Power* (Oxford, 1975), p. 38. If we conceive of intention sentences as imperatives that a speaker addresses to himself, then assertoric and intention sentences represent the two possibilities of agreement between sentence and state of affairs that are open to objective appraisal.

22. G. Gaefgen, "Formale Theorie des strategischen Handelns," in H. Lenk, ed., *Handlungstheorien*, 1(Munich, 1980):249ff.

23. Compare Ottfried Höffe, *Strategien der Humanität* (Munich, 1975): "A strategic game is composed of four elements:

1) The *players*, the sovereign units of decision, who pursue their ends and act according to their own deliberations and guiding principles;

2) The *rules*, which fix the variables that each player can control: information conditions, resources and other relevant aspects of the environment; the system of rules fixes the type of game, the totality of behavioral possibilities, and in the end the gains or losses of every player; a change in the rules creates a new game;

3) The end result or *payoffs*, the utility or value correlated with the alternative results of plays (in chess: win, lose, draw; in politics: public prestige, power and money, for instance);

4) The *strategies*, the encompassing, alternatively possible plans of action. They are constructed with a view both to heeding and exploiting the rules and to taking account of the possible alternatives open to the opponent. Strategies represent a system of instructions that determine in advance, and often only in a rather global way, how, in every possible game situation, one chooses a move from the set of those allowed by the rules of the game. In the game-theoretical interpretation of social reality, certain strategies are often favorable only for a segment of the contest; new strategies then have to be developed for other segments; individual strategies have the significance of substrategies within the framework of an encompassing overall strategy.

The rationality criterion of game theory refers not to the choice of individual moves but to the choice of strategies. Stated in the form of a maxim for decision, the basic pattern runs as follows: 'Choose the strategy which, in the framework of the rules of the game and in view of your opponents, promises to bring the greatest success.'" (pp. 77–78).

24. H. Gerth and C. W. Mills, *Character and Social Structure* (New York 1953).

25. This does not prejudge the question of whether we, as social scientists and philosophers, adopt a cognitive or a sceptical position in regard to moral-practical questions; that is, whether we hold a justification of action norms that is not relative to given ends to be possible. For example, Talcott Parsons shares with Weber a position of value scepticism; but when we use the concept of normatively regulated action we have to describe the actors *as if* they consider the legitimacy of action norms to be basically open to objective appraisal, no matter in which metaphysical, religious, or theoretical framework. Otherwise they would not take the concept of a world of legitimately regulated interpersonal relations as the basis of their action and could not orient themselves to valid norms but only to social facts. Acting in a norm-conformative attitude requires an intuitive understanding of normative validity; and this concept presupposes *some* possibility or other of normative grounding. It cannot be a priori excluded that this conceptual necessity is a deception embedded in linguistic meaning conventions and thus calls for enlightenment—for example, by reinterpreting the concept of normative validity in emotivist or decisionistic terms and redescribing it with the help of other concepts like expressions of feeling, appeals, or commands. But the action of agents to whom such categorially "purified" action orientations can be ascribed could no longer be described in concepts of normatively regulated action.

26. E. Goffman, *The Presentation of Self in Everyday Life* (New York, 1959). On p. xi of the preface he writes: "The perspective employed in this report is that of the theatrical performance; the principles derived are dramaturgical ones. I shall consider the way in which the individual in ordinary work situations presents himself and his activity to others, the ways in which he guides and controls the impression they form of him, and the kinds of things he may and may not do while sustaining his performance before them. In using this model I will attempt not to make light of its obvious inadequacies. The stage presents things that are make-believe; presumably life presents things that are real and sometimes not well rehearsed. More important, perhaps, on the stage one player presents himself in the guise of a character to characters projected by other players; the audience constitutes a third party to the interaction—one that is essential and yet, if the stage performance were real, one that would not be there. In real life, the three parties are compressed into two; the part one individual plays is tailored to the parts played by the others present, and yet these others also constitute the audience."

27. Harré and Secord, *Explanation of Behavior*, pp. 215–16.
28. Goffman, *Presentation of Self*, p. 31.
29. For the sake of simplicity, I am confining myself to *intentional* experiences (including weakly intentional moods) in order not to have to deal with the complicated limit case of sensations. The complication consists in the fact that here the misleading assimilation of experiential sentences to propositions is particularly tempting. Experiential sentences that express a sensation have almost the same meaning as propositional sentences that refer to a corresponding inner state brought about by stimulation of the senses. [Habermas uses the term *intentional experience* in the way that Husserl does, but without wanting thereby to subscribe to the phenomenological concept of intentionality. *Transl.*] On the extended discussion of expressions of pain that has been sparked by Wittgenstein's remarks on this topic, *see* H. J. Giegel, *Zur Logik seelischer Ereignisse* (Frankfurt, 1969); P. M. S. Hacker, *Illusion and Insight* (Oxford, 1972), pp. 251ff.
30. Compare the analysis of desires and feelings by Charles Taylor, "Explaining Action," *Inquiry* 13(1970):54–89.
31. Richard Norman, *Reasons for Actions*, pp. 65ff.
32. Goffman, *Presentation of Self*, pp. 17–18.
33. I shall come back to the nominalistic theory of language developed by H. P. Grice in Chapter III.
34. Benjamin Lee Whorf, *Language, Thought and Reality* (Cambridge, Mass., 1956); H. Gipper, *Gibt es ein sprachliches Relativitätsprinzip?* (Frankfurt, 1972); P. Henle, ed., *Sprache, Denken, Kultur* (Frankfurt, 1969).
35. Harré and Secord, *Explanation of Behavior*, pp. 215ff.; *see* especially Charles Taylor, *Language and Human Nature* (Carleton, Montreal, 1978).
36. F. Schütze, *Sprache*, 2 vols. (Munich, 1975).
37. For similar reasons, M. Roche insists on the distinction between linguistic and social conventions: "The school of conceptual analysis has characteristically seen no contrast between intention and convention; in their view the latter includes the former and vice versa." M. Roche, "Die Philosophische Schule der Begriffsanalyse," in R. Wiggershaus, ed., *Sprachanalyse und Soziologie* (Frankfurt, 1975), p. 187. One could say, Roche allows, "that communicative conventions are a very special kind of social convention, that the life of ordinary language and its use in social situations can be described independently of social interactions in social situations. But it would be difficult to ground this assertion, and conceptual analysis has no interest in clarifying it. Normally it assumes, rightly, that the analysis of concepts requires an analysis of 'language games' and social 'forms of life' (Wittgenstein), or that

the analysis of speech acts requires an analysis of social acts (Austin). But it then mistakenly infers from this that the conventions of communication are paradigms of the social conventions surrounding them and that a use of language stands in the same relation to communication conventions as a social action does to social conventions" (pp. 188–89).

38. Arthur C. Danto, "Basic Actions," *American Philosophical Quarterly* 2(1965):141–48, and *Analytical Philosophy of Action* (Cambridge, 1973).

39. The false impression that bodily movements coordinated with actions are themselves basic actions might be sustained perhaps by looking to certain exercises in which we intend nonindependent actions *as such*. In therapy or sports training, for purposes of anatomical display, in singing lessons, or foreign language lessons, or to illustrate action-theoretic assertions, every speaking and acting subject can, upon request, certainly raise his left arm, bend his right index finger, spread open his hand, repeat vocal sounds in a certain rhythm, make hissing noises, execute circular or linear movements with a drawing pencil, trace a wavy line, enunciate a German *ü*, straighten up his body, roll his eyes, stress a sentence according to a certain meter, raise or lower his voice, stretch his legs, and so on. But the fact that such bodily movements can be carried out intentionally does not contradict the thesis that they represent nonindependent actions. This can be seen in the fact that with these intentionally executed bodily movements the normal structure of mediation of action (as represented in 1. below) breaks down:

  1. *S* is opening the window by executing a circular motion with his hand.

For it would be artificial to say:

  2. *S* is (intentionally) raising his right arm by raising his right arm.

Of course, an intentionally executed bodily movement can be understood as part of a *practice*.

  2.′ During the gym lesson, in raising his right arm *S* is carrying out the teacher's instruction to raise his right arm.

Nonindependent actions typically have to be embedded in a demonstration or training practice if they are to be able to appear *as* actions. Instructions of this type always appear in connection with a practice that demonstrates or exercises nonindependent elements of action as such. The exercises may belong to the normal education of growing children; but they may also belong to a training practice that prepares one for special actions, for *skills*.

40. A. I. Goldmann, *A Theory of Action* (Englewood Cliffs, N.J., 1970).

41. R. Bubner, *Handlung, Sprache und Vernunft*, pp. 168ff.

42. *See* Chapter III, section C below.

Section I.4: The Problem of Understanding Meaning
in the Social Sciences

1. On the connection between Weber's ontological presuppositions and his theory of action and methodology of *Verstehen, see* Seyla Benhabib, "Rationality and Social Action," *Philosophical Forum* XII(1981):356–75.
2. Max Weber, *Methodologische Schriften* (Frankfurt, 1968), p. 170.
3. For a discussion of this proposal, *see* K. O. Apel, J. Mannheim, and R. Tuomela, eds., *Neue Versuche über Erklären und Verstehen* (Frankfurt, 1978).
4. Max Weber, *Economy and Society,* G. Roth and C. Wittich, eds. (Berkeley, 1978), p. 6.
5. G. H. von Wright, "Erwiderungen," in Apel et al., *Neue Versuche,* p. 266.
6. Weber, *Methodologische Schriften,* pp. 116–17.
7. On the controversy between causal and intentionalistic theories of action, *see* A. Beckermann, ed., *Analytische Handlungstheorie. Handlungserklärungen* (Frankfurt, 1977).
8. Compare my remarks in *Legitimation Crisis* (Boston, 1975), pp. 111ff. On the critical reconstruction of the factual genesis of a normative system, *see* P. Lorenzen, "Szientismus vs. Dialektik," in R. Bubner, K. Cramer, and R. Wiehl, eds., *Hermeneutik und Dialektik* (Tübingen, 1970), 1:57ff.; P. Lorenzen, *Normative Logic and Ethics* (Mannheim, 1969), pp. 73ff.; P. Lorenzen and O. Schwemmer, *Konstruktive Logik, Ethik und Wissenschaftstheorie* (Mannheim, 1973), pp. 209ff.
9. J. Habermas, "The Hermeneutic Claim to Universality," in J. Bleicher, *Contemporary Hermeneutics* (London, 1980), pp. 181–211; W.A. Schelling, *Sprache, Bedeutung, Wunsch* (Berlin, 1978); A. Lorenzer, *Sprachzerstörung und Rekonstruktion* (Frankfurt, 1970); T. Mischel, *Psychologische Erklärungen* (Frankfurt, 1981), pp. 180ff.
10. Alasdair MacIntyre, *The Unconscious* (London, 1958).
11. Anthony Giddens, *New Rules of Sociological Method* (London, 1976), p. 151, and "Habermas' Critique of Hermeneutics," in *Studies in Social and Political Theory* (London, 1977), pp. 135ff.
12. K. O. Apel, *Die Erklären/Verstehen Kontroverse* (Frankfurt, 1979); English trans. (MIT Press, forthcoming).
13. Hans Albert, "Hermeneutik und Realwissenschaft," in *Plädoyer für kritischen Rationalismus* (Munich, 1971), pp. 106ff.
14. Theodore Abel, "The Operation Called Verstehen," *The American Journal of Sociology* 54(1948):211–18.
15. J. Habermas, *Zur Logik der Sozialwissenschaften* (Frankfurt, 1970), pp. 142ff.; English transl. (MIT Press, forthcoming); K. O. Apel, *Analytic Philosophy of Language and the Geisteswissenschaften* (Dordrecht, Holland, 1967). For a good overview of the discussion, *see*

F. Dallmayr and T. McCarthy, eds., *Understanding and Social Inquiry* (Notre Dame, 1977).

16. *See* Kuhn, *Structure of Scientific Revolutions;* Lakatos and Musgrave, eds., *Criticism and the Growth of Knowledge;* and Diederich, ed., *Beiträge zur diakronischen Wissenschaftstheorie.*

17. Mary Hesse, "In Defence of Objectivity," in *Proceedings of the Aristotelian Society 1972* (London, 1973), pp. 4ff, here p. 9.

18. I shall leave to one side here the question of the applicability to the social sciences of the concept of paradigm that Kuhn developed for the natural sciences. *See* D. L. Eckberg and L. Hill, "The Paradigm Concept and Sociology: A Critical Review," *American Sociological Review* 44(1979):925ff.

19. Giddens, *New Rules,* p. 158.

20. A. V. Cicourel, *Method and Measurement in Sociology* (Glencoe, Ill., 1964); K. Kreppner, *Zur Problematik der Messung in den Sozialwissenschaften* (Stuttgart, 1975).

21. Richard Bernstein, *Praxis and Action* (Philadelphia, 1971), pp. 165ff.; K. O. Apel, *Charles Sanders Peirce: From Pragmatism to Pragmaticism* (Amherst, Mass., 1981).

22. H. Skjervheim, *Objectivism and the Study of Man* (Oslo, 1959), reprinted in *Inquiry* (1974):213ff., 265ff.

23. Ibid., p. 272.

24. Ibid., p. 265. Skjervheim explicitly takes Husserl's transcendental theory of intersubjectivity as his point of departure; in fact, however, his analysis is closer to the basic ideas of the dialogical philosophy stemming from Martin Buber and Franz Rosenzweig. Michael Theunissen understands the philosophy of dialogue (with which he also connects Rosenstock-Huessy and Griesbach) as a counterproposal to Cartesian—i.e., monological—transcendental phenomenology. *See* his *Der Andere* (Berlin, 1965); English transl. (MIT Press, forthcoming). On Husserl, *see* P. Hutcheson, "Husserl's Problem of Intersubjectivity," *Journal of the British Society for Phenomenology* 11(1980):144ff.

25. W. P. Alston, *The Philosophy of Language* (Englewood Cliffs, N.J., 1964); Savigny, *Die Philosophie der normalen Sprache,* pp. 72ff.

26. Harold Garfinkel, *Studies in Ethnomethodology* (Englewood Cliffs, N.J., 1967).

27. J. Habermas, "A Review of Gadamer's *Truth and Method,*" in F. Dallmayr and T. McCarthy, eds., *Understanding and Social Inquiry,* pp. 335–63.

28. Alvin Gouldner, *The Coming Crisis of Western Sociology* (New York, 1970); H. Albert and E. Topitsch, eds., *Werturteilsstreit* (Darmstadt, 1971); U. Beck, *Objektivität und Normitität* (Hamburg, 1974). I shall not take up here the question of the methodological significance of Quine's thesis of the radical indeterminacy of translation; on that

point *see* D. Wrighton, "The Problem of Understanding," *Philosophy of the Social Sciences* 11(1981):49ff. and R. Feleppa, "Hermeneutic Interpretation and Scientific Truth," *Philosophy of the Social Sciences* 11(1981):53ff.

29. In the Federal Republic of Germany they were launched with the so-called *Positivismusstreit; see* Theodor Adorno et al., *The Positivist Dispute in German Sociology* (New York, 1976).

30. D. Böhler, "Philosophische Hermeneutik und hermeneutische Method," in H. Hartung, W. Heistermann, P. M. Stephan, *Fruchtblätter: Veröffentlichungen der Pädagogische Hochschule Berlin* (1977), pp. 15ff.; W. Kuhlmann, *Reflexion und kommunikative Erfahrung* (Frankfurt, 1975).

31. Alfred Schutz, *The Phenomenology of the Social World* (Evanston, Ill., 1967).

32. Alfred Schutz, *Collected Papers,* Maurice Natanson, ed., vol. 1 (The Hague, 1967): pp. 5-6.

33. Ibid., p. 43.

34. Ibid., p. 44.

35. Ibid., p. 40.

36. Ibid., p. 56.

37. P. Attewell, "Ethnomethodology since Garfinkel," *Theory and Society* 1(1974):179ff.; D. H. Zimmermann, "Ethnomethodology," *American Sociologist* 13(1978):6ff.

38. "The features of a setting attended to by its participants include, among other things, its historical continuity, its structure of rules and the relationship of activities within it to those rules, and the ascribed (or achieved) statuses of its participants. When viewed as the temporally situated *achievement* of parties to a setting, these features will be termed the occasioned corpus of setting features. By use of the term *occasioned* corpus, we wish to emphasize that the features of socially organized activities are particular, contingent accomplishments of the production and recognition work of parties to the activity. We underscore the occasioned character of the corpus in contrast to a corpus of members' knowledge, skill and belief standing prior to and independent of any actual occasion in which such knowledge, skill and belief is displayed or recognized. The latter conception is usually referred to by the term culture." D. H. Zimmermann, M. Pollner, "The Everyday World as a Phenomenon," in J. D. Douglas, ed., *Understanding Everyday Life* (London, 1971), p. 94.

39. T. P. Wilson, "Theorien der Interaktion und Modelle soziologischer Erklärung," in Arbeitsgruppe Bielefelder Soziologen, ed., *Alltagswissen, Interaktion und gesellschaftliche Wirklichkeit,* pp. 54ff., here pp. 66-67.

40. P. McHugh, "On the Failure of Positivism," in Douglas, ed., *Understanding Everyday Life,* p. 329.

426 REASON AND THE RATIONALIZATION OF SOCIETY

41. J. H. Goldthorpe, "A Revolution in Sociology?" *Sociology* 7(1973):429.
42. A. V. Cicourel, *The Social Organization of Juvenile Justice* (New York, 1968); "Cross-Modal Communication," in *Cognitive Sociology* (London, 1973), pp. 41ff.; and *Theory and Method in a Study of Argentine Fertility* (New York, 1974).
43. F. Schütze, W. Meinfeld, W. Springer, and A. Weymann, "Grundlagentheoretische Voraussetzungen methodisch kontrollierten Fremdverstehens," in Arbeitsgruppe Bielefelder Soziologen, eds., *Alltagswissen, Interaktion und gesellschaftliche Wirklichkeit*, 2:433ff.
44. Goldthorpe, "A Revolution in Sociology?" p. 430.
45. D. H. Zimmermann and M. Pollner, "The Everyday World as a Phenomenon," p. 289.
46. Edmund Husserl, *Formal and Transcendental Logic* (The Hague, 1969).
47. Garfinkel, *Studies in Ethnomethodology*, p. 33.
48. P. McHugh et al., *On the Beginning of Social Inquiry* (London, 1974).
49. On the methodological significance of question and answer in connection with Collingwood, *see* W. Kuhlmann, *Reflexion und kommunikative Erfahrung* (Frankfurt, 1975), pp. 94ff.
50. Kuhlmann has worked out the performative character of the practice of interpretation in an energetic way; he has shown that understanding meaning is possible only by way of coming to at least a virtual understanding about the issue itself. Understanding a text requires reaching an understanding with the author, who, as long as he counts as a responsible subject, cannot be wholly objectivated. For responsibility—as the capacity to orient oneself to validity claims that aim at intersubjective recognition—means that the author must be just as capable of *being in the right* in relation to the interpreter as he is in principle capable of *learning* in turn from the interpreter's critique of his presuppositions. "Only when the other, even (and precisely) in the eyes of someone who wants to learn something about him, remains (1) capable in principle of saying something really *new and surprising*, (2) capable in principle of uttering something *superior* to the views of those wanting to get to know him—when they could in principle learn something from him—and (3) capable in principle of saying something *true*, only then is he recognized and acknowledged as a subject." Ibid., p. 84.
51. H. G. Gadamer, *Truth and Method*, pp. 261–62.
52. On the postulate of reaching agreement in an unlimited communication community, *see* K. O. Apel, "Scientism or Transcendental Hermeneutics," in *Transformation of Philosophy* (London, 1980), pp. 93–135.
53. Gadamer, *Truth and Method*, p. 255.
54. D. Böhler, "Philosophische Hermeneutik und hermeneutische Methode," pp. 15ff. Böhler describes the special case of dogmatic hermeneutics as follows: "The interpretation of institutional texts

whose validity is presupposed in the community presents the task of bridging differences between the text and the given situation in such a way that it can actually have an action-orienting effect, that is, can be applied to the present situation of the interpreter. *The dogmatic hermeneutics* that developed from Jewish and Christian theology and from jurisprudence—the Aristotelian doctrine of phronesis might be regarded as its social-philosophical precursor—reflects upon and methodically manages the task of situationally actualizing, appropriating and applying binding practical meanings" (p. 37).

55. Ibid., pp. 40–41. Böhler's critique of Gadamer follows K. O. Apel, *Die Transformation der Philosophie,* (Frankfurt, 1973), pp. 22ff.; Habermas, "A Review of Gadamer's *Truth and Method"* pp. 356–61, and "What is Universal Pragmatics?" in *Communication and the Evolution of Society* (Boston, 1979), pp. 1–68; E. Tugendhat, *Der Wahrheitsbegriff bei Husserl und Heidegger* (Berlin, 1970), pp. 321ff. *See also,* D. Böhler, "Philosophische Hermeneutik und hermeneutische Methode," in M. Fuhrmann, H. R. Jauss, and W. Pannenberg, eds., *Text und Applikation* (Munich, 1981), pp. 483ff.

56. Alasdair MacIntyre, "Rationality and the Explanation of Acting," p. 258, gives a particularly clear statement of this thesis: "If I am correct in supposing rationality to be an inescapable sociological category, then once again the positivist account of sociology in terms of a logical dichotomy between facts and values must break down. For to characterize actions and institutionalized practices as rational or irrational is to evaluate them. Nor is it the case that this evaluation is an element superadded to an original merely descriptive element. To call an argument fallacious is always at once to describe and to evaluate it. It is highly paradoxical that the impossibility of deducing evaluative conclusions from factual premises should have been advanced as a truth of logic, when logic is itself the science in which the coincidence of description and evaluation is most obvious. The social scientist is, if I am right, committed to the values of rationality in virtue of his explanatory projects in a stronger sense than the natural scientist is. For it is not only the case that his own procedures must be rational; but he cannot escape the use of the concept of rationality in his inquiries."

57. *See* the remarks by Thomas McCarthy in W. Oelmüller, ed., *Transzendentalphilosophische Normenbegründungen* (Paderborn, 1978), pp. 134–36.

58. On the soundness of transcendental arguments in Strawson's sense, see G. Schönrich, *Kategorien und transzendentale Argumentation* (Frankfurt, 1981), pp. 182ff.

59. Alan Ryan, "Normal Science or Political Ideology?" in P. Laslett, W. G. Runciman, and Q. Skinner, eds., *Philosophy, Politics and Society,* vol. 4 (Cambridge, Eng., 1972).

60. Sheldon Wolin, "Paradigms and Political Theories," in P. King and
    B. C. Parekh, eds., *Politics and Experience* (Cambridge, Mass., 1968);
    Richard Bernstein, *The Restructuring of Social and Political Theory*
    (Philadelphia, 1978).

Chapter II: Max Weber's Theory of Rationalization

1. Karl Löwith, *Max Weber and Karl Marx* (London, 1982); S. Landshut,
   Kritik der Soziologie (Leipzig, 1969), pp. 12ff.; H. Freyer, *Soziologie
   als Wirklichkeitswissenschaft* (Darmstadt, 1964), pp. 145ff. *See also*
   my remarks in Otto Stammer, ed., *Max Weber and Sociology Today*
   (New York, 1971), pp. 59–66. Still in this tradition are D. Käsler,
   ed., *Max Weber* (Munich, 1972); Norman Birnbaum, "Conflicting
   Interpretations of the Rise of Capitalism: Marx and Weber," *British
   Journal of Sociology* 4(1953):125–40.
2. S. Kalberg, "The Discussion of Max Weber in Recent German
   Sociological Literature," *Sociology* 13(1979):127ff.
3. On the following, compare Albrecht Wellmer, "On Rationality,"
   I–IV (unpubl. MS, 1977).
4. J. Habermas, "Some Aspects of the Rationality of Action," in T.
   F. Geraets, ed., *Rationality Today* (Ottawa, 1979), pp. 185–212.
5. Niklas Luhmann, *Zweckbegriff und Systemrationalität* (Tübingen,
   1968).
6. H. Strasser, *The Normative Structure of Sociology* (London, 1976),
   pp. 44ff.
7. English transl. (London, 1955).
8. Condorcet, *Sketch*, p. 55.
9. Ibid., p. 4.
10. Ibid., p. 125.
11. Ibid., p. 136.
12. Ibid., p. 163.
13. Ibid., p. 192.
14. Ibid., p. 173.
15. Ibid., p. 193.
16. Ibid., p. 200.
17. Ibid., p. 173.
18. Michael Theunissen, *Die Verwirklichung der Vernunft*, Beiheft 6 of
    the *Philosophische Rundschau* (Tübingen, 1970).
19. J. Habermas, "Historical Materialism and the Development of
    Normative Structures," in *Communication and the Evolution of Society*
    (Boston, 1979), pp. 95–129.
20. L. Sklair, *The Sociology of Progress* (London, 1970), pp. 56ff.

21. E. Rothacker, *Logik und Systematik der Geisteswissenschaften* (Bonn, 1948).
22. T. Burger, *Max Weber's Concept of Theory Formation* (Durham, N.C., 1976); R. H. Howe, "Max Weber's Elective Affinities," *American Journal of Sociology* 84(1978):366ff.; M. Barker, "Kant as a Problem for Weber," *British Journal of Sociology* 31(1980):224ff.
23. On the influence of Nietzsche upon Max Weber, *see* E. Fleischmann, "De Weber á Nietzsche," *Archives Européennes de Sociologie* 5(1964):190ff.

Section II.1: Occidental Rationalism

1. For bibliography *see* C. Seyfarth, G. Schmidt, *Max Weber Bibliographie* (Stuttgart, 1977); G. Roth, "Max Weber. A Bibliographical Essay," in *Zeitschrift für Soziologie* (1977):91ff.; D. Käsler, ed., *Klassiker des Soziologischen Denkens,* (Munich, 1978), 2:424ff.
2. "Author's Introduction," to *The Protestant Ethic and the Spirit of Capitalism* (New York, 1958), p. 25 (hereafter abbreviated *PE*).
3. *PE*, p. 26.
4. *PE*, p. 26.
5. In *Max Weber. An Intellectual Portrait* (New York, 1960), Reinhard Bendix characterizes this form as follows:
    " 1. Official business is conducted on a continuous basis.
    2. It is conducted in accordance with stipulated rules in an administrative agency characterized by three interrelated attributes: (a) the duty of each official to do certain types of work is delimited in terms of impersonal criteria; (b) the official is given the authority necessary to carry out his assigned functions; (c) the means of compulsion at his disposal are strictly limited, and the conditions under which their employment is legitimate are clearly defined.
    3. Every official's responsibilities and authority are part of a hierarchy of authority. Higher offices are assigned the duty of supervision, lower offices the right of appeal. However, the extent of supervision and the conditions of legitimate appeal may vary.
    4. Officials and other administrative employees do not own the resources necessary for the performance of their assigned functions, but they are accountable for their use of these resources. Official business and private affairs, official revenue and private income are strictly separated.
    5. Offices cannot be appropriated by their incumbents in the sense of private property that can be sold and inherited. (This does not preclude various rights such as pension claims, regulated conditions of discipline and dismissal, etc., but such rights serve, in principle at least, as incentives for the better performance of duties. They are not property rights.)

6. Official business is conducted on the basis of written documents (p. 424)."

6. Max Weber, "Antikritisches Schlusswort zum 'Geist des Kapitalismus,'" in J. Winckelmann, ed., *Die Protestantische Ethik*, (Hamburg, 1972), 2:325.

7. Ibid., p. 324.

8. Max Weber, "Religious Rejections of the World and Their Directions," in H. H. Gerth and C. W. Mills, eds., *From Max Weber* (New York, 1958), p. 355. This essay appeared as the "Zwischenbetrachtung" of the *Gesammelte Aufsätze zur Religionssoziologie*, (Tübingen, 1963), 1:536–73); hereafter, *RRW*.

9. *RRW*, pp. 350–51.

10. *RRW*, p. 342.

11. T. W. Adorno, *Ästhetische Theorie*, vol. 17 of the *Gesammelte Schriften* (Frankfurt, 1970), p. 313.

12. *RRW*, p. 342.

13. *RRW*, p. 328.

14. *RRW*, p. 330.

15. Bendix, *Max Weber*, p. 422.

16. Ibid.

17. *RRW*, p. 328.

18. Max Weber, "The Social Psychology of the World Religions," in Gerth and Mills, eds., *From Max Weber*, p. 293; hereafter, *SPWR*.

19. Max Weber, *Economy and Society*, 2 vols, G. Roth and C. Wittich, eds., (Berkeley, 1978), p. 26; hereafter, *ES*.

20. I find previous attempts to explicate his notion of rationality to be unsatisfactory: D. Claessens, "Rationalität Revidiert," *Kölner Zeitschrift für Soziologie und Sozialpsychologie* 17(1965):465ff.; U. Vogel, "Einige Überlegungen zum Begriff der Rationalität bei Max Weber," *ibid.*, 25(1973):533ff.; A. Swidler, "The Concept of Rationality in the Work of Max Weber," *Sociological Inquiry* 43(1973):35ff.; A. Eisen, "The Meanings and Confusions of Weberian Rationality," *British Journal of Sociology* 29(1978):57ff.; W. M. Sprondel, C. Seyfarth, eds., *Max Weber und das Problem der gesellschaftlichen Rationalisierung* (Stuttgart, 1981). There is a helpful essay by S. Kalberg, "Weber's Types of Rationality: Cornerstones for the Analysis of Rationalization Processes in History," *American Journal of Sociology* 85(1980):1145ff.

21. *ES*, p. 65.

22. *ES*, p. 65.

23. Starting from this concept we can introduce the concept of "technicizing" that will be used below in discussing the theory of communication media. Actions and communication processes are "technicized" when they can be repeated as desired, according to a rule or an algorithm, and can be rendered automatic, that is, freed

from the burden of explicitly taking up and formulating the requisite intuitive knowledge. Compare N. Luhmann, *Macht* (Stuttgart, 1975), p. 71; Luhmann introduces this concept of technicization by drawing on Husserl.

24. Max Weber, "The Meaning of 'Ethical Neutrality' in Sociology and Economics," in E. Shils and H. Finch, eds., *The Methodology of the Social Sciences* (New York, 1949), p. 35.
25. Ibid.
26. Ibid.
27. *ES*, p. 30.
28. *ES*, p. 85.
29. *ES*, p. 25.
30. *ES*, p. 30.
31. *ES*, p. 627.
32. *ES*, p. 556.
33. *SPWR*, p. 293.
34. *ES*, pp. 500ff.
35. *See* Eisen, "The Meanings and Confusions of Weberian Rationality," pp. 61–62.
36. *SPWR*, p. 294.
37. Weber, *Gesammelte Aufsätze zur Religionssoziologie, (Tübingen, 1966),* 3:2n.
38. J. Weiss, *Max Webers Grundlegung der Soziologie* (Munich, 1975), pp. 137–38.
39. W. Schluchter, "Die Paradoxie der Rationalisierung," in *Rationalismus der Weltbeherrschung* (Frankfurt, 1980), p. 10.
40. In his book, *Die Entwicklung des okzidentalen Rationalismus* (Tübingen, 1979); English transl., *The Rise of Western Rationalism* (Berkeley, 1981), Schluchter takes this into account by drawing upon Kohlberg's moral theory in his interpretation of Weber. There are many points of agreement between that interpretation and the one developed here. Compare W. M. Mayrl, "Genetic Structuralism and the Analysis of Social Consciousness," *Theory and Society* 5(1978):19ff.
41. *RRW*, p. 328.
42. Weber, "The Meaning of Ethical Neutrality," p. 32. As mentioned above, Adorno held a similar position.
43. Ibid., p. 34.
44. *PE*, p. 13.
45. Schluchter, *Die Entwicklung des okzidentalen Rationalismus,* pp. 36–37.
46. *PE*, p. 26.
47. *PE*, pp. 77–78.
48. *SPWR*, pp. 293–94.
49. *PE*, p. 26.

50. *SPWR*, pp. 286–87.
51. *PE*, p. 78.
52. *PE*, pp. 193–94.

Section II.2: The Disenchantment of Religious-Metaphysical
Worldviews and the Emergence of Modern Structures of Consciousness

1. J. Habermas, *Zur Logik der Sozialwissenschaften* (Frankfurt, 1970),
   pp. 74ff.; English transl. (MIT Press, forthcoming).
2. W. Schluchter, *Die Entwicklung des okzidentalen Rationalismus*, p. 30.
3. R. Bendix, *Max Weber*, p. 47.
4. Max Weber, " Über einige Kategorien der verstehenden Soziologie,"
   in *Methodologische Schriften*, J. Winckelmann, ed., (Frankfurt, 1968),
   p. 210; English transl., "Some Categories of Interpretive Sociology,"
   Sociological Quarterly 22(1981):151–80.
5. See *ES*, pp. 29–30.
6. Weber, "Die drei reinen Typen der legitimen Herrschaft," in
   Methodologische Schriften, p. 215.
7. *ES*, p. 31.
8. *ES*, p. 319ff.
9. *ES*, p. 312.
10. *ES*, p. 326.
11. *ES*, p. 321.
12. *RRW*, p. 324.
13. *SPWR*, p. 280.
14. *RRW*, p. 324. R. Prewo tries to establish a connection between the
    methodology and the sociology of domination: the construction of
    ideal types is said to be possible only to the extent that rationalized
    systems of action develop in fact (in the sense of the institutionaliza-
    tion of purposive-rational action). *Max Webers Wissenschaftspro-
    gramm* (Frankfurt, 1979). This interpretation cannot explain why
    in his sociology of religion, for example, Weber constructs ideal
    types that refer to the ethical rationalization of worldviews and not
    to the purposive rationality of actions.
15. *SPWR*, p. 267.
16. F. H. Tenbruck, "Das Werk Max Webers," *Kölner Zeitschrift für
    Soziologie und Sozialpsychologie* 27(1975):677.
17. Ibid., p. 682.
18. Ibid., p. 682.
19. Ibid., p. 683.
20. Ibid., p. 685.
21. Robert Bellah, *Beyond Belief,* (New York, 1970); R. Döbert, *System-
    theorie und die Entwicklung religiöser Deutungssysteme* (Frankfurt,
    1973), "Die evolutionäre Bedeutung der Reformation," in C.
    Seyfarth and W. Sprondel, eds., *Religion und gesellschaftliche Ent-
    wicklung* (Frankfurt, 1973), pp. 303ff. "Zur Logik des Übergangs

von archaischen zu hochkulturellen Religionssystemen," in K. Eder, ed., *Die Entstehung von Klassengesellschaften* (Frankfurt, 1973), pp. 330ff., and "Methodologische und forschungsstrategische Implikationen von evolutionstheoretischen Studienmodellen," in U. Jaeggi and A. Honneth, eds., *Theorien des Historischen Materialismus* (Frankfurt, 1977), pp. 524ff.

22. On the state of the contemporary discussion, *see* R. van Dülmen, "Formierung der europäischen Gessellschaft in der frühen Neuzeit," *Geschichte und Gesellschaft* 7(1981):5ff.
23. Weber, *The Religion of China* (New York, 1964), pp. 226–49. *See* W. Schluchter, ed., *Max Webers Studie über das antike Judentum* (Frankfurt, 1981).
24. *See* the detailed presentation by Schluchter, *Die Entwicklung des okzidentalen Rationalismus,* pp. 230ff.
25. *SPWR,* p. 271.
26. Ibid., pp. 272–73.
27. K. Eder, ed., *Die Entstehung von Klassengesellschaften;* K. Eder, *Die Entstehung staatlich organisierter Gesellschaften* (Frankfurt, 1976).
28. *SPWR,* p. 277.
29. *SPWR,* p. 281.
30. Weber, *Gesammelte Aufsätze zur Religionssoziologie,* (Tübingen, 1966), 2:326ff.
31. Ibid., pp. 173ff.
32. *SPWR,* p. 285.
33. Ibid., p. 281.
34. E. Rothacker, *Die dogmatische Denkform in den Geisteswissenschaften und das Problem des Historismus,* Abhandlungen der Mainzer Akademie der Wissenschaft und Literatur (Wiesbaden, 1954).
35. Weber, *Religion of China,* p. 226.
36. On China, *see* ibid., pp. 198ff.
37. Ibid., pp, 226ff.
38. Weber, *Gesammelte Aufsätze zur Religionssoziologie,* 2:371ff.
39. *See* the discussion of "relations to the world" in Chap. I.3 above.
40. W. Schluchter, *Rationalisierung der Weltbeherrschung,* pp. 19–20.
41. *RRW,* p. 328.
42. *RRW,* p. 325.
43. The correlation of theocentric/cosmocentric foundations of salvation with ascetic/mystical paths to salvation should be understood merely in the sense of specific affinities. Mystical currents are just as familiar within Occidental traditions as are ascetic currents with Oriental traditions. These structurally less probable combinations have been tried at the level of virtuoso religiosity but no religions of broad cultural influence have developed from them. On this point *see* W. Schluchter, *Die Entwicklung des okzidentalen Rationalismus,* pp. 238–39: "This clarifies the discussion of two

cases that exhibit at first sight a decided similarity to Protestantism: innerworldly Confucianism and ascetic Jainism. Both manifest consequences that could well lie on the same course as ascetic Protestantism. The religious ethic of Confucianism motivates its followers to deal with the world rationally; Jainism motivates its followers to capitalism, if not in the form of factory capitalism, at least in that of trading capitalism. But the innerworldliness of Confucianism is not combined with asceticism, and the actively tinged asceticism of Jainism leads in the end away from the orders of this world. It is no accident that in neither the one nor the other case did there result a religiously motivated *domination* of the world. Confucianism's relation to the world is one of adjustment, that of Jainism—as of all radical, ascetic religions of salvation —is in the final analysis indifference to the world, even flight from the world."

44. Weber, *Religion of China*, p. 228.

45. Ibid., p. 229.

46. Joseph Needham, *Science and Civilization in China*, 4 vols. (Cambridge, Eng., 1954–1970). *See* Benjamin Nelson, "Wissenschaften und Zivilisationen, 'Osten' und 'Westen'—Joseph Needham and Max Weber," in *Der Ursprung der Moderne* (Frankfurt, 1977), pp. 7ff.

47. T. Spengler, "Die Entwicklung der chinesischen Wissenschafts- und Technikgeschichte," introduction to J. Needham, *Wissenschaftlicher Universalismus* (Frankfurt, 1977), pp. 7ff.

48. Compare Hannah Arendt, *The Life of the Mind*, 2 vols. (New York, 1978).

49. Benjamin Nelson coined the concept of "universal otherhood" to designate the form of interpersonal relations made possible by an ethical objectification of the world; *see* the introduction and epilogue to *Der Ursprung der Moderne*; *see also* his *The Idea of Usury* (Chicago, 1969).

50. A. Koyré, *From the Closed World to the Infinite Universe* (New York, 1958).

51. H. Blumenberg, "The 'Trial' of Theoretical Curiosity," part 3 of *The Legitimacy of the Modern Age* (Cambridge, Mass., 1983), pp. 229ff.

52. Ibid., parts 1 and 2.

53. Compare Adorno's critique of logical absolutism, in particular of Husserl's *Logical Investigations*, in *Against Epistemology* (Cambridge, Mass., 1983).

54. Wolfgang Krohn, "Die neue Wissenschaft der Renaissance," in G. Böhme, W. v.d.Daele, W. Krohn, *Experimentelle Philosophie* (Frankfurt, 1977), pp. 13ff.

55. Wolfgang Krohn, "Zur soziologischen Interpretation der neuzeitlichen Wissenschaft," in Krohn, ed., E. Zilsel, *Die sozialen Ursprünge*

der neuzeitlichen Wissenschaften (Frankfurt, 1976), pp. 7ff.

Section II.3: Modernization as Societal Rationalization:
The Role of the Protestant Ethic

1. The idea of an institutional embodiment and motivational anchoring of structures of consciousness that develop culturally is important for the theory of societal rationalization. This model, which Weber applies to the Reformation, can also be tried out on the Renaissance and above all the Enlightenment. *See* the interesting collection of essays edited by H. V. Gumbrecht, R. Reichardt, and T. Schleich, *Sozialgeschichte der Französischen Aufklärung*, 2 vols., (Munich, 1981).

2. R. Bendix, *Max Weber,* pp. 49ff., 381ff.

3. *ES,* p. 1394.

4. *ES,* p. 1394.

5. W. Zapf, ed., *Theorien des sozialen Wandels* (Köln, 1969); W. Zapf, "Die soziologische Theorie der Modernisierung," *Soziale Welt* 26(1975):212ff.; H. U. Wehler provides an overview in *Modernisierungstheorie und Geschichte* (Göttingen, 1975).

6. Ernst Tugendhat has examined the relations between analyses in the first and third persons in connection with a theory of moral learning: "Der Absolutheitsanspruch der Moral und die historische Erfahrung," unpubl. MS 1979. G. Frankenberg and U. Rödel make use of this idea in *Von der Volkssouveränität zum Minderheitenschutz—Die Freiheit politischer Kommunikation im Verfassungsstaat, untersucht am Beispiel der Vereinigten Staaten von Amerika* (Frankfurt, 1981). *See also* J. W. Patterson, "Moral Development and Political Thinking: The Case of Freedom of Speech," *Western Political Quarterly* (1979):7ff.

7. *PE,* p. 183.

8. Schluchter, *Die Entwicklung des okzidentalen Rationalismus,* pp. 210ff.

9. J. Winckelmann, ed., *Die Protestantische Ethik,* vol. 2 (Hamburg, 1972), p. 232.

10. *PE,* p. 117–18.

11. Schluchter, *Die Entwicklung des okzidentalen Rationalimus,* pp. 250–51.

12. Ibid., p. 251.

13. *RRW,* p. 330.

14. *RRW,* p. 329.

15. *RRW,* p. 331.

16. *RRW,* p. 339.

17. *RRW,* p. 332–33.

18. *SPWR,* p. 281.

19. *RRW,* p. 355.

20. *PE,* p. 183.
21. B. Groethysen, *Die Entstehung der bürgerlichen Welt- und Lebensanschauung in Frankreich,* 2 vols. (Frankfurt, 1979).
22. Ibid., 1:17.
23. Ibid., 2:210.
24. Ibid., 2:213.
25. I would include here, among others, the approaches to moral theory of Baier, Hare, Singer, Rawls, Lorenzen, Kambartel, Apel, and myself. Compare W. Oelmüller, *Transzendentalphilosophische Normenbegründungen* (Paderborn, 1978); R. Wimmer, *Universalisierung in der Ethik* (Frankfurt, 1980).
26. *RRW,* p. 339.
27. On the connection between ethics and the theory of science in Weber, *see* W. Schluchter, *Wertfreiheit und Verantwortungsethik, zum Verhältnis von Wissenschaft und Politik bei Max Weber* (Tübingen, 1971).
28. R. Döbert, "Methodologische und forschungsstrategische Implikationen von evolutionstheoretischen Stadienmodellen," pp. 544ff.
29. Max Weber, "The Protestant Sects and the Spirit of Capitalism," in Gerth and Mills, eds., *From Max Weber,* pp. 302-22.
30. Compare Weber's remark on the "revolution of the Anabaptists" in *RRW,* p. 340. On this point *see* R. van Dülmen, *Reformation als Revolution* (Munich, 1977); he provides additional bibliography on pp. 373ff.
31. It is from this perspective that Herbert Marcuse criticizes Weber in "Industrialization and Capitalism," in Otto Stammer, ed., *Max Weber and Sociology Today,* pp. 133-51; compare the introduction to D. Käsler, ed., *Max Weber* (Munich, 1972), pp. 7ff.
32. *RRW,* p. 328.
33. See my response to McCarthy in Held and Thompson, eds., *Habermas: Critical Debates* (Cambridge, Mass., 1982), pp. 242ff.
34. *RRW,* p. 356.
35. *RRW,* p. 334.

Section II.4: The Rationalization of Law.
Weber's Diagnosis of the Times

1. On the neoconservative potential among American social scientists, *see* P. Steinfels, *The Neoconservatives* (New York, 1979); for West Germany, *see* R. Lederer, *Neokonservative Theorie und Gesellschaftsanalyse* (Frankfurt, 1979).
2. *RRW,* p. 328.
3. Max Weber, "Science as a Vocation," in Gerth and Mills, eds., *From Max Weber,* pp. 148-49.
4. Ibid., p. 147-48.
5. *PE,* pp. 180-82.

6. *PE*, p. 182.
7. Max Weber, *Gesammelte politische Schriften* (Tubingen, 1958), pp. 60ff.
8. *ES*, p. 1209.
9. *See* the excursus on the theory of argumentation in Chap. I above.
10. Weber, "Science as a Vocation," p. 148.
11. Ibid., pp. 144–45.
12. *ES*, p. 1379. Only the first part of the passage cited is translated in *ES*; the complete passage can be found in "Über einige Kategorien der verstehenden Soziologie," in J. Winckelmann, ed., *Methodologische Schriften* (Frankfurt, 1968), pp. 201–02 [Trans.].
13. Weber, "Über einige Kategorien," p. 210.
14. *ES*, pp. 760–61.
15. *ES*, p. 882.
16. K. Eder, *Die Entstehung staatlich organisierter Gesellschaften* (Frankfurt, 1976), pp. 158ff.
17. W. Schluchter, *Die Entwicklung des okzidentalen Rationalismus*, p. 146.
18. *SPWR*, p. 294.
19. Leo Strauss, *Natural Right and History* (Chicago, 1953); C. B. McPherson, *The Political Theory of Possessive Individualism* (Oxford, 1962); W. Euchner, *Naturrecht und Politik bei John Locke* (Frankfurt, 1969); Iring Fetscher, *Rousseaus politische Philosophie* (Frankfurt, 1975).
20. *ES*, pp. 868–69.
21. *ES*, p. 37.
22. Ibid.
23. *ES*, p. 869.
24. *ES*, p. 867.
25. Niklas Luhmann, *Legitimation durch Verfahren* (Neuwied, 1969); *see* my critique of this position in J. Habermas and N. Luhmann, *Theorie der Gesellschaft oder Sozialtechnologie?* (Frankfurt, 1971), pp. 243–44.
26. *See* R. Alexy, "Eine Theorie des praktischen Diskurses," in W. Oelmüller, ed., *Normenbegründung, Normendurchsetzung* (Paderborn, 1978) pp. 22ff.; R. Dreier, "Zu Luhmanns systemtheoretischer Neuformulierung des Gerechtigkeitsproblems," in *Recht, Moral, Ideologie* (Frankfurt, 1981), pp. 270ff.
27. *ES*, p. 215.
28. J. Winckelmann, *Legitimität und Legalität in Max Webers Herrschaftssoziologie* (Tübingen, 1952); J. Habermas, *Legitimation Crisis* (Boston, 1975), pp. 97ff.; K. Eder, "Zur Rationalisierungsproblematik des modernen Rechts," *Soziale Welt* 2(1978):247ff.
29. *ES*, p. 36.
30. *ES*, p. 37.

31. *ES*, p. 37.
32. Weber, "Über einige Kategorien," pp. 212–13.
33. Ibid., p. 214.
34. To fill this gap W. Schluchter (following H. Heller) introduces "legal principles" that are supposed to function as a bridge between positive law and the foundations of an ethic of responsibility (*Die Entwicklung des okzidentalen Rationalismus*, pp. 155ff.).The status of these principles remains unclear, and they are a foreign element within Weber's systematic construction.
35. *ES*, p. 892.
36. *ES*, p. 886.
37. *ES*, p. 895.
38. *ES*, p. 894.

Chapter III. "Intermediate Reflections: Social Action, Purposive Activity, and Communication"

1. M. Brand and D. Walton, eds., *Action Theory* (Dordrecht, 1973); A. Beckermann, ed., *Analytische Handlungstheorie. Handlungserklärungen* (Frankfurt, 1977); G. Meggle, ed., *Analytische Handlungstheorie. Handlungsbeschreibungen* (Frankfurt, 1977).
2. *See* Chap. I.3 above.
3. S. Kanngiesser, "Sprachliche Universalien und diachrone Prozesse," in K. O. Apel, ed., *Sprachpragmatik und Philosophie* (Frankfurt, 1976), p. 278. *See also* T. Frentz and T. Farrell, "Language-Action. A Paradigm for Communication," *Quarterly Journal of Communication* 62(1976):333–34.
4. J. Heal, "Common Knowledge," *Philosophical Quarterly* 28(1978):116ff.; G. Meggle, ed., *Grundbegriffe der Kommunikation* (Berlin, 1981).
5. H. P. Grice, "Meaning," *Philosophical Review* 66 (1957): 377–388; idem, "Utterer's Meaning, Sentence-Meaning and Word-Meaning," *Foundations of Language* 4(1968):1–18; and idem, "Utterer's Meaning and Intentions," *Philosophical Review* 78 (1969):147–77.
6. D. Lewis, *Convention* (Cambridge, Mass., 1969).
7. S. R. Schiffer, *Meaning* (Oxford, 1972).
8. J. Bennett, *Linguistic Behavior* (Cambridge, Eng., 1976).
9. A. Leist, "Über einige Irrtümer der intentionalen Semantik," 1978, Linguistic Agency, University of Trier, Series A, Paper No. 51. On the critique of linguistic nominalism, *see also* K. O. Apel, "Intentions, Conventions and Reference to Things," in H. Parret, ed., *Meaning and Understanding* (Berlin, 1981); and idem, "Three Dimensions of Understanding and Meaning in Analytic Philosophy," *Philosophy and Social Criticism* 7(1980):115ff.

10. K. Bühler, *Sprachtheorie* (Jena, 1934).
11. Ibid., p. 28.
12. W. Busse, "Funktionen und Funktion der Sprache," in B. Schlieben-Lange, ed., *Sprachtheorie* (Hamburg, 1975), p. 207; and G. Beck, *Sprechakte und Sprachfunktionen* (Tübingen, 1980).
13. R. Jakobson, "Linguistics and Poetics," in *Style in Language*, T. A. Sebeok, ed., (New York, 1960), pp. 350–77.
14. P. Watzlawick, J. H. Beavin, and D. D. Jackson, *Pragmatics of Human Communication* (New York, 1962); H. Hörmann, *Psychologie der Sprache* (Heidelberg, 1967) and *Meinen und Verstehen* (Frankfurt, 1976).
15. K. O. Apel, *Analytic Philosophy of Language and the Geisteswissenschaften* (Dordrecht, 1967); *see also* S. Davis, "Speech Acts, Performance and Competence," *Journal of Pragmatics* 3(1979):497ff.
16. J. Habermas, "What is Universal Pragmatics?" in *Communication and the Evolution of Society* (Boston, 1978), pp. 1–68.
17. K. O. Apel, "Zwei paradigmatische Antworten auf die Frage nach der Logosauszeichnung der Sprache," *Festschrift für W. Perpeet* (Bonn, 1980).
18. *See* Chap. I.3 above.
19. Ludwig Wittgenstein, *On Certainty* (New York, 1972).
20. *Economy and Society,* G. Roth and C. Wittich, eds., 2 vols. (Berkeley, 1978), p. 4. Hereafter cited as *ES.*
21. Max Weber, 'Über einige Kategorien der verstehenden Soziologie," in *Methodologische Schriften,* J. Winckelmann, ed., (Frankfurt, 1968), p. 194.
22. H. Girndt, *Das soziale Handeln als Grundkategorie der erfahrungswissenschaftlichen Soziologie* (Tübingen, 1967).
23. *ES,* p. 4.
24. *ES,* p. 26.
25. *ES,* p. 24–25.
26. W. Schluchter, *Die Entwicklung des okzidentalen Rationalismus* (Tübingen, 1979), p. 192.
27. *ES,* p. 327.
28. *ES,* p. 326.
29. *ES,* pp. 26–36, 319–33.
30. Weber, "Über einige Kategorien."
31. J. L. Austin, *How To Do Things with Words* (Oxford, 1962).
32. I shall leave aside the development that speech act theory underwent in the hands of Austin himself (see my "What is Universal Pragmatics?", pp. 44ff.) and take as my point of departure the interpretation that Searle has given to this theory. John Searle, *Speech Acts* (London, 1969); and D. Wunderlich, *Studien zur Sprechakttheorie* (Frankfurt, 1976).
33. Austin, *How To Do Things with Words,* p. 101.
34. B. Schlieben-Lange, *Linguistische Pragmatik* (Stuttgart, 1975), pp. 86ff.

35. D. S. Schwayder, *The Stratification of Behavior* (London, 1965), pp. 287ff.
36. M. Meyer, *Formale und handlungstheoretische Sprachbetrachtungen* (Stuttgart, 1976).
37. M. Schwab, *Redehandeln* (Königstein, 1980), pp. 28ff.
38. Austin, *How To Do Things with Words*, p. 118.
39. P. Strawson, "Intention and Convention in Speech Acts," *Philosophical Review* 73(1964):439ff.
40. Compare J. Habermas, "What is Universal Pragmatics?": "With institutionally bound speech actions, specific institutions are always involved. With institutionally unbound speech actions, only conditions of a generalized context must typically be met for a corresponding act to succeed...To explain what acts of betting or christening mean, I must refer to the institutions of betting or christening. By contrast, commands or advice or questions do not represent institutions but types of speech acts that can fit very different institutions. To be sure, 'institutional bond' is a criterion that does not always permit an unambiguous classification. Commands can exist wherever relations of authority are institutionalized; appointments presuppose special, bureaucratically developed organizations; and marriages require a single institution (which is, however, found universally). But this does not destroy the usefulness of the analytic point of view. Institutionally unbound speech actions, insofar as they have any regulative meaning at all, are related to various aspects of action norms in general; they are not essentially fixed by particular institutions" (pp. 38–39).
41. Compare D. Wunderlich, "Zur Konventionalität von Sprechhandlungen," in D. Wunderlich, ed., *Linguistische Pragmatik* (Frankfurt, 1972), pp. 16–17; Wunderlich also gives there a linguistic characterization of speech acts in standard form.
42. Even the use theory of meaning stemming from the later work of Wittgenstein (*see* W. P. Alston, *The Philosophy of Language* (Englewood Cliffs, N.J., 1964); Ernst Tugendhat, *Vorlesungen zur Einführung in die sprachanalytische Philosophie* (Frankfurt, 1976)) remains fixated on the solitary employment of sentences. Like Frege's theory of meaning, it takes its orientation from the non-communicative use of assertoric sentences *in foro interno;* it abstracts from the interpersonal relations between speakers and hearers coming to an understanding about something by way of communicative acts. Tugendhat justifies this self-limitation of semantics with the claim that the communicative use of language is constitutive only for special linguistic expressions, in particular for the performative verbs and for the speech acts formed with them; in the areas essential to semantics, however, language can be employed in a monological train of thought. There is in fact an intuitively accessible distinction between

thinking in propositions in abstraction from speaker-hearer relations and imagining interpersonal relations. In imagining stories in which I—the imagining subject—have a place in a context of interactions, the roles of participants in the first, second, and third persons—however internalized—remain constitutive for the sense of what is thought or represented. But solitary thought in propositions is also discursive in more than a figurative sense. This becomes evident when the validity, and thereby the assertoric force, of a proposition becomes problematic and the solitary thinker has to go from inferring to devising and weighing hypotheses. He then finds it necessary to assume the roles of proponent and opponent as a communicative relation in his thought—as the daydreamer takes up the narrative structure of speaker-hearer relations when he recalls scenes from everyday life.

43. If, for example, a promise were to take the form:

1.+ I promise you that I was in Hamburg yesterday.

one of the grammatical conditions of well-formedness would be violated. By contrast, if S uttered the correct sentence (1) in a situation in which it was presupposed that H could count on a visit from S in any case, one of the contextual conditions typically presupposed for promises would be violated.

44. Contributions to speech-act theory from philosophy and linguistics are chiefly concerned with analyzing these conditions. D. Wunderlich analyzes speech acts of giving advice from the theoretical perspective developed by Searle, in *Grundlagen der Linguistik* (Hamburg, 1974), pp. 349ff.

45. R. Bartsch speaks in this sense of "acceptability conditions" in contrast to conditions of correctness or validity, in "Die Rolle von pragmatischen Korrektheitsbedingungen bei der Interpretation von Äusserungen," in G. Grewendorf, ed., *Sprechakttheorie und Semantik* (Frankfurt, 1979), pp. 217ff.

46. Surprisingly, Searle also comes close to this view of intentionalist semantics in *Speech Acts* (London, 1969), p. 66. Compare S. R. Schiffer, *Meaning* (Oxford, 1972).

47. M. Schwab, *Redehandeln* (Königstein, 1980).

48. In the case of commands or directions, principally for the addressees; in the case of promises or announcements, principally for the speaker; in the case of agreements or contracts, symmetrically for both parties; in the case of advice (with a normative content) or warnings, for both sides but asymmetrically.

49. On these speech-immanent obligations, *see* J. Habermas "What is Universal Pragmatics?," pp. 62ff.

50. *See* Volume 2, Chap. V.1 below.

51. Because Schwab distinguishes neither between simple and normed

requests, imperatives and commands, nor between monologically and communicatively employed intention sentences—that is, between intentions and declarations of intention—he draws a mistaken parallel between imperatives and declarations of intention and distinguishes both from constative speech acts by virtue of the separation and hierarchical ordering of success in the sense of validity and success in the sense of fulfillment. *Redehandeln,* pp. 72–73, 74ff., 95ff.

52. E. Stenius, "Mood and Language Game," *Synthese* 17(1967):254ff.; compare D. Follesdal, "Comments on Stenius' 'Mood and Language Game,'" *Synthese* 17(1967):275ff.

53. A. Leist, "Was heisst Universalpragmatik?," *Germanistische Linguistik* 5/6(1977):93.

54. Ibid., pp. 97–98.

55. Ibid., p. 109.

56. H. P. Grice, "Logic and Conversation," in P. Cole and J. L. Morgan, eds., *Syntax and Semantics* (New York, 1975), 3:41ff.; A. P. Martinich, "Conversational Maxims and Some Philosophical Problems," *Philosophical Quarterly* 30(1980):215ff.

57. For other objections of this kind, *see* John Thompson, "Universal Pragmatics," in Thompson and Held, eds., *Habermas: Critical Debates* (Cambridge, Mass., 1982), pp. 116–33.

58. A. Leist, "Was heisst Universalpragmatik?," p. 102; K. Graham, "Belief and the Limits of Irrationality," *Inquiry* 17(1974):315ff.

59. Searle refers to this argument in *Expression and Meaning* (Cambridge, Eng., 1979).

60. Ernst Tugendhat, *Selbstbewusstsein und Selbstbestimmung* (Frankfurt, 1979), lectures 5 and 6; English transl. (MIT Press, forthcoming).

61. L. Wittgenstein, *Zettel,* G. E. M. Anscombe and G. H. von Wright, eds. (Berkeley, 1970), ¶404, 549.

62. Tugendhat, *Selbstbewusstsein und Selbstbestimmung,* p. 131.

63. L. Wittgenstein, *Philosophical Investigations* (New York, 1966), p. 222. Compare S. Hampshire, *Feeling and Expression* (London, 1961); B. Aune, "On the Complexity of Avowals," in M. Black, ed., *Philosophy in America* (London, 1965), pp. 35ff.; D. Gustafson, "The Natural Expression of Intention," *Philosophical Forum* 2(1971):299ff.; D. Gustafson, "Expressions of Intentions," *Mind* 83(1974):321ff.; N. R. Norrick, "Expressive Illocutionary Acts," *Journal of Pragmatics* 2(1978):277ff.

64. M. Dummett, "What is a Theory of Meaning?" in G. Evans and J. McDowell, eds., *Truth and Meaning* (Oxford, 1976), pp. 67ff.

65. Ernst Tugendhat, *Vorlesungen zur Einführung in die sprachanalytische Philosophie* (Frankfurt, 1976), pp. 256ff.

66. Dummett, "What is a Theory of Meaning?," p. 81.

67. Ibid., pp. 110–11.

68. Ibid., p. 126.
69. P. M. S. Hacker, *Illusion and Insight* (Oxford, 1972), chaps. VIII and IX.
70. A convincing example of this is P. F. Strawson's analysis of the resentments called forth by moral violations, in *Freedom and Resentment* (London, 1974), pp. 150ff.
71. J. L. Austin, *How To Do Things with Words,* pp. 150ff.
72. One should not, however, make the requirements as strong as T. Ballmer does in "Probleme der Klassification von Sprechakten," in G. Grewendorf, ed., *Sprechakttheorie und Semantik* (Frankfurt, 1979), pp. 247ff.
73. J. Searle, "A Taxonomy of Illocutionary Acts," in *Expression and Meaning* (Cambridge, Eng., 1979), pp. 1ff.
74. D. Wunderlich "Skizze zu einer integrierten Theorie der grammatischen und pragmatischen Bedeutung," in *Studien zur Sprechakttheorie* (Frankfurt, 1976), pp. 51ff.; "Was ist das für ein Sprechakt?," in Grewendorf, ed., *Sprechakttheorie und Semantik,* pp. 275ff.; idem, "Aspekte einer Theorie der Sprechhandlungen," in H. Lenk, ed., *Handlungstheorien* (Munich, 1980), 3:381ff.; B. G. Campbell, "Toward a Working Theory of Illocutionary Forces," *Language and Style* 8(1975):3ff.; M. Kreckel, *Communicative Acts and Shared Knowledge in Natural Discourse* (London, 1981).
75. One measure of the flexibility of a society is the share of the totality of available illocutionary possibilities made up by institutionally more-or-less-bound, idiomatically set, ritualized speech acts. Thus Wunderlich distinguishes speech acts according to whether they depend more on action norms or on action situations (Wunderlich, "Skizze," pp. 86ff.) Campbell uses the dimensions "institutional vs. vernacular" and "positional vs. interactional" (Campbell, "Working Taxonomy"). In this regard, the dimension "initiative vs. reactive" is also relevant (Wunderlich, "Skizze," pp. 59ff.).
76. On the speech acts that serve to organize speech, *see* E. Schegloff and G. Jefferson, "A Simplist Semantics for the Organization of Turn-Taking for Conversation," *Language* 50(1974):696ff., which draws on the work of Harvey Sacks; *see also* D. Wunderlich, *Studien zur Sprechakttheorie,* pp. 330ff.
77. For this class of speech acts the most likely thesis may still be that *S,* through his illocutionary act, informs the hearer of the execution of this act, or tells him that the act is being carried out. For a critique of this thesis (which has been advanced by Lemmon, Hedenius, Wiggins, D. Lewis, Schiffer, Warnock, Cresswell, and others), *see* G. Grewendorf, "Haben explizit performative Äusserungen einen Wahrheitswert?," in Grewendorf, ed., *Sprechakttheorie und Semantik,* pp. 175ff. It is, of course, wrong to assimilate operatives, which express the carrying out of constructive performances, to cognitive

speech acts. The speaker connects with them not a claim to propositional truth but to constructive well-formedness or intelligibility.

78. W. Kummer, *Grundlagen der Texttheorie* (Hamburg, 1975); M. Halliday, *System and Function in Language: Selected Papers* (Oxford, 1976); K. Bach and R. M. Hanisch, *Linguistic Communication and Speech Acts* (Cambridge, Eng., 1979).

79. M. Coulthard, *An Introduction to Discourse Analysis* (London, 1977); L. Churchill, *Questioning Strategies in Sociolinguistics* (Rowley, Mass., 1978); J. Schenken, ed., *Studies in the Organization of Conversational Interaction* (New York, 1978); S. Jacobs, "Recent Advances in Discourse Analysis," *Quarterly Journal of Speech* 66(1980):450ff.

80. D. Hymes, ed., *Language in Culture and Society* (New York, 1964) and "Models of the Interactions of Language and Social Life," in J. Gumperz and D. Hymes, eds., *Directions in Sociolinguistics* (New York, 1972), pp. 35ff.

81. R. Rommetveit, *On Message-Structure* (New York, 1974).

82. K. O. Apel, "Sprechakttheorie und transzendentale Sprachpragmatik," in Apel, ed., *Sprachpragmatik und Philosophie*, pp. 10ff.; J. Habermas, "What is Universal Pragmatics?."

83. *See* the critical appraisal of the formal-pragmatic approaches of Allwood, Grice, and myself in Kreckel, *Communicative Acts*, pp.14ff.

84. Classification into constative, regulative, and expressive speech acts means that we attribute a dominant basic attitude to the speaker. In admitting a performative attitude we are taking account of the fact that complex processes of reaching understanding can succeed only if each speaker undertakes an orderly, rationally controlled transition from one attitude (be it objectivating, norm-conformative, or expressive) to the others. Such transformations are based on intermodal invariances of validity. This area of the logic of speech acts has scarcely been studied. Why, for example, can we infer from the validity of an expressive speech act, $M_e p$, to the validity of a corresponding speech act of the form $M_c p$? If Peter truthfully confesses to loving Frances, we feel entitled to accept as true the assertion that Peter loves Frances. And if, conversely, the assertion that Peter loves Frances is true, we feel entitled to accept as truthful Peter's confession that he loves Frances. This transition could be justified by the rules of propositional logic only if we could assimilate expressive to constative speech acts or experiential sentences to assertoric sentences. Since we cannot, we have to look for formal-pragmatic rules for the connections among speech acts that appear with the same propositional content in different modes. The table in Figure 17 is meant merely to illustrate which transitions we intuitively regard as allowable (+) and which not (−). These phenomena cannot be explained by the familiar modal logics. On the constructivist approach to a pragmatic logic, *see* C. F. Geth-

mann, ed., *Theorie des wissenschaftlichen Argumentieriens* (Frankfurt, 1980), part 3, pp. 165–240; and C. F. Gethmann, *Protologik* (Frankfurt, 1979).

Figure 17
Intermodal Transfer of Validity Between Speech Acts
with the Same Propositional Content

From:	To: Constative Speech Acts (truth)	To: Expressive Speech Acts (truthfulness)	To: Regulative Speech Acts (rightness)
Constative Speech Acts (truth)	x	+	–––
Expressive Speech Acts (truthfulness)	+	x	–––
Regulative Speech Acts (rightness)	–––	+	x

85. This is the methodological meaning of Searle's "principle of expressibility," *Speech Acts* (Cambridge, Eng., 1970), pp. 87–88. Compare T. Binkley, "The Principle of Expressibility," *Philosophy and Phenomenological Research* 39(1979):307ff.

86. J. Habermas, "Universalpragmatische Hinweise auf das System der Ich-Abgrenzungen," in M. Auwärter, E. Kirsch, M. Schröter, eds., *Kommunikation, Interaktion, Identität* (Frankfurt, 1976), pp. 332ff.; idem, "Some Distinctions in Universal Pragmatics," *Theory and Society* 3(1976):155–67. *See also* the empirical study by Auwärter and Kirsch, "Die konversationelle Generierung von Situationsdefinitionen im Spiel 4- bis 6 jähriger Kinder," in W. Schulte, ed., *Soziologie in der Gesellschaft* (Bremen, 1981), pp. 584ff.

87. J. M. Ruskin, "An Evaluative Review of Family Interaction Research," *Family Process* 11(1972):365ff.; J. H. Weakland, "The Double Bind Theory: A Reflexive Hindsight," *Family Process* 13(1974):269ff.; S. S. Kety, "From Rationalization to Reason," *American Journal of Psychiatry* 131(1974):957ff.; D. Reiss, "The Family and Schizophrenia," *American Journal of Psychiatry* 133(1976):181ff.

88. J. Searle, "Literal Meaning," in *Expression and Meaning*, pp. 117ff. *See also* R. D. Van Valin, "Meaning and Interpretation," *Journal of Pragmatics* 4(1980):213ff.
89. G. E. Moore, "Proof of an External World," *Proceedings of the British Academy* (London, 1939).
90. Ludwig Wittgenstein, *On Certainty* (New York, 1969) ¶ 103, p. 16.
91. Ibid., ¶ 102, p. 16.
92. Ibid., ¶ 144, p. 21.
93. Ibid., ¶ 205, p. 28.

Chapter IV. From Lukacs to Adorno: Rationalization as Reification

1. Karl Löwith, *Max Weber and Karl Marx* (London, 1982); W. Schluchter, *Wertfreiheit und Verantwortungsethik, zum Verhältnis von Wissenschaft und Politik bei Max Weber* (Tübingen, 1971); Norman Birnbaum, "Conflicting Interpretations of the Rise of Capitalism: Marx and Weber," *British Journal of Sociology* IV(1953):125–40; Anthony Giddens, "Marx, Weber and the Development of Capitalism," *Sociology* 4(1970):289–310.
2. See Chap. III, above.

Section IV.1: Max Weber in the Tradition of Western Marxism

3. On the history of the Frankfurt School during the emigration, *see* Martin Jay, *The Dialectical Imagination* (Boston, 1973); Helmut Dubiel, *Wissenschaftsorganisation und politische Erfahrung* (Frankfurt, 1978), English transl. (MIT Press, forthcoming); David Held, *Introduction to Critical Theory* (London, 1980).
4. Max Horkheimer, *Eclipse of Reason* (New York, 1974); hereafter cited as *EoR*.
5. *EoR*, preface, p. v.
6. *EoR*, p. 10.
7. *EoR*, p. 5.
8. *EoR*, p. 5.
9. *EoR*, p. 12.
10. *EoR*, p. 19.
11. Max Horkheimer and Theodor Adorno, *Dialectic of Enlightenment* (New York, 1972); hereafter cited as *DoE*.
12. *DoE*, pp. 117–18.
13. *EoR*, p. 40.
14. *DoE*, p. 23.
15. *EoR*, pp. 23–24.
16. Max Weber bears witness to this heroic self-understanding of modern science in his lecture on "Science as a Vocation," in

Gerth and Mills, eds., *From Max Weber,* pp. 129-56. Karl Popper also professes this kind of subjectivism, as he bases scientific criticism not on a grounded choice between knowledge and faith but on an irrational decision between "two kinds of faith." K. R. Popper, *The Open Society and Its Enemies,* (London, 1966), 2:246. *See* my critique of this view in "Dogmatism, Reason and Decision," in *Theory and Practice* (Boston, 1973), pp. 253-82.

17. *EoR,* pp. 144-45.
18. *EoR,* pp. 137-38.
19. *EoR,* pp. 138-39.
20. Max Weber, *Economy and Society,* G. Roth and C. Wittich, eds., 2 vols. (Berkeley, 1978), p. 1156; hereafter cited as *ES.*
21. W. Mommsen, *Max Weber, Gesellschaft, Politik und Geschichte* (Frankfurt, 1974), p. 138; *see also* his *Max Weber und die deutsche Politik 1890 bis 1920* (Tübingen, 1959).
22. David Riesman, *The Lonely Crowd* (New Haven, 1950).
23. *EoR,* pp. 95-96.
24. *EoR,* p. 98.
25. Under the rubric of "options versus ligatures" R. Dahrendorf again takes up this idea of a dialectic between growing possibilities of choice and increasingly weaker bonds, in *Lebenschancen* (Frankfurt, 1979).
26. Compare the picture of the plebiscitarian leader that Wolfgang Mommsen draws in *Max Weber, Gesellschaft, Politik und Geschichte,* pp. 136-37: "The politician is obligated only to himself and to the task he has chosen in the light of certain personal value ideals. His responsibility is limited to 'proving his worth'; that is, he has to show by his successes that the unconditional surrender of his followers to him purely as a person has an inner justification. On the other hand, there are no obligations in regard to the material goals of the masses; Weber emphatically attacks any hint of the theory that the democratic leader has to carry out the mandate of those who elect him. On his view, what is proper to the plebiscitarian *Führerdemokratie* is a binding of the masses to the person of the leading politician and not their substantive conviction of the value of the aims pursued. It is not the substantive goals as such that decide the outcome of an election but the personal charismatic qualification of the candidate for leader. Only in this way can Weber conceive of the independent domination of the great individual under modern conditions, without prejudice to any constitutional safeguards. He describes *Führerdemokratie* as a continual competition among politicians for the favor of the masses. It is carried on primarily with demagogic means; a system of formal rules of the game ensures that the victorious politician has to prove himself and that if he fails he must step aside."

27. *DoE,* pp. 29–30.
28. *DoE,* p. 30.
29. *EoR,* p. 145.
30. Compare Maurice Merleau-Ponty, *Adventures of the Dialectic* (Evanston, Ill., 1973), pp. 30ff.
31. *DoE,* "Introduction."
32. Georg Lukacs, *History and Class Consciousness* (Cambridge, Mass., 1971), pp. 83–222; cited hereafter as *HCC.*
33. *HCC,* p. 83. I shall not be discussing the aesthetic and culture-critical writings of the young Lukacs. For the concept of a form of objectivity, "Die Seele und die Formen" and the "Theorie des Romans" are particularly important. *See* A. Heller, P. Feher, G. Markus, and R. Radnoti, *Die Seele und das Leben* (Frankfurt, 1977); A. Arato and P. Breines, *The Young Lukacs and the Origins of Western Marxism* (New York, 1979), part 2.
34. *HCC,* p. 153.
35. *EoR,* pp. 9ff.
36. *HCC,* p. 92.
37. Karl Marx, *Capital* (New York, 1906).
38. *Capital,* p. 83.
39. H. G. Backhaus, "Zur Dialektik der Warenform," in A. Schmidt, ed., *Beiträge zur Marxistischen Erkenntnistheorie* (Frankfurt, 1969); H. J. Krahl, "Zum Verhältnis von *Kapital* und Hegelscher Wesenslogik," in O. Negt, ed., *Aktualität und Folgen der Philosophie Hegels* (Frankfurt, 1970); P. Mattik, "Die Marxsche Arbeitswerttheorie," in F. Eberle, ed., *Aspekte der Marxschen Theorie I* (Frankfurt, 1973); J. Zeleny, *Die Wissenschaftslogik und das Kapital* (Frankfurt, 1973); D. Horster, *Erkenntnis-Kritik als Gesellschaftstheorie* (Hannover, 1978) pp. 187ff.
40. *HCC,* p. 99. I shall take up the concept of "abstract labor" in my "Concluding Reflections," vol. 2, Chap. VIII.
41. H. Dahmer develops this idea in connection with his study of the Marxistically inspired social psychology of the Freudian left: *Libido und Gesellschaft* (Frankfurt, 1973).
42. Karl Marx, *Grundrisse der Kritik der Politischen Ökonomie* (Berlin, 1953), pp. 908–09.
43. Ibid., p. 909.
44. *HCC,* p. 88.
45. *See* volume 2, Chap. VII, Section 2.
46. *HCC,* p. 93.
47. *HCC,* p. 100.
48. *HCC,* p. 101.
49. *HCC,* p. 120.
50. *HCC,* p. 121.
51. This is the point of departure for the work of Alfred Sohn-Rethel; *see* esp. *Intellectual and Manual Labor* (Atlantic Highlands, N.J., 1978).

52. *HCC,* p. 139.
53. *HCC,* pp. 136–37.
54. *HCC,* p. 142.
55. *See* the controversy between Lukacs and Adorno, Georg Lukacs, *Wider den missverstandenen Realismus* (Hamburg, 1958).
56. *HCC,* p. 148.
57. Merleau Ponty's important, but admittedly "very free," Lukacs interpretation ignores this point: "This 'philosophy of history' does not so much give us the key to history as restore history to us as a permanent interrogation; it does not so much give us a certain truth hidden behind empirical history as present empirical history as the genealogy of truth. It is quite superficial to say that Marxism reveals to us the meaning of history; it binds us to our time and its partialities; it does not describe the future for us; it does not stop our questioning; on the contrary, it intensifies it. It shows us the present worked on by a self-criticism, a power of negation and sublation which has historically been delegated to the proletariat" (*Adventures of the Dialectic,* pp. 56–57). Merleau-Ponty here assimilates the position of the young Lukacs to an existential Marxism for which what counts is not so much an objective sense of history as the removal of non-sense. Lukacs himself revoked the thesis developed in *HCC* in his preface to the new edition (1967). It is by no means necessary to accept his self-criticism on all points, even if there is one point on which we can agree: "But is the identical subject-object anything more in truth than a purely metaphysical construct? Can an identical subject-object really be created by self-knowledge, however adequate, even if this were based on an adequate knowledge of the social world—that is to say, by self-consciousness no matter how perfect? We need only to formulate the question precisely to see that it must be answered in the negative. For the content of knowledge does not thereby lose its alienated character. In the *Phenomenology of Spirit* Hegel rightly rejected the mystical irrationalistic realization of an identical subject-object, Schelling's "intellectual intuition," and demanded a philosophically rational solution of the problem. His healthy sense of reality led him to leave this standing as a demand; it is true that his most general construction of the world culminates in the perspective of its realization; but within his system he never shows concretely how this demand could be fulfilled. The proletariat as the identical subject-object of real human history is thus not a materialist realization that overcomes the idealist thought-construction; it is rather an effort to out-Hegel Hegel, a construction boldly raised in thought above all reality, and thus an attempt objectively to surpass the master himself" (p. xxiii). Compare Arato and Breines, *The Young Lukacs,* part 2; J. P. Arnasson sees the conception

of HCC as less consistent. *See* my remarks on Merleau-Ponty in "Literaturbericht zur philosophischen Diskussion um Marx und den Marxismus," in *Theorie und Praxis* (Frankfurt, 1971), pp. 387–463, here pp. 422ff.

58. Lukacs, "Towards a Methodology of the Problem of Organization," in *HCC*, pp. 295–342. Compare my critique in the "Introduction" to *Theory and Practice* (Boston, 1973), pp. 32ff.

59. Albrecht Wellmer, "Communication and Emancipation: Reflections on the Linguistic Turn in Critical Theory," in J. O'Neill, ed., *On Critical Theory* (New York, 1976), pp. 241–42. [There are some differences between the English and German versions; Habermas cites the latter, which I have translated in the text. Trans.]

Section IV.2: The Critique of Instrumental Reason

1. For now I shall leave to one side the position developed in the 1930s by the Frankfurt School and take it up instead in vol. 2, Chap. VIII, Section 3.

2. By taking the *Dialectic of Enlightenment* as my point of reference for discussing the reception of Weber, I shall be able to say little beyond a few incidental remarks about the unmistakable differences between the positions of Horkheimer and Adorno. On the interpretation of Adorno advanced by the editors of his collected works, H. Schweppenhäuser and R. Tiedemann—an interpretation that considers itself to be orthodox—*see* F. Grenz, *Adornos Philosophie in Grundbegriffen* (Frankfurt, 1974). By contrast, Alfred Schmidt maintains the continuity of critical theory in its Horkheimerian version, in *Zur Idee der Kritischen Theorie* (Munich, 1974) and *Die Kritische Theorie als Geschichtsphilosophie* (Munich, 1976).

3. Helmut Dubiel, *Wissenschaftsorganisation und politische Erfahrung*, pp. 15–135.

4. Wellmer, "Communication and Emancipation," p. 237.

5. Herbert Marcuse, *One-Dimensional Man* (Boston, 1964); compare my remarks in "Technology and Science as 'Ideology,'" in *Toward a Rational Society* (Boston, 1970), pp. 81–122, and "The Place of Philosophy in Marxism," *Insurgent Sociologist* 5(1975):41–48.

6. *HCC*, p. 101.

7. *HCC*, p. 168.

8. *HCC*, p. 172.

9. *DoE*, pp. 120–67.

10. *See* Horkheimer, "The Revolt of Nature," in *EoR*, pp. 92–127. I shall here confine myself to the social-psychological side of a theory for which the economic works of F. Pollock were also important. On the differentiated analyses of fascism in the Institute for Social Research during the years 1939–1942, see the documentary volume edited and introduced by H. Dubiel and A. Söllner, *Horkheimer, Pollock, Neumann, Kirchheimer, Gurland, Marcuse: Wirtschaft, Recht und Staat im Nationalsozialismus* (Frankfurt, 1981).

11. *EoR,* p. 109.
12. *See* the contributions to the issue of *Esprit* devoted to the Frankfurt School, May 1978.
13. *EoR,* pp. 121–22.
14. On this thesis, compare R. Dahrendorf, *Society and Democracy in Germany* (New York, 1967).
15. *EoR,* pp. 122–23.
16. Erich Fromm, *Arbeiter und Angestellte am Vorabend des Dritten Reiches. Eine soialpsychologische Untersuchung,* W. Bonss, ed. (Stuttgart, 1980).
17. T. Adorno, E. Frenkel-Brunswik, D. J. Levinson, and R. N. Sanford, *The Authoritarian Personality* (New York, 1950); compare M. V. Freyhold, *Autoritärismus und politische Apathie* (Frankfurt, 1971).
18. *HCC,* p. 172.
19. In *The Essential Frankfurt School Reader,* Andrew Arato and Eike Gebhardt, eds., (New York, 1978), pp. 270–99.
20. Ibid., p. 279.
21. *DoE,* p. 141.
22. J. Habermas, "Consciousness-Raising or Redemptive Criticism," *New German Critique* 17(1979):30–59.
23. *DoE,* p. 222.
24. See volume 2, Chap. VIII, Section 3.
25. *HCC,* p. 211, n. 9.
26. In his inaugural lecture at Frankfurt University in 1931 Adorno had already rejected Lukacs' proposed solution to the problem of the thing-in-itself because it rested on a genetic fallacy. "Die Aktualität der Philosophie," in *Gesammelte Schriften* (Frankfurt, 1973), 1:337.
27. Theodor Adorno, *Negative Dialektik,* in *Gesammelte Schriften* (Frankfurt, 1973), 6:21; English transl., *Negative Dialectics* (New York, 1973).
28. In *The Origin of Negative Dialectics* Susan Buck-Morss elaborates the genuine Adorno-line of critical theory and stresses the continuity of his philosophy from the early 1930s to the mature works, *Negative Dialectics* and *Aesthetic Theory.* In his early philosophical writings Adorno already began with a renunciation of the illusion "that it is possible to grasp in thought the totality of the real" (*Gesammelte Schriften,* 1:325). From the very start he criticized the idealism, acknowledged or unacknowledged, of identity thinking, whether in the form of the Hegelian system or in the neo-ontological thought of Heidegger. In his lecture "Die Idee der Naturgeschichte," we find the strongest version of his Heidegger critique: "For Heidegger, history, understood as an encompassing structure of being, is synonymous with the ontology of being. From this we get such feeble antitheses as that between 'history' and 'historicity'—to which there is nothing more than that some

qualities of being observed in connection with *Dasein* are removed from entities, transposed into the domain of ontology and made into ontological determinations, and are thus supposed to contribute to interpreting what is in reality merely said over again. This element of tautology does not derive from accidental features of the form of language being used; it adheres necessarily to the ontological line of questioning itself, which holds fast to the onto-logical endeavor but, owing to its rational point of departure, is not in a position to interpret itself ontologically as what it is— namely, something produced by and conceptually related to the starting point of an idealist *ratio*'' (ibid., pp. 351–52). And again: "The tautological tendency seems to me to be explained through nothing other than the old idealist motif of identity. It arises from the fact that a being (*Sein*) which is historical is brought under a subjective category of historicity; the historical being compre-hended under the subjective category of historicity is supposed to be identical with history. It is supposed to accommodate itself to the determinations stamped upon it by historicity. The tautology appears to me to be less a self-plumbing of the mythical depths of language than a new concealment of the old classical thesis of the identity of subject and object. And if Heidegger has recently taken a turn toward Hegel, that appears to confirm this reading" (ibid., pp. 353–54). It is only later that Adorno radicalizes this critique of identity-thinking into a critique of identifying thought generally, which denies to philosophy not only the claim to totality but the hope for a dialectical grasp of the nonidentical. In 1931 Adorno still spoke confidently of the "actuality of philosophy" because he still believed it capable of a polemical, nonaffirmative grasp of a reality that preserves in vestiges and remnants the hope of someday arriving at a right and just reality. *Negative Dialectics* gives up this hope.

29. *Negative Dialektik*, pp. 322–23.
30. G. Rose, *The Melancholy Science. An Introduction to the Thought of Theodor Adorno* (London, 1978), pp. 43ff. On the concept of reification in Adorno, *see also* F. Grenz, *Adornos Philosophie*, pp. 35ff.
31. *Negative Dialektik*, p. 191.
32. Y. H. Krikorian, ed., *Naturalism and the Human Spririt* (New York, 1944).
33. From the ranks of the neoconservatives, recruited in great num-bers from the schools of J. Ritter and E. Voegelin, R. Spaemann stands out: *Zur kritik der politischen Utopie* (Stuttgart, 1977).
34. *EoR*, pp. 61–62.
35. *EoR*, p. 80.
36. *EoR*, p. 77.

37. This has been taken seriously as a requirement by the second generation of critical theorists, as can be seen in the works of Apel, Schnädelbach, Wellmer, myself, and others.
38. *EoR*, pp. 81–82. On the concept of the "empirical" in early critical theory, *see* Wolfgang Bonss, *Kritische Theorie und empirische Sozialforschung* (diss., University of Bielefeld, 1981), *Die Einübung des Tatsachenblicks* (Frankfurt, 1982).
39. Richard Bernstein, *The Restructuring of Social and Political Theory* (Philadelphia, 1978).
40. J. Habermas, *Knowledge and Human Interests* (Boston, 1971).
41. *Negative Dialectics* (New York, 1973).
42. On the derivative status of exchange rationality in the work of Adorno, *see* J. F. Schmucker, *Adorno—Logik des Zerfalls* (Stuttgart, 1977), pp. 105ff.
43. Compare Schmucker, *Adorno*, p. 106: "Whereas for a member of modern exchange society the dialectic of self-preservation is constituted through the exchange process, for the structure of the Odyssean subjectivity it is rather derived from the principle of mastering nature."
44. *EoR*, p. 93.
45. *DoE*, p. 31–32.
46. *DoE*, pp. 54–55.
47. On the connection between truth and natural history in Adorno, *see* F. Grenz, *Adornos Philosophie*, pp. 57–58.
48. *EoR*, p. 175.
49. *EoR*, p. 173–74.
50. *EoR*, p. 176.
51. *EoR*, p. 177.
52. *Mimesis* does not, to be sure, denote "the form of an unmediated participation in, and repetition of, nature by men," as G. Rohrmoser thinks. *Das Elend der Kritischen Theorie* (Freiburg, 1970), p. 25. Rather, even in the terror of speechless adaptation to the experienced superior power of a nature that hits back chaotically at the interventions of instrumental reason, it *recalls to mind* the model of an exchange of the subject with nature that is free of violence. "But the constellation under which likeness is established—the unmediated likeness of mimesis as well as the mediated likeness of synthesis, assimilation to the thing in the blind discharge of life as well as the finding of likenesses in what has been reified in the process of scientific concept formation—is still the sign of terror" (*DoE*, p. 181). The fact that mimetic behavior, "the organic accommodation to the other," stands under the sign of terror does not take away from it its role as the placeholder for a primordial reason whose position has been usurped by instrumental reason. Schmucker fails to see this (*Adorno*, p. 29, n.63), as does G. Kaiser in

Benjamin, Adorno (Frankfurt, 1974), p. 99.

53. On the significance of this motif in Bloch, Benjamin, and Scholem, *see* my *Philosophical-Political Profiles* (Cambridge, Mass., 1983).
54. *EoR*, p. 177.
55. *EoR*, p. 179.
56. *DoE*, p. 77. On Adorno's philosophy of language, *see* F. Grenz, *Adornos Philosophie*, pp. 211ff.
57. *DoE*, p. 40.
58. On Marcuse's attempt to extricate himself with a theory of the instincts from the aporias—especially the quietistic consequences—of the critique of instrumental reason that he shared, *see* my "Psychic Thermidor and the Rebirth of Rebellious Subjectivity," *Berkeley Journal of Sociology* XXV(1980):1–12.
59. T. Baumeister and J. Kulenkampf, "Geschichtsphilosophie und philosophische Ästhetik," in *Neue Hefte für Philosophie* 5(1973):74ff.
60. Adorno, *Gesammelte Schriften*, 1:336.
61. Walter Benjamin, *The Origin of German Tragic Drama* (London, 1977).
62. Adorno, *Gesammelte Schriften*, 1:357.
63. Ibid., p. 341.
64. Schmucker, *Adorno*, pp. 141ff.
65. F. Grenz, *Adornos Philosophie*, p. 117.
66. Axel Honneth, "Adorno and Habermas," *Telos* 39(1979):45ff.
67. Theodor Adorno, "Der Essay als Form," in *Gesammelte Schriften*, (Frankfurt, 1974, 11:27).
68. Compare R. Bubner, "Kann theorie ästhetisch werden?," *Neue Rundschau* (1978):537ff.
69. H. Mörchen has devoted a detailed and wide-ranging study to the reception of Heidegger by Adorno, *Macht und Herrschaft im Denken von Heidegger und Adorno* (Stuttgart, 1980).
70. "Even though we had noticed for some time that in the modern scientific enterprise great discoveries are paid for with the growing decay of theoretical culture, we still thought that we might join in to the extent that we would restrict ourselves largely to criticizing or developing specialized knowledge. Thematically, at any rate, we were to keep to the traditional disciplines of sociology, psychology and the theory of knowledge. The fragments collected in this volume show, however, that we had to abandon that confidence" (*DoE*, p. xi). Helmut Dubiel provides an excellent analysis of the change in their views on the relation between philosophy and science and on the status of social theory (*Wissenschaftsorganisation*, pp. 51ff., 81ff., 113ff., 125ff). He traces through the thirties the "re-philosophizing" of the whole theoretical orientation of the Institute in its emigration to the United States. "Finally, in the *Dialectic of Enlightenment* all specialized scientific work is identified

with its technical application to production or to society and discredited as 'positivistic,' 'instrumentalist' and the like. In opposition to the 'instrumentalist' spirit of the age, which finds its exemplary palpable expression in the specialized sciences, philosophy is supposed to become encysted as a mental preserve for a shattered intellectual culture. The actual research practice of the Institute is symptomatic of the relation between philosophy and specialized science. It is true that further empirical work was done in the wideranging studies on Fascism and in the "Studies in Prejudice"; but the empirical work of Adorno, for example, stands alongside his temporally parallel philosophical reflections in a bewildering absence of any mediation between the two" (ibid., pp. 125–26). Of course, Adorno had always been secretly skeptical of Horkheimer's program for a materialist theory of society which, supported by interdisciplinary research, would take up the heritage of philosophy. In his inaugural lecture of 1931 he expressed this skepticism in the form of a parable in which sociology is assigned the role of a thief who steals treasures without realizing their value ("Die Aktualität der Philosophie," p. 340). Adorno's later critique of positivism, which amounts to a total devaluation of social science, is already prefigured here.

71. Dieter Henrich, "Die Grundstruktur der modernen Philosophie," in H. Ebeling, ed., *Subjektivität und Selbsterhaltung* (Frankfurt, 1976), p. 117.
72. Hans Blumenberg, "Selbsterhaltung und Beharrung," in Ebeling, ed., *Subjektivtät und Selbsterhaltung,* pp. 144–207.
73. Norbert Wiener, *Cybernetics* (1961).
74. Max Horkheimer, "Vernunft und Selbsterhaltung," in Ebeling, ed., *Subjektivität und Selbsterhaltung,* pp. 47–48.
75. *EoR,* p. 176.
76. *DoE,* p. 217.
77. *Negative Dialektik,* p. 192.
78. *EoR,* p. 135.
79. *Negative Dialektik,* p. 294.
80. Compare D. Henrich, "Die Grundstruktur der modernen Philosophie."
81. Ibid., p. 138.
82. Ibid., p. 114.
83. Dieter Henrich, *Fichtes ursprüngliche Einsicht* (Frankfurt, 1967); idem, "Selbstbewusstsein," in Bubner, Cramer, and Wiehl, eds., *Hermeneutik und Dialektik* (Tübingen, 1970), 1:257ff.; compare U. Pothast, *Über einige Fragen der Selbstbeziehung* (Frankfurt, 1971).
84. E. Tugendhat, *Selbstbewusstsein und Selbstbestimmung* (Frankfurt, 1979), p. 62; English trans. (MIT Press, forthcoming).
85. Henrich, "Selbstbewusstsein," p. 280.

86. Tugendhat, *Selbstbewusstsein und Selbstbestimmung,* pp. 64ff.
87. Henrich, "Selbstbewusstsein," p. 283.
88. Compare Pothast, *Über einige Fragen der Selbstbeziehung,* p. 76.
89. Niklas Luhmann, "Selbstthematisierungen des Gesellschafts-
    systems," in *Soziologische Aufklärung,* (Köln, 1976), 2:72ff.; English
    transl., *The Differentiation of Society* (New York, 1982).
90. Henrich, "Die Grundstruktur der modernen Philosophie," p. 113.
91. Tugendhat, *Selbstbewusstsein und Selbstbestimmung,* pp. 63ff.
92. K. Bühler, *Sprachtheorie* (Jena, 1934). *See* Chap. III above.
93. H. Neuendorff, *Der Begriff des Interesses* (Frankfurt, 1973).

Index

Index

Abel, Theodor, 109
Action, analytic theory of, 273-275
  defined, 96
  four action concepts, 75-96
    communicative, 94-96
    dramaturgical, 90-94
    normatively regulated,
      88-90
    teleological, 86-88
  types of, 101, 280, 285-286, 294,
    332-334
  Weber's theory of, 279-286
  See also Communicative action
Adler, Max, 150
Adorno, Theodor W., 144, 343,
    351, 353, 366
  collapse of Marxism, 366-367
  critique of Kant, 391
  culture industry in, 370-372
  and Heidegger, 385
  mimesis in, 382-390
  negative dialectics, 370-372,
    384-387
  reconciliation in, xx-xxi, 374,
    381-384, 386, 389-390
  self-preservation in, 387-394
  See also Dialectic of Enlighten-
    ment
Agreement, and validity, 287
  analysis of conditions of, 307
  See also Argumentation; Com-
    municative action
Apel, Karl Otto, 277
Argumentation, defined, 10, 18

and rationality, 249
theory of, 18-42
Aristotle, 26, 85
Austin, John, 95, 277, 288-291,
    294, 319-320

Basaglia, F., 369
Bellah, Robert, 195
Bendix, R., 163, 188
Bernstein, Richard, 111
Black, Max, 12
Blumenberg, Hans, 393, 397-398
Bühler, Karl, 275-278, 307, 397

Calvinism, 173, 223-224
  See also Protestant ethic
Carnap, Rudolph, 271
Circourel, A., 127
Communicative action, analysis
    of, ix, 94-101, 305-310
  and illocutionary force, 294-295,
    305, 327
  orientation toward reaching un-
    derstanding, 99-101, 286-288
  as reproducing and coordinating
    action, xxv-xxix, 101, 305,
    397-398
  shift toward in Critical Theory,
    392
  and validity claims, 278, 298,
    306-308
  See also Action; Language; Life-
    world
Condorcet, Marquis de, 145-151

See also Language; Semantics; Speech act theory
Media, money, xxvii-xxx, 342, 358-359
  and paradoxes of modernity, xxxi, power, xxx-xxxv, 342
  substituting for language, 342, 398
  system forming, 359
Modernity, vi, xxxi-xliii, 44, 74, 130, 211-216, 236
Moore, G. E., 310, 336
Morris, Charles, 276
Mommsen, Wolfgang, 352
Morgenstern, Oskar, 186

Needs, and interests, 91-92
  rational interpretation of, 20, 89
  in Weber, 188
Needham, Joseph, 209
Neo-Hegelianism, 77
Neo-Kantianism, 83, 108, 154, 186-188, 191, 339, 355
Nietzsche, Friedrich, v, viii, 155, 246, 247
Norman, Richard, 16
Norms, and cognitivist ethics, 230
  and consensus, 19, 189-191
  post-conventional moral and legal structures, xxix, 166, 254-256, 260-262

Parsons, Talcott, xxii-xxiii, 188, 341, 343
Peirce, C. S., 276, 387
Piaget, Jean, 3, 14, 45, 67-69, 72, 140
Pollner, Melvin, 13
Popper, Karl, 76-79
Positivism, 109, 375
Progress, v-vi, 145-155
Protestant ethic, 216-233
  dissolution of, 228-229
  in Horkheimer, 351
  methodical conduct of life, 172-175, 184, 224-225
  and purposive rationality, 217-219, 222-224
  and rationalization, 218
  as selective, 232
  See also Weber, Max
Psychoanalysis, and distorted communication, 332, 391
  and therapeutic critique, 21, 41

Rational reconstruction, counter-factual element of, 220
  internal relation of meaning and validity in, 197, 220
  logic and dynamics in, xv-xvi, 67, 195, 237-239
  performative aspect of, 192, 220
  of worldviews, 197
Rationality, and argumentation, xi, 16, 34, 249
  of action, 10-11, 17, 19, 103-105, 132, 331
  communicative, 11, 75, 140, 397-399
  context independent standard of, xi, 62
  formal-procedural conception of, 92-93, 249, 363
  and knowledge, defined, 8-11
  of lifeworld, 13, 17, 144
  phenomenological and realist conceptions of, 11-15
  and relativism, xv-xxii, 53-54, 62, 137, 249
  in social sciences, 3-6, 136-141
  universalistic claims of, xii, 2, 62, 137-138, 249
  and validity, 9, 66
Rationalization, and communicative action, xlii, 138-141, 335-343, 397-399
  cultural, 237-242
  of law, 243, 258-262
  of lifeworlds, xlii-xliii, 340-343, 398-399

paradoxes of, xxxi, 342, 362
possibilities of, defined, 237-239
and reification, 354-365, 368-377
as selective under capitalism, xlii-xliii, 180-183, 221-223, 233, 363-364
of society, 158, 166, 335
and theory of action, 145, 335-339
as universal historical process, 143-145, 158, 175, 335
of worldviews, 66, 70, 175-180
Reason, history of, 34, 135, 143, 249
impartiality of, 34
and philosophy, vii-ix, 1-2
procedural unity of, 249
See also Rationality
Reification, in Adorno and Hork-heimer, 355, 369-377
in Lukacs and Marx, 355-357
in myth, 51
paradoxes of, 399
and rationalization, 354-365, 368-377
and science, 376-377
and steering media, 358-359
as universal, 368-370
and utopianism, 73
Relativism, and rationality, 135, 180-184
in Weber, 154
Rickert, H., 186

Schelling, Friedrich J. W. von, 387
Schluchter, Wolfgang, 176, 225-226, 258, 285
Schütz, Alfred, 13, 79, 82, 121-124, 337
Searle, John, 277, 320-321, 323, 335-337
Self-presentations, and aesthetic criticism, 20, 40
and dramaturgical action, 91
as raising a validity claim, 15

as relation to world, 237
Semantics, analysis of sentence forms in, 39, 276
dependent on action context, 115
intentionalist, 95, 274-275
and pragmatics, 316-319
as replacing philosophy of con-sciousness, 316-319
truth-conditional, 276,316
See also Language; Meaning; Speech act theory
Skjervheim, H., 111-115
Social evolution, differentiation of attitudes toward world in, 49
as learning process, xv, 68
nineteenth-century theories of, 152-155
Social integration, principles of, 342
Society, subsystems of, vi, 4-6
as symbolically prestructured, 107
Speech act theory, classification in, 319-328
and communicative action, 305-307
illocutionary force, 278, 288-295
as binding, 278
illocutionary, perlocutionary and locutionary acts, 288-295
meaning in, 307
self-sufficiency of speech acts, 289
theory of action in, 288-289
See also Communicative action; Language; Meaning; Seman-tics; Validity claims
Spencer, Herbert, 151-152
Spinoza, B. de, 387
Stalinism, 367
Stenius, E., 277
Strawson, P. F., 292

Tenbruch, F. H., 195